Merry Christmas 1982

Love,
Pam

MEMOIRS

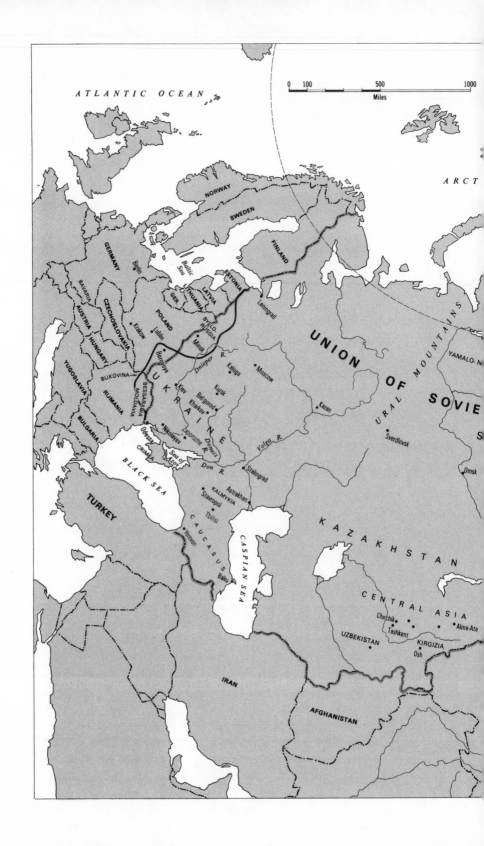

ATLANTIC OCEAN

ARCT

UNION   OF   SOVIE

URAL MOUNTAINS

YAMALO-N

NORWAY

SWEDEN

FINLAND

GERMANY

BAVARIA

AUSTRIA

CZECHOSLOVAKIA

HUNGARY

YUGOSLAVIA

RUMANIA

BULGARIA

TURKEY

POLAND

GER.

LITHUANIA

LATVIA

ESTONIA

BYELO-
RUSSIA

UKRAINE

BESSARABIA

MOLDAVIA

BUKOVINA

CRIMEA

Baltic
Sea

Berlin

Kraków

Lublin

Borgnye

Minsk

Leningrad

Dnieper R.

Kaluga

Moscow

Kursk

Belgorod

Kharkov

Kiev

Nikolayev

Zaporozhe

Donets R.

Odessa

Sea of
Azov

Don R.

Volga R.

Kazan

Sverdlovsk

Omsk

Stalingrad

Astrakhan

KALMYKIA

Stavropol

Tbilisi

Yerevan

CAUCASUS

BLACK SEA

CASPIAN SEA

KAZAKHSTAN

CENTRAL   ASIA

Chirchik

Tashkent

Alma-Ata

UZBEKISTAN

KIRGIZIA

Osh

IRAN

AFGHANISTAN

Baku

S

0   100   500   1000
Miles

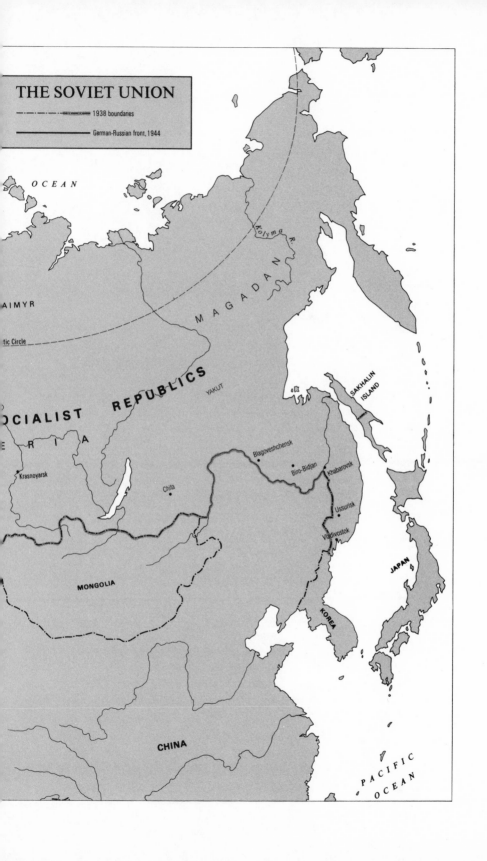

THE SOVIET UNION

—·—·—·— 1938 boundaries

———————— German-Russian front, 1944

OCEAN

AIMYR

tic Circle

Kolyma R.

MAGADAN

SOCIALIST REPUBLICS

SIBERIA

YAKUT

Krasnoyarsk

Chita

Blagoveshchensk

Biro-Bidjan

Khabarovsk

SAKHALIN ISLAND

Ussurisk

Vladivostok

MONGOLIA

JAPAN

KOREA

CHINA

PACIFIC OCEAN

MEMOIRS

PETRO G. GRIGORENKO

Translated by
Thomas P. Whitney

W. W. Norton
and Company
New York · London

The text of this book is composed in Times Roman,
with display type set in Times Roman Black and
Demi Outline. Manufacturing by The Haddon Craftsmen, Inc.

First Edition

Library of Congress Cataloging in Publication Data
Grigorenko, Petro Grigoryevich, 1907–
Memoirs.
Includes index.
1. Grigorenko, Petro Grigoryevich, 1907– .
2. Soviet Union. Armilla—Biography. 3. Generals—Soviet Union—Biography.
4. Dissidents—Soviet Union—Biography.
5. Political prisoners—Soviet Union—Biography.
I. Title. DK268.G75A36 1982   361.230924 [B]   82-7852
AACR2

ISBN 0-393-01570-X

W. W. Norton & Company, Inc. 500 Fifth Avenue,
New York, N. Y. 10110
W. W. Norton & Company Ltd. 37 Great Russell Street,
London WC1B 3NU

1 2 3 4 5 6 7 8 9 0

CONTENTS

PART III: THE FALCON CASTS OFF HIS HOOD

Photographs appear between pages 248 and 249.

AUTHOR'S NOTE

I have lived a long and complicated life, through turbulent, tempestuous, and horrible times. I witnessed death, destruction, and awakening. I met a great number of people. I searched and got involved, erred and reformed myself. I lived with the people and for the people. I accepted their help, took advantage of their good advice and instruction. Many of them left a visible mark on my life, influencing its formation. This book is first and foremost about them. Among them are those without whom I could never have been the way I am.

This book is for my parents—Gregory Ivanovich Grigorenko, my father, and Agatha Semyonovna (nee Belyak), my mother; for my first spiritual mentors—Uncle Alexander (Alexander Ivanovich Grigorenko) and Father Vladimir Donskoi, who have sown the seeds of goodness in my soul; for my wife, Zinaida Mikhailovna Grigorenko (nee Yegorova), who became my friend and support throughout my uneasy life; and for my children and grandchildren, who are destined to live.

In working on the book my aim was not to instruct my contemporaries or descendants. Moreover, I do not believe that someone else's life can be an example for others. Everybody paves his own way. What, then, was the reason for writing the book? the reader may well ask. I will answer this question with another question: "And why does one confess?" This is my confession. I have honestly attempted to tell the truth the way I see it.

But why should I confess in public? It is because my life had outgrown the bounds of ordinariness and become a social phenomenon.

Born into a working family, from my childhood onward I believed in communist ideas and later served them fanatically. I took a leading place among the ruling hierarchy and worked successfully in my chosen field. I had bright prospects. And all of a sudden I embarked on a road of struggle, something that not only deprived me of all my privileges but led me into hostile relations with the authorities. I was threatened with the strongest repressions and with execution.

How does one explain this kind of phenomenon?

The authorities gave it a very simple explanation—lunacy.

I am not satisfied with this explanation. I want the reader to accompany me on my road of life and, consequently, to draw his own conclusions.

I

THE
FALCON
RESPONDS
TO THE
LURE

CHAPTER ONE

I
DID NOT
HAVE A
CHILDHOOD

I was born on October 16, 1907, on a farm in the Ukrainian village of Borisovka in the Primorsk (then Nogaisk) district of Zaporozhe province. I have few recollections of early childhood. My mother died when I was barely three. I do not remember what she looked like nor can I recall any events connected with her.

I did not have childhood playmates. After my mother's death my father became severe, silent, demanding, and strict. He always had work for us. In summer, at threshing time, I felt as though I had been born on horseback.

Father came of a very poor family. His father had been killed trying to jump a train and had left my grandmother Paraska with no money and three small children. To support them, she hired herself out as a farm laborer, doing heavy work all year. I remember how she could barely move about, though she was not old.

After Grandmother Paraska became an invalid, my father and his brother Alexander hired out as farm laborers. Father was employed outside Borisovka by German colonists whose level of agricultural practice was much higher than that of the Ukrainians, Russians, and Bulgarians in surrounding villages. Curious, and devoted to agriculture, my father remembered everything he saw on the German-run farms; subsequently this proved very much to his benefit.

When he returned to Borisovka to be drafted into the army, he met my mother, Gasha Agafei Semyonovna Belyak at a party. They soon married. Uncle Alexander had quit working as a wage laborer, in order to support his mother and sister and operate their common farm. My mother lived with them while Father was away.

He returned from the army in late 1906 to a three-year-old son, my brother Ivan. Within a year he had bought a pair of horses and leased some land, and within two, he and Uncle Alexander, who continued to do field work together, had become relatively prosperous. They became the local authorities on farming, and fellow villagers adopted many of my father's methods.

Our lives changed drastically when my mother caught typhoid and died. My father, left with a sick mother and three small children—Ivan, seven; myself, three; and Maxim, ten months—fell silent, immersing himself entirely in farm work. He took Ivan on as his helper. Grandmother Paraska's condition worsened. She became nervous and irritable, talked constantly of my mother, and accused my father of having forgotten her. I stayed at home to help her and to look after Maxim. I took care of the cows, pigs, and chickens and got my grandmother everything she needed to prepare our meals. I weeded the vegetable garden, brought in water, and pressed dung and straw as fuel for the stove. During warm weather, I also helped with the field work. I had almost no time for sleep. I was three years old.

Grandmother Paraska's grumbling and her use of the stick on us made me dislike her. Nor was my father tender. Consequently I became attached to Uncle Alexander, who lived next door and who talked with me in a low voice, always very seriously, as though I were an adult. I liked to listen to his conversations with everyone. To me, my uncle's words were infinitely precious. Even now I cannot believe I later was unfaithful to my trust in the word of this wise man.

I was also fond of my Grandmother Tatyana, who we visited on Sundays and holidays. Everything in her house was fabulous: the gleaming, freshly varnished floors, the high table with its snow-white cloth, the tall bentwood chairs, the food, the plates, and a marvelous smelling drink named tea, unknown in our house, which we sipped through lumps of sugar.

As time passed after my mother's death, my grandmothers saw the need for someone to look after us children. They were adamant, however, in the opinion that no one ever could or should fill my mother's place. Father seemed indifferent to the possibility of remarriage, and with this same indifference he agreed to the candidate they proposed to him as a wife—Dunya, the daughter of a woman pauper who lived in a nearby village. The marriage took place in the spring of 1913, almost three years after my mother's death. From the beginning, my grandmothers picked on Dunya. Though she was industrious, they never once let up on her. I loved my stepmother. She was kind to me. But our family was not a happy one.

In the summer of 1914, into the measured lives of our hardworking villagers, as into all of Russia, burst the horror of war. When I read my contemporaries on the beginnings of the war of 1914–1918, I constantly encounter the opinion that people supported the war and that they united enthusiastically to struggle against a common enemy. My own childhood impressions contrast sharply with this view. I can still hear the awful lamentation of the women and the drunken uproar of the men during the first days of war.

My father did not drink or take part in the farewell celebrations. He worked until the last minute. Only when the column of recruits marched up to our yard did he kiss us children, mother, and wife, toss over his shoulder a readied sack of food, and step off to catch up to the other men. Grandmother lamented with the women following the column; the sound arose from all corners of the village.

Life went on. Our work was every bit as cheerless, but without Father it became uninspired. My stepmother worked with a sort of desperation. Only Uncle Alexander gave a lift to our spirits. Dropping in from time to time, he cheered us a little with his jokes or sharp comments. Whenever we needed help, he either did the job himself or advised us how best to execute it.

Sometime that fall Father came home on a few days' leave, during which he drew upon his power in Borisovka to enroll me in the first grade. I was only six, but I had looked at Ivan's books for awhile and to be a student was my greatest desire. Upon being admitted to school, I reached a peak of happiness. I loved to study.

But happiness never comes unalloyed. My stepmother, unable to endure her subordinate role and my grandmothers' attitude toward her, left our house. She took nothing, only the clothes on her back, the same she had arrived in. Both grandmothers were sure she would return. She never did.

My uncle rushed back and forth between the two farms, but things went from bad to worse with us. We had neither Father's strength nor his drive or love of farming. The farm fell into decay. Uncle Alexander was taken into a home guard formation at Berdyansk, thirty kilometers from Borisovka. We felt his absence keenly. On his own farm remained only Aunt Gasha, who was sick with tuberculosis, and her two children. Our household consisted of an invalid grandmother and three children, the oldest twelve. Grandmother Paraska named two distant relatives our guardians. Instead of helping us, the guardians began to sell some of our possessions, claiming the money was needed to put the farm in order. We never saw any of the money. Ivan tried to persuade Grandmother to dismiss them. Every time they visited us they took away whatever they could carry. But Grandmother refused to listen to Ivan and the guardians went right on ruining the farm. Ivan became incensed. Perhaps because I was so young or perhaps because I naturally trusted people, I failed to detect anything reprehensible in these people's conduct—though I actually witnessed them removing our possessions. Ivan became increasingly hostile toward them, to the point where he followed them around and blocked their way whenever they tried to take something. Eventually he drove them away by threatening them with a shovel. News of Uncle Alexander's imminent return might also have helped to rid us of them.

Beginning in the summer of 1915 Ivan and I operated the farm by ourselves. At first Ivan tried to run the threshing as Father had: to thresh in the daytime what we had hauled in during the previous evening and morning. The guardians, however, had sold our best pair of horses, which meant we could hitch up only one cart. Father had left us five working horses; we now had three. Also, we were not strong or tall enough to load a cart as high as Father could. Instead of the four large carts Father always threshed in a day, we did only two or three much lighter loads. Given this pace the threshing could have gone on until winter, and the corn, sunflower seeds, and melons would have remained unharvested and the fields unplanted.

Here Ivan showed exceptional initiative. He hauled the grain sheaves to the yard and piled them up in stacks. This method was used all over Russia, but in the Ukraine it was customary to thresh harvested grain immediately. Thus Ivan, who had never been to Russia, became an inventor. Thanks to him we harvested and brought in all of the bread grain, threshed some of it, harvested all the fall crops, and planted the winter wheat. Late that fall Uncle Alexander returned. With a great deal of difficulty he had succeeded in getting exempted from service on the grounds that he was the only person in his entire family capable of working. Uncle Alexander applauded Ivan's initiative and carried it a step further by renting a threshing machine, something we never had done.

Even today, I can say that we boys managed the farm very well during those few years. Farming did not satisfy us, though. We dreamed of distant wanderings.

Ivan and I were ardent readers. By the time I was in second grade, I had read all the books in the school library. Every time Ivan visited Berdyansk or Nogaisk, he brought home bundles of cheap dime novels, and occasionally, true adventure stories. We also borrowed books from the personal libraries of our teachers, Olga Ivanovna and Anfanasy Semyonovich. Because of this exchange, I grew quite close to the Nedoveses. I will always remain grateful to them both; it seems they brought out much of the good in me. After talking with many of their former pupils, I know that everyone who studied under them remembers them fondly—even those who neglected their studies.

In the spring of 1915 a new priest came to our church, named Vladimir Donskoi. Immediately he attracted the attention of everyone—even people like Uncle Alexander who, though they considered themselves believers, did not attend church. A missionary in Africa for forty-four years, Father Vladimir had returned to Russia because of his health. He was offered a post as senior priest of a cathedral in the city of Simferopol but asked to be given instead a small rural parish.

Father Vladimir, a widower, played a large role in my life. Maxim and I became friends with his son, Sima, my age, and his grandson, Valya, Maxim's age. Father Vladimir's daughter Anya managed the household. He had three sons besides Sima. The eldest, Alexander (Valya's father), was a colonel in the Russian expeditionary force in France. Vladimir was a captain in the army on the Rumanian front. Sasha, sixteen, was a student in the gymnasium in Berdyansk.

I listened with great interest to the theology lectures Father Vladimir gave in our school. In the winter of 1918, when the teaching of theology in school was abolished, Father Vladimir taught in his apartment, and I attended his classes there.

He and Uncle Alexander became great friends. After the Civil War began, their conversations continued, but politically the two men were in opposition. Uncle was a Red and Father Vladimir a White. And how could Vladimir be anything else? He believed that the tsar was annointed by God, and he had brought up his children to believe that service to the tsar was a Christian duty.

A strong supporter of the White Army, he was opposed to terror, especially when it was used against civilians. It was because of him that not one person in our village was shot. Several times the White Army seized villagers involved in the partisan movement, but in each instance Father Vladimir succeeded in getting them freed.

These feats, however, earned him no credit with the Reds, who said he defended local Reds only to protect himself. They claimed that Vladimir was afraid that if anyone in the village was shot, he himself would be executed when the Reds returned. This seemed nonsensical to me. Father Vladimir was merely carrying out his duties as a priest. Several times he was threatened by the Whites because of his interference with their prisoners, and once he escaped execution by the Reds only when some brave villagers rescued him at gunpoint.

I last saw Father Vladimir in 1922. Sadly, our friendship had suffered because of my involvement with the village Komsomol (Communist Youth League). He died in 1923 after I had moved from Borisovka.

CHAPTER TWO

I
LEARN
OF MY
NATIONALITY

In the spring of 1918 I completed the course of study in the village school and took the entrance exams for the secondary school in Nogaisk. On the first of September I started classes. Each day I walked the four miles from Borisovka to Nogaisk and back again. My father, a prisoner of war, had returned from camp in Hungary that spring (after having been reported missing in action in 1915) and, as he was immersed completely in rebuilding the farm, he couldn't afford to rent a cot for me in Nogaisk. Besides, he needed another working hand. To keep me company Sima decided to live at home, too. Our talks made the four-mile journeys pass quickly.

One beautiful sunny morning we got to school and found no one there. We asked around and learned that everyone had gone to the cathedral to greet the Drozdovtsy (White Guards). Sima ran ahead. For some reason I didn't want to hurry, even though I had not yet begun to dislike the White Guards. It was simply that I did not understand who they were or why they had come.

I took up my observation point on the sidewalk not far from where the city soviet (council) held meetings.

People were milling around the building. From their talk I gathered that they were relatives of the soviet members, all of whom were gathered in the hall awaiting the arrival of the Drozdovtsy, to whom they would relinquish the city government. The city soviet of Nogaisk, as with many soviets in the first election, had drawn its members from the town's most respected and educated people, who were, for the most part, also well-to-do. The village soviets took their members from among the leading farmers.

Two former front-line soldiers in the soviet were screaming themselves hoarse trying to persuade their colleagues to scatter and hide, saying, "The officers will shoot us!" Those who responded to them said only: For what? After all, we did not seize power. People asked us to lead them. So they'll hold us in jail for a few days to give us a good scare. But shoot us? I too could not understand why a person would be shot just because people had elected him to the soviet.

All of a sudden a brass band thundered on the outskirts of town, beyond the cathedral. Many people ran in the direction of the music. I started that way, but after a few dozen strides returned to where I had been standing before. From behind the cathedral, gleaming in the sun, a regiment emerged, deployed in a line of company columns (in ranks of approximately fifty persons). After a time, bypassing the regiment from the right, a small column of officers appeared, moving swiftly toward the soviet building. When this column was quite close, I saw an enormous window open in the back. Two soldiers in unbuttoned greatcoats jumped out of it and dashed across the garden to the iron fence surrounding the building.

Their plan was clear to me: They would climb the fence, run down an adjacent side street, and hide behind the secondary school building. Then they would make their way through the city to a nearby ravine, and hide. The officers approaching the building also noticed the fleeing pair. Four of them separated from the column and headed for the side street, shooting as they advanced. One of the men was hit as he reached the top of he fence; he fell to the ground inside the yard. The second was wounded, but he got over the fence and ran, limping to the school building. He was just a few steps from shelter when a boy in a student's uniform dashed beneath his legs and tripped him. The boy jumped from under the body as the pursuers ran up and began to attack the man with bayonets.

At this moment a convoy that had entered the building began to bring the soviet members out to the square. Some shouted to their relatives in the crowd: "Don't worry, we'll soon meet again!" I heard a familiar voice saying servilely: "Mister officer, don't forget please, that I knocked him over. I tripped him." Pavka Slastyonov, the son of a rich friend of my father's and a childhood idol of mine, was trying to keep ahead of the officer so that he could look him in the eye while reminding him of what he had done. The officer replied graciously: "Yes, yes, indeed, I will report your patriotic act."

I wanted to vomit. I felt disgust for the boy. Ever since then, when people use the word "patriotic" I cannot help but remember that motionless and defenseless body being pierced by bayonets. No one questioned the victim. No one judged him. No one even asked who he was.

The guard drove the soviet members across a bridge over the Obitochnaya River and on toward the village of Denisovka. A line of empty carts followed the prisoners. Civilians were not allowed beyond the bridge. Soon shots sounded from the direction of Banovskaya grove. A short while later the rattle of fire sounded again. An officer rode over and shouted: "Which of you are the relatives of the soviet puppets? You can come and get them!" The people clamored toward the grove and relatives returned, weeping. In the carts lay the dead.

Many people scattered in fear in the direction of their homes. Others returned to the soviet, myself among them, and wandered about in shock.

As I watched the soviet I saw my history teacher, Novitsky, in the dress uniform of a captain in the Russian Army, and wearing four crosses of St. George on his chest, march smartly into the building. I could not believe it. I was sure that he had been among those shot.

A few minutes later I heard a barrage of cursing. Novitsky stumbled out onto the porch. His shoulder boards and crosses of St. George had been torn off, and his tunic was ripped. An officer with a white band on his sleeve jumped out behind him and, holding a revolver to the back of my teacher's head, shouted: "Get a move on! Get a move on!" Novitsky walked down the steps. Just as he reached the bottom a shot resounded and he fell onto the sidewalk. I was in a trance. The unimaginable cruelty and inhumanity of everything taking place overwhelmed me and deprived me of strength and will. When in a moment the realization that Novitsky had been murdered awoke me, I screamed and started to run. I remembered that Uncle Alexander was chairman of the Borisovka soviet.

I ran as fast as I could, desperate to reach home and warn my uncle and his comrades before the Drozdovtsy reached them. Breathing like a driven horse, I ran into Uncle's yard, where he, suspecting nothing, was working.

"Uncle, run away!" I screamed and fell on the grass. He ran over to me, questioned me, and went to warn the other members of the soviet.

None of the Borisovka soviet members were captured by the Drozdovtsy, and the neighboring villages were warned in time.

Novitsky, an experienced front-line soldier and a man of great will power and presence, had been among those shot in the Banovskaya grove, but had managed to fall one second before the bullet intended for him reached its target. When the relatives had come to claim the corpses, he had stood up and gone home, where he had put on his uniform in order to go and protest the illegal terror. His family had begged him not to go, certain that he would be killed. He had insisted.

There was no school the next day. The city was covered with placards reading: "Beat the Jews and Save Russia!"

In the school building, I sat by a window in the mezzanine above the first floor. To my left lay the entrance to the schoolyard. Across from this entrance a gang of pupils gathered, presided over by Pavka Slastyonov. They waved white flags carrying the same legend as the posters I had seen everywhere and chanted those ugly words as well. As they did so, a Jewish boy passed by them—a pupil much younger than they. He was puny and looked sickly. The gang surrounded him: "Pray to your Jewish God! We're going to save Russia from you right now!" They formed a circle around him. Cackling, they tossed him from one side to the other, back and forth. After awhile they dropped him on the sandy path. He was sobbing.

All of the anger that had built within me over the last few days rose to my throat. I opened the window and jumped out, landing right near the gang. I began to lash out with my fists, shouting: "You White bastards!" The boys dashed off in all directions. I was in a rage against Pavka, both for helping the White officers yesterday and today for masterminding a gang attack on a defenseless child. My previous affection for Pavka made me particularly furious.

He retreated behind the other boys. Smiling maliciously he took off his belt and began to lengthen it. I guessed what he was planning and looked about for my own weapon. As I grabbed a piece of brick, I felt a horrible pain in my right arm. The belt's heavy metal name plate had landed directly on my right elbow. I grabbed the injured place with my left hand, pressed my arm to my body, and quickly went away. I couldn't run. The pain was too great. I walked without thinking, not to the city, where I could have gotten help, but to the park, which was completely empty at that time of the morning. While I made my way, Pavka pursued me and kept beating me with the buckle, on my back, my neck, and my head. I didn't respond. At the park entrance, for some reason, he let me be.

I still have a souvenir of this, my last encounter with Pavka—a floating bone chip beneath the skin of my elbow. It hurt for a long time.

On my way to school the next day I noticed a crowd of people in a yard and a carriage parked at the doors of the house. I dove into the crowd, crawled beneath the carriage, and sneaked into the house, where what I saw made me dash back outside. In the first room an old man lay with his skull split open. On the threshold of the second lay an old woman, dead also, and horribly wounded. Two men were dragging a body out from under the woman's. The rooms were spattered with blood.

Outside I was sick to my stomach. I walked among the crowd and heard rumors that the third person was a youth, still alive, that the family was Jewish, and that the commandant's officers didn't seem at all interested in the crime and might even be involved in it.

The young man was brought out, his head and face covered with bandages. The district doctor, Gribanov, was directing the youth's removal and placement in the carriage. I heard him order the driver to the hospital.

When I reached school, class had already begun. I asked permission to be seated and the teacher answered me by asking whether I had read the director's order. I replied that I hadn't and he ordered me to do so. I went to the bulletin board and read: "The peasant's son, Pyotr Grigoryevich Grigorenko, has been expelled from school for engaging in a hooligan fight with stones and bricks."*

What a blow! It was the end of a dream. I knew that my expulsion was the work of Pavka Slastyonov.

My early return home caused astonishment. Uncle Alexander was furious, and he had Father Vladimir see the director on my behalf. However, even the priest's intercession did not help. The director said that I had been expelled because I had defended a "kike." He promised to reinstate me after the whole affair had quieted down a little, and kept his promise, but not until a year and a half later, after the forces of the partisan leader Nestor Ivanovich Makhno had evicted the Whites from our district. I believe he did it more in self defense than because he had given his word; everyone knew that my older brother was serving with the Reds. I never went back to the secondary school. The students there were all on the side of the whites and they looked on me with a mixture of fear and hatred. I did not want to be among them.

On the day of my expulsion, Sima returned home and told us that many inhabitants of Nogaisk ascribed the murder of the Jewish family to the White officers and that the youth was rumored to have died. This rumor was confirmed the next day. Sima reported that officers had gone to the hospital the evening before to question the young man. Dr. Gribanov told the officers that he had died and that relatives, whose address he did not know, had claimed the body. Other rumors circulated that he had not died but had been hidden from the officers by Gribanov who feared they might have killed the young man as a witness to their crime.

Several months before these events, Ivan and I had tried to join the Red Guard in Berdyansk. Ivan was fully grown by then, and after convincing the commander that he was seventeen, he was accepted into the detachment. Father found out about our attempt to enlist and proved, by producing a birth certificate, that Ivan was only fifteen. Ivan and my father argued for weeks. Father advanced the irrefutable argument that Ivan was still very young and would see enough war in the course of his lifetime. Ivan vowed that he would not work until he had smelled gunpowder. He threatened to run away.

My father was forced to give in. However, things did not turn out well for

*Grigorenko discontinued using the Russian *Pyotr* and resumed using *Petro*—his Ukrainian given name—after his Soviet citizenship was revoked.

Ivan the second time he tried to join. He came into conflict with one of the commanders of the detachment and returned home once more. Soon after, he joined up with another group, commanded by a member of the Denisovka soviet who had escaped execution by the Drozdovtsy. Ivan fought with this detachment until the end of the Civil War, by which time it had become a regiment. When the Red Army retreated, Ivan's regiment, so as not to be too far from home territory, joined up with Makhno but retained its independence, rejoining the Red Army when it returned. All those who fought with Golikov received certification as Red Army soldiers; all the Makhno men were shot or imprisoned.

Borisovka, like all the neighboring Ukrainian and Russian villages, was Red. One hundred forty-nine men from the village served with the Reds (counting, as we did until the end of the war, the Makhno army as part of the Red forces), and only two served with the Whites. The nearby Bulgarian villages and German colonies fought with the Whites.

People in our village and those around us knew little about the struggle for Ukrainian independence or about the Ukrainian nationalist movements. We did not receive information from the Ukrainian rada (legislative body). Most of us made no distinction between the Ukrainian parliament—the Central Rada—and Skoropadsky, the hetman (cossack headman), who executed a monarchist coup d'etat. Our attitude toward both the Central Rada and the hetmans was hostile. People felt that both groups had been put in power by the Germans.

Little was known of the Petlura forces except that they, like the Hetmen, claimed to support the estate owners. But when two villagers who had been imprisoned by the Petlurists returned home with stories of torture, indifference became hostility and soviet propaganda against the "Petlurist remnants" began to find fertile soil. This hostility intensified when Petlura's name became associated with White Poland. The expedition of Tyutyunick was viewed as a bandit attack. Almost everyone was tired of fighting.

Ivan came home in 1920. It was a miracle that he was still alive. In late 1919 he had contracted typhus somewhere near the Dnieper River and had wandered ill for over two months before reaching Borisovka. When he finally got home, he was excruciatingly thin. His entire skeleton was visible. His skin, stretched over his bones, seemed transparent. I had had typhus myself in 1919 and almost died. Both Ivan and I were lucky.

Ironically, Ivan *had* smelled gunpowder. The tip of his nose had been blown off when the breechblock of his rifle burst during battle.

With Ivan barely able to stand, I was my father's principal helper on the farm, but my thoughts were elsewhere.

In March 1921 the Workers' Seven-Year School No. 1 had opened in Nogaisk in the secondary-school building and I had enrolled in the sixth grade. That year classes continued until the middle of July and resumed on September 1.

The teachers were not paid regularly, and because of inflation the money they did receive was worth nothing. Literally starving, they were forced to neglect their work and wander about the villages exchanging their possessions for food. Ordinarily there were no more than one or two lessons per day.

The demand for education, both by children and by parents, was enormous. Yet the number of places available was limited. Playing upon this demand and on the teachers' poverty, my father organized parents of children already studying in the Workers' Seven-Year School No. 1 and those who wished their children to study there in the future. Together they presented to the Department of Education a request to open the Workers' Seven-Year School No. 2 in Borisovka. The officials replied that this could be done only if teachers could be found, which they believed impossible.

My father obtained a list of the teachers required and in just two days' time he submitted the names of qualified people for the jobs. He had been able to act quickly because he had prepared such a list in advance. Back in the winter of 1920 he had seen on the street in Nogaisk a strange man, wearing a broad black cloak and a soft black hat with drooping rims, out from under which could be seen long, thick double moustaches. My father learned that his name was Mikhail Ivanovich Shlyandin and that he was a teacher in one of the Moscow gymnasiums.

Mikhail Ivanovich had no talent for practical life. He knew only mathematics and physics. After his wife died from starvation, he became possessed by one thought only: to feed his children. Taking his few valuable possessions, he brought his children to Nogaisk where he was able to get a teaching job, but his family soon was starving again. When Father met him, he had gone almost a week without eating.

Father gave him food and told him that he would bring him more the next day. Mikhail Ivanovich wept and kept asking how he could repay this kindness. Thereupon Father recruited him to help start a secondary school in Borisovka. His payment would be food. Mikhail Ivanovich undertook his task with enthusiasm. He assembled an excellent staff and, after receiving approval from the Department of Education, began classes.

Because the upper classes were attended by adolescents and young adults, the school became a cultural center. Almost at the same time the school opened, Onisim Grigoryevich Zasukha, the history teacher, and his wife, Oksana Dmitrovna, the German teacher, founded a Borisovka section of Prosvita, the Ukrainian cultural organization. In their house I first saw and heard played the Ukrainian national musical instrument, the bandore. From them I learned of *Khobzar*, written by the great Ukrainian poet Taras Grigoryevich Shevchenko. And from them I learned that I belonged to the same nationality as the great Shevchenko, that I was Ukrainian.

CHAPTER THREE

"TO BE COOKED IN THE WORKERS' POT"

Through the Prosvita, Ukrainian culture flowered in Borisovka. Readings of Ukrainian stories and poems, lectures in Ukrainian history, and performances of Ukrainian plays brought many of us a dramatic new awareness of our heritage. At the same time the October Revolution brought us new ideas. As I read the slogans, the posters, and the political leaflets of the new government, the concepts of freedom, brotherhood, and the "dictatorship of the proletariat" entered my consciousness. Love for my culture and for my people mingled in my mind with the dream of universal happiness, international unity, and the unlimited "power of labor." I wanted to build a new life, to struggle for the ideas the Communist party and Lenin were bringing into the world.

Many in our Prosvita group dreamed of creating a cell of the Komsomol (Communist Youth League), but none of us knew how to go about it.

On the evening of March 7, 1922, a lecturer from the district came to Borisovka to talk about International Women's Day. He was a young man, wore a leather jacket, and was about eighteen or nineteen years old, tall, well-built, with thick, curly, light brown hair. He seemed to us an envoy from another world.

He talked and invited us to ask questions. Not a single one of our questions had anything to do with the lecture. Almost all related to the Komsomol (he said he was a member), especially to how we could create a cell in Borisovka. The young man asked all those who wanted to join the Komsomol to remain behind after the formal session ended, when he would conduct an organizational meeting with us.

More than two dozen young women and men stayed, most of them pupils at the Workers' School and members of the Prosvita group. Almost none of us were older than fifteen. A bureau was created and I was the propagandist. Two copies of our membership list were drawn up, one for the lecturer, who promised us we would receive our Komsomol membership cards within several weeks. He gave me *The ABC of Communism,* by Nikolai Bukharin, and told me: "This contains all the wisdom of humanity. You must study it from cover to cover."

I read the book through in several days and began to study it with the group. The simplicity of its concepts shocked me. The history of humanity, it said, is the history of class warfare. Until the working class—the proletariat— entered the arena of history, society was divided into the oppressors and the oppressed. The oppressors, the ruling class, preserved their own privileges and exploited the other classes. The oppressed did not dare even to dream of the benefits enjoyed by the oppressors. They stagnated in work and in poverty. The proletariat takes power into its hands not, like the classes ruling before it, to make eternal its ruling position, but to raise everyone to its own level, to transform society into a unified collective of workers in which there will be no difference between mental and physical labor, between city and countryside, and in which everyone will serve society in accordance with his capabilities and will receive from society what he or she needs.

We received such ideas enthusiastically. The happiness of all people was our goal. To put the manifesto into practice we would sacrifice everything, even our lives.

Fascinated by our exalted purpose, we did not see that to rise up to the working class we must sink into its situation, become part of it. We did not know that this rising upwards necessitated destroying not only the estate owners and capitalists but the large class of urban and rural bourgeoisie, and that the suppression of such a large mass of people required a more powerful apparatus of oppression than ever had existed in tsarist Russia.

We believed that the attainment of universal happiness demanded the reconstruction of all society and that this must be carried out by the dictatorship of the proletariat. This resounding phrase pleased our naïve consciousness and aroused in us feelings of strength, of inexorability, of romantic struggle. We never thought about how we would change people's minds or that what would impress people most would be not our words but our reprisals against those who were unwilling to change their minds. Most importantly, we failed to ask what gave us, a minority of the people, the right to reeducate the rest and to suppress those who refused to be reeducated, to deny them the possibility not only of refuting us, but even of merely disagreeing with us.

To this very day I am astounded by the fascination we had with dictatorship. We were not evil people. We did not seek easy lives and material advantages. That we created a Komsomol cell in the village proves our dedication. So much was happening during those years, however, that we were not always able to distinguish evil from good. All of us, for example, knew of and condemned the Whites' execution of the members of the first soviets.

In spring 1920 the Cheka (secret police; forerunner of the KGB) passed through the villages, taking weapons from the people. When the Chekist troika reached Borisovka an assembly was convened. The chairman of the troika read a list of hostages (seven of our most respected elderly men) and declared that they would be shot if all weapons were not turned in by noon of the following day.

That night hunting guns, revolvers, and daggers were thrown in front of the village soviet building. After lunch soldiers from the detachment accompanying the troika searched our homes. A sawed-off shotgun was found in someone's garden. All of us suspected that the police had planted it there themselves. That night they shot the seven hostages and took seven more. Again the chairman of the troika, standing on the porch of the village soviet building, read the list of hostages and declared that they would be shot if any weapons were found after noon the next day. As he turned to leave a voice asked from the crowd:

"What did you shoot them for?"

The chairman halted, obviously caught off guard. Taking hold of himself, he stared at the crowd: "Who asked that?"

In a calm voice Uncle Alexander identified himself as the speaker.

"It's not clear to you?" the Chekist roared at my uncle.

"No, it's not clear," Alexander replied.

"Not clear?" the man roared even more loudly.

"Seize him!" he ordered, turning to the Red soldiers standing behind the crowd. "Put him in with the hostages! When he's in prison he'll understand!"

The crowd stirred. People began shouting hostile remarks at the chairman. The commotion grew. Three soldiers stood beside Uncle Alexander, afraid to act because people had surrounded them.

"Disperse!" screamed the chairman. "Disperse or I will give orders to fire!"

The soldiers raised their guns. The bolts clicked into place. The crowd seethed.

Then came the calm voice of Uncle Alexander: "Disperse, good people, disperse. It would be like them to shoot." In a few minutes people scattered and the soldiers took my uncle away.

In the morning word spread that the Cheka had left. The hostages were alive. No one knew what had happened. Some said the chairman who had left never shot less than three groups of hostages in each village. Why he shot only one group in Borisovka and then departed secretly no one could say.

A particularly large-scale shooting took place in Novo-Spasovka (now the village of Osipenko). Eyewitnesses said that blood flowed down the slopes of the ravine on which the executions took place. I did not believe this story. Novo-Spasovka villagers were heroic. In 1918 they had fought the Whites and had withstood attacks for eight months, until Makhno's army relieved them. The villagers had rewarded Makhno by providing his armies with two well-armed and well-tempered infantry regiments. How could a revolutionary government deal so cruelly with those who had fought for it?

I later learned that this and other horror stories were true. Almost half the men in Novo-Spasovka had been shot. The government thought differently than I. It believed that those who had risen against the Whites also could rise against the Reds.

All of us knew about the slaughter in Novo-Spasovka, but after only two years we had conveniently forgotten the whole thing. Today stories about atrocities committed by the Whites remain fresh in our minds. But we forget the Red terror—even though in my own village the Cheka shot seven innocent men.

By and large we did not disagree with the government. We were totally devoted to it. The first demand it made on us as Komsomols was help in collecting the recently introduced labor cartage tax. People had not yet recovered from the Civil War and the requisitioning of food supplies. Just one year had passed since the introduction of the New Economic Policy (NEP)—the replacement of food supplies requisitions by the agricultural tax—and already the government was adding this new labor cartage tax to the "one and only" first tax.

Peasant farms were ruined. People had nothing with which to pay the new tax. Still, we Komsomols went from hut to hut, taking everything of any value at all.

The villagers compared my comrades and me to a whip that the government was using to punish them. At nearly every farm we encountered sobbing women and children, reproaches and hostility. Many Komsomols complained, then refused to go to the farms, and then quit the cell. We were threatened with collapse. Our "organizer" had never been back in touch with us. We did not have Komsomol membership cards or instructions from the Komsomol authorities. In order to save ourselves, we freed the least stalwart members from participation in the collection of the labor cartage tax. Then we intensified our study of *The ABC of Communism* and our indoctrinational work through the drama circle. There were no more productions of Ukrainian classics; the stage was given over to Soviet propaganda playlets that depicted young people struggling against the kulaks (wealthy farmers), the White Guards, bandits, and the workers' lack of political consciousness. Finally, my friend Mitya Yakovenko and I decided to go to the district Komsomol Committee in Berdyansk.

Before we made this expedition, sometime around the end of March, a directive arrived at the school ordering qualified pupils to take entrance examinations for the Vocational-Technical School in the village of Molokanka, not far from Melitopol. Mikhail Ivanovich reviewed the advanced students and chose several of us to take the tests.

In Molokanka I no doubt cut a rather comical figure. I wore a military outfit and my father's red hussar's service cap. On the application I listed myself as a Komsomol member. My father had acquaintances in town. The day after the first exam he said to me: "Maybe we should go home son? The director told the teachers that he doesn't want any communist spies here."

I rejected my father's proposal. Though I felt enmity from every side, I wanted to compete. Obviously both the teachers, the pupils, and their families still supported the White movement. What kind of Komsomol would I be if I gave in to the pressure they were putting on me? Let them give themselves away. And they did. After the first examination the director summoned my father and me to his office: "Your son, Grigory Ivanovich, did not pass the written examination in mathematics and will not be admitted to the subsequent exams. He is a very talented young man and I am astonished that without having completed the required mathematics courses, he nevertheless undertook to solve the problems, though he did not get the right answers."

I was barely able to control my rage. All of the problems were familiar to me and I was convinced I had solved them correctly. Sensing a class enemy in the director, I spoke out angrily: "Show me my mistakes!"

"What's this, young man? You do not trust the teacher?" The director looked astonished.

"I do not!" I snapped back.

"Then why did you come here?" he asked sarcastically. "What you need is to create your own school." Turning to my father, he added, "I beg your pardon, Grigory Ivanovich, but unfortunately I do not have time for such an interesting conversation with your son. I have said what I have to say. Goodbye."

For the whole fifty miles home I raged over my failure to come back at the director with a sharp retort. To me he was a living example of a class enemy. Once home I dashed off to see Mikhail Ivanovich. I remembered all the problems and correctly solved them in his presence. Then and there he wrote a complaint to the District Department of Public Education. At the same time,

I wrote a letter to the district committee of the Komsomols in which I charged that the Vocational and Technical School in Molokanka was a nest of Whites. Fortunately my accusations did not have tragic consequences; "vigilance" had not yet reached the heights it would in the 1930s.

Soon afterward Mikhail Ivanovich received an official communication from the Department of Public Education stating that the admissions committee's decision on my case had been annulled and that I had been admitted to the school as the son of a working peasant. I refused to go.

At our next Komsomol political study class, I told of what I had seen in Molokanka. We concluded that as children of workers, we had to rally more closely around the government. In light of my experience in Molokanka, the danger of a counterrevolutionary coup, about which Soviet propaganda trumpeted every day, seemed a reality. We had to become official Komsomols. Mitya and I decided to go to Berdyansk at once.

We left early in the morning of an overcast April day. After we had walked about three miles, a cold, fine rain began to fall, quickly soaking through our rawhide peasant boots and making walking very difficult. Eighteen miles remained. We reached Berdyansk late that evening. Soaked, hungry, and cold, we wandered about the city for two hours before finding the District Komsomol Committee in the former home of a merchant in the center of the city. The first person we saw in the house, a young man, looked us over suspiciously and demanded to know what we wanted. I began to explain that we had traveled from Borisovka to register our Komsomol cell. But the youth interrupted me and shouted: "Boys, some kulaks want to blow us up!"

A crowd of young people appeared, surrounded us, and stared. We must have painted a sorry picture: wet hair, wet clothes, our wet service caps in our hands, untied rawhide peasant boots, and giant puddles at our feet. I protested that we were indeed Komsomols, but the group began to jostle us about. Mitya estimated the situation more accurately than I, and retreated. I began to get angry, and shoved back those who were being particularly rough. Suddenly there came the cry: "Beat them! Why fool around?"

A terrible uproar commenced. I looked about. We were cut off from the exit. The pushing had increased and I had nothing to hold on to for support. Noticing a rather steep, narrow staircase, I whispered to Mitya to run up it while I held them off. As he moved to the stairs, I heard a sharp voice:

"Brothers, what's all the noise about?"

"We caught some kulaks, comrade Goldin!" The crowd separated a bit and a young man of twenty or twenty-two pushed his way toward Mitya and myself. He wore jackboots and uniform britches and carried a leather jacket over his shoulder. His head was uncovered and his dark, curly hair was not combed back, in the style of Karl Marx, popular at the time, but forward, in an obvious attempt to cover a horrible blue scar running from beneath his hairline, across his forehead, almost to his right ear. His eyes were merry and benevolent. One could feel the respect and affection all present felt for him.

"Well, show me your kulaks," he said to the young people. He turned to us. "Where are you fellows from?"

"Borisovka," we answered together.

"What did you ride in? The weather's so bad I can't imagine what could get through. The mud must be knee deep."

"We came on foot," I said.

"On foot?" he asked, and turning to the crowd: "And you say these are kulaks? What kulak would walk eighteen miles in this weather?" He turned back to us. "You are probably Komsomols?"

"Yes, yes," I cried joyously. "We have been for two months now, but we're not yet registered. That's why we came."

Goldin ordered some of the young men to bring us dry clothes and some food. Soon we were sitting in his office. I told him about our cell. He laughed when he heard about the lecturer who had organized us. He knew him well. He was neither a Communist nor a Komsomol, and so, of course, he did not have the right to organize a cell. Goldin approved of our activities, but he told us we would need formal approval from the province committee before we could become official. He was willing to help us gain that approval. The whole time we talked I kept thinking about his scar. Before we left I asked him how he had gotten it. Had he been in the Civil War?

"No, not in the Civil War. I got this scar from the ax of the White thugs. If it hadn't been for my grandmother . . . "

In a flash I recollected. "Was it in Nogaisk?"

"Yes," he said, a bit surprised. "I owe my life to two people: to my grandmother who took the blow from the ax that was meant to kill me; and to a wonderful doctor, Dr. Gribanov. He took me to a friend's house to recover. If the officers who came to the hospital looking for me had found me, I would have been killed."

I, in turn, told Goldin of how I had been in Nogaisk during those awful days.

Mitya and I spent the night in the club and met again with Goldin the next morning. He asked me to fill out a questionnaire and to come that evening to a meeting of the district committee of the Komsomol. He planned to sponsor me for Komsomol membership. Why me and not Mitya obviously had something to do with my connection to his past, but I did not think about this. I was literally burning with pride at being the first Komsomol in Borisovka. Further, the district committee would send two more Komsomols to the village, one as secretary of the village soviet and the other as chairman of the committee of poor peasants. I would continue as propagandist. Three Komsomols constituted a cell. Consequently, we could take into our Komsomol the rest of the young people who wished to join.

After we left Berdyansk I never saw Goldin again. From the two Komsomols the district committee sent to us, I learned that he was leaving Berdyansk, having been assigned to do party work. Later I read in a local paper that he had joined the Trotskyite opposition. I do not know what happened to him, though I imagine his honesty and love of justice would have made it difficult for him to survive. In the thirties anyone charged with being a member of the Trotskyite opposition that Goldin had joined was shot as an enemy of the people.

After the cell was formalized, I continued to work on my father's farm, giving all my spare time to cultural work and the Komsomols. Aroused by the limited beneficial effects of the NEP, Borisovka, like hundreds of other villages, was undertaking the restoration of its economy. One can only be astonished by the fact that, after the horrible famine of 1920–21, the country had the necessary minimum of food supplies in 1922 and in 1923 was able to contemplate the export of grain. And all these crops were raised by the people of the ruined countryside, plowing with cows or harnessing themselves to the plow.

Labor no longer seemed like punishment to me. I was stronger and I had come to love the earth and its fruits. But more than those things, I now saw meaning in labor. I looked upon it as work for the future, as the preparation of the material basis for communism. Influenced by *The ABC of Communism*, I dreamed of men laboring on common fields with the help of machinery.

I could not understand that it was the common fields that would kill the farmer's initiative and bring on forced labor, which would transform men into slaves who would be put into prison if, when hungry, they picked up a stalk dropped on a field where they had worked. Almost my whole life passed before I understood this.

I never considered the possibility that the future would not work out as I wanted it to. Uncle Alexander argued that what I foresaw never could come to pass, but I was immersed in a dream of the "bright future of humanity," and I wanted to bring it closer. Routine farm work could not satisfy me. I wanted to do something to help convert everyone to communism. Some of the other Komsomols and I decided to create a youth commune. We would take our shares of our parents' farms and put them together. But we were too young to have our shares separately and our parents merely laughed at us when we proposed to them that they combine.

After this failure, I decided to leave the village. I felt I must go and build industry so that I could attack backward agriculture. I took the examinations for and was admitted into the Vocational and Technical School in Berdyansk, where I would be able to develop a technical specialty.

Before leaving Borisovka, I called on Uncle Alexander, but our political differences had killed the warmth between us. I did not see Father Vladimir. Nor did I say farewell to my good friend Sima. All had become, in accordance with the new laws of morality, class enemies.

The pupils at the Vocational and Technical School were from the urban intelligentsia or from well-to-do rural families. I found it hard to make friends. The young men I had met when I visited Berdyansk to formalize the Borisovka Komsomol cell refused to accept me. Often I heard the adage, in fashion at the time and directed at all nonproletarian elements who tried to enter the party or the Komsomol, "You have to be cooked in the workers' pot." Someone who had never known or seen real labor would stare at me and mutter, "What you need is to be cooked in the workers' pot." No one ever cited any facts to prove the superiority of the urban over the rural worker. I became ashamed that I had not yet been "cooked" and I stopped going to the Komsomol club.

After classes, I spent my free time in the vineyard of my landlord, Stepan Ivanovich, helping him harvest his grapes. He appreciated my help, and after I told him how unhappy I was in Berdyansk and how much I wanted to be "cooked," he got me a job as an assistant lathe operator at the Berdyansk station locomotive depot. Now I was in the "pot." But I could not make my work schedule fit the schedule for the second shift at school. I constantly missed the beginnings of classes. And at the Komsomol club, where I now thought I'd be accepted as an equal, I was accused of trying to pass myself off as a proletarian.

Nothing was working out for me. I decided to leave Berdyansk and go to the Donets coal basin (Donbas), a powerful proletarian center, a real "pot."

From my neighbors on the train, I learned that there was terrible unemployment in the Donets Basin, that Stalino, Makeyevka, and the other mining towns were crowded with hungry people. Someone told me that Komsomols often found it easier than others to find work, and I felt much better, but I wondered why I as a Komsomol should get a job ahead of someone else.

When we arrived in Stalino I went to the barracks that housed the labor exchange. These shelters have long since been torn down and the site built over. But even now I can see in my mind's eye the enormous courtyard surrounding them swarming with homespun and bast sandal—swarming with peasant Russia. There were almost no Ukrainians in Stalino. Ukrainians grew grain, tended orchards, raised livestock. I would spend many days with migrating Russia in this courtyard, until cold weather came. Work was impossible to find. As a Komsomol I had just one advantage—I did not have to wait every day in an enormous line but could go directly to the youth inspector's window. Because I had very little money, I limited myself to spending no more than five to seven kopecks a day. Usually I bought a loaf of bread and a few vegetables.

Weeks passed. Cold weather arrived, and I could no longer sleep in the

courtyard, particularly since I was dressed in summer clothes. All my money
went to buying rags to wear on my shoulders and legs. After going several
days without food, I swallowed my pride and went from house to house begging for bread. That solved the food problem. The problem of a place to spend
the night remained. The simplest thing would have been to return home or
to write my father asking for money, but I still felt I had to make my way
myself.

One day I was sitting at the weighing station hoping to get a chance at un-
loading freight cars, when a young man came up to me and asked me if I had
any food. He was shorter than I was, but he was firm, thickset, and obviously
older. I had just returned from a begging expedition and my bag was full. I
pushed it over to him and he began to eat greedily. We talked. His name was
Seryozha. I complained that I was freezing at night and he asked me to come
with him to his sleeping place, the open hearth furnaces. Relieved, I went
along.

After Seryozha and I teamed up things went better for me. The very day
we met, this enterprising fellow managed to take over an arriving freight car
for us to unload, which wasn't easy. There were more people waiting to help
unload the freight cars than there were cars. Everyone rushed to each incoming
train, pushing and shoving. Often there were fights.

Seryozha grasped economic politics better than I. He would bribe the foreman and a freight car would go to us. Almost every day we unloaded two or
three cars. We bought clothes. We ate hot meals in a dining hall. We slept
in the warm pipes under the open hearth furnaces, emerging every morning
looking like black devils.

One morning I was dashing across the railway yard from the furnaces to
one of the hot water faucets scattered about, when I heard someone call, "Hey
there, come on over here!" I looked about and saw a medium sized man with
red handlebar moustaches in the style of the Zaporozhe cossacks. The man
approached me. His eyes were kind. We talked for a while and when he learned
that I was a Komsomol, he told me that he might be able to help me if I washed
up and met him at an office in a small building near the factory.

The next day I was enrolled in the locomotive depot of the railway department of the Stalino (now Donetsk) Metallurgical factory as an assistant lathe
operator and fitter. About a month later Seryozha began to work in the depot
as a stoker. I last saw him in the summer of 1934. He had become a locomotive
engineer.

I found an inexpensive room near the factory. Solutions to the problems
of employment and housing opened the doors to social activity. The Komsomol cell of the railway department operated in much the same way as the cell
in Borisovka. The young people devoted every free minute to the cell, working,
arguing, discussing. I dove wholeheartedly into all this activity, accepting

every assignment offered me, from taking subscriptions for newspapers to preparing lectures. My enthusiasm was noted and soon I received an extremely important assignment—the organization and leadership of a Pioneer troop.

At the time I was given this task, in early 1924, it was no easy matter to gather boys from off the street and conduct a Pioneer meeting with them, let alone carry on regular work with them. I had to catch their interest in some way. After much thought, I decided to enlist the boys and the Komsomols in rebuilding an abandoned passenger locomotive. Rebuilding and later riding in "our own" railway cars held together my original Pioneer collective and attracted other children to it. When I left the railway department two years later, our cell guided not just one Pioneer troop but four.

The struggle against Trotskyism was taking place and I could not stay on the sidelines. I read *The Lessons of October* and I read the periodical press. I was uneasy. Could Trotsky possibly be right? Might the creation of a socialist society be impossible? Would we perish if the world revolution did not come to our aid? At just this time Stalin's essay "Trotskyism or Leninism" appeared in *The Workers' Newspaper*. With characteristic simpicity (today I would call it oversimplicity) Stalin refuted Trotsky's affirmations one by one. We could, he wrote, succeed at building socialism in our country. The delay in world revolution must not stop us. We were obliged to carry out the cause of the world revolution ourselves.

I agreed with Stalin's every word. He liberated me from all doubts. From then on his essay was with me always. I never tired of explaining it to my friends. It was my best weapon during arguments with Trotskyites.

Youth, friendship, social activities, and my beloved work made life interesting and full. Economic conditions also kept my good mood alive.

In the spring of 1925 I received forty-five rubles a month in wages. With two comrades from the factory I rented a room in a government apartment on Smolyaninov Hill.

This was the peak of the NEP. The markets were full of food at throwaway prices. The Communist party was forced to concern itself with the "scissors"— prices were too high for industrial consumer goods and too low for agricultural products. To close these scissors the party planned to raise the latter and lower the former, but nothing came of their plan. Prices for both industrial goods and for agricultural products increased, while the procurement prices paid farmers remained at the 1924 level right up until Khrushchev's reforms in the fifties and sixties. In other words, farmers were barely paid for the produce taken from them.

Still, those were years of abundance for me. For the entire rest of my life, including the years during which I was a general, I never lived so freely as when I was a worker during the years of NEP.

In the fall of 1925 I transferred to work as an assistant engineer on a locomotive, and some months later—on February 1, 1926—I had a serious accident at the Smolyanka mine. We were leaving for the day, when the station duty officer asked my boss if we could take on some cars in need of repair. The engineer agreed to do the job. Since the coupler brigade already had switched to a different locomotive, I was sent to couple the cars and then inspect the entire train. I discovered one uncoupling—between a box car and a freight car with a stuck side—and went back to inform the engineer of the problem. Returning to the separated cars, I inspected the coupler and whistled to indicate to the engineer that it was in order. The locomotive whistle responded and the cars began to close. They came on very slowly and at times stopped entirely. Then came a stronger push. The cars were close together. I took the coupler in my hands. Only centimeters away from a hookup, the train stopped, braked by snow.

Then came a sharp push and the buffer of the freight car slipped off the buffer of the box car and came up against its planking. The stuck side of the freight car pushed me against the box car, pressing in just below my diaphragm. Fortunately it happened so quickly that I didn't slip the coupler over the hook. I could feel myself losing consciousness.

Release came suddenly. The uncoupled cars moved apart a bit and I tried with all my strength to lift the stuck side. It moved up slightly and I slipped under the cars and lost consciousness. When I came to I was being dragged by a brake rod. With great exertion I unhooked myself and rolled from the center of the track toward one of the rails. The train kept moving slowly; if it did not stop, I would be killed. I groaned. Luckily some workers heard me and shouted to the engineer to stop. As I heard the whistle that indicated the train was stopping, I again lost consciousness. I came to in the hospital as they were clipping off my red curls and then fell back into unconsciousness.

For nearly a month I hovered between life and death, before taking a turn for the better and beginning to recover. I had hemorrhaging in both eyeballs and could not see. Gradually the blood cleared up and my sight returned. My hair grew back straight. I got out of the hospital in late March. The medical commission concluded that I should be transferred to a job that did not involve physical labor.

The district committee of the Komsomol asked me to continue work I had done previously with children, and I was assigned as a temporary political instructor to the Jewish Workers' Seven-Year School in Stalino. It became clear to me when I began work that the children's parents were upset that Yiddish was not being taught at the school. I tried to prove to them that Yiddish could be learned at a Workers' school, and that it was extremely important for the Jews to reestablish their culture. No one refuted me, but once a father asked where his son could study Yiddish after completing this school and I was unable to give him an answer.

After that assignment, I worked for a short time as a political instructor in a Workers' school in the settlement of Putilovka. Next I went, again as a political instructor, to the Children's Settlement for Juvenile Delinquents at the Zhelannaya station. In Zhelannaya I first became intimate with a woman. Nineteen, I was "cooking in the workers' pot." The theory of "nonlove" predominated among Komsomols; we believed that there was no such thing as love, only physiological need and a craving to perpetuate the human race. A whole literature was created that propagandized this rationalist attitude toward love. I, a true Komsomol, of course adopted these views.

I had been brought up, however, on classical literature, on ideals of delicate, self-sacrificing, pure love, and I had dreamed of meeting someone meant solely for me. Though all that idealism had been suppressed by rationalism, it had not left me, and it was precisely my romantic education that kept me from casual encounters. But in Zhelannaya I no longer restrained myself. A girl from the Stalino Komsomol cell came to town who was pure and beautiful. Perhaps she loved me. But she espoused all the physiological theories that I did. Left alone, we were drawn together. I liked her but I did not love her. After intimacy I had nothing to say to her. I felt as if I had committed some foul sin.

I had hoped to work in the children's settlement for quite a while, but soon after I'd gotten established there, the regional committee of the Komsomol appointed me to be secretary of the Selidovka rural district committee of the Komsomol. I accepted the assignment, toured the district, and was bitterly disappointed. Formalism and stagnation reigned everywhere. The majority of cells existed only on paper. The rest lacked enthusiasm—youthful seething—and accomplished little. Even in the center of the district, in the large steppe village of Selidovka, only about half of the Komsomols came to the cell meeting and there they discussed such subjects as "the procurement of eggs," "rabbit breeding," and so on.

I immersed myself in work, giving all my time to the cells and trying to inspire them. I drew upon my experience with the Borisovka cell and got the Selidovka Komsomols to do cultural work with the villagers, organize political instruction, penetrate into the economic and social-political life of the rural area, and help the village soviet and the Committee of the Village Poor. The young people I worked with had little initiative. All their energy went into their family farms, which were developing rapidly but without any help from the cities. They had little machinery. Old prerevolutionary tools were continually repaired. The people had little clothing, only what they sewed themselves from homespun materials and animal skins. During the years 1926–27, the rural economy was regressing. Under such conditions the Komsomol could not make a place for itself.

While working in Selidovka I kept up my ties with the factory Komsomol cells, succeeding in getting the factory volunteer brigades to visit us and repair farm equipment. I often went to the factory myself to extort metal for our village smithies.

During one of these trips I was summoned by the secretary of the party organization of the railroad department, a locomotive engineer named Ilya Razoryonov. Razoryonov told me that the regional committee was planning to merge all the transportation organizations of the city, the factory, and the nearby mines—sixteen subunits—into one transportation combine. The party and Komsomol committees within this combine would be on the same level as district committees. I was being named the secretary of the Komsomol committee and I should immediately make application to the party.

I was taken into the party in February 1927, one year from the time I nearly had been crushed between the freight cars. While the decision to create a transport combine was formalized, I continued to work for the Selidovka district committee. When I left there in summer 1927 to rejoin the railroad department, my friends and acquaintances were sorry to see me go and the plenum of the district committee praised my work highly.

At the first general meeting of the Komsomols of the transportation combine, a twenty-one-person committee was elected and I was named secretary.

Thinking about this time in my life, I always recall the enthusiasm and passion we Komsomols felt. We believed we were at last achieving our goals. The epoch of industrialization and mass collectivization had begun. So thundered the loudspeakers at the railway station. Everywhere, the press and radio reported, there were successes. Even in Borisovka over one-third of the farms were collectivized by 1928. My father was in charge of field-crop cultivation for the artel (association of independent laborers for collective work), and under him this area was a model of success.

Generally the late 1920s are portrayed as stormy years during which great works were accomplished. One cannot deny that Stalin was adroit at advancing ever new and ever larger tasks. The people were tantalized by the goals he set before us. I remember the tremendous enthusiasm Stalin's essay "The Year of the Great Turning Point" aroused when it appeared a few years after the time I am describing here. Grain was in acute shortage and long bread lines were appearing. Rationing was not far off; neither was famine. But Stalin's essay engrossed and heartened us. Yes, we believed, the liquidation of small-scale peasant farming was a great turning point. The soil that might give rebirth to capitalism had been destroyed. Directly ahead of us lay the route to the complete victory of socialism.

In September 1927 I married. My attitude toward love remained confused. Therefore I did not seek it. My wife, Mariya, was the fifth of six children of a family at the very bottom of the working class. Her parents had a dugout with a tiny garden in Alexandrovka. Our marriage lasted—and we were quite happy—for thirteen years. But the absence of love told. In the end we parted.

Late in the fall of 1927 Shura Fillipov, head of the Komsomol organization department, showed me an editorial in the city paper that began: "The secretary of the most important industrial organization of the Komsomol is the son of a kulak." The essay was about me. I read it and told Shura that there was no need for alarm. Borisovka was only 150 miles away. We could go there and disprove the charge in one day. I recommended, however, that we let the party committee check out the allegations.

That evening the city Komsomol committee assembled a plenum to discuss the editorial. I defended myself, calling the article a lie and inviting my comrades to investigate the charges. No one knew where the information supposedly compromising me had come from. The newspaper refused to reveal its source. I wasn't allowed to attend the entire meeting, but I later learned that only one person had recommended that I be removed from my post as secretary.

Immediately after refutations arrived from Borisovka, an editorial entitled, "The Kulak's Son and His Protectors" appeared in the same paper. Stating that a kulak could "buy" an official for a pint of vodka, the writer expressed mistrust of the information from my village. Our party committee sent this editorial to the Berdyansk party district committee and asked for a response. Back came an indignant letter giving a thorough description of my father and of me as the organizer of the Borisovka Komsomol. The newspaper replied with a new editorial, "The Position of the Transportation Party Committee in the Affairs of the Kulak's Son," in which it was declared that the party committee had taken up my defense and had deprived the Komsomols of the opportunity to decide democratically the matter of their unworthy leadership.

Meanwhile the party committee had not interfered with the city Komsomol committee's efforts to remove me. The bureau met six times on the subject; there were also three plenums of our committee. At not one of them did anyone except Ilyashevich, the propaganda head and the person who stood to replace me, support the city committee's proposal.

Spiritually fatigued, I handed in a statement of resignation from my post until the matter had been concluded. The next day I was summoned to the party committee, warned not to "play the partisan," and told that only the party could free me from my duties as secretary. I took back and destroyed my resignation, but I was at the breaking point.

The city committee heard about my resignation and adopted a resolution freeing me from my duties until the investigation was completed. Ilyashevich was named my temporary replacement.

Our committee rejected the decision of the city committee on the basis that no written resignation from me existed. The city committee threatened to dissolve our Komsomol committee, stating that it had become separated from the masses. In reply our committee called a general meeting to discuss the city Komsomol committee's decree at which complete confidence was expressed in our committee and in me. The Komsomols demanded that the case be dropped and made public their lack of confidence in Ilyashevich, asking for his removal from the bureau and the plenum of the committee.

After this the whole affair exploded. Information regarding my family was discovered to have been collected in Borisovka by party members who were biased against me. The city committee of the party established that Ilyashevich had claimed falsely to have been employed as a "worker" in his father's garment factory.

The whole thing ended with the handing out of many official reprimands. Only a brief statement appeared in the newspaper: "The accusations against the secretary of the transportation combine, comrade Grigorenko, were dropped." I never found out who had brought the charges against me. I only know that Ilyashevich had wanted very much to play the secretary, and that his friends at the newspaper must have been very willing to help him.

This affair confirms the fact that inner party and Soviet democracy did exist at that time—though both had one foot in the grave. Nowadays failure to submit to the demands of a higher authority is extremely unlikely. But in my case not only were lower-echelon citizens bold enough to disobey instructions from above; they also dared to express a lack of confidence in their superiors.

I must say that my year-long ordeal with the "son of a kulak" charge did me some good. Much later, before completing courses at the General Staff Academy, I was selected as the finalist for a mysterious appointment. One interview was left me—with a Politburo member. Sitting in an enormous office with the Central Committee official, waiting for a summons from the person who would decide my fate, the official asked me once more: "Do you have any penalties? Either in the party or the Komsomol?"

"No."

"Were you ever involved in anything compromising?"

"No," I replied, but suddenly I remembered the "son of a kulak" affair, and I blurted out the whole story to him.

The official got up and left. When he returned he told me that the comrade who was to receive me was busy. I would be summoned at a later date.

But a summons never came.

After the war I accidentally learned that I had been being considered for appointment as a military attaché in fascist Germany. I can only thank God that I did not get the post.

In August 1928 I began recruiting young workers into a rabfak—a school that would prepare them to enter higher educational institutions. The system's goal was the creation of a proletarian intelligentsia. As a party member and Komsomol, I was required to attend the school myself. I entered that fall as a third-year student.

One year later, in September 1929, the fourth year students at the rabfak were interviewed for admission to the Kharkhov Technical Institute. I resisted at first, not wanting to leave familiar territory, but finally was recruited to study construction. Once again I was departing into the unexplored. Was it for the better? Who could say? Certainly it would be different.

CHAPTER FOUR

A NEW
"POT"

Upon arrival in Kharkhov I went with the other recruits to a student club on Pushkin Street. The club commandant gave each of us a mattress and told us to find places in the auditorium.

The auditorium was overflowing with people. I pushed my mattress up against a wall and asked my neighbors where I could get something to eat. They told me that the only operating students' mess hall in Kharkhov was just a few doors down Pushkin Street.

"But," my informant added, "there is nothing there."

I did not take this literally, figuring they meant the mess hall offered little choice of food. But my neighbors were right; there was nothing there. Not even bread. I couldn't imagine why it was open.

I ate at a nearby restaurant, but the prices were unbelievable—five or six times those of the mess halls. The next day I tried again at the mess hall, waiting my turn on a long line, only to find out that there was no food. I was forced to return to the restaurant of the day before. Afterward I counted my money and decided that I would eat dinner each day in a restaurant and have bread and hot water for breakfast and lunch in the barracks. My money lasted for about a month. Then I went back to the mess hall where the meals, when they existed, were extremely unappetizing. I grew famished. More and more I wanted to return to the railway factory, but two things kept me in Kharkhov. The first was fear of being ridiculed by my fellow workers. I was certain that everyone would think I had flunked out.

The other reason was more serious. Like the factory, the institute was a "pot with a cover." When I told the party secretary that I wanted to leave the institute he replied:"Very well. You can leave. But we will keep your party membership card here." Thus the "cover to the pot" had clicked shut on me, but I never grasped how unfair it was. Instead, I felt that my voluntary entry into the party had given the party the right to control my fate as it saw fit. For me, observance of party discipline and unconditional subordination to party decisions were absolutely natural.

My submission was made easier when at some point the institute opened its own mess hall. Even though they fed us only miserly portions of repulsive food and even though we were subjected to the humiliating procedure of receiving a spoon on entry and surrendering it before leaving, at least we were eating.

Studies began. Shocked by my lack of preparedness, I decided to teach myself those sections of algebra, geometry, trigonometry, physics, and chemistry that I had not completed in the rabfak. I would continue to attend classes and take notes. Maybe some of it would stick in my head until I completed secondary school math. The task I'd assigned myself was difficult because of my living conditions. No fewer than two hundred students were living in the club auditorium. Huddled against my rolled up mattress, however, I became so absorbed in working my problems that I ceased to notice what was going on in the hall. The ability to concentrate and to retreat into myself that I developed at this time stood me in good stead later on in life—especially in the psychiatric hospital.

After a few weeks I made some friends and we began helping each other study. By spring, and after much hard work, we had managed to catch up with those who had begun the school year prepared.

Things went quite differently, however, for the majority of workers' recruits. For almost the entire school year they had done no studying and had attended classes only rarely—saying they understood nothing. Supplementary classes were organized to assist them. In the end the administration decided to create parallel groups from the workers' recruitment that would study a special program oriented to their actual level of knowledge. These groups began operation in March 1930. About twenty workers' recruits, myself among them, declined to participate on the basis that we no longer were behind. After this the party committee of the institute summoned me and told me they intended to recommend me as secretary of the Komsomol committee. I asked that I be left free of party duties for at least a year since I was a workers' recruit and had to concentrate on studying. The party denied my request, and in a general Komsomol meeting I was elected secretary, and delegate to the Eighth Congress of the Komsomol of the Ukraine. I had now become a part of the apparatus that managed the "pot."

Large-scale reorganization of the institute was taking place. The construction engineering faculty had separated from the Technological Institute to form the Kharkhov Construction Engineering Institute.

More than half of the first-year students in this new institute consisted of our special recruitment, most of whom had very little education and were unaccustomed to mental labor. The Komsomol committee instructed the newly-appointed chief of the institute's educational section, Vasya Fetisov, to work out specific proposals for dealing with these students. He performed his task excellently. The special recruitment students were cross-examined by teachers and then broken up into study groups according to educational level. The program was set up so that all the special recruitment groups would catch up with the basic course by the middle of the second year. The students would then be able to proceed as part of the overall program. The special groups would begin immediately and continue for the rest of the school year and on through the entire summer holiday (allowing only a two-week vacation). The schedule would be an intensive one: six hours of classroom, four hours of study hall under the guidance of a teacher, and two hours of homework.

It all sounded ideal, but I knew that people who were unaccustomed to mental labor would not be able to stand the strain. I was right. Students skipped classes or simply disappeared altogether. Summons to conscientiousness and enthusiasm did not alleviate the problem. Scolding, reproaches, and threats of punishment did. I informed the students that the Komsomol committee had decided not to fool around any longer. It would ask the administration to expel those who fell grossly behind. We would ask public organizations in the delinquent students' hometowns to ridicule them in comrades' courts at open workers' meetings. They would be scorned because they had wasted the state's money and had occupied places others could have filled more conscientiously.

The threat of expulsion never was carried out, but for at least half a year not one day passed during which someone from the committee bureau did not have to attend to a problem with the workers' recruitment. Finally the special groups caught up with those in the mainstream program. My participation in the educational adjustment of more than three hundred persons seems to me to have been one of the most useful pieces of work I ever did.

Almost half of every class at the institute consisted of students selected competitively from various social strata, principally the intelligentsia. The sympathies of the teachers and flaws in the educational system made it easy for these students to enter the institute. The Seven-Year Workers' Schools, the rabfaks, and the vocational schools did not provide the education necessary for entrance into higher educational institutions. Parents in the intelligentsia organized additional private preparation for their own children, who then took part in open competitions. But there was little, if any, competition, since there were always more places than there were applicants. Thus a consistent majority of students came from the intelligentsia.

Several of the party's "thousand recruits"—veteran Communists sent by the Central Committee to all of the basic higher educational institutions of the country—were enrolled in the second-year course. Also enrolled were several dozen of the "thousand recruits" sent by the trade unions, as well as a small number of rabfak graduates.

Deeply involved with our studies and with the affairs of the institute, we saw the life of the country as if at a distance. I received almost no news from Borisovka, and my wife and friends in Stalino contacted me only about personal matters. We took our information from the newspapers and radio, and everything we read or heard was processed by the institute so that it could be applied to the indoctrination of students and teachers—it was, in other words, used as fuel for our boiler. Our two years at the institute were intended to make us devout Marxist-Leninist-Stalinists, active warriors for the victory of worldwide socialism. Of all the events of political life, Stalin's essay "Dizzy from Success" made the strongest impression on us.

Neither I nor the majority of students knew of the anticollective farm insurrections. Vague rumors reached us, stories about individual "women's revolts." The women, it was said, had believed kulak stories that on collective farms all slept beneath one blanket and ate out of one pot. Angered by these tales, they had gone out to smash the collective farms. We heard that men had brought them to their senses, sometimes using their fists, and that everything had calmed down. Later I learned that the tactics of these insurrections were as follows: First the women were sent out to attack those at the collective farms; if the Communists, Komsomols, and members of the village soviets and of the Committees of the Poor attacked them, the men rallied to the women's defense. This tactic aimed at avoiding intervention by armed forces, and it was successful. In the south of the Ukraine, on the Don, and in the Kuban the collective farm structure was liquidated during a period of a few days and without the use of armed forces. Ignorant of this, we read Stalin's thoroughly false and hypocritical essay as a manifestation of brilliant political foresight. We believed that Stalin had seen what no one else had—that a large-scale pursuit of collectivization could isolate the party from the masses.

Actually the party and the peasantry had long been hostile toward each other. In order to gain time to prepare a new blow at the peasantry, Stalin was resorting to demagogy. But we did not know of the wave of insurrections and Stalin's instructions to us seemed brilliant. A few weeks later an essay entitled "A Reply to the Comrade Collective Farmers" appeared in the papers and again aroused our enthusiasm.

We believed Stalin to be a wise leader. He was warning us against rushing forward and at the same time pointing out the impossibility of retreat from our achievements. Behind his "wise" words were plans for an awful crime against the peasantry—a man-made famine.

I do not accept the justification of ignorance. We were deceived because we wanted to be deceived. We believed so strongly in communism that we were ready to accept any crime if it was glossed over with the least little bit of communist phraseology. We did not want to have a comprehensive view of current events. Confronted with something unpleasant, we compelled ourselves to believe that it was an isolated phenomenon and that on the whole the country's state of affairs was just as the party described it—in other words, just as it was supposed to be according to communist theory. This way of looking at things was more peaceful for the soul and, I admit, less dangerous than looking at the truth.

I could have seen the awful danger that hovered over our people. In the summer of 1930, before we as plenipotentiaries of the Central Committee were sent off to take in the harvest, the Secretary of the Central Committee of the Ukrainian Communist Party, Stanislav Kossior—a plump man with a big, round, shiny, shaved head—told us: "The peasant is adopting a new tactic. He refuses to reap the harvest. He wants the bread grain to die in order to choke the Soviet government with the bony hand of famine. But the enemy miscalculates. We will show him what famine is. Your task is to stop the kulak sabotage of the harvest. You must bring it in to the last grain and immediately send it off to the grain delivery point. The peasants are not working. They are counting on previously harvested grain they have hidden in pits. We must force them to open up their pits."

I remember how depressed his speech made me.

Kossior was a victim of Stalinist terror, but I had no sympathy for him. His speech at the instruction session proves him an organizer of the man-made famine. But at the time I did not see the larger picture. All my disgust was concentrated on Kossior himself. Later I blamed everything I discovered about the Ukrainian famine on Kossior. When he was arrested in 1937, I considered it just retribution for his activities against the people.

Others, however, judged the situation more accurately than I. After Kossior's speech, alone with Yasha Zasha Zlochevsky, head of organization of the Komsomol committee, I asked him what he was thinking.

He shrugged his shoulders, and his face was sad.

"I think Kossior is either a fool or a criminal!" I declared.

"What don't you like?"

"I believe he wants to organize a famine."

"Aha! So you also figured it out?" Yasha suddenly came alive.

"How could I not figure it out? I am from the countryside myself and I know very well that pits full of grain are a myth. They did exist in the early twenties, but they've long since disappeared."

"Kossior knows that himself."

"Then he is a scoundrel and an enemy of the people," I retorted.

"Not just Kossior. They are all corrupt. To them, human beings are nothing. They want power at any price." Yasha hurled word after word as if they were blows. His face grew angry, and his eyes gleamed. His vehemence encouraged me.

"I must immediately write to Stalin about the instructional session."

"No," he said quietly but firmly. "Do you really think Stalin is any better than the rest? Let's do our own work honestly. Let's try to help the peasants realize that they cannot wage war against the government. They have to harvest the grain, but they must find a way to keep some for themselves."

I returned to the institute and called on Topchiyev, the party secretary. I told him about the instruction session, ending my account of the meeting by saying, "I want to write to Stalin about it."

He stared at his desk for several minutes and then said, "My advice is not to be too hasty. You will be going to the countryside yourself and there you will see the reality of the situation. When you return, we will talk about whether you should write Stalin."

I had to agree with Topchiyev. I told him that I had already talked with Yasha, who had also advised me against writing but hadn't been able to convince me.

"Too bad he didn't!" Topchiyev answered. "Listen to Yasha. He's very bright. And don't let it bother you that he's a former Trotskyite. It's not important what he was, but what he is."

I was not thinking of Yasha's past. Topchiyev was wrong. Of course I had heard about Yasha's Trotskyism. He had spoken of it during the election. When Yasha and I were alone at a later date I asked him whether his renunciation of Trotskyism was a tactic or a real change of mind.

He answered me at some length. "I find it impossible to do anything insincerely. I became disillusioned with Trotskyism and I will never return to it, either organizationally or ideologically. Trotskyism is not distinct from Leninism or from the present ideology and tactic of the party. But I learned a great deal from the Trotskyites' analysis of bureaucracy and of the dictatorship of the party apparatus. Thanks to this I am able to see those distortions which the bureaucracy and the party apparatus are forcing on the party, particularly by the struggle for powerful positions. We who support the basic ideology, strategy, and tactics of the party must act honestly. We must keep the self-seeking party officials and bureaucrats from stifling the party and the people, but we must not stick our necks out by making complaints to the top. We might be mistaken for those who want cushy jobs—and then we'll be crushed."

Yasha continued to keep secret his grievances against the bureaucrats, but this didn't save him. In the late fifties I encountered Nikolai Lelichenko, then a minister in the Ukraine. He told me that Yasha had been arrested as an enemy of the people and shot in 1937. I could have learned much more from Yasha during the time when we were comrades, if I had wished to think things through. During those days there were many things that needed to be thought through. In the spring of 1930 I was in Borisovka where my oldest son, then a year-and-a-half old, was seriously ill. The doctors had recommended that we take him to the countryside where he could get milk, fresh vegetables, and fruit. I had also been summoned to Borisovka by a letter from Mitya Yakovenko, chairman of the collective farm, who wrote that my father had resigned from the farm.

What had happened? The Borisovka collective farm had been organized in 1924 on a strictly voluntary basis, and since then had been very successful. During the time when collective farms everywhere were being destroyed, the Borisovka farmers did not rebel. But when mass collectivization began, the issuing of food products in return for "labor days" came to an end. In desperation the adult men tried to earn something outside the collective farm and sent adolescents and women to work their places in the fields.

My father analyzed what was taking place in agriculture and predicted a sad future in which I did not want to believe, but I had nothing with which to refute his predictions. He based his arguments on facts, one of which was that harvest yields were falling catastrophically. I protested, citing statistics I'd read in the newspaper. But he ridiculed my objections with typically Ukrainian humor.

"I don't know, I don't know. Maybe they have learned how to grow grain on asphalt in Moscow, but here we don't have any grain."

My father explained that the people had lost interest in the results of labor and that initiative was dying off. For nothing, he said, a man could be tried in court. And the people who were tried were not those who did nothing, but those who tried to improve things and who thereby conflicted with stupid directives. A case had been brought against him for sowing the black fallow before receiving instructions to do so. It had been dropped after enormous protest, but the fact that this violation resulted in an extremely large harvest mattered to no one.

He spoke with indignation. "Who needs Moscow to give a schedule for sowing? Our collective farm was harmonious and worked well, while those nearby barely functioned at all. The local government filled its quotas with our grain and we were left nothing. Who is going to work after that? The system makes the laborer responsible for everything. If you don't carry out an idiotic directive you will be taken to court; if you do carry it out and thereby cause great harm you'll be held responsible for the loss to the state."

We had many more conversations and in all I suffered total defeat. Yet I did not turn away from communism. Instead, the facts angered me and compelled me to search for refutations. But my father's words were so convincing that they stayed deep within my mind and, with the passage of time and the appearance of new facts, surfaced and made more sense than ever.

In 1963 I wrote a leaflet in response to the Central Committee's letter on the necessity of economizing bread grains. The leaflet, called *Why is There No Bread?*, exploded like a bomb in the Central Committee and the KGB. The search for its author began the portrayal of me as an "anti-soviet type." And yet Brezhnev used this leaflet in preparing his report on agriculture to the March Plenary Meeting of the Central Committee in 1965. I deserve no credit for its creation. It was written on the basis of conversations I'd had with my father.

When I did travel into the countryside as a plenipotentiary of the Central Committee, what I saw exceeded my worst expectations. Arkhangelka, an enormous steppe village consisting of more than 2,000 farmhouses, was dead during the height of the harvest season. Eight men worked one thresher for one shift daily. The remaining workers—men, women, and young people—sat around or lay in the shade. When I tried to start conversations people replied slowly and with total indifference.

If I told them that the grain was falling from the wheat stalks and perishing they would reply, "Of course, it will perish."

I could not break through that apathy. Often I spoke to people and the only answer they gave was silence. I cannot believe that the loss of bread grains was of no consequence to the peasants. Their feelings must have been terribly strong for them to go to the extreme of leaving the grain in the fields. Even today I am convinced that no one directed their action. In essence it was not a protest. The people were so repulsed by the forced collectivization of farms that they were consumed by apathy.

However, I blamed all this on the peasantry's lack of conscientiousness and undertook a one-man struggle against the people's indifference. And like a stone thrown into a lake with a smooth surface, I made a small difference. During the month and a half I spent in Arkhangelka the tempo of threshing nearly tripled. The peasants began to harvest the corn and the sunflower seeds and to do the fall plowing. This was not all because of me. People had simply gotten bored with sitting around doing nothing and slowly went back to work. I did not feel that I succeeded in making contact with them. They listened to me politely but did not accept my arguments.

As soon as I returned from Arkhangelka the Central Committee made me plenipotentiary of the Komsomol of the Ukraine and sent me to the Donbass.

In order to increase the output of coal, which the country badly needed, the authorities did not deliver machinery or improve organization. Instead, they sent plenipotentiaries. Two of us went to the Young Commune Member coal combine. My companion was Vladimirsky, the People's Commissar of Urban Services and an old Communist. Neither he nor I had ever worked in a mine. Obviously, we could not do much good. But the bureaucrats were satisfied just knowing plenipotentiaries were at the mine. I tried with all my heart to accomplish something: I went down into the mine, I visited the Komsomol members in the drifts, I made speeches and wrote reports.

The thing I remember most about the whole trip is that our suitcases were stolen as we were leaving the mines. When I realized our luggage was gone, I jumped off the train at the Izyum station and pursued the thieves with a Smith Wesson revolver (at that time Communists were permitted to bear arms), captured them, and turned them over to the railway police. Then I caught up with Vladimirsky, who was waiting for me at Lozovaya station.

Railway travel was a real torment. The crowded trains did not run on schedule. Swarms of people boarded at each station. It seemed as if the whole country was on the move. Tattered, starving people loaded down with sacks, suitcases, and trunks all were rushing off somewhere, riding the trains, running beside them, or sitting at stations and waiting. Thievery was constant. One Komsomol member I traveled with had his shoes stolen when he took them off at night to go to sleep.

In 1930–31 the Soviet Union had a totally ruined agricultural system and a disorganized transport system. Yet people like me continued to be hypnotized by the old ideals and the new construction projects. The construction projects were not as brilliant as the newspapers described them to be. I saw many negative things, but I was unable to generalize from what I had seen. In 1930, as a trainee in construction work in Stalino, I was told to complete the construction of a bath-passage at the factory. Upon surveying the situation I saw that what had been built in no way resembled the blueprints. The construction superintendent simply had not been able to read the plans. I had to redo the entire job. The next year I saw the same sort of thing but on a much bigger scale. I was sent to receive on-the-job training in the "hasholder" section at the Yenakiyevo Chemical Factory. As with the rest of the factory, the purpose of this section was a secret. Construction of machine foundations, each the size of a four- or five-story building, was underway. Nine had been completed and several others were ready for the pouring of concrete. I compared what had been built with the blueprints and immediately noted many discrepancies. In order to draw a final conclusion I had to inspect the installation blueprints, but those in charge refused to give them to me because they were secret. Infuriated, I resigned my appointment. When summoned by the chief engineer, I easily proved to him that I had to see those blueprints, and I got them. Again I noted discrepencies. Those foundations and cement molds that had been built would have to be changed.

While working on this construction project I communicated for the last time with my Uncle Alexander, who now worked at the Yenakiyevo Stock-Raising State Farm. His dead wife's elder sister cared for his children. They barely eked out a living. They had no beds, no clothes, and little bread. I went to see him several times, always bringing my bread ration. Time had passed and we were able to abandon the sharp, irritated tone of our final conversations in Borisovka. My uncle spoke softly, thoughtfully, slowly. Even though I did not agree with him, I could not effectively disagree with him, and for the most part I just listened.

He spoke of his state farm as a shining example of the total economic mismanagement of the Soviet system. He showed me how the pigs were being maintained and said, "The miracle is that they are not dead yet. But they will be soon. And the director, the one responsible for this state of affairs, will not be penalized. 'Kulak supporters' like me will be called enemies and there will be no way we can prove our innocence."

I advised him to leave the farm. To this he replied, "Then they will surely arrest me, saying that I wanted to hide from punishment. At least while I am here I can save my pigs and fight with the director. However, not much can be gained from fighting. They all protect each other. I was right when I said 'They are not managers. We are going to go through a lot of grief with them.' Everything has proven this to me."

Though I could not agree with his conclusions, there was little I could say to him in reply.

Six months later I learned that my uncle had been arrested, and I rushed to find him, following his prison trail from Uenakiyevo to Stalino, Kharkhov, Moscow, and, finally Omsk. He had been arrested for economic sabotage and classified as anti-Soviet. In Omsk he was charged with being an "owner of gold." He died, I was informed in Omsk, of a heart attack. But if he had been accused of possessing gold, he must have been killed during questioning.

Many years later when I underwent psychiatric treatment in the Serbsky Institute, I met a criminal who had been imprisoned for thirty-four years. He remembered more vividly than anything else the Chekists' treatment of the owners of gold. Those who had no gold or those who did not confess were beaten with felt boots filled with bricks until they died. Those who confessed were granted mercy until they had given up their gold. Then the Chekists accused them of not having given up all of it and began to beat them again. If they now gave up more gold, the whole cycle was repeated. In the end each person reached the point where he had nothing more to give and was beaten to death. And that, no doubt, is how my Uncle Alexander died.

In December 1931, while a student at the Military Engineering Academy

in Leningrad, I received a telegram: "Come immediately father seriously ill."
I was able to get travel orders for a brief leave and I departed by train that
day, taking with me a ration certificate. When the train reached Belgorod I
was alarmed to see the station packed with half-dressed adults and children
who literally besieged the railway car, chanting: "Bread, bread, bread!" The
further our train traveled into the Ukraine the more starving people I saw.
When I arrived at Berdyansk, I immediately dashed to the military registration
and enlistment office to exchange my ration certificate for food. I was sent to
the military commissar, who looked at me with astonishment and said, "You
must be out of your mind. You came from Leningrad with a piece of paper
instead of food! I don't even give my own people rations and you want me
to give them to you . . ."

After a lengthy exchange he finally gave me permission to redeem my student's ration certificate. I was entitled to a two weeks' supply of white bread,
butter, fish, caviar, confectionary goods, candies, and cigarettes.

I was not surprised by what I saw when I reached Borisovka. The village
streets were empty and the few people I encountered did not even respond
to my greetings—something unheard of in a Ukrainian village. My father was
at home. When I walked in he got to his feet with great difficulty, suffering
from edema caused by a lack of protein. He was starving. The only edible thing
in the house was a small pumpkin.

If I wanted to save my father, I had to get him out of there. I told him that
I was going to the collective farm to borrow a cart and that meanwhile he
should get himself together so that we could load up immediately and leave.

There was just one man in the collective farm office, Kolya Sezonenko, the
first secretary of our Borisovka Komsomol cell, now the collective farm bookkeeper. He sat behind a desk, the top of which was completely empty except
for an ancient abacus. His head was bent slightly forward and he stared at
the desk top.

"How are you, Kolya!" I greeted him.

"Ah, Petro!" he replied, without lifting his eyes to look at me and not moving at all. "So you've come to get your father? Thank you for not forgetting
him. Take him away from here. Maybe you can save him. You won't save the
rest of us."

He continued to sit there, completely motionless, speaking in an even, apa-
thetic voice.

"I need a cart, Kolya."

"Go to the stable for it. Tell them I ordered it. They will do as you tell them
anyway."

I moved closer to bid him farewell.

"Thank you, Kolya. I knew nothing of your misfortune and came without
food. But as soon as I get back to Leningrad I will write to the Central Com-

mittee. I think they will help you. So try to keep going a bit longer."

I spoke with complete sincerity; I believed that the party would help. But Kolya replied, "What do you mean? You think they don't know? They know very well. Our leaders created this famine. Last year they drove us almost to starvation." He went on to tell the same story my father had told me earlier about the unfair and barbarous acquisition of grain.

The workers in the stable quickly readied a cart for me. On the way back to my father's house I saw two corpses on the street. When I wrote my letter to the Central Committee, I attached to it a piece of the awful bread I had received from the Berdyansk military registration and enlistment office. I described the founding of the Borisovka collective farm in 1924, its development, and its spearhead role in the organization of mass collectivization. I wrote about what a harmonious, hard-working, well-organized collective it had been and how, thanks in particular to these qualities, it was now left without grain, having delivered all of it for the fulfillment of the district plan. I sent this letter via the political section of the Military Engineering Academy. In two months a reply arrived: "The facts have been confirmed. Those to blame for the faulty organization of grain procurements have been punished. The Poor Peasant Collective Farm has been given foodstuffs."

My father received letters confirming this report. I celebrated. The Central Committee had responded to my warning; justice had been done. How could I have known that while it gave food assistance to one collective farm in the spring of 1932, the Central Committee was preparing a mass famine for the collective farms of the Ukraine, of the Don, of the Kuban, of Orenburg and of a number of other areas for the winter of 1932–33.

The Central Committee's reply concluded with a postscript in which I took great pride for many years: "The Central Committee notes that comrade Grigorenko acted as a mature Communist. On the basis of a particular fact he proved capable of drawing profound conclusions in a party spirit and of reporting them to the Central Committee."

Years passed. The Twentieth Party Congress ended. My views had progressed far from my naïve communist idealism of the 1930s. I had learned how the peasantry's resistance to the collective farms had been broken with the help of a man-made famine. Remembering that postscript, I could not stop wondering what they had been praising me for. After all, I had exposed a plan they wanted kept secret.

I thought long and hard and finally I understood. I had presented the famine in the Poor Peasant Collective Farm as an isolated situation caused by the incorrect actions of the district chiefs and, most important, by the surrounding collective farms' sabotage of the grain harvest. This was an advantageous interpretation of events for the Central Committee. It could be used at instruction meetings to depict starvation as a means of eradicating sabotage. So, in an overall sense, my complaint helped in the preparation of the famine.

I am often asked by others, and I ask myself, What would have happened if I had grasped everything during those years of famine? There is only one honest answer: If I had understood then these memoirs would not exist now. I was never able to keep silence. I sought an explanation for everything that made a negative impression on me. Since my search for explanations was always based in Marxism-Leninism, the answers which I came up with were most often orthodox Marxist-Leninist. In short, the Good Lord had not endowed me with too great a talent for profound analysis and by this token he saved me from perishing early.

In late 1930 the institute underwent major reorganization and my department was transferred to the Kiev Highway Institute. I switched my field of study to construction superintendancy, remaining at the Kharkhov Institute until late 1931, when I entered the Military Technical Academy in Leningrad as a student. By this transfer I avoided great danger.

I had risen to such a high position in the Central Committee of the Komsomol of the Ukraine that I might have reached the very top of that apparatus by 1936–37, which would have meant certain arrest and death—if not from the beatings and the bullets of the Chekists, then in the Gulag Archipelago.

I immersed myself in the life of the Academy and became a career military officer.

CHAPTER FIVE

A
PROFESSION
FOR
LIFE

T he class with which I entered the Military Technical Academy in the fall of 1931 nearly doubled the school's student body. But in spring 1932 the government decided to dissolve the academy and draw upon its students and resources to create a series of specialized institutions—academies for artillery, armored warfare (called chemical warfare defense)—for the purpose of deception. I joined the Military Engineering Academy. Its faculty was drawn from the Military Technical Academy and from the Advanced Construction Engineering School (VISU), the oldest Russian higher educational institution for advanced construction engineering. The new academy was to be located in Moscow in the VISU buildings and laboratories. A small settlement of prefab houses was hastily built on the Highway of the Enthusiasts near the searchlight factory. The VISU teaching staff and students, except for those who were sent to other institutions, received appointments and were admitted into the newly established academy.

All of this reorganization affected the Leningrad group very little. Even before we moved to Moscow, our evolving academy had branches in command, defense construction, nondefense construction, airfield construction, naval construction, construction machinery, and electrotechnics. Each branch had its own faculty, and, except for the command faculty, at the beginning of the new school year each received reinforcements from VISU graduates. We completed the school year in Leningrad, were given summer assignments in practical topographic work, and told to report to our new place of service in Moscow—5 Pokrovsky Boulevard—on October 1, 1932.

Looking back, I can see that the reorganizational activities spared me much unpleasantness. Because of them I could not travel during my vacation, and I was not forced to see the awful famine descending again on my native Borisovka and the region around it. I did my topographical training in the area of Pargolovo-Yukki, near Leningrad. During June and July I oversaw the completion of a complex of nine fortifications connected by underground passages, or posterns, in the Mogilev-Podolsky district. This front line straddled the high shore of a bend in the Dniester River for more than a kilometer. Coordinated fire held the river surface and the opposite shore under heavy artillery and machine gun exposure. I was absorbed in my work, spending whole days and sometimes nights at the construction site, dozing off for short periods in one of the many pockets of the posterns.

More than anything I wanted to complete my assignment successfully. This was more complicated than it might seem.

When I arrived at the complex, I found evidence of sloth and neglect. Doors would not close. Not one mechanism worked. Everything had rusted over, and nothing had been closed up or hermetically sealed. The buildings consisted of reinforced concrete and rooms unsuitable even for the storage of vegetables. Repair work was needed. Replacements were needed for parts that had broken and then lost or returned to enormous warehouses from which they could not be extricated except by a special expedition. Finding the materials and repairing the damage was the basis of my job for the two months after my arrival. Two well-trained men spent all their time searching for parts in warehouses and central shops. I had a turning lathe and a portable smithy and metalworking shop installed. When I finished my tour of duty at the end of July all of the various mechanisms worked. The doors and embrasures were carefully sealed. The white, level walls of the posterns gleamed under bright electric lights. Stairway cases and other metallic parts were cleaned of rust and painted. The underground power plant operated smoothly.

Walking about the complex before leaving it, I looked at each machine gun and artillery piece, aimed each at the opposite shore, and envisioned my firing line and our attacking army. Fortifications were to have reliably shielded the deployment of assault groups and repelled any attempts by the enemy to break up the deployment. When the army attacked, the fortified areas were to have supported the troops with firepower. Instead, our western fortified areas did not fulfill any of these tasks. *They were blown up without having fired even once at the enemy.*

I do not know how future historians will explain this crime against our people. Contemporary historians ignore it. I cannot offer an explanation myself. The Soviet government squeezed billions of rubles (by my calculations not less than 120 billion) out of the people to construct impregnable fortifications along the entire western boundary from the Baltic Sea to the Black Sea. Then, right before the war in the spring of 1941, powerful explosions thundered along the entire 1,200-kilometer length of these fortifications. On Stalin's personal orders reinforced concrete caponiers and semicaponiers, fortifications with one, two, or three embrasures, command and observation posts—tens of thousands of permanent fortifications—were blown into the air. No better gift could have been given to Hitler's Barbarossa plan.

How could this have taken place? Stalin's justification must be that he was insane. But how are we to justify and explain the actions of those thousands of people who prepared and delivered the explosives, who placed them, who laid out the wires and closed the switches, all under the eyes of the "great helmsman" and those many others who understood the criminality of their actions. No one took it upon himself to say that even if these fortifications were not needed today, they might be tomorrow, and therefore should not be expended so mindlessly. When I left Mogilev-Podolsky I could not even have imagined the fate that awaited the complex. I had worked so hard and was proud of all I'd accomplished.

I went next on a military observation trip to the Far East. We did not undertake standard military observation but spent our time more as if we were on a field trip. The eight-man group traveled along the border from Blagoveshchensk to Vladivostok, spending some time on "Russian" Island, where a naval defense area was being constructed. My work had taught me to look at nature from a point of view quite different from that of most people. I later described the Far East in great detail, with the help of three officers who worked under my guidance, in *The Manchurian Military Theatre,* which was published in a classified edition in 1942.

It is difficult for me to talk about the Far East with anyone who has not been there, both because of my military point of view and because many years passed between my two trips there, during which time things changed very much indeed. From my first visit I remember particularly the abandoned villages of the Amur and Ussuri cossacks. They puzzled me. Everywhere I saw signs of hurried departures. Doors were left open. Homeless cows, horses, sheep, and dogs wandered the streets. Household goods and utensils were scattered about yards, and farming implements were left in the fields. Why had these people left their native land—the homeland of the workers of the whole world—to go to Manchuria, which seemed to me a backward, half-savage country? I thought about this constantly and besieged our guide, the staff commander of the Third Collective Farm Corps, with questions. "How did they leave?"

"Very simply," he replied. "When the Amur and the Ussuri froze over they crossed on the ice, taking most of their possessions and livestock. I did not see the migration myself, of course. Our corps was sent here after the cossacks had left. The border guards told me about it."

"Why didn't the border guards stop them?"

"Just try and stop them! They are cossacks. They have been taught to fight, and they were armed. It is hundreds of kilometers from one border post to another. The cossacks knew exactly where the guards were located. They blockaded their posts. The guards were more concerned about getting hurt than they were about the cossacks leaving."

"Maybe those on the other side purposely frightened them, forced them to leave," I said, grabbing at every chance to attribute their departure to someone else's evil will and not to their own desires. My guide promptly squelched this possibility.

"Who over there would frighten them? They sent emissaries over and asked for help themselves."

"How could they throw away all the achievements of the revolution and go to an alien land?" I asked.

"What kind of achievements were here for them? Total liquidation of the kulaks was underway, with exile to the north. Would any free cossack stand for that? They left town, hid, and then traveled to Manchuria. When Stalin's essay 'Dizzy from Success' appeared, things eased up a bit. Then quietly the squeeze began once more. Again some escaped to Manchuria. News filtered back that those who had escaped had gotten land and were living just as in the old times. Meanwhile the grain requisitions here were terrible and famine seemed imminent. So, having come to an agreement with their Manchurian countrymen to be met on the other shore and to be helped in case of trouble the entire cossack people crossed on the ice in one night, abandoning whatever they could not take."

I could not accept this explanation, because it laid blame on the Soviet government. I did not ask any more questions.

From the Far East I went straight to Moscow to look for an apartment and then fetched my family from Leningrad. Studies began. Though a rationing system had been imposed, life in Moscow was relatively comfortable. As seen through the newspapers, life in the rest of the country was also all right.

During my absence the academy had developed rapidly. Instead of calm, empty classrooms and silent libraries and laboratories, instead of erect, strict, and, for the most part, elderly military men, I found hundreds of overcrowded classrooms and corridors, and youthful students, all wearing their military uniforms awkwardly and, like students everywhere, making a tremendous racket.

My final two years of study passed swiftly. I will recount the one episode from those days that influenced my entire military career.

In 1933 the Central Committee set itself the task of readying all fortified areas for battle. There were not enough technical supervisors in the fortified areas and, as I saw subsequently, most lacked experience. Many construction superintendents were civilians who knew nothing of ballistics or the characteristics of weapons. Nor did they understand chemical warfare defense. Some quit their jobs, but those who did not did nothing. People preferred receiving administrative penalties for nonfulfillment of plans than serving time in prison for sabotage—for incorrect installation of weapons and equipment.

In early spring the academy received instructions to send the Fortification Faculty's students to the fortified areas. I headed a group of six. On arrival, each group was sent to a sector, mine to Pleshchenitsy. Tseluiko, the chief of the sector and a civilian who I doubt had had even a secondary education, sent me to the Saladzinevichi subsector as deputy chief. My five companions remained with him. Within the sector Saladzinevichi was as far from Pleshchenitsy as was possible. For a large part of the year it was cut off from the sector administration because the way was impassable.

Saladzinevichi covered more than half of the total sector. It was headed by a civilian construction technician named Vasilyev, who was absolutely independent. Tseluiko never visited him. Telephone communication between Saladzinevichi and Minsk (where the administration of the whole fortified area was located), was better than between Saladzinevichi and Pleshchenitsky. Vasilyev reported directly to the administration in Minsk. Tseluiko reported only for the remaining lesser portion of the sector. Despite the division the supply system for the entire sector was unified. This created manifold difficulties for Vasilyev, for in distributing supplies, Tseluiko first took into account the interests of his own portion. His self-interest kept him from stationing trainees properly.

Saladzinevichi was a tiny village consisting of eight half-ruined huts, a neglected supply yard, a kitchen-mess hall, a stable, and an office—all half-abandoned, all bearing the imprint of mismanagement. Only the managers' small house and the barracks were more or less decently looked after. I arrived at the subsector on an overcast day in early March 1933. It was drizzling and foggy and the mud beneath my feet filled out the sad picture and depressed me. My meeting with Vasilyev did little to make me feel better, though he seemed pleased at my arrival. I spent the day talking with him and his wife.

That evening I went with Vasilyev to review the work reports of the returning brigadiers, who were supposed to turn in summaries of work completed. From time to time Vasilyev would remark:"You didn't do that. I know very well. That was already done." He would correct inaccuracies in the reports. None of the brigadiers tried to refute him, but he engaged them in a sort of back-and-forth: "Didn't you do the doors? I listed them in the work order." The brigadier would confess that he had forgotten having done them and Vasilyev would make a notation on the report.

I was astonished that he had such detailed information about work done as far as twelve kilometers away, and I asked him about it when we returned home.

He laughed. "I've been doing this job for two years. The question is not whether they did or didn't work, but that soldiers have to be fed and clothed. We have no civilian help at all, unless you count me, the stable man, and my wife, who is listed as a secretary. The work is entirely on the shoulders of the construction batallion. One hundred and fifty men are conscripted for three months. Then a second group replaces them. And then a third. Then for three months no one works. After that a new cycle begins. This is the third cycle I've been through. I took enough hard knocks from the first two, and I am not about to make any more mistakes. Mistakes in what, you might ask? It's not a question of whether I leave something out of the report or write in something extra. No one can check that out. If you took all the reports from the beginning and totaled them up you would find that every bolt had been tightened at least ten or twenty times. What I concern myself with is that the soldier earns enough for his food, his barracks maintenance, and his uniform, and that he should receive a few rubles at the end of the three months—no more."

The next day I went with Vasilyev to the morning duty detail with the brigadiers, during which Vasilyev wrote out their assignments. Once again I was astounded. He filled in the blanks without looking at any notes. When I called his attention to this, again he laughed. "That's all right. In a few days you'll be able to fill out the duty detail sheets no worse than I do." In fact, I never learned to do so.

Three days after arriving I asked Vasilyev to let me have his horse so I could familiarize myself with the subsector. I spent about two weeks studying in detail the incomplete features of each point in the firing line, soon discovering that in reality no one was doing anything. Each morning the brigades marched to the work locations assigned them during the duty detail. If the sites were not distant—say, two or three kilometers away—they might work a bit. If the site was farther away, they just marched there, turned around, and marched back.

Upon completing my tour of the subsector I reported to Vasilyev and placed in front of him a notebook in which the incomplete features of each fortification were described. His friendly attitude vanished, and he pushed the notebook aside and declared in an official tone of voice, "I am the commander of the subsector. Everything will continue being done just as it has been till now." I tried to restore the good humor of our former conversations, but to no avail. I tried to convince him that it was necessary to make serious changes or risk never completing our work. He refused to admit I might be right.

Finally I said, "I guess we will not be able to go on working together." I resolved to call Zagorulko, the chief of engineers of the Minsk fortified area.

Vasilyev helped me make the phone connection. I reported the problems I had seen and the solutions I proposed and asked to be transferred elsewhere in light of Vasilyev's opposition to any change. Zagorulko told me to wait in Vasilyev's office for a decision.

An hour and a half later a telephonogram arrived:

"Vasilyev is ordered to report immediately to the administration of the chief of engineers in Minsk to be assigned a new post. The subsector command is to be turned over to student officer Grigorenko. Zagorulko."

I took the telephonogram to Vasilyev at his apartment, thinking that maybe he'd be less harsh with me with his wife present.

To my immense surprise, however, after he had read the message he ran to the next room, shouting with joy, "Hurrah, we are going to Minsk. Hurrah!" Then he rushed back in and hugged me.

"Thank you. If you only knew how you have saved me. I'll never forget it! What am I supposed to turn over to you? Let's get on with it. I want to get out of here as soon as I can!" They left that same day.

When I went out to the duty detail the next morning I thought I knew exactly what had to be done. I would give actual assignments to the brigadiers and for once work would be accomplished. But in the first place more than two hours of working time was spent writing out assignments. In the second place, I had no conception of what a realistic assignment was. And, how was I to find the necessary parts and materials that had been procured and then lost? Most importantly, how could I supervise eighteen brigades?

I called Zagorulko and asked him to order Tseluiko to send me one of the student officers as an assistant. He sent Alyosha Glushko. I was glad to have help, but I had begun to realize that the construction batallion members were ordinary peasants who had no work skills and who had not the slightest idea of how to carry out an assignment. How could such men fulfill the delicate task of lining up a machine gun stand?

The phrase "assembly line method" occurred to me. A whole series of identical, incomplete tasks existed at each point in the firing line. All gun stands and doors had to be fitted, embrasures had to be hermetically sealed, and so on.

Instead of having identical brigades performing all tasks at a given fortification, I would create specialized groups, each of which would carry out only one task. The men would be able to perfect their skills and achieve high indices of work performance. I even worked out a special work schedule so that the groups did not converge on the same fortification at the same moment and get in each other's way.

As soon as this system was implemented we met only in the evening to verify the next day's work schedule. Morning duty details were abolished. The groups went to work right after breakfast. In addition to the work schedule,

which I revised daily with the men, I prepared a different version for myself
that was approximately one month behind the current work schedule, and a
third version for the higher ups that was a half-month behind mine. When
I sent this schedule off to the Administration of the Chief of Engineers for
approval, it landed like a bomb. No one before me had planned in such detail
or given such firm completion dates. In other words, no one had taken personal
responsibility for the achievements or failures of his sector. By setting a day
for the subsector to be in a state of complete battle readiness with no unfinished
aspects whatsoever I had broken with tradition. Pomerantsev, commander of
the fortified area, decided to take a look at the odd man who in his eyes had
hung a noose around his own neck.

Pomerantsev's automobile got stuck on the road between Pleshchenitsy and
Saladzinevichi, so he abandoned it and continued on foot—not to the subsector
headquarters but along the firing line. After receiving a report on his presence
in the subsector area I went to meet him and accompanied him on the rest
of his inspection. He seemed dissatisfied and picked at things and grumbled.
Only once did he speak in a businesslike way. While proceeding past one of
the fortifications, Bugulma, he asked me what I was going to do about it. I
told him that I didn't know, and that I would have to think about it. "What's
there to think about?" he asked. "It's half under water and its line of fire is
straight into a hillock. No doubt we are going to have to put charges under
each of its corners and blow it into the air."

How prophetic was the phrase "into the air," regarding not just Bugulma
but the entire Minsk fortified area and all of the other western fortified areas.

When we returned to the subsector headquarters that evening, Pomerantsev
warned me he would study the work schedule the next day. In the morning
he was less irritable, but as he examined the work schedule he kept muttering
agitatedly, "Drawings . . . drawings. . . . We've learned how to draw but not
how to fulfill a plan. I've been listening to promises for more than two years,
but the subsector is still not ready for battle. It's time for someone to bear
responsibility for actual completion dates. I'm going to approve your work
schedule. And I'm going to remember the completion date you set yourself.
We'll see what drawings you show me when that time comes. And just bear
in mind that I'll not let you return to the academy until you have finished.
I'll let you fall a month behind this schedule—no more. As soon as you're
done, send me a telegram. I promise you I'm going to personally inspect all
your work."

He signed the work schedule and left. I did not hurry to send the telegram.
I wanted to use the time I had saved on the different schedules to try and resur-
rect Bugulma. The fortification had accidentally been set too low. Pomerantsev
had said the lines of fire were blocked by small hillocks. In order to give the
embrasures a normal fire field, 5,000 cubic meters of earth would have to be

moved 100 meters. Bugulma's being set low also caused constant flooding of the battle compartments and filter well. To alleviate this problem the level of ground water had to be lowered at least 2.5 meters. After all the other fortifications had been brought to a state of battle readiness, I set the entire batallion to work on Bugulma.

The removal and disposal of earth would have been easy with modern equipment, but we had not even the simplest bulldozer. Everything was done by hand, with spade and wheelbarrow. Each worker had to move about fifty cubic meters of earth, an immense amount of work. But we dealt beautifully with removing the obstructing hillocks, carrying away the turf first, then the earth, and putting it into a series of pits, ditches, and depressions that we then carefully sodded over. The once-obstructing hillocks disappeared. All embrasures had an open line of fire covering the entire sector at maximum distance. And once the camouflage work was completed, Bugulma itself disappeared.

Our efforts to lower the water table were another story. No matter how we tried we could not get it to drop by more than one meter and four centimeters. This left the battle compartments dry, but the filter and ventilation well—the necessity for which had been realized only after concrete had been poured at all the fortification points—was still flooded. No one had ever taken responsibility for this extremely poor planning that we now had to overcome. Without filtered ventilation, the fortification point would be useless in chemical warfare.

We had no place to put the filters and were even considering putting them on top of the concrete when Alyosha Glushko proposed moving them into an individual battle compartment. I gave orders for the filter system to be taken to Bugulma and set up in the corner of one such compartment.

Upon inspection the filters did not seem as if they would obstruct fire. I ordered a machine gun brought in and set up. We fired it. The filters did not hinder its operation. I ordered them permanently installed.

Only then did I telegram Pomerantsev. A few days later troops arrived at all points along the firing line and Pomerantsev himself showed up. Verification of battle readiness began with Pomerantsev visiting most of the fortifications. The rest were checked out by members of his staff. Though he kept trying to find flaws, he was clearly pleased. At about noon our route took us past Bugulma and Pomerantsev, who was exhausted, had his driver stop the car. Pomerantsev got out, looked around him and asked with astonishment, "Where is Bugulma?"

"Right here," I replied, pointing to a spot about one hundred fifty meters from us.

"Why did you work on it? There was no point. It can only fire under its own nose."

We approached the fortification, and as soon as Pomerantsev entered the first battle compartment he shouted, "Dry!" He then checked out the fields of fire and at each embrasure shouted, "Marvelous! At full distance across the entire sector!"

Almost immediately he realized that he had failed to express his appreciation as commander, and he embraced me and cried, "Thank you!"

"Don't thank me too much, comrade Commander," I said. "This is the work of Glushko and Khazanov."

"I'll not forget either you or them," he said and went to the door, where he noticed the flooded well and remarked, "Too bad you could not dry it out. Such a magnificent fortification and no filtered ventilation."

I told him that we had installed the filters elsewhere and that I wanted him to inspect them and give me his opinion. We returned to the third battle compartment. He had not noticed the filters when we'd been in there before. He looked them over, checked out the system of vent and exhaust, and worked with the machine gun. Then he turned to me and said, "Do you understand what you have done? This fortification is now the best in the Soviet Union. At present all others are not ready from the point of view of chemical warfare defense capabilities. Filters outside the fortification are worthless. I know that you wish to leave Saladzinevichi. But I am not going to let you go until all filters from outside wells are moved into the battle compartments. Report on completion of your assignment and at that point I will consider letting you go."

I completed my work with the filters but again I did not depart. An order liquidating my subsector arrived. I was given charge of the entire sector and told to check out all the installations and to put them in operation. I did not leave for Moscow until October. My student training had lasted nearly eight months.

I later learned that Pomerantsev had ordered that the filters be taken inside throughout the fortified area. He had also sent a report on and some drawings of our achievements to the Chief Military Engineering Administration and to the General Staff in Moscow.

Upon my departure I was given eight times the monthly wage of the sector chief and a recommendation such as I never again received. It made me out to be a genius, if not more. I returned to the academy and submitted to the Faculty of Work Organization all three versions of the work schedules, a detailed account of the organization of work on an assembly line basis, an account of the organization of supplies and a verification of execution of the work schedule. The documents were transformed into educational materials. (The last time I visited the Academy—in 1954—these educational aids were still being used.)

Around the time of my return to the academy, the Chief Military Engineering School (GVIU) suggested the following as a thesis subject: "Construction of a Long-Term Batallion District in 14 Days." Nearly everyone grasped the difficulty of the subject, and no one elected it. One day shortly after the GVIU announcement I was summoned by Tsalkovich, Chief of the Academy. On his desk lay my recommendation from student practice work. "Pyotr Grigoryevich, I am proud that a student from our academy has earned such a recommendation. And to boot it came from the most senior and most important theoretician and practical commander of fortified areas, Pomerantsev." I had no idea what he was leading up to, so I kept quiet. "I see," he continued, "that you have great talents as a researcher and an organizer—and that you have taken a thesis subject which will not challenge your capabilities. You are putting a brake on your own powers and burying your own talent. After all, there is one theme perfectly suited to you—the eighteenth . . . "

He was referring to the subject everyone had rejected. "That is not a single theme," I said, "but a complex of themes."

"So it is a complex of themes. It is not required, of course, that all the details be worked out. It will be sufficient for you to come up with general solutions."

"I would not be able to master that thesis subject."

"But I am unable to entrust it to anyone else and GVIU says it must be worked out. In short, I am ordering you to undertake this thesis subject."

The subject turned out to be even more complicated than I had thought. First I had to work out a tactical solution for the batallion. Next I had to work out five types of defense installations that could be built in fourteen days. Then came a plan for organization of work, a schedule for supply of materials, and, finally, a schedule for transportation.

In total there were nine separate theses. I projected two more as well—building a concrete factory and central workshops—but did not get to them though I worked literally day and night. I became fatigued, but I was satisfied with the result of my work. My solution was realistic: a batallion district could be built in fourteen days without using quick-setting cement, which at the time we did not possess in the Soviet Union. My supervisor was satisfied.

No one doubted that I would defend my thesis successfully. Already the graduation testimonial had been written; it contained the statement: "He received a grade of excellent defense of his thesis, and graduated first in his class of seventeen."

The thesis defense went well. The auditorium was full. I completed my report and received applause. Then came questions. The subject was clearly of interest to many. The questions were serious and I replied to them in kind. Whenever we touched on an area in which solutions had not yet been worked out or in some cases even started, I stated so frankly. As the session neared its end, a member of the GVIU commission remarked: "Your concrete factory will not be able to produce that amount of cement." He indicated my schedule for supply of cement. "You should have worked out the concrete factory first and then seen what you could build." The remark was ridiculous and no one would have thought less of me had I evaded it tactfully. Instead, I argued. Consequently my grade was changed from "excellent" to "good," and my class rank from "first" to "fourth."

When the chief of the academy showed me the corrected testimonial he said, "These changes are not for lack of knowledge or for lack of industry, but for conduct. Learn how to conduct yourself—otherwise things may end badly for you."

I never did learn to smile in the face of stupidity or to pay deference to falsehood.

We graduated in the St. George Hall of the Kremlin on May 4, 1934, with the entire Politburo present. After the usual graduation celebrations, we reported to the academy for assignments, which, in most cases, had not yet been made. However, I was singled out by Professor Skorodumuv, the dean of the faculty of work organization. He called me aside and declared solemnly: "I congratulate you! I have managed to get my way, and the People's Commissariat of Defense has authorized you to stay on as a graduate student in my faculty."

Instead of being flattered, I was indignant. I did not feel qualified to teach. In no way did I want to stay on at the academy. I received permission from the dean to see the chief of the academy. I told Tsalkovich why I did not want to remain at the academy, and I added: "Less than a month ago the People's Commissariat issued an order stating that graduate students were to be chosen from the active army, and that any student the academy desired to keep on its staff must first serve three years in the active army."

"This is an exception," Tsalkovich replied. "The faculty is weak. It has to be beefed up."

"Then beef it up with people who have experience."

"There's nothing I can do. This is an order of the Commissariat of Defense."

"Then give me permission to appeal to the Commissar myself."

"I give permission!"

Tsalkovich phoned the Commissar's office. "Comrade Khmelnitsky, good day!" he said. I recognized the name and knew Khmelnitsky to be the Commissar's aide. "I am turning the phone over to an academy graduate. I ask you to hear him out."

He handed me the receiver.

"Comrade aide, I am requesting, with the permission of the chief of the academy, that the Commissar receive me to discuss a personal question."

"What's your question?"

"I am being named a graduate student in the academy—which conflicts with the order of the Commissar. I want to ask him to cancel his assignment and give me another assignment."

"Very well, I will report to the Commissar. You will receive your reply through the academy."

Khmelnitsky telephoned several days later to tell me that I would be received by Deputy Commissar Tukhachevsky.

I went to an enormous office at 1 Frunze Street, an office I subsequently visited many times. Behind a desk that seemed tiny in the immense room sat an aristocratic looking man familiar to me from portraits I had seen of him. I approached the desk, stopped at the prescribed distance, and loudly announced myself.

"What do you want?"

"I want the People's Commissariat Order Number 42 to be carried out in regard to me. If I am needed at the academy, let me first serve, as the order outlines, three years at construction. I have never been on a construction job."

"Your request will be considered. You may leave."

I did an about-face.

"Just remember one thing . . ."

I did another about-face.

"Just remember that you wear a uniform and that everything connected with it is for *life*. You may leave!"

I wondered why he had said that to me and understood only when the order came, signed by Tukhachevsky: "P. G. Grigorenko is named chief of staff of the individual engineers batallion of the fourth infantry corps, with the rank of T-8."

It was a very unusual posting. All other graduates were assigned to defense construction. Among career officers the opinion prevailed that all students wanted to work on construction projects so that they could get out from under the strict hand of military discipline and the obligatory wearing of military uniform. This thought must have reached the Commissar of Defense, who evidently had passed it on to Tukhachevsky. I had reminded him of it, and seemingly, had confirmed it. The order read: "To be sent for three years to army service. . . ."

Twice I had mentioned construction work; presumably, that was why Tukhachevsky had stressed that the military profession is for life. I think he intended by giving me such a posting to instill a sense of permanence in me.

CHAPTER SIX

VITEBSK

My immediate superior in the Fourth Infantry Corps at Vitebsk, Pavel Ivanovich Smirnov, commander of the engineers batallion, was both a teacher and a friend to me during the two years we worked together. Pavel Ivanovich was from Leningrad. I believe he came from an educated family, though I cannot be certain. He never spoke of his family. During the revolution he fought for the Bolsheviks when he was hardly sixteen. Later he joined the party and took part in the Civil War, rising from rank-and-file soldier to commissar of a regiment. After the Civil War he asked to be educated and was sent to the Leningrad Military Engineering School.

During his first year of school he was married in a church, and for this he was expelled from the party. Why had he done it? He was not a believer. Nor would he have agreed to a church ceremony at Katya's urging. Katya was an ordinary woman from a worker's family, not very well educated, and totally under her husband's control. No matter how one figured it, it seemed Pavel Ivanovich must have done it of his own accord, and in order to get exactly what he got—expulsion from the party. For some reason he wished to leave the party and, wisely, selected the least dangerous way out. The Bolshevik leadership did not like voluntary resignation. One might even pay for that with one's life.

Serdich, the corps commander, was completely indifferent to the affairs of our batallion. He was interested in the engineers only as manpower for his dacha (country house) and the dachas of the top-ranking commanders of the corps. Like many commanders of the time he was rude and tactless. He would dress down the officers and soldiers needlessly—often for no reason at all. Despite the fact that I did not particularly care for Serdich, I acquired from him the habit of being somewhat rude, a fault I had a hard time getting rid of later on. I regret I can't say anything good about him. In no way do I want it to seem that I am supporting the Stalinist executioners who destroyed this honored hero of the Civil War in 1937. His rudeness and his lack of restraint might have been reasons for removing him from his post but not for killing him. The army never campaigned against rudeness. On the contrary, those who were crude and of limited intelligence seemed to avoid being purged. Those destroyed were mainly cultured, tactful, thoughtful people. Serdich was arrested and shot at the very beginning of the mass repressions, indicating that he was among those suspected by Stalin of being capable of resistance to his dictatorship. Purging Serdich gave State Security the opportunity to send the whole array of the commanding officers of the corps to the firing squad. The entire corps administration was liquidated after I had completed my assignment in the corps.

Initially, I had some difficulties with certain batallion commanders of the Fourth Infantry Corps. My first conflict was with Avdeichik, an assistant. A misunderstanding arose between us because of the fact that until I arrived there had been no staffs in independent batallions. I was the first chief of staff. Naturally it took Avdeichik and others some time to get used to this.

The second person with whom I clashed was the batallion commissar, Gavril Petrovich Voronov. Voronov was a benign person, a veteran hunter and fisherman, a typical political officer—semi-literate but conceited, considering himself the highest authority and the supreme judge on all political questions.

We argued when he bypassed me and gave orders to Yaskin, even though the latter was now the assistant to the chief of staff for mobilization activity. I went to Voronov and asked him not to give orders to my subordinates. He agreed with my complaint and promised not to do it in the future, but it was obvious to me that he did not consider the issue serious. I knew the same problem would arise again, and it did. Voronov was accustomed to hunting and fishing whenever he pleased. Frequently he invited others along on his expeditions. I told him several times that there were regulations to be followed if one wanted to be granted leave from the batallion area or to requisition automobiles. One day Voronov, dressed in his fishing outfit, burst into my office with a wild look on his face. His request for an automobile had been refused, and the people he had invited to go fishing with him had not been given permission to go. I had only one reply to his fury: "This was the batallion commander's order. If he sees fit to change the order or if he gives one-time permission, then you may go all the way to Moscow with, if you wish, the entire batallion."

"I am the commissar! I give orders!" Voronov shouted.

"The batallion is commanded by one person alone, the commander. And I, as chief of staff, obey only him."

"Don't you obey the commissar?"

"I obey him but only in matters which do not concern my duties. I am not going to permit anyone to violate orders of the commander. It is my sacred duty to uphold the authority of the order and of the commander who issued it. And, as I understand it, the statute on the single chain of command is also obligatory for you as commissar."

Pavel Ivanovich Smirnov heard us and came into my office to ask why we were fighting. I told him, and he immediately adopted a conciliatory tone: "What's this all about? You need an automobile, Gavril Petrovich? And some men? Pyotr Grigoryevich, issue an order. Go wherever you please, Gavril Petrovich. But in the future, whenever you need these things tell me in advance. You have to have some consideration for the chief of staff. He answers with his head for failure to carry out orders."

Because Smirnov interceded, the problem came to an end. The outcome of this and subsequent conflicts proved to Voronov that neither the chief of staff nor the staff as a whole were subordinate to him—even though he had the title of commissar and was serving with a non-party commander.

It makes no sense to hash over all of the differences between us, but one went on for quite some time and had implications later on. A seedy soldier named Chernyayev used to hang around Gavril Petrovich. Every day he managed to evade military exercises, and Gavril Petrovich, making use of his authority, kept him at his own disposal—in other words, Chernyayev did nothing. As I sought to achieve battle readiness, I pulled all those who avoided exercises out from the nooks and crannies, Chernyayev being one of those people. But before I got him to begin normal training, I had to clash several times with Gavril Petrovich and I even had to seek help from Pavel Ivanovich. I'm sure Chernyayev was not very happy with my actions. More than once I caught him staring angrily at me.

The first years of my postacademy service career were on the whole good ones, except for a personal tragedy. Our first child, Anatoly, had been born in 1929, the year I entered the institute. My younger son was seven months old when we arrived at my new service post. We called him Georgy, in honor of Georgy Dimitrov, who not long before the child's birth had struggled heroically against the Hitlerite court. In August 1934 the child died.

My wife had taken him to Stalino (now Donetsk) to see her parents. When I received a telegram that he was gravely ill, I immediately went to Stalino, and helped bring the weakened child to doctors. It was no use; he had acute dysentery. Several days later he died as I was holding him in my arms.

For months afterward I reproached myself bitterly for not having removed Georgy from Stalino's murderous climate. I remembered how when Anatoly was very ill in 1930, I had taken him to Borisovka, where he had recovered. Why had I not done the same thing for Georgy? I saw myself as having caused the death of my son.

Man always attempts to cast blame from himself; thus thoughts of my own guilt gave way to reproaches against my wife. I thought angrily of how she had brought him to Stalino, though I knew perfectly well that if I had said even one word against the trip it would not have taken place. Yet I did not think about that. Instead I got angrier and angrier, all the time finding new reasons to implicate her in the death.

After a while I realized how much my wife was suffering, and I took pity on her. But the crack in our marriage created by Georgy's death never healed. I hoped that the birth of a new child would help us. When my wife became pregnant I prayed that she would have another son. On August 18, 1935—just one year after Georgy's death—a son was born whom we also named Georgy. The entire family opposed the name, declaring it improper to give a newborn child the name of one who had died. I insisted that it be Georgy, not in honor of the child who had died but in honor of my father who, though called Grigory, was Georgy on his birth certificate. The pain of loss continued, though it became duller with time. Even today I can remember how that tiny helpless body from which life had departed felt in my arms. I consider it a great sin that in striving to minimize my own part in Georgy's death, I blamed his mother, by now long since dead herself.

Day-to-day life in the engineers' batallion fascinated me. Most of my time was spent in battle and technical training, an activity I shaped to my own and others' advantage. Instead of begging my military superiors for materials and then using these materials to build useless objects, I found work that needed to be done within the civilian community, and, acting as a contractor, carried it out with my soldiers. Of course, we only took on projects that fit in with military engineering work. The advantages to this method were great: I did not have to use my own materials, and I received money for the work we completed. Also, I was directing the creation of things that people needed—wood bridges, for example. If building materials were in surplus, you could teach soldiers to trim beams and to fit and cut and in the end use the pieces as firewood; or, you could contract out to build a specific bridge and actually build it, thereby combining instruction with practical work. Times were such that both the civilian economy and the military needed many new roads and bridges built. Business was good. There was also a lot of work to be accomplished within the batallion. Economic activity and initiative were encouraged.

Among other projects, the most profitable were blasting operations. I consciously participated in one of the most flagrant instances of barbarism of our age—the destruction of the most important historical monuments of the Byelorussian and Russian peoples, their churches.

We received our first assignment to blow up a church in autumn 1934. The cathedral of the city of Vitebsk was to be demolished. This miracle of architecture stood on the right bank of the Western Dvina River, all five of its cupolas facing the river. People on ships saw it from afar, as they passed the town, and as they traveled onward. When passing it they made the sign of the cross and prayed, many of them on their knees. The authorities were irritated by such daily public worship, so our batallion received an order from the chief of engineers of the Byelorussian Military District to destroy the cathedral. Since I was the only batallion member who had studied the use of explosives (and I had studied it only a little), the contract negotiations with the Vitebsk city soviet, the organization of the demolition, and the execution of the explosion all were left up to me. I cannot remember how much I charged them for the blasting but I do remember that it seemed fantastically expensive. The chairman of the soviet seemed delighted at the price I quoted, and I was sorry I had asked so little.

The cathedral stood only twelve meters from a three-story building that the soviet did not want destroyed. From a lecture at the academy entitled "Demolition of Buildings" I could recall only the formula for calculation of the depth and thickness of the blast holes into which the explosive charges were put along with the "spacers" (models of explosive charges made of wood). The lecturer claimed that if the charge holes were correctly located and the packing in of chargers and spacers done properly, the building would not blow up into the air but would simply fall apart and settle. I had no time to test the theory, so I went directly to the church to see how it might work out. On learning that the church was open, and that icons, an altar, candle stands, and everything else were inside, I felt nauseous. I went to the representative of the city soviet and declared sharply, "Until all the icons and church furnishings have been removed I will do nothing. And they must not just merely be removed; the priest must be invited to do it himself in accordance with orthodox rites. Otherwise I will have no part in this. I do not want the people to accuse us of sacrilege."

With the help of the parishoners, priests from the other churches in Vitebsk organized the removal of sacred objects and church property from the cathedral. Soon after this, of course, someone accused me of organizing a church procession in Vitebsk, for which I could have been reprimanded. Soon after our demolition, however, another engineers' batallion blew up a church in Bobruisk and destroyed along with the church more than a dozen buildings, incurring fatalities as well. In analyzing the accident at a meeting, Soviet members cited the demolition carried out under my name as an example of a success. It would have been inappropriate to punish me after this.

The preparation of the Vitebsk demolition took a month and a half. The actual demolition surpassed all expectations. There was no explosion in the common sense of the term, just the roar and crackling of falling bricks. The building next door did not suffer even a single broken pane of glass. The church merely shook, let out a long groan, and settled into a pile of bricks. The demolition took place at dawn. I stood at the enormous pile of bricks and, I freely confess, admired my handiwork: You could have tossed the bricks from that pile straight into a truck for use in a new building project. The Vitebsk city soviet was impressed and paid everyone who worked on the job a bonus for "the excellent quality of the explosion."

Talk of our demolition quickly spread through Byelorussia. The Central Committee of the Communist party of Byelorussia asked the commander of the Byelorussian Military District to send those who had carried it out to Minsk to destroy a tiny church that stood alongside the recently constructed nine-story government headquarters. Fresh from my experience in Vitebsk I asked three times as much as I thought the job was worth and got it without having to bargain. We demolished the tiny church without harming the government building. Next I supervised the demolition of a church in Smolensk. Then I quit church demolition, declaring to my superiors that the brigade I had trained could carry on very well without me. In actual fact the reason was my state of mind. While preparing the Vitebsk demolition I had felt an inner sense of protest. Though I had admired the pile of bricks that remained where the cathedral had been, I didn't find real joy in the work.

It would have been to my benefit for me to continue with demolition work. It was unsupervised work, produced an abundance of money, and left one with a surplus of free time—a great life, one might think! Yet I began to study morbidly the architecture of churches that still were standing, and to admire the soul and inventiveness that had gone into the design and decoration of the buildings. The architecture of each church fit marvelously into the surrounding landscape. I had prepared the Minsk demolition disinterestedly, and in Smolensk I had found what I was doing to be abhorrent.

Sometime in late February 1936 Pavel Ivanovich came into my office seeming rather sad. He told me that although one more year of work in Vitebsk remained for me, Pomerantsev was insisting that I be posted as commander of the Fifty-second individual engineers' batallion of the Minsk fortified area.

I had no choice but to go. When Pavel Ivanovich and I said goodbye to each other, neither of us imagined it would be the last time we would meet. Pavel began the war as engineer with the Fourth Infantry Corps, and was taken prisoner during the first days of fighting. After the war the omniscient Brynzov (another graduate of the command faculty and a Bulgarian from my own area of the country) told me that Pavel Ivanovich was being labeled a traitor because he had been a camp policeman and had carried a gun for the enemy. According to Brynzov, the KGB was "setting his brains straight."

It is hard to know how much of this story to believe. Brynzov had never liked Pavel Ivanovich. In all likelihood though, he *was* having his brains straightened out. The rest was probably just the usual KGB interrogatory myth-making. I tried to locate Pavel Ivanovich's wife but was unsuccessful. Perhaps she did not survive the war. And he probably did not survive the KGB. I owe a great deal to Pavel Ivanovich Smirnov. All my strengths as a commanding officer came from him.

THE

FLIGHT

OF THE

TRAINED

FALCON

CHAPTER SEVEN

MINSK
FORTIFIED
AREA

In March 1936 I returned to the small, two-story building in the center of Minsk that I had first entered exactly three years before. From here I had received my successful posting to the subsector. Zagorulko, the chief engineer, was waiting for me. He told me that Pomarentsev wanted to see me immediately, and we went to the second floor, where the latter received us right away, saying, "I told you I would find you. And I did, as you can see."

Without giving me the opportunity to report and salute in accordance with army statutes, he reached out his hand to me. "Your batallion doesn't exist yet," he continued. "The individual engineer's company of the fortified area is to be the basis for its formation. The company commander will handle all aspects of the batallion's formation. You and I, beginning tomorrow, will tour the area. As of now you know only the Pleshchenitsy sector well. Your duties require that you become familiar with the other four sectors."

The tour took a month and a half, during which I spent some of the most fulfilling days of my life. Pomerantsev was a great theoretician and practitioner; he seemed to know everything about fortified areas. In the academy I'd taken an excellent course entitled "Attack and Defense with Fortresses," which had given me fundamental knowledge in the field, but Pomerantsev taught me new things every day.

He transformed our examination into a war game. Every possible variation of the ways in which his own armies and those of the enemy might act seemed to have occurred to him. During the war (before I knew that the fortified area had been blown up) I often wondered what would have happened if Pomerantsev had been in command. I always decided that he would have fought off any enemy attack using merely the permanent garrisons and one infantry division for reinforcements. The general plan allowed for the use of four or five reinforcement divisions, but during our tour Pomerantsev conducted the entire war game on the basis of one.

He once said, "The initial period of the war will be replete with all kinds of surprises, particularly because the assigned troops will fail to arrive in time. But one division out of five will certainly get here and I am counting on that one to give the enemy a beating. Then, after all of the assigned forces have arrived, it will no longer be time to defend but to attack."

We inspected each point along the firing line, checking especially for battle readiness. Pomerantsev had many ideas for improving efficiency, a few of which he had put into practice some time back. I sensed that he hesitated to speak of his own innovations for fear that he would manifest technical illiteracy. But I seized on each concept he presented and discussed it with such interest that he was compelled to share with me everything he was thinking. We used to argue sometimes till we were hoarse.

Pomerantsev's interests were not limited to the military. He was very well read, spoke several languages, and read English and German literary classics in the original. He could speak about any subject on which I might touch. Politics was one of the only subjects he avoided. At the time I thought this was because he was not a party member, but now I think he was not a party member only because he did not like politics or politicians.

Pomerantsev never talked about his past, either. All I knew about it was that he had studied at the Petrograd Technological Institute until World War I when he had gone to the front as a volunteer. He worked his way up to the rank of captain, was wounded two or three times, was awarded decorations, and, finally, in 1918, joined the Red Army. He fought the entire Civil War and at its end signed on as a career officer. His assignment as commander of Minsk carried with it rank in the twelfth category—three diamonds. When the first officer ranks were introduced in 1936 he received the title of brigade commander, a prestigious one for those times.

During the tour we became quite friendly, but despite Pomerantsev's frequent requests that I address him by name and patronymic, I addressed him in the official manner, comrade Commander, and continued to do so after he had received the title of brigade commander. No doubt that is why I cannot remember his name and patronymic today.

After the tour I began organizing the new batallion.

A division arrived at the fortified area. The post of commander of the division was combined with that of commander of the fortified area, and the position of divisional engineer was combined with the post of chief of engineers of the fortified area, and so on. Even the machine gun and artillery batallion of the fortified area was made subordinate to the regiments of the newly arrived division. The old command was incapable of fighting for power; they turned it over to people who had no experience with fortified areas and the type of battles that would be fought.

The commander of the new division, the Thirteenth Infantry, was Brigade Commander Vishnerevsky, a conscientious man who had never even heard of a fortified area. In addition to this handicap, the Red Army mistrusted him. He was an officer of the old army, not a party member, and he came from a nonworking background. Because of his poor relationship with the army, he did not show initiative or take on new responsibility.

Pomerantsev was summoned to the General Staff Academy in Minsk. Before his departure he tried to break in Vishnerevsky. He took him through the fortified area, pointing out and explaining things of importance. In order to understand a fortified area, however, you have to work in it. And you need assistants who know the area, especially military engineers. All of Vishnerevsky's staff had come from field service.

When I said farewell to Pomerantsev, he told me, "It is going to be very difficult for Vishnerevsky. I just hope there will be no war in the near future. Even without war it will be hard. Particularly now, when it is so dangerous to make a mistake."

This last phrase was the first and final political utterance Pomerantsev made to me. He must have been reacting to the recent executions of Mikhail Tukhachevsky, Uborevich, and Yakir and to the arrests of their associates. I did not understand his remark at the time. I could not understand why people at the peak of power should enter foreign intelligence services. Though Pomerantsev may not have understood the full scope of what was taking place, he obviously grasped that many other heads would roll.

I missed my conversations with Pomerantsev. There was no one to talk with when things got difficult. Zagorulko had left. Vasilyev, the new chief of engineering, was good-natured but unassertive. He did not try to make changes in the way things were run and he did not hinder ongoing projects, but it was absolutely useless to go to him with a problem concerning work—particularly when a firm and definite decision was needed.

I'd always been concerned that the right flank of the fortified area had never been secured. Pomerantsev and I had toured that district together. Between the fortifications and the swampy basin of the Berezina River lay a gap of about six kilometers that would be excellent terrain for all types of armed forces. In order to secure the flank we needed to establish two more batallion districts within the fortified area. After my tour with him, Pomerantsev had instructed Zagorulko to request funding for the construction of these two new districts from the chief engineer of the Byelorussian Military District. The request had never been acted on. When Vasilyev arrived, I told him about the problem and advised him to have the technical section work out a detailed plan for the proposed districts and to make a second request for funding. He did neither.

Once he broached the subject to Shalayev, chief of the technical section, and Shalayev immediately said to him, "Is this something Grigorenko advised you to do? Since 1933 that's been his *idée fixe.* The fortified areas were planned by intelligent people on the General Staff and their boundaries were fixed precisely. Grigorenko's whole notion is a sham and people know it."

Without even checking the situation out for himself, Vasilyev agreed with Shalayev.

Vasilyev was one of the first of the 13th Division to be arrested in the spring of 1937. I cannot imagine how such a simple person could have caused any harm. But the divisional counterintelligence reported that he had been arrested as "an enemy of the people." After Vasilyev's departure, I was appointed to his position. I reported to Vishnerevsky, descended to the chief engineer's office to take up my new duties, and in the doorway came face to face with Chernyayev, the "seedy" soldier who had played up to Gavril Petrovich in the engineers' batallion. His appearance had changed radically. He wore a new, perfectly fitting officer's uniform. In each tab was a rectangle.

"How did you get here?" I asked, looking him over.

"I am the counterintelligence operations chief in the administration of the chief of engineers. I would like to talk to you."

"I haven't taken charge yet. There's nothing I can tell you."

"Well, there's something I can tell you which will be good for you to know before you begin your duties."

He had nothing useful to tell me, as I had already guessed. He spoke of vigilance and he stressed more than once that *the first enemy of the people had been discovered in the administration of the chief of engineers.* He was so insistent about this that I wondered whether he had not organized that arrest himself. He was obviously flaunting his position and even hinted rather transparently that I was now more dependent on him than he had ever been dependent on me in the batallion. He obviously enjoyed the situation and was extremely proud of himself. I was able to stand him for only a short time.

"Do you have anything more to say to me?" I asked him drily.

He was indignant: "I just wanted to warn . . ."

"Thank you for the warning and for the advice but right now I have a lot of work. Goodbye."

When he left I went to see Shalayev. "How are things going with the Plesh-chenitsy batallion districts?"

Shalayev began to stammer. I interrupted him, saying, "Take charge of this project yourself. Put the entire section on it. Work twenty-four hours a day if you have to, but see to it that the basic materials are on my desk by the day after tomorrow at nine o'clock in the morning. I hope to be off to Smolensk by ten for a personal report to the chief of engineers."

I left, taking with me the map of the Pleshchenitsy sector, and went again to Vishnerevsky. A field army man, he immediately grasped the danger of hav-ing an open flank. Because he was not an expert in fortifications, he had failed to attribute any significance to the open flank when he first studied the map of the fortified area.

"I thought," he said, "that our neighbors would adjoin us on our flanks."

"No," I began. "The fortified areas are built along the important operational paths in order to prevent the development of an enemy attack in those direc-tions. Our strong defense will force the enemy to seek out the flanks and to try to go around them. Fortified areas must be prepared for this and are obli-gated to take measures to counteract the encirclement of the flanks. Our plan of defense does provide for this. I think that even in our present situation the enemy's attempts to encircle our flank will fail. But why permit the enemy to carry out an encirclement of the flank on favorable terrain? Force him to move along the woodsy, swampy Berezina basin or else to cross to the other side of the river."

The brigade commander agreed at once with my conclusions. I told him that Pomerantsev had appealed unsuccessfully for funds to resolve the problem and that I believed we should set up two batallion districts—or, I knew, a fu-ture investigation would blame us for their absence. Having come to an agree-ment with him on the essence and tone of the document to be sent to the Dis-trict, I asked permission to take it there myself the day after tomorrow. He agreed to this.

As I was leaving, Vishnerevsky called out in a dry, official voice: "Comrade Chief Engineer! Why have you come to see me out of uniform?"

I turned to him and declared with astonishment, "I don't understand."

"You have not changed your insignia," he said.

I had not, in fact, put on insignia appropriate to my new duties. When I graduated from the academy my appointment to a seventh-category job (one rectangle) stated that it was "with designation of T-8"—two rectangles. My last order had not indicated any exception, which meant that instead of two rectangles I was to wear one diamond—K-10.

At the time Vishnerevsky called my insignia to my attention, the assigning of officer ranks was taking place. A few people had not received appointments, and I was one of them. My order might arrive at any moment, but in the meantime I had not wanted to change my insignia and risk getting myself into a foolish situation. The actual insignia for rank remained the same as that for duty (squares, rectangles, diamonds). But the insignia of the new career officer ranks did not denote what they had in the past. There were even cases in which a person who had worn three diamonds in accordance with his duties was now forced to wear three squares according to his new career rank. Pomerantsev himself no longer wore three diamonds but one, in accordance with his career rank. Instead of two Vishnerevsky now wore one. Both these men were fortunate. In many cases a person had to don not only insignia denoting a lower rank but also quartermaster status—an insult to command officers. Many tried to hide their new insignia. During the colder times of year we saw many overcoats with fur collars on which insignia could not be worn.

Only those who had continually been in command posts received high command ranks. Years of study, service on staffs and in rear echelons, and teaching work not only were not taken into account when alloting ranks; they had a negative influence. The ranks were granted by central commissions whose decisions sometimes seemed quite arbitrary.

Budyonny, "the icon with moustaches," and Timoshenko, "the oak general," headed the commissions that decided on ranks. They and others like them used this important work to make people dissatisfied and to discover who was capable of disagreeing with the higher-ups, capable of not saying "thank you" after he had been demoted. Many arrested officers later remembered that one of the charges against them was "Manifested dissatisfaction with rank received and uttered critical opinions."

I was not afraid of receiving my own career rank. I knew that to the Budyonnys I was nearly a civilian: I had had two years in the academy; two years on staff; and one year in command of a batallion. I would not receive more than senior lieutenant in the command line. Yet I held a high position and had the qualifications of a military engineer, which meant that they would give me a military technical rank of one or two rectangles—in other words, a military engineer of either third or second rank. Of course, something unexpected could occur. When decisions are in the hands of people like Budyonny and Timoshenko anything can happen. Therefore I did not want to change my insignia until I had received my career rank. Still, an order is an order, so I put on my diamond. I did not have to wear it for a long time—no more than fifteen or twenty days—before the order came. I received a commission as a military engineer of the third rank and put my new rectangle in the hole in which I had worn my diamond.

However, I was able to deliver the plan for the two new batallion districts to Smolensk wearing a diamond. I later surmised that this was a calculation on Vishnerevsky's part. Knowing that the insignia of permanent ranks of the military technical services did not differ at all from the insignia worn in correspondence with duties, he evidently wanted me to seem more prestigious than I really was as I sought to advance our proposal. Perhaps this was not what motivated him. Perhaps he simply wanted the old order to be observed. One way or another, on the basis of insignia I appeared to be the highest-ranking person in the administration of the chief of engineers. Even the chief himself had only three rectangles, though they were command corps rectangles, which meant he was a colonel. Everyone addressed me as if I held the rank of brigade engineer, and everything was done for me with the utmost haste. I was received by the military district chief of staff and the next morning by the commander, at that time Timoshenko. I departed with orders to begin construction immediately of two batallion districts.

The day I returned from Smolensk I was visited by a remarkable being. Imagine a human skull with the thinnest writing paper stretched tightly over it, and glassy, completely immovable eyes of light blue touched from within by a bit of milkiness. The ears and nose had the same papery quality as the face. The skull was covered with whitish hair combed flat and parted on the left. When this being talked or smiled his thin lips drew back, disclosing yellowish teeth. His smile was awful; not one facial muscle moved and the eyes remained expressionless. When he "smiled" it seemed as if someone was jerking an invisible string to move the lips that were glued to the skull.

It took great effort for me not to reveal how the sight of this phantom made me feel. He walked into my office with lips open wide and, approaching me, reached out his hand. It was Kirilov, the chief of counterintelligence (we referred to counterintelligence as "Smersh") of the Minsk fortified area. I had heard his name but I had never met him. Looking at him, I thought of Vasilyev. To be entirely in the power of such a ghost must have been a frightening thing. I decided that in order to defend oneself against this monster one had to avoid reacting to him. Thus I forced myself to converse with him normally. However, each time an arrest was made I could not help but imagine the arrested person in a dungeon face to face with him.

Speaking in a businesslike voice, I told Kirilov that I needed help from counterintelligence. "We are going to be building two batallion districts in the Pleshchenitsy area. The work is urgent. Most important, we must hide what we are building. I have thought about pretending to begin work in three or four areas, when really we will be building in only one of them. Each area will be put under guard, but the most vigilant guard will be in the true building area."

He talked with me in a respectful and concerned way. I asked him to help me in selecting guards and people who would be doing the work in the sham areas.

He said, "I will turn that over to Chernyayev."

I decided to meet him head on. "I do not consider Chernyayev very reliable. He does not like to work, and this job requires attentiveness, conscientiousness, and industry. In addition, I do not think that he likes me. This could cause trouble."

"Very well!" he said. "I will keep all this under consideration. I hope that we will do things in such a way that everything will work out for the good of the Party and of the people."

I had an uneasy feeling during this last period of my stay in the Minsk fortified area. On one hand I felt satisfaction that I had made such an enormous advance in the service and had encountered success in a new work situation. On the other hand I no longer had that joy in creative work I had had as a student trainee. I was doing useful work, and certainly it was on a higher plane than things I had done before, but I took no pleasure in it. I was quite unhappy. I always felt as if someone was looking over my shoulder and surveying everything I did. The feeling intensified with each new arrest. I had traveled over the entire fortified area many times. I knew all of the commanders of the regiments and of the artillery and machine gun batteries and I had become friendly with many of them. One by one they were arrested, and those who remained changed overnight. Frankness and openness disappeared. People looked at me suspiciously, some of them with fright.

Colonel Kulakov, commander of the Thirty-ninth regiment, was a good friend of mine and, in my opinion, an excellent leader. Gradually, though, he became less and less communicative. Then he was called before a divisional party commission and accused of "having contact with enemies of the people," all because he had served with people who had been arrested. The party assumed these people were guilty. Kulakov claimed that they had been conscientious commanders and that he had not known at all about any dishonorable activity. He was expelled from the party. Furthermore, he was intercepted by Kirilov's men, who put him into a Black Maria and, without letting him see his family, took him back to Minsk—to prison.

The commander of the Thirty-eighth Regiment, Colonel Kutsner, was hauled off to a divisional party commission and had similar accusations made against him. Like Kulakov, he was expelled from the party for "having contact with enemies of the people." Many years later I learned what happened after such expulsion and imprisonment. In prison the interrogator charged the subject with the crime and demanded that he talk about his hostile activites. Torture followed. The number of enemies of the people multiplied. After one person was arrested, all those connected with him were arrested. Soon after Kulakov's arrest, the chief of staff of the regiment, the commander of the artillery and machine gun battery, and many others were arrested. As a result, men began to be afraid to go to their chief, even when summoned. I felt an emptiness all around me. When I came to a unit, all the officers would scamper off, just in case: I might be arrested tomorrow and then they would be made to answer for connections with me. Kulakov's regiment, the best in the division, fell apart completely. The soldiers talked openly, not in defense of the commanders who had been arrested but just the opposite: "Who is commanding us! Enemies of the people are intentionally putting us in danger of slaughter. All the officers ought to be punished. After all, Kulakov received them. He knew whom he was receiving. He sent those he didn't want out of the regiment."

Things worked out differently in the Thirty-eighth regiment. When Kutsner was expelled from the party, Kirilov's men were waiting for him at his home station—the Dzerzhinsk station of the Moscow-Negoreloye railroad line—but Kutsner did what no one expected him to. He got on this same line and traveled in the direction of Moscow. That autumn I bumped into Kutsner there and he told me how he had outwitted Kirilov. None of us back at the fortified area had known where he was. Kirilov, of course, did have Kutsner's new address, but he'd not wanted to broadcast the facts of his own failure. Therefore, he led all of us to believe that Kutsner was imprisoned somewhere.

Kutsner told me: "I went to the station certain that I would be arrested in Dzerzhinsk. I knew I had to get to Moscow. If the orders originated there, I decided, let me be arrested there. But if this is just local stuff, why walk into their trap? At the station I spied one of Kirilov's men. In a loud voice I asked for a ticket to Dzerzhinsk and then went out and strolled up and down the street. The man was reassured and disappeared. I was not being tailed. Orders must have been given only to follow me to the station. Just in case, I kept walking until the Negoreloye-to-Moscow train arrived, and then went into the toilet, threw my service cap down the hole, unbuttoned my service jacket, waited until the train started moving, and, just as if I were a passenger, jumped into a moving car, and walked through the train, pretending to look for my seat. I found the chief conductor and paid him off, and he got me a place in a second-class car."

In Moscow Kutsner had gone to the Chief Personnel Administration and told them he would agree to any appointment but would not go back to Minsk. They named him a teacher in the Frunze Academy. At that time a person who felt that arrest was imminent could go to another town and, as a rule, avoid being seized. In order to apprehend such a person, it was necessary to present proof of his "criminal activity," but such proof came into existence only after a person had been arrested. Therefore, the authorities preferred to take those who were sitting in place, rather than running down "fugitives." In most cases people who were well worked over would volunteer self-incriminating "evidence."

I did not understand any of this at the time. I believed that there was a fifth column in the country. I felt that most of those arrested were actual "enemies." They had arrested almost half of the officers in Kulakov's regiment, but in Kutsner's only him. At the time I did not know that Kutsner had thwarted Kirilov's plan. Kirilov and his underlings knew that Kutsner was in Moscow, but they didn't know what connections he might have at the top. Therefore, they were afraid to touch the Thirty-eighth Regiment. In all likelihood Kutsner's evasion held back a general flood of arrests in the Minsk fortified area at the end of 1937 and the beginning of 1938.

Later, when I learned much more about the events of 1936–37, I often asked myself whether I had been afraid of arrest. I always answer No, even though I now understand that if I had not been summoned to the Academy of the General Staff in Moscow I almost certainly would have been arrested in Minsk. Not for nothing was Kirilov so attentive to me, and not for nothing did he keep Chernyayev in the post of security officer of the Administration of the Chief Engineer of the fortified area. Yet I never felt myself to be in any danger and I continued to do my work responsibly and determinedly, free from worry.

I was able to use much of what I'd learned while writing my thesis in the construction of the two Pleshchenitsy batallion districts. Of course, I did not try to complete the work in fourteen days. Lacking practical experience and the technical capabilities I had cited in my thesis, it would have been risky to try, but in three months both batallion districts were finished, and all permanent points along the firing line were camouflaged and completely equipped for battle.

If I had been worried about arrest, it would have been impossible for me to carry out such work.

During all this time Kirilov was particularly friendly to me. He dropped in two or three times a week, rather often for my tastes. We didn't talk about anything special. He made no attempt to recruit me as a secret informer. Was it simply that our offices were near each other? Or was he "playing" with me? Perhaps he was preparing me for a special role outside the boundaries of the Minsk fortified area as an expert witness at an upcoming trial on "sabotage" in fortified areas. Anything was possible. All I know is that he related to me in what seemed like a kind and honest manner.

On one occasion his corpse's face carried an expression of particular satisfaction. Seating himself—as usual without an invitation—he said: "I have a little surprise for you. Would you like to hear it?"

"Why not? If it is for me, let me hear it."

Kirilov began reading from a typescript document that he never let me see for myself. Thirty years have passed and I cannot remember word for word exactly what I heard. But I am convinced that what I do remember is entirely accurate.

"The new chief of engineers of the Minsk fortified area Grigorenko, Pyotr

Grigoryevich," Kirilov read, and then paused. He read some detailed bio-graphical material, all of which was correct. He paused again and then said, "What comes next is the most interesting. Listen carefully:

> Grigorenko belongs to the so-called Stalinist generation. He is high-principled. He is loyal to Stalin and his regime not out of a desire to make a career but out of conviction. He is intolerant of criticism aimed at the re-gime, but he does not write denunciations and he passionately tries to per-suade his adversary of his error. He accepts his dizzying advance in the ser-vice as exactly what he has earned, and despite a lack of experience, he has taken his work firmly in hand. He takes initiative and is decisive. He is not afraid to take responsibility on his shoulders. No significant faults have been noted as possible approaches for recruitment. It may be possible to reach him via a woman, although it is difficult to hope for success."

Kirilov finished and stared at me. "How do you like that recommendation?"
"I like it."
"Why don't you ask who wrote it?"
"I am waiting for you to tell me yourself. After all, you people like to ask questions but don't like to be asked."
"It's an excerpt from an intramural report to the chief of Polish intelli-gence."
"They certainly are well informed. What is Smersh doing? If you'll excuse the question."
"You'll find out about that when the time is right. But there is something there for you to keep in mind, the references to women. After all, Zagorulko has collected quite a flowerbed here. I wouldn't be surprised if one of them began to study you close up . . . . But if I were you I wouldn't wait for that. I'd set off on my own. For instance, there's a girl named Zozya in the materials section. You could begin with her. She's an interesting type."
"You can undertake that kind of study yourself. I have enough of my own work."
He never spoke to me again of this report.
Once Kirilov told me that Chernyayev had been collecting derogatory infor-mation on me but that he, Kirilov, had taken the materials away from him and had told him to occupy himself with questions of the administration of the chief engineer without involving me personally. Another time Kirilov pro-posed to me, "How would you like me to arrange a special appointment for you with your friend Kulakov?" I told him that I could wait until the Kulakov affair had been investigated completely. "All right, we will see," he said rather enigmatically, and never brought up Kulakov again.
In August the sector project was completed. I was preparing to leave to de-liver my report in Smolensk when a telegram from the chief of engineers of

the Byelorussian Military District arrived and ordered me to a meeting of chief engineers of the fortified areas. The atmosphere at the meeting was one of alarm. Something seemed to be threatening us. Perhaps this was due to the fact that three of the four chief engineers participating in the meeting were new; their predecessors had been arrested.

When I did go to Smolensk, I was summoned by the chief engineer of the Byelorussian Military District. As I entered his office, a colonel handed me a telegram from Vishnerevsky addressed to the chief engineer. "I ask you to return Grigorenko immediately to Minsk in order to avoid great misfortune."

Greatly alarmed, I left and went directly from the Minsk station to my administration and called Vishnerevsky. "Come to my office immediately!" he shouted in an hysterical voice I had never heard before.

When I arrived, he was running nervously from one corner to another. He did not respond to my salute or my greeting but ran to his desk, grabbed a sheet of paper, and waved it in the air, shouting, "They've cut our throats! They've cut off our heads! I trusted you more than myself. You are an experienced fortifications specialist. Pomerantsev recommended you as a conscientious officer. And what do you do? You've had so much time, and still you didn't put the fortified area into battle readiness. And all the time you fed us your reassuring reports."

In the midst of Vishnerevsky's tirade Telyatnikov, the political commissar of the fortified area, came in, evidently having been summoned by Vishnerevsky after my call. Telyatnikov was pale and excited. When Vishnerevsky saw him, he began shouting even louder and more hysterically, "You muddled our heads with those two battallion districts, and all the time you were forgetting about battle readiness of the entire fortified area. But don't you dare think that Telyatnikov and I are going to prison alone. They won't forget you either!"

I stood there flabbergasted, not understanding at all what was going on. Vishnerevsky kept shouting. Finally I was able to ask Vishnerevsky what the problem was. "A commission from the Commissariat of Defense came to verify points from various sectors of the fortified area, checked them out, and rated every one of them unsatisfactory in terms of chemical warfare defense," he told me. "In twenty minutes the major, the chairman of the commission, is going to come to sign the formal report. I refused to sign before you had returned. Now I have to sign—and then go to prison. As you know, the directive states that the commander and the political commissar of the fortified area are personally responsible for putting the fortified area into a state of battle readiness. The commission came from Mozyr, where it also found the fortified area unready for chemical warfare defense." There the commander and the political commissar have both been arrested." He stood up and added caustically, "And the chief of engineers was imprisoned also."

"Give me the list of fortifications checked out by the commission," I said.

Vishnerevsky gave me the sheet of paper which he was holding in his hands. I looked over the list and said calmly, "Every one of these fortifications should receive a grade of 'excellent.' "

"Just what are you trying to tell me!" Vishnerevsky screamed. "They didn't make the inspection alone. Your deputy, military engineer of the first rank, Shalayev, and the chief of chemical service of the fortified area participated in the commission. The inspection and grades accorded with instructions set forth by the Commissariat of Defense. Our own officers can verify this."

I replied, "I'm sorry, but I believe myself to be correct. I personally checked out, using those very same instructions, every battle installation in the fortified area, and I affirm that all of them—I stress *all* of them—can be graded 'excellent.' "

The directive on putting the fortified areas into a state of battle readiness had been issued in spring 1937, before my appointment as chief of engineers. When I became chief of engineers, I immediately grasped its importance and selected several fortifications to be worked on. Most crucial was the removal of all leaks and cracks in the concrete and the hermetic sealing of the doors and embrasures so that adequate pressure could be maintained inside the fortification while the ventilation was working. The minimum pressure (measured in terms of millimeters of water column) was seventeen Chemical warfare defense capabilities were rated "satisfactory" at seventeen, "good" at nineteen, and at twenty-three, "excellent."

I supervised several brigades that removed cracks and cavities in the concrete and sealed up the doors and the embrasures. After this, a different brigade inspected and graded the chemical warfare readiness of each one of the fortifications. The hermetic sealing work had been carried out so conscientiously that in the entire fortified area no fortification had a pressure of less than twenty-seven millimeters. Though it demands a tremendous amount of detailed work, achieving a state of battle readiness for chemical warfare is a simple matter, fully within the powers of any conscientious person. While we had never clearly been filled in on exactly how the pressure would be measured and while the bureaucratic instructions had been written by careless nonspecialists, eventually I had figured out that pressure could be measured with the help of a U-shaped pipe. I knew that at least one such pipe must have been shipped to the fortified area along with the filter-ventilation equipment. After much searching we located an instrument labeled "a device for measurement of pressure inside battle installations" and with great difficulty got it to work.

Anyone who could read figures could measure the pressure accurately, but the process of arriving at the figures was still very difficult. I doubted whether everyone was up to this work and whether all fortified areas had overcome the implicit difficulties. Concerned about the situation, I reported it to the chief engineer of the military district in a special letter. I do not know how my letter was put to use, but standing there with the hysterical Vishnerevsky, I wondered whether this entire catastrophe was caused by a misunderstanding.

At a certain point during my conversation with Vishnerevsky, the chairman of the commission and the chief of chemical warfare services of the fortified area entered the office. With them was Shalayev, chief of the technical section of the administration of chief engineer of the fortified area, deputy chief of this administration, and military engineer of the first rank. The chairman handed the official readings to Vishnerevsky, who looked at me questioningly.

"I have to study them," I said sharply.

"You, evidently, are the chief of engineers," the major said to me, handing me the document.

"Yes, I am chief of engineers of the Minsk fortified area, military engineer of the third rank, Grigorenko," I said in a severe and official tone and sat down to read the document. Immediately I realized that the pressure had not even been measured because, according to the report, each fortification had failed the preceding test, which was for penetration of smoke into the installation. I was astounded. This was impossible. But here was an official report signed by five experts including two fortifications area specialists—one of them my own deputy—who claimed that they had seen smoke in the installation.

Kirilov entered. "Aha, crow, you smell carrion," I thought as I greeted him. Vishnerevsky, seeing that I had finished reading the report, asked me, "What are we going to do?"

"I would begin by taking all copies of this report away from the commission, by ordering its Moscow members to leave the fortified area immediately, and by assigning investigators to discover why those members of the commmission from our own sectors have signed a saboteur's document."

"Be more careful in your words!" the major called out to me. "I did not call you a saboteur, even though you reported the 'battle readiness' of installations which were unready for chemical warfare defense."

"Prove the unreadiness of even one installation and you can call me whatever you want. Until it is proven, however, I have the right to consider this a saboteur's document, since without any basis whatsoever it undermines the faith of the garrisons in the battle readiness of their installations. Comrade Brigade Commander," I said, turning to Vishnerevsky, "I affirm that all of the installations verified by the commission have a grade of 'excellent.' I am prepared to bear full responsibility, including criminal responsibility, for the correctness of my assertions. I ask you to designate a repeat verification of those same installations by the same commission—but this time in my presence. If their conclusions are confirmed, comrade Kirilov knows what to do with me."

The major agreed to stay for another day to recheck four installations. It did not matter to me which ones he checked; we selected the four nearest. We set a time to meet at fortification 25. When I arrived there a sergeant I'd asked to attend, head of a brigade of measurement specialists, saluted me. I presented him to the Moscow major, and informed him that the measurement specialists were here at my orders. Then, with everyone present listening, I asked the sergeant, "What grade in chemical warfare defense does this fire point have?"

" 'Excellent.' The pressure stands at forty-five millimeters." No one responded to this claim.

We decided to begin the inspection. The major took charge. "We will bypass the test for disturbance of a candle flame at the joints of hermetically sealed doors while the filter and ventilation system and the exhaust are working. All of the installations passed this test for the first time."

"No," I objected. "We must conduct all of the tests in exactly the order and on the scale prescribed in the instructions."

Fortification 25 passed the first test. It also passed the second test—for penetration of smoke into the installation when the filter and ventilation system are working and the exhaust is off. The third test was exactly the same as the second but with simultaneous operation of the compressing ventilation and the exhaust. Everything was in order. The fourth test was exactly like the third but with the ventilation and exhaust completely shut off. Again the fortification passed easily. The fifth and last test dictated by the instructions was measurement of pressure. I was eager to conduct this test.

"No, there is one more before that!" the major objected.

"What?" I was astonished. "The instructions do not provide for any other."

"The instructions have omitted this test. And those to blame are going to suffer severe punishment, but we are going to carry it out now."

"Tell me about this test."

"When we begin it you will see."

"Please be so kind as to tell me about it now, so that I may decide whether I will permit you to carry it out."

"What do you mean, you will permit me!"

"It's simple. I am the one who has the forces here. If you do not obey I will order the garrison to arrest you and to convoy you to an appropriate place for further investigation."

"Very well, I will tell you. But I will also remind you of this conversation later on. It's a simple test for penetration of smoke into the installation when only the exhaust is turned on."

I was flabbergasted. Even now I know that this test could only have been instituted by ignorance. On the basis of this test all of the leaders of the Mozyr fortified area had been arrested—and we had almost been arrested ourselves. I could not pardon him for his ignorance.

"You conducted tests like that in Mozyr?"

"Of course."

"You must understand that by all rights I ought to end this conversation with you here and now, but since the garrison of this fortification, the measurement experts, and others as well are listening to us here, and since you have slandered the defense characteristics of the battle installations, I am going to tell them why I will not permit this test to be carried out. Then they can spread the news throughout the entire fortified area that the battle installations *are* reliable. Let us carry out the second test again. Everyone put on gas masks and go beneath the camouflage. Turn on the compressor ventilation. Set off the smoke cartridges. Direct your attention to the smoke by the walls. It remains three or four centimeters away from them. Now turn on the intake. The smoke gets nearer the walls but does not touch them. Now turn off both the ventilation and the exhaust. The smoke moves right up against the wall but does not enter the interior. Now everyone come outdoors."

As we emerged from under the camouflage I asked, "Do you all understand why the smoke does not touch the walls of the installation? It was kept away by air leaving the installation through the concrete. Concrete is penetrable by air. This is the fact on which the first test is based. The second test clarified whether the garrison men would be endangered by a chemical warfare attack during which land forces were not attacking. In such a situation the men do not have to fire from the installation; therefore the exhaust is not required. Only the pressure ventilation system needs to be working.

"The third test is to discover whether the garrison will be incapacitated by a poison gas attack while enemy land forces are attacking. In order for the men to attack from the fortifications the exhaust has to be turned on. Thus the third test is carried out with the filter-ventilation system and the exhaust both turned on.

"The fourth test," I continued, "establishes whether the garrison will be incapacitated if the enemy undertakes a sudden gas attack at a time when neither the filter and ventilation system nor the exhaust are in operation. Under such conditions interior pressure equals exterior pressure and air does not move in any one single direction. But air-exchange through the concrete is still taking place. That is why the test takes only five minutes—time enough for the filter-ventilation system to be put into operation. During these five minutes neither smoke nor gas must penetrate the installation. And now let's imagine under what conditions it would be necessary for *only* the exhaust *to be turned on.* Is there such a situation?"

No one spoke.

"Comrade Major, I ask you to tell me: Under what conditions would only the exhaust be turned on?"

He could have refused to reply. He could have interrupted me. He could have said that he had not come here to take an examination but to carry out a test. Nevertheless, he answered me. "Well . . . if the men light up cigarettes? and in order to get the smoke out turn on the exhaust. . . ."

His reply told me that he was not a saboteur but an ignoramus. Somewhat condescendingly, I said, "The exhaust can be turned on by itself only when the ventilation system is not operating. But in that case the doors are to be opened and the men must wear gas masks."

I explained that no rational man would do anything to lower pressure artificially in the installation, particularly if a poison gas attack was taking place, because he would create a vacuum in the battle compartments.

"Therefore," I said, "I will not permit the test you propose. What is the point of sucking poisoned air into the installation through the concrete? We will act according to the instructions. Measure the pressure!"

The commission members looked at one another in embarrassment.

"Well, let's have your measurement instrument!" I demanded sharply.

"We don't have one," the major said.

"Sergeant, give them yours!" I ordered.

The sergeant produced the instrument.

"Who on this commission knows how to use this instrument?"

No one moved.

"Do you really mean to tell me that no one knows how to use this instrument? Just how did you intend to undertake the measurement! Sergeant, measure it!"

The sergeant attached the instrument and it read precisely 45 millimeters, just as he had reported to me earlier. I summoned the major and the commission members to each take a reading. When everyone had seen for himself that the pressure in the installation was above "excellent," I said to the commission members, "And now leave the area of battle installations immediately. In view of your complete lack of qualifications, I will not carry out any further tests with you."

The major's arrogance melted away instantly. When he realized what a dangerous situation he had gotten himself into, he became totally desperate. He fell on his knees before Vishnerevsky and begged him to cover up the whole thing. Vishnerevsky asked my advice. But could I tell him to lie? Should we accept the major's offer to write a new document that would grade as "excellent" the entire fortified area? What, then, of the arrests in Mozyr? Did the major intend those arrested never to know of the commission's lack of qualifications? Should they simply be made to remain in prison? And what about Kirilov, who, of course, knew via Chernyayev precisely what had taken place at the fortification? I saw only one way out. Vishnerevsky must write the chief of chemical warfare forces of the army that he had removed the commission from testing because it had been established that it was unqualified. And on his arrival in Moscow the major must confess that he had been unprepared to make the inspections and, as a result, had made mistakes.

I do not know what the major did. Whatever, it did not help him. When he returned to Moscow he and two other commission members were arrested and their fate is unknown to me. Shortly after this incident, we received a telegram from the chief administration of personnel stating that myself and another man, Ivanchikhin, were to be sent to the General Staff for entrance examinations.

Vishnerevsky, who trusted and depended on me even more after the conflict with the Moscow commission, was terribly disturbed. After checking with me he sent a telegram to the chief personnel administration, urgently requesting that I be permitted to keep my position at the fortified area for at least one year. In reply a telegram arrived from the commander of the armies of the district: "To Vishnerevsky. You are personally responsible for the prompt arrival of Grigorenko at the General Staff Academy for entrance examinations. I hope you understand that the selection of worthy candidates for this academy is an urgent state task."

I sometimes wonder what would have happened if the chief personnel administration had gone along with Vishnerevsky's request. Would I have taken the same path as Petrov, a rather untalented graduate of the Military Engineering Academy who replaced me in the fortified area? In less than three years he made a brilliant advancement in service, and soon after he had taken up his duties the fortified area was taken over by an infantry corps—so that besides being chief engineer of the fortified area, he also became the corps engineer. Later the Minsk area was taken over by the army, and Petrov became chief engineer of the army and of the fortified area. Nor did his rise to power not stop there. Arrests were swiftly clearing the way to the top for those who survived and soon Petrov was appointed Chief Engineer of the Armed Forces of the USSR.

Could I have achieved the same success as Petrov, or would I have shared the fate of the rest of the leaders with whom I served? I'll never know. As I left for the General Staff Academy, I had no idea that most of those who saw me off soon would face heavy suffering and even death. I learned of their fate in September 1938, at the Voroshilov Sanatorium in Sochi. The swimming season was in full swing and I spent a lot of time on the beach. One day I heard: "Pleasant holidays, Pyotr Grigoryevich!" I would have known that voice anywhere. It was Kirilov. For several days he was with me almost constantly. He spent the whole time telling me about the great work his department had carried out in purging the fortified area of enemies of the people. Often he would repeat himself. We would be walking or lying on the beach in silence, and all of a sudden: "Did you know that Kulakov was the military head of the center for rebellion in Minsk? That's the kind of person he was. You had too high an opinion of him. For a long time he refused to confess, but we forced him to. He was shot." Or: "And Vishnerevsky. He was an inveterate fiend. He entered the Red Army in 1918 on the orders of The Union to

Save Russia. All along he was connected with the White emigration and with foreign intelligence services. He had the rank of full general in the Polish Army." Or: "Do you remember that major from Moscow? How Vishnerevsky 'fought' with him? It turned out they were both trying to undermine the faith of the garrisons in their fire installations—so the men would be afraid to be in them. Vishnerevsky was also shot."

Listening to him talk, I could barely restrain myself. By this time I had lost some of my earlier naïveté. I had learned a great deal from Bogdanov, a class-mate at the Military Engineering Academy. A Chekist in the Civil War, he graduated from the academy with me and was put in charge of an enormous construction project in the Far East. There he was arrested. But after Nikolai Yezhov's fall (Yezhov had been secret-police chief), he had been released. We met by chance. He was already wearing a colonel's uniform and was working in the military group attached to the Council of Ministers of the USSR. From him I first heard of the Chekist torture chambers called fascist torture chambers. He was the first to weaken my belief that most of the arrests were justified, telling me that he had met not one guilty person—except for those conducting the interrogations. However, he did not object—why, I do not know—when I said, "Praise the Lord that all is now being corrected. Lavrenty Beriya is a reliable Communist."

Having talked with Bogdanov I did not believe one word Kirilov said. Even had I not had the knowledge I did, I could hardly have believed all his rhetoric. It became more and more difficult for me to be civil to him. But either he did not notice my state of mind or else he wanted to force me to lose my temper. I did. We were lying on the beach without talking. All of a sudden, in a quiet and rather thoughtful voice, full of bitter regret and malice, he said, "But what I'm really sorry about is that Kutsner, the bastard, got away from me!"

I jumped like a released spring. "You are the bastard!" I grabbed him by the throat and squeezed so that his glassy eyes nearly popped out. I shook his head and slapped him. "He got away!" I whispered angrily, gripping his shoulders. "Got away where? I see him in Moscow every day. But he got away from you. I did, too. You would have put us in your torture chamber, executed us, and then you would have slandered us after we were dead. Vishnerevsky was not an enemy. And neither was Telyatnikov. Kulakov was a very honor-able man. Don't worry, they'll get to you. Now scram—before I change my mind and choke you."

I pushed him away and he disappeared. I never saw him, nor did I ever hear anything about him again.

CHAPTER EIGHT

THE GENERAL STAFF ACADEMY

Ivanchikhin and I arrived in Moscow on a beautiful, sunny day with autumn already in the air. We asked at the station information desk for the academy address and were told it was on Bolshoi Trubetskoi Lane in the Zubov Square area. As we proceeded down Kropotkin Street by streetcar, we glimpsed someone wearing a general staff uniform. We pushed our way out of the overcrowded tram, but the officer had crossed the square. We rushed after him and caught up with him on Bolshaya Pirogovskaya.

"Comrade Commander!" I called out. It was my beloved brigade commander, Pomerantsev. He, too, was going to the academy, so we walked with him. On the way I told him about the fortified area situation. The news of Kulakov's arrest disturbed him, but he was particularly interested in my story about the chemical warfare tests. He said thoughtfully, "Yes, things are going to be difficult for Vishnerevsky without you. These are bad times. God grant he should survive. But all this ignorance and trembling before high rank has consumed us. A man from the center can get away with anything."

We parted at the academy entrance and I took his address. Ivanchikhin and I turned in our travel orders and went to the admissions committee to get the exam schedule. There we ran into a man in a leather jacket who was trying to look important and who introduced himself as Academy Political Commissar Furt. We presented ourselves. I noted he had not named his military rank. Later we learned that he was a "batallion commissar," not a low rank then. He asked us to stop in and see him after we'd gotten the schedule. When we did he plied us for biographical details. He was especially interested in any deviations from the party line, connections with "enemies of the people," and relatives under arrest or abroad.

During the two weeks of exams, I talked with Furt often. He obviously cast himself in the role of Latvian and Chekist. Always in his leather jacket, he was clean-shaven and wore an expression of importance on his not at all important-looking face.

Things went badly for me in the exams. The most important test, tactics, I failed miserably. I did just as poorly on the foreign language test. I passed only service regulations, Leninism, contemporary politics, and geography. Ivanchikhin passed all of his exams with grades of "excellent" and "good." Before we returned to Minsk we were told that all those accepted would receive orders.

In Minsk I buried myself in work. I did not expect a summons and was glad to return to a milieu in which I felt comfortable. Thus I was shocked when the telegram arrived: "Grigorenko ordered to Moscow for study in General Staff Academy."

While getting my documents, I ran into Ivanchikhin and asked him what he had heard, to which he replied, "Nothing."

"Maybe you will later on. You passed the exams."

"No, I won't. The exams were merely to keep us busy while they checked out our families. I know I did not pass *that* test. What I'm worried about is what will happen to me now." Ivanchikhin and I lost touch when the war began.

My family and I, all five, left Minsk together. Our third son, Victor, had been born that summer. Unfortunately, the relationship between my wife and me continued to deteriorate.

When I arrived at the academy Furt had left for good. I didn't know where he had gone and didn't much care. I ran into him again in 1945 at the Frunze Academy and approached him, saying, "Comrade Furt, if I am not mistaken!"

His face took on a pained look. "Furt? I am Furtenko! Please keep that in mind, Comrade Grigorenko."

"But I knew you as Furt."

"That was a mistake. I found my birth certificate and reconstituted my real name."

Not only had he "reconstituted" his family name; he had grown cossack moustaches. These failed to make him look Ukrainian and in fact made him look even more Jewish. He had become one of the most energetic exposers of "Zionists" and "cosmopolites" and taught military history at the academy.

Furt told me that he had been fired as political commissar of the General Staff Academy precisely becuase his name was Furt. Regimental commissar Gavrilov replaced him for a while, until a second high-ranking political officer, batallion commissar Nikolayev, arrived to head the political section. Both Nikolayev and Gavrilov used most of their ample free time seeking out enemies of the people. During the rest of it they engaged in a feud.

Nikolayev was a short, broad-faced, big-boned peasant type. His speech was clumsy and ungrammatical. No one in the academy took him seriously. He seemed to like me, and used to invite me in for chats. At first I thought he was trying to grasp the educational process through me, but soon I realized he was merely recruiting me as an ally in his fight against Gavrilov. He began to urge me to speak out against Gavrilov and to that end supplied me with "facts."

In no uncertain terms I told him what I thought of their feud and advised him to end it. But it kept on. Once, when they quarreled at a general academy party meeting, I could not contain myself, and I got up and dressed down both of them. Everyone laughed—not so much at my speech as from the release of tension. Arrests were widespread and the atmosphere gloomy. Any statement that did not call for vigilance or that ridiculed those who spread the "vigilance" psychosis could serve as a release valve.

Because of this incident everyone in the second-year class and all of the teaching staff got to know who I was. Among my friends from the second-year class, in addition to Pomerantsev, were Division Commander (later, Lieutenant General) Alexander Vasilyevich Sukhomlin and Brigade Commander (later, a marshal of the Soviet Union) Ivan Khristoforovich Bagramyan. Arrests of teachers were constant.

There were no arrests in our class. At first I thought naïvely that this was because everyone had been carefully checked out. Only later did I realize that two other factors were involved.

First, the higher command cadres had been so decimated that it would be foolish to destroy the replacements. Second, pure luck kept us safe. This was the autumn of 1937—the very height of the repressions. That they would end on their own was nearly impossible, but they simply were not permitted to develop and gain momentum in our class. This we owed to two men: Major Safonov, the secretary of the class party organization, and Colonel Geniatullin, deputy secretary. For some reason they believed that the diabolical machine could be stopped in its tracks.

I participated in the first and the most decisive battle against the attempt to begin arrests in our class. Arriving at a regular party bureau meeting, I was surprised to see two high-ranking guests present—academy political commissar Gavrilov and the academy Smersh chief. The meeting commenced. In an even voice, Safonov read the agenda, which consisted solely of routine matters. When Safonov was done Gavrilov asked: "What about the case of Sharokhin?"

Not until then had I seen Colonel Mikhail Nikolayevich Sharokhin sitting in a far, dark corner of the room looking crestfallen.

Though Safonov seemed astonished, in the same even voice in which he'd read the agenda he asked, "What case, comrade Gavrilov?"

"What do you mean, what case?" Gavrilov spoke more loudly. "What about the declaration?"

"Oh, the declaration." Safonov continued speaking evenly. "We will consider that last."

"What do you mean?!" Gavrilov leaped up. "I propose it be considered first."

"Comrades, you have heard my proposal for the agenda. Comrade Gavrilov, for a reason unknown to us, proposes we change our regular order. I see no reason for this. Whoever is for the agenda as I have announced it, raise your hands? Who is against it? No one. Who is for the change proposed by comrade Gavrilov? No one. Who has any additions to or changes in the agenda? No one. Let us proceed to consideration of the first matter."

Looking dissatisfied, Gavrilov and the Smersh chief sat through the meeting without opening their mouths. Finally, Safonov picked up a document and read that Sharokhin had served with certain individuals who had been arrested. When he had completed reading it, he asked, "Is there a proposal to take cognizance of this declaration?"

"What do you mean, take cognizance of?" Gavrilov jumped up.

"What do you propose we do?" Safonov's voice took on a serious tone.

"We have to call to party account a Communist who failed to observe enemies," Gavrilov said.

Very quietly the Smersh chief uttered an aside: "I'm sick and tired of having to arrest party members."

As if he had been burned by this remark, Geniatullin jumped up and spoke with his strong Tatar accent.

"Listen here, comrade, do you have specific facts against our party member? If so, set them forth!"

"I don't have to tell you everything I know."

Geniatullin exploded. "Where do you think you are? You are in a party organization! You are a Communist? You are talking about a member of our organization. It is your duty to put all facts out on the table. Otherwise we will charge you with disrespect for the party."

Safonov motioned him to stop and said, "Comrade Gavrilov, and partner, this is a party bureau meeting. We are considering a party member's declaration which informs us that people with whom he served have been arrested by security organs. That is, of course, unpleasant, but our comrade is not guilty, so all we can do is take cognizance of his declaration. This angers you and you even hint at possible arrest. Either you inform us of everything compromising in relation to Sharokhin or else we will report your conduct as not befitting a Communist."

Both our "high-ranking" guests looked put out. And when Geniatullin proposed a resolution to report to the Smersh party organization that its chief had been guilty of conduct unbefitting a Communist and of insult to the party bureau, his arrogance disappeared and he began to apologize and explain. But the resolution was adopted. Later we were informed that he had been subjected to a party penalty—a rebuke. And later on he was dismissed or transferred to another post. At any rate, he disappeared from the academy. From then on any declarations about a member of our class were taken into cognizance— including my own. Our party organization did not consider even one case of "ties with enemies of the people," and no one in our class was arrested.

My class, the first-year class, ran quite smoothly, thanks to Safonov and Geniatullin. Things were worse in the second-year class. Because access to us had been cut off, Gavrilov and Nikolayev did everything to stimulate "vigilance" in the second-year students. They expelled Ivan Khristoforovich Bagramyan from the party as an alleged Dashnak (member of the Armenian revolutionary federation), though he proved with documents that he had participated in the overthrow of the Dashnaks. Awaiting arrest, Bagramyan was unable to find support or understanding anywhere, and he became deeply depressed, saying he only wished they'd arrest him soon so that he could get it over with.

I told him to appeal, and he did, though unwillingly. The threat of arrest was staved off, and then came complete rehabilitation.

Things also worked out for Alexander Vasilyevich Sukhomlin, whose brother Nikolia, an important government official in the Ukraine, was arrested and shot in 1936.

Pomerantsev was arrested and imprisoned for four months. When he was freed in the spring of 1938 he'd lost his mind and was delivered to the chief military hospital. The authorities told his wife and son that the charges against him had been dropped and that perhaps he'd get well if only they could make him understand this. But Pomerantsev recognized no one and realized nothing. At his wife's request I visited him once myself. He did not recognize me either. He was not violent. He lay there quietly, calmly, occasionally muttering something which made no sense. He looked awful—deathly pale, like a corpse. In no way did he resemble the energetic, searching and bright Pomerantsev. And so without ever becoming conscious of his surroundings he died.

Yan Yanovich Alksnis was also a victim of "vigilance." He'd been in danger for a long time—since the arrest of his brother, commander of the Soviet Air Force, in 1936—and lived always with the fear of arrest. During the few days before they took him, we often walked about the city together. As if he would soon be bidding farewell to the whole visible world, Yan noticed and appreciated everything. I could not help him. He had not been expelled from the party and he had been presented with no charges. But all knew he would soon be arrested. He tried to forget what lay ahead of him. I learned a great deal about the military from Yan Yanovich. He was the last of the constellation of military theoreticians Kuchinsky had assembled when he organized the academy. Almost all were liquidated in late 1936 and early 1937.

Though not a young man—he'd been a tsarist officer and commander of a division during the Civil War, and, before his academy appointment, chief of the mobilization administration of the Red Army General Staff—Yan took a ballroom dancing course with many young people and got me to take it, too. One day he did not show up at the lesson, and I went straight to his home. His wife tried to send me away, but I went in anyway and was told he had been taken at dawn. She showed me the ransacked apartment and, weeping, told me how rudely they had treated him. For several days I visited her and comforted her, but one day I found the door sealed. I have never learned what happened to either of them.

As far as we students were concerned, the academy suffered a great loss. Yan Yanovich's lectures had been wonderful. Excellently delivered, bright, and informative, they had transformed that most boring of subjects—"the mobilization and organization of armies"—into a fascinating thing.

I later learned that the General Staff Academy was Tukhachevsky's idea, intended to upgrade the military cultural level of the Red Army. Under him, military schools were reorganized, the length of studies doubled, and the leadership and teaching staffs improved. The number of military academies grew rapidly. The General Staff Academy was at the top of this structure of military educational preparedness. Tukhachevsky himself selected the entire teaching staff and chose the academy building. He wished to take the position of chief of the academy, but when he was not released from his job as chief of the General Staff, he selected as academy chief one of the youngest of the highest-ranking officers—the talented military leader, organizer, and teacher, Kuchinsky. Such "stars" of military affairs as Svechin and Verkhovsky were brought in as professors. Brilliant theoreticians like Alksnis were common within the academy.

No sooner had the academy taken its first halting steps than the trumped-up trial of Tukhachevsky, Uborevich, Yakir, and others cast suspicion on all things planned by Tukhachevsky. Stalin saw the academy as an "anti-Stalinist military center," and the pogroms commenced. Arrests began in winter 1936 and intensified in 1937. The highly qualified teaching staff assembled by Tukhachevsky was almost totally annihilated.

Positions were taken by untalented or inexperienced people. In turn, some of the new teachers were arrested, which frightened the rest and left them with little enthusiasm for their new jobs. Texts that had been written by "enemies of the people," the first teachers, now could not be used. The new teachers wrote a hasty conspectus of each of their lectures, but fearful of being accused of proferring views hostile to Stalin, they filled their lectures with faddish dogmas.

For almost a year after Kuchinsky's arrest the academy had no chief. Then in early 1938 Brigade Commander Shlyomin was given the job, which he was obviously not up to. He was able to handle the administrative functions, but dissatisfied people kept comparing him with Kuchinsky, who had possessed a comprehensive military and general outlook and who was tremendously erudite as well.

Shlyomin was not stupid. During the war he successfully commanded an army. But as academy chief he failed to distinguish himself.

A man named Isserson was head of the faculty of operations, a field in which Shylomin took a great interest. Though Isserson was not a dynamic lecturer, his exposition was so logical that one did not want to miss even one link of his chain of unity. Shlyomin tried to compete with Isserson, both as a lecturer and in the organization and conduct of war-operational exercises, but Isserson stood his ground. He possessed excellent insight into the character of contemporary battle, at a time in the USSR when the outdated war-of-position theoreticians, mostly officers who had served in Spain, were in power. Spain had been a war of position, and those who had fought there affirmed that the coming war also would be. They felt that the armies must be taught to wage positional defense and to strive for breakthroughs by "grinding down" strongly fortified zones. These theories also suited the party and government leadership because they justified the country's lack of preparedness for modern warfare.

The theory of battle in depth worked out by Tukhachevsky, Yegorov, Uborevich and Yakir was cast aside. Great bravery was required of proponents of this theory. Isserson possessed such bravery. His lectures, problems, and war games were permeated with the concepts of battle in depth, even though he never called the theory by name. The German-Polish War of 1939 caught the Soviet political and military leadership off-guard. When they recovered from the shock, they blamed the blitzkrieg defeat of Poland on the fact that its political regime was rotten. Isserson was not satisfied with this explanation. Immediately after Germany occupied Poland, he wrote and managed to publish a small booklet called *New Forms of Battle,* based on the war. While cleverly sidestepping the government's explanation of Poland's defeat, he concentrated on proving that old warfare had disappeared for good and that wars of the present would resemble that which had rolled over Poland. Even now this book is relevant.

Isserson's future was mixed.

After the Soviet-Finnish War of 1939–40 had passed its zenith, the great military theoretician who headed the leading military faculty of the top military educational institution in the country was appointed to an ordinary military post—chief of staff of one of the armies fighting on the Finnish front. All Isserson's former pupils viewed this as revenge for his criticism of the "Spanish experience" and of the "Spaniards" themselves—those officers who participated in the Spanish war. None of us fully realized the danger Isserson was in. We did not know that he had a personal enemy and that his new assignment had delivered him into the hands of this enemy, Marshal Timoshenko.

For a time Isserson had commanded a division in the Byelorussian Military District when Timoshenko had been assistant commander there. Several times he had sharply rebuked Timoshenko for stupid remarks, sometimes even making him appear ridiculous, and not only when they were alone, but in front of commanders of all ranks—at various conferences and analyses of training exercises and war games. Timoshenko had come to hate Isserson with a passion. Now Timoshenko was commander of an active front, and his hated enemy was serving in one of the armies subordinate to him. All he needed was an excuse for taking revenge, and it turned up quickly enough.

Timoshenko, considered by certain authorities a great strategist, with Stalin's blessing, decided to bring Finland to its knees with one blow. To this end a division of the front was sent through completely roadless, forested, swampy territory that was covered with snow—into the deep rear of the Finnish forces.

Only Isserson opposed this mindless venture. He predicted that the Finns would move against this division with ski troops, cut the column into pieces by sniper fire, and piece by piece destroy the entire division. But the great "strategists" refused to heed his warning.

When Isserson's predictions proved correct, it became necessary to find scapegoats. The division commander and several other divisional officers were shot, and Isserson was removed from his post "for not having given the division direction." His rank was reduced to colonel. At the beginning of the war he was arrested as a disguised German, but somehow he managed to survive till he was rehabilitated and restored to membership in the party and to the military rank of colonel. He did not return to the army but was hired as an editor of the magazine *Voyennaya Mysl (Military Thought)*. I last saw him in 1960. His mind was still sharp, but what could he do with his interesting thoughts and observations? He could be fully honest only with former students such as me, those who remembered and still respected him.

Writing about this period, I find I keep referring to the fate of people involved with politics. The country's political climate was the background against which our study proceeded. My group did not have a permanent leader for about a month. Then Colonel Fyodor Ivanovich Trukhin arrived. Nothing distinguished him particularly except for the fact that he was not a party member—a rare thing among young commanding officers. During the war he would win notoriety as chief of staff of the Russian Liberation Army (the ROA) commanded by A. A. Vlasov.

Personally I did not like Trukhin. I was the only man in the academy with a technical military commission. Upon entrance I had shown a total lack of knowledge of tactics and therefore I thought that military subjects would be difficult for me. But Karl von Clausewitz, the Prussian general and military writer, was right when he said that the science of war is simple and accessible to a man of common sense; it is waging war that is complex. We were not waging war, and I swiftly mastered military science and felt in every way equal to my comrades. However, in summing up the results of our very first assignment, Trukhin said, "Comrade Grigorenko . . . studied tactics until he came to the academy. But he works hard and I hope he will soon catch up with us."

On Red Army Day, February 23, 1938, many students in our class received promotions out of turn. My own rank of military engineer third rank became a command rank of major. In Trukhin's class I had received the highest grade on the final exam. Only after that did his attitude toward me soften somewhat.

Truhkin was executed along with Vlasov—as reported in the TASS communiqué of August 2, 1946, published in the Moscow papers. In 1959 I encountered an officer friend from before the war. Our conversation touched on the Vlasov people and I told him that Fyodor Ivanovich Trukhin had been my group leader in the General Staff Academy.

"Trukhin!" He nearly leapt into the air. "I saw him off on his last journey."

"How was that?"

"Well, as you know, when Vlasov was arrested, a communiqué was published in the press stating that the ROA leaders would be tried publicly. Everything was ready, but the Vlasov men spoiled the whole plan by refusing to confess to treason against the motherland. All of them declared they had fought against the Stalinist terrorist regime and therefore were not traitors— but Russian patriots. They were tortured but to no avail. At that point it was decided to 'attach' a friend from the past to each of them. I 'worked' with an old friend of mine. Trukhin's cell was not far from mine. I talked a great deal with him. Our one assignment was to persuade Vlasov and his companions to confess to treason without saying anything against Stalin. For such a confession they were promised life. A few of them wavered, but most, including Vlasov and Trukhin, did not. Promises of rewards had no effect on them. Nor did threats. We told them that if they did not confess, they would not be tried but tortured to death.

"There was no open trial," my friend ended. "They were tortured for a long time and hanged when half-dead. How and by what they were hanged I will not even tell you. . . ."

That was in 1959. By then I had already changed my mind about the Vlasov movement. At first I had believed it to be German-provoked. I was not personally acquainted with Vlasov but I knew a lot about him. In 1940 hardly a day went by when *Red Star* did not write about the Ninety-ninth Division, which, under Vlasov's command, was a model of infantry training. I heard Vlasov again described as an outstanding commander in November 1941 when his Twentieth Army freed Solnechnogorsk from the Germans, and again when he defeated German forces besieging Leningrad.

I could not believe this man to be a traitor, but the reports turned out to be true. With German help, Vlasov was recruiting war prisoners into a Russian Liberation Army. The question of why he was doing this was painful. After all, Vlasov was a career officer, a Communist, and a pure Russian from a working peasant family. My heart ached. Then I learned that Trukhin was the ROA chief of staff and that his deputy was Colonel Andrei Georgiyevich Neryanin.

Neryanin had been a member of my class at the General Staff Academy. He was a serious, intelligent officer who quickly grasped new ideas and was not afraid to speak his opinions and criticize the higher-ups. At party meetings his speeches were sharp and businesslike. He often raised acute, timely questions and I usually supported him—or vice versa. An authority on tactics, he was among us one of the best prepared in politics and philosophy. Now this man whom I had taken as a model had turned up in the Vlasov movement. No one could convince me that he had joined the movement out of dishonorable motives. He might have made a mistake, I thought, but he would not act without what he thought was noble conviction.

In short, Neryanin's actions forced me to think. When the ROA leadership was executed, I became even more concerned. If they were traitors, why had they been sentenced secretly? After all, such crimes should be tried in public. Intuition told me that something was amiss, but I had no facts. Only when I became an émigré did I come to understand the history of the Vlasov movement and its tragic and hopeless character.

Late one evening in early 1938, after the children and my wife had gone to bed, my elder brother Ivan came to my Moscow apartment, led me into the bathroom, and turned on the faucets full strength. He told me that yesterday he had been released from the police ministry (NKVD) interrogation prison in Zaporozhe after being held there for a month. Upon his arrest he had been thrown into a cell that literally was packed with "enemies of the people." Ivan had been working at the Kommunar Combine Factory as an engineer in the foundry. Until he was imprisoned he had seen no "enemies of the people" but had heard about them in speeches made at the factory. Realizing the company he had fallen into, he decided to isolate himself and for several days refused to talk to his cellmates.

With horror he had observed how they dragged men back to the cell after interrogation. He had heard whispered stories of the methods of interrogation. He himself was called in to an interrogation cell at 8:00 P.M. and taken out at 4:00 P.M. During that time the interrogator told him to write out a detailed autobiography and then left him alone. In the cell next to him they were torturing prisoners. My brother could hear every word, cry, groan; the interrogator went in and out of the torture chamber through the door joining the two cells, and the torture masters came into my brother's cell to smoke and take a breather. Meanwhile the door was either open all the way or only half-closed.

When Ivan returned from the interrogation a man crawled up to him who had returned from "standing torture" just before Ivan had been taken to questioning. Standing torture consisted of forcing a man to stand for a very long time in a special small locked closet in which he could not turn or change his position. Gradually, from a lack of air and from fatigue the prisoner would lose consciousness and sink downward. Then he would be taken out of the closet, aroused, and once again locked in. From standing up for so long the circulation in his legs would be interrupted and they would swell with stagnant blood. This man had those horribly swollen legs. He spoke in a whisper. "Do not be afraid of people here. I know what you are thinking: 'They are all fascists, enemies of the people, and I got here by accident, by mistake' . . . I thought that too. But now I know: there are no enemies here. Someone is compelling us to call ourselves 'enemies of the people.' " He told Ivan about his interrogation. He was an engineer from the Zaporozhe Steel Works; subsequently he signed a confession saying that he had been planning to bomb the factory. After subsequent interrogation the man said to Ivan, "They are not yet torturing you. That means you may be released. They need that for some reason, too. If they let you out, try not to forget anything you've seen here."

My brother carried out the engineer's request. I was astonished at the number of persons whose names, cases, and tortures he remembered. We sat in my apartment till it was almost morning, and I wrote down everything he told me. He talked about trumped-up sabotage, terrorism, and espionage charges, the biographies the "enemies" were forced to write, and the tortures used—beatings, crushed fingers and sex organs, cigarette burns on the face and body, standing tortures, and torture by bright lights and with thirst.

I told Ivan I would take his story to the Prosecutor General of the USSR, Vyshinsky. We both tended to believe that this was something purely local, but we were not convinced. Because arrest might ensue from my statement to Vyshinsky, we agreed on a code for communication. We would write each other not less than once a week. If everything was all right, we would send post cards with run-of-the-mill content. But if one of us was arrested his wife was to send a telegram saying that he was seriously ill. Ivan, however, was afraid he might not be able to contact his wife. Before he'd been released from prison the interrogator had warned him: "Well, Ivan Grigoryevich, we are parting for now. Here is your pass and you can go home. It goes without saying that whatever you have seen and heard here is not to be told to anyone. We shall meet again soon."

"What about my passport and a certificate saying I have been freed?" Ivan had asked. "Everyone knows I was arrested. How am I going to be able to show up at work?"

"We will tell them," the interrogator had answered. "And we will talk about your document when we meet next time. Here is an address. Memorize it. When the time comes I will call you at work and tell you to go to the doctor. When I do, come to this address at 10:00 P.M. Then we will talk about your documents. Meanwhile, do not be concerned. No one will touch you so long as we trust you—even though there are very serious accusations against you. But we will speak of them later as well."

Obviously they were trying to recruit Ivan. Both of us knew that they would pick him up and put him back in prison if they found out that he hadn't gone home but had come to Moscow. We agreed that he should write me a post card as soon as he reached Zaporozhe. If I didn't receive one, I'd know he'd been arrested. On that note we parted.

The next day I attempted to make an appointment with Vyshinsky. His reception room was packed, but I was a major, at that time a person of magnitude, and the duty officer of the reception room quickly brought me to the small office of Reutov, the investigator for very important cases.

"Well, tell me what has brought you here?" Reutov asked me.

I began to tell him, but just as soon as he understood what the matter concerned he stopped me with a movement of his hand.

"We will not speak of that here." He pointed at the plywood partitions separating his office from the others, picked up the phone, and dialed a number.

"Lidochka! Are there receiving hours on Monday? Do you have many appointments? Fifteen? What's the quota? Well, you will have to add a sixteenth. This is just like the Minsk case. There's a very pleasant major here—a General Staff man. I am going to ask you to see him first, Lidochka. It is a very important matter. His name is Grigorenko and he is a Muscovite. He wants to talk about Zaporozhe. His brother just left there yesterday. So the major's information is very fresh."

On Monday I went to keep my appointment and, as Reutov had requested, Vyshinsky received me first. I know what an awful role he played in the Stalinist terror. But at the time, I must confess, I left his office feeling he was a worthy man. To be sure, his appearance was not pleasant. He had a prominent chin, thin lips, and his narrow, almost slitlike eyes gleamed sharply. He reminded me of a beast of prey.

As I sat down, Vyshinsky smiled cordially and said, "Do not hurry, Major. We have time. Tell me calmly."

I immediately felt reassured and free to speak my mind. In less than five minutes I told him the whole story. I did not name names or describe the tortures, though I told him that I knew all of these details. I finished speaking, and he asked his secretary to get someone named Nina Nikolayevna. He asked me several questions, and presently an elderly woman wearing a uniform with Chekist insignia entered. Vyshinsky said, "Nina Nikolayevna, the major here has very important facts from Zaporozhe. Please protocol his story in detail and report to me with recommendations. And, please, comrade major, tell Nina Nikolayevna everything, names and descriptions of everything that took place."

I left Vyshinsky with a feeling of deep gratitude and respect. He seemed to have taken to heart the violations of legality recounted by Ivan and wanted to take decisive action to bring them to an end. This appointment convinced me that tortures were local abuses. True, I recalled Reutov's statement "Just like Minsk," but I concluded that though there were many outrages in the provinces, Moscow was struggling against them.

In Nina Nikolayevna's office I wrote the whole story down. She questioned me about things that were unclear. I left exhausted but felt I had fulfilled my duty.

I sent Ivan an encoded letter with a report on what I had done. Some mornings afterward I awakened before daybreak, feeling quite alarmed, and saw the door of our apartment silently open and my wife slip through it. I jumped from bed and raced into the corridor. She was running down the staircase, headed for the street exit. I caught up with her and found she was crying. "Mariya, what's wrong?"

She sobbed, "Let me go."

Trying to calm her, I insisted that she and I go back to the apartment and that, once there, she tell me what was the matter. We returned and I said, "Well, what is it?"

"What's this?" She showed me a letter.

"A letter from Ivan," I said, looking at the postmark.

"What's in it?"

"I haven't read it. When I do, I'll tell you. Since when have you been reading my letters?"

"You know I never read your mail, but in this case something made me. I opened it but couldn't understand a thing. It was in code."

"Where were you going with it?" I had some idea and felt frightened. She forced her answer out. "To the NKVD, to the Lubyanka."

I sat down. I could imagine her at the police ministry: "My husband received a letter in code. Here it is." She would be forced to write out a statement and then would be questioned about my suspicious actions. From the time I had been in military service and involved in secret work I naturally had had to hide a lot from my family. All this she would report. And while her excitement brought back more and more memories, the Yezhov-Beriya boys would be dashing through the empty streets of Moscow toward our apartment on Bolshoi Trubetskoi to take me "warm," right out of my bed.

"How could you do that?" I said, nearly weeping. I decoded Ivan's letter and read it to her. In it he reported that the Dnepropetrovsk prosecutor had arrived in Zaporozhe to investigate my report. He had summoned the people I had named, asked them if they knew how information on them had reached Moscow, and then forced them to deny it all. When they summoned Ivan, they took his pass away from him and put him in the same cell from which he had heard the howls and groans of the tortured prisoners. By this he knew that the arrival of the Dnepropetrovsk prosecutor had changed nothing. Then they questioned Ivan:

"Whom do you have in Moscow?"

"My younger brother."

"Who is he?"

"A major."

"What does he do?"

"I don't know. He doesn't tell me."

"How does he know what happened to you?"

"I told him."

"How did you do that?"

"I went to see him."

"When?"

"As soon as I left here."

"Maybe you want to end up in the other room yourself?"

"That's your business. I want to warn you, however, that before I came here I sent my brother a telegram saying that I'd been summoned here. If he doesn't get another telegram from me tomorrow morning he'll know I have been arrested and will take measures."

Then they'd signed his pass and he had left.

When my wife learned what the letter said and listened to my story of what Ivan had been through, she asked my forgiveness. I myself would never have denounced a family member to the NKVD. Yet the party held up Pavlik Morozov (who had denounced his own family) as an example; therefore you might say that my wife had turned out to be more reliable. My heart, however, was not soothed by this logic. I simply could not understand her actions. If she actually had gone to the Lubyanka, I would have been destroyed. I thought of this every time I saw her.

Ivan's letter inspired me to return to Reutov. I had raised the alarm, but no changes had been made in Zaporozhe. People were still being tortured.

I was unable to see Vyshinsky—he'd gone to Byelorussia—so Reutov sent me to Vyshinsky's first deputy, Rogovsky. In his reception room were the secretary—a young girl—and two young, athletic-looking men who were dressed like one another. The secretary asked for my pass and put it in a folder. Someone from an internal office rang for her and she went in, taking the folder with her. When she emerged, she told me to go in. In the office, Rogovsky sat in an armchair with a high back. He did not even look up at me when I entered. Next to Rogovsky's armchair stood a weak-looking little man who was a whole head shorter than the back of the chair. This was Roginsky, the chief military prosecutor and a military jurist. His presence was probably supposed to put pressure on me.

"Well, what do you wish to say?" Roginsky asked, still not looking at me.

"Nothing has changed in Zaporozhe. They are torturing people there just as before."

"How do you know?"

"I have a brother there."

"But the Dnepropetrovsk prosecutor reported that though there had been individual violations, they had been eliminated and legality totally reestablished."

"This is not true. Only a week has passed since my brother personally heard them torturing prisoners."

"You believe your brother and not the provincial prosecutor?"

"Yes."

"You see," Rogovsky turned to Roginsky, "the provincial prosecutor is not an authority for him."

"For him evidently there are no authorities," Roginsky said. "He sees a person of senior rank, a person of the highest command corps, and he pays no attention at all."

"You ought to read how he writes, without respect, without restraint. Listen." Rogovsky got out the statement I had written for Nina Nikolayevna and read from it: " '. . .that is not Soviet counter-intelligence but a fascist torture chamber.' "

I interrupted him sharply: "To whom was it written?"

"What do you mean, to whom? Wasn't it you who wrote it?"

"I wrote it but I ask you to whom I wrote it. To the *New York Times* or to comrade Vyshinsky?"

"Of course to Vyshinsky. But the tone . . . "

"I can write to Vyshinsky in any tone. I didn't only write like that, I talked to him in that tone. And he did not rebuke me. Vyshinsky also began our interview by asking me to sit down. He put me at ease and listened to everything I wanted to tell him. Here in your office I am left standing like a schoolboy.

Maybe you are not interested in my business? Then let me leave, comrade Ro-govsky. I can find some other channel to answer my question."

"I beg your pardon, comrade Grigorenko. You must not take offense. Sit down. The question is complex. I am not entirely up to date on the business, so perhaps I did not put the question correctly. Tell me what you want."

"I want my statement to be checked out, tortures to be brought to an end, and those guilty to be punished."

"Very good. I shall send a telegram to the Dnepropetrovsk provincial prose-cutor ordering him once again to verify the entire matter carefully and report back."

"I've already told you that I do not trust the Dnepropetrovsk prosecutor. In my opinion things are no better in Dnepropetrovsk. He is not going to ex-pose in his neighbors' jurisdictions what he is hiding in his own. I ask you to appoint someone else."

"But then you might discredit that person, too. Perhaps it would be better if you named your own candidate." Rogovsky laughed ironically.

"All right. I would like comrade Reutov to make the investigation."

"We can come up with a candidate ourselves. What else do you have in mind?"

"Nothing."

As I opened the door to leave there was a ring in the reception room. The secretary, taking the file folder with her, walked past me into the office. A short while later she emerged and signaled to the two young men, who both depart-ed. The girl opened the folder, got out my pass, stamped it, signed it, and turned it over to me.

Soon after this I got a letter from Ivan, not in code, in which he reported that a new inspection commission, headed by Reutov, had arrived and was working in the building of the city prosecutor. The interrogators who had taken part in the tortures had been arrested as had the Zaporozhe city prosecu-tor and the Dnepropetrovsk provincial prosecutor. Those prisoners I had listed had begun to be freed.

I was satisfied and was finally convinced that the party would not permit tyranny. We rank-and-file Communists should not ignore local outrages, we must report them to the center immediately. Only years later did I come to understand that the situation had cleared up thanks only to the fact that my statement had coincided with the change in leadership of the NKVD. Beriya was sweeping aside those who had worked carelessly and permitted exposure of the internal secrets of the NKVD. At the time I also did not realize how much danger I had been in, but I was reminded of it one day in an auditorium on the second floor of the academy building, when a high-ranking official from the NKVD gave a lecture on "The Evil Methods of Foreign Intelligence Ser-vices Aimed at Undermining the Soviet Rear." During the intermission I went to the back of the hall to have a cigarette and heard someone talking behind my back: "Could you point Major Grigorenko out to me?"

I turned around and saw that it was the lecturer speaking. "I am Grigorenko."

"Would you mind if I asked you a few questions?"

I did not answer, and he asked, "You remember your reception at Rogovsky's office?"

"Yes, of course."

"Was Roginsky there from the very beginning or did he come in afterward?"

"From the beginning."

"Who was in the reception room?"

"A girl—Rogovsky's secretary. And two other men—in civilian clothes."

"And they took your pass from you when you came in?"

"Yes, the girl took it and put it in a folder."

"Yes, yes, that's all as it was supposed to be. Why, in your opinion, didn't they arrest you?"

"I didn't even know that they intended to arrest me. For what?"

"Yes, they were to have arrested you that day. Roginsky was there to sign the warrant as the chief military prosecutor. The question of arrest had been definitely decided. But they had not agreed on one thing—whether to receive you first or to arrest you when you first walked into the reception room. Evidently they decided to receive you and then arrest you when you left them and returned to the reception room. But something stopped them. Something frightened them. What was it?"

"Why don't you ask them?"

"They were not asked soon enough and now it's too late. Both were shot."

"Perhaps my boldness put them off. I did not think about arrest. I was convinced that I was right and there was no place in which I would have been afraid to defend my demands. Perhaps they felt that my daring meant that I had someone very strong behind me."

"Yes, of course, that is possible. You did conduct yourself . . . carelessly . . . as if you had strength behind you. But in fact you were acting alone. And even though you have not helped answer the question that interests me, I do want to give you some wise advice. Do not meddle in those dangerous affairs again unless you do have firm backing, and remember that any support you get may be here today and gone tomorrow. Think it over, Pyotr Grigoryevich. You have a restless character. Restrain it."

I have never known whether this was the friendly advice of a well-wisher or a serious warning from a powerful organization.

I cannot complete my story about the General Staff Academy without telling of an event that influenced the rest of my life.

In 1938 on party assignment I was sent to head the propaganda collective at the construction organization of the Palace of the Soviets, Stalin's proposed monument to Lenin. As everyone knows, the Palace was never built. For nearly two decades thousands of workers were busy with this project and billions of rubles were squandered on it. In the end, instead of the five hundred-meter-high Palace of the Soviets, all we had was a swimming pool.

The people who worked on the Palace of the Soviets were capable of great things, but the system was not. The only thing the system was capable of was demolishing that architectural wonder—the Cathedral of Christ the Saviour —that had stood on the site which that genius of a leader, Stalin, had chosen for the palace.

When I arrived at the construction site, people were not aware of the blind alley into which they had been led. They still dreamed of the realization in concrete and steel of a great architectural work. I was infected by the same enthusiasm.

Occasionally the propaganda group I led admitted new members. One day a beautiful and lively young woman arrived. What drew me to her was not so much her beauty but her eyes. They were full of sadness and contrasted markedly with her external gaiety. One day I joined a group of my students after one of our study sessions. This young woman—Zinaida Yegorova—was among them. All of us walked along the Kropotskinskaya, dropping out one by one to take a street car or go home. Finally just she and I were left and we were both going in the same direction.

Alone, we could be more open with each other. She told me that she had recently lost her husband, arrested as "an enemy of the people." Because of his arrest, she too had been arrested and only recently had been freed from the Butyrka prison in Moscow. We walked for a long time, the first of several such walks. She had not been exposed to torture and so I remained under the illusion that such atrocities were not committed in Moscow. But she had seen other things—mothers taken away from their children, even nursing infants. She herself had been arrested while her son lay ill with meningitis, with a temperature of 104. She told of three hundred women packed into a cell intended for thirty. She told me how any discussion of children was forbidden—how a chance violation of this taboo led to mass hysterics.

As she talked I wondered again and again why these women had been punished so horribly. From time immemorial a person has been held responsible only for his own crimes. But our humane workers' government had managed to think up the concept of punishing an entire family—wife, children, parents, even mistresses—for the crime of one man.

I was furious. But thanks to my recent experiences, I was frightened as well as angry. I was beginning to realize that one or two men could not successfully attack the awful machine of suppression. Thus I began to suppress my own feelings of outrage, to seek justifications for any atrocities I heard about and

to struggle, not against evil as a whole, but against its particular, partial manifestations only.

One day Zina introduced me to her family. My heart went out to them. Two
old people, her mother and father, a sick son who could only be understood
by his mother, and two nephews, the children of her sister who had been arrested in 1937. Of them only Zina could work, and, despite her higher education, she was employed as a technical secretary and receiving extremely poor
pay. After her arrest she had not been permitted to engage in teaching or any
other work for which she would be well compensated. She also took in sewing
and laundry, which she did at night.

Our long evening walks were taking up her time, and she wasn't getting
enough sleep. I began to stay away from her. And then I realized that the love
I had dreamed of in my youth had come to me. It had come late. No, I did
not have spiritual ties to any other woman. But there were the children. Zina
and I began to see each other less often, but that only made things harder.
I was so proud of her, having heard her argue publicly against the arrest and
slaughter of innocent people. She had a brilliant, analytical mind, and she was
brave.

This was the spring of 1939, and I was working on my thesis. But I could
not seem to get anything done. Zinaida simply would not leave my consciousness. Finally I went to her and told her that I loved her, but that I realized,
given the pressures of my career and my family, that mutual love was impossible for us.

And I left. Now I began to work furiously. I completed my thesis nearly
a month ahead of time, a lucky development because I received an immediate
assignment—to a battle site in the Far East, on the Khalkhin-Gol River. Before I left Moscow I submitted my thesis to the brigadier commander Kirpich-
nikov, and in my absence he reported on it to the state commission. The work
was graded "excellent," and I received a diploma with honors. Had I not completed the thesis before receiving the assignment, I never would have graduated.

Though I had very little time to prepare for my departure, I managed to
see Zinaida for a few moments. I told her—so she would know—that the
woman who lived under the same roof with me, though the mother of my children, was no longer my wife.

CHAPTER NINE

THE
FAR EAST

Thus in June 1939 I traveled with about two dozen of my classmates and a group of Japanese to an area in Mongolia where fighting had broken out.

Half of us were assigned to the newly established Front Group, led by Army Commander Second Rank Shtern, in essence the chief command in the Far East, and half to the First Army Group, led by Corps Commander (later, Marshal of the Soviet Union) Georgy Konstantinovich Zhukov.

We left Moscow on June 11 on the Moscow-China express. Our trip was scheduled to take five days, but it took eleven. We were lucky. The regular passenger train that had left just before us took not eleven days, as scheduled, but over a month. An insignificant military skirmish had paralyzed the Transiberian trunkline. It seemed to me that we stood still more than we moved.

All the young general staff officers like myself realized that our enormous country was totally unprepared for war. Our worries increased when we arrived at our destination and found that only eight trains a day were available to supply the needs of the warring army group and that two divisions were being moved, one after another, at a snail's pace, on four trains a day. In short, there were only twelve military trains a day—less than had been used on this same trunkline to supply the needs of the Russian armies in Manchuria during 1904–5.

Our train got in at about 10:00 A.M. We went straight to staff headquarters and reported for duty to Brigade Commander Kuznetsov, a former teacher at the academy who had just been named chief of staff of the Front Group. He had arrived several days before us and as of yet had no staff. We received our assignments immediately. Kuznetsov knew me and asked me to step forward first.

"Here is the order of the day of the First Army Group. Post it on the map." He handed me an enormous stack of onion skin paper.

Surprised, I asked, "All of this is an order of the day? For an army?" I checked and saw that the last sheet was numbered 25.

"Yes, it's an order of the day for an army. Post it on the map. And do it quickly. The commander and the military council member and I have to be able to analyze the situation before we go to army headquarters."

I went to my assigned room, trying to guess how an order of the day could possibly fill twenty-five typewritten pages. Two or three pages maybe, but not twenty-five! I unrolled the map and began to read. Instantly I understood. The order of the day was not devoted to army units but to various temporary formations: "Such and such a platoon, such and such a company, such and such a batallion, such and such a regiment, such and such a division, such and such a platoon, such and such a battery, such and such a regiment, such and such a front line," and so on. The entire order was written in this manner. To sum it up, there was no army. It had dissolved into detachments. The army commander was not commanding divisions, brigades, and separate regiments, but detachments! Little flags on the map denoted divisions, brigades, regiments, and batallions, and all around them was a sea of detachments subject directly to the army commander. At this point I recalled the Russo-Japanese War experience of commander Kuropatkin.

In 1904–5 the Japanese were very active. When they attacked a particular sector Kuropatkin would jerk elements from a sector not under attack and create a temporary formation—a detachment—and rush it to the sector under attack. Soon after this the Japanese would attack the sector from which that detachment had been taken. Again Kuropatkin would attempt to save the sector under attack with a temporary detachment. He would not, however, use the one he had first created but another, one that was easier to get to the attached sector. In this way the army lost its organization and turned into a conglomerate of detachments. Every experienced officer was familiar with Kuropatkin's tactic. It had been so caustically ridiculed in the literature of military history that it was hard to imagine anyone would ever repeat it. But Zhukov, who had never studied in the academy and who evidently had never studied the lessons of the Russo-Japanese War, was following Kuropatkin's methods exactly.

In 1939 the Japanese were again very aggressive. And once again the war was being waged with temporary detachments.

I took the map to Kuznetsov and told him of my suspicions. He agreed with me; together we went to see Shtern, who also agreed with my conclusions.

The next day Shtern flew to the First Army Group headquarters with several other officers. He spoke to Zhukov alone for a long time. Zhukov emerged from the conversation irritated. He gave orders for his forces to regroup—all detachments subordinate to army headquarters were to return to their regular units and regular command.

Regrouping took place at night over the course of a week. The Japanese did not know what was going on; they got nervous, and were continually shelling us with mortar and cannon fire, shooting off rockets and spraying us with machine guns. I came under mortar fire several times as I moved about with Shtern checking on the regrouping. There is nowhere to hide when you're under mortar fire. It's as if you were naked on a smooth surface. No matter how hard you press yourself to the ground, no matter what little hole you crawl into, you still feel completely visible.

It was not for nothing that I feared mortar fire. A shell fragment caught me just below my left shoulder blade. They removed it at the nearest field medical post, and washed and bandaged the wound. That was my first christening with the blood of battle.

After the regrouping had been completed, Shtern prepared to encircle and destroy the Japanese armies that had invaded territory we considered Mongolian. According to old Chinese and Mongolian maps, the boundary was along the Khalkhin-Gol River. But a newer map showed the boundary in one small sector to be on the other side of the river. The Mongolians used this map and since the boundary was not guarded on the Manchurian and Inner Mongolian side, the Outer Mongolian forces had put the boundary markers where they pleased without meeting any resistance. Conflict had arisen when the Japanese decided to put their forces on the boundary along the Khalkhin-Gol River, chasing off the Outer Mongolian border guards. Soviet forces had intervened and bloody battles had ensued for almost four months over a tiny bit of land consisting only of sand dunes.

Now Shtern was preparing to decide the issue by battle. At the same time he was resolving a multitude of problems Zhukov had created, one of them being death sentences. Shtern had gotten the Presidium of the Supreme Soviet to give the Military Council of the front the right to grant pardons. Seventeen prisoners were to die by firing squad. Everyone was astounded at the indictments. Each man's file contained either an official report from a commander stating that the man had failed to execute an order and should be court mar-

tialed, condemned, and shot. Or, it would contain a personal note from Zhukov stating that the man was to be court-martialed, convicted and shot for
not executing an order from Zhukov. There was nothing else: just one small
piece of paper. The following story will illustrate what lay behind such a deadly
piece of paper.

Major T. and I both left the Academy on June 10, 1939. That same day he
flew on a TB-3 heavy bomber to Khamar-Daba, the location of the headquarters of the First Army Group. He arrived on June 14 at about 5:00 P.M. and
reported to his immediate superior, the chief of the Operations Section brigade,
Commander Bogdanov, who ordered him to take his bearings. Naturally, any
man who finds himself in battle for the first time and who has not been assigned
a specific task simply bobs about among the entrenchments. How long Major
T. did this I do not know, but Zhukov soon put in an appearance with his
service cap cocked over his eyes as usual. The major saluted and reported to
him. Zhukov said nothing and went over to Bogdanov. They stood in a trench
and talked for a while, glancing now and then at the major. Then Bogdanov
motioned the major to come over. Zhukov looked at him and declared grimly,
"The 306th Regiment abandoned its positions and fled from a platoon of Japanese. Find the regiment, restore it to order, and return it to its position! You
will get the remainder of your orders from Comrade Bogdanov."

Zhukov left. The major looked questioningly at Bogdanov. But Bogdanov
only shrugged his shoulders, said he had no idea where the regiment was, and
told him to take an armored car and look for it. When the major found the
regiment, he was to send the armored car back and have the chauffeur report
where and in what state it was.

By then the sun had set. The major got in the armored car and thought for
a while about where he might find the regiment. He did not take a map. Bogdanov had told him that all available maps were useless. The war had caught
the topographical service unprepared. All the major knew was the general area
in which the regiment had been in action. He ordered the chauffeur to drive
in that direction, paying no attention to the roads. The clay soil of the Mongolian steppe was like asphalt and permitted traffic in any direction. The major
found the regiment rather quickly. Unarmed men were dragging west to fords
on the Khalkhin-Gol, more like a mob of civilians than soldiers. Most had
been sent into battle without equipment. Only officers who had been called
up from the reserves had uniforms. Most of the soldiers had thrown their
weapons away.

Leaping from his car, the major shouted, "Halt! Halt! I will shoot!" He
jerked out his pistol and fired at the sky. At that point someone hit him over
the head and he fell into a sand pit. Lying there he realized he would get nowhere with threats. He got up and began to call, "Communists! Komsomols!
Officers! Come here!"

While yelling, he marched ahead with the disorganized mob, and gradually a group of men gathered around him, most of whom had weapons. With their help he was able to stop the rest and by morning the officer staff of the regiment had been assembled and the soldiers had managed to retrieve many of their weapons. All surviving officers were from the reserves and were greatly confused. They could not even remember who was in their unit.

The major himself divided the regiment into units and named the commanding officers. He ordered the entire regiment to halt and be seated and ordered the officers to draw up lists of their men. After that he intended to move the regiment by units back to its original position. While the men were making up the lists he lay down to try to recover from his troubled and sleepless night, but he got no rest. An armored car drove up and a major jumped out and showed Major T. an order making him the commander of the 306th Regiment.

"You are to return to headquarters," he said to Major T., and when Major T. tried to tell him what he had done and what was still left to do, the latter ignored him.

Major T. went to the armored car and was met there by a lieutenant and junior officer. The lieutenant presented the major with a warrant for his arrest and ordered him to surrender his gun.

Major T. was taken to a small settlement of tents and dugouts, where he was interrogated by a counterintelligence officer. Asked why he hadn't carried out the corps commander's orders, the major told him everything he had accomplished during the night. His answer was not written down. Soon after this his trial was held and he was convicted on the grounds that he had not fully carried out the order he had been given, though he'd been in the process of carrying it out.

He was sentenced to death by firing squad but appealed this fate.

Thanks to Shtern, in the name of the Supreme Soviet the Military Council of the Front Group pardoned Major T. and the other sixteen of the First Army Group who had been condemned by court martial. All seventeen subsequently showed courage in battle, and each was decorated for heroism.

Kuznetsov soon recalled me to Chita. I had been assigned to the Separate Red Banner Far Eastern Army (OKDVA) and my presence in staff headquarters was necessary since it was possible that the Japanese, to divert our attention from Mongolia, might unleash a conflict elsewhere. Though I returned to Chita, I kept informed of everything that went on in Mongolia. Things were relatively quiet until September, when the First Army Group attacked, surrounded, and destroyed units of the Sixth Japanese Division that were on Mongolian territory. The Japanese never surrendered or moved. In the first place, they never received orders to retreat from their positions. In the second place, we had far more men and equipment than they did. Still, we suffered enormous losses mainly because of our commander's inexperience. In addition, Zhukov did not care about any losses we suffered. I was only in his army for a short time, but I'd earned his dislike with my reports to Shtern. He was a cruel, vengeful person and throughout the war I was afraid I might have to serve under him again.

The battles at Khalkhin-Gol were studied by a large group of specialists in operations from the staff of the Front Group and the First Army Group. Their report, which was released as a book, disclosed deficiencies in the preparation of enlisted men and officers. Military actions were described and thoroughly analyzed. Zhukov was not directly attacked nor Shtern praised, but anyone who read the book could draw his own conclusions. Zhukov understood this himself.

The book was warmly approved by the General Staff. At the time Zhukov was commander of the Kiev Military District. While the book was being prepared for publication he became chief of staff. The first thing he did when he took this post was to demand the book on Khalkhin-Gol. He read it and relegated it to the archives.

Thus a book that revealed through the study of one small military episode the basic defects in the battle preparation of enlisted men and officers was hidden from commanding officers. Consequently, these defects manifested themselves again in World War II.

When the battles at Khalkhin-Gol ended, the half-decomposed corpses of the Japanese dead were carried over the border, piled up in mounds and burned. The ashes were put into urns. We saw the whole thing.

I had never realized that the odor of corpses is so persistent. It followed us all the way to Chita. And even there it haunted me for half a year.

In Chita we were put up in the physiotherapeutic branch of the district military hospital and fed sanatorium meals. We lived there for several months until the apartment buildings were ready and our families began to arrive. Now we found out what life in Chita was really like. The bread lines were so long that either my wife or one of our elder sons was on one at all times. And even in winter, when the temperature dropped as low as fifty and sixty degrees below zero, the lines formed outdoors.

In the spring a rumor began circulating that the Front Group was to be dissolved. Then we learned that it would not be dissolved but reorganized into a Front Administration. The Far Eastern Front was created, consisting of four armies: the Second, the Fifteenth, the First, and the Twenty-fifth. The administration and staff were to be located in Khabarovsk. The Trans-Baikal Military District and the First Army Group in Mongolia were removed from the Front Group and made subordinate directly to Moscow.

In May 1940 we traveled with our families to Khabarovsk by military trains. This was the first such organized move I had made in my life. Khabarovsk was a different world from Chita. At the time the Far East had priority supplies. The stores were full of all kind of baked goods—bread, rolls, buns, pastries, and cakes.

The Front Administration was housed in a solid, comfortable building that had been the military administration of the Amur and Ussuri Cossack District during tsarist times. The crew that had prepared the building for our arrival had cleaned out everything deemed "unnecessary." The criteria used in determining what was unnecessary were very simple. They asked, Who needs tsarist books?—and the richest library of the district was destroyed. Who needs company orders from years back?—and the district archive was thrown away. We, as experts in operations, tried to save what we could.

After reading several volumes of company orders, we knew more about the Amur and Ussuri Military District of tsarist times than we did about our immediate predecessor, the OKDVA. In its time the OKDVA had possessed nearly legendary fame. Its commander, Marshal of the Soviet Union Vasily Blyukher, had enjoyed universal admiration before he was arrested as an "enemy of the people," tried in a closed court, and shot. The entire OKDVA administration was destroyed. Out of several hundred officers only two were released, and they both had been saved by Shtern.

I saw for myself the aftermath of the destruction of officer cadres in the Far East. Almost right after my arrival in Khabarovsk I went with Shtern to review his forces. Two years had passed since the mass arrests had come to an end, but the command pyramid had not yet been restored. Many positions remained unfilled because there were no men qualified to occupy them. Batallions were commanded by officers who had completed military schools less than a year before. Some batallion commanders had completed only courses for second lieutenants, and their experience had been limited to several months of command of a platoon and a company. How could anyone have thought that such a gap could be filled? If only two officers were left on the army staff, in divisional commands the situation was even worse. In the 40th Infantry Division not only had the officers of the divisional and regimental administrations been arrested, but also the commanders of batallions, companies, and platoons. Just one officer in the whole division was left—a lieutenant—and obviously he could not act as even temporary commander of the division. The corps commander, Colonel (later, Marshal of the Soviet Union) V. I. Chuikov, had phoned this lieutenant and told him that he was responsible for everything until the divisional commander arrived.

The divisional commander failed to arrive. Two or three were sent, but all were arrested either en route or on arrival. Only after the battles at Khasan began did Mekhlis arrive and appoint Brigade Commander Mamonov from his own reserve as the commander.

Everywhere we went we met people who admired Shtern. His arrival in the Far East in 1938 had marked the end of the wave of mass arrests and had resulted in the liberation of a number of senior officers from prison. Shtern had written a very daring report to Stalin with an analysis of the dangerous situation in the Far East created by the destruction of the officer corps. Beriya presented this report to Stalin and undertook himself to "correct the situation." Of course, we were simply making a transition from the Yezhov terror to the Beriya terror. But at least in the Far East something positive resulted from the transition. The arrests came to an end and some individuals were released and restored to their posts. That such improvements were related to Beriya's schemes does not in any way lessen Shtern's courage and nobility.

Shtern was attractive, handsome, and dark-haired. When he walked he leaned forward a bit, in the style of weight lifters or wrestlers. He spoke in a slightly muffled voice, stressing his "o's." During a year with him I never once heard him raise his voice at anyone, interrupt anyone, or react arrogantly to something said to him—though he certainly heard many things that tried his patience.

In Biro-Bidjan he was admired because of his Jewish origin. Jewish manual workers, white-collar workers, and intellectuals used to come to his railway car in order to greet him, give him gifts, or just look at a Jewish commanding officer.

Army Commander of the Second Rank (later, Marshal of the Soviet Union) Ivan Stepanovich Konev, commander of the Second Army, differed greatly from Shtern. He was swift in his decisions and actions and unrestrained with his subordinates. I had met Konev back in the mid-thirties when he was commander of the 2nd Infantry Division stationed in Minsk. There his behavior was acceptable, if at times somewhat frightening for the target of his wrath. But now, in a luxurious general's office, his conduct seemed inappropriate.

One time Konev's behavior caused even me to get into a conflict with him. A staff exercise was being readied by Konev. The staff of the front, led by me, was sent to assist him in the exercise. When I approached him with the solution to a problem that came up, I could see that he was irritated, but I spread out my maps and started to report. He listened halfheartedly and all of a sudden burst out, "What kind of nonsense is this?" He began shouting louder and louder, and getting increasingly worked up. I started to roll up the maps.

"What are you doing?" Konev shouted at me.

"I am rolling up the maps."

"Why?"

"I see you are out of sorts. I can come back when you are in a better mood."

"I already am. Spread out the maps."

I did, and we proceeded to discuss the exercise calmly.

The next day Konev came to the room in which I was working.

"Pyotr Grigoryevich, I ask your pardon for what happened yesterday."

"There's no need, Ivan Stepanovich. It happens to all of us."

From that day on Konev always treated me respectfully. However, those who fought under him all commented on his temper. Still, they did not accuse him, as they did Chuikov, of being insulting.

The commander of the First Army, Corps Commander (later, Army General) Markian Mikhailovich Popov, was yet another distinctive individual. Popov was tall, with good posture, blond hair and fine features. He was young-looking, communicative, and jolly, and an ardent sportsman. Popular with both officers and enlisted men, he had a quick, logical mind; yet he was unlucky in the war. Yes, he met with success on the battlefield, extraordinary success at times, but he was not liked by those close to Stalin. Perhaps Stalin himself did not like him. Popov was twice removed from command over a front and for the rest of his life he served under the most talentless, tactless, and crude of all commanders, Chuikov. I encountered Popov more than once after service in the Far East. During the war I served for a time in the armies of the Second Baltic Front, which he commanded. After the war I worked in the Frunze Academy where I often met him, as he was chief of staff of land armies—of which the academy was a part. I retain the greatest respect for this man.

Shtern did not command the Far Eastern front for very long before he was summoned to Moscow and named commander of antiaircraft defense. On the first day of the war, after he had received the report of the German attack, he set out for his post. Within a few days he was arrested as a "German" (he was Jewish), and shot. In 1956 I met his wife in the sanatorium of the Ministry of Defense in Kislovodsk. She had only recently been freed from a camp in which she had served a sentence as "the wife of a disguised German carrying out espionage assignments for the Abwehr." At first I didn't recognize her. When I did ask her whether she was Shtern's wife, she smiled and said, "I recognized you a while ago, comrade Colonel, but I did not wish to put you in an awkward situation. I thought that perhaps you would rather not recognize me." But that type of "forgetfulness" was an illness from which I never suffered!

Even before Shtern was called to Moscow, Konev, Popov, Chuikov, and many other high-ranking commanders were sent west. Army General Iosif Rodionovich Opanasenko came to the Far East to take Shtern's place.

CHAPTER TEN

INTELLIGENCE
SUMMARY
NUMBER
EIGHT

On June 21, 1941, a Saturday evening, I was awaiting the soldier who would take over the guard of the vault room, when the telephone rang. I hesitated before picking up the phone. Such a ring could only mean trouble and tomorrow was supposed to be my day off.

It was Vasily Georgiyevich Kornilov-Dugov, lieutenant general of artillery. He asked me to stop by his office on my way home. Kornilov-Dugov was not my immediate chief, so I knew I would not lose my day off.

I enjoyed talking with Vasily Georgiyevich. He was one of the most interesting officers in the front administration. Others—Iosif Rodionovich Opanasenko, for example—were skilled in placing good men in the administration. All the leading officers were people of broad military scope who did their jobs well and were willing to take initiative. They included: chief of staff, Colonel General Ivan Vasiliyevich Smorodinov; his deputy, and my immediate superior, Chief of Operations, Major General Arkady Kuzmich Kazakovtsev; commander of aviation, Colonel General Zhigarev; and chief of engineers, Lieutenant General Molev. Yet even against this distinguished background, Kornilov-Dugov stood out, not only because of his broad range of military interests but because of his intellect. Only my own chief, Kazakovtsev, with whom he was friends, could bear comparison with him. I was attracted to these men, but I approached them only when work required it. Still, they constantly stressed their good feelings for me and tried to become friends with me outside of work. This particular telephone call clearly was not of a service nature.

When I entered Kornilov-Dugov's office, he stood up and asked with a slightly embarrassed air, "Pyotr Grigoryevich, are you sure you do not have to hurry away? I don't really have any serious business in mind. If you have to go, I'll understand."

I reassured him I had no plans for the evening and we went into the back of his office and sat down in comfortable armchairs. Kornilov-Dugov enjoyed indisputable prestige, the respect of those who served with him, and the affection of his subordinates. Legends circulated about his firmness and wit. Like only a few others, he was not afraid of arguing with Opanasenko himself.

Kornilov-Dugov began our conversation. "To tell you the truth I have only one thing on my mind: the West. What do you think? Will there be a war there?"

"Absolutely!"

"Soon?"

"Tomorrow!"

We both fell silent. Then I continued, "You, of course, understand that my 'tomorrow' is not to be taken literally."

"I understand," he replied.

"War is imminent," I spoke again. "If the Germans have decided to attack us they cannot delay further. I feel they are already somewhat late right now. If it is to be, it will be soon. Intelligence summary number 8 reports an attack group in a take-off position. How can it be otherwise? Hitler has to find a way out of the war he started. He can only move against England or against us. He would have to be crazy to attack England. What would he gain by even a successful airborne/amphibious operation? The best part of his army would be tied down on the British Isles. And then a weakened Germany would be face to face with the powerful Soviet Union. No, if Hitler is going to continue the war, he first of all must conquer the Soviet Union. That is why he has positioned all his forces on our borders. Not for rest, as the TASS communiqué says. They could have rested very well in France, Belgium, Denmark. . . ."

"Do you think our government does not understand all that?" he asked. "And if it does understand, why was that reassuring TASS communiqué published? Why reject the possibility of a German attack?"

"I think," I said, "that you have failed to understand the TASS communiqué correctly. I imagine it is the personal work of Stalin. It reflects his Caucasian cleverness. He wrote it to egg Hitler on to action against England. The language is Aesopian: 'We realize that you have drawn up your armies on our borders and we are ready to meet them there as they deserve to be met. But if you are smart and remove them, we are prepared to pretend we never noticed them there.' "

"I hope to God that's how it is," Kornilov-Dugov replied. "But I get a different feeling, one that upsets me greatly. I think the authors are hiding their heads in the sand."

"Why, then, was there intelligence summary number 8? No heads in the sand there. If one read the TASS communiqué without knowing about the summary, one would have to feel as you do. But if you compare these two documents, it seems to me that you have to interpret the communiqué as I have."

"I wish it were so," Kornilov-Dugov said. "But it seems too wise. Who knows about intelligence summary number 8? The command staffs of military districts, fronts, and armies. What about the armed forces as a whole? Or the people? They only heard the communiqué. It reassures them, puts them in a complacent mood. I do not think that is good. Should we, in order to warn Hitler, deceive the entire country? We could warn him some other way and tell the country the truth . . . or else say nothing."

But I was unable to agree with him. I had not been brought up to criticize. To me words of the party leadership, especially those of the "great leader," were the height of wisdom; thus they merely had to be understood and elucidated for those who did not understand. I interpreted the TASS communiqué in a positive light. And I believed so strongly in my interpretation that my conviction was communicated to my hearers. I even shook the doubts of Kornilov-Dugov.

How ashamed of myself I was when I later heard the true story of intelligence summary number 8. Vasily Georgiyevich was right, and I had merely deceived myself in the interests of supporting my faith in the "infallible" leader.

I learned the complete story behind that document only in 1966 when visiting my friend and teacher, Alexei Kostyorin, who'd told me he'd like to introduce me to a very interesting person.

I was always glad to have an invitation from Alexei. He was an excellent conversationalist. I sat with my back to the door of the apartment and was so engrossed in our conversation that I barely noticed the knock at the door and Alexei's "Come in!" Therefore it was a complete surprise when my host, smiling widely, declared, "All right, service comrades, get acquainted."

I leapt up and stared in astonishment at my no less astonished classmate at the General Staff Academy and my service comrade in Mongolia and the Far East, Vasily Novobranets. We had been good friends during the last year of our joint service. The Writers Union had sent Vasily Novobranets with his memoirs to Alexei, and Alexei had very swiftly realized that the two of us knew each other well and decided to bring us together. We began reminiscing almost immediately. That afternoon Vasily gave me a copy of the manuscript of his memoirs and told me in full of the disaster that had taken place in military intelligence.

Before entering the General Staff Academy Vasily had worked in field intelligence, and then he had done operational work. A year before the war began he was reassigned to the intelligence administration of the academy and subsequently was appointed chief of the information administration. This dizzying promotion had been one of those "bold appointments" recommended by Stalin himself. Vasily Novobranets had taken firm control of the administration. When Beriya's intelligence service reported to the Politburo of the Central Committee and to the academy the "Yugoslav scheme" of battle order of German forces in Europe, Vasily studied it carefully and said, "Dezo!" meaning "misinformation"—a "plant." He reported to the chief of intelligence administration that the scheme was based on the reports of agents and had been checked out by "travelers"—people who knew nothing about the disposition of enemy forces but were sent out along specific routes with instructions to report on whatever they observed en route.

"Even without the travelers' reports," Vasily told us, "the scheme was definite. The battle order of the enemy was clearly an attack battle order. Not only did the 'Yugoslavs' not even notice almost one-fourth of the German forces, but they reported most of them in senseless patterns near the Atlantic Ocean. They showed German forces on our own borders where we know there were none and they gave no operational meaning. The Yugoslavs explained this absence of meaning in the battle order as a clear sign that the German armies were there only for rest. But this was a childish explanation. Even if those German armies shown to be at the Atlantic Ocean were really preparing, as the Yugoslavs affirmed, for an airborne/amphibious operation against England, then at least those armies on our borders, even if they were there for rest, had to be disposed in a defensive grouping. I did not believe that there were idiots in the German general staff who would plan an offensive operation against the west without taking all measures to cover their rear against the east."

The chief of the intelligence administration agreed completely with Vasily. But the Politburo was unwilling to listen to him. Instructions were given to disseminate the Yugoslav scheme, which Stalin liked, as the basis for evaluating the composition and grouping of the German armies. And it was on the basis of this scheme, not on intelligence summary number 8, that the TASS communiqué was written. The TASS communiqué deprived the army of elementary readiness for battle and disoriented the entire people; and the Yugoslav scheme struck a blow at the most knowledgeable, experienced, and heroic officers of the higher leadership of the armed forces.

Evidently because he felt many lacked confidence in the Yugoslav scheme, Stalin assembled a special session of the Politburo devoted to its defense. After several persons had spoken out in its support Proskurin, the chief of the intelligence administration of the Soviet Army and lieutenant general of aviation, asked for the floor. Despite several nasty comments by Stalin and Beriya, he delivered a convincing, broadly based and well-illustrated speech that tore the Yugoslav scheme to shreds and impressed the Politburo. Even Stalin seemed to waver.

But the next day Proskurin was arrested and shot. The new chief of Intelligence was Colonel General (later, Marshal of the Soviet Union) F. I. Golikov. A short while earlier, Army General (later, Marshal of the Soviet Union) G. K. Zhukov had replaced Marshal Meretskov as chief of the General Staff. Both Zhukov and Golikov commenced to carry out the Yugoslav scheme Stalin liked so much.

In the meantime the information administration was readying its regular intelligence summary. Novobranets submitted an outline for the project to Golikov, who took it to Zhukov. When he returned from Zhukov he summoned Novobranets, returned the outline to him, and said drily, "You didn't understand a thing. You must use the Yugoslav scheme as your basis!"

"But that's 'dezo'—'misinformation,' " Novobranets said.

"Don't be smart," was Golikov's reply. "Stalin himself believes in this scheme. Carry out orders!"

What could Vasily do? Was he to call in his officers, order them to rewrite the "dezo," and send it out to the armies in the name of the General Staff as the most recent information from intelligence? This was the worst crime imaginable. Then he thought of a plan. It would not be easy to carry out and it meant almost certain death. But he would not sign his name to a lie. For the next two days he did not go out of his office and did not receive anyone. At the end of the second day, Rybalko, lieutenant general of tank armies (later, Marshal of Armed Forces), one of Vasily's closest friends, visited him. Vasily told Rybalko of his plan, and though Rybalko warned him that carrying it out would mean death—or worse—he did not sway in his intention.

After Rybalko left, Novobranets put one copy of the outline for summary number 8 in the safe and took the other copy back to his desk. On the first page, in the upper left-hand corner, the words "I confirm this. Chief of the General Staff Zhukov, G. K." were typed.

Vasily took his pen and before the word "Chief" wrote "p/p," which in Russian means "signed the original." Then he turned to the end of the summary, where lines for two signatures had been typed in, the upper one for Golikov and the second for Novobranets himself. Vasily wrote "p/p" next to Golikov's name and then signed his own name in the proper place. This document thereby acquired the force of a signed original. Vasily's own signature indicated that the copy in the safe had actually been signed by Zhukov and Golikov.

Novobranets summoned the head of his chancellery and told him to have the document set in type immediately. When ready, the whole edition was to be marked urgent and delivered. The man was to confirm that it had been received at all locations and report back to Novobranets.

In a few days all summaries had reached their destinations. The urgency of its dispatch and the request for confirmation of receipt attracted attention. People talked about the document in military districts, at the fronts, and in the armies.

When Novobranets received confirmation that all copies of the summary had been delivered, he took the first copy and went to see Golikov. He put the document on Golikov's desk, opened it to the last page, and said, "Sign it."

"What is it?" Golikov looked up.

"It is the summary. It is too late to correct it. I turned it over to typesetting without your signature."

"Get it back!" Golikov screamed.

"It has already been printed."

"Bring the entire edition to me here!"

"Impossible. It has already been delivered, and in every case I have received confirmation of its receipt."

Golikov fell silent, and then with great effort said almost in a whisper, "You are going to be sorry for this!" Grabbing the folder containing the summary he dashed off to Zhukov.

The next day a major general came to Novobranets's office and told him that he'd been appointed his replacement. Novobranets called Golikov, and Golikov confirmed that he'd been replaced and that the chancellery had given orders for him to go to the Odessa sanatorium and take a cure.

The Odessa "sanatorium" was a secret prison of preliminary detention. Everyone in the army knew about it. Intelligence service operatives who were to be arrested were sent to this sanatorium several days before being formally detained.

Vasily described his stay in Odessa. "The first day I explored the entire place. It was well fenced and vigilantly guarded. I did not see any other prisoners that whole day. I had been tailed on the train, but my bodyguards had disappeared as soon as the sanatorium Ford picked me up at the station.

"I wondered where they would take me when they arrested me and thought they might finish me off right there. The sanatorium was filled with nooks and crannies. Maybe they wouldn't bother with arrest. Just a bullet in the head from behind a bush. No one would hear the shot. And no one would ever find out about it. I had merely told my wife I was off on an urgent assignment.

She would not guess what had taken place until they asked her to leave my officer's apartment for the day. I walked about the sanitorium park thinking these gloomy thoughts.

"On the fourth day I awakened to the sound of distant bombs. It seemed to be coming from the direction of the military airdrome.

"I got up and quickly dressed. When I opened the door, an ugly guard was standing in front of me. After some argument, he led me to the telegraph room. The duty officer was also alarmed by the explosions and he accepted my telegram to Golikov. It said 'I consider it a crime to be resting in a sanitorium when war has begun. I ask to be sent to the front in any capacity.'

"Viacheslav Molotov's speech at noon confirmed that war indeed had begun. Later that day I received the reply to my telegram: 'You are named chief of intelligence of the Sixth Army in the Kiev Special Military District. Report immediately to Lt. General Muzhichenko. Signed Golikov.' "

Despite confusion everywhere, within three days Vasily was with his army.

The foregoing—and much more—was described in Vasily's memoirs, which never were published. My copy was confiscated by the KGB. A copy in Kostyorin's literary archive was also confiscated by the KGB. And the remaining two copies were confiscated from the author himself.

Because his story may never be available to the public I want to recount an abbreviated version of the rest of it.

Vasily's Sixth Army was encircled by the Germans. It broke out of encirclement but soon was surrounded again. Without ammunition, food, or supplies the fight was hopeless. Finally the army broke up into small detachments, each of which tried to make its way back to Russian lines. Novobranets was in one of these detachments and he was captured by the Germans and condemned to be shot. Although, miraculously, he escaped, he fell ill soon afterward. He kept losing consciousness but finally reached the viilage in Poltava province where his wife's family lived. They hid him. He changed his name for fear of being recaptured by the Germans and questioned as a high ranking intelligence officer. It was lucky for him that he did so; when he was recaptured his identity remained unknown to the Germans. He served four years in prisoner of war camps and he became a resistance leader. He spent his last year of imprisonment in a severe regime camp in Norway, where he organized an uprising that freed the camp. Then Vasily joined the Norwegian resistance as the commander of a large contingent of liberated and armed Soviet war prisoners who played an important role in the liberation of Norway.

By the end of the war Vasily Novobranets was a hero to all Norwegians. When he and his resistance fighters were taken back to the Soviet Union on Soviet ships, they did not receive the hero's welcome they deserved; rather, all were arrested as traitors. Vasily then spent eight years in the most severe of the northern Gulag camps.

In 1954 a delegation of Norwegian workers visited the Soviet Union. Among them were leaders of the Norwegian resistance who demanded during their audience with the Soviet premier to see their friend and companion-in-arms Vasily Novobranets. In two days' time Vasily was brought by special plane to Moscow, where he was restored to his position in the army, given the rank of colonel, and taken to meet his Norwegian friends. This was not what had originally been intended for him. Logic and the wishes of the Soviet leaders would have had him in his grave by now.

CHAPTER ELEVEN

THE WAR

BEGINS

June 22, 1941, was a beautiful summer day. I'd begged my superiors to let me take off—I'd promised my sons a trip along the Amur River—and reluctantly they agreed. Early that morning, Anatoly, Georgy, Vitya, and myself crossed the river by boat to a beach on the right bank. We had lunch, and for the rest of the day we played on the beach and swam. These were wonderful hours. All of us felt free and I experienced the joy of communicating with my children, something my duties as deputy chief of the operations administration of the front did not let allow me too often. The next day I was to go to the Baranovsky artillery range to prepare for a large-scale training exercise. I realized this might be my last free day all summer. I did not know it would be the last such day I'd have for a long time.

When we returned to the apartment my wife let us in. I began to greet her but when I saw the look on her face I fell silent. Her eyes were full of fear, grief, and confusion. They shocked me and I remained quiet, waiting for some awful news. The children froze, too, and looked back and forth from their mother to me.

Finally she spoke: "Petya, it's war."

"How did you find out?" I asked her skeptically, though inside I believed she was speaking the truth.

"Molotov just finished speaking."

"What did he say?"

"The German-Fascist armies perfidiously violated their treaty and crossed the borders of our motherland at dawn on June twenty-second."

"Did he say anything about our planes?"

"I don't think so."

I looked at my watch. It was 7:30 P.M. local time. The battles had been going on for at least seven hours.

"Get me my suitcase!" I ordered Anatoly, and at the same moment began to take off my civilian clothes and don my field uniform. When I was dressed, Anatoly handed me the suitcase and I dashed off to the staff office of the front.

Kornilov-Dugov caught up with me there. In passing he shook my hand and joked gloomily,

"Now I *know* you are a dishonest person. You said you didn't mean it literally—but it turns out that it was literally true." He was referring to my prediction, made only yesterday, that war would begin "tomorrow."

Once inside, I was greeted by my subordinate, Lieutenant Colonel Andrei Oleinikov, one of the recently appointed emissaries of the operations administration.

I asked him what he'd heard from the General Staff, and he replied, "Nothing!"

"Have you requested information?"

"Yes!"

"What is the situation along our borders here?"

"For the time being quiet. No movements are observed on contiguous territory. Our forces have been brought up to a state of heightened battle readiness."

"Did you hear Molotov's speech yourself?"

"Yes."

"Tell me about it."

Andrei reported to me exactly what I had learned from my wife. As he spoke, my indignation rose. When he finished, I asked him the same question I had asked her: "What did he say about the activities of our air force?"

His answer was the one I most feared: "Nothing!"

Even though I had heard the same thing from my wife, only now did I accept what I believed to be true. I'd hoped that perhaps my wife, as a lay person, might not have remembered some technical aspects of Molotov's speech. Molotov had said nothing about our air force because there was nothing to say. It had been destroyed by the enemy.

I sat down on my chair. "They messed up the whole thing!" I said in a desperate voice. "Now we'll be fighting without an air force. That's the 'wise policy' for you. Wise indeed."

"What do you mean—without an air force?"

"Why should I have to explain it to you? We studied in the same academy. Do you remember how the Germans began in Poland, France, and Norway? Everywhere they first destroyed the air force. Then they went on to destroy the land armies without interference. You don't have to be wise to see this and to take measures to ward off such an attack. But our Supreme Command gave no thought to this at all—and now the entire western front of our air force has been annihilated."

"But Molotov said nothing about bombings of our airdromes. He said only that German air forces were bombing Odessa, Kiev, Smolensk, and Riga."

"Yes, and why do you think he didn't mention our air force? As military men it should be perfectly clear to us that no one would begin a war by bombing cities. It's the air force that has to be destroyed first. Only after that is it time to deal with the land forces, and only after that can the population be frightened by bombings of cities and columns of refugees."

Andrei tried to protest, but I had no time for a discussion with him. In any case, he was not an interesting person. His military knowledge was of a formal sort, learned by rote. He lacked the talent for analysis, for reaching his own conclusions.

I had a lot to do. As I left I said to him, "Ask Moscow again about the situation. If you hear nothing new within the hour then ask Shevchenko [emissary of the Far East] to come to the phone. I will talk with him myself. After all, the war has been under way for at least nine hours now."

I left and commenced my work. Putting into effect the plan for concealment of our forces took all my time. I forgot about the conversation with Oleinikov. At about two in the morning I finished up and, after giving instructions to the duty officer, went home. Instructions and further information had never arrived from the General Staff in Moscow. Colonel Shevchenko had told me that he could add nothing to what Molotov had reported in his radio address.

When I reached the apartment I opened the door quietly so as not to awaken my family, but my wife was waiting up for me. She looked alarmed and began speaking immediately,

"L.'s son came here twice and said that his father asked you to come to see him no matter when you come home."

L. was one of the most important party chiefs of the administration of the Far Eastern front. From the very first we had been friends. He lived in our building. I ran to his apartment and knocked quietly on the door. L. opened it immediately and silently motioned me in to his office. Once inside he shut the door tightly and immediately whispered, "Did you speak with Oleinikov today?"

I told him the entire conversation.

"First of all," L. said after listening to me, "remember that you and I have not talked. I gave you no advice. You can conduct yourself however you please and say whatever you please, but if you should ever say that you doubted Stalin's wisdom, I cannot help you in any way."

"I did not mention Stalin's name."

"That does not matter. There is just one person in our country who is 'wise.' Therefore remember that you did not speak at all of 'wisdom' in the way Oleinikov says you did."

"But that's not true. I did."

"I ought not to be trying to help you. I did not see you. You and I did not speak with each other. I did not give you any advice. You can conduct yourself as you please and say whatever you like but if you should say that you had doubts of Stalin's wisdom, I cannot help you in any way." After he had finished delivering this torrent of words, he added, "And remember, too, that this matter concerns not just your party membership but your life. I will do my best not to permit your arrest until the completion of the party investigation. But if that investigation concludes that you had doubts about the wisdom of the leader, I will wash my hands of you. That's it! Be off with you! And think hard before tomorrow. In the morning you will be invited to an investigating committee whose members I have named. Do not forget when you come in to see us that you have no idea why you have been summoned there."

I couldn't sleep that night. In the morning the investigation commenced, and I "easily" proved that I had had no doubts about the wisdom of the "wisest of the wise" and that my comments had been directed at the military command that had ignored the preparation of Hitler's attack.

The investigation went on for a long time. At each stage I had to repeat my lie. My conscience protested, but my mind said that L. was right. And then, behold—man is master at calming a troubled conscience. At one point I was particularly upset by having to repeat my lie and I said, "I have condemned the views which were uttered in my conversation with Oleinikov. I consider them to be harmful, particularly at the beginning of a war when it is every Communist's duty to strengthen the trust of the people in the leadership of the party, the government, and the command of the armed forces. Repetition of these mistaken views here can only sow doubts among the people. Therefore in the future I refuse to repeat my conversation. . . ."

The committee members fell into confusion and broke off the meeting. When we reassembled, their attitude toward me had changed sharply. I had made the best move possible. The top political command of the front had agreed that continued repetition of my "dangerous" news constituted disseminating politically harmful information.

From then on things moved swiftly. I was examined by a party bureau and at a general party meeting of the entire front administration. A decision on my case was delivered: "Grigorenko, a Communist of many years, possessing a party education, and a participant in the struggle of the party against deviationists, has been guilty himself of a crude mistake for which he might well have been expelled from the party. But, taking into consideration his sincere repentance, his past work in the Komsomol and the party, and his positive party and service recommendations, we will limit ourselves to deliver a stern rebuke with a warning and with registration of this incident in his party record."

I remembered my conversation with Oleinikov on that first day of war for a long time. Perhaps, in fact, it represented the point at which I turned from my youthful dream about a bright communist future.

As a result of the conversation I spent the entire war serving in positions normally held by generals and colonels, while remaining in rank a lieutenant colonel. It was only a matter of chance that at the very end of the war, on February 2, 1945, I received the rank of colonel. My conversation with L. was to cause conflict between me and Leonid Brezhnev in late 1944. I heard about it again when I spoke out in 1961 against the personality cult surrounding Nikita Khrushchev.

CHAPTER TWELVE

1941–43

Opanasenko, who replaced Shtern several months before the war as commander of the Far Eastern Front, was reputed to be a petty tyrant of little education and intelligence. Physically he looked as if he had been hacked out of an oak log by an ax. He had a powerful but seemingly untrimmed figure and his features were crude. His loud, hoarse voice lent everything he said a mocking tone. He profusely swore and often lost his temper.

Those closest to Opanasenko, however, soon discovered his poor reputation to be in many respects unfounded. First of all, he had a colossal natural intelligence. Though uneducated, he read a great deal and was skilled at evaluating his subordinates' proposals. Secondly, he was daring. If he decided to do something, he did it, assuming all responsibility. Never did he put blame on a subordinate for carrying out his orders. If a subordinate actually was at fault, Opanasenko would not turn him over to the minister or to a court-martial, but would mete out the punishment himself.

Opanasenko personally ordered many high-ranking officers to the front, among them the new chief of the operations administration, Major General Arkady Kuzmich Kazakovtsev. One day Kazakovtsev, having just reviewed his predecessor's operations plan, delivered an oral and written report on it to the chief of staff and then to the commander. The report began with the plans for screening. This being my responsibility, I spoke first. When I began to talk about the disposition of the front reserves, Opanasenko exclaimed, "Righto! If a threat is created here, we will move our reserves over here"—he motioned southward with his hand. "And if one is created here we will maneuver in this direction," he gestured to the west.

Kazakovtsev, who had remained silent when Opanasenko gestured southward, now remarked, "We'll maneuver, you mean, if the Japanese allow us to."

"How's that?" Opanasenko seemed distressed.

"On this railway there are fifty-two small tunnels and large bridges. If just one is blown up, we will not be able to move anything anywhere."

"Then we'll switch to automotive transport. We will maneuver on dirt roads."

"No!" Kazakovtsev exclaimed. "There are no dirt roads parallel to the railway."

A red patch appeared above Opanasenko's collar and spread upward. His face flushed, he barked, "How can this be? They tell me: 'The Far East is a fortress! The Far East is locked up tight!' And it turns out that we are sitting here in a mousetrap."

He ran to the phone picked up the receiver, and summoned Molev, lieutenant general of engineers, who rushed in, frightened.

"Molev! Did you know that there is no highway from Khabarovsk to Kuibyshevka?" Opanasenko exclaimed.

"Yes."

"Why didn't you say something? Maybe you thought the Japs would build it for you. In short, you have one month for preparation and four months to build it!

"And you," Opanasenko turned to me, "on September 1 you are to drive to Kuibyshevka-Vostochnaya and phone me when you reach there."

Again he addressed Molev. "If he doesn't get through, I don't envy your fate, Molev. In that case you will give me a list of those to blame for failing to build the road in time. That way you won't be so lonely where I will send you. Now make a list of everyone who will participate in the construction—army units and local population. Allot each of them sectors and set schedules. Make a list of all materials you'll need. I'll get you everything. I want to see a communiqué of plan fulfillment every day. And separately—a list of those who fail to fulfill the daily plan."

On September 1 I rode in a Gazik truck—a Soviet-made Ford—from Khabarovsk to Kuibyshevka-Vostochnaya, a distance of 946 kilometers (587 miles). I was amazed at what had been done and felt that plaques honoring Opanasenko should be put at the beginning and the end of the new highway. A more highly educated individual would have been stopped by the difficulties of the task. Opanasenko saw only the necessity of the road and sought the means to build it. Ironically, the building of the highway only added to the legend of his petty tyranny. During construction he demoted two district party secretaries to rank-and-file soldiers—something later cited as proof of his dictatorial ways.

Within the first days of war we received an order to send our entire mobilization reserve of weapons and ammunition to the west. Smorodinov, long our leading mobilization officer, was indignant—at any moment we might be engaged in battle ourselves. Together we went to see Opanasenko. But as soon as we told him our doubts about this order, his face grew flushed and he roared, "What are you talking about! There's a rout. Do you understand, a *rout!* Begin loading up immediately!"

Opanasenko's honesty distinguished him from those who provided us with information from the General Staff in Moscow. "Information" is not exactly the right word. In essence they continually tried to misinform us. They never indicated what map the operations communiqués referred to and in indicating the line of the front they enumerated the most obscure points. For example, they would cite a tiny place or maybe a high point alongside a large city. And this tiny place or high point would be called by different names on different maps. We would have to spread out maps of all scales, and one man would read the communiqué while the other operations officers searched the maps. Usually it took us some time to find the point in question. How could we know that the author of the communiqué was referring to a place just outside the captured city, instead of to the city itself?

Besides the problem of locating points, the communiqués were written in such a way that it was difficult to know whether our armies were attacking, on the defense, or in full flight. "With crushing blows our armies dealt serious losses to the enemy and, driving him back, our advance units are conducting battles on the line. . . ." Naturally, after reading such language, we would look for the line of the advance units out in front of the front line of yesterday. Not finding it, we would look for it back a bit, but not far. Finally we would find it forty to sixty kilometers back. Certain armies that we christened "marathon" armies managed in the course of a day to retreat by one hundred or more kilometers. We realized, of course, that these armies no longer existed, that the front line the communiqués outlined for us was occupied by rear units or by no one at all. All we knew for sure was that for the time being there were no Germans there. One general later wrote that when the officers of the operations administration of the General Staff prepared an operations communiqué, they would telephone nearby collective farms to ask whether the Germans had arrived there or not.

All understood the nature of this kind of information, and Opanasenko spoke out against its dissemination. He was not a passive critic, a grumbler. He had to take action. His first idea was to take all of the training rifles, machine guns, mortars, and cannons from the units and put them in fully working order. The chief of armaments reported that training rifles, machine guns, nonworking cannons and mortars, and weapons of both out-of-date and foreign design were available at warehouses in significant quantities. This gave rise to arms production in the Far East. By this time Opanasenko had been named representative of the Council for Labor and Defense, as well as representative of the staff of the Supreme Command in the Far East. The party committees of the provinces, the Executive Committees of the Provinces, the enterprises of all peoples' commissariats, and even 'Goglidze'—the plenipotentiary of the NKVD for the Far East—were subordinate to Opanasenko, who used his power fully.

The workers began by remaking into real rifles more than 300,000 training rifles found in warehouses. They then undertook repairs and restoration of other weapons and organized production of new mortars, and artillery and mortar shells. As a result of all this work, we would at least be able partially to arm new formations in the event of mobilization. Then Moscow came to its senses and recollected the danger threatening the Far East. Before receiving even half our mobilization reserves of material, Moscow stopped all further shipments, though they still required us to send weapons and ammunition along with army units sent west. An order arrived to dispatch immediately eight fully staffed and armed divisions to Moscow. At once the units left their camps for the dispatch stations. This happened so quickly that men who were away from their units failed to get there in time for departure and some units didn't have full complements of arms and transport.

Moscow insisted on full staffs and complements of equipment and Opanasenko was not one to permit violation of an order. Kuibyshevka-Vostochnaya was the seat of the staff of the Second Army, and there a reserve of all types of armaments, transport and traction equipment, soldiers and officers was set up. With the help of train commanders and specially appointed officer inspectors, the commanders of departing divisions and regiments compiled lists before reaching Kuibyshevka-Vostochnaya of all missing items in each trainload. This information was reported by telegram to the Second Army and on arrival at Kuibyshevka-Vostochnaya all missing components were delivered to the trains. Every train left the verification and release station with a full complement of men and equipment.

I nearly left for the front with the 78th Infantry Division myself. The commander of this division, Colonel (later, Army General) Afanasy Pavlantyevich Beloborodov was a particular friend of Opanasenko. When he came to bid Opanasenko farewell, I was in the reception room and Opanasenko was in with someone else. I talked with Beloborodov for a few minutes and he mentioned that he was going to remind Opanasenko not to forget to provide him with a chief of staff. His own had left to command a division and the chief of his first branch was not up to the job.

An idea flashed through my mind and I said, "Ask for me! Opanasenko likes you and will agree to it."

"Would you really go? You will accept a demotion from Deputy Chief of the Operations Administration to chief of staff of a division?"

"Why not? I need to be on the front."

"If you're serious, I will ask him."

Soon after, he was summoned into Opanasenko's office. A short while later they called me in.

"Do you really want to go to the front?" Opanasenko asked.

I assured him that I did and was sent to my apartment to pick up my suitcase. It was settled.

My family had been evacuated to the Altai. I left my next-door neighbor the key to the apartment along with a note to my wife, and departed. Beloborodov and I spent two more days in Khabarovsk during which time I adjusted to staff work. When we left, I regretted that I had not been able to bid farewell to Kazakovtsev. He was down south dispatching trainloads from the Maritime province.

We arrived at Kuibyshevka-Vostochnaya at 5:00 P.M. I was getting ready to go out to look for Vavilov, the chief of staff of the Second Army, when he arrived with a major.

"Where are your things?" Vavilov asked me, smiling. "I brought your replacement with me. Kazakovtsev raised such objections when he found out about you that Opanasenko phoned me himself and demanded that I see to it that you did not leave."

So my first attempt to get to the front ended ingloriously.

I returned to Khabarovsk angry with Kazakovtsev. When I got to his office he was writing at his desk.

"Sit down!" he muttered.

I sat down. After a time he pushed aside his paper, put down his pen, and looked up. "I suppose you're angry because I didn't give you the chance to perform heroic deeds for the glory of the motherland? Don't worry. There'll be time enough for that. This is just the beginning of the war. You know history. You know that the Germans are still fighting in non-Russian areas of our country. I have no idea whether Russians will fight for communism—but they'll not surrender Russia. Hitler is going to break his neck on Russia just as Napoleon did. Your turn will come. Though they are carrying on their backs the main load of the war, those fighting right now will only fertilize the earth. The glory and the decorations will go to those who end the war alive."

"I am not looking for either glory or decorations. I want to defend my motherland."

"Do you want death?"

"I am prepared for it."

"But you see, I am not prepared for your death. You hold a very important post. The work you and I do will determine whether or not the Japanese enter the war on Hitler's side. If they do enter, our cause is hopeless."

I never found out how Kazakovtsev persuaded Opanasenko to return me, but that he did showed that the unshakeable Opanasenko would on occasion retreat.

I learned something else about Opanasenko soon afterward. Without asking permission of anyone, he had begun to form new divisions to replace those that had been sent west. Universal mobilization of all men to age fifty-five was proclaimed. But this was still not enough. Opanasenko sent me to Magadan with an order, directed personally to Nikishov, the uncrowned king of Magadan province (including the infamous concentration camp center, the Kolyma), to check out all concentration camps and to free a maximum number of prisoners and send them to Vladivostok. Nikishov, a small, rather repulsive colonel, received me in a luxurious office located in a house with pillars that contrasted strangely with the barren northern landscape and the camp watchtowers. Immediately he began lecturing me on Magadan, saying that no unimportant criminals were kept there, and that he, if a threat arose, would personally order all prisoners to be shot and would not allow any of them to have weapons. I informed him that I was carrying out orders of the representative of the staff of the Supreme Command and the Council of Labor and Defense and that he had a copy of this order and it was his duty to answer it. The colonel, who throughout the whole conversation never once removed his papakha—a tall gray hat worn by high-ranking officers—evidently because he felt wearing it would make him taller and more impressive, saluted me and said he would prepare a reply. I never saw what he wrote. I only know that when he received Nikishov's reply Opanasenko summoned Goglidze, Nikishov's chief, and spoke with him for a long time. I also learned from Kazakovtsev that because of this trip and another one like it to Sakhalin, where we organized armaments production, I became the subject of a phone conversation between Stalin and Opanasenko. Opanasenko knew ahead of time when such talks would take place and he always invited someone from his suite to be present. During one such conversation, Kazakovtsev was present and heard Opanasenko say, "Grigorenko? Yes, Iosif Vissarionovich [Stalin], there is a Grigorenko."

Stalin replied and Opanasenko answered, "Iosif Vissarionovich, all that is a concoction. My subordinates, when they travel on my orders, carry out my instructions in the most precise way. Grigorenko, too, was carrying out my orders and I bear responsibility for whatever he did."

Stalin spoke again, and again Opanasenko replied, "No, no, Iosif Vissarionovich, there is nothing to be checked out. I already know that Grigorenko carried out my orders effectively."

He put down the phone and said: "Those sons of bitches! What they cooked up could only mean a firing squad."

Evidently if Opanasenko had conducted himself differently, I would not be writing these memoirs.

The war made time pass swiftly. Things that seemed important only yesterday were quickly buried beneath the weight of the present. Organizational matters alone could have kept busy an administration with twice the staff of ours. First came the super-urgent request for eight divisions to save Moscow. Then orders were given to send four more, and then one or two at a time, until they had requested six more. In all, they took eighteen out of the nineteen divisions constituting our front. Only the Fortieth Infantry Division remained to us—and that because it would have been difficult to move it from Posyet. In place of each division sent west Opanasenko ordered us to form a local replacement division on our own.

Moscow knew about these new formations but was convinced that it was impossible for the Far East to set up formations of any value without Moscow's help: There were no men; there were no weapons; there was no transportation equipment; there was, in fact, nothing at all. Therefore while knowing about the efforts at organization of new formations by the Far Eastern front, Moscow feigned ignorance. Opanasenko mobilized all men through age fifty-five, including those in all concentration camps located on highways or railways. He even got a certain number of recruits from Magadan, including officers. Thus he solved the problem of men. Some armaments and transportation equipment were obtained from the developing local arms industry and were indeed provided by Moscow: horses from Mongolia, artillery and transportation equipment from Siberia. Later on reinforcements were even sent from Central Asia. True, the reenforcements were totally unsuited to combat.

So second-string divisions were formed to replace all the dispatched divisions. In the end, two or three more divisions were formed than we had had originally. When the new formations became a reality, the General Staff at long last "made itself heard." All were confirmed and given numbers. And suddenly Moscow had so much faith in these new formations that it took four of the second-string units to the western front.

Thus from July 1941 to June 1942 the Far East sent twenty-two infantry divisions and several tens of thousands of reinforcements to the fighting armies in the west. Today we know that during the first year of the war German intelligence affirmed that the Soviets were pulling divisions right out from under the noses of the Japanese and sending them west. Japanese intelligence, how-

ever, claimed that not one Soviet division had left its station. It is difficult to
know how things would have gone in the Far East if the commander had
merely obeyed orders. He would have sent off all the forces demanded by Moscow and would not have created new units in their place because commanders
were forbidden to create new formations on their own. It would have been
impossible for the one remaining division, three army staffs and one front staff
even to observe the enormous Far Eastern border, let alone to defend it. In
this whole affair Opanasenko manifested statesmanlike intelligence and great
courage. His principle of replacing each dispatched division not only strengthened the entire front's capacity for defense, but, as the General Staff in Moscow
later realized, also was an excellent means of camouflage. When the west took
its last four second-string divisions, we did not have the capability or the material to form third-string divisions to replace them and formed infantry brigades
instead. Among these four brigades was the Khabarovsk 18th Independent Infantry Brigade. I was named its commander.

My command was one of the most satisfying experiences of my life. From
a group consisting mostly of officer-candidate students whose training course
had been interrupted when they were sent to serve as rank-and-file soldiers
in my brigade, and with almost no heavy arms and transport equipment, I
formed an effective, mobile, and alert battle unit that was kept almost constantly in motion and that learned to cope with the mountainous Far Eastern
terrain, winters, and absence of roads. My men liked and respected me and
I acquired a great affection for them. I worked with them for over a year.

In late January 1943 we had a big war exercise with our forces divided into
two sides—assigned, respectively, the tasks of attacking Khabarovsk and defending it. Opanasenko led the exercise himself.

My unit distinguished itself by swiftness of maneuver and flexibility of operation, and when the official study of the exercise was completed Opanasenko
wrote me a very strong recommendation. Thus I was sent along with a group
of other Far East officers to the western front for training in battle conditions.

We arrived in Moscow on March 21, 1943. I immediately wanted to go look
at Zina's apartment house but decided not to. The next day, however, I went.
A man always seeks justification for his actions and I justified this one with
the thought that I was, after all, on my way to the front and that I did not
want to die without seeing her again.

Rationalizing in this way, I went to Khamovnichesky Square. The idea that
I would merely look at the apartment house from a distance was forgotten
the very moment I saw the building. I'd recently been separated from my wife
and we were in the process of getting a divorce. I climbed with sinking heart
to the third floor. Aleksandra Vasilyevna, Zinaida's mother, opened the door.
She recognized me—though she had seen me only twice before, and that almost four years earlier—and greeted me warmly seeming to grasp my state

of mind when she said, "Take off your coat. Zina will be here in a minute."

I took off my greatcoat and greeted Zina's father, Mikhail Ivanovich. I looked about but in no way did I sense the presence of another man in this apartment besides Mikhail Ivanovich. Zinaida soon entered.

"Whose military greatcoat and service cap are these?" she called as she shut the door.

I went into the corridor. She saw me.

"Oh!" was all she managed to say.

Then we rushed into each others arms. After a while she said, with a bit of embarrassment, "I have to go and see someone. He arrived only today. We were going to get married."

Her words made me shudder and I said, "No, no, you are going to marry only me."

Zina fell silent and then slowly pronounced, "Very well. I will not marry him—but you and I will make an agreement: I am going to await your return from the front. If you haven't changed your mind, we will go through life together."

Thus with a feeling of celebration I went to the front. And the whole time I was there this bright feeling stayed with me, though the situation was not one that would incline a person to gladness.

We first toured several sectors of the front and met and spoke with experienced battle commanders. After this we were sent out on specific field assignments. I was appointed understudy to the commander of the 202nd Infantry Division. This was a rather complex situation. The instructions on my probationer status specified that I take charge of the division in order to gain experience at command of a division in a battle situation. But the official divisional commander was not freed of responsibility for the division. Therefore, though the subordinates listened to me, they kept their eyes on him. But we managed to work things out. When an important decision had to be made I consulted with Major General Poplavsky, the regular divisional commander. We did not have a single misunderstanding during the whole month of my probationer status. For more than half of that time the division stood on the defense. Then it went into attack, or rather, pursuit—the enemy had commenced the withdrawal of his forces. But since the enemy did not withdraw in a hurry (in one week we advanced from thirty to forty kilometers), we were able to describe our movements as an attack. My acquaintance with Poplavsky was, in my opinion, the most noteworthy aspect of my practice training.

Poplavsky had graduated from the academy in 1935, one year after me. He was a member of a "fortunate" class that was present when Stalin delivered his famous speech "Cadres Decide Everything." After this speech, Poplavsky immediately found himself to be of interest to the cadres department—which is to say the personnel department. They wanted to know whether he might be a Pole because his family name ended in "sky." Poplavsky told them that he had no Polish ancestors.

They watched him more and more intently and, though they saw nothing suspicious in his behavior, dismissed him from the army without giving any reason. And if the army did not trust him, how could the party? So Poplavsky was expelled from the party for concealing his Polish descent. The army discharge and subsequent expulsion from the party saved his life. During the mass arrests Poplavsky was not to be found in his regular milieu. His sole occupation at the time was regaining party membership. Finally the party collegium of the Central Committee admitted that the mere presence of "sky" at the end of a name did not prove Polish descent. To be a Pole, a person would have to be able to speak Polish. And so Poplavsky was restored to the party. By then it was 1938 and the ranks of the commanding officers had grown so thin that some of them were even being let out of prison; Poplavsky was also taken back into the army. He began the war as a commander of a regiment with the rank of lieutenant colonel. When I met him in April 1943 he was commander of a division and had the rank of major general. He would have continued with his service, but once again that worrisome "sky" at the end of his family name caused trouble.

After the Polish leader Anders had withdrawn his own army, consisting of real Poles, to Iran, those in charge decided to assemble all people whose names ended in "sky." And so Poplavsky was once again declared a Pole—but this time he was regarded as our own Pole—a positive sort of Pole. He was assigned to the First Polish Army and there achieved the rank of general. He might still have been serving faithfully and honorably in Poland, but then the Poles had the same thought that Poplavsky had once had himself: It was not enough for one's name to end in "sky" to be a Pole. Thus Poles like Marshal Rokosovsky and Poplavsky had to end their "useful" activity in Poland and return to Russia.

After finishing my practice training, I flew to Moscow, where I remained for a short time before going to the Far East. Zina and I lived in a little house in the cantonment of the brigade then out on the Amur River. The brigade encampment was located on the majestic Ussuri River. We spent many fine hours on its broad expanse in the staff speedboat or lying on the sand after bathing in the cold water.

The news at this time that the Council of Labor and Defense had "freed" Opanasenko of his duties as commander, as plenipotentiary of the Council of Labor and Defense and of the staff of the Supreme Command shocked and dismayed us all. For a full week Opanasenko kept to himself. Then he boarded a railway car and left, without bidding us goodbye and without waiting for the new commander—Army General Purkayev. What hurt Opanasenko most was that the decision concerning him was communicated in writing. Stalin did not wish to speak to him.

On Moscow's orders Kornilov-Dugov traveled in the railway car with Opanasenko. Later he told me: "Opanasenko was depressed the entire journey. He drank a lot but did not get drunk and hardly spoke to anyone. We arrived in Moscow in the afternoon. That night Opanasenko was received by Stalin. They spoke for more than two hours. When he returned to the railway car in the early hours of the morning he was elated. He told me in detail about his meeting with Stalin and talked about it constantly during the several days we spent in Moscow."

Following is the story of Opanasenko's meeting with Stalin, as told to me by Kornilov-Dugov.

Stalin greeted Opanasenko standing up and immediately asked, speaking throughout in his strong Georgian accent, "Well, now, tell me—were you angry with me? No, no. You don't have to reply. I know myself. You were angry. After all, you tried so hard—and Stalin didn't appreciate it. He didn't trust you. He removed you from all your posts. He believed all the slanderers. That's what you thought when you sat there all alone in your apartment and drank for a whole week? Don't answer! Sit down! You'll tell a lie anyway! You'll tell me that you never were angry at Stalin. Maybe that's true—but not all of it. Maybe you didn't get angry at Stalin as a human being. But you were angry at his actions. Every person gets angry if he tries hard and is mistrusted.

"But I did not mistrust you. Tell me who did I trust as I trusted you? Just tell me! You can't name anyone! There is no one. You were given more power in the Far East than a tsar's governor general. I put everyone under you. I put Borkov under you. I put Pegov under you. I put Goglidze himself and Nikishov under you, too."

(Borkov was the party chief of Khabarovsk region. Pegov was the party chief of the Maritime province. Goglidze was the plenipotentiary of the NKVD for the Far East. And Nikishov, whom I have already described, was the chief of Dalstroi—the tsar and god of the Kolyma concentration camp hell.)

Stalin continued, "Who didn't I put under you? I put all of them under you. And you think they liked that? Do you think they didn't want to get out from under your power? They wanted to! And they worked at it! They wrote things against you. Oh, what things they wrote! They even said you wanted to split the Far East off from Russia and become king in the Far East.

"And did I believe them? No, I did not believe them! I know you are loyal to the party . . . and to Stalin. And you never thought of the trust Stalin had in you. You forgot it when I freed you from all your posts. I know that I could have called you on the phone and said, 'You know, the party needs you some-where else.' Then you would not have even thought about objecting or getting angry. You would have gladly accepted even a demotion. But I didn't want that. I wanted to teach you a lesson. You thought that Stalin had forgotten the good, and I did what I did to teach you not to forget Stalin's good, not to forget that enormous trust which was put in you.

"Now I will explain to you why we freed you from the Far East. In the first place the Far East is no longer in the same situation it was in at the begin-ning of the war. An attack by the Japanese in the Far East can practically be excluded. We owe this, first of all, to our victories on the Soviet German front, and also, not the least, to your own activity in the Far East. And in conditions of relative security on the Soviet-Manchurian border there is no sense in leaving there a leader of such scope as you. We can get along with Purkayev as commander of the eastern front. And now we can 'let loose' Borkov and Pegov, Goglidze and Nikishov. But the main thing is that I do not want to lose such devoted men as you from the leadership. What would have happened if we had left you in the Far East? We still would have had to free Borkov, Pegov, Goglidze, and Nikishov from under your supervision. Circumstances do not require the retention of an intermediate person between them and Moscow. And what would they have done once they were free of you? Certainly they would have caused you all kinds of trouble. And here the war is coming to an end. It has already passed its midpoint and who are you? The commander of a nonfighting front. Yes, and a commander against whom no fewer slanders have been written than Dumas wrote novels.

"Therefore I have decided to give you the chance to command on an active, fighting front. You will end the war as a marshal who headed one of the deci-sive fronts of the last period of the war. But you'll not begin with the command of a front. You have to begin by getting used to battle situations. Therefore you will first become deputy commander of a front under Rokossovsky. I know he was once a subordinate of yours. But don't be put off by that. He has been fighting for three years. He is an excellent army commander, one of the strong-est of the commanders of fronts. You can learn a lot from him. And I am con-vinced that you will not let pride get in your way. I will not keep you in the rank of a deputy for long. Therefore learn as quickly as possible."

Within this whole story only one thing is not clear to me: Why did Stalin feel he had to give such a circumstantial explanation to Opansenko, an expla-nation that was more like a justification?

Perhaps it was one of Stalin's traits to try to make people like him. I do not know. I never encountered Stalin directly. But I have heard the stories of other people who did meet alone with Stalin and who left him feeling not only esteem but also warmth for him as a person. One of these stories was told me after Khrushchev's report on Stalin at the Twentieth Party Congress, a time when it was more advantageous to criticize than praise Stalin. The man who told it to me, Lieutenant General Pyotr Panteleimonovich Vechny, was very modest. Even those of us who were close acquaintances of his had never heard him say that he had worked in Stalin's immediate suite for a lengthy period at the beginning of the war—though any self-seeking careerist would have talked constantly about such an experience. But after we had read Khrushchev's report, Vechny sighed deeply and said: "This is not the Stalin I knew."

And he commenced his story, a simple human story about ordinary events and conversations. But out of his words arose the picture of a human being both great and humane! I am convinced that Vechny was sincere and honest. Stalin, he explained, actually made him feel that he could freely discuss with him the situation at the front and even calmly contradict him. And Stalin evidently did not forget him after this. How else can it be explained that Stalin took only Vechny's name off of the order in which he was named as one of those to blame for the failure of the 1942 Kerch operation? When reading the order, Stalin crossed out Vechny's name any time he came to it, never explaining to anyone why he did this.

I recount all this so that the reader will understand that my anti-Stalinist utterance on the first day of the war did not at all reflect a condemnation of Stalin and Stalinism. Ideologically, I remained a Stalinist, and even if I had some individual doubts, the cult of the leader was something in which I partook. Like most people with whom I associated, I connected the turnabout in the course of the war with Stalin, and stories of him as a human being encouraged the magnification of his charisma. Therefore, though I had begun the war with doubts about the "wisdom" of Stalin's leadership, I ended it believing that we had been very lucky, that without Stalin's genius, victory would have taken much longer to achieve and would have entailed far greater losses, had it come at all.

At about the same time that Opanasenko left the Far East, I realized that the war might end and I would have had no battle experience. I submitted a request to the new commander, General Purkayev, that I be assigned to the front. A short time after that my request was granted. I was ecstatic.

CHAPTER THIRTEEN

UNEXPECTED
REST

Zina, who was employed as a nurse in the medical unit with the rank of senior sergeant, decided to accompany me to the front. On December 2, 1943, we left Khabarovsk for Moscow. After a short stay with Zina's family, I received orders from the Chief Personnel Administration to proceed to the Tenth Guards Army of the Baltic Front as commander of the 66th Infantry Division. With great difficulty, Zinaida left her invalid son and elderly parents.

Our journey was sad. In Velikiye Luki, where we left the train to proceed further via auto transport, we saw total devastation. Not one building was undamaged. Most often all that was left standing were the big Russian stoves and their chimneys.

We arrived at the Tenth Guards Army headquarters in early January. The commander, Lieutenant General Aleksandr Vasilyevich Sukhomlin, a friend of mine in the General Staff Academy, greeted me warmly and told me that he had had kept open for me a position as deputy chief of staff for the auxiliary center for direction of operations. I agreed to take the position, pending almost certain approval from the Chief Personnel Administration. I knew that in two days' time the army was going into attack and I did not want to take on responsibility for a division I had not myself prepared. A post on the staff would allow me to gradually get used to battle conditions.

The attack was a failure. The troops got bogged down in front of the advanced boundary of the enemy's defensive positions and had to return to their departing points. Punishment followed swiftly. The army commander, the chief of staff, the chief of the operations section, and the chief of artillery were removed from their posts. In short, the entire leadership of the army administration was removed. Only I was left untouched, evidently because of my very short stay in this army. However, what seemed lucky to me turned into a disaster as soon as the new command arrived.

They saw me as having been left behind only by chance. I was engulfed in mistrust and prejudice. I gritted my teeth and with great difficulty was able to carry out my assignments and remain firm in my own opinions. Gradually the chief of staff, Major General (later on Colonel General) Sidelnikov, began to listen to me and to take what I said into consideration. However, the chief of the operations section, Colonel Malinovsky, viewed me as a competitor and from time to time tried to trip me up. After some time we were able to work things out and several years later at the Frunze Academy we became friends.

I was not so lucky, however, in my relations with another commander, Colonel General (later, Army General) Mikhail Ilyich Kazakov.

On one occasion an out-of-breath adjutant ran into my dugout. "The commander orders you to follow him."

"Where?"

He dashed out without replying. I followed him and saw the commander's car speeding off in a northerly direction where there was no road. I leaped into the front seat of my own car and found a reconnaissance officer sitting in the back.

"Get going, Pavlik!" I said to my driver. "Don't lose him!"

Pavlik accelerated.

"Where are we going?" I asked the reconnaissance officer.

"I don't know. Kazakov never tells me where he's going."

I unrolled a map and began to follow our course. There were no obvious orientation points. Villages and farms had been destroyed and snow covered everything. There were no roads. Tire marks went in all directions. Forests, groves, and copices had lost the configurations they'd had when the topographic photographs had been taken and therefore were no longer fully useful points of orientation. The only real points of reference were to be derived from the relief of the land, a task in which I'd had a great deal of experience.

We drove for about forty minutes in the direction of the advance outposts of the enemy defense. The commander's car was rushing along at top speed in a tank track.

I had no idea where he was going, but I knew that we'd soon fall under

German machine gun fire. I noticed a hillock ahead of us and ordered Pavlik to catch up to the commander before we reached it. He broke out of the tank track and raced up alongside the commander's car.

"Follow me!" I shouted to the commander's chauffeur.

My order must have been compelling. Without even looking at the commander, the driver followed Pavlik, whom I had directed down into a hollow in which we could move along and remain hidden. Suddenly German machine gun fire commenced. They must have been waiting for us to appear on top of the hillock, but seeing that we had turned away, they had opened fire on a narrow sector where we were visible. Though we raced across it, several bullets pierced the commander's car, one through the gas tank.

We reached the forest and stopped. I got out and walked up to the commander.

"How did the Germans get here?" he asked in astonishment, looking over his map.

"Where else would they be?" I asked. "Here is the German advance defense line. Here's where we began to turn back. Here is where we were fired on. And here is where we are standing right now."

"Do you mean we are not here?" he pointed at a totally different location.

I directed his attention to the relief of the locality and he realized his mistake.

From that day on Kazakov would go nowhere without me. He sent me to search for those who had lost their way and to check up on the reports on the location of our forces. All this took an enormous amount of my time.

I remember clearly the tremendous amount of work I did in correcting mistakes in orientation. On one occasion the 66th Infantry Division was ordered to move during the night into a new district, closer to the first echelon of the army. The division made its move and reported back that it had occupied the indicated area. In the morning the army communications officers could not find the division staff. Attempts to radio it were useless. Kazakov ordered me to find it. But how? I studied the area in which it had been before and I found such a plethora of roads made by armed force units that it was conceivable the division had gone not toward the front but toward the rear. Indeed I found the division twenty kilometers back in the rear, outside the army sector.

From incidents like this I drew the conclusion that most of the commanders in our army were incapable of orienting themselves without roads, easily distinguishable local landmarks, and particularly a local population of whom they could ask directions. I advised our commander to conduct a few exercises with all officers on orientation using relief. But we were continually engaged in marches and battles and there was no time for assemblies of officers. The only hope was that they would learn on their own.

During the two months I spent with it, January and February 1944, the battle activity of the Tenth Guards Army was most unusual. I arrived before the beginning of an attack operation that, as I have mentioned, failed totally. After this we carried out two more attacks, both of which were also unsuccessful. I left at the end of a fourth operation that resulted in a small, local success. Each of these operations was carried out after regrouping in a new direction. Therefore the attacks alternated with extended marches. There was no time for rest. The weather was bad too. A cold wave would come and felt boots would be issued and regular boots would be taken back—and there would be a thaw. Then the army soldiers would slog along in soaked-through felt boots. I will never forget those roads of war and the tormented, dispirited men squelching along them. Then, just as soon as regular boots were issued and the felt boots taken away, a cold spell of twenty or thirty degrees below zero would hit. This cycle went on and on. The men would be exhausted and ill. Many had been frostbitten. On top of all of this, the Germans seemed to know our every movement beforehand.

Our front (the Second Baltic, formerly the Kalinin) lay in a direction of secondary importance, and as such, we had neither the ammunition nor the reinforcements necessary for frontal attack operations. Under such conditions, other fronts dug themselves in and prepared their troops only for warding off enemy attacks.

Our commander, Markian Mikhailovich Popov, was an intelligent, enterprising person not afraid of taking initiative, and he selected a different mode of operation for us. He put the whole front on the defense—except for the Tenth Guards Army—ours. We were given all of the reinforcements and most of the munitions reaching the front. The plan was that we would secretly move in one direction, deal a sudden blow to the enemy, break through his defense, and develop a success in depth while drawing enemy reserves into the area. After turning over all conquered territory to our neighbors, we would withdraw and move in another direction. Thus we were supposed to disrupt totally the enemy's front.

Obviously the heart of this plan was surprise; but surprise was not something we specialized in. Before the first operations, the Germans showered leaflets on the attack launching area: "Tenth Guards Army! You are going to attack us here? Go ahead, get skinned! We'll skin you tomorrow!" They did. The only results of our first attack operation were enormous losses.

The second attack operation was likewise preceded by German leaflets. The wording was changed only slightly: "Tenth Guards Army! You have come over here? That's all right, we'll skin you here, too." Popov thereupon ordered us to postpone this operation by one day and to feign regrouping in another direction. The result was a bit better. We suffered fewer losses and moved from two to eight kilometers ahead.

When we were in the launching position for the third operation, the Germans again greeted us with leaflets. The men were indignant. All believed there must be a traitor on the staff. Those on the staff believed the same thing. Most of us, including Popov and the army commander, Kazakov, felt that the information was leaking from Bulganin (a member of the military council of the front) or his entourage.

Each operation was prepared as follows. In code the front gave us the launching point for the coming operation and the routes to be followed for regrouping in the launching position. Simultaneously the army commander was summoned to the front commander. He was supposed to be accompanied by his chief of staff or one of his two deputies. For the first operation Malinovsky accompanied Kazakov and I worked out the plan for regrouping. With the next two operations, I accompanied the commander and Malinovsky planned the regrouping. When Kazakov and I reached the headquarters of the front commander, the chief of staff of the front, the chief of operations administration, the chief of intelligence, the commander of the artillery, and the commander of the air forces all were assembled. There the plan for the coming attack operation was finalized. Bulganin had been informed of the processing of the plan, but if he was not present at the finalization, Markian Mikhailovich Popov would telephone him and Bulganin would then either come to the headquarters or order us to bring the plan to his official residence for his signature. During my first trip with the commander, Bulganin ordered the plan brought to him. The chief of operations administration and I carried out that mission. The documents were in my custody.

The procedure for approaching Bulganin was impressive. After we had completed a half-kilometer forward march, we heard a muffled order to stop. An officer in NKVD uniform came out of the bushes. We sensed the presence of one or two others who were presumably watching us.

"Identification!" demanded the NKVD man. He checked our identification documents, comparing our names with those on a paper he carried. "Follow straight behind me. It's dangerous to step to the side."

We marched. Once again: "Stop!" And then a new checking of our identification. Our guide disappeared. "Move along," we were told.

The last officer to check our identity pointed out a building, a kind of movable palace. We marched to it. At the entrance our identification was verified one more time and then we were led into a reception room. A colonel pointed to a table by the wall and gave orders. "Open your maps up here!"

Right then a girl walked in, evidently a member of Bulganin's harem, about which the whole front used to gossip. She smiled sweetly and put a tray of cookies and sugar on the table.

"I cannot unroll my maps here," I said.

"Why not?"

"Outsiders have access here."

"No one else will come in!" The colonel pushed the door partly shut.

"For me you are an outsider. The only person I have the right to show the plan to in this house is the member of the military council himself."

The colonel was obviously taken aback. My companion winked at me in warning, trying to keep me out of trouble. Finally he said, as if to excuse himself to the colonel: "The comrade lieutenant colonel does not know you face to face, comrade colonel!" Directing himself to me, he declared, "Meet the colonel aide to the military council!"

But it was too late to stop me. I replied to the general, in a firm but restrained voice, "I know who he is. But the colonel is not on the list of those permitted to see the operations plan."

Bulganin came in. He seemed sober to me, though I'd heard stories about his constant drunkenness. I presented myself to him. He greeted us cordially and declared, "Well, get on with it. Unroll your maps."

"I cannot do that while there are outsiders in the room."

"Who here is an outsider?" He smiled.

"The colonel is not on the list of those authorized to see the operations plan."

"I authorize him to. Do you need that in writing?"

"No, your oral orders are sufficient for me. I will open up the maps and make a full report—but I will be obliged to report to the General Staff that the operations plan has been compromised."

"Well, if things are as strict as that, we will not violate the rules. Everyone has to respect the laws. Even a member of the Politburo."

He emphasized the last word.

"Leave the room," he said to the colonel. The colonel left.

When we returned to the front commander's hut, he greeted us with laughter. He knew me from the Far East, and he said, "So, Far Easterner, you've been instructing us how to observe the rules? Bulganian phoned me. He didn't seem too happy about what you did, but in words at least he praises you."

The operation in question was essentially unsuccessful. On the first day we advanced only ten kilometers. Likewise on the second and third days we met with no success. But one thing in particular interested everyone—the leaflets addressed to the Tenth Guards were not delivered until the second day of the operation. Beyond a doubt this demonstrated that the leak existed in Bulganin's entourage, a fact that was taken into consideration for the future. The last operation undertaken while I was still there was prepared with particularly strict enforcement of military secrecy.

During the finalization of this last operation Bulganin arrived at Popov's headquarters very drunk. His swollen face was mottled with dark blue and red and he had huge bags under his eyes. He walked up to Popov, shoved out his hand, and sank down on a chair beside him. Popov saw the approach of

Bulganin's entourage through the window and covered up the map and other documents. When all had entered, Popov said to Bulganin, "Nikolai Ivanovich, ask all those who came with you to go to the reception room."

"I am not permitted to leave the Politburo member," a thug in NKVD uniform growled threateningly.

"Nikolai Ivanovich, I ask you once more. I cannot work while even one outsider is here."

"How suspicious everyone has become!" Bulganin remarked. "You have to understand—the comrade is my chief bodyguard. He also has instructions he cannot disobey. I will give him orders—and he will report immediately that I am interfering with his duties. . . ."

"I don't know anything about that, Nikolai Ivanovich, but I will not discuss the operations plan in the presence of outsiders."

They continued their argument for a while and finally Bulganin ordered his men to leave the room. He then proceeded to sleep for the remainder of the meeting. In the end he signed everything without looking at it.

This operation was the most successful of the four I have mentioned. Our forces advanced more than thirty kilometers and broadened the front of the breakthrough up to twenty kilometers.

On the twenty-fifth, one day before the fourth offensive was to begin, I went to the auxiliary center for direction of operations to check on preparedness for the next day. One section of the road I traveled was under German fire. A semiautomatic 37 mm. German cannon let fly while we were racing down this section, and a shell exploded right behind our jeep. I decided not to tempt fate on the way back and I went through the forest and bypassed this dangerous stretch. Two days later, on the twenty-seventh, the commander of the 101st Guards Infantry Corps and I were reviewing army units as they entered battle. We stopped where the road passed over some German defense positions that we had previously broken through. The wheel of a 45 mm. cannon got stuck in a hole. As the wheel sank in, the cannon suddenly jerked to one side and we saw that its barrel was pointed right at us. Both of us instinctively dodged and there was a terrible roar. I fell down deafened. When I came to, I heard a groan. I got up and saw that it was the corps commander: Both his feet had been shattered. We bandaged him up as best we could and sent him to the hospital.

The next day Kazakov and I went to a different auxiliary center, just the two of us, the commander's adjutant, and several signal men. En route to the center Kazakov said, "You know, I think you are going to have to take the position originally intended for you. I can't leave Dmitriyev in charge of that division any longer. When we finish this operation you'll take command there."

"I'm ready," I replied.

We arrived at the center. A ten-minute artillery preparation had been sched-

uled for 5:00 P.M. and after it the attack. At a quarter to five, Kazakov said
that he would like someone to observe the artillery preparation and attack.
I volunteered and immediately telephoned the division command point, asking, "Where can I find you?"

He replied, "You see the water tower on the map? The Germans blew it
up. But we have located our command point in the crater formed at the bottom
of the tower. You'll find us there."

Driving over, I realized that if I tried to cover the approaches to the water
tower (which were under enemy fire) on foot, I would not get there before
the artillery preparation began or even before it ended. I said to Pavlik, "Drive
right up the hill. Don't stop there—turn around and speed right out of the
zone under fire. I will jump out while you are slowing down on the turn."

I jumped from the jeep while it was still in motion and dashed to the top
of the hill. Pavlik drove back at full speed to the rear. Even before I reached
the high point I wondered why they'd chosen to locate the command in such
a dangerous place.

The hill on which the water tower had once stood was much higher than
anything around it. It resembled an enormous burial mound. The blast had
formed a crater about twenty meters across and three meters deep. The earth
thrown out by the explosion had formed a raised edge around the crater—a
sort of breastwork about two meters in height. The crater was like a mass
burial pit; it was crammed full of artillerymen, signal corps men, and engineers. No fewer than five periscopes stuck up out of it—all looking to the west,
where the sun was now setting. A chill crept up my spine as I realized that
these periscopes were flashing blazing reflections at the enemy. I tried unsuccessfully to find the staff officers of the division. Then I lay down in the western
portion of the breastwork to observe the artillery preparation. It was very thin.
In ten minutes it fell silent. No attack could be seen. Suddenly everything
began shaking. The German artillery was opening fire, a whole storm of it compared with ours. It seemed as if the Germans were going to attack and as if
we were going to have to defend our positions. The crater fell under fire. A
210 mm. battery began to work us over with a running curtian of fire. Most
of the shells struck the raised edge around the crater, but some flew past us.
Suddenly there was a loud explosion and almost immediately I felt a blow on
the bone of my right leg. I slowly turned my head, afraid of what I would
see. There was nothing, yet I felt a tremendous pain. I tried to move my leg—it
moved. I looked to the side and saw that a shell had lodged in the rear of the
eastern breastwork. I saw a dead sub-machine gunner, his back torn out from
his shoulder down to his waist, his gun completely smashed. Then I felt something hot and wet in my felt boot and I realized I was wounded. I pulled off
the boot, tore open two bandage packs, and began applying them with the help
of a soldier.

We descended and took shelter in a burrow that had been dug into the eastern side of the hill. There I met the divisional commander and his staff and saw for myself how little they could observe from that dark hole. When I returned to the auxiliary center and told Kazakov about our pitiful artillery preparation, about the attack that had not taken place, and about the Germans' powerful reply, I told him also about how I'd found the commander and staff of the division in hiding. He laughed. "What a troupe of actors! You should have heard what they reported to me!"

It took a long time to get me to the hospital. Reinforcements and artillery were moving in the opposite direction. At the hospital the chief surgeon ordered me straight to the operating table. I knew him only casually, but he treated me like a long-lost friend. When they had me stretched out and were preparing for the operation, he approached me and said, "Pyotr Grigoryevich, we are going to have to amputate your leg below the knee. It would be dangerous to try to preserve it. The joint sac has been destroyed and the shin and foot joint are damaged. Bone marrow might get into your bloodstream and then we won't be able to save you. I recommend amputation."

I had to agree with him. Indeed, my leg would have been amputated had not my wife learned of the wound and where I had been sent and arrived to be with me. She protested vigorously against the plan for amputation and won.

They operated on me and immediately sent me to Moscow, where I was put into an evacuation hospital in Marinaya Roshcha. Zinaida spent almost every day with me, bringing me home-cooked food each visit.

One operation was not sufficient. The chief surgeon of the Moscow military district, Dmitriyev, operated to prevent osteomyelitis and recommended that I convalesce in a sanatorium. So Zinaida, myself, and our son Oleg (from her first marriage) were sent to the Kislovodsk Sanatorium. There I had one more operation, again to prevent osteomyelitis.

In Kislovodsk a military medical commission examined me. Their verdict was: limited service, second degree, which meant that I was suitable for military service only in wartime and in the rear. After the war I would have to begin life all over again. I left Kislovodsk for Moscow, greatly distressed. I carried an order for ten days' leave. I was also instructed to report to the Chief Personnel Administration for further service appointment.

Evidently the doctors thought no one would willingly conceal a verdict that would save him from front-line duty, but I did. I gave my orders to the Chief Personnel Administration and kept the medical report in my pocket. To this day I have kept it.

The colonel who received my orders instructed me to begin my leave. Those ten days were both happy and bitter: happy because I was again in good health and with my family, and I loved and was loved; and bitter because the thought that we would soon part, perhaps forever, hovered over us all. When my leave ended I went to the Personnel Administration and received my new post—"At the Disposal of the Fourth Ukrainian Front." I phoned friends at the General Staff and was told that two officers would be traveling by car to the front head- quarters in a few days. They could take me with them. Early in the morning of August 8, 1944, we left.

My wife drove with us as far as Podolsk. Neither of us uttered "goodbye." As our car moved down the road, I sat there and thought to myself that it was always harder to remain behind than to leave.

My companions kept looking back at Zinaida, urging me to turn around myself. I wasn't going to; I had the presentiment that if I could only keep my- self from looking back, I would remain alive and would live with her many long years. I did not look back.

When we met again she asked, "Why didn't you look back at me?" I ex- plained why, and she said: "I thought so all along."

CHAPTER FOURTEEN

THE FOURTH UKRAINIAN FRONT

I was taken straight to personnel administration for the front. The chief there, Colonel Karpeto, sent me to the commanding officers' dormitory.

The next morning he brought me a note from Karpeto: "Come immediately to the commander."

In his reception room Karpeto greeted me by saying, "Because of you we have been delayed. The commander has asked for us several times already."

I was puzzled. "What's this all about? Why me in particular?"

"I don't know a thing. I reported your personal case history to him, and he said: 'Get him here.' "

Karpeto was summoned in by the commander. A few moments later, he stuck his head out and said to me, "Come in."

I went in and made my formal introduction. I immediately liked the commander, Army General Ivan Yefimovich Petrov. Perhaps my admiration was partly due to his fame as organizer of the defense of Odessa and subsequently of Sevastopol.

But though Petrov was one of our most talented military leaders, he also had a large number of failures in his career. Stalin did not like him. More than once Petrov had been demoted. Later he was removed as commander of the Fourth Ukrainian Front, just before the end of the war. His replacement, Yeremenko, was presented at the victory parade as the "Hero of Carpathia," though he had commanded the front for only eighteen days. Petrov, who had led his forces through the whole Carpathian chain under the most difficult conditions, was never mentioned at the parade.

I was impressed by everything about this "talented failure"—his thickset figure, his peasant face that had a bristly, short, trimmed mustache, his muffled but firm voice, even the constant twitch of his head.

He said, "Opanasenko writes that you and your brigade performed very successfully in Khekhtsir. I know Khekhtsir. Those mountains are worse than the Carpathians. So I want to ask you what you consider the main element assuring success of troops in mountain conditions?"

I replied, "Mobility and endurance—those are mountain requirements. All weapons and ammunition must always be with you. You have to operate with maximum exertion of strength. The soldier must always be laden down like a mule, have as much endurance as a donkey, be as mobile as a mountain goat, and as quick-witted and courageous as the snow leopard. When necessary a mountain infantryman must be able to carry on without rest and without sleep for two, three, and even more days. Lost time can never be made up."

"Correct!" cried Petrov. "That's what I want you to teach the 27th Guards Infantry Corps and the Eighteenth Army. Would you accept a post as chief of staff of a division?"

"Of course," I responded.

He raised his head, and looking at me with a direct and an open expression he pronounced, "Now that's the right way to answer. Given your service record, you deserve more. But you can show your talent in any position. I keep my eyes on people and at the first chance I will give you a post you deserve. For now you will be chief of staff of the 8th Infantry Division. You will replace Major General Podushkin. And before you take up your post, you are to do a little instructing. I will call Zhuravlyov, commander of the Eighteenth Army, and tell him you're coming. He can use you to lecture his troops on waging war in the mountains."

Zhuravlyov barely used me. I'd only spoken at two conferences, when I left for the 8th Infantry Division. And Zhuravlyov had tried to send me off even more quickly. Nonetheless, I stayed there long enough to leave my mark. I participated in a conference at which Leonid Brezhnev, chief of the political department of the Eighteenth Army, spoke also. A full-length photograph published some thirty years later in *Pravda* depicted the chief making his speech. At the time, I was modestly sitting on my heels making notes for my upcoming speech. Somehow I got into the picture. The publication of the photo in *Pravda* was an obvious oversight. But then how could the editors

possibly have been expected to recognize the face of just another dissident—
and for that matter, the way he had looked in 1944?

I left the Eighteenth Army by car, riding from the Stanislav region to Delyatin, where the division staff office was located, via Kolomyia—where the corps
staff office was located. Because he is not the top person in the division, the
chief of staff is not obligated to present himself to the corps commander. But
I believed, as the saying goes, that "You can't spoil porridge with butter." I
felt even more this way because the corps commander, Gastilovich, had been
a student at the General Staff Academy and subsequently a teacher there. Even
though we had not been friends in the academy, we had been respectful and
well-disposed toward each other.

Our meeting was cordial. We talked a long time about business. I was a pupil
and he the teacher. He ordered dinner. We ate and drank. New themes crept
into our conversation. I began to realize that relations between Gastilovich
and my division commander, Major General Smirnov, were strained, to put
it mildly. Gastilovich remarked several times that he would prefer to see me
in Smirnov's post. He seemed to be trying to set me against the division commander. I found this unpleasant and I thought for a long time how I could
change the subject without making him my enemy as well.

Finally I said, "Comrade Lieutenant General! You know my attitude toward you. Back in the academy I trusted your every word. And right now
I am convinced that you are speaking only the truth about my divisional commander. But you do have to understand my situation: I am chief of staff—not
only the head of the organization that runs the division but also a *reflection
of the divisional commander.* It is my duty either to act as the divisional commander does or to leave the post. Therefore please permit me to forget everything I have heard here about my divisional commander and to maintain my
neutrality. This does not at all mean that I will support the divisional commander if he wishes not to fulfill your orders or if he acts against your directions. In such cases, I can assure you, I will do my duty and report to you."

Gastilovich agreed with me and we parted that night on friendly terms.

Major General Podushkin, the man whom I would be replacing, was delighted to see me. He had not performed well in the post, and my arrival meant
his penalty period was over. We'd been at the academy together and we remi-
nisced about our mutual classmates. He told me that Neryanin had gone over
to the Germans. I did not believe it, but he insisted that his information was
correct. After he left the next morning, I met the officers, visited units, and
was introduced to the commanders and staff officers. The division was doing
battle with the Hungarians. That evening I reported to Smirnov on what I
had done, and I concluded, "I consider that from this hour on I have taken
over my assigned duties. So I ask you to consider me responsible in full."

"Thank you," he said warmly. "Go along now and rest up."

When I awakened the next morning I ordered my breakfast, called the operations branch, and asked for Volodya Zavalnyuk, the chief of the branch.

"He's not here," I was told.

"Where is he?"

"He and the division commander have gone off somewhere."

"Report to me when he returns."

A few hours later Zavalnyuk entered my office, saying, "Did you ask for me?"

"Yes. You went out this morning without my knowledge. I hope that this will be the last time that happens."

"It was the commander. . ."

"I do not need any explanations. I have told you what I expect. If anything like this is repeated, then we will not be able to work together."

Zavalnyuk left and I immediately went to see Smirnov.

"Come in, come in!" he said cordially.

I adhered to a severely official tone. "Comrade Major General, this morning you took my deputy with you on what I am sure was an important piece of business. But I beg of you, if in the future you intend to issue orders to my subordinates over my head, send me back to the corps. I will not be chief of staff in a division where the divisional commander does not respect me."

"Forgive me, Pyotr Grigoryevich. Please sit down. Podushkin had no interest in his work and didn't want to do anything. I got used to working with Zavalnyuk. So today I called on him as usual. I will not do so any more."

Smirnov kept his word. We became quite friendly and met three times a day to talk during meals.

Things didn't work out as well with Zavalnyuk. I had forced him as a subordinate to keep silence, and he left me firm in the conviction that I suspected him of wanting to "take over my position." Though I later loved him like a son, he remained convinced that I thought him hostile toward me.

Several months later Zavalnyuk was made commander of the 151st Regiment. During one of my visits to the regiment he invited me to dine with him and his girlfriend. It was April 18, 1945. I accepted the invitation with pleasure. The three of us had a wonderful dinner together. Zavalnyuk drank more than usual that evening. He told me that he felt uneasy, that he had a presentiment of misfortune. We finally talked openly about the misunderstanding between us, and I tried to convince him that I had never thought he was out to get my job. I'm afraid he did not believe me.

On the morning of April 19, 1945, Zavalynuk was killed by an enemy shell.

When in late August 1944 I was getting used to my new command, I unexpectedly encountered an acquaintance at the front. In the Kislovodsk Sanatorium a lieutenant colonel and Hero of the Soviet Union and his wife had stayed in a room next to us. And now Ivan Mikhailovich Leusenko commanded a regiment in the same division in which I served. We were delighted to see each other again. Vera, his wife, was with him and their presence made the whole division seem like a better place to me. I had a lot of work. My first task was to check out the disposition of the troops in defense and to organize the absorption of reinforcements into units. The division had suffered greatly in preceding battles and little by little was being built up again. Twice in the short time I had been there, reinforcements had been distributed among regiments. When I examined the second reinforcement list I noticed that the 129th Regiment, as had been the case the first time, got the largest number of men; the 151st got less; and Leusenko's 310th got none at all.

"Why do you distribute them this way?" I asked Major Belenkov, chief of the organizations branch.

"It's the commander's order."

I went to see Smirnov and direct his attention to this abnormality.

"Yes," he said, "those are my instructions. Alexandrov of the 129th has hardly anyone left in his companies and Leusenko's regiment has its normal complement."

"Have they had different combat tasks or did the 129th not get reinforcements before?"

"No, Alexandrov got more reinforcements the last time, too. People simply disappear in his regiment."

"Perhaps he is incapable of husbanding his men?"

"That might be—but still he carries out his assigned tasks successfully."

"Much might depend on how he carries them out. I personally believe that the correct principle of distribution of reenforcements is equal distribution. Assignments have to be executed with the forces and means you have been given. Those who bury people without reason ought to be given less of them. They have to learn how to husband their men."

Smirnov agreed to think about what I had said. Just before I left him, he mentioned that Leusenko also was unhappy with the distribution of reinforcements.

My respect for Leusenko grew. I enjoyed visiting with Vera and him at his home not only because of our friendship, but also because I needed advice on practical matters, one of which was helmets.

The entire Soviet Army was contemptuous of helmets, and our division was not an exception. Inspecting units, including those on the front line, I did not see one man wearing a helmet. Professor Kostenko, a Kiev surgeon who'd operated on my leg, had told me (during the operation, I might add) that almost eighty percent of those who had been killed on the field or who later died of wounds had head wounds, and all were people who did not wear helmets.

Death from a wound in the head through a helmet was unusual. Thus I was forced to conclude that many of our men were dying from a lack of discipline. In essence, they were suicides: suicides of negligence.

I discussed with Leusenko what Kostenko had told me and added, "And look at the Germans. Have you ever seen even one German in the front line without a helmet. I have not seen one . . ."

"The Germans have discipline. Our men even flaunt their open heads. I support your idea, but I do not intend to introduce helmets into my regiment on my own initiative because I will be known throughout the army as a coward. But if an order is issued, I will be able to force them to wear them."

Neither of us knew then how strict the Germans were about helmets. For appearing in the front line area without one, the punishment was identical to that for self-mutilation.

After my talk with Leusenko, I prepared an order requiring all enlisted men and division officers (except for staff officers) to wear helmets and to carry their assigned weapons at all times. Officers, in addition to sidearms, were to have pistols. The staff and rear personnel when with units or during alarms were to wear helmets.

It was easy to issue an order—Smirnov gave me no argument and signed it right away—but it was difficult to put it into effect. Every day I spent several hours in advanced positions wearing a helmet and with a pistol strapped on my chest. I spoke with rank-and-file soldiers and officers about the importance of helmets. I handed out penalties. But Leusenko was right. The rear echelons pegged me as inexperienced in battle and a coward, an eccentric who by wearing a helmet and pistol wanted to look like an old veteran fighter.

I soon learned where most of this bad press was originating. The chief of the division's political branch, Colonel Parshin, was naturally arrogant. An old political officer, he considered himself to be the most important element in the army. Old political officers demanded obedience and subordination from everyone. They even believed that those superior to them in rank or position should honor them.

When I arrived at the division I called on everyone, Parshin included. Not realizing that I was merely making the rounds, he was very pleased with my visit and "rewarded" me by telling me about the "moral and political state of the division." Two or three days later I called him and asked him whether he would like to familiarize himself with the general operational situation. We got into an argument when I realized he expected me to come to him, as had been done in the past. I put my foot down. He would have to come to me to get information—and he did, but not without beginning to spread gossip about me.

Meanwhile, relations between Gastilovich and Smirnov worsened, causing nervousness in the division. I tried to keep peace between them, not always successfully. Soon they were not even speaking. If Gastilovich had something to communicate to Smirnov, he phoned me. If Smirnov had to relay something to Gastilovich, he called the corps chief of staff, Shub.

While all this was going on, I was trying to whip up enthusiasm in the units, to prepare them for battle. Almost every night our troops took prisoners and seized portions of trenches and individual strong points. The enemy saw this as preparation for attack. The division occupied defensive positions over thirty kilometers in length, with an open right flank. Leusenko's 310th Regiment held the defensive position on this flank, and manifested the most intense level of activity among our troops. The enemy riveted most of its attention on that section. But what interested me most of all was the mountain, called Makovitsa, located on the left flank within the 129th Regiment sector. At its crown was a small plateau, which could accommodate only one side—and even then, no more than a pair of sections. But from here all land to and including the highway from Delyatin to the Czech border was visible. The plateau kept changing hands. When I arrived it was the enemy's. The mountain slope on our side was very steep. Anyone giving up the top had to slip down all the way to the bottom.

When the squad from the 129th was once more driven out of the trench along the edge of the top on the enemy's side, the entire squad had to slide all the way down. The regiment commander, a tall, handsome, twenty-eight-year-old major named Aleksandrov, wore a service cap for most of the year and another type of hat in winter, both rakishly pushed forward on his forehead, letting his luxuriant forelock hang down on his left temple. His authority in the regiment was indisputable. The bosses also liked him. He valued their positive response to him a great deal and did everything he could to strengthen it. Aleksandrov could not tolerate knowing that his men had abandoned Makovitsa. He summoned his first sergeant who commanded the squad that was defending the mountain and gave him orders: "Get Makovitsa back."

The sergeant, assembling his eighteen or so men, climbed back up to the top, where they found something totally unexpected. After occupying the squad's trench on their own side, the enemy had gone no further and the entire tiny flat spot at the top, with a breadth of about thirty meters, remained a no-man's land. On the eastern edge of the plateau, toward us, there was a very shallow trench. When the squad was driven from its main trench on the enemy side and had fled, three soldiers located in the eastern, or rear, trench—which constituted the squad's reserve—had opened fire on the enemy and forced them to lie down in the trench they occupied. The squad commander had forgotten about this reserve; it was still in place. The entire squad now dug themselves into this eastern trench and reported to the regiment commander that they had scaled the mountain and were digging in. Aleksandrov reported to the division that Makovitsa had been taken by the enemy in a night attack, but that the situation had been restored that same night.

On taking up my duties I decided to begin my study of the advance positions with Makovitsa. Major Aleksandrov tried hard to dissuade me. First by telephone, and subsequently in visits to the division staff, he tried to prove to Smirnov and myself that it was dangerous for me to visit Makovitsa and that my visit might attract the special attention of the enemy to this mountain. I did not change my mind, though I agreed that there was some danger in scaling the mountain since in two places I had to cross enemy fields of fire. I therefore planned to go in the evening or at dawn. In order not to attract attention I would take with me only one soldier and would dress in rank-and-file uniform.

According to Aleksandrov's report the plateau at the top was in our hands, and the advance units of the enemy were located in two continuous trenches of full cross-section on a ledge about 150 meters below the summit.

When we reached the top the squad commander, First Sergeant Pavlychko, asked us to get down in the shelter fast because our men occasionally exchanged grenades with the enemy.

"From where can I see the enemy's defenses?" I asked Pavlychko.

"Nowhere right now," he replied. "We used to be able to see them when we had that trench over there."

He pointed across the top of the plateau.

"Did you know about this?" I asked Aleksandrov.

At first he was surprised, and then he realized I was catching him in a lie. Several times, evidently wishing to remain in good favor with the chiefs, he had reported to the division staff: "I am going up to observe on Makovitsa, so I will be out of direct communications with you. If an emergency arises, communicate with me through my signal group."

Now I found out that we had no observation point on Makovitsa at all. The enemy in the first trench prevented us from seeing anything, but we did not hinder him.

I was disgruntled. "We came here for nothing. This little trench has no value for the division. It's only good for deceiving the chiefs: 'Makovitsa is in our hands.' I am going to apologize to the division commander and tell him that Makovitsa has long been surrendered to the enemy. I'll let him decide what's to be done."

Aleksandrov was crestfallen. Even his gay forelock seemed to have lost its verve. He stood there silent and finally said, "Comrade Lieutenant-Colonel! Don't report this to the division commander. By morning Makovitsa will be ours."

"You're in too much of a hurry. This has to be thought through. I am leaving now and you are to stay here with Pavlychko and consider the whole thing. I will tell the division commander that we didn't reach Makovitsa because of strong enemy fire. But if you don't get the mountain back in three days' time

I will tell him everything. Call me as soon as you have taken the peak and I will come myself to observe and report after that."

Aleksandrov kept his word. The next night he took the top. Then counterattacks began. An enemy company was deployed to retake the peak. To ward off the counterattack a whole batallion had to be engaged. It was true that from Makovitsa the enemy's whole defense was laid out on the palm of a hand. Not for nothing had month-long battles been fought over this mountain in World War I. Once I saw a German leaflet from World War I in which Makovitsa was depicted as an enormous, open gullet into which an unbroken column of Russian soldiers marched. The legend read: "Makovitsa will devour you all."

We knew the enemy would do his best to retake the peak. If he couldn't get it, he would withdraw to the other side of the highway; with his second echelon lower than his first he could not maintain a reliable defense. Aleksandrov was ordered to devote all his attention to Makovitsa in order to thwart a sudden attack or to prevent the enemy from leaving his positions quietly.

Then I remembered a story from World War I about a trick used successfully on the Russo-Turkish front. One of the Russian units that was higher than the Turks forced the enemy to retreat by rolling barrels full of gunpowder and stones down onto them. I told this story to the officers and soldiers on Makovitsa and mentioned that they might employ the same tactics. They did, and the enemy soon abandoned the trenches in which they'd been attacked by the barrels. That night Aleksandrov sent out a reconnaissance detachment to secure the abandoned sector and to try to clean out the whole first trench of enemy by attacking it on the flanks. Forty minutes after action began, an unexpected report arrived: enemy retreating.

The division commander issued an order: "The 129th Regiment is to go on the offensive immediately. The 151st and the 310th are to carry out reconnaissance by means of battle."

After Makovitsa, the 129th Regiment advanced swiftly, taking prisoners and capturing the orders of the commander of a Hungarian brigade. From these orders we learned that the enemy had planned withdrawal not from the first trench to the second trench, but from the first trench to the second ledge, while still occupying the second trench on the first ledge. But the Hungarians had bad luck; a reconnaissance detachment of the 129th got into the first trench at the same time that the Hungarians were withdrawing from it. Inspired by the sight of the enemy retreating, the reconnaissance detail pushed forward in pursuit. The enemy panicked. Instead of moving calmly along the prearranged retreat routes, they ran in every direction back to the second trench and caused a panic among the troops there. The panic spread further into the rear, and even into neighboring units. As a result, the 129th occupied both ledges and secured territory all the way to the highway. When daylight came the enemy began to organize resistance. But their defense had been broken along the entire front of the division. The 151st and 310th, which had met with some success during their night battles, put their main forces into battle in the morning. During the day the offensive proceeded along the entire divisonal front.

Smirnov and I decided to take advantage of the success that luck had granted us. The enemy had no operational need to withdraw troops on this sector of the front. Nothing was threatening enemy flanks. There also was good reason to hold the Carpathian mountain chain, like a knife buried in the body of the Soviet offensive. The Carpathians were important, too, as a storehouse for battle supplies and material supplies and as an important military-industrial area. Consequently, only a major effort could rout the enemy from the Carpathians—and in no way were we up to such an effort.

When I joined the division, it had less than four thousand men. Reinforcements brought it up to six thousand—that is, to fifty percent of normal complement. Companies consisted of only thirty to forty men, and Aleksandrov's regiment was even smaller. We had no means of increasing our strength. Artillery and mortar units had full complements of weapons, but we had little ammunition and no hopes for regular ammunitions supply. We had no air force support. We had no neighbors to help us with military actions. In fact, the corps flanks were open: It was about thirty kilometers to our nearest neighbor on our right and on the left even farther.

Obviously, we could achieve success under such conditions only by maneuverability. Only surprise, swiftness, and decisive action could make up for our lack of striking force. The broad front for maneuver and the concealment possibilities of the forested mountain locality favored our emerging on the enemy's flank and in the rear and undertaking a sudden and decisive blow. But the entire corps was not ready for such maneuvers.

Our division had no desire to go up into the mountains; when we came to places where the enemy was strong, we kept slipping back to the roads. In order to drive the enemy off the roads we needed powerful artillery fire, tanks, and air force support. Not having any of this, we continually ordered our troops to leave the roads and to head up into the mountains again in order to go around the nuclei of enemy resistance. Smirnov spent an entire day with the troops, demanding that they attack along mountain routes, bypassing the enemy resistance points.

That evening we moved the staff into Yaremcha, which we had just occupied. The division commander arrived fatigued almost to the point of collapse. After he'd washed up and sat down to dine, he said, "Prepare an order for tomorrow which shows the direction for attack and states that only artillery with a small infantry cover and the rear echelons are to move along the roads."

At that point Smirnov received a call from Gastilovich. They argued for several minutes and he hung up exasperated. "What do you make of that?" he began. "Gastilovich thinks the enemy, threatened by flank strikes of the Third Ukrainian Front and the First Guards Army of our front, has begun a hasty withdrawal of troops. And so, in order not to let the enemy get away, we are supposed to create a strong advance detachment, put it in automobiles and move it along the road to Yasinya and on to Rakhovo. The purpose of this detachment would be to force the retreating enemy troops from the road back into the mountains, thereby creating an open road for unhindered advance of the corps troops. A good order! Its only shortcoming is that it doesn't suit this situation. Go ahead and give our troops my orders."

During the night our forces occupied launching positions away from the road and in the morning we began our attack. The first reports indicated strengthened resistance. The enemy had set up well prepared defense blocks on the roads—with artillery, self-propelled guns, machine guns and mined approaches. Again Smirnov went off to the regiments.

At ten o'clock Gastilovich called. "Where's that bull-shitter?"

What could I say? I couldn't join sides with Gastilovich and I couldn't admit that it was proper to speak of my commander like that. So I feigned ignorance and asked, "Who?"

"What do you mean? You don't understand?"

"No, comrade Lieutenant General. I do not understand. I don't know whom you want."

"What a schoolgirl you are!" He cursed me repeatedly.

Finally I couldn't control myself any longer and I hung up on him. When the phone rang, I picked it up and, desperately trying to keep my temper, said in a calm voice, "Soldatov here!" (Soldatov was my code name for the day.)

"Soldatov hell! Soldatov shit!" Once more the torrent of cursing and epithets poured forth. I put down the phone. After a time it rang. I again answered, "Soldatov here!"

Gastilovich's voice was extremely low. He sounded official and restrained. "Grigorenko! Do you want to be court-martialed?"

"No, comrade Commander." I permitted myself a bit of flattery. "I certainly don't want that."

"Then why don't you want to listen to my orders?"

"Comrade commander, I not only will listen to your orders but I will carry them out without regard to my life."

"I am not yet the commander," he querulously but good-naturedly corrected me.

"Well it won't be long now," I said.

"You mean you've already heard about it?"

"I did hear something."

"Well nothing should be said for the time being. Now write down my orders."

I wrote his orders down, energetically exclaiming "Yes, sir!" after each phrase.

(Soon after that he was named commander of the Eighteenth army, and the corps ceased being a separate entity and became a part of Gastilovich's army.)

The morning after the phone calls, Gastilovich arrived at our command point. The division staff was quartered in an enormous, prosperous peasant homestead that was surrounded by a fence. Most of the buildings surrounding the home were located on a flat piece of land, but many stood on a grassy slope, at the very top of which was my hut.

Through the window of this hut I saw a jeep drive into the yard and pull up to the lower part of the main house. I raced out of my hut and ran down the slope to the jeep. While Gastilovich was clambering out of it I began to report to him. He did not let me finish.

"Where is Smirnov?"

"Out in the front line with the regiments, as usual. I can connect you with him."

"That's not necessary. Are you familiar with the situation?"

"Of course."

"Let's go to your place then!"

We walked along, conversing as we went. When we reached the entrance to my hut, I signaled the adjutant there that he was not to follow us. As soon as Gastilovich and I entered the room, I said to him, "Comrade Lieutenant General! While there are no outsiders present I ask you to hear me out on a very important matter."

"All right, come on. Out with it."

"I sincerely ask you not to rebuke me, particularly in an insulting tone, in the presence of others. After all, you know what kind of a person I am. I might lose my temper and do something irrevocable. . . ."

As I spoke Gastilovich glanced at the pistol that lay on my desk. I continued, "Do you really want me to get court-martialed? It would be better if you waited till we were alone, and then rebuked me if I have deserved it. You can even strike me. I esteem you so highly that I will stand for it. But cursing in public I might not be able to stand."

"Well, in that case, out of respect for me, don't shoot beneath my feet but in my chest." Obviously he remembered a story I had told him once about an experience I'd had in the Tenth Guards Army, one that very nearly cost the lives of two men.

I was returning to the army staff office from one of my visits to the troops when I suddenly met with an impenetrable traffic jam. I got out of my jeep and, after telling Pavlik to catch up with me when the cars got moving, I went ahead on foot. Soon I found the cause of the jam. A car had smashed up a small wooden bridge that provided a crossing over a swampy little stream.

Other cars had tried to go around the bridge and had gotten stuck themselves. About thirty or forty cars were piled up. All that needed to be done was to haul off the car that was blocking the bridge, fix up the bridge itself, and then pull out the cars that had gotten stuck in the stream. I gathered the drivers together and together they were easily able to remove the car which had caused the whole mess. They then repaired the small bridge and traffic finally started to move again. Beyond the small bridge the road ran along a hollow for a distance. I left the drivers of the two last cars in line to direct traffic at the bridge, and I climbed to the top of the hollow from which I could see everything. It was drizzling and I pulled the hood of my raincoat over my helmet. The line of cars was moving and no further supervision was required. Reassured, I turned around to light a cigarette. Suddenly a heavy blow fell on my helmet. I turned around and saw a man lifting up his staff for a new blow. I remember only it and a papakha. Involuntarily I grabbed my pistol from my chest and pressed on the safety pin. At exactly that moment, somone pushed down the barrel of the pistol and my whole volley went into the ground by the feet of my assailant. It was my orderly, Petya, who thus interfered in a most timely way and thereby saved the lives of two men: the man whom I would otherwise have shot; and myself, as I would have been shot after being court-martialed for killing a general. I pulled the pistol back toward me, but Petya literally clung to it. The general dashed down the slope and leaped into his jeep, which sped away. At that point some drivers came up and told me what had occasioned the incident. The general—they claimed it was a colonel general—had pulled up to the tail end of the line of cars and had begun to curse, demanding that his car be let through immediately. The drivers pulled over and allowed him to pass. When he reached the bridge he asked the traffic directors who was in charge, and one of them pointed to me.

The general had left his jeep, run up the slope, and hit me with his staff, whereupon the incidents I just related ensued. When I returned to army headquarters, I went immediately to Kazakov and told him what had happened. An order was issued to the army demanding that my assailant turn himself in to the commander. No one showed up. It was this incident that Gastilovich was remembering and in light of which he promised never to rebuke me publicly again.

From that time on the signals men of the entire army knew, and through them the officers as well, that the hot-tempered army commander refrained from rebuking only me. Many decided that I was a relative of Gastilovich.

The offensive continued. To be sure, we advanced only from four to six kilometers a day, because we were not using the roads. On the other hand, after two days of unsuccessfully attempting to break through the enemy's front line, the division to our left suddenly moved ahead at high speed and on the third day caught up with us. The enemy simply retired in front of them. Gastilovich proposed that we institute a system of advanced detachments, but the divisions trying to keep up with us rebelled against this because it was clear that we would encounter organized resistance when we emerged from the mountains to the road. At the time a rumor was circulating about the corps that along the Czech border lay the outposts of a fortified area in which were stored some type of mysterious battle equipment capable of destroying everything alive.

Unwittingly the General Staff encouraged this rumor. A special intelligence communiqué on fortifications in the former Polish-Czech state frontier charted and described a fortified area with many permanent fortifications and barriers. This information terrified the army and lessened the troops' determination. The regiments obviously did not want to reach the frontier or to cross it but preferred continued action on former Polish territory. The rumors had originated among the rank-and-file soldiers and the local population, but after the special intelligence communiqué arrived from the General Staff, the commanding officers also began to believe them.

After thoroughly analyzing the chart of this awesome fortification, I made a report to Smirnov: "If there are permanent fortifications in our direction, and I am not convinced that there are, they are located immediately southwest of Yasnina. I do not believe that there is even one permanent fortification on the boundary itself. No one would stretch a fortified area along a 130-kilometer front when the same effect could be gained by concentrating along a front of three to five kilometers."

Smirnov agreed with my conclusions and gave orders that the regiments were not to be informed of the general staff chart. But he refused to sign my analysis of the chart for the corps. He advised me to send the report to the corps with only my own signature, thus indicating that he as division commander had been presented with the report, but that he had doubts and therefore was permitting my conclusions to be transmitted as my personal opinion.

He said, "Given my relations with Gastilovich my 'doubt' will serve the cause, whereas my signature on the document would have a negative effect."

Smirnov was right. Gastilovich agreed with the report and directed the division to end the hysterical rumors about mythical fortifications and to begin a decisive offensive. His orders were timely. We were only three kilometers from the state boundary. The units now began to advance, but slowly. Miraculously, the legend about a fortified area on the boundary began to turn into a reality.

The corps reported that our neighbor on the left, the 137th, had captured twelve permanent fortifications. The 151st Regiment reported two more and the 129th and the 310th Regiments each one. The number reported captured by the 137th kept increasing, stopping, I think, at forty-two. Meanwhile I visited the first captured permanent point. It was only a long abandoned infantry blockhouse with reinforced concrete walls no more than six inches thick. In all four walls there were slits for machine gun fire, but there were no embrasures. Evidently the blockhouses were not set up for occupation by garrisons but as temporary places in which border guards would conduct moving battle with small invading enemy detachments.

Despite the actual existence of a fortified area, Gastilovich was inspired—by the seizure of a large number of permanent points along the firing line—to return to his advance detachment concept. Either he did not really believe my reasoning on the fortified area or else he imagined that it would be advantageous ex post facto for him to support the General Staff charts, since the corps's breakthrough of a fortified area was extremely significant. Therefore, believing—or pretending to believe—he wrote reports that the troops of the corps had broken through a deeply-echeloned fortified area on the border, captured about fifty permanent reinforced-concrete fortifications, and were engaged in an ongoing attack. Because of these developments, we were ordered to create a strong advance detachment that would move forward and dislodge the enemy's screening and would develop a decisive attack on the road from Yasnina to Rakhovo. The main forces of the division were to attack in the same direction as the advanced detachment and were to establish contact with the advancing troops of the Third Ukrainian Front in the area of Sighet, Rumania, not later than the end of the third day.

Before this order was executed, while we were breaking through the fortified area, the front commander recalled Smirnov and named as his replacement Colonel Nikolai Stepanovich Ugryumov, up to that point the deputy corps commander in our own corps. Gastilovich was pleased.

From the first I did not get along with Ugryumov. My relations with him were tense. It was precisely at this juncture that Gastilovich's order about the advance detachment came through. On receiving orders from Ugryumov I undertook the formation of the detachment. As I did, I formed the opinion that a fortified junction lay just beyond Yasnina. Having received permission from Ugryumov, I went to the 151st Regiment in order to talk with the man who was to command the advanced detachment, a batallion commander, Zayats. In Russian his family name meant "hare," and this fit his character. He was extremely careful. Zayats and I went to the regiment's observation outpost. There I told him, "In my opinion you are going to encounter fortifications right after Yasnina. Look there! I believe those are well-camouflaged reinforced concrete antitank obstacles. If I were you I would carry out a thorough reconnaissance before going in there. A divisional reconnaissance has already been into Yasnina. But don't go further without good reconnoitering."

Battle reconnaissance indeed showed that before us lay a fortified area with powerful reinforced concrete antitank obstacles and electrified barriers in front of the advanced outposts. The reconnoitering was carried out so skillfully that only two men were wounded—yet we had uncovered the entire advance area. We were helped by good luck. At the very beginning of the reconnaissance, a local inhabitant named Yura Kandush who worked in this fortified area came to us as an informant and reported that there was a place from which he could point out all the fortifications. He took Ugryumov and myself to this spot and from it we were able to see all of the barriers. We observed the turning on of the electrical obstacles and the grass burned by them, saw four points where fire had been opened on our reconnaissance, and the rest of the points as well.

Ugryumov, who was well acquainted with the Finnish fortifications in battles on the Karelian Isthmus in 1939–40, was delighted with the well-executed reconnaissance, and he began being slightly more pleasant to me.

When we returned to the staff headquarters after having been with Yura Kandush, Ugryumov tossed off his service cap and picked up the phone. Inspiration burned on his face. I knew what would come of his inspiration and I even felt, somewhat maliciously, that it served him right and that perhaps he'd learn something from what was about to happen.

Ugryumov began speaking. "Comrade Lieutenant General! I have in front of me a permanent fortified center of defense. We . . ."

He was permitted to say nothing more. His face fell and he looked confused. I could imagine what Gastilovich was saying. He had already reported to the front his breakthrough of a fortified zone and was now impatiently awaiting information on the rapid forward movement of the advance detachment—and now to hear that we'd located a permanent fortifications center.

Ugryumov hung up and said slowly, "I'll never talk with him on the phone again." He sat there a while and continued, "What are we going to do now? He just ordered us to push ahead with the advance detachment to Rakhovo. That is sending them all to their death."

"Will you permit me to offer some advice, comrade Colonel?"

"Yes, in fact I am asking you for it."

"Don't push ahead."

"You mean don't carry out the order?"

"Not at all. Orders have to be carried out or we'll be court-martialed. But they have to be executed intelligently. What will happen if we order Zayats to move into the fortified center?"

"They'll all perish on the electrical barriers and the antitank obstacles."

"Well, that is how you have to report it—so Gastilovich understands it. And if he does understand it he'll cancel the order."

"How can I report it to him if he won't listen?"

"Don't worry. He'll listen. Comrade Colonel, there is a concept called 'telephone war.' We are convinced that the fortified area exists. We know what will result from an attack on it by cars. Let's report as if it had already happened. It won't be a lie, just a playing out of the future on a map."

I picked up the telephone and asked for Colonel Shub.

When I heard his voice, I said, "I wish to report some information, comrade Colonel!"

"Go ahead, I am ready."

"We formed up the advance detachment as the corps commander ordered. But we slipped up a bit. You see, we thought the fortified area had already been broken through, and without reconnaissance we pushed out of Yasnina. But the detachment ran into antitank obstacles and electrified barriers. A permanent fortification went into operation. Two cars were destroyed. Twelve men were caught on the electric barriers. The rest retreated, dismounted, and turned the artillery about. They assembled to attack in battle order, but the division commander is ordering them to attack in their cars."

"Your division commander is an idiot!" Shub seemed to be speaking in Gastilovich's voice. "And what about you—don't you understand anything?" He seemed ready to attack me, but he managed to restrain himself. "You must drop the idea of a frontal attack. You don't have the forces to break through permanent fortifications. You'll have to try to find a way around the barriers—and not sacrifice people on electrical wire."

"It's clear to me. Can I communicate this to the division commander?"

"Yes! And ask him to phone me himself. I'll clean out his brains for him. I'll teach him how to fight in the mountains."

I reported the entire conversation to Ugryumov.

"Well, Pyotr Grigoryevich! You are some . . . liar." (This was the first time he had called me by name and patronymic.)

"No, I did not lie. Such losses definitely would have been incurred if you had carried out Gastilovich's orders. I merely told Shub about them as if they had already happened."

From that time on our relations improved. We developed a strong battle friendship. I was attracted by Ugryumov's directness, his frankness, and his knowledge of the military trade. I emphasize the phrase *military trade* as opposed to military profession. Ugryumov was not a theoretician or commander of broad military scope, but a rank-and-file worker at war. I was astounded when I saw him for the first time in the bath. His body was literally covered with scars. He began his military career as a batallion commander in the Soviet-Finnish War, where he was wounded several times and granted the highest decoration—Hero of the Soviet Union. He began the war of 1941–45 as commander of a home guard's division below Leningrad. Then fate and his wounds took him from one front to the other.

In the end the permanent fortified junction of Yasnina was taken by outflanking. With the help of Yura Kandush we put this junction on a large-scale map and sent it to the corps. Twelve days later we received an intelligence summary from the General Staff in which there was a copy of our map bearing the legend: "Permanent fortifications junction at Yasnina (according to information from the 8th Infantry Division)."

Our division spent a long time preparing to outflank this fortified junction. The situation was complicated, because the division's left flank was covered by field forces, and important enemy troops were grouped above its right (or outflanking) flank. We worried a great deal about the location of the enemy troops and were forced several times to surrender territory we had occupied, leaving behind weapons and other materials. Because of these losses we were unable to seek an outflanking by moving to the west of the junction, but we had to outflank directly along the flank of the junction—so that our division would always be in a fist, its outflanking and frontally attacking elements always acting as a team. While we were undertaking to outflank the junction we also had to attack the Hungarian mountain infantry units who were covering the flanks. These battles lasted days. Our chief weakness was that we had less men than the enemy. To compensate for this, we dragged up mortars, heavy machine guns, and batallion and regimental artillery into the mountains. Divisional artillerymen were taught to choose positions in mountain localities and to fire on mountain targets, including targets at maximum distances.

Gastilovich demanded we carry out the outflanking maneuver. To encourage us, he cited the achievements of the 137th Infantry Division, which had two regiments operating in a more difficult locality and which already had penetrated far into enemy territory from the rear. We did not believe what Gastilovich told us. If those regiments actually were located where the corps showed them, why had they not descended to the highway and cut off the grouping in front of which we were marking time. I put this question to the chief of staff of the 317th Division and his reply that the enemy had self-propelled guns, while all we had was antitank grenades and batallion mortars, told me how bad things really were for those regiments Gastilovich called "triumphant."

Battles continued incessantly. Although we kept pressing the enemy, we were unable to force him out of our way by outflanking him. Still Gastilovich urged us on. The forces in the mountains had no ammunition or food and were exhausted. One afternoon Gastilovich ordered us to strike and join up with the mountain forces. Otherwise, he said, the entire operation would end tragically.

That very night we pushed one batallion into the valley of the Charna Tissa River. Our batallion cannon were located on the upper slopes of the heights along the road. As soon as we started firing on the Germans who carried self-propelled guns and were patrolling the highway, the latter retreated. The Hungarians, located in front of us, heard the noise of battle, saw the Germans re-

treating, and themselves retreated into the mountains. At this point most of
the garrisons of the fortified junction of Yasnina abandoned their positions
and, without destroying their weapons, fled into the mountains. Those who
did not flee were taken prisoner. Thus the division got a firm grip on the highway. Now was the time for the "advance detachment" to begin its long-desired
work. Without stopping, and moving swiftly, it took Rakhovo, Slatin, and even
Sighet, a city not in our area but that was rich with supplies.

The regiments of the 137th presented a pitiful picture as they came down
from the mountains. They had spent almost two weeks in the most harsh
mountainous and forested terrain, without ammunition and rations. Our combined experiences forced us to conclude that outflanking in contemporary war
cannot be carried out by infantry alone. To the end of the war this thesis was
extremely influential in the battle actions of our division.

When the Yasnina-Rakhovo road opened up for us, the enemy grouping
hovering over the flank and rear of the division remained in place, and it was
decided to leave one infantry batallion behind to watch over it. Again Captain
Zayats was chosen as commander. He was assigned the difficult task of maintaining watch over the enemy grouping and reporting once a day to the division, or immediately in urgent cases; he was ordered to maintain a high standard of communication—this at a distance of up to one hundred kilometers
and sometimes more from the main forces.

This batallion was the only Soviet force arrayed against the enemy grouping.
The enemy could have destroyed Zayats and his men and then burst upon the
open rear of the division. It could have destroyed the rear, defeated the division, and deprived it of supplies, or it could have swiftly moved along a parallel
road and put itself in a position to attack our division. But the enemy group
did neither of these two things. For two days it remained in place, and then
slowly proceeded south, stopping at times to try and "catch" Zayats, whose
batallion had to flee four times, once for twelve kilometers. But as soon as the
hunt for him was called off, Zayats pursued the enemy closely. Throughout
all this his communication with the division was not broken off. As a result
we knew precisely where the enemy grouping was and met it when it emerged
from the mountains. Battle never took place. "Caught" between the division
and Zayats's batallion, the two Hungarian brigades surrendered without resistance.

The capture of these two brigades completed our rout of the eastern Carpathian grouping of the enemy. No enemy forces now lay in front of the 27th
Guards Infantry Corps. The front commander used this opportunity to take
the personnel of the 239th Infantry Division and a tank killer regiment, put
them in jeeps, and disperse them along our sector of the front. Though the
enemy soon began to bring fresh troops, the positioning of men along the front
permitted the offensive to be developed for several more days.

The corps troops took Berehovo, Khust, Mukacevo, and Uzhorod and were brought to a halt only on the approaches to Kosice. The 239th took Chop but was immediately thrown back by a tank counterattack. The suddenness and strength of this blow caused panic. Infantry fled in disorder. The tank killer regiment, left without infantry cover, abandoned its weapons and fled.

When panic broke out and the flight began, the batallion commander, Major Vasilyev, created an infantry cover out of his own artillery batallion and met the enemy tanks emerging from Chop with fire. After several tanks were set ablaze, the enemy hid behind some buildings and continued firing from there. Seeing that our troops had retreated, Vasilyev began the withdrawal of his own batallion. At this point he received a report that cannons had been abandoned a short distance back. Vasilyev ordered that they be hauled out by his own tractors. Using his batallion for cover, he was successful. The enemy was satisfied with their recapture of Chop and went no further. Vasilyev, with his booty, rejoined his batallion.

Major Vasilyev was named a Hero of the Soviet Union, one of three in the division who had received this decoration for the battles on the Dnieper; but he, like Leusenko, another from that troika, never bragged about his honor.

The 229th fled right through our battle formations, but Vasilyev was not among them. We heard stories about how tanks had crushed people and guns but neither I nor Ugryumov believed that our own artillery batallion had perished or fled. Both of us were convinced that Vasilyev would lead them out, and he had. Immediately he wanted to know where the commander of the tank killer regiment was, so that he could warn him not to report the loss of his weapons and material since Vasilyev himself had gotten everything out.

Vasilyev survived the war, and, I believe, left the army. I never saw him again after the division was dissolved in June 1945.

The battle at Chop ended the first period of my participation in the battles for the Carpathians. Strangely enough, I remember this time, during which blood was shed and friends perished, as a good one. I felt triumphant that we had captured almost without loss a powerful permanent fortified junction of enemy defense. After the capture we undertook what amounted to a victory march along the attack routes. Few of the scattered enemy groups located along these routes gave any resistance—and those that did fought in an unorganized way, without determination. Soldiers and officers of the defeated units emerged from the mountains and surrendered to us. All this was topped off by the capitulation of the two Hungarian brigades. During this entire period we took more than ten thousand men prisoners and acquired a great deal of material goods.

We were most impressed by the attitude of the people we encountered during those days. Wherever the Germans had destroyed bridges and roads, the local inhabitants, usually led by their priests, were laboring to restore what had been wrecked even before we got there. All of them said they were undertaking the reconstruction on the instructions of the Czech government in London. Wherever our troops went, people greeted them with celebration.

The city of Berehovo was captured by an envelopment maneuver of the 151st Regiment, while the main forces of the division remained twenty kilometers away. When the regiment commander, Lieutenant Colonel Melnikov, reported on the taking of Berehovo, he said in conclusion, "Wine is flowing in rivers here—enough types to suit any taste. Place your order and I will have it ready on your arrival."

I immediately grasped the danger in this situation and interrupted his joking to say, "I appreciate your sense of humor but I am telling you seriously that the division commander has named you commandant of Berehovo, with your main duty being to prevent drunkenness—even if you have to use weapons."

A bit later Melnikov called again and reported, "The local inhabitants won't leave us alone. They are besieging the soldiers and officers with wine and food. They want to drink with us. Am I to use my weapons against them?"

"Don't ask silly questions. You know what to do. Explain to them that you are carrying out a battle assignment and that anyone who gets drunk can get court-martialed. People feel responsibility for others more than for themselves. And don't offend the populace. Accept their presents in any organized way. Set up a special reception point."

"I have the situation under control right now, but I am concerned about when you come to Berehovo. If the whole division comes to town I won't be able to maintain order. Can't the division go around Berehovo or, at least, not stop here?"

I understood his fear and agreed with him that bringing the entire division into Berehovo would be disastrous. Orders were given that, though we would march through Berehovo, there would be no stopping. No one must leave the columns of march. No gifts from local inhabitants must be accepted.

But when the division entered, both sides of the central street were already full of people. From time to time baskets full of wine and food appeared and then disappeared into the soldiers' columns. A short while later empty bottles and baskets would be tossed onto the street. The column escort guard was powerless: Of course, they could not shoot at people who were expressing their good will. I tried to influence the populace personally. Moving along in my jeep beside the column I spoke to them in their native language, Ukrainian, requesting that they not give the "warriors" wine.

The people only continued to shout: "Hurrah for the Colonel!" and went right on supplying the column. Soon even my jeep was piled high with bottles of wine and all kinds of food—in particular, fruits and vegetables. So I abandoned my useless reproaches and hurried the columns along. Many of the soldiers were already staggering, singing drunken songs, even dancing as they marched.

With much difficulty we moved four kilometers beyond the city and halted.

The men lay right down on the road and fell asleep. Fortunately, the weather was excellent and continued to be so during the entire September offensive, putting us all in a holiday sort of mood. Already we could feel the approach of victory. How could men who had marched all the way from the Caucasus to the Carpathians not be gladdened by having done so!

After checking out the guard, I returned to Berehovo, where the division staff was quartered. Melnikov and I went around the city, surveying the riches of the Carpathian land. We were astonished by the enormous, full wine cellars, by the piles of fruits and vegetables, and by the abundant poultry in the homes. We were delighted to meet the hard-working and hospitable Carpathian Ukrainians. Here I first heard about the Carpatho-Russians. "We are not Ukrainians," these people told me in the purest Ukrainian. "We are Russians, Ruthenians, Carpatho-Russians."

I objected: "What kind of Russians can you be if you speak Ukrainian?"

"We only speak it in our homes," they responded. "Our books are in Russian and we write in Russian also."

I never understood this Carpatho-Russian movement, but they didn't understand me, either. They were very interested in life in the USSR, most of all in collective farms. I tried to satisfy their curiosity but they did not understand our systems and did not accept them, even though the picture I painted was somewhat brighter than reality.

During those days I saw the marvelously tended Carpathian forests. I spoke with foresters, who told me about the methods they'd devised for taking timber from a forest for years without depleting the resources of the forest at all. Today the Carpathian forests have been destroyed, and irreversible erosion of the mountain soils has taken place.

I spoke with many rural working people and found out that their lives were not easy. The Carpathian soils bore no comparison with our Tavrichesky black earth. But the people worked hard, from dawn to dusk, and they achieved results. They lived much more prosperously, much more richly, than did the collective farmers in my native village, Borisovka.

Yura Kandush, the man who'd helped us in reconnaissance of the permanent fortified complex of Yasnina, caused me great consternation when he told me how he used to earn 135 Czech crowns a day working as a blaster at a fortifications construction site. Just one day's pay would have him dressed from head to toe.

Units that had entered the Trans-Carpathian Ukraine territory were permitted to enlist volunteers from among the Trans-Carpathian inhabitants, so Yura Kandush remained with the division. We enlisted also a deserter, Ivan Andre, even though he was a Slovak and had a family in Slovakia. However, his village was only two kilometers from the borders of the Trans-Carpathian province and, consequently, it was easy to pass him off as a volunteer. We needed him badly. Ivan understood German and knew nearly all the Balkan languages: He was an excellent translator. Soon after he became a volunteer, his village was occupied by our troops and Ivan became a Soviet soldier. When he visited his home on leave, his mother was overjoyed. She had received notice that her son had died in battle. Ivan invited Zina, who was with me again, and me to visit his family.

Zina had arrived in the division in the middle of September and immediately had begun working as a nurse. She brought my elder son, who had threatened to run away to the front if he was not sent to be with his father. I set him up as a student soldier in a training regiment and let him experience all of the "delights" of front-line life—in the hopes that he would soon ask to go home to his mama. But my hopes were not borne out. He was a good student. He completed the course on a sniper team and himself became an instructor of snipers. Soon after, he was awarded with an Order of Glory Third Degree and a medal for bravery. After the war he attended and graduated from the Frunze Academy. Beyond a doubt he had more than a little military talent and he advanced successfully in the service until my arrest in 1964. After this he received an assignment without any future and, having lost all hopes for advance, served out his time till his pension. He is now a reserve colonel who performs the drudgery of a petty Soviet bureaucrat. He lives near Moscow with his wife, son, and daughter.

Ivan Andre served with the division until it was dissolved. He was demobilized and left for Slovakia. I never heard from him again.

Yura Kandush was less fortunate. He was assigned to reconnaissance in an engineers batallion. That October our engineers discovered a widespread mining of roads and adjacent territory. They set up barriers and stationed observers there, one of whom was Yura. Soon the tanks of the Third Ukrainian Front rolled up and Yura tried vainly to halt them. To avoid being crushed he leaped aside, and a mine blew off his leg. After he recovered, he was demobilized and sent back home to Yasnina. I never encountered him again, but I doubt that he ever lived as well as he did when he was a blaster at the fortifications complex.

My wife was not long at the front. In early February she visited a doctor, as she had become terribly afraid of artillery shelling, the noise of battle, and air attacks. The doctor attributed her problems to pregnancy. Just before Christmas 1944 she left.

The division had spent the autumn getting used to mountain terrain. Gradually everyone came to understand that mountains were our allies and that with our weak armaments, our small numbers of troops, and our shortage of ammunition it was advantageous for us to move along roads only when the enemy was not present or was fleeing. Now, as soon as the enemy grew strong and took to the roads, our units did not hesitate but immediately went into the mountains and began to press the enemy on his flanks and rear.

The division also got used to helmets, and on one occasion I was rewarded for my persistence on this question. I was moving along a mountain trail with a group of eight soldiers and officers, all on horseback, en route to the 310th Infantry Regiment. The trail sometimes went through forest and at others emerged into clearings. Evidently enemy observers had discerned our path. When the lead man of our column emerged into a clearing a mortar attack rained down on the edge of the forest. My horse cried out and a crushing blow on the head knocked me out of my saddle. When I came to, my face was wet. I touched my hand to my cheek—it was blood. There was a ringing in my head. While an orderly and a guard bandaged me, they told me that two horses had been severely wounded and had had to be shot. Two others were lightly wounded, but the men were all whole.

They put me on a horse and after we had already started to move, I suddenly realized that I no longer had my helmet. My orderly, an elderly Siberian named Vasily Maksimovich, rushed back to find it. A short while later he returned and, in a strange voice, said, "Just look!"

My helmet had been penetrated by a shell fragment as large as the palm of a hand. The fragment was still stuck in the helmet. Vasily Maksimovich paused and then said, "It was God who made you wise about helmets."

A doctor in the medical company of the 310th Regiment examined my head. The shell fragment had bruised and burned only the skin. To this day I have the scar.

I decided to preserve the helmet as a souvenir and ordered that it be packed up along with the shell fragment. For some reason rumors about this incident spread swiftly. Many officers came by and asked to see the helmet. Finally I had to unpack it and set it up so that it could be inspected without me present. Then Leusenko asked whether he could show it around his regiment. Of course, I could not refuse him; he was a friend. When he returned it, commanders of other units began to ask for it and it was difficult to turn them down.

Leonid Brezhnev himself asked to see my helmet, saying it had become famous throughout the whole army.

At the time, the helmet was in one of the units of the division. I telephoned and it was quickly brought over. Leonid Ilyich inspected it and with deep meaning pronounced, "Yesss!" Then he said, "Let me have it for a time. I have to show it to the higher-ups." I told him I wanted to keep it as a souvenir, and he replied, "Well, I will return it after I show it about. For you it is a souvenir. For me it's only a matter of business. I will show it and return it."

How could I not believe the chief of the political branch of the army? Yet he didn't keep his word. My helmet disappeared. I tried to find it but did not meet with any success. The political branch people said they thought that excessive handling had caused the shell fragment to fall out and that the helmet had been thrown away.

By late autumn 1944 the end of the war seemed near. No more men were to be had in our country. The class of 1927—seventeen-year-old-boys—was already being mobilized, but we were promised none of these reinforcements. The Fourth Ukrainian Front was supposed to get its manpower by means of the mobilization of men of all combat ages in the Western Ukraine, the enlistment of volunteers in Trans-Carpathia, and the return to units of those ill and wounded who had recuperated. The lack of manpower was so acute that mobilization became like hunting and trapping, like the work of slave traders in Africa.

Voluntary enlistment was organized in more or less the same way that a one hundred percent turnout of Soviet citizens at Soviet elections is organized. I never dealt with either the mobilization or the recruitment of "volunteers," but troops from our division did. One officer told me in detail the story of such a mission: "We surrounded the village at dawn. We had orders to shoot, after one warning, at anyone attempting to flee. Next, a special team entered the village and went from house to house, herding all men—regardless of age and health—into the village square from which they were taken, under guard, to special camps. There they were given medical examinations and politically unreliable persons were singled out and taken away. After receiving primary military instruction in these special camps, the men were sent out to units, again under guard, where they received further military instruction. Supervision was very severe because officers from whose subunits men escaped faced court-martial. Desertion was discouraged by threats of punishment to the families of 'deserters.' The area near the front was policed and any person found wandering was detained. A deserter, whether one of the mobilized or the volunteers, was either shot or put in a penalty company.

"Volunteers were enlisted by different methods than the mobilized. They were invited to an assembly in such a way that no one could refuse. At the assembly the potential enlistees listened to organized speeches. Anyone who objected was forced to explain his behavior and at his first poorly chosen word was declared to be an enemy of the Soviet government. The KGB men worked it out so that no one remained free after such an assembly. Everyone ended a volunteer or an arrested enemy of the Soviet government. From this point on the volunteers were processed in exactly the same way as those mobilized."

Our division received reinforcements from both these sources and, understandably, these reinforcements were not very reliable. In order to transform mobilized Western Ukrainians and Trans-Carpathian volunteers into reliable soldiers, they had to be rallied into a battle collective by a core of experienced warriors who were loyal to the Soviet Union. These warriors, and reinforcements from hospitals, were the existing personnel of the division. The latter were the most valuable manpower we had and there were never enough of them. So that recuperating wounded and sick soldiers did not settle down in the rear or linger too long in the hospitals, the front gave the medical service directives on time allowed in hospitals for recuperation and quotas on numbers of recuperating men to be sent to the front. For failure to comply with the established norms or for tardiness in dispatching those who had recuperated, strict penalties were meted out to the medical service. Therefore doctors often sent men back to the front who were nowhere near ready to leave the hospital. These men came to us in extremely weak states—just barely off stretchers.

Still, the reinforcements from the hospitals were valuable. The division commander and I personally met them, looked them over, and gave them their assignments. In each group we invariably found men whom we sent to our own medical batallion to complete their recuperation. Such doctors who prematurely discharged these wounded men and sent them to the front certainly obeyed the Hippocratic oath in an unusual way.

Once, while examining the men from one of the reinforcement groups whom our surgeon had held back for further medical treatment, I noticed an elderly soldier who held his left shoulder rather strangely. I asked and learned that this man was fifty-one. To me, at that time thirty-six, he seemed almost an old man. After talking to each man, I finally reached this one who had so intrigued me. "Surname?" I asked.

"Kozhevnikov."

"Name and patronymic?"

"Timofei Ivanovich."

"What's wrong with your shoulder?"

"A shell fragment hurt it a bit."

"Where are you from?"

"Near Moscow."

When I questioned whether he had been fighting a long time, he replied, "A very long time. I fought the whole First World War. And this one, too—I joined a home guard's unit on the first day and have served throughout."

"In which branches have you served?"

"Only in the infantry."

"How many times have you been wounded?"

"Four times in World War I. And in this war, this wound here," he cocked his head in the direction of his left shoulder, "is the seventh."

"Comrade Major," I addressed the surgeon, "please examine Kozhevnikov's wound."

The major did and reported to me, "The wound is still open. He should go to the medical batallion for at least a month."

"Timofei Ivanovich," I said to him, "the major says that you need another month of recuperation—but if you can wait for the end of the inspection, I would like to talk to you. You can leave the formation and sit or lie down. But if you find it hard to wait, I will give orders for you to be taken to the medical batallion."

"I'll wait."

After I had completed the review I went up to him once more. "Timofei Ivanovich, I think that you've done enough fighting in the infantry. One of the soldiers from my personal guard has been badly wounded and will probably not be able to return before the end of the war. If you are not against it, I will keep that job for you. You can complete your recuperation and then take up duties."

"Well, if I am going to be working on the staff, why do I need to go to the medical batallion? My wound will heal anyway. If you take me as a member of your guard, I am ready to begin my service right now."

Thus Timofei Ivanovich Kozhevnikov joined my guard. We quickly became friends. Our relationship was strange. Kozhevnikov was a silent chap. Almost every word had to be dragged out of him, except when he told me how much he liked me. For a long time I did not know the reason behind these outpourings. Finally I realized that Kozhevnikov was communicative after he'd been drinking. He could drink an extraordinary amount without ever showing the effects. I was always astonished when I learned of one of his heavy drinking bouts and then saw him at work.

He and I became attached to each other. One the very first day of his service with me, we got into a complex situation. We were going to the observation point of the 129th Regiment when suddenly a Hungarian unit infiltrated the area. The trail along which we were climbing—up a rather steep mountain, the top of which was the regiment observation point—had not yet been cut off by the enemy. Aleksandrov sent scouts along the trail we had taken. They were fired upon by Hungarians.

Soon after our arrival at the top the Hungarians attacked the heights, moving up along the steep incline and firing their machine pistols continuously, using explosive bullets. The explosive bullets frightened the men and someone cried out that the Hungarians had broken through at one point. Kozhevnikov stuffed his pockets full of cartridge clips. He growled, "Child's play! They want their crackling bullets to make us panic. Let me go to the trench and help out. They need every man they can get. And there's nothing to do here. If they get into the trench my guard duty isn't going to do you much good."

"What good can you do with your rifle?" I asked him. "At least take my machine gun."

"What would I do with that? I can beat off any mountain attack with a rifle. While they're climbing up the slope, I'll pick them all off."

At this moment Aleksandrov received a report that the Hungarians had lain low under our return fire but that they seemed to be preparing for a new attack.

He ordered all his men into the trench and asked my permission for him to leave me with his own signals man and a scout, as well as Kozhevnikov.

"No," I said. "I'm also going to the trench. Come on, Timofei Ivanovich."

Kozhevnikov immediately led me to a most convenient position within the trench. Was it intuition or had he already managed to look about the whole place? In a few minutes the Hungarians started up the slope.

"What would you do now with your machine gun?" Kozhevnikov asked me. "It's not less than two hundred meters to the enemy. Only greenhorns and cowards use a machine gun at distances like that. As for me, I am going to pick off that little officer over there."

I no sooner had made out his target than the officer fell.

"And now that one over there. . . . And that one . . . and that one, too."

After every single shot he fired someone fell. Putting in a new clip he informed me as if it were a most important secret, "I won't even finish this clip, before the part of the line I am shooting at lies back down."

Infrequent rifle fire that never misses causes panic and fright. His second clip knocked down a significant part of the enemy chain. The officers ran along, shouting orders for the men to rise. When the third clip went into action the officers themselves began to lie down.

The entire sector of the enemy chain within Kozhevnikov's fire line had gotten down on the ground.

"How many widows and orphans you made today, Timofei Ivanovich!" I declared thoughtfully.

"Not a single one."

"How's that?"

"I don't kill them. I only wound them. In their leg, their arm, their shoulder. Why kill them? All I need is for them not to kill me. Let them go on living. A bullet is a tender, clean thing. The wounds are not serious—they'll heal swiftly and they won't leave any damage behind. Not like a shell fragment."

Then I understood that this was a highly experienced soldier, one who not only knew his business, but who looked upon it like any other form of labor, with esteem and affection. He didn't joke, did not brag, and did not exploit the power he had. I had enormous confidence in him. After that incident, I never again went to the advance posts without Kozhevnikov.

Timofei Ivanovich looked after me until the end of the war. He was demobilized when the division was dissolved and he and I went together to Moscow and from there, home. After the war he and his wife visited us several times and once Zina and I visited him at his home. Eventually we lost touch.

By January 1945 our division was so worn down by the months of almost uninterrupted battle that we were unable to overcome the heightened resistance of the enemy and we went into a temporary defensive pose. An old wound of Ugryumov's had opened again and he had to go to the medical battalion. Left as division commander, I concentrated all my attention on reconnaissance. There was no continuous front on our side or on that of the enemy and the flanks and rear of our division were open—a deplorable situation. In order to keep anything unexpected from happening, reconnaissance constantly checked out the surrounding areas and eventually established the fact that the enemy had no reserves anywhere around the Czech city of Poprad. The only enemy troops in the area were those in immediate contact with us. Therefore we decided to take Poprad by a deep envelopment operation that would cut off from the rear and rout the enemy located in the battle line. I talked with Ugryumov in the medical battalion about the route we planned to take to carry out the envelopment and told him that I thought we could cover it in two days. Ugryumov approved the plan but advised me not to push too far ahead. If a dangerous situation should arise for the rear of the division then the front should return. The army should not be informed of our intention ahead of time. If Gastilovich became enamored of our plan, he would drive the division ahead—despite the threat of destruction.

So we went ahead on our own. For almost two straight days the division moved along the mountain paths, dragging artillery and battle supplies. On January 30, 1945, in the middle of the day, we occupied Poprad, meeting with almost no resistance. The small rear units of the Germans stationed there surrendered. We captured warehouses full of valuables and freight cars stocked with goods.

Leusenko was named commandant of Poprad and he was ordered to post guard over all the captured goods and to preserve order in the city. The 129th Regiment was assigned to guard the railway. The 151st was ordered to advance fifteen kilometers westward along the highway to take the town of Zavadka. Reconnaissance patrols were sent out in all other directions. Artillery was set up in firing positions. Only after I was convinced that we were threatened by no immediate danger did I report to Gastilovich, by phone, that I had taken Poprad.

Just before sunset Gastilovich arrived in Poprad with a group of staff officers and a guard. Pointing to a spot on the map, he ordered, "By morning you must get to here."

I looked at the map—the place he'd indicated was at least sixty kilometers away. "My men are utterly exhausted. They've gone for two and a half days without sleep or rest."

"Pyotr Grigoryevich, you must! Look, the highway runs along a narrow gully, almost a canyon. It can be shut off by a mere company. Before the enemy even begins to recover, you will have reached the beginning of this broad plateau. No one will be able to hold us back there."

Gastilovich was right. He had an extraordinary mind and a talent for war. Too bad the system spoiled it all. He had a liking for clichés, and, worst of all, he imitated the rudeness and crudity of his superiors.

Now, however, no one was around before whom he had to perform and he said softly, cordially, "Tell the regiment that when they get to the plateau they will be able to rest. I have already ordered the 24th division to advance behind you at forced tempos. It will replace you. You'll get a week of rest—and decorations too, of course. You must get there by morning," he stressed again. "Think of how many men we'll lose if the enemy shuts off the valley!"

"Very well, comrade commander, we'll get there."

I left Gastilovich and called the 151st Regiment in Zavadka, personally ordering the commander to advance by morning to the plateau. When he complained of the great fatigue of his men, I echoed Gastilovich and told him that he had no choice. I promised rest and decorations and demanded that he set out immediately. When Aleksandrov and Leusenko arrived, I ordered the 129th to follow along on our left and the 310th to follow on our right, both along mountain trails, keeping a close watch over the situation on the highway. If the enemy approached and halted the advance of the 151st Regiment, the 129th and the 310th were to strike the enemy in the flank and in the rear and free the road so that the 151st could move forward.

I ordered them to get under way immediately and released them. My eyes kept closing and I realized that the soldiers were in no better shape than myself. I felt I had to recommend that the officers set an example for their soldiers, proceeding with them in the general column. In order to wake up I washed and dined. I would have given anything for just one hour of sleep. I dismissed the idea of a stolen nap, shook myself, and left, driving to Zavadka just to make sure that everyone had left. When my car was almost through the town, I noticed a soldier with a mess tin. I turned my car about, approached the soldier and asked him, "What regiment?"

"The 151st, comrade Colonel."

"Where is the regiment staff office, do you know?"

"Over there." He pointed to a house and we drove up to it. In the first room a lieutenant colonel lay on a couch in his overcoat and his straps, with his cap beneath his head, fast asleep. I peered at his face in the dim light of the kerosene lamp. It was Tonkonog—the commander of the 151st Regiment—named to this post after Melnikov was wounded. I was furious. I took the sleeping man by his collar and jerked him upright to the floor. "You're asking for a court-martial!"

All sleep disappeared from his face. He grew pale and pleaded, "Forgive me, comrade Lieutenant Colonel. I don't know how it happened. It's as if I sank down into the earth after your telephone call. We will catch up."

My wrath faded. I remembered how I had felt only half an hour before and I realized what had happened to him. He had become impossibly exhausted and there was no one to keep him from falling asleep and no one to awaken him. Not only the commander of the regiment was sleeping—the entire regiment was.

"Get your men up and get moving as soon as possible," I said.

The regiment carried out its assignment. As I had done during the preceding two days of marching to Poprad, I drove beside the general column and checked out the condition of the men. Many were falling asleep on their feet and were marching with closed eyes. Some Germans drove in front of the column in a jeep. They fired on us and dropped a mine on the road. The men just walked along, stepping over the mine in a half-somnolent state. Yet by morning they had reached the point assigned to us by Gastilovich.

The division command point was set up in a fortresslike manor house located three kilometers from the advance detachments of the 151st Regiment. I was elated. I wanted to wash up, and ride out and congratulate the units, whatever state they were in.

There was good reason for all of us to be proud. In just three days we had marched more than 150 kilometers, coping beautifully with Gastilovich's assignment. The advance detachments, having traveled through the mountains, already had arrived on the plateau. Gastilovich had moved the division just in time. The Germans had failed to catch us in the narrow valley. Only after we reached our destination did enemy troops appear and begin firing at us. The 24th division was late in arriving and I could see that the enemy was establishing himself firmly in his positions. I had to tell Gastilovich.

Just then the telephone rang. I picked it up and heard "Grigorenko?" It was Kolonin—a member of the military council of the front—who modeled himself on Gastilovich, by disregarding all "call letters" or code names. "It's I, comrade member of the military council," I replied in a satisfied tone, convinced that I would soon hear congratulations. The chief political official in the army was certainly an appropriate person to express thanks for the masterful way in which we'd carried out such a difficult assignment.

Instead of praise, I heard a threatening voice: "Do you know what's going on in *your* area in Poprad?"

"No, I don't know what's going on in *your* area in Poprad."

"So that's it! And you are a smart-ass on top of it all! Do you know that the local populace is plundering booty in your area here?"

"I'm telling you once more: I don't know anything about what is going on in Poprad."

"So that's how it is! You even consider yourself right! You're going to a court-martial."

"If I do it will be with you," I replied. "You left the booty batallion in Sighet just to guard your own skin, and now I am supposed to guard your booty instead of carrying out battle tasks. Go ahead, turn it over to a court-martial!"

I put down the phone, my hands trembling. I went off to the regiments, and returned two hours later, still angry. At the very moment that I sat down to breakfast, three jeeps raced past the window and turned into the yard. Obviously they were full of important people. I grabbed my jacket, shoved one arm into a sleeve, and the door swung open. Mekhlis, member of the military council of the front, entered. I finished putting on my jacket.

"Don't bother to dress, don't bother!" Mekhlis ran up to me, grabbed my right arm, shook it, and spoke. "You were having breakfast? We won't keep you long. I came especially to congratulate you. You saved the front! We had a failure at Moravská Ostrava—and your success saved everything. I want to thank you personally and communicate the gratitude of the command of the front to the whole division."

I was touched by his words but they reawakened the hurt that Kolonin had only recently caused me to feel. "Thank you, comrade Mekhlis, for coming hundreds of kilometers to say a good word to us! In our army you have to wait a long time for it!" I looked to see who was standing behind Mekhlis: Kolonin, Brezhnev, and Dyomin (chief of the political branch of the corps). "You came to thank me, but others here are going to turn me over to a court-martial."

"Who? What for?"

"Just two hours ago comrade Kolonin threatened to court-martial me because inhabitants of Poprad were stealing booty."

"Look here, comrade Kolonin, it's up to a battle division to guard booty. It's your own problem."

Mekhlis was restrained but still one could sense how furious he was. I decided to continue. "For that matter our army generally replaces good words with obscenities. I'm not even going to talk about the army commander. Perhaps in his job he has the right. But the political branch officials often use obscenities. Kolonin does. And Dyomin too—he shouted obscenities at me the other day. And for this entire operation no one from our army has even said 'thank you.' "

"That's no way to conduct yourself, comrade Kolonin," said Mekhlis in an angry tone of voice. Ironically, though, he let loose his wrath on Lieutenant Colonel Dyomin, an officer who generally was not harmful.

"Comrade Dyomin, you are to make your apologies to the division commander!"

I had not yet finished. "You can also judge the attitude toward people in our army, comrade Mekhlis, by this fact," and I showed him my shoulder with my rank insignia. "I began the war as a lieutenant colonel and I am a lieutenant colonel today—though all along I have been occupying posts belonging to colonels and generals. And I have been successful in them, too."

As Kolonin watched Mekhlis listen to me he grew pale. Everyone knew that Mekhlis had a terrible temper, and that he was quite capable of striking without bothering to think things through. Kolonin, fearful of this, butted in. "Comrade Mekhlis, it's not our fault. I will talk to you later about what the problem is. But it's not our fault. Several times we have asked for promotion for comrade Grigorenko. But all our requests have been turned down."

"Very well, comrade Grigorenko, I will work this out. You will get your promotion."

I, of course, knew that the army was not to blame for the delay in my promotion. But how else could I speak about this matter to Mekhlis?

As Kolonin and Mekhlis left, Brezhnev spoke to Mekhlis. "Let me stay behind to help the division commander." He didn't have to ask Mekhlis; Kolonin was his superior. But Brezhnev, assuming a servile expression and tone of voice, had appealed to the more superior of the two, thereby showing his own loyalty and zealousness. When just Brezhnev, Dyomin, and myself were left in the room, Brezhnev immediately asked me, "Aren't you angry at me, too—or is it just that you haven't yet got around to complaining about me?"

"No, I had no reason."

"Good. And as far as you are concerned, comrade Dyomin, you must carry out comrade Mekhlis's instructions. Apologize to comrade Grigorenko." Brezhnev put on a look of extreme seriousness.

Smiling with embarrassment, Dyomin asked me, "How can I apologize to you? Of course, I am sorry. . . ."

"Consider that you already have," I said, "and for that matter, you can swear at me if you have to. I won't complain about you again. It just popped out this time. You suffered because of someone else."

"That's good! Peace is better," declared Brezhnev, trying to look like a good, decent chap and speaking in a familiar tone.

It is not gratuitously that I describe Brezhnev's many facial expressions. His smile reminded me of the smile of a marionette. During my nine months of service under the party leadership of Brezhnev I observed on him a whole repertoire of expressions. The first was an obsequious, servile smile: he donned this in the presence of higher-ups. It covered the area between his ears, the end of his nose, and his chin, and it looked as if it had been glued on or as if somewhere someone was pulling strings, since it suddenly would appear in full scale without any transition; then someone pulled a different string and it disappeared just as suddenly.

He could assume a severely edifying expression when instructing his subordinates; it involved his entire face, and, like the servile smile, also appeared without warning. Suddenly his face would become severe, but somehow not in a genuine way. This was a put-on expression, like the grimace on the face of a doll.

The third was the face of a good, decent chap, which appeared from time to time in the course of conversation with soldiers and junior officers. In this case his face, while remaining immobile, was enlivened by a wink, a half-smile, or a sly squint. Likewise, all of this looked doll-like. The artificiality of his facial expressions and his voice caused people to think of Brezhnev as a lightweight, a dullard, a simpleton. In the army he was given the condescending nicknames "Lyonya," or "Lyonechka"— our "politleader."

I imagine that this attitude toward him continued after the war as well. At the Frunze Academy graduation in the Kremlin, I encountered Dyomin, by this time a lieutenant general and member of the military council of the Baltic Military District. We had a drink together to celebrate our reunion. During our reminiscing he asked me, "Do you ever visit Lyonya?"

"No," I said, "I don't know him well enough and to be perfectly honest, I don't like to pester the big bosses."

(By this time Brezhnev was the Chairman of the Presidium of the Supreme Soviet of the USSR and was counted as one of the pupils and closest comrades-in-arms of Khrushchev.)

"You certainly ought to," he said. "Lyonya likes to have his army companions pay him visits. And it's easy to get to him, too. Just call up, give him your name, and they will give you an appointment. I always pay him a visit when I am in Moscow. We have a drink and talk."

My encounter with Brezhnev after the division had reached the plateau was not my last, but it was the only time that I knew him to be in the front-line area or even at the army command point. His place as chief of the political branch was in the army's second echelon—where party documents were handled. He usually visited troops and personnel in order to meet with Communists only when battles were not going on. A chief of the political branch would only be a hindrance to have around during battle.

Everyone knows that Brezhnev did not see battle, but still they depict things as if Brezhnev had himself led an attack. He, too, remembers the past rather poorly. If he had a better memory, he would be ashamed to have received the order of Hero of the Soviet Union for participation in the battle actions of an army in which not one of the commanders or members of the military council received such an honor. They were the ones who directed the troops—not Brezhnev, whose duties were to sign party membership cards and to turn them over to new Communists. Signing battle orders was the duty of the army commander and the members of the military council.

Consider: Brezhnev was a rank-and-file chief of a political branch of an army. There were hundreds like him in the Soviet army forces; none participated in the direction of troops; none understood anything about such business; none would have been able to command even the lowest of all military units, a section, let alone an army. Now, if some twenty years after the end of the war one such man commences to be depicted as a great strategist and is ascribed almost the decisive role in the victory over Hitler's Germany—even though the army he served in during the whole war only served in minor ways—then the role and glory ascribed to him is such drivel that it is shameful even to have to refute it. But when such drivel is disseminated and the hero himself accepts it with gladness and begins to believe in his own outstanding role, it says something both about the intellectual capabilities of the "hero" and about the rottenness of a system that permits such utter lies about the most powerful man within its hierarchy, one whose wartime past was totally insignificant to the functioning of the army and the winning of the war.

So why had Brezhnev come to Poprad the day after we took that city? He was present during my conversation with Mekhlis, smiling his obsequious and servile smile, demonstrating to Mekhlis his zealousness by announcing that he would stay behind "to help" the division commander, "reconciling" me with Dyomin and thereby bringing his mission to a successful completion. As he departed he said, "I am going to leave these two instructors from the political branch to assist you. Just provide them with transportation and escorts as they go about the regiments."

That's how Brezhnev "helped" me—by giving me political instructors whom I did not need in the first place and by making me responsible for their transportation and guards.

In general the political organs of the army did not have any important function, and thus it was useless to expect any help from them. But within the Soviet system they are necessary. They make political reports, denounce various soldiers and officers, and thus they work to indoctrinate people into total loyalty to the leader. The political branch particularly valued those who kept close track of the conduct, opinions, and thoughts of people and reported anything suspicious, even about their own bosses. Devotion to the leader was stressed by every political worker. Political workers began everything they did by praising the "leader" just as a true religious believer begins everything with a prayer. Brezhnev was no exception, as I soon saw.

Mekhlis did not forget my complaint. On February 2 I received a telegram from him congratulating me on my promotion to colonel, and on the same day I received a telegraphed order actually promoting me to colonel.

Though I was glad to receive this promotion, I decided to submit a declaration requesting the removal of the party penalty from my record. In my declaration I wrote that at the beginning of the war I had made an incorrect utterance in connection with the attack by Hitler's Germany and as a consequence had been given a "strict reprimand with a warning and an entry in my registration card." Finally, I pointed out that though Oleinikov had alleged that I had expressed doubts in the wisdom of Stalin, the party investigation had not confirmed this. I asked, in view of the time that had passed since this mistake, and in view of the fact that I had admitted my error and since then had demonstrated my devotion to the party and to comrade Stalin, that the penalty be annulled.

Brezhnev was present at the meeting of the army party commission that handled my case. I mention this because he usually was not present at such meetings, as the party commission was subordinate to him. It was his duty to confirm the commission's actions. Thus it was impossible that a decision could be made that was unacceptable to Brezhnev, even in his absence. Nevertheless, he was present at the meeting in question.

My case was the third to be taken up. The first was that of a deputy commander of a rear regiment who had been stealing valuable food over a long period of time, hundreds of thousands of rubles worth. He had been caught in the act. The case had gone to a court-martial and it seemed likely that he would face a firing squad. But the bosses intervened and the case was handed over to the party commission for consideration. He was given a "severe reprimand with a warning" (not to be entered onto his registration card). Six months had passed since this reprimand, the minimum time period for raising the question of annulment of a reprimand. To me it seemed obvious that he had not stopped stealing—he had to continue, if only in order to pay off those who had saved him from trial. This must have been clear to the party commission and to Brezhnev, but the the decision was unanimous: "Reprimand annulled."

The second case was that of the commander of a signal corps regiment who had been reprimanded for "exploiting his service position for the purpose of forcing subordinates into sexual relations with him." In other words, he had his male subordinates bring him young female soldiers and he raped them.

Looking at his fat, stupid, bull-like face and swinish eyes, I realized that he would never stop exploiting his service position. But six months had passed and the party commission, which also knew he would never stop, wiped his record clean. During the discussion of both cases, Brezhnev sat in a back corner of the room, his face like a graven image.

Discussion of my case began. The commission secretary read my declaration. With the two other cases, the order of things had been questions, speeches, proposals. Now suddenly and unexpectedly, Brezhnev himself spoke: "Lack of respect for comrade Stalin?! No, for that let him continue to bear his reprimand! Let him continue to bear it!"

His face wore a mask of most severe edification. He poked his index finger in my direction, punctuating each of his sentences. What an actor! I thought. He came here especially for this, to demonstrate in front of all these party officials how concerned he is for the authority of "the great Stalin." How much he loves him. However, as it later became apparent, even his love for Stalin could not compel him to labor conscientiously. The most useful work for Brezhnev was work for show.

I submitted my application for annulment of the reprimand again in 1946. In my statement I wrote approximately what I had written in my first appeal. A month and half later the chief of the political branch of the Frunze Academy, where I was serving at the time, summoned me. "What sort of a penalty was imposed on you?" he asked.

"A strict reprimand and a warning and entry onto my registration card."

He handed me a card that read: "The Central Party Archive reports that by decision of the front party commission of the Far Eastern Front comrade

Grigorenko was meted out a party penalty: 'A reprimand.' "

"As you see, there is no 'strict,' no 'warning,' and no 'entry.' Therefore your case is in the hands of your own primary party organization. Make your appeal there. The party commission will not consider this declaration."

I recollected Brezhnev's "Let him continue to bear it!" and I realized that he had either not inquired into the Central Party archive or else had hidden his findings from the party commission in order to have the chance to utter his own dramatic words of condemnation. There was always hope, given the Soviet system, that such a statement might reach Stalin himself and prove to him the total loyalty of Leonid Ilyich Brezhnev.

CHAPTER FIFTEEN

THE WAR
ENDS

Gastilovich was not able to keep his promise to give the division a week's rest after we took Poprad. After only two days the situation changed sharply. One of the tank armies of the First Ukrainian Front that was developing a western offensive along the Czech-Polish border encountered strong enemy resistance near the village of Khyzhne. The front command shifted the tank army in a new direction. By forced marches our division occupied the area now left open, a strip approximately thirty kilometers long. Though both our flanks were now open, we really only had to defend ourselves against attacks along the ten kilometers of highway running to the village, and along a highway through the small city of Trstena. Both roads moved westward. The breadth of this front was five to six kilometers. Between the two highways was a swampy forest almost entirely flooded with spring water. Thus maneuvering was difficult. It was possible to move only along roads that circumvented the forest, and this involved distances of more than sixty kilometers. The terrain in the Trstena direction was comprised of a mountain valley that rose up on our side and was convenient for defense. In the direction of Khyzhne, however, the enemy had the definite advantage.

After much back and forth between Gastilovich, Ugryumov, and myself about how we could surmount these obstacles, we settled on a plan for taking both Khyzhne and Trstena. I was to concentrate especially on the attack of Khyzhne.

We had difficulty in deciding on a location for the Khyzyne command point. It had to have reliable communications and transport lines both with the 151st Regiment and with the artillery and machine gun batallion. Reliable command of the artillery and machine gun batallion could be provided from the existing command point—but from there it would be impossible for me to command the regiment. For a time we could see no easy solution to this problem. Then one day our division intelligence chief, who had carried out reconnaissance in the area of Khyzhne and the forest, ran into an abandoned trail that originated at the Trstena highway, quite near advanced outposts. He followed this trail and emerged at an abandoned forester's hut, located on a dry, elevated clearing. From there it was about two kilometers to the southern edge of Khyzhne and no further away from the edge of the forest. The forester's hut could be set up as the point of command. Two kilometers through a flooded forest was no obstacle. We also established this hut as a supply point from which ammunition could be delivered to the 151st Regiment during the course of the battle. Engineers worked on the trail and made it passable for carts and even for jeeps.

At dawn on March 2 our engineers dismantled the mine and rocket fields between the forest and the southern edge of Khyzhne. As they ended their operation one of the displaced rockets blew up and illuminated our advance subunits. Because of this the regiment commander decided to attack before the time previously agreed upon.

During the first stage of battle each of the two batallions in the village captured three houses. And, in accordancee with our plan, they moved into the houses and prepared to repel enemy counterattacks. I had spent a long time indoctrinating Tonkonog—telling him over and over again that he should not be hasty but should advance in short spurts.

With the commencement of the 151st Regiment's attack, the artillery and machine gun batallion also moved forward. The enemy opened fire from its installations along the crest of the hill, but our artillerymen, moving in battle formations and firing accurately over their sights, soon crushed these installations. The enemy troop cover retired behind the crest and back into the trench and into the village. The artillery and machine gun batallion emerged on the crest but did not advance any further. The artillerymen dug into position and began to prepare to fire. In case of an enemy counterattack on the strip in front of the village, the commander of the artillery and machine gun batallion had been ordered to destroy all counterattacking enemies. Patience, viligant observation, and precise fire would be demanded of the men. If there was no counterattack, the batallion would be given a new task.

I spent till about ten o'clock in my forester's hut. In the village Tonkonog moved forward bit by bit, occasionally repelling counterattacks. The stream batallion had seized the small bridge on the highway and had assumed defensive positions. Per orders, the artillery and machine gun batallion did not fire on the trench or on the village. For several hours all I heard was the exchange of rifle shot—not the sounds of a full-scale attack. At ten o'clock I reported the situation to Ugryumov and to the army staff. A few minutes later the phone rang. I picked it up, and before I could say my name Gastilovich began speaking. "Grigorenko, how long will it take you to get to me?"

"A half hour."

"You know where I am?" he asked, obviously astonished at my reply.

"I know very well. If necessary I can be with you in half an hour."

"Yes, it's necessary. You are to take command over the division. I have removed that jackass Ugryumov for trying to pull the wool over my eyes."

Bumping along the forest trail and watching the jeep move like a speedboat through the water in the flooded sections, I kept wondering what could have happened. I was certain that Ugryumov would never deceive the army commander.

Arriving at Gastilovich's command point, I immediately reported to him.

"Take command of the division," he said. "Find out what is going on and report to me. That jackass told me that we'd taken the little railway station. I have been observing the action since the very first shot and I saw that Ugryumov's infantry never left their starting position. Vasilyev's got moving but then lay back down—Ugryumov's never moved. And here he's telling me: 'We occupied the station.' Go and put things straight."

"Yes, sir!" I saluted and went out.

The situation was already clear to me. But it would have been unwise for me to contradict the army commander when he was convinced he was right and I had been ten kilometers away from the disputed action. Gastilovich's command point was perfectly located. Its views were unlimited. The strips of attack of both divisions were visible to Trstena itself. I knew that the division's departing position was at the beginning of several kilometers of irrigated fields. The deep ditches and high crests between the individual fields ran in the same direction as our advance—and could be used as cover from enemy fire. But neither the ditches nor the crests were visible from Gastilovich's command point. What he saw was a smooth, lifeless plain. Moving around, I finally found one spot from which the ditches and crests were clearly visible. Unfortunately, I had never told Ugryumov about the problem with visibility of the ditches and crests from Gastilovich's command point.

When I arrived at the division observation point, Ugryumov said, bitterly, "Well, take over! Come on over to the periscopes and I will show you the soldiers whom Gastilovich can't see."

I looked through the scope and, indeed, I could clearly see men moving along the ditches, in the area of the station. They were our own soldiers. "I knew it all along," I told him. "Now tell me exactly what took place."

"What's there to say?" he answered me. "Gastilovich phoned me and asked: 'Where is your infantry?' I told him they were attacking. He said I was lying. Half an hour later I called and reported to him the occupation of the station. He cursed me, accused me of trying to deceive him, removed me from my post, and summoned you."

"Well," I said, "the worst thing is that he is absolutely convinced he's right. *He* has the bad command point. He cannot see the men moving along the ditches. If I try to prove to him that he was mistaken, no doubt he will remove me, too. Which regiment did he turn over to you? The 129th? Let's carry out his orders. Go to the railway station with an engineer. Take Zavalnyuk, exactly whom you'd take when the first echelon command point is being shifted. When you get to the station, call and I will come down. Then the command point will be at the railway station. *That's* when we'll talk to Gastilovich—don't bother with him till then."

Zavalnyuk phoned forty minutes later to say that they had arrived at the station. I immediately called Gastilovich. "Comrade Commander! I've worked everything out. The troops did move forward. But they can't be seen any longer from this observation post. Permit me to shift the command point. Zavalnyuk already has chosen a new location. He is there right now and confirms that he can see all our troops from it."

I avoided naming the railway station as the new command point. I was afraid that this news would anger Gastilovich, but he didn't even ask where it was. "How much time do you need for the shift?" he asked.

"About forty minutes."

"Go ahead! Move!"

When I got to the railway station I presented my plan to Ugryumov: "Call Gastilovich and present yourself as division commander. Report the situation and in conclusion tell him that the chief of staff of the division has also arrived here."

Ugryumov resisted, not wanting to talk to Gastilovich, but when I reminded him he would be known forever as a general who was removed during battle, he made the call, gave his name, reported the situation, and ended with, "The chief of staff has arrived and reported your decision to change the command point."

"Give the phone to Grigorenko," Gastilovich growled.

"Are you really at the station?" he asked me.

"Yes sir! Our subunits have made use of irrigation ditches and therefore they can't be seen from your command point. At this moment our first subunits have advanced two kilometers, but have been halted by the division commander because the enemy is preparing to launch a counterattack. Therefore it has been decided to hold the infantry back until the arrival of antitank weapons. In fact, Vasilyev and his tank-killer batallion are moving past us right now."

A short while later the enemy's tank counterattack began. Our artillerymen performed superbly, destroying four tanks and two self-propelled artillery pieces. During the battle I kept up a running commentary to Gastilovich—and he finally became convinced of our division's actual advance. He then turned his attention to General Vasilyev's division, which had not yet moved beyond its departure point. After repelling the enemy tanks, our regiments—the 129th and the 310th—had gone over into an assault and at approximately 1:30 A.M. had entered Trstena and were threatening to cut off the highway. The enemy began to withdraw its troops into the strip of our neighbor on the left, the 137th Infantry Division. Concentrating on Trstena, we somehow forgot about Khyzhne. Then, at about two o'clock the clatter of machine guns and the roar of cannons began.

Gastilovich phoned me. "What's going on in Khyzhne?"

"I don't have any reports from there yet—but I'm assuming that the last battle is in progress. I think it would be wise for me to go there and personally take charge of all further actions."

"You're the division commander. You decide where it is best for you to be."

Pretending not to understand him, I said, "Yes, sir! I will decide that question with the division commander," and I put down the phone. I waited nervously to see whether he would correct me, but the telephone was silent.

Ugryumov agreed with me that we should return to Khyzhne. I called the old command point and ordered my driver to proceed to Khyzhne and look for me in the 151st Regiment or in the artillery and machine gun batallion; furthermore, I informed Zavalnyuk that the auxiliary command point was to be shifted into Khyzhne and was to be in contact with the 151st Regiment and the artillery and machine gun batallion. Accompanied by five scouts, Timofei Ivanovich and I went straight from Trstena to Khyzhne, traveling across territory only recently occupied by the enemy. It took us an hour and a half to get to Khyzhne and by that time the village had been cleared of the enemy and dinner was being brought to the subunits. Scouts had been sent to patrol the highway to Trstena and Bobrov. With everything under control, I reported to Gastilovich. He gave orders for the entire division to turn toward Bobrov and to develop an offensive to the west along a highway that was parallel to the one running through Trstena. The enemy was retreating along this road and one division would be adequate.

I made a point of informing Gastilovich of the losses suffered by the enemy. I told him that I had never seen so many dead Germans. Corpses covered the entire field to the east of Khyzhne. On my orders a count was made, and there were 832 corpses in that field alone. There were also many dead along the village street. We took more than four hundred prisoners, and much ammunition, food, and other material. I went around the entire battlefield and, frankly, I admired the work of the artillery and machine gun batallion. After talking with the batallion commander, I was even more pleased. He told me, "They came from the highway, from the northern edge of the village, marching in two dense columns. At first they moved rather timidly, as if they were afraid of an ambush; then they became bolder, marched more quickly, and began to move away from the village and approach the trench. After one column crossed the trench to the east, they began to deploy.

"Tonkonog was nervous and wanted me to act. But I was waiting for all the columns to emerge into the open. I recalled your instructions—'Patience is the chief weapon of the fortified area artilleryman.' And so I decided that I would have patience. Finally, the columns stopped emerging from the village. Those out in front had deployed and kept marching more and more quickly. Tonkonog shouted that they were already approaching the rear, but I kept thinking: 'No, it's not yet time.' Most of the Germans were on the run, going into an attack, but some were still marching, even though it was a quickstep. Finally those, too, began to run and at that point I let loose and everything went as planned.

"I had never, the whole war long, known such gladness. The machine gunners trembled as they completed their jobs, their eyes burning. 'Now that is work for you,' one said. 'I unburdened my soul for the whole war.' The artillerymen also performed superbly. They struck the enemy in flight as if worried they would get away. And the enemy! They must have forgotten all about us. When we struck, they were paralyzed. Instead of running into the village or jumping in the trench or falling on the ground, they stood stock still. After a minute, they began to whirl around and only when half of them had been downed did they rush into flight, not rationally, but in every direction, running into each other, colliding and falling beneath the machine gun fire and the cannon fire. We cleaned them out so effectively that when we rose and moved as a unit into the village, not one single shot was fired in our direction."

I walked among the piles of corpses and felt nothing but satisfaction. The thought never entered my mind that these were human beings, that they had mothers, wives, and children, that they had had dreams and expectations, that they had had hopes. I did not see the faces frozen by horror, torment, and pain. I did not pay any attention to the hands, legs, and bodies curled up in death. For me these were nameless, faceless units of production—just corpses—as logs would have been to a woodcutter. And I felt the same as a woodcutter who had managed to cut an enormous quantity of wood. I was proud of myself and I wanted to brag about what I had accomplished. I called

Gastilovich and asked him to come over and take a look.

His artillery commander came over. And he, like all who saw it, was awed by the "work" of the fortified area artillerymen.

He said, "The only thing I've seen like this was in World War I—but then the corpses were ours."

He turned out to be such a good storyteller that not only did Gastilovich come to take in the sights, but also the entire army leadership, including those from neighboring divisions. Even Petrov sent representatives. Talk about this battle—exaggerated naturally—spread along the entire front. All of the field fortified areas sent representatives and throughout the units a recommendation was circulated that everyone should strive after this type of action we had undertaken.

I was not decorated for that battle, but that was my fault. When Gastilovich asked me what decoration I wished to receive, without thinking I replied, "I want an order for outstanding military leadership. I feel that what was done in Khyzhne fits the requirements for the Order of Suvorov: 'A victory over large forces of the enemy as a result of which a turning point in operations has been achieved.' We destroyed a division with a regiment. If our troops had not cleansed Khyzhne, the divisional reserve that perished there would have counterattacked the 129th and 310th Regiments and would have turned them back—then the 137th would have failed."

Gastilovich agreed with me but added, "You are not going to receive the Order of Suvorov. Decorations for outstanding military leadership are given out only by Moscow. And Moscow isn't going to give you any decoration. I think you know that yourself. Therefore you should take a modest Order of the Red Banner. That I can guarantee you. Petrov will sign my personal report immediately."

"No, for this operation I must get either a decoration for outstanding military leadership—or nothing at all."

"Very well. I will write Moscow and recommend you for the Order of Suvorov. And Petrov will sign my recommendation. But those who issue decorations never even glance at the recommendations. They look only at the signatures, and the signatures from our front are not very weighty. If Zhukov, Vasilevsky, or Rokossovsky signed it, they would hand it out. But if Petrov signs it—it's not certain. Therefore you have only yourself to blame if you end up with nothing."

And so I got nothing.

Tonkonog and the commander of the artillery and machine-gun batallion also requested decorations for outstanding military leadership. Both received Orders of Alexander Nevsky.

Thus it was not just a matter of signatures.

This had been Tonkonog's last battle in our division. A few days later he

was badly wounded and had to be hospitalized. Ugryumov had gotten himself
into a complex situation. Because of our passive resistance he was not removed
from his position during the course of battle. But Gastilovich did not let him
return to his command, either. He kept him in the medical batallion and tried
to arrange, as he had earlier done with Smirnov, to have him transferred to
another army. Luck saved Ugryumov. As the end of the war approached, an
old promotion request for him went through and he was awarded the rank
of major general. Gastilovich was forced to retreat.

After his promotion Ugryumov said to me, "If you weren't an idiot, you
would long since have commanded the division."

I knew what he meant, but I was not sorry for what I had done. In fact,
I am proud that even when our heads were being banged against each other
by those in charge, we still managed to retain our soldiers' friendship.

Since first coming to the front I had had an overwhelming faith that I would
survive the war to return home to my family. The events that threatened my
life only intensified this faith. In them I saw the hand of providence, though
I was a party member and truly believed myself an atheist.

Several times at the very end of the war death brushed me. Each time it
was fended off by what I call a miracle.

On a sunny, warm day in early spring I drove to the division headquarters
set up in a small Czechoslovakian mountain village. I found the division commander in a beautiful little house with gleaming windows. Immediately I realized that though the house was lovely, it was too much or too obviously so,
and we would have to leave it.

Upon entering the house, I found Ugryumov and the artillery regiment commander, Shafran, in the first room.

"Well, are we in session or is someone missing?" I joked, and approached
the round table behind which Ugryumov and Shafran were sitting, studying
a map.

"No, you're not present," Shafran answered me in the same joking tone.

These were the last words I heard. A terrible blast descended on me and
buried everything in darkness. When I came to, blood was flowing from my
nose and there was a buzzing in my head. Beside me, beneath the window,
an enormous hole had been blown in the wall, right next to the table at which
Ugryumov and Shafran had been sitting. The table had been tossed to the opposite corner of the room, shattered. The doors to the house had been flung
open. Ugryumov lay unconscious in the middle of the room, his face yellow,
the map he and Shafran had been studying wrapped around his chest. Shafran
was nowhere to be seen. The entire room was strewn with shell fragments.
I began to examine myself for wounds. It seemed almost impossible, but I had
none. I crawled over to Ugryumov and examined him. He also was not wounded. In my head the buzzing increased and then all was silent. I felt I was going

to lose consciousness again. I was dizzy and nauseous. Crawling to the door to see if I could get some help, I saw a pair of legs—Shafran's; he was lying half outside and half inside the entryway. I looked him over, too, and found no wounds. The last thing I saw was Kozhevnikov and the artillery regiment physician. I lost consciousness and came to on a stretcher being loaded into an ambulance. Ugryumov, unconscious, was already in the ambulance. I ordered the medics to take me out. I could not hear my own voice, but they understood me and did as I asked. Sitting up on the stretcher and supporting my head with my hands, I began to hear voices, though they were faint.

Captain Gusev arrived. He helped me into the jeep and we drove to the operations branch. There I issued an order reporting the shell shock of the division commander and my own assumption of division command. I sent a similar message to the army commander. In general, I was able to function normally. After a week my nausea and dizziness went away, and I forgot about my own shell shock.

When I was arrested in 1964, I underwent a psychiatric examination, and it was discovered from a look at my medical record that I had suffered "traumatic cerebropathy" at the end of the war—in other words, shell shock. On the basis of this they sent me to the Serbsky Institute for examination. And there, of course, they found it necessary to "cure" me—twenty years after the shell shock.

I consider it a miracle that I, who was right next to the explosion, was not killed and was the least shell shocked of the three of us. Ugryumov could not return to duty until after the war had ended. Even later, he still suffered acute pain from strong headaches.

Late one night in April 1945, I was returning, exhausted, to the division command post after touring the units. We had arrived at this particular settlement during the evening. Kozhevnikov went off to sleep and my guard was assumed by his relief man, Solovyov. Solovyov was only about twenty-five, but his long, thick mustaches made him look like one made wise by life's experience. He had come to the army from the partisans, which made him the target of constant kidding from Kozhevnikov: "Partisans, shmartisans! They collect food for the winter and hide in a den like a bear. Let someone else go fight!"

As if to confirm these jokes, Solovyov was unable to hide his fear of flying shells and trips to the front line. When the command post was shelled, Solovyov would leave his own post and run off to the best shelter he could find. More than once Ugryumov advised me to send him off to the regiment, fearful that he would let me down in a dangerous situation.

But I felt sorry for him. I was certain that a man like him would die in almost any dangerous situation. I knew that if I sent him to a regiment, I would feel guilty after his death. Thus I kept him with me.

I ordered Solovyov to wake me at 7:00 A.M. and quickly went to sleep. At dawn, when the sky had just begun to get gray, I suddenly awoke, completely alert, feeling as if someone had awakened me for an urgent piece of business. This had never happened to me before. I always slept until awakened by someone else. Uneasy, I lay in my bed wondering what was happening. I couldn't think of anything I might have forgotten to do. I got up, pulled on my trousers and boots, and went out. Solovyov was standing exactly where he should have been. I asked him where the toilet was. He pointed to the yard behind the house, and as he began to speak I heard a distant cannon shot. No sooner had I closed the toilet door behind me than I heard a tremendous blast nearby. I didn't know what was happening, but somehow I connected the shot in the distance with this blast.

Solovyov was not at his place when I returned to the little house. (I later ascertained that he had fled in terror. I merely gave him a disciplinary penalty.) Entering, I saw that the door to my room was wide open. I knew I had closed it. I walked cautiously up to the door and peered into the room. The first thing I saw was an enormous hole in the corner, in which the head of my cot stood. The end of a ceiling beam had fallen onto my cot; the room was strewn with shell fragments. I heard steps behind me, looked around, and saw it was Kozhevnikov, who told me he had been awakened by the explosion. He took hold of my shirt, which had been hanging at the bottom of the cot, and was now all cut up by the shell fragments. He surveyed the hole, walked about the room, and finally asked, "Where were you?"

I told him.

"It was God who saved you," he said with deep conviction. "If you had been asleep when the explosion took place, your head would have been torn off by the blast, you would have been punctured by the shell fragments that cut up your shirt, and the falling beam would have broken your back."

There had been only that one distant shot and the one explosion. Someone had awakened me, I thought, and forced me to leave the place of the explosion before it happened. That morning artillerymen came and inspected the blast site. They determined the type and system of the cannon but they were unable to determine where the shot had come from. Most importantly, they could not imagine why just this one shot had been fired and why it had been directed at an unimportant Czech village.

On May 7, the first day of the peace, we, like other Soviet units, communicated to the German troops opposing us an ultimatum to capitulate by midnight. At about 10:00 P.M. our subunits in advance positions reported to us that explosions and shooting were taking place in the formations. By midnight we had not received any reply to our ultimatum, so we went into attack. The enemy resisted briefly and retreated. Beyond our foreposts we encountered almost immediately an awful scene. I had seen more than enough dead soldiers, but I will never forget what I saw at these artillery positions. Alongside the blown-up guns lay the bodies of the enormous German Percherons—all the horses had been shot. It was cruel and inexplicable killing that cannot be forgiven—carried out on the orders of Field Marshall von Scherner, who had refused to capitulate.

We continued our attack for the entire next day, putting soldiers on carts and advancing swiftly. By the end of the day we had covered eighty-four kilometers and caught up with the 129th Regiment. When I readied the regiment staff, they told me the regiment commander was up ahead. We drove on and eventually overtook a batallion. Personnel there told me that the regiment commander was with a second batallion directly ahead of this one.

We drove on. Ahead of us we saw a column, which we approached boldly. When we were just fifty meters from its end, the driver turned to me, his face pale: "Germans!"

"Do not slow down!" I shouted at him. "Blow your horn!"

It was a German column in complete military array, but I was not afraid; the only thought that went through my mind was that it would be stupid to be killed after the war had ended.

The column parted for us and we drove on through, staring at the Germans who stared back at us—maybe out of curiosity and maybe out of fear, probably both.

I joked, "Now in this case, Timofei Ivanovich, your rifle is of no use. You would hardly be able to finish off one of them with it, before they would have finished dealing with you. I advise you to take the driver's machine gun. As long as his hands are on the wheel, he won't need it. And when they shoot the wheel from under him he won't need it either."

We passed through the column and continued driving ahead.

"Where are we now?" the driver asked.

"Let's turn off on the first road," I said.

"There's another column," Kozhevnikov suddenly cried out.

"What should I do?" the driver asked, obviously terrified.

"We'll have to catch up with it," I told them. "We can't turn back into that other column." We drove forward and as we got closer to the new column we were relieved to see that it was ours. Aleksandrov came forward. We exchanged greetings and I told him that there was a column of Germans three kilometers back. He hadn't known. I gave orders for our men to immediately get into ambush. We would let the Germans come right up to us and then we would disarm them without bloodshed.

Aleksandrov and I hid in the bushes, at a spot from which we could see the road clearly. According to my calculations the Germans ought long since to have appeared in our field of vision, but they had not. A liaison man from the party of scouts we had sent out could find no Germans anywhere.

Aleksandrov, the liaison man, and I got into the car and pursued the scouts. When we reached the place where we had caught up with the German column, no Germans were to be seen. Kozhevnikov was convinced that they must have gone off into the woods.

We drove along the entire area where the column had been, inspecting both sides of the road. I noticed that Kozhevnikov had left, and then we heard him calling us.

He had gone in the opposite direction and had found tracks of the column on a cart path that ran off the right side of the highway into the forest. I ordered the scouts to reconnoiter a patch of woods that was visible from the path. A short time later the sergeant chief of the scouting party called us over to the woods and we saw the remnants of the German column. The column had marched in threes, halted in threes, and, with typical German precision, disposed of all their equipment. In place lay knapsacks, uniforms, boots and machine guns. Missing only were the men.

"Where did they go?" Aleksandrov asked. "Did they leave in their underwear?"

"No!" I said. "They must have had civilian clothes with them. Look—the knapsacks are empty."

"The only reason they didn't kill us," Kozhevnikov said, "was that they were afraid of the noise. They had planned ahead how to get out of the war and any noise would have worked against them. That's why they let us live. Thanks to them for that."

He bowed his head in the direction of the column.

"I wish them all luck in getting home safe."

We all looked at the ground. It seemed as if each of us was giving a warm send off to the missing Germans.

The last episode about which I shall speak also took place after the war was over. On May 12, 1945, our division conducted its last battle. It was with the troops of Field Marshal von Scherner, the commander who refused to capitulate.

We had just occupied Pardubice without battle and our regiments were driving toward Prague. Soon we heard an intensive artillery exchange. On our side 85 mm. cannons were firing—field cannons and antiaircraft. From the Germans came the sounds of firing tanks and self-propelled guns. I decided to see what was happening for myself. I got into my jeep and we drove in the direction of the cannon fire. The road was quite empty. When we neared the sounds of battle, I told the driver to pull off the road and conceal us. He drove about ten meters down a cart path into a rather deep hollow. I stopped the car, ran up the slope, and began surveying the area with my binoculars. All of a sudden, at a distance of about thirty to fifty meters, I saw a sinister ring—the throat of a cannon. I did not see the cannon itself, only the mouth that was slowly moving, targeting on me. Before I could do anything, someone knocked me down and together we rolled down the slope. Immediately an antitank shell landed right where I had been standing, whistled malevolently, and ricocheted off the ground.

"Excuse me, please!" a junior lieutenant artilleryman said to me, getting up and brushing himself off. "That was a self-propelled gun. If I had taken the time to shout at you, you wouldn't have managed to get out of the way."

I thanked him but didn't ask his name. I never did find him again.

That afternoon the division received orders to rest in Zwickau, Germany. The next day I was unable to get out of bed. My temperature was 104 degrees and at the hospital I was diagnosed as having pneumonia, but the disease had almost run its course. In other words, I had had pneumonia for quite a while and had not even noticed that I was ill. As soon as my élan dropped, the illness came to the surface. On my third day in the hospital my temperature fell to normal and on the fifth they discharged me, with the recommendation that I be given twenty days of rest and recuperation.

CHAPTER SIXTEEN

A
DECISIVE
TURNING
POINT

The war ended most favorably for me, both physically and emotionally. I had suffered only a wounded leg, and fate—in the person of my wife—had saved me from an amputation. The war's end also brought me complete spiritual reassurance. Doubts I had had now disappeared. To me, Stalin was once again the "great infallible leader" and the "brilliant military commander." I forgot the stupid mistakes and the crimes, or I saw them in a new light, as manifestations of Stalin's brilliance.

Now the leader himself taught us that the suddenness of the German attack was not our fault but had been a natural instance of the "law" of aggressive countries. The aggressor always attacks suddenly. All the attacked country can do is to liquidate as soon as possible the advantage the enemy has gained through surprise. The ancient Parthians had succeeded in doing this—they lured the enemy into the depths of their own country and there massacred him. Like Kutuzov with Napoleon, Stalin had drawn Hitler all the way to Moscow and there defeated him.

All this, of course, was nonsense. But the fascination with victory and the glorification of the leader was such that we accepted it all as revelation.

I was not a protestor, a critic of the system, or a member of the opposition, but a man who was dedicated to and loved his work, who devoted to it all his energy and time. Without hesitation I accepted everything that was said about Stalin, about the party, about the country, as truth. I spoke as a passionately convinced propagandist. Nothing could disturb me. Were people starving in our country? Well, that was natural—we had just come through a terrible war and had suffered unheard-of destruction. Were trainloads of Soviet prisoners being sent to the camps? Why not—if they had betrayed the motherland in a critical hour? Were they arresting civilians who had remained on occupied territory? Naturally! They weren't imprisoning all of them—they would release the innocent. They imprisoned my elder brother Ivan, held him for two or three months, and then released him *without my intervention*. Thus I drew the conclusion that what had happened in 1937–38 was not happening again.

At the victory celebration in 1945 Stalin delivered a toast to the great Russian people. His words gave free rein to those already in power and reduced the dignity of other peoples, including my fellow Ukrainians. Still I perceived this as natural.

In general, no clouds loomed on my political horizon. I was hopeful and optimistic about my postwar future.

In late May 1945 my division and the Eighteenth Army were dissolved. Those who made this decision clearly did not look to the future. To dissolve an army in which such a "great" political leader and strategist as Leonid Ilyich Brezhnev had served was an obvious case of carelessness, of failure to think things through. Today the justification is that Brezhnev was no longer serving in the Eighteenth Army at the time of its dissolution. In the last days of the war he headed the political branch of the Fourth Ukrainian Front. But still that is no justification. The Eighteenth Army should have been allowed to live. What better place in which to create a memorial to Brezhnev and from which to disseminate the light of the "unique strategic genius?" To be sure, those responsible for this mistake could say that during the war they never noticed any special military and political talents on the part of Leonid Ilyich, that they only learned about how special he was some twenty years after the war. But this, too, only makes obvious their own political and military nearsightedness.

I failed to perceive the significance of the Eighteenth Army and was indifferent to its dissolution. I received orders to report to the personnel branch of the Fifty-second Army, into which the Eighteenth had been assimilated. Before leaving I went in to bid farewell to Gastilovich. He seemed happy to see me, and we drank one for the road. Before I left him, I took out the hospital medical comission's recommendation that I be given twenty days leave for rest and recuperation.

"Give me your permission to spend those twenty days in Moscow."

"How can I when you no longer are under my command?"

"All you have to do is to write: 'I give permission for twenty days in Moscow,' and then sign it—and postdate it."

He seemed to understand what I was getting at, and he laughed, saying as he wrote, "What an operator you turned out to be."

"Sometimes it's necessary," I replied. "My wife is going to give birth soon. And after all, the war is over and there are more than enough officers in the reserve."

Shortly after this conversation I traveled to the Fifty-second Army to talk about a new appointment.

The chief of the personnel branch there told me that they intended me to command the division that had absorbed my former Eighth Division. The present commander of this division was due to return home soon because of age and illness.

I told him that I would think it over and would give him my answer after my leave. He conceded to my taking this time and I left for Moscow.

My twenty days flew by like a single moment. I was horrified at the thought of leaving my wife again. She was weak and pale. There was not enough food in her large family, and her pregnancy had been extremely difficult. My leave was almost over, and she had not given birth. I could not leave her in such a difficult situation. I knew that I wouldn't be of much help to her, but just my being there would give her greater strength. I'd have to be an "operator" again. My leave papers were written on the stationery of my dissolved division and I was registered in Moscow with the city commandant. Two days before the expiration of my leave I went to the emissary of the Carpathian Military District at the Chief Personnel Administration. I told him that I was in Moscow on leave for illness and that my leave was over, but I had just received a letter announcing that my division had been dissolved. Where was I to go now?

I was ordered to report to the reserve of the Chief Personnel Administration. I did, and one week later they called me in and offered me several different assignments. I kept insisting that I would only accept a post as division commander, thinking that no one would offer me such a position since hundreds of division commanders with seniority had been let go at the end of the war. I was wrong. Several days later I was sent to the emissary of the Far East, an old acquaintance, Colonel Antsyferov. I had known him as a captain. He offered me a post as commander of a division in the Fifth Army. I smiled and said, "You know, Antsyferov, when I left the Far East in 1943, I didn't leave anything behind."

I did not believe that war would break out in the Far East. If I had known it would, my reply might have been different. When the war began in Manchuria, I was sorry that I had not accepted Antsyferov's proposal. After I turned him down we talked a bit. He observed with a laugh that I was in no hurry to leave Moscow.

"Yes," I replied, laughing along with him, "we want to die near Moscow like our brothers did."

"But you have to understand," he said, "that I don't get paid for sitting here in the reserve. I have to find you a position that pleases both of us. Let me send you to the administration for Assimilation of War Experience on a temporary assignment. You graduated from the General Staff Academy. So go there and work on scientific problems."

The head of the administration was Colonel General Mikhail Nikolayevich Sharokhin, a classmate of mine at the General Staff Academy. He received me very warmly and said, "I am going to send you to the Service Regulations administration. I am thinking about a permanent staff appointment for you there. It's still in the planning stage now and it will take time to get it approved, but meanwhile you can work there as a temporary assignee."

A month later I was offered and accepted the position of deputy chief of the Service Rules and Regulations administration. I heard nothing for a time, but people's formerly pleasant attitudes toward me had somehow changed. My superior, Major General Esaulov, who had already begun treating me as if I were his formal deputy, took me aside one day and told me, "Unfortunately, we are not going to be able to work together. I am telling you this in confidence. You will be informed of it officially, through the personnel branch. They will come up with some reasons for the turndown, but I can tell you that counterintelligence refused to approve of you *because of your wife.*" He continued, "This is strictly between the two of us. I am very sorry this happened. You were the person I wanted for the job."

So once again I had to return to my old acquaintance, the emissary of the reserve.

"What happened?" he greeted me with this question.

"I don't know. In any case it wasn't my fault. I worked conscientiously."

"Yes, everything was going well. Your chiefs thanked me. They praised your work and then suddenly told me that they were sending you back. Well, where are we to send you next?"

"Are there any positions in the academies?"

"Would you accept?"

"Of course."

"Why didn't you say so earlier? There are all kinds of positions in the academies. No one wants to go there. That's why I hadn't offered you one before. Do you want to go to the General Staff Academy or the Frunze Military Academy?"

"Frunze."

In just a few minutes I had orders to be presented for approval to the Frunze Military Academy.

At that time the deputy chief of the Academy for Scientific and Educational Work was my old friend Aleksandr Vasilyevich Sukhomlin. He was enthusiastic about my working there, but first had to consult with the chiefs of the operations and tactics courses, a colonel general and a Hero of the Soviet Union, Nikolai Nikolayevich Bogolyubov—brother of the well-known Soviet scientist Aleksandr Nikolayevich Bogolyubov—who had been a year ahead of me at the General Staff Academy. During the devastating purge of the teaching cadres at the academy he, like Gastilovich, had been transferred to teaching duties before he completed the academy and had taught until the beginning of the war. Though I had never been a member of his group, he was now very friendly to me. Bogolyubov quickly approved my joining his general tactics faculty.

On December 8, 1945, I began my sixteen years of creative work in military science and pedagogy as a senior teacher at the Frunze Academy, and took my first step on the path that led me to where I am today.

I have often asked myself why I chose to go to the academy at a time when life was pushing me in another direction, one to which I was more attracted. Teaching had never inspired me.

What had attracted me was a career as a commander, but when it all of a sudden became a reality, I pulled back from it. I knew that teaching was hopeless in terms of promotions and high ranks. To command a division in the Fifty-second Army at the age of thirty-eight would almost have guaranteed me continued promotions.

All I had to do was telegram the army commander and I would have gotten a division. Today I would be just one more little-known colonel general or army general in the Soviet armed forces, or maybe even a Marshal of the Soviet Union—but in that case I would have had to begin my postwar path with a crime.

The Fifty-second Army later participated in the suppression of the rebellion in the Ukraine. Some of those who had served under me in the Eighth Division visited me in Moscow and with indignation and pain told me how they had burned and destroyed the homes of those suspected of aiding the rebels. They told me how they had sent to Siberia families from these homes, women and small children; how they had cast people out of villages and off farms; how they had trapped the rebels.

After one of my speeches in the United States, I was asked whether I had fought against the Ukrainian Rebel Army. I replied, "God kept me from it."

That was true. It was a miracle that I did not accept a position I had always wanted when it actually was offered to me.

If I had accepted, I would have fought against the Ukrainian Rebel Army and against my own peaceful fellow Ukrainians. At the time, I was capable of such actions, and once I had begun to commit them, I would have moved farther in the direction of inhumanity. I thank God that He did not set me on that path, that He helped me find another.

I do not believe that a man's life is predestined. A human being constantly has to decide where to go and what actions to take. I have had to make choices many times. My postwar choice was perhaps the most important of them all.

CHAPTER SEVENTEEN

THE
FRUNZE
MILITARY
ACADEMY

On my first day of work at the Frunze Military Academy in Moscow, I met the chief of the general tactics faculty, Lieutenant General Ivan Stepanovich Shmygo. He was a short, homey sort of person who radiated kindness. He kept a tight rein on the faculty, which numbered over one hundred teachers. All the other faculties combined—more than a score—had fewer teachers than Shmygo's single faculty in general tactics.

The staff was divided into several groups, each headed by a senior leader. Shmygo put me in the group for the first-year class, headed by Major General Prostyakov.

That year the rebirth of normal education commenced. During the war the academy's only courses were for improvement of officers' qualifications. Students participated now in a full three-year program. Admissions requirements were strict. Stalin admitted to the Frunze Academy one thousand officers who before the war had graduated from higher educational institutions and who during the war had risen to at least the rank of major. The various fronts presented us with over 1,300 such candidates for admission. All were enrolled and together became known as the "Stalinist thousand."

As is normal in Soviet higher educational institutions, the school year began on September 1. I was therefore more than three months late in beginning my new career. I was nervous about my first class, but it was not as difficult as I thought it would be. I communicated easily and clearly with these experienced front-line soldiers, most of whom possessed a critical frame of mind.

I became absorbed in my work. While I never mastered the art of teaching, my natural inclination toward research was stimulated by the academy atmosphere. On my own, I began work on a candidate's dissertation entitled "Attack by a division in mountainous forested terrain." Though I never officially submitted the dissertation, my bosses evidently noticed my love of research, and they drafted me into a group of officers assigned to write a textbook entitled *The Infantry Regiment in Basic Aspects of Battle.* I was extremely excited about this project, so much so that I completed my assignment before the others had even begun theirs. The head of the group, Lieutenant General Sergatskov, gave me an additional assignment that I likewise completed quickly and in the end I wrote the whole text myself. At the same time I began writing for military journals and working out assignments for studies in general tactics.

Money was an added stimulus to my undertaking extra writings and other work. The honoraria I was paid helped to support my family, which at the time consisted of nine people—five sons, two parents, my wife, and myself. Most of the family had ration cards for dependents and children, which provided only forty-four grams of bread a day—and nothing else. We had to buy extra food on the open market from the so-called "commercial" stores, where prices were high. My salary alone could not cover such purchases, so I spent much of my spare time earning extra money.

I also spent a great deal of time standing in lines: for my own rations—in the commissary—and for purchases in the "commercial" stores. In both places colonels had the special privilege of forming a line separate from the regular one, but lines for colonels were long as well.

My wife was ill and was breast-feeding our son. She was always exhausted. My night work and the fact that I was not helping her at home irritated her and she let me know it. Because I was afraid of sounding self-righteous and reproving, I was unable to object to her complaints, to tell her that without my work at night we would starve.

I also couldn't utter such a reproof because every adult in the family was working hard to make our situation easier: Zinaida's mother helped her look after the family, Zinaida took in sewing, and her father earned a bit by repairing shoes for neighbors. These were terribly difficult times.

If I had accepted an appointment as division commander in the Fifty-second Army, my wife, children, and I would have gone to a military cantonment where we would have had more than enough of everything we needed. We would never have known how ordinary Soviet people were living. The Soviet system was set up so that a man worked only among people of his particular social group, lived only among them, shopped only among them, and socialized with no one else.

In this respect I was fortunate. I lived in my wife's old apartment house. Because she had been there since childhood, the more than two thousand neighborhood workers and lower level white collar workers and their families accepted me as one of their own. I was, so to speak, a member of their "corporation." They could talk with me just as frankly as with people who'd lived there longer. We became so much a part of this milieu that when I was offered a bigger and better apartment in a building for the professorial and teaching staff of the Frunze Academy, my wife refused it.

Thus I worked in an intellectually stimulating professional collective and still was able to communciate freely with ordinary workers during my non-working hours. I was also fortunate in another respect. Soon after I moved to Moscow, I became friends with two remarkable men who had known my wife for many years: Vasily Ivanovich Teslya and Mitya (Moisei) Chernenko.

Vasily Ivanovich Teslya was four or five years older than I. He had fought in the Civil War and subsequently became a party official. Vasily Ivanovich was working in Sverdlovsk when arrests began in 1936 among his colleagues at the Institute of the Red Professorate. The terror might have passed him by, but he spoke out in defense of friends and was arrested. He managed to survive but became a total invalid. In 1941 he was brought to Moscow, at which point the charges against him were dropped; but he was not one to be dumbly delighted by this "justice" that had been extended to him. Vasily Ivanovich never ceased believing in communism, but he came to the conclusion that communism did not exist in the Soviet Union and that the men ruling the country were ordinary gangsters who would commit any crime whatsoever if it helped them stay in power.

I loved talking with Vasily Ivanovich Teslya. Knowing that I was a Stalinist, he led my thoughts with the greatest of caution in the direction of criticism of things as they were. He knew Lenin's theories forwards and backwards and constantly compared them with existing practice. Under his influence I began to critically analyze Lenin's theoretical heritage. This set me on that path by which people with communist convictions move into the dissident movement.

Leninism, like Marxism in general, is a doctrine replete with contradictions—not only in tactical matters but also in basic matters of principle. Contradictions can also be found in Marx's economic teachings. A particularly large number of conflicting statements exists concerning political matters. Some writings characterize Marxism-Leninism as a democratic and humane movement, but from that same Marxism-Leninism have come extreme totalitarian, dictatorial, and antihuman theories and affirmations. When we read, we notice only that which excites us. A kind human being with democratic inclinations will find all that is good about himself in Leninism. But Stalin, too, found in Leninism confirmation of all of his thoughts, justification of all his actions.

In order to shed their ideological chains people of communist convictions must first see the contradictions I speak of. Only then will they begin to see life as it is and only then will they understand that in one sense there are no contradictions in communism: It is, in fact, a well-constructed system of extreme dictatorship and extreme totalitarianism, in which democratic and humanitarian deviations serve to mask the truth, in which such deviations are used for democratic and humanitarian demagogy, for the deceit of the masses.

Vasily Ivanovich Teslya launched me on the path of liberation from communist ideology. At that time, Teslya was director of a state farm, and, naturally, he talked most about agriculture. However, he did touch on other subjects, including his memories of prison and camp. Once, when we were discussing fascist atrocities, I said, "What beasts they must have been and how absolutely corrupt to have thought up gas wagons."

In reply Teslya said, "Are you aware, Pyotr Grigoryevich, that we invented the gas wagon for use on the so-called kulaks?

"In the prison in Omsk one day a fellow prisoner called me over to a window which opened on the inner court. There was a shutter on the window, but through a crack we could see a door into another prison building.

"In a short time a Black Maria rolled up. The door in the building opened and guards drove people into the open doors of the prison van. Well over thirty prisoners jammed into the Black Maria standing up. The doors were forced shut by the guards and the van departed. I was going to leave the window but my cellmate said: 'Just wait a bit. They will come back soon.' And they did. When the van doors were opened black smoke poured into the air and corpses fell out onto the ground. Those which did not fall out by themselves were pulled out with hooks by the guards. Then all the corpses were dropped into a nearby basement sewer hole. Every day for a week we watched this happen. That other wing of the prison was known as the 'kulak' wing."

Vasily Ivanovich Teslya's story filled me with horror.

The other remarkable man whom Zinaida introduced me to—Mitya Chernenko, a journalist—had been a friend of hers for years. We were friends from our first encounter. Mitya was easy to talk to. He was one of those who understood, as the saying goes, that you can't chop wood with a penknife, but still he did not feel that you had to submit abjectly to the government. Journalists like Mitya tried to write about things that were important to the people and that could be reported without resort to lies. Such journalists were tolerated for their skill and their intelligence—but never were trusted. Mitya had worked for a long time as a correspondent for *Komsomol Pravda* and then joined the staff of *Pravda*. During the thirties he acquired special distinction as a correspondent of the Papanin epic, after which he had ghostwritten Papanin's memoirs and thereby earned his support—something that evidently had saved him and his family from arrest.

Mitya knew the country not by hearsay but on the basis of personal observation and conversations with those who really did know what was going on. He taught me to understand current events, to get to the truth, and, in reading the Soviet press, to read between the lines.

Mitya's attitudes toward Stalin were differently displayed than Teslya's. He, too, refrained from making accusations against the "great leader." But he asked me questions about my own views, from which I could sense he doubted Stalin's genius as a military leader. There is no point in detailing my answers to these questions. The fact that I was a Stalinist at the time by itself defines the nature of my replies. Today I feel differently.

Following the lead of Nikita Khrushchev, the vision of Stalin as an untalented military leader was widely disseminated. Stalin was alleged to have been no more than a nominal commander-in-chief. In the West the conviction was widely held that the actual wartime commander-in-chief had been Marshal Zhukov. Even Abdurakhman Avtorkhanov, one of the most serious students of the Stalinist period, who disclosed its essence in his outstanding work, *The Technology of Power,* was swayed by this fashionable opinion. An essay of his published in New York, ("The Mania for Decorations of the General Secretary," in *Novoye Russkoye Slovo* May 13, 1979) stated that "Marshal Zhukov . . . was the factual commander-in-chief during the War of the Fatherland."

Such an opinion fails to take into account the personalities of Stalin and Zhukov. Can one even imagine that Stalin would tolerate for a moment a person superior to him? In posing this question one immediately realizes that not only was Zhukov not Stalin's superior but he never tried to be such—for if he had, he would have disappeared not only from the army but entirely.

Neither Stalin nor Zhukov had any military training. Zhukov's peacetime command of a regiment, a division, a corps, and a military district could not replace military education—as Khalkhin-Gol certainly demonstrated. Zhukov's mistakes there were so childish that it is embarrassing even to analyze them. He was even more helpless in the role of General Staff chief, distinguishing himself only after he, at Stalin's orders, had taken command of the western direction and managed to stabilize the front outside of Moscow. This he did not by employing any original concepts, operations, or plans but merely by putting more and more new forces into battle and by drawing on his unparalleled ferocity. This latter quality attracted Stalin most of all. It was the reason why he "loved" Zhukov and gave him his full trust and why, throughout the whole war, he deployed him in all decisive directions as the representative of the General Staff.

Of the many wartime documents of the Supreme Command that I saw, not one was signed by Zhukov in the name of the General Staff. If the words "General Staff" appeared at the bottom of a document, beside there always was written: "Stalin, Vasilevsky," or "Stalin, Antonov"—in other words, the Supreme Commander and the chief of the General Staff. Zhukov is encountered in such documents only as the representative of the general staff. Vasilevsky, Voronov, and even Voroshilov, Budyonny, and Timoshenko were, likewise, representatives.

Perhaps Zhukov was more talented than the other marshals, but he did not rise above their level. He could not have been the commander-in-chief. It was a war of coalition and for such a war Zhukov simply did not have the breadth. The commander-in-chief had charge not only of the battle outside Moscow, the battle of Stalingrad, and the battle of the Oryol-Kursk arc, but of the "battles" of the Teheran Conference, the Yalta Conference, and the Potsdam Conference. Zhukov did not participate in these meetings. The obtaining of arms and raw materials was one of the chief concerns of the commander-in-chief, but Zhukov never was involved in this. Stalin was—to a great extent. A look at the correspondence between Stalin and Churchill and Stalin and Roosevelt shows that this was one of the decisive responsibilities of the leadership of the war.

Unfortunately for the West, and perhaps for all of humanity, after Stalin lost his head at the beginning of the war and abandoned power for a short time, he took it up again and showed himself to be a brilliant student of events. After fearing for his life and being threatened by a total loss of power, he understood that he needed specialists to conduct the war successfully, and in his search for them he even turned to those he had arrested. Men were freed from prison and sent to high command posts—Rokossovsky and Gorbatov, among others; but this did not, of course, solve the entire problem. It was impossible to fill with individual bricks the enormous gaping hole that Stalin's insane terrorist activity had made in the leadership of the armed forces. Nonetheless Stalin succeeded in gathering the minimum number of worthy military executives. It was Stalin who found, in the person of a modest General Staff officer, Major General A. M. Vasilevsky, an outstanding General Staff chief and a future Marshal of the Soviet Union. It was Stalin who defined Zhukov's role, sending him, as his plenipotentiary, wherever decisive operations were being carried out. Under Stalin's leadership a whole galaxy of front and army commanders was selected and under him the command cadres of all levels were prepared and taught.

Operational and strategic moves—the rout of the Germans at Moscow, coordination of the efforts of the fronts and of the various branches of arms and of aviation—are beyond serious criticism. These things, no doubt, were achieved by more than Stalin alone. But it would be wrong to say that they were done without his participation. After he had gotten over his confusion and panic at the beginning of war, Stalin not only understood the necessity for military specialists, but he learned also to listen to them and respect their opinions. At the same time he remained involved in operations and strategic activities. His participation can be sensed everywhere. On each operation lies the shadow of his mind. All were carried out under his inhuman standard: "Don't spare the men!"

Though Stalin was the commander-in-chief, it was not he who won the war. He was not a military man, though he adorned himself with the uniform of a generalissimo and tried to assert himself as a "great military leader" and to ascribe to himself all of the achievements of the victorious Soviet armed forces. Was Roosevelt a military man? or Churchill? or Hitler? Today's wars are conducted by entire states. The leaders of states have to take upon themselves the role of commander-in-chief, a role not suitable to military men. And Stalin, as a commander-in-chief, had no equal either among our allies or among our enemies. To the present moment, Europe is the way Stalin left it. Even now the knots he tied in the Far and Middle East remain untied.

The criticism of Stalin as a military leader in Khrushchev's report at the closed session of the Twentieth Party Congress is on the level of small-town gossip. The one serious criticism of Stalin it contained was that he did not call a halt to the operation near Kharkhov when a threat to our flanks arose, and this criticism misses the point. In the case of Kharkhov, Stalin acted as the serious military leader. During the moment of crisis, persistence was what was most required. Stalin's conduct, his unwillingness to come to the telephone, was geared toward calming his nervous subordinates, and it underlined the fact that he was convinced of the operation's success. Khrushchev acted like a child. He was frightened by the prospect of being encircled and he failed, along with his commander, to provide any protection for his threatened flanks.

Such is the truth. I can and I do hate Stalin with all the fibers of my soul. I know that he brought my people death, torment, suffering, famine, and slavery. I know very well that his untalented leadership almost brought the country defeat in 1941. But I cannot help seeing that the brilliant offensive operations of Soviet troops are models of military art. Many generations of military men the whole world over are going to study these operations and no one will ever imagine that they were prepared and carried out without Stalin's participation or against his will. Historians will be astounded at the skill with which Stalin forced his allies not only to conduct those military operations in the most advantageous way for him but also to work for the strengthening of the Stalinist dictatorship—for example, by turning over Soviet war prisoners to Stalin's repression, and by assisting in the occupation by Soviet troops of advantageous strategic positions in Europe and Asia.

In 1942 a tall, broad-shouldered, slightly stooped lieutenant colonel of medical services had appeared at Zinaida's apartment.

"I want to see Malva's aunt," said the officer as he entered. (Malva was Zinaida's niece who had died in Stalin's camps.)

"I am Malva's aunt," replied Zinaida.

He laughed, lifted her up by her arms and whirled her around. "So that's what kind of an aunt she is!"

Zina was thin and frail and, despite her thirty-three years, looked like a twenty-year-old. She was about to take offense at such familiarity on the part of the stranger when he carefully set her down on her feet and said, "You see, I am your 'nephew.' My wife is Kostya's sister." (Kostya was Malva's husband.)

So from that time on, though he was not a blood relation, we thought of Aleksandr Grigoryevich as our nephew. He was an exceptionally skilled doctor and a profound religious believer. Knowing of my atheism, he never touched on questions of faith in our conversations. Out of respect for his religious feelings, I also avoided these questions. Sometimes I did ask him whether the authorities bothered him because of his beliefs. He always answered that he had an extended armistice with them.

I understood what he meant. Grigory Alexandrovich's faith was so sincere that one had to respect it. I myself felt such respect, understanding what bravery it required in those years to openly declare oneself a believer. Though Grigory Alexandrovich never once spoke to me of God, he was already leading me to Him in 1942. Subsequently, he played a decisive role in my return to the Russian Orthodox Church, but this was years later, after I had already gone through the first circle of suffering—the Lubyanka, the Lefortovo, and the Leningrad prison and psychiatric hospital.

My first years in the Frunze Academy were good ones. I was immersed in my classes and research and I enjoyed the people I worked with. I was optimistic about the future of my country.

Postwar life dealt me its first blows in 1948. Difficulties with my dissertation, the death of my close friend Mikhail Ivanovich Yegorov—Zinaida's father— and an encounter with anti-Semitism together destroyed that ivory tower I had created when I arrived at the academy after the war.

Everyone at the academy seemed friendly and benevolent, and I considered it out of the question that anyone might try to trip up a comrade. I imagined that if someone disagreed with another's opinion, he could speak out openly. I failed to realize that those who did not feel able to make a competent reply might hold a grudge against you and at the first opportunity try to harm you.

A month before the day set for my dissertation defense a comrade told me he'd heard that certain negative aspects of my dissertation were to be discussed by the chief of the political branch at the party conference. He advised me to see the person who held that post, Major General Bilyk, and try to clarify the matter.

I did, and Bilyk read out to me the relevant section of his report: "Certain of our comrades have become so fascinated with science that they have forgotten about the principal of the party character and are taking lessons from tsarist generals. For example, in the list of basic sources for his dissertation, comrade Grigorenko cites such 'pillars of science' as the tsarist generals Svechin and Verkhovsky."

With his negative recommendation, my dissertation surely would perish, but it was not this that angered me most of all. It was the fact that his evaluation maliciously twisted the facts. My dissertation had criticized, not supported, Svechin and Verkhovsky's theories on battle in mountainous regious. In particular I had pointed out the folly of those who continued to preach out-of-date theories. I explained this to Bilyk and he promised to leave this portion out of his report. Whether he forgot his promise or whether some of his superiors advised him to leave it in, the accusation was made at the party conference.

The next day I was summoned by the chief of the academy, Colonel General Tsvetayev, who said to me, "In the second chapter of your dissertation you criticize respected men and undermine their authority. Omit that chapter or I will be unable to approve the defense."

No matter how I tried to prove to him that criticism of out-of-date theories could not undermine the authority of respected men, Tsvetayev held to his opinion. I also stood firm: I refused to drop the second chapter.

After this memorable conversation with the academy chief I abandoned my dissertation and tried not to think about it at all.

A year later Alyosha Glushko, a man I considered a close friend at the time, paid me a visit and asked me about my dissertation. I told him the whole story, emphasizing that I was particularly indignant that the interests of science could be sacrificed for the sake of the personal arrogance of the chiefs. Alyosha heard me out, and after I had finished, asked me a question I found shocking: "What do you want? Do you want to get a degree or to make scientific discoveries?"

"I should think that the two should coincide," I said, confused.

"Not at all. First you get your degree, and after that you make your scientific discoveries. Only an idiot would keep a completed dissertation in a desk drawer. You could have been engaged in creative work for a whole year. Go tomorrow and ask them to permit you to defend your dissertation without that chapter."

One week later, in April 1949, I defended it. Evidently the members of the council were pleased by my retreat. Many of them clapped as I made particular points within my defense. When the results of the vote were announced as "unanimous" there was stormy applause.

Despite this triumph and despite a good libation after it was over, I did not have any sense of accomplishment. My interest and pride in my dissertation were completely destroyed. I had been forced to bow to opinions that undermined my views. Of course, I had encountered such situations before—but it was only now that my idealistic evaluation of people and facts began to topple. This experience showed me that seemingly decent people are not averse to tripping up idealists—and the idealists are always the losers.

My father-in-law, Mikhail Ivanovich, had been a typical idealist. He idealized, first of all, the communist party. He joined the revolutionary movement in 1904, and after the October Revolution continued as a rank-and-file communist party member. He brought his children up to be idealists in his own image. His two sons and his four daughters all joined the party. And the party "rewarded" their father richly. His elder son was shot in 1934 in the Far East. His younger son was forced into hiding during the mass arrests in 1936–38. Two of his sons-in-law were arrested in 1936. One was killed during interrogation and the other was shot. His eldest daughter perished in camp. Another daughter languished for months in prison. Despite all this he kept right on idealizing the party and its members and people in general.

I was amazed by his naïve, even sacred, faith in the cause, and in people whom he saw as his comrades-in-arms.

When he died in 1948 at the age of seventy-seven, his mind was still completely clear. With his death I lost a vital ideological support. Though I was by no means such an idealist as he, I could not help but respect his selfless devotion to that cause with which he had begun his adult life.

The episode of anti-Semitism I mentioned earlier occurred after Mikhail Ivanovich's death and concerned my faculty comrade, Colonel Vaisberg. He was charged by the party bureau of the faculty with making "slanderous statements on the Jewish question." Vaisberg, in a conversation with his comrades, had declared that anti-Semitic measures were being implemented and encouraged from above. In the discussion at the bureau, Vaisberg literally was terrorized. The questions, charges, and statements put to him were intended to force him into "confessing his mistakes" and into admitting the "slanderous" nature of his statements. I, too, participated in the attack on Vaisberg, deeply convinced at the time that he was mistaken, that he was distorting the facts and giving them a nationalistic interpretation. Under this pressure, Vaisberg finally "repented" and as punishment for his statements on the question of nationalities, he received a "severe rebuke."

I observed that Vaisberg had not really admitted his errors, that he had repented only after being threatened with expulsion from the party. I decided to help him in understanding the entire extent of his errors and to prove to him using concrete facts what a happy life the Soviet government had created for the Jews.

Intent on doing so, I left the bureau office with Vaisberg. When the two of us were alone, I began my speech, but he backed me up against a wall. I could not argue with the facts and examples he cited. We walked about Moscow for several hours. In the end I was overwhelmed by his irrefutable proof of the presence of out-and-out anti-Semitism in the USSR.

"I'll have to write a letter to the Central Committee," I said. "I must bring all this to the attention of comrade Stalin."

"What makes you think he doesn't already know about it? If we write, they'll simply compel us to repent—or maybe worse. I'm not going to write. And I am not going to give testimony as a witness if you write. I told you about this only because I saw that you really believed what you were saying before."

The next day I ran into my party secretary. He seized my hand and shook it. "You sure gave that kike what he deserved yesterday."

Still under the spell of my conversation with Vaisberg I exploded, called the secretary an anti-Semite, and wrote a denunciation of him that I sent to the political branch. It was to no avail. They simply forced the secretary to apologize to me. In the meantime, I began to observe more and more displays of anti-Semitism. Therefore, to me the January 1953 Doctors' Plot was no surprise. It and the struggle against "cosmopolitanism" clearly indicated that a big anti-Jewish campaign was being readied. I realized this and awaited each further development with alarm. But the death of Stalin brought the whole thing to a halt. The punishment given those "guilty" of the organization of the Doctors' Plot gave the impression of impending justice. This reassured me and once again I stopped noticing the anti-Semitic actions of the government, which, however, they continued.

Jews were purged from the party apparatus, from the Ministry of Foreign Affairs and the Ministry of Foreign Trade. They were purged from the organs of repression of the people—the KGB, the MVD, the Prosecutor's Office, and judicial organs. Gradually they were also removed from the army. In higher educational institutions a percentage quota was established, and on and on.

This encounter with anti-Semitism dealt a blow to my sociologically naïve views of people. Until then, the world had seemed simple to me. The worker was the ideal, the repository of the highest morality. The kulak was a beast, an evil-doer, a criminal. The capitalist was a bloodsucker, an exploiter, a parasite. The communist party was the one and only repository of the new morality, the one and only truth common to all humanity. Even though I witnessed many deviations from these ideal rules, in my heart I was convinced that they were only accidents and that in reality life was the way I wanted it to be.

The death of Mikhail Ivanovich took from me the only example I had of the communist idealist. At the same time my experiences with my dissertation and with anti-Semitism forced me to acknowledge that most of the negative things I was seeing were coming from people who ought to be examples of high morality. For the first time I began to wonder whether a man should be judged by himself alone and by his deeds—not by his social origins or adherence to a social group. But much time would pass before that thought matured and affirmed itself in my consciousness.

Before I left on vacation in the summer of 1949, I gave my consent to be named a staff professor of the faculty of general tactics. When I returned in late August, I received an order from the minister of defense appointing me to the post of deputy chief of the academy's Scientific Research Branch. I refused to accept this appointment.

After my refusal, I was summoned by Colonel General Bogolyubov, who said, "Pyotr Grigoryevich! Your refusal has put me in a difficult position and has caused insoluble conflicts in my plan for personnel shifts. I'm sorry that I did not ask your permission—at least by telegram. But I was afraid that you, not knowing the nature of the work, would refuse. Therefore I decided not to ask your permission ahead of time—particularly because the position of deputy chief of the Scientific Research Branch exactly corresponds to the duties of a faculty career professor—a position to which you had already given your consent."

"No, it does not—not in everything. Scientific research constitutes most of a faculty professor's activity; the Scientific Research Branch does not conduct any research at all, but occupies itself with organizational questions of science, and is really a scientific organizational branch."

"Well, after all, work depends on people. In name and in staff it is the Scientific Research Branch—so go ahead and make it that in reality."

We talked for a while longer without coming to an agreement. Before we parted Bogolyubov said, "Think about it a bit longer, Pyotr Grigoryevich. I hope that you will take the academy's interests into consideration. Now please go see Shabalin." (Shabalin was the chief of the Political Branch.)

When I entered his office, Shabalin said directly, "Don't be put off by Bogolyubov. We advised him not to telegram you for permission. It is easier to make an appointment without the appointee's opinion, than it is to make one when he has already turned it down. You would have been appointed to the post in any case. Even if you had turned it down. *You are our candidate for this post.* We consented to the appointment of the nonparty General Markov to the position of chief of the Scientific Research Branch only on the condition that you would be named his deputy. A refusal on your part is out of the question. When party interests are involved, we have the right to oblige a Communist to consent."

His words made it clear that any attempt to change the order would fail.

Therefore, I steered the conversation toward a different aspect of the business at hand. "If I am your candidate, then I ask you to support me in reorganizing the work of the branch. I want to transform it from the scientific organizational branch it is now into an actual Scientific Research Branch."

Shabalin approved my intention and agreed to support me in this reorganization.

As long as he was at the academy, he kept his word. On September 3, 1949, I assumed the position of chief of the Scientific Research Branch from Lieutenant General Pyotr Panteilimonovich Vechny, who left to become the academy's Learned Secretary of the Council. At the time, the newly appointed chief of the Scientific Research Branch—Major General Georgy Mikhailovich Markov—was on leave for the purpose of editing a large collective military-theoretical work. Thus he did not assume his duties for some time.

I knew Markov from my work on the faculty. He thought and spoke in clichés. Possessed of a remarkable memory, he knew all the statutes and directives. During those years, when all real ideas were being suffocated, his talent for smoothly formulating his thoughts gave him fame as a theoretician. He had the ability to take any text and make it read relatively smoothly, even though it might not contain a single living thought. Though this work imparted no knowledge whatsoever, it also did not arouse objections from the "party-thinking" censors—an extremely important fact at the time. For these reasons Markov was simultaneously editor of a military scientific work and chief of the Scientific Research Branch. His jobs were to write a theoretical work that contained no military theory and to transform the Scientific Research Branch into an organ that would plug up all the cracks and crevices through which the academy's vital military scientific thought might slip. Markov was most suitable for both these roles.

However, as my old tactics teacher Major General Prostyakov used to say, it is impossible to take hold of everything with one hand. Thus while Markov worked at his editing for almost an entire year, I managed, with the support of the political branch, to turn the Scientific Research Branch in the direction Markov, as it was intended, would cut off completely. By the time Markov finally came to the branch, the academy had a new head.

Colonel General Ivan Semyonovich Zhadov (later, Army General) himself had creative abilities. He perceived my reorganization as natural and urged me to make it more thoroughgoing. When Markov arrived and tried to return to the old situation, he was in conflict not with me but with the chief of the academy.

Markov did not look for means to carry out assignments—but for justifications not to carry them out. This made conflict inevitable. Zhadov, who was full of plans and ideas, had no need for this kind of a helper. He'd been inspired by the work our branch had carried out before Markov's arrival. Markov was not capable of working with the rest of us. He was retired.

At this point I formally became chief of the Scientific Research Branch, a job I'd been doing for three years. My hands were now free. The chief of the academy and the chief of the Political Branch supported me, and, as a result, I could carry out my planned reorganization without having to keep looking behind myself. Nineteen-fifty-two was a good year for me, full of creative work that I was glad to do.

One event took place that, while unimportant at the time, was later used against me. During the summer, while staying at the military sanitorium in Gurzuf, I simultaneously became ill with shingles and paresis of the right facial nerve. For several days I was unable to sleep or even dress. The tormenting pain wore me down totally. Both illnesses eventually came to an end.

Yet, twenty-two years later, in the hands of the falsifiers from the Serbsky Institute, my shingles were transformed into cerebral thrombosis and the paresis of my *right* facial nerve became a lesion of the *left* side of my body, accompanied by paralysis of my *left* hand and destruction of my speech patterns.

Here is what was written in the history of my illness composed by the Serbsky Institute in 1973 to be shown to foreign psychiatrists in place of the genuine history that had been written up in that same institute during my first psychiatric examination: "In connection with the lesion of the left side of his body, Grigorenko underwent treatment for more than two months in the neuropathological department of the military hospital. He became irritable and he began to have failures in his work."

In 1953 Stalin died. The year was notable for the Scientific Research Branch in the enormous upsurge of work we accomplished, an increase best described by the publication of "Works of the Academy." In 1949, the year I began work in the Scientific Research Branch, not a single issue of the journal appeared. During the preceding postwar years—1945 to 1949—two issues had been published. In 1950 we managed, with difficulty, to publish one issue; in 1951–52 we published four, and in 1953 eleven. Undoubtedly, this increase partially resulted from my reorganization of the branch's work—but, as I now realize in analyzing this period, no small role was played here by the death of Stalin. Merely the departure of his malevolent figure from the political arena took an enormous weight off scientific research. Authors no longer needed to fear that Stalin's role had been inadequately shown or, even worse, insufficiently valued in their studies. Thus liberated, the effectiveness of their work grew.

At the time I did not understand this. I perceived Stalin's death as a great tragedy and I thought with alarm about what would come of our country without him. I was not involved with the farewell to his body—a free-for-all in which hundreds of people were suffocated and crippled. We, his "true pupils," were delivered in an organized fashion to his decorated corpse.

Time passed. Though we did not yet understand that the death of Stalin had let in fresh air, even if only in small amounts, we still felt its results. True, we ascribed this new feeling of freedom not to Stalin's death but to the fact that the Beriya terror had been liquidated, along with Beriya himself and my Far Eastern acquaintances Goglidze and Nikishov. We continued to think of Stalin as faultless, though tales of Stalinist terror kept reaching us ever more loudly. The Commission of the Central Committee, headed by Lieutenant General Todorsky, was reviewing the cases of arrested military men, and many who had managed to survive the Gulag archipelago were freed. From them new horror stories emanated. But most of my comrades and myself stubbornly persisted in justifying Stalin, accusing only Beriya and his henchmen. We were even ready to accuse Stalin's closest comrades, most of whom now were flourishing—but not Stalin himself.

Then we began hearing rumors about the Twentieth Party Congress. When the report itself finally reached us, all the academy Communists assembled in the largest academic hall—auditorium number 928—and the entire report was read to us, a deadly silent audience. The reading ended; the silence persisted for a while, and then people began to rise and leave. Hundreds of us left that room, all silent, all alone.

The staircase outside the auditorium was crowded with people I knew from the party, but I continued as before, alone. At the second landing, I felt someone's hand on my shoulder and I jumped. It was Vechny, from, as I've mentioned, the academy council. A good-natured and intelligent man, Vechny smoked makhorka, enormous cigars twisted from pieces of newspaper. He looked at me and said, "What is it, Pyotr? Are things bad?"

"Very bad!"

"Well, how do you think I feel! Maybe the report contains truth, but I knew a different Iosif Vissarionovich myself."

We walked to my office, and Vechny began to tell me his story. We sat down and I brought him an ash tray from the reception room. As he rolled his astounding cigar, I involuntarily turned away.

Vechny smiled and said, "That's exactly how Iosif Vissarionovich reacted to my cigar when he saw it for the first time. We were working on the battle regulations—Stalin, Vasilevsky and I. We began work at midnight. Stalin was astounded when Vasilevsky announced that several thousand suggestions, corrections, and additions had been received. Vasilevsky had anticipated this reaction, and he told him that there were actually only around a hundred real suggestions and proposals, of which only about twenty were serious."

Here Vechny recounted the conversation that had ensued when Stalin exclaimed, "Do you mean to tell me they were written by illiterates?"

"Well, not illiterates," Vasilevsky had objected. "But in order to write battle regulations one must have extensive battle experience and military men as experienced as that don't often possess a high degree of literary talent."

"That's natural," Stalin had agreed.

"We worked for more than two hours," Vechny went on with his story. "Stalin was sucking on his pipe the whole time and Vasilevsky was lighting up now and then himself. I sat there, nearly dying without a smoke. I held back and held back but in the end I could not stand it any longer." Vechny continued recounting their conversation for me. "Comrade Stalin, is it all right if I smoke, too?

"Of course, of course!" and he had pushed his box of 'Hertsgovina Flor' over to Vechny. (These were high-quality cigarettes that Stalin used to break up and use in his pipe.)

"No, I prefer my own," Vechny had said, rolling a makhorka that might have been even larger than the one he held now. Stalin was astonished; Vechny had always refrained from smoking within his sight.

"We continued working on the battle regulations," Vechny said. "By 4:00 A.M. we had dealt with all the suggestions and proposals. Stalin sat back in his chair and said, 'Is that all? Have it printed and sent to the troops.' "

As Vechny reported it to me, Vasilevsky then said, "There is one more question. The majority of officers who have worked on the regulations have proposed that they be classified as secret. They are afraid that the Germans will quickly get their hands on the regulations and in that way will find out all about our tactics."

"What do you think yourselves, comrades?" Stalin had responded, directing his question to Vasilevsky.

"The way I see it, Iosif Vissarionovich, it might not be a bad idea to classify the document. But in that case, how will the troops study it and how can the commanders of squads and companies make use of the regulations? They don't have security units."

"What do you think?" Stalin had said, turning to Vechny.

"It's my opinion that classified regulations will fall into German hands just as quickly as unclassified regulations. If the Germans get just one copy, they'll publish their own nonclassified edition and their officers will be familiar with our battle regulations—while our own officers will not."

"You are right!" Stalin had exclaimed. "The battle regulations must not be classified." Then, to Vasilevsky: "Comrade Vasilevsky, the Germans are going to fight by their own rules, not by ours. Our tactics cannot be disclosed through our regulations—because the tactics of a specific battle are based on the specific situation. On the other hand, our commanders might hand the regulations out carelessly and we'd never be sure that everyone necessary had seen them. Comrade Vasilevsky, let's number the copies and issue them along with the field pouch. Then they'll be registered in the property inventory and we'll know exactly where they are and we'll be able to establish a penalty for losing them."

And that was what was done during the whole war.

Recalling Khrushchev's statements about Stalin's military illiteracy, Vechny said, "No, Petro, it is untrue that Stalin did not understand military affairs. He might not have been able to command a company, but he grasped things better than any of us who worked alongside him. He never hesitated to speak out if a particular matter was unclear to him, and he would ask several different people the same question so that he could choose the best of the proposals or assert his own original decision."

We talked until late that evening, not about a leader but about a human being. This was how we received the Twentieth Party Congress. Despite the fact that we had just heard a report on the awful crimes of Stalin, we sat there and recalled only the good in him, trying to overcome the serious doubts evoked in us by the report.

The real turning point in my thinking began after that congress. The very next day I requested a copy of Krushchev's report from Kolesnichenko. He gave it to me for two hours and I worked with it for that whole time. I reread the important sections, copying extracts in a notebook. I had been promised it for another two hours, but subsequently I was permitted to have it overnight, during which time I was able to master the report's contents. I was horrified and revolted, but my party indoctrination was so strong, and the traditions of Stalinism so rooted in me, that though I did not argue against the evaluation of events, for a long time I continued to affirm that the Central Committee did not have the right to make its accusations public.

It took a significant amount of time and many conversations with Vasily Ivanovich Teslya and with Mitya Chernenko before I began to grasp that crimes like Stalin's cannot be corrected in silence, that it is in silence that they arise, develop, and grow. In order for such tyranny to end, the leading party and state organs must be under the control of the masses.

An important aide to me in forming these thoughts was Anya Zubkova, an old friend of Zinaida's. During the thirties her husband had been the deputy director for science at the Scientific Research Institute for Orthopedics and Traumatology in Moscow. In 1937 he was arrested and died during interrogation. Anya was arrested for being related to an enemy of the people and got ten years in the Gulag from a special interrogation board, the OSO. Subsequently they increased her term and then sentenced her to exile. She returned to Moscow only in 1956. One had to be astonished by this dear, beautiful woman's love for life. She was lively, gay, and full of joy—despite her nearly sixty years of age, her almost twenty years of suffering, and a serious heart disorder that soon killed her.

She had suffered the unbearable loss of the husband she passionately loved. Her two children, ten and four at the time of her arrest, had brought themselves up. Oleg went to work in a dining hall. He provided food for his sister, Renata, and enabled her to study medicine and become, like her mother, a doctor. He even put himself through school.

When Anya returned, she found her children fully grown and herself unable to dote on them. She was immensely proud of them.

Anya did not preach to me. She did not like to talk about the camp or to discuss politics. She enjoyed being with our family and always brought us laughter. Her life served as an example for me. How could a quiet person, a doctor who devoted her whole life to people, be dangerous to the Soviet government? Nonetheless, she was. I finally came to understand this—though to reach that understanding I had to make an about-face. She was dangerous because she intrigued me and others with her optimism and her loyalty to truth. Anya cast a bright light on the dark hearts of the Soviet potentates and the blackness of torture chambers. What she revealed educated those of us who had never experienced the horrors ourselves.

Her actions were illuminating as well. Once she needed to have a reference for her dead husband. I can't remember now whether it was for her own pension or for his rehabilitation. She went to the Institute of Orthopedics and Traumatology and asked Nikolai Priyorov for the reference. Priyorov, director of the institute when Anya's husband had been arrested, still held that position. He had received the additional title of Academician in the Academy of Medical Science, after the extensive arrests among academicians. In a grim voice, Priyorov announced, "I do not know anyone by that name."

At the moment his office was being cleaned by a woman hospital orderly, who heard the conversation and butted in: "What do you mean, Nikolai Nikolayevich? You don't know Fyodor Fyodorovich? Everyone in the whole Institute knows Uncle Fedya."

Thereby Priyorov was forced to recollect him.

When Anya told this story in our home, I made a connection between two events. Not long before the time of the events Anya described, Zhukov had issued an order demoting Colonel General of Engineers Galitsky to the ranks and retiring him from the army. What for? The daughters of a former chief of engineers of the Moscow Military District were seeking the rehabilitation of their father who had been arrested in 1937 and shot by decree of the OSO. They requested a reference from Colonel General Galitsky—who at the time was deputy chief of engineers of the district—and he issued a very positive one. In reply to this the KGB sent to the minister of defense a copy of a declaration made by Galitsky in 1937. The arrest of the chief of engineers of the district was based on this declaration; Galitsky had accused him of sabotage.

I had read Zhukov's order demoting Galitsky with satisfaction and thought of Zhukov as a principled man who had undertaken the exposure of provocateurs regardless of rank. Now everything became clear to me. This was not an exposure. It was a warning to all those like Galitsky, and Priyorov had heard it so clearly that he had even "forgotten" his own deputy. When he was forced to remember him, all he wrote was that he recollected him as a deputy. That Zhukov's demotion of Galitsky was indeed a warning was given away by the fact that very soon after this a new order was issued that annulled the preceding one. Galitsky was not to be reduced to the ranks. He was instead demoted to lieutenant general and retired to the reserves. After all, Galitsky was not a dissident. So he had made a little mistake. He thought that time had covered up everything—but it turned out that the KGB forgets nothing. In light of the second, Zhukov's first order did not look so noble to me. It was more like participation in a litle bit of KGB-organized theater. The West is wrong when it attributes special qualities to Zhukov and ascribes to him plans for the overthrow of the existing order. In terms of both knowledge and psychic make-up, he is not to be distinguished from the other military leaders of his circle.

How did Zhukov survive the thirties? Was he just lucky or was someone protecting him? It is difficult to say. The only thing we know definitely is that his circle of colleagues was thoroughly purged. We also know that two years before the war he made a dizzy, unmerited climb in rank. In 1939 he was an army commander in Mongolia. Then he was made commander of the Kiev Special Military District, the equivalent of a front; and in 1940 he was named chief of the General Staff. He was not promoted again during Stalin's lifetime. In fact, at the beginning of the war he dropped one step—he became commander of a front.

After Stalin's death and the liquidation of Beriya, Zhukov became minister of defense. But his fate was decided at that "historical" session of the Politburo when Politburo members Khrushchev, Mikoyan, and Suslov became a "majority" of three, while the other members turned out to be a minority. Even Shepilov, who took their side, could not increase their weight.

The crisis came when Khrushchev protested a vote on the basis that it was a matter that should be decided by the Plenum of the Central Committee. The objection was made to him that the Politburo has the right to prepare the question for the Plenum—and the vote was started. At that point Zhukov, then a candidate member of the Politburo, declared that he would bring the army onto the streets if the question were decided at the Politburo and not at the Plenum. This was a bluff. I do not believe that the army would have followed Zhukov. But the members of the Politburo who opposed Khrushchev did not know this and they fell for the bluff. Thus the matter was decided in favor of Khrushchev. At the same time, it decided Zhukov's fate as Zhukov was not a politician and did not understand that it was dangerous to bluff in politics. Khrushchev believed that Zhukov could lead the army. Consequently he saw him as a dangerous enemy, one he was not about to tolerate.

Soon afterward Zhukov was removed from his post as minister of defense. The degree of Khrushchev's belief in Zhukov's capabilities can be demonstrated by the circumstances of his removal. The removal was presented as an antimilitary coup. Zhukov had been in Yugoslavia. When he returned to the Ministry of Defense building he was denied admission. Evidently it was assumed that he would encounter allies within. He was told to return home and to stay there. The political organs of all the military districts were directed to hold meetings of party activists to discuss "the state of party indoctrinational work in the army." Orally, directives were given to subject Zhukov's activities as minister of defense to unlimited criticism. Criticism was also ordered for the commanders of the military districts, especially those who were considered protégés of Zhukov. This plan was counted on to expose those who might be thinking like Zhukov.

The fear of opposition to Zhukov's removal was great, as the following incident will show. Army General Luchinsky, commander of the Central Asian Military District, always played things extra safe and was perpetually playing up to the party organs. At the time of Zhukov's removal he was in a sanitorium. The military council member from his district informed him of the meeting of the party activists. Luchinsky, still unaware of the removal, liked on every convenient and inconvenient occasion to demonstrate his special devotion to the party and political work. He replied with a telegram: "Postpone the party activists meeting until I arrive."

The military council member reported this telegram to the Chief Intelligence Administration. An order immediately followed: "Luchinsky to be removed from his post. Meeting of party activists to be convened on schedule."

When Luchinsky received this information he panicked and rushed to Moscow. He spent a long time repenting his lack of political foresight. Finally the higher-ups realized that his telegram expressed only his special devotion to the party, and that it was not an attempt to defend Zhukov.

The meetings of party activists are frequently used by higher jurisdictions to attack the prestige of individual party leaders, making it easier to remove them from high positions, to frighten them, or to demonstrate to them the weakness of their situation and their dependence on the chiefs. Occasionally it happened at these meetings that criticism might touch on one of those with whom the higher ups were quite satisfied. In that case, the criticized individual would express gratitude for the harsh words and would then thumb his nose at the critics.

At meetings following Zhukov's removal, party activists "criticized" Zhukov and the commanders of the military districts for "failure to give sufficient importance to party and political work and for neglect of the party and political apparatus." Zhukov in particular was charged with liquidation of the institution of political officers of companies—even though everyone knew that he could not have done this without the agreement of the Central Committee, as demonstrated by the fact that this institution was never restored. As a result of the campaign against Zhukov, the commanders became more dependent on the political officers. Frightened by the specter of a military coup, Khrushchev and his entourage let loose their watchdogs—the political officers of the army. The meetings of the party activists made this development not only possible but necessary-seeming.

Army opinion had been stifled for far too long. When people finally were allowed to speak out, things got out of control. The meetings of the party activists were especially stormy in the Kiev Military District. For two days men mounted the platform and spoke about one thing alone—the rudeness, lack of tact, vengefulness, and crudity of then-Marshal of the Soviet Union, Vasily Ivanovich Chuikov.

Khrushchev invited Chuikov for a chat on this subject, but what could he do? Chuikov was one of his own men, a loyal servant. All that resulted from their chat was a slight decrease in profanity—and an increase in the revenge Chuikov took on his critics.

Two years later Chuikov had forgotten the lesson he'd learned and again got completely out of hand. Minister of Defense Marshal R. Y. Malinovsky tried to remove him. Maneuvers were taking place in the Kiev Military District. P. A. Kurochkin, head of the Frunze Academy, was Chuikov's own referee. I was referee for Chuikov's staff. Kurochkin, who received his instructions directly from Malinovsky, told me to grade men without regard for rank.

I tried to do so. In communications with the staff officer, I saw how the commander kept picking at the staff and disorganizing its work. The officers told me that these were their usual work conditions. I summarized all of this, carefully analyzed it, and wrote my report. What resulted was a thorough reference report on Chuikov's operational and strategic knowledge, on his ability to command operations, communicate with people, and make good use of their experience and skills. Much attention was devoted to his unpleasant and unprofessional personality. Malinovsky was satisfied.

When the report reached Khrushchev, he called in Chuikov and said, "It's impossible to leave you in your district. People are dissatisfied. I have decided to move you to the post of commander-in-chief of the land armies."

Thus it happened that even as I helped rid Chuikov's subordinates of him, I actually helped him rise even higher. Kurochkin signed my reports without changing even a single comma. Things took a further and an unexpected turn when Chuikov got to the staff office of the land armies. As commander-in-chief he demanded to see all the documents of the referees and, on the back of the first page of the report of the chief referee, found the names "Major General Grigorenko and Colonel Tetyayev." Soon after, Tetyayev was fired, even though his only involvement was that I used his notebook when I gave the report to my secretary.

Commanders who did not have such powerful protection as Chuikov got their wings clipped after the meetings of the party activists. Everywhere the party political apparatus became more active. I felt this myself. Obviously guided by directives from above, the chief of our political branch, Major General Kolesnichenko, decided to show the power of the party political apparatus in the academy and decided on me as the subject of his attention. As allies he chose some of those with whom the Scientific Research Branch had most concerned itself—the advanced students.

As soon as I had come to the Scientific Research Branch, I had sought and obtained the creation of the advanced student program and devoted most of my time to it. The academy had a large group of teachers—experienced officers and generals—but only a few writers.

I idealized the advanced students. In my mind they offset the "pure" teachers—those who were incapable of conducting scientific research and who by virtue of this fact were prejudiced against "scientists." But my idealization was mistaken. Among the advanced students were no few for whom the status of an advanced student was not a path to science but merely a means of getting an academic degree and a teacher's post. After completing their work, these advanced students became pure teachers themselves and swiftly found the road that led to senior faculty positions. They also adopted attitudes even more hostile to those who were engaged in scientific work than did the older teachers.

Still, most of the advanced students were enthusiastic about becoming scientists. Over the years many of them worked zealously in the field and came to love hard, thankless scientific labor.

Those who had been time-servers had no time for scientific work after the defense of their theses, and they were angry with those who urged them to keep working. They did have time to arrange all kinds of "plots" and engage in all sorts of intrigues. As they saw it, I was a most harmful person. They did not attack me directly but instead took advantage of the political branch's need for "critical" activities. To be sure, they did everything "scientifically." Not for nothing had they defended their dissertations.

One day an instructor from the political branch, Lieutenant Colonel Grigoryan, arrived in order to check up on the state of party work in the Scientific Research Branch "on the orders of the chief of the political branch." The secretary of our party organization, Major Nikolai Ivanovich Anisimov, who had recently been a political officer himself, immediately suspected trouble. He told me after several days that in his opinion the checkup was directed against me.

Two weeks passed. The chief of the Political Branch, Major General Kolesnichenko, summoned Anisimov and gave him Grigoryan's report, adding that there would be a discussion of it in the Political Branch office that very evening.

Anisimov brought the report to me and I studied it carefully. He was right; it was entirely directed against me. In spirit and in style, it was a collection of insignificant gossip derived principally from former advanced students.

At the meeting that evening Kolesnichenko skipped over some of the more ridiculous points from the report. When we reached an accusation of nationalism, he attempted to remove it without calling attention to it. I refused to go along with that.

"No!" I said. "Grigoryan has to be punished by the party because he not only levied an accusation of nationalism but tried quite consiously to inflame national hatred in the branch."

After a long and drawn out back and forth, our decision was formulated thus: "The accusation against Grigorenko of nationalism was not based on facts. The materials which served as a basis for this conclusion were selected in a tendentious fashion and were falsified. The party organization of the Scientific Research Branch demands that comrade Grigoryan be punished by the party for his attempts to inflame anti-Ukrainian attitudes."

Thus it was that one by one *all* the accusations against me were dropped. As a result, things ended badly for Kolesnichenko. Kurochkin, head of the academy at the time, was fully informed of the political branch's checkup. He did not like to stick his neck out for anyone, but he was not pleased with the way Kolesnichenko's attitude had changed after Zhukov's removal. Previously cautious in his relations with the academy chief, Kolesnichenko had recently become more self-assured, even unduly familiar. He had begun to drop in on Kurochkin unannounced. He would enter his office despite the presence of other visitors. Kurochkin didn't like this—but he was not a man to do open battle. He preferred to wait for a convenient moment to strike, and usually he used someone else's fist.

The day after the meeting, Kurochkin ordered me to write down my account of it. I described it in one page, supporting my words with the report and the statement signed by Kolesnichenko.

Kurochkin read it and put it in his briefcase. He had an appointment with Malinovsky, the minister of defense, and, just in case, was taking my material with him. During the meeting he mentioned how political officers had begun to stick their noses into commanders' business. Citing my case as an example, Kurochkin emphasized that under the guise of verification of party work and without the knowledge of the chief of the academy, the Political Branch had launched a crusade against the chief of the Scientific Research Branch using lies, slander, and gossip. Dissatisfied himself with the expanded interpretation by political officers of the rights of the political organs, Malinovsky decided to use my case to teach a lesson. Kolesnichenko's fate was sealed. A few days later he was replaced by Lieutenant General Nikolai Vasilyevich Pupyshev.

I had first encountered Pupyshev at Khalkhin-Gol in 1939. Then a brigade political commissar, he was deputy chief of the Political Branch of the front group. I remembered Pupyshev as communicative, jolly, and bright, and when he arrived at the academy we became great friends. Immediately after his appointment the Central Committee decree "On Technical Progress" was promulgated—and in connection with it the Political Branch undertook a campaign that deeply involved me.

As early as 1953 I had heard of Norbert Wiener's work in armed forces research operations. Though cybernetics had been declared a "bourgeois false science," I directed a portion of the Scientific Research Branch capabilities to study everything connected with it. We established a translation bureau that summarized works on cybernetics and the analysis of operations. I personally established contact with Academicians Berg and Kolmogorov and began to collect information. The General Staff Intelligence Administration (GRU) supported us in these efforts. The Scientific Research Branch became the leader in this field, accumulating more and more material until, in 1959, we created a faculty of military cybernetics.

Cybernetics deals with new methods of control based on electronics. It was natural for me to join in the campaign for technical progress and to draw the attention of both students and leaders to the new technology behind the direction of the armed forces. But in the USSR, campaigns can end swiftly.

Pupyshev lived on campaigns. I soon came to understand that he resented everything new. Only people who want to show off in front of the bosses can find the time to participate in useless campaigns. All such people grouped themselves around the political branch and supported it wholly. If they had only stuck with putting on their insignificant campaigns, we could have tolerated them. But no, in their struggle to survive they spread gossip and came out in opposition to all changes. I tried to keep away from the Political Branch members; then I began to get into hostile conflicts with then.

Soon after Pupyshev's arrival the Political Branch was reorganized into a party committee and Pupyshev was elected its secretary. Two years passed. The gap between the party committee and me had widened. I went to their office only when summoned.

One day I was called in by Pupyshev. Thinking that he must want something from me, I remembered that he had had an affair some time ago with the secretary of the academy's deputy chief for scientific and educational work. The woman's husband, a lieutenant, found out about the affair, got his hands on irrefutable proof of it, and made a big scene. Everybody knew about it. Particularly scandalous was the fact that the lovers met at Pupyshev's secretary's apartment. She'd gotten the apartment in an utterly illegal way—applying for it through a civilian employee on a requisition form normally reserved for military personnel—and Pupyshev had arranged the whole deal.

When all this came out in the open, it seemed as if Pupyshev's song had been sung. The Chief Intelligence Administration named a committee to investigate the matter. It seemed clear that he should be fired, but in view of the upcoming elections and the committee's findings, it was decided not to consider the case immediately. The committee was in no hurry to complete its work and by the time of the elections still had not reached any conclusions. The cuckolded lieutenant and his wife had been sent far from Moscow and the gossip had quieted down. Pupyshev was preparing to go through with the elections, and that is why he had summoned me. He had decided to lay it on the line with all those who might speak out against his reelection and to try at the very least to neutralize them.

When I walked into his office he got up to meet me and, smiling, shook my hands with both of his. He took me over to a far corner, where we both sat down in armchairs. He'd set the stage for "a frank discussion."

"Pyotr Grigoryevich," he said, "you are aware that elections are approaching. The new party committee will have to take on those vital questions on which the existence of the academy depends. I want to get the advice of the heads of the most important faculties. Your own faculty is one of the most advanced and up-to-date of all and I would like to hear from you your own primary needs and wishes."

"Nikolai Vasilyevich," I said, "I don't think you give a damn about my faculty and its desires. What you really want to know is how I feel about your candidacy for the post of secretary of the party committee. Well, here's my frank advice to you! I could care less about who you sleep with and where. But in the struggle against your candidacy, I will make use of your liaison with Kolganov's secretary. I am no moralist but I do consider you harmful in the post of party secretary. You continually support the most reactionary elements, you constantly hinder the introduction of new ideas. Because of that I will do everything I can to get you thrown out."

I stood up. "I imagine, Nikolai Vasilyevich, that there is nothing more for us to discuss."

He gave me his hand. "Thank you, Pyotr Grigoryevich, for your frankness. I am sorry I could not come to terms with you earlier. And now it is too late."

Pupyshev was nominated for the post of party secretary. When the discussion of his candidacy was underway, I brought up the love affair and all its attendant illegalities, dwelling especially on Pupyshev's moral unfitness for the post. His candidacy was voted down overwhelmingly.

This incident established the first connection between Boris Nikolayevich Ponomaryov, a secretary of the Central Committee of the Communist Party of the Soviet Union, and myself. When the defeat of Pupyshev was reported to him he asked, "Isn't the man who defeated Pupyshev the same man who 'devoured' Kolesnichenko? We are going to have to take a closer look at this destroyer of political officials."

This was in the spring of 1961. That autumn Ponomaryov and I met at the party conference of the Lenin District of Moscow. This conference was decisive in shaping my future.

These years were very strained, in both my service and civilian lives. My attitude toward the actions of the leaders became increasingly critical. It was more and more difficult for me not to react to the illegalities and pompous trivialities of the rulers of my country. When we went through the second post-war currency reform (devaluation), I protested. Stalin's devaluation, which was openly extortionate, had not aroused a protest in me, but I had changed. Khrushchev's declaration that no one gained or lost anything by his reform angered me. Things were nowhere near so simple as Khrushchev said they were. He assured us that though the mass of currency had been lessened ten times, its purchasing power had not been reduced because prices had been lowered by ninety percent. This was a lie. Even the example he cited was false, though at first it seemed convincing: A box of matches that used to cost ten kopecks now cost one kopeck. I directed my attention to the fact that the gold backing of the new currency had been reduced by fifty percent.

I wrote to the magazine *Kommunist* and asked them to explain this discrepancy. In reply I received a confusing letter, the main theme of which was that gold backing has no meaning in a socialist society. Supposedly our currency was backed by the entire wealth of the Soviet Union.

In reply to this reply I wrote: "If gold backing has no significance, why reduce it? Why not leave it where it was—or for that matter, why not increase it?"

To this question they did not reply. I sent the same letter to them several times, but they remained silent. In the meantime the general population began to react to the devaluation. The first to speak were the poor. A woman neighbor of mine, a pensioner, said, "Pyotr Grigoryevich, this money is deceitful. I used to get along on ten rubles a day. Now I can't even go to a store with just one ruble in my hand."

One day in a trolleycar an Armenian shouted so that the whole car could hear, "What a rascal! A box of matches—one kopeck! You think a man can live on matches? He arranged a burglary and wants to cover it up with matches."

At the same time I began to hear account after account of how difficult it was to get any backing for new inventions. However significant and innovative an idea arose, the government seemed to prefer sticking with the old. Technologically we were about fifteen years behind the United States. I couldn't believe we weren't doing everything possible to catch up. It angered me.

I had many acquaintances from various strata: directors of big enterprises, officials of the State Planning Commission, heads of agricultural organizations, teachers, workers, collective farmers—all were dissatisfied. All talked about instances of inefficiency, illegality, bureaucracy, and stupidity. There was no agency or bureau to which we could report our dissatisfaction, and so it began to appear in ordinary conversations. Once after I'd complained particularly bitterly in front of a large group, my wife said to me, "You can now expect a denunciation." *But no one denounced me.*

Though my friends did not turn me in, they also did not really listen to me. I was doing something wrong. I decided to continue speaking on the same topics, but to do it more accessibly—to employ the political jargon of the Soviet Union. But for the time at least, I ceased all political conversations. I also tried to suppress my doubts and dissatisfactions, burying myself in my work.

Nineteen-fifty-eight to fifty-nine was an especially difficult year for me. I had been put in charge of a group of authors who were having trouble writing a basic theoretical work entitled *Combined Forces' Battle.* Simultaneously, we were preparing to instate a military cybernetics faculty. I had been selected as its head. Colonel Mikhail Mitrofanovich Kiryan was running the Scientific Research Branch in my absence. He was only forty, and had never commanded anything other than a company. He had been deputy head of the Scientific Research Branch for only a little over two years. Faced with ending our partnership, both of us were worried but for different reasons. I was concerned with the fate of what I had created. Kiryan was worried that he wouldn't be able to do the job. Still, I supported him, knowing he would carry on the work I had begun. After talking it over with Malinovsky, I had presented his name for appointment.

Despite a small uproar over the large promotion, Kiryan had received the job. I followed his work for years and always was impressed.

I loved my work at the academy, just as I had loved every kind of work I had ever undertaken. But the academy was especially important to me. The creativity of the people I worked with there and the creative nature of the work itself gave me enormous satisfaction.

After the Twentieth Party Congress and all the hypocritical conversations about the cult of Stalin, a new cult was being created and I was uneasy. I found it difficult to tolerate the hypocrisy of the rulers, but at the same time I knew that speaking out would ruin my entire way of life, one which suited me perfectly. Therefore I strove to suppress my moods of protest by my own strength of will and with the help of my work. The theoretical work I have already mentioned, the composition of a course of lectures for the new faculty, work on my doctoral dissertation, and service activities absorbed me completely. In 1960 my theoretical work was published. The study materials for the 1961–62 school year were completed by the faculty in early August. In the last days of that month I submitted my doctoral dissertation to the council of the academy. I felt liberated.

At this point the thought that had long been haunting me returned with new strength: "You must speak out. You cannot keep silent. Now you have a platform from which your words will resound far and wide."

During my dissident years I was often asked about the horrors that I experienced in insane asylums and prisons. Yet I experienced my worst horrors in the academy and at home in August and September 1961. I was bidding farewell to the institution in which I had experienced the best years of my life, and where I had written eighty-three scientific works. I knew my name would disappear from them, but I also knew that my teachings would be carried on by my students. I felt that I was undergoing a death of creativity.

I also bade farewell to the people I loved. Even as I write these lines, they seem to stand in front of me just as they did during my goodbyes. I would like to name those who were particularly dear to me but, as always, I am afraid of bringing someone harm. My declaration would cost me dearly! At the time, I exaggerated the dangers that would ensue from my actions. I was prepared for the worst. I had no fear, but what I felt was more painful to me than fear—it was pity for the people I knew, the kind of devastating pity you feel when you see a loved one tormented and are unable to help him. Desperation would seize me and I would think: "To hell with it! Forget about making declarations! Forgive me, my loved ones, for wanting to subject you to evil."

Time passed and my thoughts changed again, often becoming sarcastic: "I'm tired of my general's insignia, of my high pay, of my special refreshment bars and stores. What do I care about some collective farmers or workers who are rotting in prisons and concentration camps? I'll go on living as I please. Enjoy my life." And then: "What a rat you are, Pyotr Grigoryevich!"

And so it went on from one to another extreme. I kept seeking an answer.

There was none, right up until the conference itself, right up until I was on the platform.

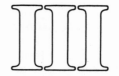

THE

FALCON

CASTS OFF

HIS

HOOD

CHAPTER EIGHTEEN

MY
DASH
TO
FREEDOM

Septer 7, 1961, was our son Andrei's sixteenth birthday. It was also the first day of the party conference of the Lenin District of Moscow at which I was an academy party organization delegate. The secondary school for mathematics that Andrei attended was a twenty-minute walk from the Moscow University club building in which the party conference was being held. Zinaida and I had agreed we would go to the school and surprise him with birthday greetings.

The conference opened at 10:00 A.M. As soon as they announced the agenda, I entered my name to speak on the first topic—"The Party Program." Official lists of speakers are drawn up ahead of time, and those who wish to be added to the lists sign up later. Usually only those on the original lists get heard—anyone else has to fight to be included. I hadn't decided yet whether or not to fight about this. I didn't want to think about it. The reader of the report droned on; the document contained not a single original thought. It was a simple repetition of the published project for the program. As I sat there, I thought about the academy. Today was the second day of the new school year. I wondered how things were going in our faculty. The previous evening I had delivered my introductory lecture to the first class. Yesterday's installment had been two hours; I would deliver two more hours on the same subject for the entire academy course tomorrow—September 8. The lecture yesterday had ended unusually—with a thunder of applause.

I thought about Andrei and my wife; about Ugor-Zhilov, where Andrei was conceived. I was so deep in thought I didn't notice that the report ended, even though I applauded with everyone else. Discussions began. The longer they continued the more alarmed I grew. I had to decide. If anyone had known of my intention it would have been quite simple to prevent me from speaking, but I had not told anyone. I was not certain I would, but I knew that anyone to whom I might turn would advise me to keep quiet.

An hour passed. Another, and still I had not made a choice. Finally the decisive moment came. In announcing the last scheduled speaker the presiding official failed to mention who would follow him, indicating that discussion on this report would end. They had no intention of going beyond the official list of speakers. If I wanted the floor I had to ask for it.

The hall was enormous, filled with people who for the moment seemed to me both faceless and hostile. I kept thinking that the simplest way out was silence. Those at the meeting would make their decisions and so be it! If the discussion on this point came to an end, it meant that I wasn't fated to speak out today. Only if they let it continue would I speak. This was a clear case of hypocrisy on my part. I knew very well from experience that whatever the presidium of the conference proposed would pass—no one would oppose. Everyone was sick of listening to the rubbish that had resounded from the speaker's platform for about four hours already. The custom of going along with leadership would also prevail: They would pass the presidium's motion unanimously. In order to ease my conscience I could vote against the motion—but such a vote would change nothing.

The last speaker left the platform. The chairman stood up and said, "Comrades! Fourteen people signed up to speak in the discussions and twelve have spoken. Since all basic questions of the party program have been covered by the speakers, there is a proposal to end the discussions."

At that moment someone seemed to pick me up and stand me on my feet. Thus it was that I declared loudly and clearly, "I would like to speak on this question."

"Yes, comrade Grigorenko, go ahead and speak." The chairman pointed a pencil in my direction.

He had recognized me at a rather considerable distance, and we were not closely acquainted. I said, "For my part I consider that those who spoke said very little about the program. They spoke mostly of local matters. I propose that the other two who wished to speak be allowed to do so. Perhaps they will deal with the important questions of the program."

I sat down. The chairman acted as if he had not heard what I said, and answered, "Comrade Grigorenko asks to speak."

"Let him!" resounded throughout the hall.

"Are there any objections?" the chairman, Grishanov, asked.

"No!" the audience replied.

"Comrade Grigorenko, you have the floor for ten minutes."

I got up and walked to the front. What was going on inside me at that moment I will never be able to recount. I had no feelings. It has to be the same with someone about to be executed. Or perhaps this was a special feeling aroused by the hypnotic influence of the mass in the hall that had concentrated its entire attention on me. In any case it was awful—the most terrifying moment of my life—but it was also a fateful moment. I concentrated on just getting to the speaker's platform, and, once there, I spoke without being conscious of anyone or anything.

I am not going to include here what I said and I am also not going to cite the text I prepared ahead of time; I made use of it only in part, and then mostly from memory. I prefer to cite the stenographic record, probably the most objective version both of the speech and of the atmosphere at the conference. Here is the report: "Comrades! I have pondered long whether to rise or not to violate the calm course of this conference. But I then thought to myself that if Lenin had wished to say something he would most certainly have stood up." [Applause.]

"Comrades! The project for the program of the Communist party is a document of such enormous resounding impact and such colossal mobilizing force that it almost seems improper to criticize it, but it is precisely its great scientific and mobilizing resounding impact which obliges each of us to look more attentively at the details and to consider what is necessary and permissible to suggest to the party congress which is going to discuss this program. I myself consider that in the project of the program the questions of the withering away of the state, the possibility of the emergence of a personality cult, and the methods of struggle for the realization of a moral code for a builder of communism have been completely elaborated.

"Why do I wish to speak about this? Because we always must turn to our experience. To decide on something is not such a complex thing. To study our experience from all aspects is more complicated.

"What is our experience in the question of the state and of the personality cult? Stalin put himself above the party. This the Central Committee itself has established. Even more importantly there is in the experiences of our party the case of a man who was not only alien to the party but who was hostile to our entire system and who turned out to be in charge of the highest organ of the government, the state, and the party. I am thinking of Beriya. If his was an isolated case we might not have cause for alarm. But we have also the case of another Communist party coming to power—in Yugoslavia—and turning out to be under the heel of a man who broke away or who is hostile and who changed the composition of the party, transformed it into a very negative and exclusively cultural-educational organization which is no longer a fighting revolutionary force. He is now leading his country along the path to capitalism. This too might be considered a matter of chance—but we also know that the Albanian leaders have set out on the same path, and we no longer have a strong, authoritative Albanian party to oppose this.

"The question arises: Does the fact that such actions are committed mean that there are shortcomings in the organization of the entire party? What has taken place in our party?

"Let us imagine Khrushchev had been destroyed like Voznesensky and others. After all, it was pure coincidence that at the moment of Stalin's death strong men were present, men capable of raising up the party with the strength of Lenin. It was pure coincidence that Stalin died so early. He could have lived till ninety." [At this, noise and stirring in the hall.]

"We are approving a project for a program in which the personality cult is condemned, but the question arises: Is everything possible being done to prevent the repetition of a personality cult while the personality itself is perhaps arising? If Stalin was nonetheless a revolutionary, some other personality could have arisen." [Noise in the hall.]

At this point Marshal Biryuzov, a member of the presidium of the conference, said, "Comrades! It is my opinion that there is no point in listening further to the comrade. There is a definite and clear decision of the congress on this question. And what do all these statements have to do with the building of communism? I think he should be deprived of the floor." [Noise in the hall, and voices from the audience: "Incorrect! Let him continue!"]

Grishanov (chairman and secretary of the district party committee): "There has been a proposal. I put it to a vote."

From the hall: "Biryuzov's proposal has no basis."

"Correct!" "He was given the floor—let him speak."

Grishanov: "I put it to a vote. Who is in favor of continuing? A majority. Comrade Grigorenko, you have five minutes left. Continue."

"I consider that the principal paths along which the development of the personality cult took place were, in the first place, the abolition of the party maximum, and that very few people returned to work at production, that they became bureaucrats, that they allowed the struggle for the purity of the ranks of the party to weaken. Just look if you will: How often it is written that someone stole or deceived customers, and then it is reported that so and so has been given a party penalty. Is it permissible for such people to be kept in the party?

"I consider that comrade Biryuzov's proposal that the floor be taken from me is in conflict with Leninist principles. That method of repressing criticism has been condemned, and in the party statutes it is proclaimed that a member of the party has the right to set forth all questions in any organization. And I am speaking here at a party conference.

"My concrete proposals are the following: to strengthen the democratization of elections, and to strengthen similarly the wide-scale replacement of officials and also our responsibility to voters. We must abolish all conditions which give rise to violations of the Leninist principles and norms, in particular high salaries and lack of replacement of officials. We must struggle for purity within the ranks of the party.

"We must write directly in the program about the struggle against careerism, against deceit of the party and the state for the sake of personal advantage, something which is incompatible with party membership. If a Communist in a leading position cultivates bureaucracy, philandering, servility, nepotism, or in any way suppresses criticism, he must be subjected to a severe party penalty, obligatorily removed from the position he occupies, and sent to do physical work in industry and agriculture." [Applause.]

Grishanov: "Comrade Kurochkin asks the floor for a matter of information."

Kurochkin (colonel general, and chief of the Frunze Academy): "I wish to give a brief piece of information. Comrade Grigorenko is a member of the party organization of the Frunze Military Academy. Comrade Grigorenko did not speak in our own party organization on the question which he has raised here today. So this matter was not voted on in our party organization and it is not the opinion of the party organization of the academy. All this is the personal opinion of Comrade Grigorenko. I wanted to make this clear." [Noise in the hall and a voice: "He didn't say it was."]

An intermission for lunch was announced. The foyer was seething. Loud conversations were taking place. The largest group was gathered in front of Grishanov, who was pushed up against a wall. As I walked past the group I heard a short, stocky man with gray hair and a young face shouting into Grishanov's face, "Oh, they've been allowed to get too far out of hand! They pull rank even at a party conference. The general was speaking as a Communist—and then they let loose the big star—that marshal—in order to shut his mouth. Those big shots have gotten out of hand. . . ."

I strode through the foyer, hearing conversations about my speech all around me. It seemed that the reigning emotion was indignation at Marshal Biryuzov's interruption. Instead of gladdening me, this disturbed me, and I became increasingly alarmed. The thought flashed through my mind: "They will not forgive me for this. They will accuse me of arousing past hostility toward the top-level military commanders."

I hurried to meet my son and my wife.

After lunch, a report on the project for the party statutes was given and discussion began. When the first two speeches were finished, an intermission was announced. I noted that the program did not state who would be speaking when we resumed.

I sat in the foyer chatting with Colonel Boris Fedotov. As we talked, another colonel ran up and said to Fedotov, "Boris Ivanovich, Argasov is asking for you." (Argasov was the secretary of the party committee of the academy.)

Fedotov got up and left. I remained sitting and opened up a newspaper. Soon I noticed that I was the only one in the foyer. I had no idea where everyone had gone. I went to the buffet area, but no one was there. The same was true of the dining hall. I returned to the foyer, which began to fill up with people.

I went into the hall and took my seat. The stalls in front of me were nearly empty. Obviously the delegates were in no hurry to return, though the time alloted for the intermission had long since passed. Once again I opened up my newspaper.

All of a sudden I heard something rustling behind me and then a woman speaking quietly: "Comrade General, they are going to take you to pieces."

I turned around. Behind me stood a young worker from the Red Rose silk mill. I lived beside the mill and always used to walk past it on my way to work. Over the years I'd become familiar with many faces at the mill, one of which was this woman's. When those elected to the presidium had climbed up on the stage at the beginning of the conference, I'd immediately seen her. She spoke swiftly. "They want this attack on you to be unexpected. But I decided to tell you about it myself. They said that if you repent nothing bad will happen to you. And if you don't repent, they'll expel you from the party and from the army. Please repent—it won't be so bad." She completed her warning in an imploring tone of voice. There were tears in her eyes.

"My dear girl," I smiled at her, "thank you very much for your warning. But don't worry. I am able to look after myself."

The conference reconvened. Grishanov announced, "The Frunze Military Academy asks that its representative take the floor in order to make a statement which is not on the agenda."

The academy representative was brief: "Our delegation has discussed the speech of the member of our delegation, comrade Grigorenko, and determined it to be politically immature. We ask the conference to deprive comrade Grigorenko of his delegate's credentials."

Immediately after our representative finished, representatives of two other delegations spoke in turn. They repeated his statement almost word for word.

As soon as the second of the "hired assassins"—which is what wags in the party call those who speak in order to make proposals set up ahead of time by the party apparatus—had finished speaking, Grishanov said, "We have before us a proposal to end debate and to vote. Who is for. . . ."

A gravelike silence reigned in the hall. And in this silence I said, without standing up, and in an ordinary conversational tone, "For the sake of decency you might at least offer the floor to me."

Grishanov heard me and, stumbling over his "Who is for . . ." cried out, "Ah, comrade Grigorenko, you wish to speak? If you please."

This time I walked to the platform with a measured pace. I was composed and wanted to give a worthy rebuff. Here I cite my statement from memory. They refused to give me the stenographic record. Why? It is difficult to say; the official reason was that I had no need of the record, since I was not penalized for the statement.

"It is impermissible to punish a person for political immaturity. No party rule permits such punishment. Political immaturity is dealt with by political instruction and political indoctrination.

"No one has demonstrated the political immaturity of my speech. It has simply been given this label. On what basis? What specific accusations are there against me? For the conference to be able to make such a harsh decision, the accusation must be formulated specifically and I must be given a chance to offer my own explanations and objections to all the accusations.

"If the conference approves this decision, it will be simply illegal. In the first place, the statutes forbid the discussion of essential questions by delegations or at group gatherings. Specific discussion of the matter can take place only at the conference as a whole. The leadership has violated this principle. As regards me a decision has already been made—lawfully—by the conference. It has voted on the proposal of comrade Biryuzov that I be deprived of the floor. In order to annul this lawful decision, the presidium has broken the conference into delegations which, after assembling without me, adopted a decision without discussion.

"In the second place, the decision will be illegal because the conference does not have the right to deprive anyone of his delegate's credentials. I can be recalled from the conference only by those who sent me here. Therefore I ask the delegates to vote against the unlawful and politically immature proposal of the Frunze Military Academy delegation."

I departed from the speaker's platform calmly, conscious that I had done my duty. I realized that things were bound to end badly for me, but I also saw that my speech had penetrated the hearts and minds of the listeners. A normal person is quite sensitive to nobility and courage. These were normal people who, though they had party cards in their pockets, had realized that this enormous and cruel machine was going to roll over me and that I was not retreating but instead was standing up firmly for my rights and, by this token, for their rights too. Most of them sympathized with me. This was my first speech in defense of civil rights, and, like all the rest I eventually gave, it was received sympathetically by many people.

The entire hall was silent. The presidium itself was in a state of shock. I reached my seat and the silence prevailed. If a vote had been taken right then, I am not convinced that the presidium would have managed to get a majority. But they, too, realized this. The Central Committee secretary, B. N. Ponomaryov, leaned over toward Grishanov and whispered something to him. The latter nodded servilely and ran to the speaker's platform. I cannot even paraphrase his speech. It would be interesting to read the stenographic report of it, but I doubt it exists. If it does it would show that he spoke nonsensically, without meaning, merely to talk.

Evidently his chatter was supposed to cleanse the hall of tension. He gabbed for at least twenty minutes and in the end the audience, tired of trying to find meaning in meaningless speech, stopped listening and began to yawn and chat among themselves. Then the shock tactics were employed.

Ponomaryov himself went to the speaker's platform. His speech was almost as empty as Grishanov's, but it was nonsense on a higher ideological plane. He spoke of how the proposed program represented a high point for, and worked out some of the basic questions of, Marxism-Leninism. He accused me of bringing up petty matters and he made a point of saying that "the best minds of the party" had created the project. (To be sure, he was overmodest—he didn't explain that these minds had worked under him.) He explained that Nikita Khrushchev himself had devoted many hours to the project.

At this point I shouted from the audience, "So what do you mean—that we can't even discuss it?"

He ignored me and continued grinding away. "The party long ago decided the question of the cult of Stalin."

Someone from the audience shouted, "He wasn't talking about the Stalin cult—but about a new one."

Ponomaryov was an experienced demagogue. He continued on his own line and gradually the delegates slipped into the customary tone of a party conference. He was, after all, a secretary of the Central Committee, and no matter how stupidly he spoke, he was supposed to be applauded—and he was.

Ponomaryov left the speaker's platform, and Grishanov said, "Who is in favor of condemning as politically immature the speech of comrade Grigorenko and of depriving him of his delegate's credentials?"

I sat in the fourth row of the circle, the entire auditorium in front of me. When Grishanov said the words "in favor of," I thought with anguish: "Everyone knows that I am right but everyone will vote for my destruction."

But there was no forest of hands. Individual hands were raised, but not immediately or boldly—slowly, one after another. When less than a third of the hands in the hall had been raised, I thought: "People are, after all, better than I had thought they were."

Then Grishanov asked, "Who is against?"

I looked around the hall: Not one hand was raised.

"Who abstains?" Grishanov asked.

Once more not a single hand was raised. Grishanov concluded in a joyful voice, "The proposal has been adopted unanimously. Comrade Grigorenko, surrender your credentials."

I marched to the table of the presidium and placed my credentials on the table. Looking Grishanov in the eye I declared, "I submit to the decision of the conference, but I remain firm in the conviction that it is illegal and that it was adopted with illegal *unanimity.*"

As I walked through the hall there was an oppressive silence. When I approached the exit, I heard someone near me whisper to his neighbor, "Good for the general! He refused to crawl."

This whisper resounded throughout the entire hall.

It was dark outside and drizzling. My feet sank in the slush. All was in tune with my mood. I didn't want to see anyone. For a long time I wandered aimlessly around the city. I wanted to exhaust myself. I didn't want to think about my family or how they would react to what I had done. My own life and theirs had come to a turning point. My eldest son, Anatoly, was an officer. How would things be for him now that that his father had fallen into disfavor? How would Anatoly feel about me? My second son, Georgy, was also an officer and a pupil at the artillery academy. He loved me and his stepmother and lived with us. How would his career go now? My third son, also from my first marriage, Victor, was a tank officer. Victor would not be badly hurt by my disgrace. He didn't want to serve in the army anyway, so my failure would play into his hands. How would my wife and her children take it? The eldest, Oleg, an invalid, was always with us. How would sixteen-year-old Andrei take it? And how would it affect my relations with my wife, whose difficult life would now become even more difficult? How would she react to my "immature" performance? I hadn't even hinted to her that I would speak out.

I walked for a long time, getting soaked to the skin. I was frozen. When I got home I immediately began insulting my wife. I haven't the slightest idea why I did this.

It was not the first time that she repressed her hurt feelings. She asked me what had happened and gradually I began to talk. I told her the whole story and talked of the possible consequences for all of us. I felt her beside me as a friend.

When I finished talking Zinaida asked, "Why didn't you ask my advice?"

"What would you have advised me?"

"Not to speak."

"I knew that. And since I wasn't very firm in my own decision to speak out, I didn't want that kind of advice."

"You always think you know everything," she said acidly. "But in this case you didn't. If you had asked me, I would have told you that it was unwise to speak out without having reinforcements backing you up—but at the same time I would have understood your anguish and would have known that you were unable to keep silent any longer, that you were suffocating. In that case I would have gone to the conference myself and organized support for you there."

I stared at her with astonishment and thought, Yes, things could have turned out differently. All I had needed during the vote was one brave comrade. The tension was so great that one person standing up and shouting: "What are we doing? The man made an honest, heroic speech and for that we want to devour him!" would have made all the difference.

If something like this had happened, the presidium's entire scheme would have collapsed. Not only my observations after talking with Zinaida but facts I learned later pointed to this conclusion.

In the first place, I saw and spoke with several heads of delegations. All of them told me how much trouble they'd had getting their delegates to agree to condemn my speech. Only the threat that the district party committee would somehow punish those who refused to vote against me compelled them to submit. One man, head of an industrial enterprise delegation, told me that his delegates rebelled after my second speech and refused to vote for condemnation. All leaders had been told that they'd lose their party cards if the vote for my condemnation was not unanimous, and so he persuaded them simply to abstain from raising their hands at all.

In the second place, I met Demichev, at the time first secretary of the Moscow Committee. What a hypocrite he was! He began our first encounter by saying that he was indignant at my being repressed. "If I assembled all my instructors right now, they would confirm to you that when we assembled that same evening to talk about the district conferences, I told an instructor who had been present at your conference that it was stupid of them to have made such a big deal about the whole thing."

I hadn't the slightest wish to have Demichev assemble his instructors. I said I believed he had told them that the reaction at the conference was stupid. What I was more interested in was what he would say to me about the illegal decision and how it was made. "After all," I said, "the delegates did not vote. Less than a third of them raised their hands for 'yes.' "

He agreed. "Yes, a majority did not vote. And, in fact, many of the delegates sent a declaration to the Moscow Committee in which they reported their nonparticipation in the voting and their disagreement with the final decision."

This surprised me. Together with the stories told me by the heads of delegations, it showed the tenuous outcome of the vote. More than likely my wife could have affected that outcome in my favor. I was surprised at her foresight and boldness. In the future I would discover other such qualities in her; again and again I would be astonished. I was astonished, too, that the delegates were not afraid of sending a protest to Moscow, but that they were unwilling to vote the same way in public. The entire system works to this end. As an individual you can make any complaint whatsoever to bureaucratic institutions. As a rule they will not answer you, but they also will not punish you—unless you bother them further. Collective actions that don't suit the higher-ups are punished cruelly.

I asked Demichev, "You know that the proposal that I be condemned for a politically immature speech and that I be deprived of my delegate's credentials actually did not pass at the conference? And yet on the basis of this decision I am being investigated by the party. What, then, may I do now?"

"Nothing. The decision was formally adopted. No one voted against it. As a result, the decision is being deemed lawful."

"But you have written declarations from a majority of the delegates stating they did not vote."

"We aren't going to reassemble the conference for the sake of reconsidering your case," he said. "Why assemble it? As the highest jurisdiction, the Moscow Committee can use the written declarations of the delegates as a basis for annulling an unlawful decision."

I persisted with my argument, and he soon adopted a different tactic. "I cannot do anything, because the military men are very angry at you and Ponomaryov is supporting them. He was at the conference and can always respond to my intereference by reminding me that I wasn't. Why don't you try to talk directly with Ponomaryov?"

"I already have, and he told me he had nothing to say to me."

At that point Demichev said sympathetically, "In that case, you're in a bad way. The only person who can help you now is Nikita Sergeyevich Khrushchev."

"How can I get to Khrushchev?"

"You'll have to find out yourself."

"But the party system makes no provision for meetings between the leaders and the rank-and-file. There isn't even anyone to whom I can apply for an appointment."

"Nikita Sergeyevich has an assistant. Call him."

When I called for the first time Khrushchev's secretary was very polite. He wrote down my name and asked, "Does Nikita Sergeyevich know you?"

"Yes."

He told me when I should call again, and I phoned at the designated time. As soon as he heard my name he replied very sharply, "Nikita Sergeyevich is not going to speak with you. Who gave you my number?"

"That's unimportant. Since Nikita Sergeyevich does not wish to talk to me, the number is no longer important to me, and likewise it is not of any importance to you how I got it."

So my attempts to circumvent the customary party investigation of my case—my efforts to enlist the attention and assistance of the higher powers—ended. If I could not reach Khrushchev, it was time to stop. If Khrushchev, Ponomaryov, and Malinovsky all refused to see me, my fate must have been decided. I had been turned over to the party bureaucratic machinery to be repressed. This had become especially clear when Malinovsky had refused to see me. After all, it was he who had said that I was "the one and only candidate" for the post of head of the cybernetics faculty. Now he would not even speak to me, though he understood that by this he was sanctioning my expulsion from the academy and assuring the death of the cybernetics faculty. At the time, I did not think he would act this way unless he had received instructions to do so from the Politburo. Much later, a reliable source told me that in fact these instructions were given personally by Khrushchev. Malinovsky's refusal to speak to me clearly indicated that I should be prepared for the very worst.

True, I had never expected any personal good to come out of my actions. One of the first persons whom I wanted to talk with following my speech at the party conference was Mitya Chernenko. I went to his tiny, crowded office, where he was at work on an issue of *Pravda*.

"Pyotr!" he cheerfully exclaimed as I walked in. "Sit down for a few minutes, and I'll be with you shortly." Several minutes later he joined me and, smiling warmly, said, "I already know from Zina and Andrei about your 'feat.' You aren't very bright, Pyotr. On whom are those in power going to depend for support if generals start speaking out against the state of the nation? And what do you do? You speak out and say: 'If Lenin rose from his grave and saw you, he would die all over again on the spot.' "

"I didn't say that."

"No, you didn't. But I have heard it already from several people. Well, what did you say in reality?"

I took the text of my speech out of my pocket and handed it over to him. Mitya read it attentively and then read it again.

"Well, well! You certainly did say a lot. You will be lucky if you are only expelled from the party and dismissed from the army."

"Mitya, you must be exaggerating. It is a lightweight and, to be honest with you, cowardly speech. You think I couldn't have said more than that?"

"The problem is not what you could have said but what those who listened to your talk actually heard. How did they perceive you? Tell me in detail."

I told him.

"That's not so bad. The majority accepted your speech. That means it was on a high plane. You say it was fainthearted? No, it was reasonable. All speeches are in party jargon and include defensive themes. You were smart to stress that the program will be adopted only by the congress, and that until

Grigorenko's father, Gregory Ivanovich Grigorenko (left), and a peasant of the village of Borisovka.

Grigorenko's stepmother, with his father and their grandson and daughter.

Grigorenko on the left at seventeen.

Chief of staff of a sappers battalion, 1935.

Grigorenko and his wife Zinaida, when he was senior lecturer at Frunze Military Academy, 1948.

Grigorenko and Zinaida with their son Andrei at the Arkhangelsk sanatorium, 1950.

On maneuvers with the Soviet
Fifth Army, 1963. Grigorenko
was head of the operations
section.

Grigorenko in 1964.

Grigorenko, Lev Kopolev, and
Grigory Podyapolsky.

Zinaida, Father Sergei Zheludkov, and Grigorenko.

With Kharkhov supporters of the Initiative Group. From left to right: Arkady Levin; Genrikh Altunyan, who previously taught at a military academy in Kharkhov with the rank of major; Grigorenko; Vladislav Nedobora, an engineer; and Nikolai Ponomaryov, an engineer. Because of their human rights activities the Kharkhov men were imprisoned from 1969 to 1972, after which they were able to find jobs only as ordinary workers.

Mikola and Raisa Rudenko with the Grigorenkos.

The Grigorenkos' apartment in Moscow, 1975. From left to right: Nina Bukovskaya, Grigorenko, Igor Shafaryevich, and Zinaida.

The Grigorenkos' birthday at their apartment in Moscow, 1977. It falls on the same day for both, October 16.

Kennedy Airport, New York, November 30, 1977.

Petro and Zinaida, 1979.

it is adopted all sorts of proposals can be made; it is wrong to punish you for that. But they will find a way to. And they cannot stop at simply punishing you. You made the rank-and-file delegates understand things which the higher party bureaucracy cannot accept. You connected the question of a cult not with a particular individual, as the Politburo does, but with the system. This they will not forgive you—just as they will not forgive your declaration on the inadequacy of measures taken against the cult and on the possibility of the emergence of a Khrushchev cult.

"For that matter, your statement that the party was lucky that Khrushchev and others survived and that Stalin died early sounds like pure irony, pure mockery. But the most painful of all is your declaration that the personality cult originates in high salaries, lack of replacement personnel, and bureaucratization. Also painful are your proposals on the democratization of elections, on the responsibility of those elected by the voters, on the abolition of high salaries for elected officers, on institution of broad-scale replacement of officials, on the struggle for purity in the ranks of the party and on the expulsion from the party of careerists, bribe-takers, and other rascals. That's a lot to pack into one speech, Pyotr. And all of that was accepted by the mass of delegates and will be disseminated by a thousand mouths. What you must think about now is how to emerge from the battle with the least possible losses.

"Biryuzov is an idiot. His speech only focused more of the audience's attention on you and helped you to defend yourself. You will not be punished for the essence of what you said, all of which was rooted in idealized Leninism. What they will do is to rebuke you for specific formulations. And in that regard you must blame Biryuzov for creating an atmosphere in which you were misinterpreted. As to how your speech should have been written, remember in the future to write in such a way that nothing can be said against you.

"Their second crude error was their attempt to deprive you of the floor, because of which they had to put a previously decided question before the conference for a second time. This they did by a blatant violation of party statutes: A question which had already been settled at the conference was then transferred to individual delegations. What you have to do is to seize upon that violation and complain about it to the higher-ups. Try complaining first to Ponomaryov. After all, as the representative of the Central Committee he is responsible for the violation. But your chances of getting anywhere with him are small. He is a terrible son of a bitch. And in addition he is very much trusted by Khrushchev. Your chances are better with Demichev. He is a younger official—but a clever one, a diplomat. He will try somehow to squash the whole affair or to drag it out, but he is certain not to want a public scandal over a violation within his organization of the party statutes. Yes, and you must try to get to Khrushchev as well. Sometimes he has bursts of democracy. But remember that while you are trying to deal with the higher-ups, they will

be dealing with you at the lower level. This, of course, will make it difficult
to attack the top. Our leaders are quick to cite the 'leading role of the masses.'
Now they will tell you that though you are complaining about the conference,
you have already been condemned by a primary party organization, your own
comrades.

"You must try to slow things down at the lower levels as best you can. But
make haste in the higher echelons. Remember you do have one other option—
repentance. Then you might get off with only a minor party penalty."

"That's not for me, Mitya."

"That's what I thought. If you intended to repent, then you would not have
spoken out in the first place. If you attack above and delay things on the lower
levels, you might be able to stay both in the party and in the army. If you
can do that without repenting, you will have gained double the advantage by
speaking out."

I did as Mitya advised, but in the upper echelons things did not develop
as he had predicted. My principal ace—the violation of the statutes—had no
impact. I understood why this was only after I learned about the provincial
party conference at Kursk on the very same day— September 7, 1961. At that
conference the writer Valentin Ovechkin spoke on the party program. He devoted his speech to the subject of the virgin lands,*presenting a scene of total
failure. The speech was based on convincing figures and examples and his proposals were reasonable and well-founded. As he spoke, he was frequently interrupted by applause. No one hindered him. Everyone left for the dinner break
peacefully. But after the report on the statutes things developed in the same
way that they had with me: Separate delegations were assembled to which
Ovechkin was not invited, and finally his speech was condemned as politically
immature and he was ordered deprived of his delegate's credentials.

Ovechkin surrendered his credentials and left. Everything, it seemed, had
proceeded as he should have expected. But Ovechkin's nerves had given out.
When he got home, he shot himself. Doctors managed to save his life, but he
never fully recovered. He left Kursk for Tashkent, where he became seriously
ill and soon died. When I learned of Ovechkin's case I realized that the Politburo must have dictated this mode of treating dissidents, since I had been handled in the same way. Much later I learned that in preparing for the Twenty-
second Party Congress Khrushchev had worked out this tactic to protect himself from criticism.

Therefore, my "attack" on the higher-ups was useless. I found unexpected
allies on the lower levels, however.

The day after my speech, September 8, at 10:00 A.M. I was supposed to deliver the second portion of my introductory lecture at the academy. I arrived

*A program inaugurated by Krushchev. Crops were sown on millions of acres of semiarid
land in the steppes of Central Asia in an effort to solve the agricultural crisis.

an hour early and began to review the visual aids. I felt awful. I had hardly slept at all the night before. Still, I was eager to give my lecture. At 9:30 the chief of the educational branch, Major General Belsky, called me. "Pyotr Grigoryevich, your lecture has been cancelled. I will let you know when it has been rescheduled."

I put down the phone. Everything was clear. They didn't want me to meet with my students. I could do nothing. Suddenly I felt ill. My throat was sore and I felt feverish. Yesterday's walk was taking its toll. I went home.

I took my temperature, and the thermometer read 100.6°. I lay down in bed.

That evening an acquaintance who had been at the conference came over. To her the party was never at fault. She was convinced I would be severely punished for my speech, but she was also convinced that I deserved such punishment. At the same time, because she was a friend, she wished to make our lot easier. "All of the district committee people are saying that the only thing that can save you is a diagnosis by a psychiatrist that you did not know what you were saying. I went to the director of our district psychiatric clinic, Bugaisky, and he confirmed that this was the best way out for you. I asked him whether he could give me such a diagnosis right then and he told me you'd have to come and see him yourself. I told him I would talk with you and that tomorrow we would go see him together."

I replied that she would have to go without me, as I was ill.

Late that evening I got a call from the secretary of the party organization of the faculty, Colonel Zubaryov, asking me to attend a meeting of the bureau of our party organization the next day at 9:00 A.M. I told him that I was ill but that if I were able to move about at all I certainly would come.

I felt somewhat better the next morning and attended the meeting. As I'd expected, it concerned my speech. A report was delivered by the secretary of the party committee, Colonel Argasov, that consisted entirely of bandying about the phrases "politically immature" and "deprived of his delegate's credentials." Not one word was said about the content of my speech. The bureau decided to turn the matter over to discussion by the faculty.

The submission of my case to the bureau and to the faculty was an unlawful act. According to the rules of party organizations of the Soviet Army, individual cases are to be discussed by party committees on the level of district committees of the party—in other words, my case should have been discussed by the party committee of the academy. I knew this but remained silent. I was convinced that they were trying to provoke me, and I believed that their line of reasoning was: "Grigorenko is a person who insists on the letter of the law. Therefore he will protest against discussion of his case at the faculty level. We will then accuse him of being afraid of the people."

Argasov left immediately after the session ended, as did the bureau members. I stayed behind and used this time to tell Zubaryov, a senior faculty member and one of the leading officials, the contents of my speech at the party conference. The phone rang. It was Argasov. Sitting beside Zubaryov, I could hear every word.

"When is the meeting to take place?" Argasov asked.

"Tomorrow or the day after tomorrow after classes," Zubaryov answered.

"That's not satisfactory. I am supposed to send our decision on expulsion to the Central Committee by five o'clock this afternoon. After all, in addition to your meeting it is necessary to convene the party committee. Therefore you must hold your meeting before three."

"I don't know how I can do that," Zubaryov said. "The members are at classes with their students. I will ask their advice and then phone you later on." He turned to me. "Did you hear that?"

"Yes, I did. He may need the decision quickly, but I am in no hurry. I came here only to meet with the members of the party bureau. For that matter, I am sick and I am supposed to be in bed. I am going to get a medical excuse right now and I am not coming to the party meeting until I am well."

At the medical unit my regular doctor, Yefim Ivanovich Kovalyov, a fine therapeutist and cardiologist, examined me, took my temperature, and exclaimed, "Where did you get such a cold? You must go to bed immediately. I assume, as usual, you won't need an excuse. . . ."

Though I never took excuses, right now I could not risk anything. I asked Yefim Ivanovich for one and told him why I needed it. He immediately turned sour.

"Pyotr Grigoryevich, you must pardon me, but I am going to ask you to drop in on the duty doctor. Your grippe is so obvious that they will give you an excuse without me, but if I give it to you alone, they would think that I did it out of friendship."

I immediately got up. "So that's the kind you are!" With those words I bade him goodbye forever. The duty doctor gave me a medical excuse without any conversation.

Before going home I dropped in on the chief of the personnel branch, who'd earlier requested that I see him. He handed me an order from the minister of defense: "Major General P. G. Grigorenko is freed of his duties as chief of faculty number three and is to be listed in the reserve of the commander-in-chief of the land armies." No reason was given.

I was ill for ten days. When I returned to the academy a new secretary of the party committee had already replaced Pupyshev. Argasov had been shifted to the position of deputy secretary. I talked for a long time with the new party secretary, who seemed to be a good man. As I left he handed me a form to be filled out by any member called to account by the party, with the instructions, "When you have completed it, bring it back to me."

In answering the questions on the form I made a mistake in replying to one,

"For what are you being called to account?" I should have written exactly what had happened: "For speaking out at a party conference." I should have forced them to call me to account for that. But failing to realize fully the hypocrisy of the political apparatus, I decided that this might drive my case into a blind alley. I went back to the new party secretary and, indicating which question I meant, asked him, "What am I to write here?"

"You mean you don't know why you are being called to account?"

"Of course I do. It is for my speech at the party conference."

"Oh, no! You cannot write that!" He grabbed the form from me.

"I know that it is impermissible for me to be brought to account for that. That's why I came to you," I said.

"Leave the form with me. We will think about it."

He and all the chiefs of the social studies faculties worked at formulating an answer for two weeks. Several times they went to Ponomaryov to get the approval of the Central Committee. Finally they worded it this way: "For distortion of the party line on the question of the personality cult and for underestimating the activity of the party in the liquidation of the personality cult of Stalin."

Their formulation affected my whole case but did not play a role at the party meeting of the faculty, a meeting worth telling about. As I have already explained, it was out of step with regulations. But the party summit wanted to sanction the illegality perpetrated at the conference by means of approval of the party mass—in particular, approval from the organization in which I worked. On September 9 they held the first series of party meetings on the results of the conference. These party meetings embraced approximately one-half of the student party organizations and included a joint meeting of the party organizations of the leading faculties. At each meeting a proposal was moved to "condemn the politically immature speech of General Grigorenko." Nothing was said about the content of the speech. The unexpected took place: At every meeting the proposal was turned down. The only place this was done tactfully was at the party meeting of the faculties led by Zubaryov, who reported that I was ill and proposed that the question be considered only after I had recovered. Everyone agreed with him.

As far as the students' organizations went, a scandal seemed to be brewing. Everywhere students were demanding that the stenographic report of my speech be read—and in several organizations it was moved that I be invited to the meeting so that the question could be considered with me present.

Several blunt speeches were made against the decision of the conference. Those who spoke out were indignant. Thus the condemnation did not succeed. In the next series of meetings this matter was not only not debated—it was repressed. To questions from the audience about my speech the reply everywhere was: "According to instructions to party organizations of the Soviet

Army, individual cases of generals are to be considered in party committees which are on the plane of district committees of the party."

Despite this widespread refusal to pursue the question of whether my speech should be condemned, our own party organization was ordered to discuss the matter. The reason was clear to me. The higher-ups, having failed to induce students to turn against me, wanted the faculty to condone the decision made at the conference. The calculation was simple. Against a chief (any chief, but particularly a chief of a faculty) hostilities accumulate. To speak out against an overthrown chief is not only safe but in this case advantageous. The chiefs thought that by merely reporting the conference's opinion of my speech, they could goad the teachers to talk about their grievances against me. This plan had generally worked in the past. But our faculty was made up of enthusiasts who had come to the academy to create a new subject, one that even they did not know well. For them I was not so much a chief as a teacher—one whom no one could replace. If misunderstandings or impossible questions had arisen, there was no one outside the faculty to turn to for explanations. There was no one outside to complain to or about whom to complain. Everything, no matter how difficult, had to be decided right there at the faculty, in our own circle, and all of us were accustomed to that.

The atmosphere among the faculty was creative and friendly. Only Major General Yanov, deputy chief of the faculty, did not fit into this milieu. He was not occupied with cybernetics but was in charge of "battle documents" of the old form, battle orders and reports, operations and intelligence communiqués, and so on. Yanov had felt isolated and uncomfortable at the faculty ever since he realized that his "documents" were gradually disappearing into the past. He was the only one who spoke out in condemnation of me.

The remaining eighteen members of the faculty collective took the only possible position in my favor. They did not condemn my speech. Instead, they stated that they were "in favor" of such condemnation but first considered it necessary to read the stenographic report. And that was precisely what the leadership could not permit. For five straight hours the argument went on. Those present who were not members of our organization—the chief of the academy, the deputy secretary of the party committee, three chiefs of the faculty of social sciences, and two representatives of the Chief Intelligence Administration—kept trying to persuade our Communists to condemn me. Each of these eight spoke several times to our own eighteen party members, but the latter, as if they had previously agreed on it, continued to demand the stenograhic report before they could make a decision on my case.

There seemed to be no way out until suddenly the youngest advanced student, also the junior in terms of his party membership and his time on the faculty, spoke out. "In my opinion," he said, "two proposals have emerged. The first is to condemn the speech of General Grigorenko as politically immature. The second is to request the party committee of the Academy to acquaint the Communists of the faculty with the stenographic report of comrade Grigorenko's speech, and after this to decide the question of his being called to account by the party. I suggest a vote on these two proposals."

All of the outsiders immediately attacked the idea—but the faculty Communists defended it. Then someone proposed to end the discussion and vote, and all of the faculty Communists except Yanov voted in favor of the student's proposal.

The chairman spoke. "The proposal to end the discussion and to vote has been passed. We will proceed to a vote. Who is for. . . ."

At that moment the voice of the secretary of the party committee was heard. "Just a minute! We can't vote. According to the instructions of the Central Committee, matters regarding generals can be discussed only in party committees on the level of district committees. We did not bring this matter before you for a solution, but for the purpose of giving you information. Inasmuch as the purpose of information has been achieved, we will bring this meeting to an end and will transfer the decision on Grigorenko to the meeting of the party committee."

Thus the effort to get the masses to defend the Central Committee's tyranny failed. I thank the academy for this and I thank my own faculty. They couldn't have done more. Their actions gave me strength.

A few days later a session of the party committee was held. The sole item on its agenda was "A Consideration of the Individual Case of P. G. Grigorenko." Almost all the members of the party committee condemned me for my speech, but no one touched on the speech's basic meaning. They accused me of not having set forth my views within my own party organization. I was accused of comparing myself to Lenin. They said that I did not perceive the program as a "document of great theoretical significance" and that I was trying to impose petty details on important questions. They made a point of saying that I had underestimated the party's work in liquidating the consequences of the cult of Stalin and that I had failed to understand party policy on this question.

In my own speech at this meeting I reasserted the views I had set forth at the conference: 1) I had the right to speak out and no one had the right to punish me for that; 2) No one had formulated exactly what the mistakes were in my speech; 3) Even if the speech had contained mistaken views, it was still wrong to punish me for them. Such views could only be refuted, but I had the right to defend them (Paragraph 3 of the Statutes of the Communist Party of the Soviet Union) until the approval of the program by the Twenty-second Party Congress; and 4) The presidium of the conference did not have the right to transfer consideration of a matter already decided by the conference (that I should be deprived of the right to participate in the conference—as per the proposal of Biryuzov) to consideration by delegations, especially in my absence.

Based on these facts I considered that my own rights as a member of the party had been crudely violated. I asked the party committee to report this to the Central Committee.

During the debates two new proposals were put forth: 1) to deliver me a severe rebuke with a warning to be entered into my party record; and 2) to deliver me a reprimand.

After my speech the chairman asked if there were any other proposals. There were none, and it was decided that a vote be taken. Subsequently Kurochkin, chief of the academy, asked for the floor. He had not yet spoken, and he proposed now that I leave the hall during the voting. This was standard procedure and I did not oppose it.

What took place while I was gone? Kurochkin evidently did not want me to know, but he must not have realized that when a person appeals a decision of any party jurisdiction, he has the chance to acquaint himself with the entire protocol and all materials attached to it. In my case, just the protocol report told me all I needed to know. After I left, Kurochkin took the floor and attacked the proposals made.

Ivan Alexeyevich, the party secretary, took the role of chairman. He said that since there were now three proposals, he was afraid that the vote would be split and that it would not be convincing.

The party committee consisted of twenty-one persons. Ivan Alexeyevich proposed that in addition to the alternative proposal—to expel me—only one of the first two proposals be retained.

He asked whether those who had proposed that I merely be given a simple reprimand would be willing to withdraw their proposal. Those members refused and he failed as well to get the other proposal recalled. He then suggested that the two proposals be replaced by a new one—that I be given a "severe reprimand." The group agreed. Kurochkin and the chief of the first faculty, Major General Petrenko, were the only members to vote for expulsion. Despite Kurochkin and Petrenko's votes, I again say "thank you" to the academy. The party committee could not save me from punishment, but it had the courage to make it a minimal one. This unquestionably put a brake on further repressive measures against me. The party bureaucracy was forced to take into consideration the fact that the academy's sympathies were with me. It thus became advantageous for them to bury my case quietly.

I now went back over to the offensive and submitted a complaint against the decision of the party committee to the Chief Intelligence Administration, in which I demonstrated the illegality of reprimanding me for exercising my rights. Before the party commission met, the complaint was considered in my presence, first by the party investigator and then by the secretary of the party commission, Colonel General Shmelyev. At this point I finally came to understand the hypocrisy of the persons who had drawn up the accusations against me. They continued to maintain that I was not being punished for my speech. When I demanded to know what I was being punished for, they opened my file and read: "For distortion of the party line on the question of the personality cult and for underestimating the activity of the party in liquidation of the personality cult of Stalin."

I was infuriated. "And just where did I do this distorting and underestimating?"

"In your speech at the party conference."

"So that means I was punished for my speech," I said.

"No, you had the right to speak."

"What, then, did they punish me for?"

In reply they again cited the formulation already given.

We argued back and forth, each side deaf to the other's points. At another session of the party commission they turned down my complaint and endorsed the decision of the party committee of the academy. I then appealed to the party collegium of the Commission for Party Control of the Communist Party of the Soviet Union (CPSU).

The party collegium of the CPSU is a unique institution. As with all Central Committee institutions, its officials are well taken care of. Its membership is divided into two groups. In the first echelon—on the facade, so to speak—are the party investigators. These people are cordial, gentle, attentive, and sensitive. Whether they are naturally this way or whether they are trained to be this way I do not know. At any rate they greet those who make complaints at the collegium in a classy way, showering them with attention and concern and thereby attempting to bolster the prestige of their institution. They are not the decision makers. The citadel of this institution is the party collegium itself. Here, members are chosen quite differently. Those in the Party Collegium are culled from among the second secretaries of provincial party committees who have fallen to such moral depths that even under our election system, they cannot be put up for any elective office whatsoever.

My own party investigator was a short, thin man by the name of Vasily Ivanovich. I have forgotten his last name. He had very sympathetic eyes and he seemed almost literally to overflow with good wishes. He listened so attentively and nodded his head so often that he made one want to be completely frank with him. Fursov, Vasily Ivanovich's boss, was portly and of medium height. His face was expressionless and his eyes stupid and indifferent. Because of bribery he had been removed from a post as second secretary of a provincial party committee and was now working at increasing the moral stature of the party.

Party collegium members worked at the most four to five hours a week, which is how long their weekly sessions were. They arrived an hour before the meeting and left immediately after it. During the hour prior to the meeting they heard the conclusions of the party investigators on cases scheduled for the upcoming session. Fursov heard my case in this manner. Vasily Ivanovich summarized it for him in two or three minutes, after which Fursov called me into his office, looked at me indifferently, and said, "Just behave yourself in there and everything will be all right." He asked me no questions.

I do not know how many such parasites there are in the party collegium. About twenty heard my case. The session took place December 19, 1961, in an enormous hall. Entering on the right I saw four large old-fashioned windows stretching almost from floor to ceiling. To the left was a long table covered with green cloth, where the members of the party collegium sat. At the head of the table was a high-backed armchair beside which stood a portly, broad-faced person in a very fine suit of dark cloth. It was Serdyuk, the first deputy chairman of the collegium. My party investigator sat to his left. An open file lay in front of him and he seemed more than ready to jump up and begin his report. Fursov was seated in the center of the opposite side of the table. As I strode across the room Serdyuk indicated I was to sit at the foot of the table. A row of chairs lined the wall closest to me. Three were occupied by Colonel Argasov, Colonel General Shmelyev, and a man I didn't know.

I was wearing a civilian suit in an effort to stress that I was here only as a party member and that I acknowledged only party laws and party discipline. After the gentle, concerned Vasily Ivanovich and the lazily indifferent Fursov, I was ready for anything—anything except a hardening of attitude toward me. What took place surprised even Vasily Ivanovich and Fursov.

I hadn't even gotten to my seat before Serdyuk's voice resounded. "So you talked out of turn!"

"I don't understand."

"You don't understand? How naïve can you be! You understood everything very well indeed. It's only here that you're so polite. But just as soon as you got among people who like a fuss you started gabbing. High salaries don't suit him—can you believe it! Why didn't you think about your own high salary?"

"I don't distinguish myself from the party," I interrupted.

"You don't distinguish yourself! Don't play at being holy! You differentiate and distinguish in everything very well indeed. You thought about your own high salary when you gave your speech. You were convinced that as a highly trained specialist you had a right to such a salary. But you know you were thinking about *my* high salary."

He stressed the word *my*—and throughout the tirade he insulted me by using the familiar rather than formal address.

He continued, "You want to have removability in high positions—don't you! Well, you didn't think about your own removability. You are a specialist and don't need to be removed and replaced. You didn't think about being removed yourself. You want to have *me* replaced." With that he fixed his gaze on the seat of his armchair. "He wants democracy, you see! So every good-for-nothing can meddle in the work of government and party institutions and hinder the efforts of conscientious officials.

"He wants free elections, you see, so that all kinds of demagogues can slander conscientious Communists and can hinder the people from electing those who are most worthy. He spouted demagogy like that and then he had the effrontery to complain! We didn't deal with him lawfully, you see. Well, we aren't going to waste our time on your clever manipulations. We aren't going to listen to your demagogy here! You can go!"

I remained silent. I wanted to pick up my chair and beat all of them over the head and wreck everything in the room. If I had opened my mouth torrents of cursing would have poured out of it. I clenched my jaw until I felt pain in my teeth and walked away from the table. Serdyuk continued to rant, and when I was at the door he shouted at Argasov, "Why didn't you expel him? We would have confirmed the decision. We can't reform him. We'll have to expel him."

I could control myself no longer. "What gangsters!" I yelled as I stepped into the reception room. "They have the right to make expulsions from the party. But still they want us to expel each other so that all they have to do is to confirm it. What gangsters!"

Vasily Ivanovich ran into the reception room. He was embarrassed and at a loss as to what he should do. I had lost faith in his decency during Serdyuk's tirade, but seeing his dismayed face I felt sorry for the man. He walked ahead, inviting me to follow him and handing me my pass. He said, "I don't understand what just took place. Nothing like that has ever happened before. But they didn't expel you from the party after all. It's just a severe reprimand! Six months from now we'll wipe it off your record. Don't be downhearted, comrade Grigorenko!"

"I'm not downhearted. Thank you for the sympathy. Goodbye!"

I went out onto the street. The sun was shining, highlighting a recent snowfall. I felt I had escaped from a cellar and breathed in the fresh, frosty air joyfully. Walking along the embankment to our apartment house in Khamovniki, I could not stop thinking about what had just happened. A knot formed in my throat. I was irritated that I had kept silence when Serdyuk mocked my ideals. Profound responses now occurred to me, but I realized that they had come too late and that even if they had come in time I would not have benefited by saying them. However evil it was, I kept imagining crushing Serdyuk.

When I got home my wife was waiting and I told her my story in detail, concluding with, "They were gangsters! They are dissolute, demoralized men!"

"You've only just found that out? I've known it for a long time. But now that you know about it, conduct yourself accordingly. Don't put your head in the beast's jaws."

I had learned something from the hearing. At the same time my disturbed party affairs had stabilized somewhat. I could begin seeking a service appointment, which until now, no one had been willing to talk to me about. Even Chuikov, who had always responded positively to my requests for appointments, had told me, "Solve your party problems, and then we will talk about your appointment."

So I went to him again. We discussed what had happened at my investigation, and he said, "What are you asking for now?"

"Well, it's clear that they won't make me head of a faculty. But I am not proud. I would agree to take a post as a senior teacher in my own faculty."

"There can be no talk at all about a teaching position. It is impermissible to let you get close to young people."

"Well, then, as a senior scientific worker in the Scientific Research Branch?"

"No, the academy will not accept you in any position."

"As a senior scientific worker in any of the computer centers of the Ministry of Defense."

"No, we are not going to let you stay in Moscow."

"In that case pick my position yourself."

"Very well. As soon as we choose I will summon you."

He summoned me a week later. "I am offering you three positions—the choice is yours: one, provincial military commissar in Tyumen; two, deputy chief of the operations branch of the Novosibirsk Military District; and three, chief of the operations branch of the army staff in Ussurisk."

I immediately rejected the first position; my party problems definitely would keep me from being accepted in such a post. Chuikov agreed. The second job did not appeal to me; I did not want to go to Siberia. So I accepted the third offer, though it certainly was a step down.

In early January 1962 an order was issued making me chief of the operations branch of the Fifth Army. The order stated my title as "chief of the operations branch," whereas the accepted full title was "chief of the operations branch and deputy chief of staff of the army." The second phrase—"deputy chief of staff of the army"—was missing. At the time I did not attach any importance to this. Only after I arrived at my post did I understand that the omission was not accidental.

Thus in early February 1962 I returned to the Far East, where I had first served as a nonspecialized general army service career man. Now I was going into exile, but the tricks of fate are strange. Unexpectedly, the simple departure of a penalized general turned into a triumph. At the station senior officers began to come up to my railway car—at first, friends from work; then closer to departure time, the papakhi of high-ranking officers filled the railway platform. Many of my more distant colleagues did not approach my car and even acted as if their presence had nothing to do with me. But I understood. Even from a distance people wanted to see me off.

At first I pretended not to understand the meaning of this gathering. My wife, however, gestured toward the platform and said, "Nikita is not going to forgive you for this."

I couldn't argue with her.

CHAPTER NINETEEN

FOR THE
REBIRTH
OF
LENINISM

My friends, relatives, and wife all remained in my beloved Moscow as I traveled east, back into the past. Almost every day we set our watches back an hour, sometimes more.

I made a stop in Novosibirsk. Perhaps I would feel better if I saw my old friend, Ivan Alexeyevich Manuilov, my comrade-in-arms in the 18th Separate Infantry Brigade. Perhaps the past would return for me. The energetic, quick-minded, decisive chief of staff had aged and become corpulent.

Standing on line to buy vodka and bread, we talked about the present and I told Ivan Alexeyevich my story. He said, "You were lucky. It doesn't matter that you were demoted. You are still in the army—that's the main thing. Stay there for as long as you can. Don't be as stupid as I was: I was offended when they didn't give me a promotion, and so I applied for retirement. There are many shocking things in the army. But at least there isn't repulsive bribery. In the civilian world bribery runs rampant. I'm chairman of the district commission of party control. I do my work and it's taken away from me. Few cases, if any, are ever pressed."

I stayed with Ivan Alexeyevich two days and had time to browse through his library. He had collected Russian proverbs and sayings and recorded interesting thoughts and episodes from his life. I thought, "All this should be published." Clearly, though, this was unrealistic. There wasn't a single Soviet publishing house that would have taken it on.

Two days later the train took me past Chita, where I had served on the staff of the front group for about a year, in the late thirties. It had been our departure point for battles on the Khalkhin-Gol River, and the place where I had recuperated from my first wound. We traveled on into my past. Here was Boryza—the supply station of Zhukov's First Army Group during the Khalkhin-Gol battles. We traveled farther and farther along the Manchurian frontier.

I stayed a few days in Khabarovsk, where the 18th Separate Infantry Brigade had been deployed, and then spent almost the last six hundred kilometers of the journey standing. Was I nervous? I do not know. I only remember looking out of the window, trying to recollect the terrain of the districts through which I had traveled during the years of my training. At the Ussurisk station I was met by a group of my future subordinates, headed by my deputy, Colonel Savaseyev.

Our meeting was warm. I could not help but react positively to the way they honored me. At work I was welcomed by chiefs of the various branches of the army and by their subordinates. They accepted my suggestions with enthusiasm and understanding, no doubt because they'd heard legends of my speech at the party conference and of my conflict with Chuikov. The "explanatory" material and the warnings against me that had been disseminated by the political branch of the army before my arrival at Ussurisk played a role contrary to intentions: They aroused sympathy for me. I was perceived as one who had suffered unjustly.

In addition to explanations and warnings, measures were taken by those in Moscow to make my work difficult. On my second day we received a new staff schedule for the army administration. After the heading were the words: *For the administration of the Fifth Combined Forces Army solely.* How was this staff schedule distinct from others? In only one respect. The position of "deputy chief of staff" was crossed out. Correspondingly, opposite the position "deputy chief of staff" the position "chief of the operations branch" was also crossed out. These two deletions indicated that the duties of deputy chief of staff were to be distinct from the functions of chief of the operations branch, and that a special position—deputy chief of staff—had been introduced. This was done specifically to reduce my rights, but since it is impossible to define a position without regard to the individual who operates it, emending the staff schedule was stupid and only created confusion. Several times the chief of staff, Major General Vasily Ivanovich Petrov, and I conflicted over the assignment of duties supposedly mine.

Petrov, I am convinced, got genuine satisfaction from stressing his service superiority. In order to underline the fact that he, a recent academy graduate, was my boss, he discarded every one of my proposals for innovations. At first I tried to prove to him that I was right, but seeing the satisfaction it gave him to reject all my arguments, I tried a different approach.

As soon as he had rejected my proposal and began to joke about it, I would say indifferently, "It's my duty to propose and yours to accept or reject. The essence of my proposal is this. . . ."

And I would quickly set forth my proposal in several sentences. Vasily Ivanovich had a high opinion of his own talents. As a result he often made decisions without thinking them through. Heaven help anyone who objected to such a decision. Vasily Ivanovich would become offended, arrogant, and stubborn. On the other hand, if you simply expressed your doubts, he was capable of changing his mind.

As soon as I began taking the position "It's my duty to propose and yours to decide; I do not insist on my proposal," each one of my proposals was accepted.

Our army commander, Alexander Fyodorovich Repin, was stocky and had a broad, simple face. He was much loved by his subordinates, who always tried to carry out his orders in the best way possible. I cannot recall a single case in which he raised his voice or punished anyone. Despite this, or perhaps because of it, he maintained a high level of discipline.

I'd known Repin briefly before coming to Ussurisk, but there we actually became friends. He was the only person who got around the instructions that I should be isolated from the other generals. As a rule I was invited to all his meetings of the high-ranking army leaders. At these meetings he invariably asked my opinions and always found something useful in them. He emphasized my ideas when he stated his conclusions, simultaneously pointing out my teaching and scientific experience and my authority.

Not one training exercise led by Repin was carried out without my participation as chief of staff of the command. During such exercises, we talked quite a bit, often about my military experiences. Never did we touch on politics— even in passing. In this, Alexander Fyodorovich Repin showed extraordinary tact. He wanted to help me regain the status I'd had before my speech. I later learned of the reports he'd written about me to the commander of the forces of the Far Eastern Front, Army General Kreizer, in which he spoke glowingly about my work in the army and pressed for my return to the academy.

Repin was an outstanding military leader. He would have achieved positions higher than that of lieutenant general, had he not lost his life in a senseless accident. Several years after I finished working with him, his head was severed by a helicopter propeller. This tragedy launched V. I. Petrov's career. On Repin's death he became commander of the army, then was named chief of staff of the Far Eastern Military District. Later, as chief military adviser, he was sent to help Mengistu stifle the Ethiopian people. Subsequently he achieved the rank of army general, and was made commander-in-chief of the Far East.

I worked hard at Ussurisk, reorganizing the activities of the branch on the basis of cybernetics research I had carried out at the Frunze Academy, but my work no longer absorbed me. Cybernetics was still important to me, but I was now concerned with weightier matters—the fate of my country, the fate of communism. More and more, the idea entered my head that the social structure created in our country was not a socialist one, that the ruling party was not communist. Where we were going, what would become of the country and of the cause of communism, and what had to be done to return us to the right path—these questions plagued me.

Out of habit, I went to Lenin for answers. Once again I sat down with his works, seeking proof that the present party line had diverted from Leninism, seeking the means by which we could correct ourselves. Lenin began to appear to me in a new light. What had seemed absolutely clear and totally acceptable now seemed contradictory and wrong. I knew that the dictatorship of the proletariat was democracy for the majority of the workers, but I saw that in his "Leftism as an Illness of Childhood . . ." and in "The Proletarian Revolution and the Renegade Kautsky" Lenin defined dictatorship as "governmental power basing itself not on law but on violence." This formulation perfectly suited the present government.

When Demichev, the Central Committee secretary, had talked to me about my speech, he had brought my attention in particular to this formulation, stressing that "Leftism as an Illness of Childhood . . ." was modeled after "The State and Revolution." But this fact did not satisfy me. I read and reread, trying to find a formula which would reconcile my new concepts with Lenin's definitions. But no sooner did I resolve one contradiction than another would arise.

Take the question of "freedom of the press." How well and how simply Lenin wrote before the elections to the constitutent assembly: Freedom of the press is not only the abolition of censorship but also the just distribution of paper and of printing presses, first to the state for the needs of the people at large; then to large groups; then to smaller groups; and finally to any citizens who can gather a number of signatures. Was this Leninism or not? I had considered it so, but I reread the decree of the Council of Peoples Commissars written by Lenin on the abolition of freedom of the press, and his essay entitled "On the Deceit of the People with the Slogans of 'Freedom of the Press,' and 'a Party Press,' and 'Party Propaganda,' " and he seemed to be saying that freedom of the press was of no importance to the people; it was for the bourgeoisie.

There were even more obvious contradictions. Take the question of democracy and of Lenin as a classical example of a democrat. I read "We will win the majority over to our side; we will convince the majority; and we will *compel* the minority, we will *force* them to submit."

Feverishly I returned to "One Step Backward—Two Steps Forward," in which Lenin proved that he was right in defending the rights of the minority. He wrote that it was not necessary to defend the rights of the majority. The majority will defend itself because it is the majority, but within a country's statutes it is necessary to have a guarantee of the rights of the minority, to assure it protection from the tyranny of the majority. Obviously when Lenin was in the minority he believed that the majority had no right to force its will on the minority; only later did he say that the majority has the right to suffocate the minority.

Who is to determine what the majority and the minority are? How do they manifest themselves in society? I looked on this phenomenon from the heights of my past experience, from the speaker's platform of the Twentieth and Twenty-second Congresses, from the recollections of friends who knew Stalin's dungeons. What I saw was that the majority was formed out of terror of the repressions to which the minority was being subjected and to which everyone who refused to join the majority could be subjected. People supported the government because they were afraid and because they were deceived by the avalanche of propaganda. The constant suppression of the minority, and the incessant lying of the party and state guarantee a permanent popular majority of those supporting the government. Lenin's formula is false. It does not defend the rights of the people—but seeks to make the people's lack of rights eternal.

The materials of the Tenth Party Congress made a tremendous impression on me. Previously I had looked upon them as a model of the party approach, as a brilliant Leninist plan for preservation of the unity of the party in the face of a struggle between factions. Now I saw with horror that the decisions of the Tenth Party Congress were suicidal. This was not a document against factionalism but a weapon for one faction to win power within the party. Stalin did not have to be original in his climb to the top. All he had to do was create his own faction, and this he did by creating a strictly centralized party apparatus with its own internal factional discipline with whose help he seized power within the party.

The decisions of the Tenth Party Congress gave a legal basis to Stalin's actions. All this was now clear to me. However, I still could not reconcile myself to accepting such a concept.

I kept looking for something else in Lenin and "found" it in his remarks on the resolution of the anarchist-syndicalist deviation and on the proposal of Ryazanov to forbid future voting on platforms. Speaking from his seat, Lenin sharply criticized this proposal. How can we establish the rules for future congresses? What if circumstances require voting by platforms! From this I drew the conclusion that all of the decisions of the Tenth Congress were in effect only until the Eleventh Congress, and that Stalin, consequently, had violated Lenin's will when he extended the decisions of the Tenth Congress to the future. At the time I did not have the courage to view Lenin's speech against the Ryazanov proposal as an ordinary demogogic trick, exactly the same as the one about freedom of the press. Lenin was very generous in passing out democratic rights in the future. Someday there will be freedom of the press! Someday money will disappear! Someday we will cease detaining people in prisons and concentration camps! Someday the state will wither away! All in the future! But for the time being we are seizing control of the machinery of state and, using it as our own weapon, we will destroy the old world totally.

All this was said only two years after he had written: "The proletariat does not need just any kind of a state, but a state which is withering away, which *would begin to wither away immediately* after the proletarian coup d'etat and *which cannot but wither away.* "

Things did not seem to "add up" in Lenin. But, I repeat, at the time I did not have the courage to understand this. I cast aside the "state as a club" and continued to hold on to the judgments of "The State and Revolution." I began to "sort out" Lenin unconsciously, selecting to retain only that which suited my own views and totally bypassing some of his most important opinions. Thus I skipped over the matters of the masses, the party, the leaders. Too obviously Lenin had substituted for the "dictatorship of the proletariat" the "dictatorship of the leaders." True, Stalin wrote about this more thoroughly, but it was Lenin who provided him with a theoretical basis.

Thus by reconsidering Lenin and analyzing the internal and external policies of the party and the state, I worked out my own evaluations of events and my own ideas of the problems that lay before the country and the world communist movement. I began to devote all of my free time to this work, leaving my job promptly each day, no longer working each night on cybernetics. Gradually I conceived a plan for realization of my ideological-political explorations. I decided to elaborate on it and then to send a series of letters to the Central Committee.

I composed two letters. The first was essentially an introduction in which I wrote that I considered my speech at the party conference to be a mistake because it is foolish to try to raise broad questions of principle in five to ten minutes. I said that I had now studied the question more thoroughly and, making use of the right of a party member to write on all questions to any party jurisdiction, including the Central Committee, I had decided to write a series of letters for the Politburo, hoping by this means to help it in its difficult work. Further, I set forth the content of all the letters I had planned.

I sent just one letter before abandoning this series. In the first place, I am not one to write unanswered letters. In the second place, my wife, who had joined me in Ussurisk, fell ill. The climate turned out to be damaging to her bronchial tubes. She developed asthma and the Ussurisk military hospital was unable to control her attacks. For days at a time she was barely able to breathe. She couldn't eat or sleep. The doctors decided to move her to the Khabarovsk military district hospital, hoping that she would receive more skilled medical attention there and that the new climate might play a positive role in her recovery. Once there she did feel better. No doubt the climate helped, but the main thing was the attentiveness and concern of a skilled doctor, Vasily Nikolayevich Tsvetkovsky.

Nineteen sixty-two was an unfortunate year for us. As soon as Zinaida felt somewhat better, I tried to reserve time in a sanatorium for us. I arrived in Khabarovsk myself on November 5 and registered at the hotel for generals, awaking at dawn the next day with a feeling of suffocation. Things grew dark in front of my eyes and I couldn't breathe. I jerked open the door to the balcony and in my underwear went outside, where the temperature was below freezing. I went back into the room, put on my bedroom slippers and greatcoat, took a chair, returned to the balcony, and sat there for about two hours. Although I got thoroughly chilled, eventually I felt better. Back in bed, I quickly warmed up and went to sleep but awoke again just after seven. It was too early to go to the hospital and I didn't feel like going to the dining hall, so I dressed slowly and went out again onto the balcony.

At nine-thirty I went to the hospital. As soon as I entered my wife's room, she asked what was wrong with me. I told her that it was nothing in particular, just a general feeling of malaise. We talked for awhile and then Tsvetkovsky came in on his morning rounds and I had to leave the room. After her own examination my wife urged me to ask Vasily Nikolayevich to examine me.

He performed more than the simple checkup I'd expected and asked me to stay afterward, saying, "What are your plans, Pyotr Grigoryevich?"

"On the ninth I am leaving for Ussurisk, where I will spend a couple of days turning over my duties. Then I will come back here. By that time you will have prepared Zinaida Mikhailovna for release from the hospital. I will pick up our sanatorium reservations at the Medical Administration and fly with Zinaida to Moscow. After a couple of days there we will proceed to Kislovodsk."

"Pyotr Grigoryevich," Tsvetkovsky said, "in your present state of health *I do not have the right* to let you leave the hospital. I have clearly diagnosed in you an infarction. If you do not stay here voluntarily, I will be forced to report you to the commander of the forces of the military district."

"Well, go ahead and report to him! I am not going to stay in the hospital." I finished dressing and went back to my wife's ward. A few minutes later Tsvetkovsky dropped in on me there.

"Comrade General! The commander asks to speak to you."

I picked up the phone. "This is Kreizer. Do you think you have the right to dispose of your own health as you please? Follow Tsvetkovsky's instructions. Occupy immediately the place allotted you and undergo treatment. Do not leave the hospital until you have recovered and received the doctor's permission." And then, more gently, "I wish you a quick recovery. Please don't deprive Repin and me of the satisfaction of being present at the banquet celebrating your return to the faculty. Alexander Fyodorovich and I are working to this end and I hope that our efforts will not be in vain. Go ahead and get well."

I had to cancel our sanatorium reservations. We did not get to Moscow until December, and after this went to the clinical sanatorium called Arkhangelskoye. As always, it gleamed with cleanliness and magnificent care and service. It snowed a great deal and I spent a lot of time on skis, something my doctor didn't like at all.

I had the chance while there to meet and talk with people a generation older than I, many of whom made veiled criticisms of the direction our country was taking. I especially recall conversations with a retired hero of the Civil War, Lieutenant General Sharaburko. He had been close to those who later headed the Soviet armed forces—Voroshilov, Budyonny, Kulik. He was a simple person of little education but, like Opanasenko, naturally intelligent, quick to grasp things, and attracted to the new.

One evening I entered the Arkhangelskoye dining hall and saw a young couple—unusual in this primarily old folks' sanatorium. The woman looked like a nineteenth-century merchant's wife, rather pleasant looking but somewhat overweight. The man was a colonel, quite tall. He seemed to look down with a certain air of superiority on those around him.

Seeing that I kept staring at this couple, a major general who sat at our table said to me, "That's the son of a very highly placed government official. He's an interesting type. He raped a nine-year-old girl. As you know, the penalty for seduction of minors is the firing squad! But this fellow got sent up for psychiatric diagnosis and was found to be insane, and they sent him to a special psychiatric hospital in Leningrad on Arsenal Street instead of sending him to prison. They kept him there for half a year as a "cure." And now he is among us once again. Just look at the triumphal look with which he is surveying us all."

I listened to this indignant appraisal of the fact that a psychiatric hospital had been used to protect a criminal. I was just as indignant as my tablemate, but I never even thought about the fact that if it is possible to hide a criminal with the aid of psychiatry, that same method can turn a well man into an allegedly insane man and thereby shut him up in a special psychiatric hospital; and, of course, I didn't know that before little more than a year passed I would be at the Arsenal Street asylum unprepared to accept psychiatrists as executioners. I put the conversation about the rapist out of my mind and remembered it only much later.

After my return from the sanatorium my work in the Fifth Army continued as successfully as before. My prestige kept rising. Correspondingly the activity of my defenders, those proponents of my return to the faculty, intensified. I later learned that I did not return to the faculty in 1963 only because of the strong opposition of Kurochkin and Ponomaryov. Kurochkin's furious opposition to me got him in so good with Ponomaryov that he eventually attained the rank of army general. Without Ponomaryov's support he would never have received this rank. Both Malinovsky and Chuikov knew his real worth.

Evidently the support for me was also very weighty. Judging from Chuikov's speech at the annual scientific conference of the academy in the spring of 1963, he was in favor of my return. Knowing him, I imagine that he was not alone. Chuikov would not have expressed an opinion that contradicted that of the Minister of Defense. He expressed himself so definitely that those at the conference immediately understood his speech as a vote in favor of my return. All of a sudden I was flooded wth letters from the academy.

I might have returned to the Academy in 1964, but I had already chosen a different path for myself.

My work on Lenin proceeded successfully, but I did not write to the Central Committee any more. I imagined the faces of the Politburo members, even the face most friendly to me—that of Nikita Khrushchev—and they all seemed angry, stupid, and hostile. There could be no dialogue with such monsters. They needed not to be persuaded but thrown out. I pondered creating a revolutionary organization whose theoretical basis would be selected opinions and teachings from Lenin.

I had thought of doing this for more than twenty years. During the war I had been close to one radical officer and we had talked a great deal about the country and the party. I did not agree with many of his conclusions but concurred with his idea that after the war it would be necessary to change the course of the party sharply. During one conversation he mentioned that some people felt preparations for such changes should be taking place right now. There was an organization, he said, calling itself the "Alliance of True Leninists," which was organized on the principle of a chain. Each member of this alliance knew only the person who had enlisted him in it and those whom he himself had enlisted. You might enlist ten members, but each would know only you. They would not know each other. It was impermissible also to know anyone outside your own cell, or group. If another member whom you did not know should try to enlist you in the alliance you had to agree to enlistment, without revealing that you were already a member. If one member was arrested, all those connected with him would act as end links of the organization. If a member moved, those members who had been connected with him in his former location would become end links and act as such, and the member who had moved would found a new chain in his new location. The organizers of the alliance believed in infiltration of like thinkers into all of society, without creating any organization, inasmuch as any organization would be easily discovered through connections within it and organized activity.

At the time I did not agree to join the alliance, but the idea intrigued me. Such a chain seemed indestructible, and it could accomplish quite a bit since it combined ideological unity (true Leninism) with the broadest sort of initiative.

Now at Ussurisk the thought of such a mass ideological organization simply would not leave me. If I had known one of the alliance members I would have joined right then. The officer who had attempted to recruit me died at the front, and I never met any other members. Several times I met people whom I suspected of alliance activity, but I never strove to enter into permanent contact with them, though I believed the alliance still existed and believed also that "democratic trends" in the CPSU arose from such a movement. I believe the organization may still exist today, and it is precisely for this reason that I do not name the officer who proposed that I join the alliance. I do not want to give even one small bit of evidence to the KGB.

By the summer of 1963, having completed my ideological and theoretical work, I was convinced that it was necessary to battle the leadership of the CPSU and not try to propitiate it with loyal requests. Still I had not decided on any organized actions. I knew creation of an organization that would be called anti-Soviet could cost me my life, but this did not frighten me. What held me back was fear for my family. I had not the slightest doubt that they would be persecuted. The ruling clique had no fear of resorting to past methods. I do not know how long I wavered, but a petty occurrence disturbed my equilibrium. An article appeared in *Komsomol Pravda* directed aginst the poet Yevgeny Yevtushenko. Like all such articles it was woven out of lies, tendentiously presented half-truths, and unscrupulous distortions.

Somewhat later, when I had already rejected the concept of an underground struggle and had decided to act out in the open, I took three lines from one of Yevtushenko's verses as my motto:

> Without stooping, and in front of all,
> Unarmed I reach out for arms,
> Without friends, I reach out for friends.

The impudent and brazen attack by nonentities and scoundrels on my favorite poet of the moment (Yevtushenko has changed since then) enraged me, and in one session I wrote a very sharply worded lampoon entitled "Lackeys'

Pravda," which I mailed anonymously from Vladivostok. This action led to others. That fall I took my leave in Moscow and with my son Georgy started organizing the Alliance for Struggle for the Rebirth of Leninism. The organizational work rested entirely on Georgy, who, as I've mentioned, was a student in the Artillery Engineering Academy. I worked only on leaflets and in less than a month had written seven.

1) The introductory or foundation leaflet. It reported that on the forty-sixth anniversary of the October Revolution, the "Alliance for Struggle for the Rebirth of Leninism" had been formed. The organization, I said, recognized the degeneration of the Soviet system and the betrayal of Leninism by the leaders of the party and the government. I elaborated our organizational principle— the chain. We called on all Soviet citizens to create chains of their own and to follow our leaflets closely.

While in theory we sought to keep to the principle of chains, Georgy brought into the organization friends and acquaintances from among the young officers and students. These people either were already acquainted with each other or else quickly became acquainted. The upshot was not an elusive chain but instead a large group that began its activities with the dissemination of my first leaflet. The alliance received unexpected reinforcement one day when an embarrassed Georgy informed me that my younger son, Andrei, by this time a student in an institute, had created an underground circle with two of his friends. Georgy and I had agreed not to involve any of his brothers in our cause. When he learned of Andrei's undertaking he came to me. Georgy felt that it was better to enlist Andrei and the others in our alliance than to leave them on their own. In any case, he knew he would not be able to dissuade them from revolutionary activities. If I were to object to Andrei's organization, he and his friends would go into the underground—away from Georgy and myself. Thus Andrei's group participated in the dissemination of the first leaflet, more than a hundred copies of which were handed out primarily in the area of factories.

2) The second leaflet was devoted to the present Soviet government, which was characterized as a state dominated by the bureaucracy.

3) The third leaflet dealt with the Soviet people's lack of rights and the omnipotence of bureaucratic power. It reported, in particular, the shooting of workers in Novocherkassk, and also mentioned the shootings in Temir-Tau and Tbilisi.

4) The fourth was entitled "What Are We to Struggle For?" My reply was that we should struggle for the ousting of the government bureaucrats and parasites, for free elections, for control over the government by the people, and for frequent replacement of all persons of high position, including the very highest.

5) The fifth dealt with the fact that the Soviet trade unions are not an organ

for the defense of workers—but a weapon for their exploitation.

6) The sixth asked: "Why is there no bread?" It was a reply to the letter of the Central Committee that had claimed that the bread shortage existed because slices were cut too thickly in dining halls. The leaflet discussed the real causes: low harvest yields, high losses in harvesting, loss of bread grains as a result of poor storage. Behind all this was the absence among farm workers of interest in the results of their labors. Figures were cited in this regard—figures not published in the Soviet press.

7) The seventh leaflet, "A Reply to Our Opponents," was actually a brochure. It discussed the question of the state. Our basic opponent turned out to be the son of our family friend, Dr. Grigory Alexandrovich Pavlov, the son being a scientist in one of the institutes of the Academy of Sciences. When our organization was discovered, the KGB accused him of collaborating with anti-Soviet elements. He conducted himself with dignity, insisting on his right to discuss political questions of importance. In connection with this case he was long threatened with arrest and dismissal from his institute. The family suffered greatly.

Our alliance grew swiftly and extended its activities outside Moscow to other cities. The young people involved were pleased, but I was worried. When my leave ended and I prepared to return to Ussurisk, I advised Georgy temporarily to halt the dissemination of leaflets and to go into hiding. All the same, the young continued their activities when I was not in Moscow, and I was away for quite a while.

In mid-January 1964 I received an urgent summons to the General Staff. It arrived during a general meeting of our administration, and when it was announced that I was to leave in answer to an urgent summons from Moscow, everyone applauded. Alexander Fyodorovich Repin shook my hand firmly, smiled warmly, and said, "I hope that you will not return."

Little did he suspect in what manner his wish would be realized. Like all of those applauding me, he thought that I was being summoned to return to the academy. Even I thought so. I flew to Moscow in a fine mood that disappeared with the first conversation I had with Georgy.

The story he told me was alarming. From the very beginning of the alliance's activity he had rented a room where he kept a typewriter, which he used to prepare leaflets. One morning he was summoned at ten o'clock to the academy commandant and detained. No one told him why he had been called. After he had waited two hours in the reception room, a subordinate of the commandant told him he could go. Naturally Georgy suspected something was wrong. He immediately went to his room, which clearly had been searched. Indignant, he accused his landlady of messing about in his things and told her that some valuables were missing. Frightened at being made responsible, the landlady told him that two men who'd identified themselves as KGB agents had searched the room. Still, Georgy told me, there had been nothing suspicious in his room at the time. Thus we relaxed a little. We were both so inexperienced that we never thought they might have found what they needed. Neither of us paid the least attention to the landlady's report that the KGB men had used the typewriter.

Georgy had what he felt was encouraging news. A number of leaflets had been circulated in Vladimir, in Kaluga, and among the troops of the Central Asian and Leningrad Military Districts. He and Alyosha Yegorov, Zinaida's nephew, reported with particular enthusiasm how the leaflets had been disseminated in one of the technical secondary schools in Vladimir in which Sasha Grossmer, Zinaida's nephew and Alyosha's first cousin, was studying. This report affected me quite differently than it had Georgy; the same leaflets had been discovered in Moscow, and the KGB would realize that someone at the school was connected with the Moscow organization.

The next day I reported to the General Staff. The chief of the operations branch and the emissary of the Far East had an assignment ready for me. While reading the job description, I occasionally sensed one or the other of them glancing curiously at me. Still, I attached no particular significance to this, thinking simply that my speech had not been forgotten. I set to work. My assignment was interesting and worthwhile—it required a highly skilled officer to carry it out. I was given plenty of time to execute it, and naturally I did not put in overtime. I worked for five or six hours a day. Why should I rush if they did not rush me? Life with my family was far more pleasant than my Far Eastern loneliness.

My worries abated. The questioning of the pupils at the secondary technical school in Vladimir had ceased. Intent on preserving the alliance, I entrusted Georgy with the task of liquidating the closeness of the Moscow group. He would reorganize the group into a chain system and temporarily halt its activity by going into hiding himself.

When it seemed that everything had quieted down, I thought about trying to verify what attitude people had toward an underground opposition. I hesitated for a long time, believing that a favorable outcome was probably impossible, but in the end I decided to proceed.

I went to one of the entrances of the Hammer and Sickle Factory in Moscow—taking with me thirteen leaflets. In our family thirteen is considered a lucky number. I had thought about whom I should pass them out to. It seemed to me that those going to work would be afraid to go through inspection with such a dangerous item on their person or to actually have it at work, where it might by chance be discovered. Therefore it seemed a better idea to pass them out to people going home. Before handing out a leaflet I would first ask each man if he would like to take one.

With my heart in my mouth I offered one to my first customer, who nodded and, without stopping, took it and hid it in his pocket. The second was successful, too, and the third. The fourth was a misfire. In response to my question he grimly shook his head and put his hands in his pockets. The next was successful. I swiftly gave away ten. At that point I decided to offer them to people going to work.

My first offer was a failure as was the second. I began to feel that maybe I should stop. It seemed too risky. A blond, blue-eyed, friendly looking young fellow came who resembled a friend I'd had as a boy—Misha Pozhidayev. Involuntarily smiling, I asked him, "Would you like a leaflet?"

"Give it to me!" Without stopping he smiled, seized it, and left, waving it at me.

An elderly worker came up to me and held out his hand for a leaflet. I gave one to him and then decided I would give the last to the next person who passed by. A tall intellectual-looking man walked out of the factory and I pushed the last leaflet into his hands. I then walked swiftly away from the factory along the high board fence. I had not taken twenty steps when I heard someone coming behind me and a voice: "Hey, fellow!"

I turned around. I was being pursued by a worker approximately my age, though his moustaches made him look older than he probably was.

"Are you talking to me?" I asked.

"Yes, you! Have you given them all away?"

"All."

"That's too bad. I wanted to read it." He walked alongside me. "Aren't you afraid?"

"I'm tired of being afraid. After all, someone has to begin."

"That's true," he said seriously. "But people are afraid."

We walked along talking. He was interesting company, but distributing the leaflets had worn me out. I had been at the factory for a maximum of ten minutes, but it had seemed like hours. The man wanted me to come home with him. He assured me that he lived nearby. I didn't feel that he had any dishonest intentions—but reason told me to get out of there as fast as possible.

I told him that I did not have time to talk and ran to a streetcar and boarded it. After a few stops I got off and got into a taxi and then went to the metro.

I allowed this experience to prove to me that industrial workers were eager for truthful information. I wanted to distribute a leaflet to the public at large. I decided to take just one leaflet, a large one, "The Reply to Our Opponents," to the Paveletsky station. This time I wore my general's uniform.

I found a seat in the main hall of the station, took out the leaflet and began to read it. I read it from beginning to end. During this time, the hall half emptied. Evidently many people boarded the same train. My bench was empty. I left the leaflet and went to the other end of the hall, sitting down so as to be able to see the length of it. Soon a young fellow I had noticed earlier sitting with a girl walked up to me. The two had been closely pressed to one another, talking absorbedly. He took the leaflet and carried it over to the girl. They scanned it, talked heatedly for a few seconds, and then got up and came over to me. I was reading the magazine *Ogonyok* and pretending I did not see them.

"Comrade General!" the young man said, "isn't this yours?" He showed me the leaflet.

"No, it's not," I said firmly.

"But . . . we . . . thought we saw you reading it."

"Yes, I read it. But it was not mine. I read it and left it where it was before I came in."

Embarrassed, they walked away. Suddenly the young woman—almost a girl—broke away from her companion and ran to me. "Comrade General! Maybe you have another of these? We are going in different directions and we both want to take it with us."

"No, my dear girl! On my word of honor I don't have any more!" I smiled at her sympathetically.

"Well, then, excuse me." She ran off.

This experiment, too, showed me that people wanted the truth.

CHAPTER TWENTY

THE

SERBSKY

INSTITUTE

My work at the General Staff ended and I received orders to return to the Far East. Before leaving I discovered that I was being followed and that our apartment was bugged. Obviously the KGB knew about the alliance. Too late I realized that they also knew about the typewriter Georgy had had. I decided to remove it from Moscow.

My eldest son, Anatoly, had traveled from Germany to Moscow with his family. He had an enormous trunk of goods that he wanted delivered to his wife's family in Ussurisk. This trunk could carry my typewriter.

On February 1 Andrei, Zinaida, and I went to the parking area in the Moscow hotel building twenty minutes before the bus for the airport left. Several well-built young men began to help us very efficiently: They checked the baggage and helped get the tickets written up. Zinaida said quietly, "Look at them! In my opinion they are your 'escorts.' "

Presently another young man appeared. He was dressed in a sheepskin coat and skin boots. He talked a great deal in a loud voice and made fun of himself. He told us he was a correspondent on his way to Magadan and Kamchatka. He had never been in the north and had dressed as advised by friends.

The correspondent kept trying to amuse us during the trip. Our farewells at the airport had been sad. I keenly felt the distance between Moscow and Ussurisk. If I had only known that tomorrow I would be even farther away—but still in Moscow—at the Lubyanka in the embraces of the KGB; but I did not even entertain the possibility. Zinaida seemed to, however. During the excitement at the bus station she had fallen silent and hidden her eyes, pressing her head against my shoulder.

Finally I was in the air, beginning the nine hours of nonstop flight to Khabarovsk. My place in a four-seated compartment by chance was shared with the correspondent and the two young men who had carried my luggage in Moscow. The buffoonery had ceased. We all sat there silently. I went to sleep and woke to see that we were flying over clouds. It was still two hours to Khabarovsk. Time passed. When we landed, the passengers rushed to the exit. I, too, got up.

"Why are you in such a rush? Let those who are in a hurry go first," cried the correspondent. As we approached Khabarovsk, he had resumed his joking. Paying no attention to him I quietly pressed toward the exit. He was right behind me, always peering over my left shoulder. When we emerged on the upper landing of the stairs, the correspondent said, "They are probably meeting you, comrade Major General!"

"No one is meeting me here," I said.

"But they are," he persisted. "That major over there is probably meeting you."

I looked in the direction he was pointing and saw the commandant of Khabarovsk, who waved and smiled, met me at the bottom step, saluted, asked for my baggage checks, and gave them to the sergeant behind him. He invited me to come into the room reserved for deputies of the Supreme Soviet, so that I could rest while someone brought my things. He told me that I was being met on the orders of the chief of staff of the military district.

When I entered the deputies' room I found the spirit of the KGB. In the center of an enormous hall stood a general—the chief of the counterintelligence branch (Smersh). Four interrogators from counterintelligence and the prosecutor's office sat at small tables. Another ten stood in groups at the edges of the room.

"Pyotr Grigoryevich!" proclaimed the chief of counterintelligence, "I must carry out an unpleasant task in fulfillment of my service duties. Here is a telegram from the Committee on State Security [the KGB]. Read it."

It said: "We have information that Major General Grigorenko is carrying anti-Soviet materials. You are to search General P. G. Grigorenko and if such materials are found on him you are to seize them and send them to Moscow."

I signed the telegram, confirming that I had been made acquainted with its contents, and the search began. All they took was the typewriter, claiming that they had information to the effect that anti-Soviet materials had been printed on it. They found nothing else of a criminal nature on me. I learned later that our Moscow apartment was searched simultaneously and that all the undistributed leaflets were confiscated.

Next the counterintelligence chief declared that, though it was unpleasant, he had one more duty to carry out. He handed me a second telegram, which read: "You are to detain Major General Grigorenko and to send him by return trip back to Moscow." He said, "I have the right to put you, as an arrested person, in a cell for preliminary detention, but I am not going to do that. Instead I will arrange for you to spend the night in one of the service rooms of our branch; I have ordered your lunch in our own dining hall."

After lunch, I was led to a cot in a private room and was told, "You can lie down if you want right now. Someone will be on duty all night in your room. And the light will be on all night too. Those are our regulations."

I was afraid that after what I had just been through I would not be able to sleep; that these bastards would think I was frightened by my arrest, though this was not true. When they had handed me the first telegram, I had known I was being arrested, and I was ready for it. Everything had seemed to be taking place somewhere outside of me. Only once had I come to life, when the thought occurred to me: "What will happen to the gift from my son and his bride to her parents?" I had asked the question of the chief of counterintelligence, who'd replied that by sending the package he would be breaking the law (the possessions of an arrested person are supposed to stay with him); but he agreed to do it for me.

My fears about sleeping amounted to nothing. I had always been able to sleep under any conditions and the habit did not fail me now. No sooner did my head touch the pillow than I was out.

The next morning they took me to the airport. I was put on the plane before the other passengers, and I met the same young men who had accompanied me the day before.

We all sat in the same positions as on the flight to Khabarovsk. As if by orders, the buffoons had fallen silent. I myself had no desire to joke. But I hadn't been able to restrain myself when I saw the correspondent for the first time that morning. He was dressed in a magnificent civilian suit and he was clean-shaven and had changed the style of his hair.

"Whatever did you do with your fine northern outfit?" I asked him.

He looked at me in astonishment and said, "What outfit? You must be confusing me with someone. . . ."

"I'm confusing nothing, citizen correspondent. I am merely sorry that such a remarkable wielder of the pen did not travel on to his destination, and that therefore Kamchatka and Magadan will not be worthily depicted in the central press."

In reply he merely shrugged. For some reason he was not supposed to admit to his false identity. The appearances of the other young men had also been altered but less radically than the correspondent's.

The nine-hour flight was uneventful. I slept for most of it, not wanting to think about the future; nor did the past come to mind as I slept. At Vnukovo Airport, I was led out after all the passengers and packed into one of four cars. The correspondent sat in the front seat with the driver. I sat in the back between the two other young men. I had been hoping to see someone familiar, so that I could shout to them to let my family know about my arrest. Since chances were good that no one I knew would be present, I decided to shout out my name and address to no one in particular. Surely someone had done so before, because the "servants of the people" who were escorting me took great pains to isolate me.

We dashed along the highway and then through Moscow without stopping once. In Dzerzhinsky Square we drove to the back of the Lubyanka Internal Prison and pulled up to a pair of enormous iron gates. A toot of the horn, and the gates opened. We drove in, proceeding on through several small internal courts, got out, and, via stairways, passages, and an elevator, walked to the main building. There they took me into an interrogation room that contained nothing but a small writing table by the window and a stool in the center of the room.

"Sit down!" I was told. I picked up the stool, placed it against a wall, and sat down with my back up against the wall.

"That's impermissible! It's forbidden to move a stool," my escort cried out. I ignored his outcry.

"Citizen! It's forbidden to move the stool!"

"To whom are you talking?"

"To you . . . citizen . . . general."

"I am not moving it. I put it where it was more comfortable for me, and I am sitting."

A sergeant major entered and reported that he had arrived to guard the prisoner. My former escorts left. I remained sitting with my back to the wall. The sergeant major made no demands of me. He stood almost motionless at the door for about six hours. During that time I got up more than once, walked back and forth, sat down again, and moved the stool to a new place. He said nothing. At 4:00 P.M. they brought me lunch—a decent one.

By what I estimated to be seven o'clock I was led out of the room and down a broad, carpeted corridor into a large office where there were two men in civilian clothes—one I recognized from his portrait: Semichastny, chairman of the KGB—and two men in uniform. The second man in civilian clothes stood beside an armchair behind a large writing desk. He introduced those present. In addition to Semichastny there was his first deputy, Lieutenant General Zakharov; and the interrogator, Lieutenant Colonel Kantov. The speaker was Major General Bannikov. As I looked at him I thought that his name really should be Barinov—from the word "barin," meaning a gentleman landowner of tsarist times. His corpulence, his graying hair, and his contemptuous glance all suggested a barin. His own name suggested a bath attendant—there was something to be said for that as well.

All of us, obeying the broad, gentlemanly gesture of Bannikov, had seated ourselves: Zakharov and Kantov, behind the long table, on the side toward the window; I, in the middle on the opposite side. Bannikov occupied the armchair and Semichastny sat by one of the windows that opened out on Dzerzhinsky Square.

"Well, just what have you gotten yourself into?" asked Semichastny, directing himself to me.

"I don't understand your question."

"What is there to understand? You probably think that we don't know anything. Show us, please, Georgy Petrovich." Kantov pushed over to me several leaflets that appeared to have been picked up off the streets or torn off walls.

"Are you going to deny your part in this activity?" Semichastny again directed himself to me.

"No! I mean to deny the right of the KGB to participate in the consideration of this matter."

"How so?" he exclaimed with surprise.

"Very simply. I have a conflict with *my* party. And I insist on my lawful right as a member of the party. Inasmuch as people are trying to hinder me in this by unlawful, nonparty methods, I am intensifying the struggle. Perhaps in some way I have overstepped the bounds permitted by the party statutes. For this the party can punish me. But what do the police have to do with this? This is purely a party affair."

There was an awkward silence. Zakharov broke it. "Pyotr Grigoryevich, it is unforgivable for you to speak in such a way. You declare yourself a Leninist, and Lenin says that the Cheka is first of all an organ of the party."

"This does not apply to you. In the first place, you are not the Cheka but the KGB. In the second place, yes, Lenin said that, but he also affirmed that if the Cheka retained the character of the secret police it would degenerate into an ordinary counterintelligence agency. And in fact we saw this happen in Stalin's time."

Semichastny collected himself. "You are going very far afield there. All that is theory. But you are not conducting a theoretical argument. You have created an underground organization which has set itself the task of overthrowing the Soviet government. Dealing with that is the task of the organs of state security and not of party commissions."

"You are exaggerating. I did not create an organization which set as its purpose the overthrow by force of the existing structure. I created an organization for the dissemination of undistorted Leninism, for the exposure of its falsifiers."

Semichastny said, "If the matter only concerned propaganda of Leninism why have you chosen to go underground? Teach it within the system of party and political education and at meetings."

"You know yourself that this is impossible. That Leninism has to be preached from the underground is best evidenced by the fact that the present party leadership has departed from Leninist positions and thereby lost the right to leadership of the party. Thus Communist-Leninists have the right to struggle against that leadership."

"Pyotr Grigoryevich!" Bannikov interrupted. "No matter what you say, the fact of the matter is that you were engaged in anti-Soviet activity. You created an underground organization which, basing itself on garbled Leninist theses, wants to achieve the removal of the present Soviet structure. It is not important what methods it wishes to use to attain this end. Today you may use peaceful means, but tomorrow it could come also to violence. It is not necessary now to get ourselves deep into theoretical intricacies. Let's simply set forth what is indubitable. You are a meritorious man who took offense at the party and adopted a mistaken course.

"I am not saying that you didn't have cause to take offense. Without doubt you were treated unjustly. But no good can result from your continuing to nurse your wounds. We will give full speed to your case, and within the Soviet Union not one single judge would find you guilty. You have a family. You have sons with their lives ahead of them, and your fate cannot but affect their fate. You and your wife are not young people. What good will result from you going to camp, losing your rank as general, and all your privileges? It is in your own best interest not to let the case go forward, to find a reasonable way of bringing it to an end before it ever begins. Now you are only a detained person and you will retain that status for two more days. We can free a detained person quite simply. And this person even has a right to deny the fact that he was ever arrested. During the subsequent seven days, when you become a suspect, things will be more difficult. Therefore I am proposing to you that you act immediately, without delay. It's in your own interests."

"I don't know what you are proposing to me. But I am convinced that you can offer me nothing good. You said that I was mistreated. I could forgive the party for mistreatment. I would not undertake a struggle against the party because of a personal offense. But they wished to crush me and force me to serve an unjust cause. I believe that right now they are also trying to manipulate me by threatening me with imprisonment and telling me I have the power to avoid it. But in actual fact I believe I will in any case have to suffer through the categories of suspect and accused and defendant in court and sentenced—

and in addition have to swallow a humiliating repentance and pardon."

"Why obligatorily suspect people of baseness?"

"It's not that I suspect but that I see. You utter starry-eyed words and act illegally. But I know my rights. A general may neither be arrested nor detained without the permission of the Council of Ministers of the USSR, and you have detained me and you want to make some sort of a deal with me by frightening me with what lies ahead. An honest deed is never begun with deceit."

Once again Semichastny intervened. "Georgy Petrovich, show him."

Kantov got up, came over to me, and put in front of me an open file folder. I read: "A Decree of the Council of Ministers of the USSR: To permit the KGB to arrest Major General Pyotr Grigoryevich Grigorenko, born in 1907 in the village of Borisovka, the Maritime District of Zaporozhe Province of the Ukrainian Republic."

I said, "Still, citizen Bannikov, you have been authorized to arrest me, not to detain me for three days. So let's each of us busy himself with his own business. My business is to prove my innocence. I think that if each of us executes his duty honorably then I shall be the one to succeed. And if not, then I will travel the whole path—from being detained, to being sentenced, to being imprisoned. This will be the final proof of the betrayal of Lenin's heritage by the leadership."

While I was talking, Semichastny made a sign to Kantov, who opened the door and admitted the sergeant major. "Do you have any requests?" Semichastny asked me.

"Yes, I ask you to have my wife send me a civilian suit. I don't want to strut around prison in a general's uniform."

"We can find civilian clothing here."

"I also will not put on a prison uniform. I am not yet sentenced."

"Very well! Your request will be considered."

I was relieved to realize that my wife might soon learn of my whereabouts.

"Do you have any other requests?" Semichastny asked again.

"No!" I replied.

"To the cell with him," Semichastny said quietly, looking at Bannikov.

The latter nodded and said to the sergeant major, "Take him away."

I wondered if there was really any alternative. If I had behaved differently, would it have been possible for me not to spend the night in a cell? No! Common sense cast aside this question. Most likely this was all a game. They wanted to break my will, to force me to make an agreement with the prosecution. They would not get it. I would not endure the humiliation of a false repentance!

Ten minutes later I was in cell number 76. (The Lubyanka Internal Prison was still in operation at this time.) I thought of my wife and what she must be going through. Later, when she stood outside that prison in defense of me and other prisoners of conscience, I felt bitter . . . and ashamed.

The day after being imprisoned I had my first meeting with Kantov, the interrogator. He was in his mid-forties and came from a poor peasant family in northern Russia. I imagine that he had a difficult childhood and that he climbed the ladder ruthlessly. Such men serve with particular devotion. They cling to an advantageous position with all their strength and are willing to do anything for the sake of advancement. Kantov had not yet, however, totally quelled the voice of his conscience. Whenever I demonstrated with particular conviction the falsity and the inhumanity of the cause he was upholding, he became embarrassed and blushed, continuing, nonetheless, to hold to his own point.

At our first encounter he asked all the routine questions about autobiographical details, party, service and scientific experience. As we ended he said that he had not planned official questions for the near future; he merely wanted to chat about the leaflets. In order to conduct a succcessful investigation, he considered it requisite to understand the beliefs of the person being interrogated. I told him that it was a matter of indifference to me how he conducted the interrogation. I did not consider myself to be a criminal and I was ready to prove this in any way presented to me.

And so our conversations began. Kantov was skilled at questioning and was a first-class listener. I tried hard to set forth my views intelligently. In several improvised lectures I discoursed on the essence of Leninist teachings about the state, basing what I said on "The State and Revolution" and casting aside the version of the state as a weapon, which came from Lenin's lecture "On the State." I described in detail the Soviet state, demonstrating its oppressive role and its bureaucratic structure. From my point of view everything seemed to be proceeding well. I pondered the probable themes of our conversations in advance and prepared for possible questions. I was ready to give an answer to most of them.

One question concerned my leaflet "The Dispersal by Shooting of the Workers' Demonstration at Novocherkassk." I was expecting to be asked: "What makes you think that someone was fired upon at Novocherkassk and that there was an antigovernment demonstration there?" This question seemed inevitable. What could I reply? I believed absolutely everything I had been told by an acquaintance who had seen it with his own eyes and who had also read official reports on the events. I was unable to name that person—just as I cannot name him now. Even today he might suffer if the authorities learned he had disseminated information on the events at Novocherkassk. In considering my reply, I concluded that the only way I could answer was as follows: "I am convinced that everything took place exactly as I described it in my leaflet. I cannot name my sources because that would be a violation of their security. If you are in disagreement with my descripion, let us go and conduct a public investigation with my participation."

I didn't have to resort to this. Georgy Petrovich did not risk denying the shooting. He put his question this way: "You write in your third leaflet that the troops shot down workers in Novocherkassk, but, after all, the whole matter was quite different than you say it was."

"How?"

"Well . . . violations of public order had taken place."

"There were violations of public order *in your version,* but in actual fact the Novocherkassk workers went out on the streets *in a peaceful fashion.* If there were hooligan or terrorist gangs which could only be dealt with with guns, why was this not reported in the press?"

"It was reported. . . ."

"Where? In what newspaper? I did not read any such reports anywhere."

"In the local press," said Kantov, quite embarrassed, and added, "They convicted the troublemakers. And the local press reported it. . . ."

"Well, of course! They merely finished beating to death those who had not been shot on the streets. I know all about that. The local press briefly reported that there had been a trial of the initiators of public disorders and that fifteen persons were convicted in order to frighten the entire population of the city. Out of the fifteen, nine were sentenced to execution and the sentences were carried out. What interests me is not that—but who was guilty of firing upon a demonstration; who was guilty of the murder of several hundred people, including women and children. And in particular I would like to know why the members of the Politburo—Miloyan and Kozlov—preferred bullets to words in their communications with the workers. This was a heinous crime. The bloodshed on the streets of Novocherkassk, Tbilisi, Temir-Tau, Priluki, Alexandrovo and other cities, has become an insurmountable obstacle between the party and the workers."

My success with this most dangerous question inspired me and in all subsequent conversations I conducted myself with self-assurance. Feeling myself victorious, I did not restrain myself and set forth everything I thought and dreamed about. I saw my interrogator not as an enemy but as a soldier who was sincerely confused and who I must help to see the truth. It never entered my head that these restrained conversations were leading toward my own civil death. On the contrary, the further we went the more self-assured I became. After each talk I said words to this effect: "You can see there are no bases for the investigation. You will become confused; in fact, you already are in a blind alley. You have nothing with which to begin the investigation."

Today I am ashamed to recollect what a rooster I must have seemed at the time. I suffered a great deal before I realized that I had no sympathizers at Lubyanka, that not a single person I dealt with was guided by conscience and honesty, and that to feel oneself superior to the interrogator, to hope to be able to outwit him in the investigation is, at the very least, a mistake. No matter how inexperienced and unintelligent the interrogator is, he is more powerful than the person under investigation. In the first place, he is working in an environment that favors him. He is not torn from his regular milieu and isolated from the entire world. In the second place, he conducts the questioning in accordance with a previously conceived plan. He ponders the formulation of each question, and often his most innocent questions have a purpose far beyond their appearance, a purpose that must always remain unknown to the person under investigation. Thirdly, the interrogator knows what is going on outside the interrogation room. He knows every aspect of the case and each witness's testimony. The person under investigation is totally ignorant of such facts and developments. For that matter, the interrogator can intentionally lead astray the person under investigation.

Taking all of this into consideration, many civil rights advocates in the Soviet Union have come to the conclusion that in investigations of political cases the only correct tactic is not to give testimony, not to help the investigation prepare a falsified trial. I did not understand this at the time. I was still a Communist, and I believed that the officials of the investigatory and judicial branches were Communists. Not until 1965 did I learn that all my statements had been taped and that the tapes had been heard by all the Politburo members.

There is no question that my case earned Kantov a promotion. During the time I spent in the special psychiatric hospital he rose in rank from lieutenant colonel to major general.

On March 10 Kantov summoned me, and with an indifferent expression on his face—as if the matter was unimportant—he put before me a typewritten sheet and said, "Acquaint yourself, if you please, with this decree and sign it."

At a glance I read the heading: "A decree on the dispatch of Pyotr Grigoryevich Grigorenko to ambulatory psychiatric diagnosis in the Serbsky Scientific Research Institute for Forensic Psychiatry."

I read no further, but raised my eyes to the interrogator and quietly and reproachfully said, "This means they found a way out of that blind alley?"

Georgy Petrovich blushed and with fake horror cried out, "Pyotr Grigoryevich, what are you thinking! That's just an empty formality. I haven't the slightest doubt that you are psychologically normal. And I would not have sent you to diagnosis at all, had it not been written in your medical record that you had experienced traumatic cerebropathy.*But since that's the case, it is my duty to send you for a checkup. Without it, the court will refuse to accept the case."

---

*As I have mentioned, in actuality I experienced shell shock.

"In order to present a case to a court, you must first of all have a case. And I have not yet been questioned on the essence of the matter, nor has any proof been presented that I am guilty. And yet you are already stating that I may be insane."

"I can have a diagnosis made at any stage of the investigation. In any case this is an ambulatory diagnosis—you will be returned here within several hours and we will then continue the investigation."

"You don't believe yourself what you are saying. You and I will not meet again—you have nothing with which to charge me."

"You are wrong, Pyotr Grigoryevich. You and I will be working together for a long time yet and we will clarify all of the questions."

"All right!" I said. I took the pen and right across the lines of the decree (which I still had not read), I wrote: "I am outraged to the bottom of my heart by the dispatch to an insane asylum of a psychologically healthy man. This diagnosis is a formality. The KGB has decided, and the psychiatrists will obey."

Kantov, seeing that instead of signing I had begun to write, ran over to me but did not try to grab away the paper. He only said, "Why did you do that? It isn't going to help you."

In all likelihood, even for such a man as he it was not easy to send a healthy person to an insane asylum.

On March 12—thirty-six days after my arrest—a Black Maria from the Lubyanka delivered me to the Serbsky Institute. My home was not more than a ten-minute walk. Yet it had never seemed so distant. The ambulatory diagnosis consisted of my future doctor and diagnostician, Margarita Feliksovna Taltse, asking me several autobiographical questions and several extremely stupid political questions and thereupon writing on my chart: "He requires in-patient investigation."

I had never felt a more intense enmity toward a person in my life. Margarita Feliksovna was a peroxide-blond with a long, dry face, nasty eyes, and thin lips. She reminded me of a skinned cat. Only with extreme difficulty was I able to suppress my hostility toward her; and my revulsion grew constantly. I stayed at the Serbsky Institute from March 12 to April 19, 1964, and conversations with her are my most painful recollections of that time. She constantly pried, wrote incessantly in her notebook, and was forever asking multitudes of stupid questions about my leaflets. Her political outlook was moronic and she was incapable of grasping anything above the simplest statements. She asked the same questions over and over again, listening each time to my same answer and never comprehending what I was saying. Instead she would arrive at a conjecture comprehensible to her alone and then jot a few words in her notebook.

Her general stupidity wore me down. It was not just her lack of understanding but the fact that she was incapable of comprehending the significance of moral values. I spent hours attempting to prove to her that it was impossible to enjoy the good things of life if all around you people were living in poverty.

Dozens of times she asked: "But just what was it that you needed—given your high salary and your special privileges? What affair was it of yours?"

All my replies were evaluated as the judgments of an abnormal person. She also could not understand historical analogies, and she evaluated them only in psychiatric terms. If I referred to Chernyshevsky she would write: "He compares himself to Chernyshevsky." If I referred to Lenin she would write: "He compares himself to Lenin."

I became unbelievably fatigued after such sessions. They were tortures capable of driving a man insane. She simply existed in some other mental space.

On one occasion, after several hours of torturous conversation with Taltse, I was sitting with my back to her, my hand supporting my head, my eyes shut, trying to rest. She was writing in her notebook. Suddenly her revolting voice creaked out, "Nonetheless, Pyotr Grigoryevich, I cannot understand you fully. You have been close to many highly respected people. It is only natural that if you did not respect someone before, then you do not now. But you even speak disrespectfully of Nikita Sergeyevich Khrushchev *himself.* Nikita Khrushchev *himself!* How can that be, Pyotr Grigoryevich?"

Irritated, I decided that if this hen would listen to nothing I said, then at least I could tell her something that would shock her. And so I said, firmly and deliberately, "So what is Nikita Sergeyevich Khrushchev? He is an *ordinary zero,* who accidentally became the head of state. But he will not remain in power long. He'll be out by this autumn."

This was something she could grasp. In the first place, this was lack of respect for the supreme leader of the state. I had called him a zero—which meant that I considered myself superior. And in the second place—and this was entered duly in the history of the illness—I was prophesying: I was predicting that Nikita Khrushchev would soon be removed from power. Her record of this actually played a decisive role in my premature release.

Any thinking person, even one who definitely thought me insane, would have asked why I thought Nikita would soon lose power, would have wanted me to explain. If Taltse had been normal and had pressed me for further details, she would have realized that this was not an uninformed prophecy but an intelligent conclusion based on an estimate of the political situation in the country. Nikita's libertarian experiment, in particular his constant attempts to shuffle those at the higher levels, made him persona non grata in the highest levels of the bureaucracy. Despite the fact that he was the only human being in the whole post-Stalin galaxy of leaders, Nikita did not have the support of the people. His fate, one could say, had already been decided. The only question was when he would be removed, and the best time was autumn—after the harvest. If it was a good harvest, supplies would be more plentiful and the new rulers would take credit for the changes. If the harvest was poor, they would blame Khrushchev's libertarianism. Any normal person would have understood this.

Without a doubt Taltse's insensateness wore me out, and her diagnosis seriously harmed my psyche. Paradoxically, my experience at the Serbsky Institute strengthened my spirit. Earlier I had become convinced that dissatisfaction was more common among educated people than among the uneducated. But at the institute I heard people from various localities, social groups, and professions express approximately the same dissatisfaction I did.

All these people had been acting in isolation, but when circumstances brought us together, we immediately understood one another. Every evening we would gather on the floor in my room and I would talk to them about politics. The initiator of these meetings was a fifty-year-old professional prisoner who had spent thirty-four years in children's colonies, camps, and prisons. He was functionally illiterate and could only read by spelling things out laboriously; he wrote in a scrawl. But he was extremely inquisitive. During our conversations he stared at me and showered me with questions. It was clear to me that had these people met outside, they would have become friends. Yet they would not have met, because conditions would not have permitted them to find those who thought like them. In ordinary life, the lie reigned supreme. Fearful of repression, people would not risk expressing their disagreement with the ruling elite. So they tried to seek like-thinkers by using leaflets.

During this time I began experiencing a doubt: Was it right to have gone into the underground? I suspected I would not find people who thought like me there. I had to look for like-minded people among the population as a whole.

My speech at the party conference had not been particularly biting. In comparison, my leaflets were profound political works. And the results?—the entire country learned of my party conference speech almost immediately. More than half the conference delegates sent letters of protest to Moscow. Many of my old service comrades wrote me letters of congratulation. In the Far East, all knew of my speech and greeted me with sympathy. As for the leaflets, on the other hand, at the most several dozen people had known about them; and all copies had been destroyed.

My conclusion was that whoever wanted to struggle against tyranny had to destroy within himself the fear of tyranny. He had to take up his cross and climb Golgotha. Let people see him, and in them the desire to take part in his march will awaken. Let others see those who follow him and they themselves will follow. Open speeches attract new forces, whereas retreat into the underground increases the danger of arrest without guaranteeing any growth in numbers. Such new convictions might have prompted me to tell my captors that I considered my earlier actions misguided. I would not have been lying; I also would have been opening up an almost certain path to liberation. I never admitted my change of mind, however, and thank God. I cannot imagine where they would have hidden me away if I had mentioned to Kantov my new preference for open struggle.

On April 19, 1964, a commission of experts presided over by Academician Snezhevsky, with the special participation of a Professor named Lunts, determined that I was insane. They did not, of course, tell me this, but I had no doubts that the commission's decision would confirm previous ones. However, I wanted to hear this directly and therefore asked for a meeting with Lunts and Taltse. Neither received me. Previously they had seen me any time I so requested. It was probably to avoid such an encounter that they sent me to prison the next morning.

After being told the decision I did not return to the Lubyanka. They had closed it down and thus took me instead to Lefortovo, where I was put in cell number 25. I was taken to neither questionings nor conversations. I could read and think in peace. I demanded more walks in the fresh air and received permission to go from one to two hours. A few days after I entered Lefortovo they allowed me a visit with my wife.

The visit was unusual. After lunch they called me out for a walk. A few minutes later I felt ill. I asked them to take me to my cell. They said they would, but didn't. I felt I was going to fall asleep while I was in motion. Once again I asked them to take me to my cell. Again they did not do so. Just before the end of the walk period, the escort guard appeared and led me away. On the way to my cell we encountered the duty officer. He announced, "You have a visitor."

I tried to pull myself together as best I could and went along with them. I remember nothing about the visit; nor do I remember returning to my cell. Later my wife told me that I made grimaces, that I shouted out "Rot front!" and jerked like a marionette. At one point I tossed a note to her, which fell short. Bending in front of the guard, I picked up the paper and reached into her pocket. When the meeting came to an end the guard demanded the note of her. She gave him something but found when she returned home that she had the note. I don't have the right to disclose the art of this deception; while there are still prisoners they must be allowed their special secrets.

They then informed my wife that she had been invited to see the interrogator. At that moment it dawned upon her that our visit had been staged. The interrogator would want to know what she thought. Did she now believe that her husband was insane? Understanding this, she nearly hurled herself upon the interrogator when she entered his office, demanding to know what they had done to me and whether they had given me drugs. When she said that she was going to complain—to let the whole world know—the interrogator offered to let her visit me again the next day.

The next visit went very well. My wife told me a great deal of family news. I kept looking at her; I felt I couldn't get enough of seeing her. Then she asked me, "Do you remember my last visit?"

"No! I went to sleep afterward, and in the morning everything that had happened the day before, beginning with my walk, seemed to have happened in a fog. I remember asking them to take me inside. Everything else is like a dream—I don't know whether it really happened or not."

It was at this visit that my wife told me I had been declared insane.

If judged by events, my life flowed on monotonously, but a human being lives not by events alone. Always, and especially in prison, one is introspective, concerned with the past, relationships, politics, and the spiritual world. More and more, I returned to the question of defense against the tyranny of the ruling authorities. My belief that it is possible to achieve something only by open and daring struggle grew even stronger. People love truth, nobility, and honor. They follow with fascination the example of a bold, heroic battle for justice and good; against evil, falsehood, and deceit. It is the duty of all who are capable to openly set such an example. Then the army of the heroic, honorable, and just will grow.

What form of organization must this movement take? I thought about this for a long time and then firmly decided, none at all. In the first place, as soon as even small groups came together they would be liquidated by the KGB. In the second place, I did not want to belong to a party. I was through with parties! Each assures the death of the cause it stands for. A party is a struggle for power; it replaces communication with bureaucratic intrigues, and is necessary simply as a forum in which to struggle against what you would never accept for yourself.

Such thoughts were not new to me. The Alliance for Struggle for the Rebirth of Leninism was an unorganized organization. In essence I continued to support the concept of a chain—except that the chains I now foresaw would not be secret and would unite all honest, just, courageous people on the basis of love and on the basis of the inseparable rights given us by God.

In the prison quiet the past unfolds before the mind's eye in an incessant stream. Books are read in a new way: What interests you is not so much the plot as the author's philosophy, and light reading simply does not satisfy. One takes a different attitude toward events. Nothing is insignificant.

My first evening at Lefortovo prison, I heard a bell that aroused memories of my childhood, my father, my Uncle Alexander, Father Vladimir, Sima, Valya, church holidays, and in particular Christmas, Easter, and church services. At the time I was an agnostic—indifferent to the teachings of religion. Now I heard the voice of the church. During the war I had spent almost two months in the chief military hospital, in the very same district in which I was now serving time in prison. Then I had not heard the bells. When I heard them ringing for the first time, I was astonished. I wanted so much to be in that church. No, I did not believe in God, but in my heart that church was a living being emitting a living voice. Right then I decided that if I was freed, I would go there. (I did so after my release. A friend, Grigory Alexandrovich Pavlov, told me that the bells I'd heard were from the Church of Peter and Paul, a church built by Peter the Great for soldiers. Together we attended a beautiful service.) While in Lefortovo I had come to know when the bells would ring and would put everything else aside to listen. The first chime always brought blessedness into my soul, and each time the ringing stopped I was terribly sad.

One day, shortly after breakfast, my cell door opened and a short, frail, bearded man, who looked to be in his early twenties, entered. He told me his name was Alyosha Dobrovolsky, then ran all about the cell, inspecting. Tossing his bag down on the cot furthest from the door, he asked in a barely audible voice, "Is this a hospital room?"

"I don't know," I replied.

"And what about you? Have you been judged insane or are you going to be tried?"

"I have been judged insane."

"What kind of bread do they give? Black or white?"

"White."

"Aha, so this is a hospital room. God be praised! I won't get sent to camp. That means I have been judged insane."

"Why are you so glad about it? Do you think an insane asylum is better?"

"Of course. In camp there is heavy work and bad food, and you sleep on boards in barracks where it is cold and they don't let you go to Moscow after you have served out your term. I've already been in camp. True—not in a severe regime camp. I got off with six months. This time, of course, as a repeater, they are going to keep me in longer and probably send me to a special hospital—but nonetheless not to camp."

We spent more than a month in the same cell. When he was released from the insane asylum shortly after me, Alyosha Dobrovolsky helped me a great deal. He introduced me to such outstanding civil rights defenders as Vladimir Bukovsky, Aleksandr Ginzburg, and Yuri Galanskov. But Alyosha had a weak little soul, despite the fact that he used to pray very energetically in the cell, crossing himself and whispering prayers. The KGB understood him. They knew he was afraid of camp and when he was arrested for the third time they did not classify him as insane. He broke down. In court he gave false testimony against Ginzburg and Galanskov and as a reward received a short term of two years. At the end of his term, he left the movement.

The time I spent in Lefortovo prison, from April 20 to August 14, 1964, was one of spiritual rebirth and of intensive liberation from communist habits and ideas. I thought every day about the system of psychiatric pressure and soon became firmly convinced that there was a secretly authorized plan for the transformation of dissidents from the Soviet system into lunatics.

On one occasion, while taking a walk, Alyosha and I heard: "You're young and healthy and you sit up there on a watchtower like a poll parrot. Do you at least understand whom you are guarding?"

I would have known this voice anywhere. It came from the opposite end of the court, and from such a distance even a shout might not be clear. This particular person, though, had a voice like a foghorn. It was the bookkeeper at the Serbsky Institute, Borovik. At the institute I had predicted to him that he would be imprisoned in an insane asylum. He had become indignant and declared that obviously I thought he was crazy. I insisted that he would be sent to an insane asylum not because of illness, but because there was no case against him and because they could not risk freeing him He could not understand this. He'd returned from the expert's commission to proclaim to me, "Pyotr Grigoryevich, you were not right. They classified me as sane and are sending me to be tried in Kaliningrad."

"I am very glad for you," I replied. "I congratulate you from the bottom of my heart. But I don't understand."

Now in the court at Lefortovo he cried out, "The sons of bitches deceived me! They classified me as insane."

So my conviction that there was in effect a precisely worked out criminal psychiatric syndicate was strengthened. My own case bears witness to this. On June 17 I was tried by the military collegium of the Supreme Court of the USSR. Because I was "insane" I was not present at the trial; my wife, too, was barred. My "interests" at the trial were "represented" by a lawyer, Korostylov, who had never once seen me. This lackey could say anything at all—except statements that went against the KGB. As the theme of his speech he picked the Russian novelist Garshin's story about the lunatic who went mad over the red flower.

The trial was a mockery. Of the six people present—the chairman of the collegium, two members, the prosecutor, the lawyer, and an expert in psychiatry—only the latter had ever seen me. It was Professor Lunts—and it was unlawful for him to speak in such a capacity. Speeches concerning persons in the armed services are the duty of the chief psychiatrist of the armed forces. The man who held this position at the time, Major General of Medical Services, N. N. Timofeyev, was not even notified that there was an "insane" general within his area of responsibility. Thus I was "convicted" of insanity. On August 14 I was shipped off to the Leningrad Special Psychiatric Hospital. I arrived late at night.

Such hospitals as the Leningrad Special Psychiatric Hospital can be visited by anyone, even foreign tourists. The most trusting of them may even be impressed by it. In order to understand the system, though, we have to ask whether psychologically disturbed people are present at all within these institutions. A person is sent to a commission of psychiatric experts in the notorious Serbsky Institute of Forensic Psychiatry on the basis of a decree of an interrogator. This institute is nominally part of the system of the USSR's Ministry of Health, but I saw the head of the department in which I was diagnosed, Professor Lunts, coming to work in the uniform of a KGB general. True, when he made his rounds he always wore a white doctor's robe as well. However, I saw other doctors of this institute in KGB uniform also. Precisely what the relationship is between these KGB men and the Ministry of Health, I never managed to establish. Some claim that only those who diagnose political prisoners are connected to the KGB. In my opinion the influence of the KGB extends throughout the entire institute.

I arrived in the political department of the Serbsky Institute on March 12, 1964. Before this I had not heard of such a method of repression as the classification of a healthy person as insane—except in the case of Pyotr Chaadayev, the early nineteenth-century writer and philosopher. It never entered my mind that a system of "Chaadayevization" might exist in my own country. I came to understand this only from my own experience.

When I arrived in the department nine persons were there. During the next five to six days, two more arrived. Guided by my own concept of the purpose of the diagnoses, I predicted the diagnosis of all eleven persons. I based my predictions only on the character of each case—on whether the crime had been proven or not—and not on the individual's mental state. In my opinion, only three of us would be sent to an insane asylum: myself, Pavel Borovik, and Denis Grigoryev, an electrical repairman from Volgograd. Each of our three cases had no basis for prosecution, and no means by which the prosecution could manipulate it to its own advantage.

All the rest, I felt, would be judged normal, though three were very skillfully faking insanity and one, Tolya Yedamenko, was insane. I had doubts about only one person—Yuri Grimm, a crane operator from Moscow, who had disseminated a leaflet bearing a caricature of Khrushchev. I told him, "If you do not repent—you will go to the loony bin. If you do repent—you will go to camp." Several times a week the interrogator came to see him and promised him all kinds of benefits while trying to persuade him to "repent." In the end Yuri "repented" and got three years of severe regime camp. His case was particularly instructive to me. When I demanded to see my prosecutor and interrogator, I was told that during a period of diagnosis these two were not allowed access to the person in question. This rule was not observed with Grimm—a fact that clearly illustrates that the so-called institute was nothing more than a tool of the investigation.

All my predictions about patients with whom I had entered the hospital came true.

One particularly sad case at Leningrad was the engineer Pyotr Alexeyevich Lysak. For giving a speech at an assembly of students opposing the expulsion of several of them for political unreliability, he was put into the Leningrad Special Psychiatric Hospital. By the time I was admitted, he had been there seven years. Outrage at this horrible repression and his crippled life had flooded his mind. Every day he wrote angry letters that naturally went nowhere except into his medical case history, where they served as a basis for his further "treatment." (The Special Psychiatric Hospital rarely released those who refused to admit they were ill.) I kept trying to convince Pyotr Alexeyevich of this. But though in all other questions he had normal judgment, on this point he was not to be convinced. We argued and argued.

Once during a conversation, when Pyotr had gotten himself into a particular tizzy, I said with irritation, "Your judgment is so abnormal that I begin to have doubts of your normality."

He stopped, looked at me in a way I will be unable to forget till my dying day, and quietly, very quietly, in a bitter voice asked, "And do you really think it is possible to stay seven years here and remain normal?"

This is the horror of our inhuman system of forced treatment. A healthy person confined among the insane knows that in time he may become one of those he sees suffering around him. This is particularly frightening for people with sensitive psyches who suffer from insomnia, who are incapable of isolating themselves from a hospital's sounds.

The Special Psychiatric Hospital is located in the building of a former women's prison, alongside the notorious "Kresty"—Leningrad's principal prison for political prisoners. Here, as in regular prisons, there is a normal partition only on the ceilings of the cells. The middle of the building is hollow. From the corridor of the first floor you can see the glass skylight of the roof over the fifth floor. Sounds intensify and reverberate as they travel up and down this well. During Stalin's time, this fact was used to carry out psychic torture.

Luckily I was able to ignore most of what went on in the hospital. I could get used to and not notice the incessant tap-dancing over my head for whole days at a time—with intermissions coming only when the dancer fell into total insensibility. The one thing that I cannot forget and that sometimes awakened me at night was a wild nighttime cry, mingled with the sound of breaking glass. In sleep evidently the nerves are not protected from such stimuli. I can only imagine what a person must suffer whose nervous system takes in everything around him.

A patient in a Special Psychiatric Hospital does not have even the wretched rights of a prisoner. He has no rights. The doctors can do whatever they please to him and no one will interfere, no one will defend him. None of his complaints will ever leave the hospital. He has left only one hope—the honesty of the doctors.

I believe in the honesty of some doctors, but I also know that courage is necessary for this honesty to emerge. I said then and I still insist that *a system is no good* in which one's only hope is the *honesty and courage of the doctors.* There are many examples of dishonesty—simply in the practice of diagnosing completely healthy people as insane. If the authorities want to worsen the situations of those who are falsely imprisoned as insane, they will evict the honest doctors and replace them with those who, for the sake of money and position, are ready to do anything. And one must believe that among psychiatrist-physicians there are the same number of people like this as there are in other professions.

Another frustrating fact is the total lack of definition of the term a healthy person will get in a psychiatric hospital. The doctors have minimum norms. I do not know them. However, I do know that those who have committed a murder are held for at least five years. Supposedly, political prisoners are equated with murderers in this regard. But if political prisoners do not "repent" they can be detained longer.

But even the honesty of physicians does not help. The KGB maintains secret agents in these institutions and their denunciations play a no less important role than the conclusions of the physicians. There have been cases in which the court refuses to confirm a medical commission's recommendation for release from a hospital on the basis that the "term of treatment does not correspond to the seriousness of the crime committed."

Under such conditions as these, where rights are absent and release almost impossible, it is likely that individuals with vulnerable psyches will swiftly fall psychically ill. Such a person may first become suspicious of the physicians, believing that they are intentionally carrying out a scheme of treatment directed at destruction of the normal psyche. And he may very well be right.

One of the first problems that arose while I was in the Special Psychiatric Hospital was my dismissal from the army and the deprivation of my pension. Under the law, criminal cases against those diagnosed insane are dropped. Servicemen diagnosed as insane are retired to the reserve "without the right to wear uniform," or are enlisted in the reserves until cured. They are paid from the day of arrest to the day of trial, when their release from the army is formalized. On release they are paid a release bonus that amounts to two months' wages and a pension is designated for them in correspondence with the statutes on pensions of servicemen.

My wife was invited to the Chief Administration of Personnel where she was informed that the Council of Ministers of the USSR had deprived me of my rank as general. Because of this she was not entitled to any money at all. Before telling me this she told the chief of the hospital, Colonel Blinov, a specialist in servicemen's rights. He declared, "This is impossible. I ask you not to say anything to Pyotr Grigoryevich until I check this out myself."

But Zinaida told me. After hearing what she had to say, I said, "Our government is not rational. It is guided by malice, not mind. They sentenced me to insanity and many believed that I was. There is nothing worse than being insane—but by depriving me of my rank, they discredited that very punishment. Things have gotten better."

The entire hospital commiserated with me over my dismissal. Everyone was dismayed and the attitude toward me changed sharply: "How can they take bread away from a sick man?"

What had taken place was highway robbery. If a person against whom a criminal case has been dropped is supposed to be paid a salary, it should be paid. If a pension has been earned, then even if you have committed a crime, it must be paid. There is no such punishment on the books as deprival of a pension. This crudest of all tyrannies was so obvious and so infuriating that I decided to tell in full detail what had taken place. In conversations with the doctors I told them what had happened, and, emphasizing that my family consisted of helpless invalids who now had not a piece of bread, I implored them to release me as soon as possible for the sake of my family.

I later learned how I had come to be dismissed from someone who was present at the Council of Ministers meeting that decided my fate. According to my informant, Marshal Malinovsky placed in front of Khrushchev a legal decree for my retirement into the reserve without the right to wear a uniform. Khrushchev stared silently at the draft for a long time, and then said, "What is this? Grigorenko has reviled us in every way, and he gets off with a slap on the hand. He's now going to receive his pay for half a year, a general's pension, and he will continue to live at ease and spit on us."

"Not at all. He is in an insane asylum. This is for his family," Malinovsky declared.

"All the more so! The husband has misbehaved. His wife helped him. And now she gets a reward for all that. No, he has to be degraded."

"That's not in accordince with the law, Nikita Sergeyevich. The criminal case against him has been dropped. And he is already in the insane asylum," Malinovsky spoke again.

"What do you mean in accordance with the law! Does or does not the Council of Ministers have the right to deprive a man of his rank as general!"

"It does," Aleksei Kosygin (who was to succeed Khrushchev as premier of the Soviet Union) interrupted. "But if you wish to do that, the case should have been turned over to the courts. We changed it about entirely. We turned our right over to the military collegium, and it decided in favor of retirement from the army, without demotion."

"That's nonsense! The court did as much as it could. If it failed to complete the job, we can make use of our own right." Khrushchev was irritated. Turning to one of his assistants he ordered, "Draw up a decree on demotion." When they brought the decree, Khrushchev, just as he had the first time, stared at it for a long time. Finally he got up and said, "He doesn't deserve for me to sign it! You sign it!" He shoved it over to Kosygin—and Kosygin signed it.

The person who told me this story remarked, "This was a classic example of a Khrushchev ploy. He wanted to strike a blow—but in such a way as to stay himself on the sidelines. All Kosygin had to say was, 'No, Nikita Sergeyevich, this matter involves a violation of the law, so sign it yourself.' Khrushchev probably would not have signed it."

My demotion shook up the whole hospital. Blinov wrote several times pointing out the need to correct the "mistake" but the Ministry of Internal Affairs maintained silence. This angered the physicians. One of them told me, "They have deprived us of the moral right to retain anyone behind these walls. We are constantly being reproached with your case. They keep asking: Is he ill or is he healthy?"

In connection with this development, my own regime was relaxed a bit. When the chiefs were absent the nurses offered me real tea. The jailers directed political questions to me. I was permitted to go out in the corridor for two hours each day to do cleaning work. I was even allowed to polish the rails of the staircase between our second floor and the first floor. This represented great trust. For a few moments every day I was allowed in a different department. And there was a most strict taboo on communication between departments. But it was precisely such communication that commenced for me.

Several days after I had begun to polish the staircase handrails, I heard a whisper when I reached the first floor. It was Alyosha Dobrovolsky, who I had known in Lefortovo: "Hello, Pyotr Grigoryevich!"

From that day on there was not one evening when we did not succeed in exchanging a few words.

Alyosha had adapted astonishingly well to the insane asylum. How he managed to leave his ward at the very moment when I was on his floor, how he managed to avoid being observed, and where he concealed himself while he conversed with me, I could not imagine. During one of our encounters he said to me, "Tomorrow I am going to introduce you to Volodya Bukovsky. When I go to the toilet, take note of the man in a dark worker's suit who will be right behind me. That will be Volodya."

Alyosha had spoken to me about Volodya Bukovsky back in Lefortovo. He loved Volodya and had advised me that I must make his acquaintance soon. The very next day Volodya and I exchanged glances, nods, and gestures of greeting. Soon after we were able to meet in person. I, too, came to love this young man who was so courageous and enterprising. In the future we were destined to pursue our common cause together.

In October 1964 Khrushchev was removed from his posts. People were disturbed by this change of leadership. Every evening one person or another asked me whether it was for the better or the worse. I answered that on the whole things couldn't be worse—but that I could see no way open to an improvement. More likely, I commented, things would continue to deteriorate; at least, I was sure they would for me.

But on December 2 a commission from Moscow arrived to finalize the release of those who had recovered. I asked my doctor, Alexander Pavlovich, "Are you going to ask the commission to give me a hearing?"

"I can't, Pyotr Grigoryevich. To be granted a hearing by the commission, a patient has to have been under our observation for at least six months. And you have been here for less than four."

The next day, though, they came to get me, "to see the commission." They took me to the office of the chief of the hospital. In front of the office on the opposite side of the corridor was a bank of theater seats. I sat down in the one furthest to the left and didn't look to either side. However, after a time I noticed a man walk up to the bank of seats from the right side. I recognized him immediately. He had been present at the meeting of the commission of experts of Snezhevsky that had decided the question of my insanity at the Serbsky Institute. His name was Shestakovich and he had taken a degree as a candidate—later, doctor—of medical science. I pretended not to notice him.

He sat down next to me. "How do you do, Pyotr Grigoryevich!"

I turned my head in his direction. "How do you do!"

"Do you know me, Pyotr Grigoryevich?"

"You were one of the members of my commission at the Serbsky Institute."

"Well, well, well," he nodded cheerfully. "Can I ask you a few questions? Not to check up on anything but just as a matter of ordinary conversation. If you would prefer not to talk with me just tell me—I will not take offense."

"Why not? Go ahead."

"Tell me, how do you feel about your diagnosis? What is your opinion of it? Just be frank with me."

I thought for a moment before answering. If I told him the truth, he would be against releasing me at the commission meeting. I didn't know that he knew he would have no opportunity to be against my release. He was merely trying to measure what to be expect from me. I perceived him as a fully empowered member of the commission. Thus I was not willing to risk telling him the whole truth. At the same time I am unable to lie. I had to come up with a formula or reconciliation, and I did: "I consider that the members of the commission wanted to do the best they could for me when they reached their decision. . . ."

"That's precisely it. We were seeking a solution which was in your own interests."

He seemed happy to see I comprehended. But I had not finished yet. I continued, "But unfortunately while you were concerning yourself with me, you forgot to ask me what would be best for me. . . ."

"Now see here, Pyotr Grigoryevich, there's no question about that. Do you really think you would have been better off in camp? You are not a young man. Frankly, your health is not that good. In camp you would have suffered heavy labor, inadequate nourishment, and difficult living conditions. Then, too, you are a person who has earned honors—and if you had gone to camp you would have lost them all. Here you keep both your honors and your privileges. The fact that you were treated unlawfully is an entirely different matter. But that, I imagine, is going to be corrected in the near future."

"Nothing can wound a man so painfully as the deprivation of his human rights and dignities."

"Were you badly treated?" He looked at me with alarm.

"By no means! I will be eternally grateful to the personnel of the hospital for understanding my state and doing everything in their power to ease my situation. I am especially grateful to Alexander Pavlovich. He never gave me the feeling that he perceived me as a being with a damaged psyche. But I always felt that under the law I had been placed outside society. If the commission had asked my opinion I would not have elected insanity for the sake of any benefits whatsoever."

"You have never been in camp, and you don't have sufficient knowledge to reach a judgment on life there. I am convinced that in time you will realize that the way things were done was better for you. Let's end our dispute. I hope you will someday send us your thanks. Now I want to ask you one more question. And let me remind you again you do not have to answer if you don't want to."

"Ask me."

"In early April, in a conversation with our physician, you predicted that Nikita Sergeyevich Khrushchev would be removed from his positions in the autumn. On the basis of this statement she diagnosed prophecy as a psychic illness. Now that your prophecy has come true in full, we cannot, of course, leave that diagnosis intact. But if possible, please tell me how you determined that Khrushchev would be removed."

"So that's it," I thought. "They believe that the démarche against Khrushchev was planned and that I was involved in it. In that case, let them go on thinking as they do. I will not affirm their beliefs or refute them."

So I said, "You must understand that in addition to medicine and psychiatry, other sciences do exist, including social science. Social science in particular sometimes permits predictions of the course of events. I know a little about this science. You, however, are not familiar with it at all. Therefore I am afraid that it would be very difficult for me to explain to you how it was possible for me in April to foresee the events of October."

"Please, please, Pyotr Grigoryevich, you don't have to explain anything at all."

And with that he took his leave.

A few minutes later I was summoned to the hospital chief's office. Present in addition to Blinov, the chief himself, were my physician, Alexander Pavlovich, and a Major General of Medical Services with whom I was not acquainted. Blinov introduced me to him. He was the chief psychiatrist of the armed forces, chief of the psychiatry faculty of the Academy of Military Medicine, Timofeyev. Blinov and Alexander Pavlovich soon left, and Timofeyev and I were left by ourselves. He listened to my tale with great sympathy, saying that he had not known anything about my case. He also had not known about my incarceration in this hospital—even though he was the chairman of the local commission on release. He told me that he felt the matter had been concealed from him intentionally. That crafty courtier Blinov had undoubtedly received some instructions to this end, I thought to myself, although at the present he was depicting it all as an accident. Before we parted, Timofeyev asked me, "So will the release be on the basis of recovery or of annulment of the diagnosis?"

"Which will get me home faster?" I asked.

"There's no question at all that that would be via recovery. We can annul the diagnosis after release, too, but that takes much time. It would be better for you to wait out this procedure at home than while imprisoned. It will also be easier for me to work out your pension and other material matters that fall under my jurisdiction while you are still in my hands."

Timofeyev then told me that he had been informed of my case by my wife. Zinaida had heard of an official with the title of "chief psychiatrist of the armed forces"—Timofeyev. She got his telephone number and called him. He consented to meet with her, immediately took her story to heart, and actively joined in the defense of my interests.

Knowing our bureaucratic system well indeed, particularly the bureaucrats' fear of the top-level bosses, Zinaida had undertaken a furious campaign after the removal of Khrushchev. She had enlisted a group of our friends to phone her several times a day: "Zina! How are things going? Everything will be all right now. We know that Pyotr is a friend of Brezhnev. Have you approached him yet?"

"No, I don't want to try him right now. I will wait a while. I hope he will remember Pyotr by himself."

Zinaida had no doubts that the bugs that had been installed on our phone and in our entire apartment would nibble at this bait. The KGB would begin to check up on this "friendship" between Brezhnev and me, and the only definite fact they would come up with would be our joint war service. Friendship—

that was another question. But if my wife spoke of friendship, then she must
be basing it on something. One day she received a call: "Zinaida Mikhailovna,
this is the adjutant of General Petushkov, First Deputy Minister for Preservation of Public Order.* Would you be able to pay a call on the general?"

"Of course. I will leave immediately."

"By no means! Why should you tire yourself out on public transportation?
I will send you a car."

A short while later someone knocked at the door, and Zinaida heard a
hearty greeting: "Lieutenant Colonel Pyotr Mikhailovich Rybkin, chief psychiatrist of the Ministry for Preservation of Public Order, has been placed at
your orders. Where is your coat, Zinaida Mikhailovna?"

When Zinaida arrived at the Ministry, she got red-carpet treatment from
Petushkov himself, who welcomed her in his enormous office. "No one is to
smoke. Zinaida Mikhailovna has asthma." He began to express feigned indignation and astonishment: "Do you realize, Zinaida Mikhailovna, that I just
learned today that they are keeping a general in one of our hospitals. And that
his rights have been violated!"

"My, my, my!" Zinaida jokingly wagged her head.

"Yes. But I have now taken this matter under my personal supervision.
From now on please don't deal with anyone other than us."

This did not suit Zinaida. Rybkin had already told her that they could not
raise my case at the December commission meeting because six months had
not passed from the date of my arrival in the Leningrad Special Psychiatric
Hospital. Zinaida informed Timofeyev of this, and he quickly found a way
around this regulation—my case would be reviewed by an experts commission,
but the question would be decided not through release but through transfer
to a local commission. Only the central (Moscow) commission is empowered
to make releases. But if they have doubts or if, as in my case, the period of
observation had been less than the established minimum, the Moscow commission can turn the case over to a local commission. Then the latter has the right
to release the patient any time after the minimum period of incarceration. The
local commission could, for example, have released me February 15, but they
did not. Blinov, the experienced bureaucrat, did not want to take that risk.
I was too big a fish. He'd received no direct instructions to release me and
he didn't put much stock in the rumors about my alleged friendship with
Brezhnev. Like any careerist he didn't want to take the risk of being made
the fall guy by those in Moscow.

To everyone's dismay, Zinaida involved a completely new jursidiction. She
applied to the Military Collegium of the Supreme Court of the USSR for a
writ to free me from "compulsory treatment." Even Blinov was astonished.

_____
*Now the Ministry of Internal Affairs.

Despite his bureaucratic "wisdom," he now fell flat on his face. Under the law, compulsory treatment can be annulled—either on the basis of application by relatives to the court that sentenced the individual to such treatment, or on the basis of a representation by the Special Psychiatric Hospital to its local court. This is law. It is tradition, however, that releases only take place on the representation of the hospital. Relatives had completely given up trying to apply directly themselves.

Zinaida, however, applied—and the court accepted her application and then sent an inquiry to the hospital about my mental state. Blinov panicked. Why was the Supreme Court inquiring? Did it want me released quickly or kept in confinement longer? Blinov wasn't sure. In order not to trip himself up, he wrote in a manner described even by tsarist bureaucrats as double-talk—he tried to confuse the question of whether he was in favor of release or in favor of my continued confinement. He hoped the answer he would receive would clarify the matter. Then he would be able to respond more clearly himself.

Much to Blinov's surprise, one of the military collegium officials was sympathetic to Zinaida! He told her of Blinov's reply and said that with such a reply the case would get nowhere in court. She went to Rybkin, who immediately placed a call to Blinov. "Prokofy Vasilyevich! What's happened? Has Grigorenko gotten worse since we saw him in September?"

"Not at all!"

"Then why did you send a document to the Supreme Court which does not make it clear that we are recommending him for release?"

Zinaida could not hear Blinov's reply. Pyotr Mikhailovich replied in turn, "Yes, of course! Rewrite it immediately—and send it to the military collegium."

And Blinov was thereby convinced that these were instructions from the top.

On April 14, 1965, the military collegium decreed the annulment of my compulsory treatment. At their session, Major General Timofeyev spoke very effectively as an expert in favor of my release. The decision went into effect the twenty-second. On that day, my wife arrived at the hospital at exactly 10:00 A.M.

Little did we then know how lucky it was that I left the hospital immediately. About two weeks after my liberation Brezhnev actually did recollect me.

As he had promised, General Petushkov assembled all materials connected with the illegal deprivation of my rank of general, and in the presence of his minister presented these materials to Voronov, chairman of the Council of Ministers of the Russian Republic. Voronov expressed indignation at the tyranny—the "libertarianism"—of Khrushchev, and he ordered Petushkov and his minister to make this same report to Kosygin the next day. The material was reported to Kosygin, who ordered Petushkov to prepare by the next day a draft decree of the Council of Ministers on restoration of my rank, and my retirement from the army in accordance with established norms, including payment of pension and all other monies to which I was entitled.

That evening the "leaders"—including Brezhnev—met at Lenin Hills. Opportunity arose to cast a slur on Nikita Sergeyevich Khrushchev. Kosygin added, "Yes, and he behaved oddly with a certain general. They classified him as insane and sent him to a sanatorium. At the same time they took away his rank. I gave orders to prepare a draft of a decree and I want things put in correspondence with the law."

"Just a minute," Brezhnev interrupted him. "What general are you talking about? Grigorenko? I know him. Don't be in such a hurry. Show me the whole case folder."

He looked at it and asked, "Where's Grigorenko now?"

"At home."

"They let him out too soon. Too bad!"

My wife was right to get me released as soon as possible.

CHAPTER TWENTY-ONE

FIRST SWALLOWS OF FREEDOM

We did not immediately set off for Moscow. I was not ready to see other people. Zinaida was the only person in the world with whom I wanted to communicate. Even with her I was shy. I felt like I had arrived from another world and that it would take some time for me to get used to life in this new world. I was glad when Zinaida suggested that we stay in Leningrad several days.

I shall remember those days forever. Gradually I became accustomed to being with my wife. I bathed in her warm concern and ventured into public with her. By the end of our Leningrad vacation, I could visit stores, and I was even so bold sometimes as to pay for purchases myself. When we finally left for Moscow, the train did not bother me at all. I spent the entire trip looking out the windows, greedily taking in the swiftly changing pictures of nature and of human creativity. When we began passing the copses and country villages near Moscow my heart swelled and my eyes filled with tears.

The joy of meeting my children and friends, of being in the home in which I had known both happiness and grief, filled my first days in Moscow. But after this first bliss, an uncontrollable bitterness began to creep more and more

305

into my thoughts. Here I was, returning, having suffered, according to the official version, a serious illness, and the army to which I had given thirty-three of the best years of my life, in whose ranks I had twice shed my blood, and the country to which I had given *all* of my life, my mind, my energy, and my heart, did not utter even one word of sympathy, and did not give me one kopeck to help me subsist as even a pauper.

What if my wife had followed the foul advice of the deputy chief of the Personnel Administration, Colonel General Trotsenko, and had divorced me and remarried after my dismissal from the army? What if she, following the hints of advisers sent to her from the KGB, had made a deal with this organization, and after getting a pension for her first husband who had been killed in the Yezhov-Stalinist torture chambers, had renounced me? What if she had turned out to be just as helpless and unsuited to life as many of the wives of military men? What, then, would I have done? What would I have lived on, and how would my family have survived?

The "socialist" state did not think about these things or, rather, if it did, it thought about them with malicious pleasure. But we had all survived. For fifteen long months, Zinaida had supported the entire family with her sewing. She had also managed to visit me and bring me food and she had planned how our lives could be better when I was freed and had coordinated a celebration in honor of my homecoming.

But the joy of my return was overshadowed by grief. The doctors found that Zinaida had breast cancer and needed an urgent operation. My first wife had died from breast cancer. Life seemed to be repeating itself. Fortunately the operation went well, although, of course, my wife was out of commission for a long time.

Luckily we received some unexpected assistance. My closest friends at the academy visited us and gave us a small sum of money that they had collected for us. And though their visits and help soon came to an end, we will always remain grateful to them. We know that they broke off relations with us not of their own will but under direct pressure from the KGB.

I now realized how difficult it had been for my wife to earn money for food while I was in the hospital. Naturally we could not count on her earnings any longer or on the gifts of friends. I had to find out what the Ministry of Defense was thinking, and if they presented me with no immediate prospects, I had to look for any kind of work. To my great surprise, I was received immediately at the Chief Personnel Administration. I was led into the office of the chief, Lieutenant General Maiorov. There with him were four other generals, among them, no doubt, one or two KGB men. As soon as we began talking, I realized that I could expect nothing good to come of this meeting. Either a decision had not yet been reached on my case, or else it was being concealed because it contained an illegality.

"Just why did you come to us?" began Maiorov after we had all greeted each other and sat down. "After all, you have been expunged from our lists."

"What do you mean, expunged? What do you think I am? Some Johnny-come-lately off the streets who has signed up to be a soccer player and not made the final cut? I am a general of the Soviet Army. I was judged to be ill—and against my will was put in a special mental hospital. Now I have been deemed recovered—and have been released. Just where am I to go—other than to the Chief Personnel Administration?"

"Of course, you were right to do so, Pyotr Grigoryevich, and I did not refuse to receive you," Maiorov replied. He seemed slightly embarrassed. "We are going to sort the whole matter out. Here, you see, I have your criminal case." He opened one of his desk drawers and took out a thick volume and shook it in the air. "All of us have assembled here," and he glanced around the room, "solely in order to speak with you and to report your matter to the chiefs."

Thus began a lengthy but somewhat incoherent and slippery conversation. No one seemed to want to come out and state what we were really talking about. I kept citing the fact that I had been declared to be ill but that I had been dealt with as if I were healthy. They kept trying to prove that I had committed criminal actions and that I must either condemn those actions or bear punishment for them. We parted dissatisfied. I realized that they wanted me to repent and that my own unwillingness to do so would cause their report on me to be negative. I had to divest myself of my status as an invalid and go out and look for work. But first I wanted to visit the academy.

Though Pavel Alexeyevich Kurochkin, the academy chief, always went out of his way to avoid decisions that involved risk, he agreed to see me. "Come in tomorrow," he said. "There is a meeting of the Learned Council and you will be able to see everyone at once." I was surprised. Kurochkin was incapable of changing so much as to permit such an odious individual as myself to enter the academy. The matter must have been previously decided. Someone wanted me to visit the academy. So what! I would go anyway!

I visited my faculty, both the libraries, the open one and the secret one, Frunze's office, and the Scientific Research Branch. Then I went to Auditorium 301, estimating that I would arrive at intermission time. I was right. A few minutes after my arrival, the doors opened, and members of the Learned Council began to emerge. All recognized me immediately and greeted me. Some congratulated me on my recovery, pronouncing "recovery" with obvious irony. And then they dragged me away from the doors, "Well, tell us about things. How was it there? How are things at home? What prospects do you have?"

I told them my situation in brief. It was not a joyful story and evidently it aroused in all of them an inner protest. Lieutenant General Petrenko, who had been promoted during my absence (he had been the only one to support formally Kurochkin's proposal that I be expelled from the party) exclaimed in astonishment, "You mean they have not restored your rank? They haven't given you your general's pension?"

"Of course not!" I confirmed.

"How can that be!" he cried out, even more astonished than before. "That is illegal. If a man is ill, the law applies to all. Anyone can see that this is illegality. It can't be concealed. And who, then, after learning about this, will ever believe he is insane?"

"They could care less about that," a general said. "They aren't concealing anything. They let him come here so that we could all see that the law will help no one who tries to act against the government. Without laws there will be repression. That's what they're showing us today. He has done his part. He told us himself what they did with him. Now we have to believe the rumors. You can bid him farewell. They'll not arrange any more meetings with us."

And so we all said a final goodbye. This was my last visit to the academy, and my farewell to the army. The Chief Personnel Administration did not receive me again either.

The Soviet state and its armed forces were finished with me. For all they cared, I could die of starvation.

The last "privilege" accorded me was a KGB watch over me.

Naturally, I did not wish to starve to death. I began to look for work. At first I investigated opportunities within the highest civilian professions for which I was qualified. My prospects seemed good since all over Moscow the bulletin boards carrying job announcements were covered with notices: "Construction engineers needed!" I began to respond to these notices. At each office I had the customary talk with the chief of the personnel branch. When I reported that I had been dishonorably discharged from the army, they always found a reason to turn me down. I then learned not to mention either my arrest or my discharge. As a result, they began to give me job application blanks. On these, it was difficult to conceal arrest, discharge, and in particular expulsion from the party, and they invariably caught me at this stage—and refused to give me a job.

In the end I learned how to fill out the job application in such a way that my whole biography looked quite decent—and then they would put my name on a schedule for job assignments. But only once was I assigned a job. In all other cases those who watched over me prevented this from happening. Even in this one case, I did not manage to go to work either. The director of the institution called me at home. "Unfortunately they sent us a young engineer in your place."

It soon became clear that I would not get work in engineering. I was not proud. I would take any job. As a youth, I had been a lathe operator and a locomotive engineer. True enough, locomotives had been modernized since the days I'd worked on them—but it was not that complicated to learn how to use nonsteam locomotives! And for that matter steam locomotives were still being used in some places. In addition, I had an automobile driver's license, and I had three construction skills—carpenter, bricklayer, plasterer. But none of these skills were of any use to me, either. Though I kept rushing all about Moscow, everyone always found a reason for refusing me work. I encountered so many rejections I cannot possibly detail all of them here; besides, it is always repulsive to have to do so. Therefore, I will cite just two turndowns, which, though they were also degrading, were at least original.

In the first instance I had an interview for a job as a locomotive engineer with the chief of a locomotive depot located outside Moscow. His first question was, "What military rank do you have?"

"I already told you—none."

"That's now. What rank did you have before?"

"That doesn't have any bearing on our talk today."

"Yes, it does. If the workers know that the locomotive engineer on the only steam locomotive left here is a general, there will be a scandal. They are youths who will run to see you working on your steam locomotive. Come now, Pyotr Grigoryevich, get into a nonworkers' profession. Otherwise, you might incite some sort of antigovernment demonstration."

"But what can I do if they refuse to take me in a white-collar profession?"

"I don't know, but I am not going to hire you as a manual worker."

"I guess I'm supposed to find a fence and die under it?"

"I don't know, I don't know, but I cannot accept you in the position of a locomotive engineer."

The second rejection occurred at the Likhachev Automobile Factory, where I had found a man who, as a result of pressure from a dozen of my acquaintances, had undertaken to fix me up with a job. This man was so influential that the chief of the personnel branch did not dare to turn him down. But the latter was sly. He said to my sponsor, "It's not difficult for me to fit him to a job—but I am asking you to speak to the secretary of the party committee. Comrade Grigorenko has been expelled from the party. It is our established procedure to send all those expelled from the party to the secretary of the party committee."

My sponsor and I went to him. He quickly grasped the essence of my case. More particularly, he recollected my name. "Weren't you the one who spoke at the party conference of the Lenin District in 1961?"

"Yes it was me."

"You see, your name is so notorious that I remembered it immediately. And do you think workers have less of a memory for it? No, you'll not be able to get around that. Just try to explain how a man rose from worker to general—and then returned to worker again. For that matter, you should not even be trying to get work in a large enterprise. They are the citadels of the working class and they must be kept pure."

There was nothing more to be said.

I continued searching for a job almost without hope. I had a constitutional right to work. This was trumpeted to the whole world as the greatest triumph of socialism. But I had no chance of getting work if the one who had it did not want to give it to me. And there was only one source of work in the Soviet Union—the state, the party-state bureaucratic apparatus. How could anyone get through the barricades set up by this apparatus? I became desperate. My wife and I were no longer young. We had a helpless son. For the time being, my wife could meagerly support us with her work as a seamstress. But before us lay old age, total helplessness—and no one to aid us in any way.

But again fate took pity on us. One day I was walking along Komsomol Prospect and saw an announcement: "Watchmen needed for a teachers' tourist base (Secondary School No. 11)." I went to the school and enlisted both my wife and myself as janitors at a salary of sixty rubles a month each. The director of the school and the tourist base told us to go to a specific personnel branch and take our work orders with us. When we got to the branch, the director there looked us over and said, "If you are able, you can begin right now."

We hadn't worked long as custodians before I was recognized. Our tourist center had been set up for teachers from the provinces who wished to spend their vacation or part of it in Moscow. They often came with their families. One teacher brought her husband, an army major who had studied in the academy during the time of my whole party drama. He, of course, might very well not have deigned to notice a general, one who had not been very close to him, in the guise of a doorman, but by the time of his arrival at our base, the tourists had already become attracted to us. My wife is a communicative person and she quickly became friendly with the teachers. Since she knew a great deal about literature, the theater, and music, the more curious of the tourists grouped themselves around her and often conversed with her. During these talks, Zinaida occasionally was asked questions to which she did not know the answers. At this she would turn to me and I would help her if I could. People wondered aloud how the custodians could be so literate. This led the major to look more closely at me. When I was cleaning a carpet in the corridor, I heard a quiet voice behind me: "Comrade General!" I did not react. The major then came around in front of me, looked at me, and asked, "Is that you, comrade General?"

"No, it's not," I replied and I kept on with my work.

He was unwilling to drop the matter. Soon all the tourists knew that the janitors at their center were a general and his wife and that we were there because the general "had spoken against Khrushchev at a party conference."

All were indignant at the injustice that had been shown us. A group of the tourists went to the All-Union Central Council of Trade Unions and complained. "Why is it that cultured and honored people are being held down in posts as janitors—while the guides all lack culture?"

Two things resulted from the tourists' interference. In the first place, we were both promoted from janitors to guides—and by this we gained some thirty rubles a month. In the second place, we were not rehired the next year. This, in spite of the fact that we were given marvelous recommendations and that we made our applications long before the opening of the tourist centers, which, even when they opened that year, were still lacking a full staff.

I discovered that there were places where one could get work without presenting a passport—stores, for instance. On my last day of work at the tourist center, I was walking along the street and dropped into a vegetable store. I asked for the director and was sent to the cellar, where I found a short, lean, quick-moving Jewish man. "Are you the director? I am looking for work."

"For how long?"

"For however long it lasts. For as long as my own strength holds out."

"You mean you want permanent work?"

"Yes, of course."

"Do you have your passport with you?"

"Yes!" I reached for it in my inner pocket.

"I don't need it now." He made an impatient gesture. "Just go in to see the chief clerk and have him put you on the list of employees. When can you begin work?"

"Whenever you want. Tomorrow."

"Could you begin now? There are four hours until the end of the work day, but I will give you a full day's pay. The evening delivery is coming in right now and I have no help at all."

And so I became a worker at the Fruit and Vegetable Store number 7. I worked twelve hours every other day and the pay was sixty-five rubles a month. In addition, I was given a free lunch, paid for by the director's fund, and all the spoiled fruit and vegetables I wanted. On top of all this, there was legalized "taking." I saw this going on—but I could not permit myself to take part in it. Call it what you will, I considered it thievery.

Once when I was leaving the store after work Semyon Abramovich, the director, stopped me. "Pyotr Grigoryevich, come with me!"

I followed him to the cellar. He took my shopping bag, put some fruit in it and said: "You can take this quantity home with you every day after work."

"I am not going to do it, Semyon Abramovich."

"That's what I thought. I know who you are. But I am asking you to take it. If you don't, I can't have you working here. What I have just offered you, I have offered to all workers—but people sometimes get carried away and exceed my norms. From time to time we have to search those who get carried away and punish them. So if you don't do what everyone else does and take something home from work with you, the other workers will consider you an informer—and your life will become unbearable."

"All right. Since you know who I am, then I can tell you frankly that for me it is much more dangerous to take fruit than not to. People other than you may search me when I leave here—in order to compromise me."

"Pyotr Grigoryevich, don't concern yourself with that. If it did happen, I would always say that I gave it to you personally as an official bonus."

That's how I became a "taker"—in other words, I did what everyone else does in the Soviet Union who does not receive enough to live on.

Materially, our lives became easier. The fresh vegetables and fruits greatly improved our diets. But sixty-five rubles a month was an impossibly small amount for three people to live on. Even if we added to that sum the fifty rubles earned by our youngest son Andrei, 115 rubles for four was still tiny. So Zinaida had to continue her work as a private seamstress, though on a smaller scale.

I began to ponder the fact that people regularly used to work twelve-hour days. So I got a job in a second store, a grocery store. This brought in another sixty-five rubles and another three free meals for me. I was earning 126 rubles after deductions, which was exactly how much I had been paying in the form of income tax and party dues when I was the head of a faculty. This was Soviet equality for you.

In the course of one month I became so exhausted and lost so much weight that my clothes hung off of me. When I got home in the evenings I did not even have the strength to wash up. As soon as I had undressed, I fell on the bed and immediately was asleep.

Zinaida urged me to give up one of the jobs. "What good is it to us if you are going to destroy your health?" she reasoned. But I did not want to do this. She made another proposal, concerning our invalid son: "Drop one of your jobs—and work things out so that Oleg can work alongside you under your supervision." I was so utterly worn down that I agreed to her plan. I agreed to it, but I can never forgive the Soviet government for putting us in this position.

Semyon Abramovich met me halfway. He accepted Oleg as an employee and let him rest when he needed to. But I was perpetually anxious with Oleg at the store, fearful lest he have a sudden epileptic fit, perhaps even when he was carrying a load or was standing by an open hatch or on a stairway.

While Oleg and I were laboring away, Zinaida occasionally "amused herself" by conducting a one-sided correspondence in regard to my being illegally deprived of my pension. She wrote again and again to the respective organizations involved, but they maintained their silence. After my visit to the Chief Personnel Administration and to the academy, I had told her that I would do nothing further in connection with gaining back my rights. But in October, after listening to my wife's talk about her correspondence, I got angry and wrote Minister of Defense Malinovsky this note:

Rodion Yakovlevich!
According to rumors,* I have been demoted from general to the ranks. I am inclined to believe those rumors because half a year has already passed since I left the Special Psychiatric Hospital and I have still not been returned to the service and I have not been appointed the pension I have earned. I ask you to restore my lawful rights. And if, in violation of the law, I have been demoted and dishonorably discharged—then at least have the courage to tell me this to my face. During the course of my own service I never once demoted a corporal behind his back. P. Grigorenko.

My letter worked. Malinovsky went once again to the central committee secretariat and asked them to decide the matter of my pension. The response was that since Malinovsky was the minister of defense he should decide it on his own. Malinovsky then stated that he had already granted me everything his authority allowed—a rank-and-file soldier's pension of twenty-two rubles a month, which I had refused to accept. And at this point the secretariat adopted a decision: "To permit the ministry of defense to grant Pyotr Grigoryevich Grigorenko a pension of 120 rubles a month." In late December 1965 I received a registered letter. The envelope contained my pension booklet and nothing else. The next day I received a phone call from the Moscow Military Registration and Enlistment Office, and after I told the person calling me that I had received the pension booklet, he informed me that I would receive my pension in the Lenin District division of the State Bank. I wrote a sharp protest against the granting of such a pension, though I accepted the money. It allowed us to stop working.

Time passed and my son Georgy, who had been expelled from the party, was summoned to the Central Committee. The summons was allegedly motivated by the necessity of talking with him about the letter my sons had sent to the Central Committee back in 1964 protesting my being classified as insane. Their intent was in fact to request that my sons attempt to induce me to change my views. "Your father conducts himself very incorrectly. Generosity was shown him. His question was taken up by the minister of defense and by the secretariat of the Central Committee," a Central Committee official said and then told Georgy how the decision on granting me a pension was adopted.

---

*I used the words "according to rumors" because neither I nor my wife had ever seen the decree on my demotion and dishonorable discharge. I was afraid that they might try to provoke me by saying: "He affirms that he was demoted and dishonorably discharged—but where is the document to this effect? This is a clear symptom of his insanity." Therefore I always spoke of my demotion and dishonorable discharge very carefully.

He added, "Almost all the secretaries signed it."

The other official present interrupted, "No, all of them signed it. Look." He put the decree on the table in front of them.

"Yes, yes, all of them," the first official confirmed, showing the decree to Georgy.

My son's story only confirmed my old belief in the Soviet government's methods of operation. They violate the law and instead of correcting the violation add to it a new violation.

Nineteen sixty-five ended. Neither prison, nor the special psychiatric hospital, nor the effort to break my will and that of my family by making survival so difficult had forced us to bow down or compelled us to renounce the right to make judgments, not by government dogmas, but as we understood things ourselves.

CHAPTER TWENTY-TWO

FEELING
MY
WAY

In early 1966 I was not yet part of the collective in the human rights movement, but I was doing everything I could alone. The story of my "insanity" had been widely spread among the teachers who passed through our tourist center, and it had aroused indignation against the authorities.

Twice I appeared before the All-Union Commission of Technical Experts on Psychiatry. The psychiatrists listened to my story, astounded. They were surprised that I was classified as a group two invalid ("invalid on the grounds of insanity") upon my release. I explained that the hospital could not reconcile itself to the fact that I had been deprived of my pension; by putting me in group two they had wished to force the Defense Ministry to reach a decision on it. I asked them to repeal my status so that I could get work and feed my family. It was obvious, I told them, that the Defense Ministry did not want to grant me a pension.

The psychiatrists sympathized with me and cautiously expressed indignation at the illegality, but they refused to change my invalid status, saying that too little time had passed since my release from the Special Psychiatric Hospital. They did, however, agree to move me from group two to group three—and promised to remove me from there as well in six months. In mid-November I appeared again before the commission. They were expecting me. It turned out that my first appointment with them had aroused a storm of discussion. Someone had brought up my speech at the party conference and most had agreed that I had been committed to the Special Psychiatric Hospital as punishment for that speech.

Now, in November, a heated discussion went on for about an hour, during which I told the psychiatrists that I would not make promises to the government in exchange for a pension. I wanted to remain free; I wanted to be able to speak out when I saw injustices.

The commission listened to what I said as if it were a great revelation. I saw that I could speak out not only with teachers but with psychiatrists as well. In this I found confirmation of the views I had formulated during my imprisonment: I had to speak openly and honestly with everyone. In other words, I had to explain and evaluate events as I understood them myself, without trying to conform to others' opinions or to official directives and interpretations. I would not force my opinions on anyone, and I would not recruit followers. I would not create a formal organization. I began to picture instead a spiritual community, and I imagined how this community's activity could lead to the rebirth of society.

Having adopted such a credo, I was unable to select a particular person as the object of my propaganda. I was like a blind man feeling his way through a labyrinth. Circumstances had forced me to go to the Chief Personnel Administration of the army. I had talked there and beyond a doubt I had made an impression on those who heard me. I had gone to the academy—and I think my talk there was also useful, as were my discussions with teachers and psychiatrists.

But these initial contacts had to be developed. I had to communicate with more people about socially significant questions. At work places there was no time for conversation. And even if we set a particular time to talk, what would we talk about? Most of the workers in stores were women overwhelmed by daily concerns. Almost all worked at two jobs—like I had—twelve hours a day every day. One widow who had four small children worked at three jobs! She worked twelve hours daily either in a store or in a mess hall as a dishwasher. In addition, she worked four hours each day as a charwoman in an institution. That meant a total of sixteen hours' labor per day, not counting her own housework. For all of this she was paid 180 rubles a month—not very much for five people. What could I say to this woman when she talked to me about the tremendous hardships of her life?

I couldn't try to convince her of the need for a revolution, let alone lead her toward a spiritual rebirth. She had no strength for anything other than her three accursed jobs. How could I help her? Here a revolutionary would have had no problem. He would seize upon the example of this woman and at the top of his lungs would condemn the system. But I did not take advantage of this opportunity—not because I personally feared persecution by the authorities, but because I saw that little good would come out of this for the woman herself. What reward would await her in return for my big noise? Nothing. Yes, she would get a chance to sleep; they would let her have only *one* job, her legal one in the dining hall. She'd be immediately fired from her other two jobs, without termination pay, because she had been working "illegally." That's what would happen. A worker in conflict with the administration was always wrong. Throughout the Soviet Union, poorly paid manual or white-collar workers take second jobs from among those positions for which there are not enough candidates. No one tries to stop them. But as soon as you complain, you are an outlaw and you will be fired. They will punish your illegal employer for improperly accepting you for employment: They will give him an official rebuke or reprimand. But then and there he will accept some other person to do the job in exactly the same illegal way—because his store or his institution still has to be cleaned. It was not for me to expose social ulcers—if by such exposure I was going to harm even just one worker.

On February 10, 1966, the trial of the writers Yuli Daniel and Andrei Sinyavsky commenced. For a while I toyed with the idea of going to the trial, but then I decided not to, knowing they wouldn't admit me to the courtroom anyway. Only two years later, at the trial of Galanskov and Ginzburg, did I understand what I had missed. If I had gone to the first trial, I would have gotten into Daniel and Sinyavsky's circle two whole years earlier. At the time, I did not understand the significance of being present *outside a courtroom.* I was only beginning to understand such concepts, partly because I was isolated.

Early in the spring of 1966 Alexei Dobrovolsky, who had just been released from the insane asylum, arranged a meeting between me and Volodya Bukovsky, who introduced me to Sergei Pisaryev.

In the autumn three of our closest friends died: my unforgettable mentors, Vasily Ivanovich Teslya, Mitya Chernenko, and Anya Zubkova.

Vasily Ivanovich Teslya was granted a physically easy death—as if in reward for his torments in prison. Teslya's son Yura, who had spent most of his life in expeditions in the Arctic, was home, which made his father happy and very solicitous. Vasily died at evening tea. He was boiling water when Yura heard a wheezing sound, rushed into the kitchen, and found him slipping to the floor, trying to hold on to the stove. He lost consciousness almost immediately and was dead when the emergency squad arrived. Thus Vasily Ivanovich was not fated to survive until the coming of the "bright future" he had worked for.

Mitya Chernenko's death was drawn-out; he suffered greatly. The Kremlin Hospital doctors, the best in the USSR, could not help him; the worst torment

he had to endure was blindness. His funeral took place at the Moscow crematorium. Everything was solemn and pompous—in the Soviet style. I kept feeling
that Mitya had always been very melancholy among this crowd. We returned
from the crematorium in a bus with Mitya and Zinaida's friends from *Komsomol Pravda*. The person responsible for arranging the social aspects of the funeral, Yuri Zhukov, was also on the bus, and he was making it so obvious
he did not want us at the postfuneral gathering that Zinaida and I got off at
Crimean Square. We felt that Mitya did not go on with them—but instead
joined us.

In death Anya Zubkova remained just as modest and concerned as in life.
Her daughter Rena, a doctor, had taken her to her hospital with an infarction.
The next day she was gone.

Despite the loss of these three good friends, we were far from being as lonely
as we had been during the period immediately after my release from the insane
asylum. We had begun to find new friends, both among creative young people
and people of our own generation.

My first meeting with Volodya Bukovsky outside the psychiatric hospital
took place in Neskuchny Park. It was almost too dark to be sitting on park
benches without arousing suspicion, but it was also not yet warm enough for
the general public to be strolling there. We greeted each other and I said, "One
of us came with a tail."

I pointed to two figures awkwardly hiding behind the bare trees.

"The hell with them, let them hang around!" said Volodya.

We began to talk. From that first encounter I took away an impression of
determination, vigor, and swiftness. When I asked Volodya what type of action
he preferred—open struggle or organized underground conspiracy, he replied
forcefully, "Open struggle! Why should we hide? The law is on our side. People
will hear public statements and the honest and brave among them will join
us. What methods could one use for underground conspiracy? Given the corruption of our morality, I am convinced that from the very first one would
encounter a provocateur. Only an idiot would go underground."

How my opinion of Volodya changed in this brief encounter! In the Leningrad Special Psychiatric Hospital, thin, with his work clothes hanging on him,
and with his cropped hair, he had seemed to me a mere boy. Now he captivated
me, and I ceased to feel the difference in our ages. Before parting, we agreed
to meet at Pushkin Square in order to visit Sergei Petrovich Pisaryev. I will
always remember how Volodya, after saying just a few words about Pisaryev,
remarked as if it were a matter of course, "You and he are going to create
a club of Soviet political prisoners."

Of course, I had no intention of creating any clubs or other organization,
but I liked his straightforward energy; while I grinned inwardly, I did not
argue with him.

Sergei Petrovich Pisaryev was an extremely interesting man. He became a friend of our whole family. Honest, courageous, determined, kind, and almost childishly naïve, he had retained the idealism of his younger years. He also was almost fanatically devoted to the Communist party of the Soviet Union. He had been expelled from the party eight times, always on the same charge—"lack of confidence in the ruling party organs." Actually, it was for defense of arrested party comrades. Pisaryev succeeded in achieving the rehabilitation of his friends and his own restoration to the party seven times. During Stalin's rule he was imprisoned twice.

During his first imprisonment he was subjected to forty-three interrogations, thirty-eight of them with torture. The ligaments of his spine were torn, and he suffered severe pain from this injury till the end of his life. Once released, he tried to bring his interrogator to justice. At the same time, he continued the struggle he'd begun earlier for the liberation of the Chechen-Ingush Bolshevik leader Zyazikov. He continued this struggle for twenty years and eventually succeeded in obtaining the posthumous rehabilitation of Zyazikov, who had been executed by firing squad. As far as his interrogator was concerned, Pisaryev was informed that he had been expelled from the party and dismissed from the KGB.

Pisaryev's second arrest took place after the war. Despite his spine injury he had been at the front as a political commissar throughout the war; during the heavy battles of the first period, he managed to carry a seriously wounded comrade to safety. In 1953 he wrote a letter to Stalin in which he described the sensational "Doctors' Plot" as an obvious provocation. Such impertinence astonished even Stalin, and he gave orders for Pisaryev to be imprisoned in the Leningrad Special Psychiatric Hospital. Pisaryev persistently attempted to prove his sanity and finally achieved liberation. He brought out with him a written record detailing hundreds of cases in which psychiatry had been abused for political purposes. Using these materials, he wrote a convincing appeal to the Central Committee.

To investigate his charges a commission presided over by the Central Committee official, Alexei Ilyich Kuznetsov, was set up. Among its members were two leading Soviet psychiatrists, the director of the All-Union Scientific Research Institute for Psychiatry, Professor Dmitry Dmitriyevich Fedotov, and the chief physician of the Donskoi Psychiatric Hospital, Professor Anatoly Borisovich Alexandrovsky. The commission investigated both of the special psychiatric hospitals existing at that time—in Kazan and in Leningrad—and confirmed all the facts reported by Pisaryev. An enormous number of new but similar cases was discovered as well. Citing the results of the investigation, the commission proposed the liquidation of the special psychiatric hospitals as institutions of political repression—not hospitals that were curing the mentally ill. The commission's conclusion was reported to Politburo member N.

M. Shvernik. He kept this report and all the materials accompanying it in a desk drawer for two years, after which he turned it over to the archives of the Central Committee.

For more than two decades the naïve Pisaryev kept on writing to the Politburo insisting that a decision be reached to put into effect the proposals of the commission headed by Kuznetsov—though it was quite clear that the Politburo itself, or at least its most influential members, had taken measures to make sure that the commission's report did not receive any attention or action. For this reason, soon after the delivery of the report to Shvernik, the members of this commission were subjected to unfounded administrative persecution. Kuznetsov was removed from the Central Committee and for a lengthy period was denied employment. Professor Alexandrovsky was slandered and removed from his position as chief physician of his psychiatric hospital. He died soon after. Professor Fedotov was removed from his position as director of the All-Union Scientific Research Institute of Psychiatry and was appointed as a consultant on psychiatry to the Sklifasovsky Emergency Medical Aid Institute. The special psychiatric hospitals were *not* destroyed. Instead their number kept growing. In addition to those in Kazan and Leningrad, others were opened in Sychyovka, Chernyakhovsk, Oryol, Dnepropetrovsk, Smolensk, Alma-Ata, and Blagoveshchensk, and departments for forced treatment were opened in all of the provincial psychiatric hospitals.

Pisaryev kept on writing to the Central Committee until he died. He did not recognize any other means of struggle against tyranny in the country except for letters to the Central Committee and to government organs. Though I do not approve of bowing endlessly before someone who ignores you, I valued this man's friendship and felt respect for him—a warrior and a martyr!

I met the writer Alexei Yevgrafovich Kostyorin through Sergei Petrovich. Kostyorin and I saw each other almost every day; my family came to love him. He was happy despite the trials he'd undergone and a serious heart ailment he'd had for years.

Himself a worker, Alexei Yevgrafovich was from a worker's family. All were Bolsheviks. His eldest brother had been in the party since 1903; his father, since 1905; his middle brother, since 1909; and he, the youngest, since 1916. His mother was the last to join the party—on the eve of the October 1917 coup d'etat. Each met a tragic end. Alexei's father had starved to death in the winter of 1931–32. His eldest brother was arrested and shot in 1936. His middle brother was expelled from the party, fired from his job, and threatened with arrest, after which his nerves gave out and he took to drinking and died. When her eldest son was arrested, his mother put her own party card on the desk of the secretary of her party organization and declared that she was unable to remain a member of an organization that could permit such injustice. After the death of her middle son and the arrest of her younger son, she too died.

So Alexei was left alone. In addition to his three years in tsarist prisons, he'd spent seventeen years in Kolyma camps and exile. When we became friends, he already had the feeling that he had little time left—and he hurried to sum up his life in an autobiography. Unfortunately I was never able to read this manuscript. He intended to give it to me so that I might arrange for its publication if the opportunity ever arose, but he died before he could finish the work. The woman whom he'd married while in exile did not heed his instructions, which were to hand over the manuscript to me. Instead she turned it over to the KGB.

Alexei Yevgrafovich was able to make his personal declaration of resignation from the CPSU before he died. In a brief letter he set forth a short history of his own time in the party, citing proof of its corruption, particularly of its degeneration into a bureaucratic organization.

Kostyorin helped me comprehend the needs of the country and the many ways in which the people were suffering. Having spent the Civil War and the first postwar years in the northern Caucasus, he had been bound by a multitude of ties to the small groups living there. He had suffered their deportation and the concomitant death of many of these peoples' sons and daughters as if it had been his own misfortune. He instilled these feelings in me and connected me with representatives of those small nations that continued to suffer discrimination and genocide—the Crimean Tatars, the Soviet Germans, the Meschi, and others. From then on I participated in these people's struggle for their equality and among them I gained a multitude of friends.

My friendships with Sergei Petrovich Pisaryev and Alexei Yevgrafovich Kostyorin led me into a new world made up of fascinating recollections, friendly, interesting conversations, previously unavailable books, and samizdat (the network of secretly circulated, uncensored political writings). All of this altered my horizons. I could feel myself changing and I enjoyed it. I became particularly close to Alexei Yevgrafovich. Sergei Petrovich was somewhat dogmatic and not without fanaticism. Kostyorin had more of a sense of humor.

Spring and summer passed quickly. My wife's asthma had become much worse, and the doctors recommended she go to the Crimea, but we had no money. I realized, though, that if I could get a job as a stevedore in Moscow, it might be even easier to get one in the Crimea. We decided I would go to Yalta alone, get my bearings, and either summon the family or return home. My first day there was spent trying unsuccessfully to get a job as a construction engineer. The next day I went to the fruit and vegetable trade organization. While I was filling out documents, a young man approached who'd been listening when the personnel officer asked me why I had been in prison.

"You want to work in a store?"

"Yes," I replied.

"Why? You probably don't know how to steal. I can see that already. And in a store you have to steal. The pay is only sixty rubles a month. You would be better off coming to our group."

"What kind of pay do you get?"

"We do group piecework and we manage to make up to 200 rubles a month. And we are good people, too. All of us have seen heaven through bars."

So I applied for a job at his warehouse. I got a work order and had it signed by the warehouse manager and foreman. I began the next day and also found a room in a good apartment house. It had a kitchen and a bath, could accommodate three, and cost ninety rubles a month.

I sent a telegram to my wife: "Come!"

I worked the entire season in that brigade. My fellow laborers were not just a work brigade to me—they were my family. On my first day of work, at 12:30 everyone emptied his lunch basket and bag. What variety! Chicken, eggs, pork, beef, lamb, sausage, and various kinds of fish. I won't even try to list the vegetables. I can't remember what I had brought with me, but it was very, very little. I sat at the end of the table and tried to be inconspicuous, but the foreman noticed and urged me to join everyone else. No one kept to the contents of his own parcel. Rather, everyone shared. One man didn't even have a food parcel of his own and was happily eating out of everyone else's. It was a marvelous group. Of the twelve in the brigade, eleven were former zeks (prisoners).

On the second or third day I slipped and sprained my foot. For ten days someone worked in my place. I thereby got paid every day. Soon after my leg healed and I had begun to work again, the foreman came to me. "Pyotr Grigoryevich," he said softly, "there are some men following you."

I was grateful to him for telling me. Several days went by. Once again the brigadier approached me.

"Why didn't you tell me that you are a general, Pyotr Grigoryevich?"

"Former."

"Well, it's the same thing. A general! Why didn't you tell me?"

"What's to brag about?"

"Not to brag. Just so as not to make us look like fools. The man who's on your track came up to me, stuck a police card under my nose, and said: 'Come on now! Tell me all about the general.' 'What general?' I asked him. And he: 'Don't try to play the fool with me! You mean he didn't tell you he was a general?' "

I had to tell the brigadier the whole story. I don't know whether it was the brigade that helped me, or whether the KGB itself was so "kind" as not to demand that I be fired. At any rate, I worked to the end of the season. The other men couldn't help me enough. They wanted to show me ways of hiding from surveillance. I just laughed, thanked them, and said that I had nothing to hide.

So all summer long the five of us Muscovites assisted the vegetable trade in Yalta. One sixty-year-old man carried vegetables about, and four athletic young men kept watch just to see that this old man did not, in his free time, overthrow the Soviet government. Our country must be rich! It seems to have plenty of money for guarding the government's enemies.

I visited Alexei Yevgrafovich Kostyorin nearly every evening, often with Zinaida, who became friends with his daughter, Lena. My wife's friendship with Lena spread out to me and to our sons. Nowadays we all look on Lena, her son Alyosha, his wife, Lyuba, and their small son, Seryozha, as members of our own family.

I will never forget those evenings. In accordance with the zek tradition, there was always strong tea on the table. The heart of the matter was conversation. For people outside of the Soviet Union, it is difficult to imagine how hard it is to crawl out from under the pile of communist dogmas in which you have believed and that have long guided your actions. And no one is going to haul you out from under there except yourself. The Russian writer Vladimir Galaktionovich Korolenko's description of the Russian peasant whom the Bolsheviks planned to transform into a collectivist was very apt: The peasant, he said, must first of all outlive the private property owner *inside himself.* And that is precisely how it was with us former Communists. We had to outlive our communism inside ourselves. Our encounters and conversations helped us do so. Each talk seemed to remove years of ideological stratification and help us feel better and see more clearly what was taking place. After such a talk I would go home in a joyful and energetic state.

Others besides us were drawn to Alexei Yevgrafovich—Valery Pavlinchuk, Genrikh Altunyan, and Ivan Yakhimovich. The young people jokingly called those of us who gathered around Kostyorin "our communist faction." We were of all ages—from the thirty-year-old Pavlinchuk to the seventy-three-year-old Kostyorin—and all of us felt completely at home together.

It was at Kostyorin's that I met the writer Arkady Belinkov. Actually, we only bowed to each other from a distance and parted. I considered myself to be in bad favor politically and therefore did not pursue people, especially those who obviously held back as Belinkov and his wife did. I later learned that they had been preparing to flee the Soviet Union at the time we met and had not wanted to arouse suspicion by making new acquaintances. I was curious about them both. Kostyorin described Arkady as a courageous figure. He had twice been sentenced to death for his literary works. In the camp, disease had almost killed him. His illness continued after his release. People spoke of his wife as the person to whom Arkady owed everything. She was physician, nurse, mother, and wife to him. He was always by her side.

I also met at Kostyorin's Ernst Genri Rozhdestvensky, a well-known Soviet publicist considered to be almost as far left as Roy Medvedev. Ernst Genri even published works in samizdat, occasionally as a co-author with Medvedev.

One evening at the apartment in early fall 1966, Alexi led me over to a man in a dark cloak. He looked at me malevolently, and when we were introduced, I offered my hand with extreme reluctance. His touch was definitely unpleasant. This was Genri.

I left him and followed Alexei, who was holding a piece of torn newspaper. I asked what it was and he handed it to me, saying only, "Read it."

Ernst Genri tried to grab it from me—as it turned out, he'd brought it—but I held it tightly, and in order not to tear it more he released it, muttering with irritation, "I must go. I am in a hurry."

I hastened to read the article. It was from a two- or three-year-old issue of *Evening Moscow* and said that someone named Alik Ginzburg (at the time I didn't know who he was) had been found "guilty" of contacts with foreigners and had disseminated "anti-Soviet" material, and, when caught "red-handed," had "confessed" and "admitted" his mistakes. Because of his "repentance" he had not been punished. What could I say? A typical Soviet newspaper slander that an honest person had no means of refuting.

"Why are you carrying this around with you?" I asked Ernst Genri.

"I chanced to see it in an old newspaper and I brought it along to show my acquaintances so they would recognize people like that. This Alik is now running around all over the place. People have to know about him when he comes to see them."

I was unaware that Ginzburg was collecting signatures on a letter to the Supreme Soviet petitioning against the addition of the new sections 193–1 and 193–3 to the criminal code, sections that multiplied the possibilities of repression. Arrest no longer had to be tied to an intent to subvert the Soviet government. Demonstrations (though the articles did not use that word) and the dissemination in any form of material aimed at disrupting the state were punishable, respectively, by three years' imprisonment and three years' labor camp.

In his book *To Build a Castle,* * Vladimir Bukovsky writes of the difficulties people encountered in organizing a protest against these sections:

> "We found ourselves in a vicious circle. Although they obviously encroached upon constitutional liberties, the articles didn't formally contradict the Constitution, so that it was difficult to call them anticonstitutional. Such an assertion would itself be considered slander. One could only demonstrate that the very intention of the authorities in bringing in these articles was anticonstitutional after their application had become clear in practice. And even then the authorities would be able to say that one couldn't generalize from individual cases.

*Bukosky, Vladimir, *To Build A Castle: My Life as a Dissenter,* translated by Michael Scammel (New York: The Viking Press, 1979, pp. 274–75).

However, they aroused such universal unease that a group of writers, academicians, and Old Bolsheviks appealed to the Supreme Soviet not to accept this amendment to the Criminal Code. Among the signatories to this letter were such prominent people as the composer Shastakovich, the writers Kaverin and Voinovich, the academicians Astaurov, Engelhardt, Tamm, and Leontovich, and the film director Romm. The signature of A. D. Sakharov also appeared for the first time on this letter. The letter was cautious in its phrasing and merely pointed out that these new articles were "contrary to Leninist principles of socialist democracy," "opened the way to the subjective and arbitrary interpretation of any statement," and could "form a potential obstacle to the exercise of liberties guaranteed by the Constitution." No reply was received by any of the signatories, and at the end of December 1966 the decree was confirmed by the Supreme Soviet.

Subsequently I learned of Ginzburg's role in the composition of this particular letter. Genri constantly talked of Ginzburg, everywhere hinting that he could not be trusted, that he might be engineering a provocation. How many people failed to sign the letter because of his warnings it is hard to say.

Each time Ernst Genri wanted to visit Alexei Yevgrafovich he phoned ahead and asked whether I was going to be at the apartment. He did not want to see me. And I didn't want to see him. When we ran into each other on the street we did not exchange greetings.

After my first encounter with Ernst Genri I very much wanted to see Alik Ginzburg. Aleksei Dobrovolsky (a defendant in the Ginzburg-Galanskov case) often mentioned him, and Vera Lashkova (likewise a defendant), whom I had met after my return from the Crimea and who had already typed some papers for me, spoke of him with great admiration.

My initial impression of Alik was disappointing: He was young, short, thin, frail, and shy. At first his only positive traits seemed to be his infectious boyish laugh and his wise and thoughtful eyes. But with each meeting he became more and more interesting to me. I now saw the boy to be a man and we became friends. Once I met his mother, Lyudmila Ilinichna, I came to know Alik even better. These two had a tremendous love and concern for each other that was easy for others to feel. Even though they lived in an uncomfortable room, in a building falling into ruin, things were warm there; there was a warmth of souls.

On December 26, 1966, I visited Alik at the Russian Literary Museum on Bolshoi Yakimanka, where he worked. We walked, chatting, across the Crimean Bridge, which was near my home. Presently Alik had to return, even though much remained unsaid. We recrossed the bridge and crossed it a third time. Finally he said that he had to run.

We didn't meet again for eight years. At the end of August 1967 Alik was imprisoned for five years. Two and a half years after that I was imprisoned also—for over five years.

Through Alik I met Yura Galanskov and his family in their home. Their living conditions were worse than the Ginzburgs', but they, too, seemed happy. When we bade each other farewell, we also said: "Till we meet again." Yura was sentenced to seven years. He died in camp after an operation for a stomach ulcer, a martyr and a hero of the struggle for human rights!

By the end of 1966 I had made many new friends. Our finances were also taken care of for the time. My Crimean experience had shown me that I could get decent work. I soon got a job in a Moscow vegetable warehouse, right near the Kiev station.

The arrangement there was the same as at Yalta—it was collective piece-work for which I got a monthly wage of about 160 to 200 rubles. The brigade was almost the same size as the Yalta brigade, fourteen persons. Eleven of us were former zeks; I had spent the least time in prison. Here, too, everyone worked together amicably. In one respect the situation differed drastically from the one in Yalta—the brigade received almost open-handed extortion from freight recipients. At the end of the day the brigadier distributed among us, in proportion to our daily earnings, from three to five and sometimes up to seven rubles each—tips, so to speak.

CHAPTER TWENTY-THREE

GUERRILLA WARFARE

I now had friends who acted outside the prescribed framework and who made their own judgments, but I was not yet fully involved in their activities. I see myself during those days as loitering somewhere backstage, while up front conflicts boiled, passions flared, and people sacrificed their lives.

In the second half of January 1967 the arrests began. Among those arrested were Dobrovolsky, Lashkova, Ginzburg, and Galanskov. Volodya Bukovsky organized a demonstration in their defense and the demonstrators, too, were arrested, Bukovsky included. I was not frightened, but it pained me to imagine these young people in prison. I had to do something, but what? . . .

From conversations with Bukovsky and Ginzburg I had managed to divine that my new friends were different from me. Ten years later I learned why and how. In the booklet "Our Workdays," I wrote about my Soviet friends, who in the West have been christened "dissidents," and I said that they are not part of an organization, that they have no leaders—each is an individual personality. No one teaches them how to act or recruits them into the movement. Any person who feels himself to be an individual and who does not want to submit to the will of the authorities, may join the movement of his own initiative, and may act in accord with whatever he sees fit for his own defense.

But when I observed Volodya, Alik, and Vera Lashkova in 1967, I suspected the existence among them of some sort of an organization. I did not comprehend the community of individuals nor did I realize that the only way I could join them was of my own volition and by means of my work. Still prisoner of my old psychology, I was waiting for instructions, and in my heart I was even hurt that there had been a demonstration and no one had told me about it. Though I knew Volodya, Alik, and Yura, I was not part of their common cause.

For the time being I visited with Alexei Yevgrafovich and Pisaryev, arranged my personal affairs, and read samizdat. Making use of her old connections among construction people, Zinaida found a man who agreed to hire me—not as an engineer, because to give me such a post was beyond the scope of his authority—but as a foreman. Even this was a tremendous help. At the vegetable warehouse I worked in a cellar with closed doors. The dampness and the drafts had given me a bad case of radiculitis. Several times I had returned to work from sick leave only to fall ill once again. My doctors warned that if I did not leave my job I would end up a complete invalid.

The foreman's job saved me. Spring had arrived—it was the end of April. Working in the fresh air, in the university district outside the city, had a good effect on my health. For that matter, I was tired of work that made no demands on my brain. I set to my new job enthusiastically.

In samizdat at this time, two "events" appeared. I use the term "event" as it was first used among human rights defenders by Alik Ginzburg, who would say: "There is run-of-the-mill samizdat, just another action in defense of human rights—and then there is an *event.*"

When we met after years of imprisonment he said to me, "Of everything you have done there are only five *events:* your essay about the initial period of the war; your speech to the Crimean Tatars on the seventy-second birthday of Alexei Kostyorin; the funeral of Alexei Kostyorin; your part in the creation of the Helsinki groups; and your preface to the book by Rudenko, *Economic Monologues.*"

Though the vast bulk of everything I have written and done may pass into oblivion, I am gratified to know that in the eyes of others, at least some of my work was outstanding.

Alik himself worked much more productively. His own events included: "The Letter of Writers, Scientists and Old Bolsheviks" on the proposed sections 190–1 and 190–3 of the Criminal Code of the Russian Republic; the "White Book" on the trial of Daniel and Sinyavsky; his part in the creation and work of the Moscow Helsinki group; and his part in the organization and leadership of the Solzhenitsyn Fund.

I must say, however, that an individual's importance to the human rights movement is not determined by the "events" he has created. The community of those who defended human rights was miraculous. No matter what losses the authorities dealt it, I never observed any project or piece of work come to an end. On the contrary, from year to year new directions seemed to be before us. Though no one was engaged in recruitment or in filling "positions" that had become "vacant" or that had "been created," someone always appeared to take on a particular duty, quietly and without fuss. That's how it was with, for example, the *Chronicle of Current Events.* How many of those present at the birth of this immortal publication, like Natalia Gorbanyevskaya, Ilya Gabai, and Anatoly Yakobson, departed—but the *Chronicle* lived on.

After the arrests of well-known individuals whom they labeled dissidents, the foreign correspondents would proclaim the movement dead only to eventually find out that our work was going along just as before. And not only were particular projects or tasks continued—they were developed and expanded. More people entered the movement than left it. And none of the new arrivals wanted to be idle. Once in, they acted on their own and found new directions in which to work.

An event began my total involvement with the human rights movement. Two prisoners arrived from the Mordovian camps: Yura Grimm and Anatoly Marchenko. The latter burst onto Moscow samizdat as more than an *event;* he was a phenomenon. His book *My Testimony* was excellent in a literary sense and it opened up a new world to those of us who read it.

By this time many books about Stalin's camps had appeared in samizdat and in censored official publishing. These books spoke about the evils only in the past tense, leaving one with the impression that everything was different now. All were read as if they were novels with happy endings. Into this complacent milieu burst a heroic, determined voice: "Wake up! It's too early to relax! Just look what goes on in contemporary camps! In some respects they are better, but in some respects they are even worse than Stalin's camps."

Marchenko's story begins with the shooting of three escapees. The men were surrounded, and they surrendered, approaching the soldiers with hands above heads; and when they came to a halt, almost touching the muzzles of the machine guns, they were shot down point blank. Step by step, scene by scene, in excellent language, Marchenko depicts the horror of inhumanity. Stalinism had not disappeared! It had gone right on living and . . . being perfected. That was the only conclusion one could reach. It was clear that *My Testimony* would cost Marchenko dearly. They would not risk convicting him for the book. How could they refute the indubitable facts within it? But our hypocritical system would find something for which to convict him.

Yura Grimm was an event himself. In the first place, he had remembered my address through three years of camp and, when he was freed, he came to

meet my family, to thank Zinaida for the parcels she had sent to the Serbsky
Institute for my comrades in misfortune, and to learn what had happened to
me. He had not counted on finding me. Yura himself had been sentenced to
"only" three years. And since his leaflets were anti-Khrushchev, they began
to reconsider his "crime" after the removal of Khrushchev and then suggested
that he write for a pardon. "Pardoned" he was— three months before the end
of his sentence. But these three months and the pardon that gave them to him
were precious.

A pardon erases a conviction—thus Yura again had the right to live in Moscow, where he had an apartment, family, parents, and friends. Without the
pardon, he would have had to move to an entirely different part of the country,
which would have meant finding a new apartment, a new job, and a totally
new group of friends. It is hard for a non-Russian to understand how difficult
all this would be, but I can assure you that in such cases, released prisoners
usually have to leave their families in Moscow. Life in two separate residences
is difficult; often the family breaks up.

Yura realized all this, but at first he refused to ask for a pardon, maintaining
that he was innocent and had been convicted illegally. He told them that he
was willing only to file a complaint, requesting that his unlawful sentence be
annulled.

He finally did write for a pardon, but only after his comrades had told him
to—primarily Yuli Daniel and Alexander Ginzburg, with whom he had served
time in the same camp. Now, on the outside, he was glad to see me there, too.
We often met and talked, not just the two of us but our families. Yura, his
wife Sonya, and his son Clyde became our intimates. Through the whole de-
cade to come, they were at our side, a reliable pillar of strength, particularly
during the difficult period when I was serving my second term in a psychiatric
prison.

In the meantime it had become more and more obvious that the government
had firmly set the course of the ship of state in a backward direction. The Stalinist methods of leadership that had been somewhat shaken by the Twentieth
Party Congress and to some degree by the Twenty-second, were resurrected.
This was manifested most obviously and crudely in the penal policy against
the developing human rights movement. The trial of the participants in the
January 22 demonstration in Pushkin Square protesting the arrests of Galanskov, Ginzburg, Dobrovolsky, and Lashkova was a clear example. But Stalinism was also on the attack in literature, art, science, and other areas. To these
punitive, tyrannical policies my new friends counterposed a resistance, which,
though not powerful, was stubborn. The human rights movement still had not
penetrated into other parts of the country, or if it had, we were not aware of
it. Fate cast me into one of the sectors of the Stalinist offensive not previously
embraced by the human rights movement.

The September 1967 issue (no. 9) of the magazine *Questions of History of the CPSU* contained an article entitled "In Ideological Captivity to the Falsifiers of History," which dealt with Alexander Nekrich's book *July 22, 1941,* which had appeared in 1965 and had been very well received. But now, as seen in the title of the article, the evaluation of this work had changed drastically. The names of the article's authors were alarming in themselves. They were Major General (of political services) B. S. Telpukhovsky and Professor Colonel (of political services) G. A. Deborin. I knew them well. There was no reason to expect any original thoughts in their work, but certainly they could be counted on to express the latest military-strategic "truths" of the Central Committee.

As I studied their article, with pencil in hand, I tried to repress my indignation. I purposely held back several days and then calmed down and set to work planning an essay in response. I seemed to be unable to reduce my ideas to a single thesis, which in writing for a journal is preferable. Two purposes outlined themselves: to protest against the defamation of the author of a truthful book, who, considering our conditions, was courageous; and to disclose the causes of the rout of Soviet forces at the beginning of the war and to point the finger of blame at those who deserved it.

This double purpose emerged because Nekrich had not presented a completely realistic picture in his work and no one had ever taken him to task for this. Most historians and military people understood how difficult it was to write in a censored edition a work about the war that is more than a blatant exercise in patriotic braggartism. Nekrich was the first to try to present a truthful picture of the initial period of the war, but still he had to make concessions to the censor, smooth out the rough corners, fail to tell the whole truth about some things, and keep silence entirely about others. After all, everyone knows that the first step is the hardest. After this booklet had taken its place on library shelves, it would be possible for other works to discuss what it had not. This was why everyone defended the book so vociferously in 1965. Nevertheless, the book's shortcomings remained a fact. And now, when there had been a totally traitorous attack on the book, it was nearly impossible to defend it— precisely because of the partial and unspoken truths it contained. A traitorous attack can be exposed only by truth, complete and wholly unconcealed.

What I had to do was write a letter exposing the false attack on Nekrich and demonstrating also the incompetence of the national and military leaders, their criminally stupid management of war preparations and of the war itself. After carefully analyzing the article and proving that it did not accurately criticize the Nekrich book but slandered it baselessly, I asked the reader to forget for the moment both the Nekrich book and the article condemning it and to recall what had actually taken place at the front.

My essay dealt in detail with the beginning of the war, and with the inane handling of the Kiev encirclement of our forces and the resulting rout of our southwest front. I analyzed the myth of the enemy's overwhelming technological superiority—a myth created by Stalin himself and one perpetuated today by many historians. Our initial defeat was, I wrote, caused by those in the very highest positions. Thousands of capable army commanders had been purged, our border airdromes were poorly developed, we had inadequate antiaircraft defense, our tank units and antitank defense had been sharply reduced (at Stalin's whim) immediately before the war, our fortified areas had been blown up, and our troops had been trained on a peacetime basis. We were not prepared. We paid for this criminal unpreparedness both during and after the war. I pointed to Stalin as the chief culprit, but I also mentioned Voroshilov, Timoshenko, Golokov, and Zhukov. Our failures could not be blamed on the fascists but on ourselves.

And now the organ of the Institute of Marxism-Leninism had published an essay supporting the men responsible for our early defeats. Those who fought and those who died were the heroes, I wrote, not those who led us. The "falsifiers of history" must be punished.

This section of my essay also defended Nekrich's book, since by a careful comparison anyone could see that Nekrich, in a less obvious manner, had cited the same causes as I now did. There was only one cause we both bypassed. I do not know whether Nekrich sensed it at that time, but I omitted it consciously. If I had cited it, I would immediately have been sent back to a psychiatric prison.

This cause was the large number of those who refused to fight for the Soviet system. The enemy could never have taken such a staggering number of prisoners if these people had not wanted to surrender. By its policy of terror against workers and peasants the party had led masses of people to the point where they preferred to be prisoners of war to living in such a country. I first reached this conclusion solely by studying prisoner-of-war statistics. I did not then know, as I do now, that masses of Soviet war prisoners preferred death to returning to their homeland, that Soviet forces, assisted by the allies, had undertaken complete military operations for the sole purpose of returning to their "beloved" motherland the sons who had "strayed."

I mailed my letter to the journal's editor and a week later called him.

"Come, come, Pyotr Grigoryevich, do you really think a letter like yours could be studied in such a short time?" And then he added, with a note of flattery: "This is a scientific treatise. You really can't compare it to Nekrich."

"No, it is only a letter defending Nekrich against dishonorable reviewers. And I do expect that since you gave space to that review you will be willing to give space to its refutation."

"But you understand, of course, that I cannot decide that question by myself. You will have to wait a while."

Two weeks later I visited his office, where he said once again, "But you have to understand!"

"What do I have to understand?"

"You understand very well. You are an old party member!"

"I am nonparty."

"That's only a formality. You are a Communist in spirit."

"Perhaps. But I wrote a letter dealing with an important matter of principle and I am counting on its being published."

"Personally I feel that you only used our address as a formality and that you were actually writing it for samizdat."

"Evidently, you wish this letter would appear in samizdat so that you could refuse to publish it yourselves. But I have taken reliable measures to see that this does not happen, and I intend to keep on demanding that you publish it."

"But you must remember that I do not decide that matter alone."

Several days later, Pisaryev visited our apartment. A copy of my letter to the editors of *Questions of History of the CPSU* lay on my desk. He noticed it and asked me to give it to him to read. I didn't want to refuse him, but I told him that I was trying to get the letter published in the journal and that for the time being I was not going to disseminate it through samizdat. I made him promise that he would not give it to anyone else to read and that he would not make a copy of it himself.

He returned several days later with the letter, very excited about it from the point of view of both style and content. After praising it profusely he said, "And that is not only my opinion. I gave it to one of my acquaintances who is a doctor of economics. When he returned it he said that he had not slept the entire night. He realized that he needed to have a copy of it for his own library. So he stayed up all night and typed ten copies of it. He gave me one as a gift."

"What have you done, Sergei Petrovich? In effect you have disseminated it in samizdat. You have deprived me of the opportunity to pin the journal up against the wall. As soon as they find out that the letter has gotten into samizdat, they will refuse to publish it."

"Please forgive me, Pyotr Grigoryevich, I forgot about that entirely. But I will go to my friend right now and get all his copies."

Two days later Pisaryev informed me that all of the copies made by the economist had been rounded up.

A few days later I received a letter postmarked Arzamas, from a retired colonel who said that a copy of my letter to the editors of *Questions of History of the CPSU* had come his way. He had read it and had been shaken. Had I really written that letter? Was it perhaps not a counterfeit created by some imperialist intelligence service center?

I replied that I had written such a letter but that I had not disseminated it and could not answer for the contents of a copy that had not been proofread or signed by me. In reply I received a card without any signature or return address on which were written only these words: "Thanks for the letter."

For which letter? For the letter answering that of the colonel or for the one which I had written to the editors? I will never know. I will also never know how my letter got into samizdat. I have to believe Pisaryev. If he said that all the copies had been gathered up, they must have been gathered up. Perhaps someone made copies from one of the copies typed out by the economist before returning it to him. Perhaps the leak started out at the journal itself. Such a leak could have been accidental, or it could have been engineered by one of the employees of the journal, maybe the editor himself, in order to forever end the question of publication. Soon after the Arzamas letter the editor phoned me and said, "You see, your letter *was* written for samizdat. I have already received four samizdat copies of it. So we aren't going to publish it. We are not in the business of popularizing samizdat." He added caustically, "This isn't China. We can get along without wall posters."

The routes into samizdat are varied. For the entire time that I lived and struggled in the Soviet Union I never ceased to marvel at the miracle of folk creativity—samizdat. By what means do classified materials turn up in samizdat? How is it that, given the nearly total absence of duplicating equipment, samizdat works spread throughout an enormous territory in a very brief time and become available to a multitude of people? The five or six typescript copies that might originate with an author are soon transformed into hundreds and thousands of copies, each of which is read by many people. I also could never understand why one work would suddenly burst out like a bright flame and then swiftly die down, while another would seem to flare up quietly and then not leave the stage for many years.

Most interesting is the rejection reaction to alien samizdat. The KGB frequently disseminates in samizdat its own creations, many of which have the appearance of genuine samizdat both in form and content—but to my recollection there has not been a single case of KGB materials remaining in samizdat and receiving at least the normal dissemination.

My own letter was distributed across the country. Not only from the Volga area (Arzamas) did I hear news of its travels, but from Novosibirsk, Tashkent, Alma-Ata, Simferopol, Vladivostok, Kharkov, Kiev, and even from Chukotka.

In Moscow this letter paved my way into the dissident world. Students sought me out and I met with groups of them from the Moscow University on Lenin Hills four times. These encounters were very special. Everyone understood that I was speaking there illegally. I could never have gotten permission to give lectures on World War II in the university. But everyone pretended the lecture was an official one. Complete groups were present, headed by their party and Komsomol organizers and senior representatives. The organizers took care that my name was nowhere on record. They set it up so that I was admitted without a written pass and referred to me by a pseudonym. I myself was careful that no one followed me to the university. On each of the four days when I lectured I left my building five to six hours before the talk was scheduled. I spent all of this time losing my tails and verifying that I was not being followed. When it was absolutely necessary that I hide I went to a certain section of the city where there was simply no place for any "tail" to conceal himself. If by this time I had not succeeded in losing him, I would go home.

No matter how careful we were, the case of the "general's lectures" threatened to become public. Those who had heard the lectures would talk about them to comrades who had not been present. Suspicious people, including obvious informers, began to perk up their ears at these conversations. Those who had organized the lectures decided to end them in order to avoid trouble, and we began to conduct talks in private apartments. It was a rare evening in the fall of 1966 and the early winter of 1967 that I was not engaged in such a talk. I never ceased to marvel at how many people were interested in military questions. After thinking about this phenomenon for a while, I realized that people simply needed to hear the truth. Therefore they seized eagerly upon the Soviet economist Eugene Varga's works in the field of political economy, on the economic notes of Academician Agagebyan, and on Djilas's essay "The New Class" (1957). I myself launched into circulation a work that immediately occupied an important place in samizdat—a place which it occupies right up to this moment—Avtorkhanov's *Tekhnologiya Vlasti—The Technology of Power.*

Avtorkhanov's work turned my entire world outlook upside-down. Graphically and convincingly the author depicted Stalin's rise to power, showing that he had had no other purpose than to gain power. All his talk about communism meant nothing to him and was intended solely for naïve idealists. I decided to do as much as I was capable of to propagandize and disseminate Avtorkhanov's book. Before returning it to its owner, I made a copy of it and then began to make copies of this copy in turn—by photocopying and on a typewriter. I had my own typewritten copy and it was in circulation full-time. At the same time the people in charge of duplicating it were constantly busy. We always had buyers, even though the book was very expensive because of our backward methods of reproduction. For my own typescript copy I paid fifty rubles, exactly what it had cost to reproduce it.

My lectures, my talks, and the dissemination of Avtorkhanov kept expanding my circle of friends. At one of my apartment talks I became acquainted with Slava and Rita Luchkovy and their friend Pavel Litvinov. We came to know and love Pavel and befriended his large family, including his grandmothers, both now deceased—Ivy Lee, the widow of Maxim Litvinov, former People's Commissar of Foreign Affairs of the USSR, and Polina Mironovna; his mother and father, Flora Pavlovna and Mikhail Maximovich Litvinov; his sister Nina, her husband Genya, and their son Artem; his friend, subsequently his wife, Maia Kopolev, her sister Lena, and their father, the well-known Soviet writer Lev Kopolev, and his wife, the writer Raya Orlova; his aunt, Tatyana Maximovna, and her daughters, Masha and Vera.

I have listed those we met through merely one person; in fact, there were more. Pavel has a son, Seryozha, who himself has a child. He also has a stepson, Dima, a most remarkably kind and bright young man; and a daughter, Lara.

I made the acquaintance of Larisa Bogoraz, Tolya Marchenko, Lyudmila Alexeyeva, Natalia Gorbanevskaya, and Tolya Yakobson. Tolya and I became very close, and even today the memory of his tragic death causes me great pain. Though Jewish, Tolya was so Russian that he could not live without Russia, without Russian literature, without communication with the Russian people.

Meeting two young teachers from Moscow University, Seryozha Kovalyev and Sasha Lavut, was also important. The three of us liked each other a great deal. They were so pure that it seemed nothing could contaminate them. The two of them always went about together, Seryozha usually walking just a bit ahead of Sasha. In the very same way, Seryozha went to prison first while Sasha remained free. Without his comrade, Sasha remained the same, quietly restrained and always ready to help others in any way he could. He and Seryozha had made use of their teaching positions by trying to help the students who wanted to organize in defense of human rights. Seryozha visited the Komsomol security detachment office and asked to be made acquainted with what was done there. The detachment commander told everything to this teacher who was so interested in their work: how they kept a dossier on every student. He showed him the card catalogue and several personal cards on students who had been involved in politically prejudicial activites, and reported that a KGB official had been attached to his detachment, that this official visited them regularly, gave them instructions, and checked up on them. Seryozha publicized this information—and paid for it in prison.

I had one more important friend during this period—a long-distance acquaintance. Andrei Dmitriyevich Sakharov sent me the first version of his well-known work *Progress, Coexistence, and Intellectual Freedom,* with a request for my comments on it. The manuscript made an enormous impression on me. I immediately sensed that Sakharov had thought and suffered deeply. It was not so much the knowledge he set forth, it was the man himself, his soul, his heart, his mind. His work became important to me, and I scrupulously studied and analyzed it all, transmitting to him by mail my detailed comments. When

I subsequently read the final version of this work, I was delighted to discover a number of places in which I could clearly discern the influence of my comments. I thought that if he had been so attentive to my comments, perhaps he had kept a copy of them for himself. My own copy had been taken away from me during a police search. He did, in fact, have the document, and he was so kind as to make a copy of it.

The pain that I and my new acquaintances were suffering on behalf of our friends compelled us to meet daily to talk about continuing violations of the law. Galanskov, Ginzburg, Dobrovolsky, and Lashkova were under interrogation. Khaustov was sentenced in February and Bukovsky in September. Influenced by all the ongoing persecution, I decided to disseminate in samizdat a document that would expose the anticonstitutional character of section 190 of the criminal code of the Russian Republic. I wrote it in the form of a letter to the Chairman of the Supreme Court of the USSR and to the Prosecutor General.

In the meantime, Pavel Litvinov had been compiling a collection entitled "The Case of the Demonstration on Pushkin Square on January 22, 1967." I had not known of this and had been simultaneously composing my own aforementioned letter. Subsequently *The Chronicle* (no.5) published both documents, calling my letter the "logical continuation" of the Litvinov collection.

By writing this letter I had graduated from the "guerrilla warfare" stage of my defense of human rights and had begun participating along with the "regular troops."

CHAPTER
TWENTY-FOUR

HEAD-ON
BATTLE

The authorities had planned the trial of Sinyavsky and Daniel to be the event from which we would return to Stalinist methods of leadership: Nothing would be permitted without prior approval from the authorities. For dissemination of ordinary literary works without such approval authors would receive long terms of imprisonment at hard labor (seven and five years of severe regime camp)—then people would understand that the authorities would no longer just fool around with those who disobeyed them.

But from the very start, things went wrong: The prisoners did not repent and did not admit their guilt, and a small group of those who sympathized with them raised a fuss and began to undertake something very unpleasant for the authorities—namely, publicity. Not only did they speak out against the Sinyavsky and Daniel sentence but also *against every sentence not founded on the law.*

The first demonstration in the Soviet Union since 1927 took place on December 5, 1965, its participants rallying for publicity and legality for Sinyavsky and Daniel. A campaign of protest continued after the trial. This bit of "impudence" caught the authorities off guard.

A literary collection called *Phoenix* and a "White Book" were issued. The latter contained an account of the Daniel-Sinyavsky trial that detailed the government's monstrous violations of its own laws and of universal human laws. And where was this published? Right under the nose of the central authorities in Moscow. And who published it? Some "mere boys"—Yuri Galanskov and Alexander Ginzburg. What a piece of impudence! These "boys" must be flogged immediately—and so badly that even their grandsons would remember. Less than a year after the sentencing of Daniel and Sinyavsky, Galanskov and Ginzburg were arrested and with them the typist, Lashkova, and Dobrovolsky who had run errands for them. The rationale was simple: The Soviet government would punish not only those directly to blame but also those who helped them, however insignificantly. At the same time the authorities hoped that the "accomplices" might, out of fright, "slander" the basic defendants. Those arrested were so unknown that even the KGB knew little about them. Thus their arrests would not give rise to the sort of big racket that had been raised over the sentenced writers, or so they thought. But no sooner had the KGB arrested the last of the quartet—Ginzburg—than something happened that was quite unusual for the Soviet Union: The participants in the newly emerging human rights movement went over to the offensive. In Pushkin Square, people demanded the liberation of those arrested, a reconsideration of Section 70 of the Criminal Code of the Russian Republic, and the repeal of the anticonstitutional decree on supplementing the Criminal Code of the Russian Republic with sections 190–1 and 190–3. As a result, the world press and radio spoke out and the authors of *Phoenix* and of the "White Book" became well known. Publicity was won.

The arrest of five participants in the demonstration—Bukovsky, Gabai, Delon, Kushev, and Khaustov—and the subsequent cruel sentencing under Section 190–3 of Khaustov and then of Bukovsky increased the publicity and made clear the anticonstitutional nature of Section 190–3.

By the beginning of 1968 the protest had so intensified that the situation in the *court* had become worse than during the trial of Daniel and Sinyavsky. The attention of the world press and of the progressive element of Soviet society had been drawn to the trial. The trial of Galanskov, Ginzburg, Dobrovolsky, and Lashkova took place from January 8 to 12, 1968, and it was a battle in which we were on the attack—"we" meaning those against whom the trial was directed. We stood at the closed doors of the "public" trial for four days.

Entrance to the courtroom was firmly denied us. A chain of militiamen stood five or six steps from the main entrance. At the main entrance itself were two KGB plainclothesmen wearing red armbands. Inside the building, the corridor leading to the courtroom was blocked by two more men in civilian clothes. At the courtroom entrance stood another two men, and six to seven more patrolled the foyer—reinforcements, so to speak. On the first day, we tried to get into the courtroom but failed.

It was very cold all four days of the trial—below freezing. On the first day we stood in the court building vestibule until they evicted us. The same thing happened the next morning. At about noon we discovered that it was possible to warm ourselves in the entryway of an apartment building across the street. By the end of the day they had evicted us from there as well. The "inhabitants" of the apartment house asked that outsiders leave the building since they were afraid of trouble.

For all four days the foreign correspondents stood with us. Our eternal gratitude to them! They were our disinterested bodyguards. If they had not been there, we would have been chased away immediately. My walking stick, played up in some of their news reports, would not have helped us.

In this way our group participated in the struggle unfolding at the trial inside. It was not we who hid from them. They hid from us. This was our victory.

Inside the courtroom, the defendants and their lawyers destroyed the prosecution's structure of fabrication. Because the court was not able to prove even one point of the indictment, it was compelled to play a dirty trick that it hoped would impress the public. The prosecutors brought in a so-called "tourist" named Broks-Sokolov, who had come from Europe and been arrested by the KGB. Ecstatically they passed around a "spy's belt" that he had allegedly been wearing at the time of his arrest—a belt in which there was literature and money. Ginzburg's lawyer, Zolotukhin, asked a very modest question: "What relevance does all of this have to my defendant?"

To this pertinent and tactful question the judge replied crudely, which made further questions on the matter impossible. But when the representative of the Ministry of Foreign Affairs of the USSR, who from time to time provided information, or more correctly, misinformation to the foreign correspondents, came out and announced the story of Broks-Sokolov and his belt, the correspondents immediately asked, "With which of the defendants was Broks-Sokolov attempting to make contact?"

The spokesman stammered, "That's a secret of the investigation."

All of us roared with laughter, and someone shouted, "Why did you drag him into the trial? You can make a belt like that and stuff it full of anything you please without even leaving Moscow." Once again everyone laughed and the official spokesman left, offended.

The whole official spokesman bit was also a dirty trick. Because of a "lack of seats," not a single foreign correspondent was admitted to the courtroom—and since all emphatically demanded information on the trial, the Ministry decided to provide an official spokesman. He did not report what went on in the courtroom but simply repeated KGB stories. As the trial started we learned from a reliable source that the courtroom was not more than twenty-five percent filled. There were at least 170 empty seats. We and the foreign correspondents together numbered no more than a hundred.

So we assaulted the judge with applications for admission to the courtroom for this allegedly "public" trial. A KGB representative, claiming to be the court commandant, told us that all the seats in question had been reserved for "representatives of the workers." But as usual when one or another enterprise, institution, or establishment sent people to public functions in which they had no interest, these workers used the time off for their own affairs. The number of people in the courtroom fell off as the trial continued. By the end, the room was nearly empty. Meanwhile we stood shivering in the cold.

For the authorities all this was a total fiasco. It was obvious to everyone that the trial had been held in secret. Future political trials were held in ordinary chambers that could accommodate twenty or maybe thirty people and in which the public could be strictly controlled. Passes to the courtroom no longer were issued. Instead, the authorities gave out summonses to appear as witnesses. Witnesses were paid only if they showed up in court. There ceased to be announcements in the press of the place and time of trials, and the interval of time between the announcement of a trial and the actual trial was reduced. Finally the authorities even ceased informing the defendant's relatives and witnesses of the trial until after it had begun.

Our open battle for human rights, and for observance of the law, had compelled the courts to retreat into the underground. When the trial of three Armenians who were accused of setting off an explosive on the Moscow subway took place, no one knew where or when it was held (we still don't today), and no relatives or defense attorneys were present. Yet it was declared a public trial and it was announced that those present greeted the death sentence with unanimous approval.

Still, the KGB always failed in spreading misinformation about the trials. Their failure became evident during the trial of Daniel and Sinyavsky. Not only people abroad but Soviet citizens refused to believe in unsupported accusations; all demanded proof—precisely what the KGB did not have. The fabrication published in the Soviet press stuck out like a sore thumb. With his "White Book" Alexander Ginzburg had nailed the false concoction of the KGB to the wall. This experience ought to have taught the KGB to use lies sparingly. But what else could they do when the racket about the trial kept growing? The attempt to create a distorted picture with the help of the official spokesman of the Ministry of Foreign Affairs did not succeed. The foreign correspondents only listened to what was reported from directly inside the courtroom.

The totally false articles about this trial published in *Izvestiya* (no. 15712) and in *Komsomol Pravda* (no. 13089) forced me to take up my pen. It is well known, I wrote, that this trial, though proclaimed public, was kept closed to outsiders. It was a typical provocation, analogous to those that took place in the times of Yagoda, Yezhov, and Beriya. Then, however, they spoke of "enemies of the people" without indicating concrete guilt—whereas now the purest sort of fabrication is used as the basis for an unjust sentence. For example, Broks-Sokolov's presence at the trial and his possession of the notorious belt actually made material proof seem to be in existence.

An enormous number of letters similar to mine and exposing the KGB lies were addressed to the press and the authorities and disseminated in samizdat; some went abroad. The principal rebuff to the KGB was the publication of a collection entitled *The Trial of the Four* in which the trial was illuminated step by step, from beginning to end. This forced the KGB to retreat somewhat.

However, the principal success we met with in the course of the Daniel-Sinyavsky trial came from our standing outside in the sub-zero weather. By doing so we demonstrated our determination and stimulated activity within our circle. Here was born the appeal of Larisa Bogoraz and Pavel Litvinov, a turning point in the development of the human rights movement.

The principal strength of the Bogoraz-Litvinov appeal lay in the fact that theirs was the first public and international expression of a lack of confidence in the Soviet government. Typically, one appealed for justice only to the authorities. Now at the top of our lungs we named the Soviet public as the principal mover and gave a precise definition of that public on which we were counting: "We are appealing to all of those in whom there lives a conscience and who are sufficiently courageous."

For what did we appeal? "Demand the public condemnation of this shameful trial and the punishment of those guilty for it!

"Demand the liberation of the defendants!

"Demand a retrial with observation of all the norms of the law and in the presence of international observers!"

Bogoraz and Litvinov had sensed the maturing demands of the Soviet public—above all, its desire to think for itself. Their appeal touched the soul of this public and it responded. I remember the hundreds of letters the two authors received from all over the Soviet Union, from Communists and from all sectors of the population. People were obviously tired of being afraid. They gave their addresses and places of work and openly expressed their approval of the appeal. Letters came from the Ukraine, from Novosibirsk, from Latvia, from Pskov, from Moscow, letters signed by 79, by 13, by 224, by 121, by 25, by 8, by 46, by 139, and even one signed by 24 schoolchildren.

Those who signed the letters lost their jobs, were deprived of their academic degrees and titles, and were persecuted in newspapers and at meetings. Here and there one or two repented, but the numbers of those protesting grew. A social movement had begun. The authorities were furious. There were new arrests and new trials, but always new protests followed. Repressions became a fact of life and the movement continued to grow. Throughout the country trials became the same as they were in Moscow—cruel sentences behind closed doors; but at those doors stood crowds of like-thinkers.

The first bursts of publicity disclosed a whole mass of problems: legal, national, social, religious. Every day we learned of new persecutions, new arrests, and new repressions. Somehow all of this had to be regularly reported to those interested in it, so *The Chronicle of Current Events* was born. No one sat around planning ahead, working out programs, or determining the frequency of publication. It was requisite to take stock of and publicize the struggle that had unfolded after the appeal of Bogoraz and Litvinov. We were willing to suffer the consequences. The concept of *The Chronicle* turned out to be so vital that no measures taken against it by the KGB were effective. *The Chronicle* grew stronger and began to appear on a regular basis.

The appeal inspired new forces in samizdat, and samizdat ceased to be a purely literary matter. Open letters, essays, leaflets, treatises, research, and monographs began to be published. Centripetal forces also grew stronger after the appeal. Groups of other nationalities became anxious to communicate with the outer world via the foreign correspondents. Ukrainian samizdat was passed about in Moscow: verses by Simonenka, Stus, Svetlichny, Svyatoslav Karavansky, Ivan Dzyuba's book *Internationalism or Russification,* B. Chernovil's book *Wit from Wisdom,* and the essay by V. Moroz, "Reports from Beriya's Game Preserve." Personal ties were established between Muscovite and Ukrainian human rights defenders. We learned about the movement of national rebirth that had developed in the Ukraine in the early sixties, the so-called movement of the "men of the sixties," and about the cruel attacks on it by the KGB.

The time had come for Zinaida and me to establish personal contacts with the human rights defenders of my own nationality—Ukrainians—and to that end we met with Nina Strokatova and Vyacheslav Chernovil. News from the Ukraine poured in upon us: a policy of Russification, the repression of Ukrainian culture, cruel repressions of the outstanding people of the Ukrainian renaissance. We heard in particular of the tragedy of Ivan Dzyuba, who, along with other important Ukrainian cultural leaders, had appealed to the then-secretary of the Central Committee of the Ukrainian Communist Party, Shelest, protesting the oppression of Ukrainian national culture. Shelest had asked Dzyuba to document his claim. Dzyuba had eagerly taken up the cause and the aforementioned book appeared. When Shelest was removed, Dzyuba was arrested. By means of lengthy psychiatric torture they forced him to "repent"—and a talented man was destroyed. Nowadays he is not imprisoned, but he is incapable of any creative work whatsoever. Nina Strokatova told us about her husband, the poet Karavansky, who had been imprisoned for two terms, and she read us some of the poetry he had sent her from the camp. He had been convicted back in Stalinist times, and then, during the Khrushchev "thaw," had been given amnesty. But since he was an active participant in the rebirth of Ukrainian culture and since his verses did not suit the authorities, he was sent, without trial, merely on the basis of a prosecutor's decree, back to camp to serve out his previous term. As I write these words—in August 1979—he has been imprisoned for twenty-six years.

Zinaida and I made a pact with Nina Strokatova: We would maintain contact with her and help her send materials abroad, and we would support the Crimean Tatars in their demands for return to their homeland.

In March 1967 we met for the last time until 1975. Over those eight years she would serve four years in a severe regime camp and I, more than four years in a psychiatric prison. When we met she was in exile in the Russian city of Tarusa, 130 kilometers from Moscow. She lived there under administrative supervision—in essence, under house arrest. A microbiologist, she was working in the local museum, where she received wages of sixty rubles a month. It was the only work they would let her have. Even now she is deprived of work in her field, separated from her people and from her native culture—in an alien land, living under police supervision. We did not see Chernovil again. He served out a sentence of seven years of severe regime camp and is now in exile in Yakut.

The fates of Nina Strokatova and of Vyacheslav Chernovil are typical of the fates of participants in the Ukrainian human rights movement. In order to understand this, let us look at certain historical facts.

During the Middle Ages the Ukraine, one of the most powerful and enlightened of the states of Europe (Kievan Rus) fell beneath the Mongolian-Tatar assault. With time it began to struggle for statehood. But lengthy wars with powerful Turkey and the Khanate of the Crimean Tatars and the struggle against such powerful neighbors as Russia and Poland exhausted the nation. Summoning all its strength, the Ukrainian people reestablished the Cossack Republic in the war of 1648–53—but lacked the strength to go beyond this and were forced to seek a powerful protector. In 1654 they concluded the Treaty of Pereyaslav with Russia. Peace commenced, but soon after, as a result of the perfidious violation of this treaty by Russia, the Ukraine lost its statehood and was divided between Poland and Russia. In the course of subsequent struggles Poland itself fell and the Ukrainian lands that had been subjugated by Poland were divided between Austria-Hungary and Russia. Both occupying powers tried to make their territorial annexations permanent—and to transform the people who lived within them into their own subjects. The Austrians set out to Germanicize the Ukrainians and the Russians to Russify them. The enormous difference between the German and Ukrainian languages aroused strong resistance to Germanification—and in Austria-Hungary a Ukrainian national movement developed that, even after the dissolution of Austria-Hungary, did not disappear. It merely relocated in Poland and Czechoslovakia, the two countries that were heirs to the Ukrainian lands of Austria-Hungary.

Things worked out quite differently in Russia. Mass terror campaigns were carried out against the Ukrainian population together with a cruel system of serf exploitation. As a result, in one century a country of universal literacy was transformed into a dark and forgotten province. At the same time the linguistic closeness between the Ukrainians and Russians led to the relative success of Russification. During the centuries they spent in the Russian imperial state, the Ukrainians began to forget their national name and became accustomed to the name their colonizers had bestowed on them—the Malorosi, or Little Russians; or the Khokhly, or "Topknots." They also got used to speaking the Russian language in school. And for the most part the Russian intelligentsia even came to believe that there was no such language as Ukrainian, that it was only a dialect of Russian. This conviction was reinforced by the directives of the Russian Minister of Internal Affairs, Valuyev (1863) and the Emsky Decree of Tsar Alexander II (1876), which forbade the use of the Ukrainian language in literature, in schools, and in theaters and even forbade the import of Ukrainian books into the Ukraine from abroad.

The extremely low level of national self-consciousness of the Ukrainian people and the Bolshevik intervention from Russia were the basic reasons for the defeat of the national revolution in 1917–20 in the Ukraine and the fall of the Ukrainian People's Republic, which was created by free elections on January 21, 1918. Nationally self-conscious Ukrainians either perished in battle or were forced to emigrate. The Ukraine received its right to nationality not by winning a battle but as a "gift" from the Russian Bolsheviks, but the Russian Communist Party of Bolsheviks, subsequently renamed the All-Union Communist Party of Bolsheviks and then the Communist Party of the Soviet Union (the CPSU), always ruled in such a way as not to release the gift.

It was permitted to shout about national freedom of the Ukraine and to thank the Bolsheviks for giving it, but it was impermissible to make use of it. Cruel repressions rained down on anyone who actually attempted to exercise his or her national rights. Demagogically, the struggle was conducted only against "bourgeois nationalism"—but in fact every kind of national self-consciousness was suppressed. Even Ukrainian Communists were deemed dangerous and the Ukrainian Communist Party was physically annihilated. The purely cultural national organization Prosvita was also destroyed and after that they began to liquidate Ukrainian members of the Russian Communist Party who defended the national rights of Ukrainians. They then proceeded to destroy physically such outstanding figures of the Bolshevik leadership in the Ukraine as Nikolai Skrypnik, Khvylyov, Zatonsky, Kotsyubinsky, and many party officials of lower rank.

The central authorities did not stop at even this. The portion of the Ukrainian population that was conscious of its nationality, even though it was loyal to the Soviet government, represented a potential danger to the unity of the Soviet empire. After the rout of the national revolution in the Ukraine and

the destruction or flight abroad of the most active nationalists, there still remained in the country a small group of the prerevolutionary national intelligentsia who, under the conditions of Soviet rule, wished to awaken the national
self-consciousness of the people. These people sincerely believed the words uttered by the Bolsheviks, which summoned the intelligentsia to work among
the people.

The intelligentsia did labor, giving all their strength to the national rebirth.
Their self-sacrificing work was noticed by the people and their power increased. At the same time, the national self-consciousness of the people rose.
The central authority, however, sensed the danger to itself in this and went
on the attack, organizing in the early thirties a trial-provocation of The Alliance for Liberation of the Ukraine (the SVU). People from the most peaceful
professions and of the most noble character were accused of setting up terrorist
acts—explosions, murders, inciting foreign intervention, and making way for
a revolt in the country. By torture, by falsifications, and by promises of easy
punishments people were forced to "confess" to crimes they had not committed.

The sentences, in relation to the "horrible" crimes for which they were
given, were genuinely light. But a precedent had been set. Now, without publicized trials, and leveling the same charges, the authorities began wiping out
the Ukrainian national intelligentsia, including those who, as I've mentioned,
had come of age under Soviet rule. They rearrested and physically destroyed
all those who had received light sentences in the trial of the SVU. Thus the
national movement in the Soviet Ukraine was destroyed completely. It is possible to gauge the extent of the terror by the fact that about 90 percent of all
Ukrainian writers, including those who were Communists, perished. When the
Western Ukraine was occupied in 1940, the entire apparatus of terror from
the Soviet Ukraine was unleashed there. Not only the "bourgeois nationalists"
but the entire visible intelligentsia were arrested, including members of the
Communist Party of the Western Ukraine, especially those who had been imprisoned in Poland for nationalism.

The subsequent heavy partisan warfare that furrowed the Ukraine repeatedly wounded the Ukrainian nationalist leadership. In the postwar period the
organs of terror, under the guise of punishment of "war criminals," cruelly
repressed those warriors of the Ukrainian Rebel Army (the UPA) who had
not managed to or who did not wish to flee to the West. As a result the Ukraine
seemed so purged of active nationalist elements that it was possible, without
fear of being exposed, to talk about the "flowering of Ukrainian national culture." A certain portion of the young people in schools took all this big talk
seriously. Others who understood its demagogic character pretended to take
it seriously and began to study Ukrainian folklore, Ukrainian handicrafts, and
folk art. A whole constellation of young poets emerged. Presently the authori-

ties began to take measures. In the first half of the sixties a wave of new arrests rolled through the country—of the so-called "men of the sixties." They did away with or imprisoned all of the most active participants in the cultural rebirth and isolated individuals who had been scattered across the Ukraine. This was what made them dangerous to the authorities: They were like sparks scattered on a soil that held within itself a mass of incendiary material and they had to be extinguished, at any cost. Nina Strokatova and Vyacheslav Chernovil were just such sparks. Thus the authorities tried to extinguish them.

At the very time that Zinaida and I were talking with the last of the "people of the sixties"—Nina and Vyacheslav—a new wave was rolling in. The "people of the seventies," isolated individuals like the people of the sixties, were joining the battle.

In Lithuania, where we also had connections, the struggle had developed somewhat differently. There it had taken the form of defense of the Roman Catholic Church. Naturally, such a movement was larger, more organized, and more stubborn than the Ukrainian movement. It had leaders—and it was at them that the KGB struck first.

The Crimean Tatars conducted their struggle in still another way. Their common woe was deportation from the bountiful Crimea into the deserts and arid lands of Central Asia, the Urals area, and Kazakstan. This cruel, senseless deportation in which over 46 percent of the Crimean Tatars had perished had rallied the people. Their struggle began with petitions from individual settlements. From these it spread to neighboring settlements, and from there to entire districts, and so on. At first, the petitions carried hundreds of signatures. Subsequently they came with thousands. And in one case the signatures rose to 127,000. In 1967 the number of signatures gathered on petitions during the year was 3,000,000. Conceivably the entire adult population—200,000 people—had each signed an average of fifteen petitions.

The leadership among the Crimean Tatars was also quite original. Settlements elected representatives, who were grouped by district and took turns appearing in Moscow. Petitions, letters, and telegrams were sent to the group on duty in Moscow and that group transmitted the documents to the institution to which it was addressed and then reported the results. If a large-scale démarche was planned, several groups journeyed to Moscow simultaneously. There was even one case in which all the groups assembled in Moscow—about eight hundred people—and the Moscow militia had to carry out a large-scale operation in order to disperse the demonstrators and expel them from the city.

The representatives were ordinary people, and they were frequently replaced. The group on duty in Moscow elected a manager but his authority was limited. He could designate a time for an assembly. He could appoint people to deliver mail that had arrived from the Crimea. He could appoint someone to write up a report or a communiqué. Each report was signed by all members of the group. Therefore, no matter how many trials they conducted, the KGB was unable to label any one person as leader or organizer.

The scale and organization of the movement forced the government to retreat, to maneuver, to lie, and to make what seemed like concessions. Three times a commission of the Politburo of the Central Committee of the CPSU received a delegation of Crimean Tatars, heard them out, and then left things just as they had been before. The last time a delegation was received was in connection with the decree of the Presidium of the Supreme Soviet of September 5, 1967. This was the most false, the most hypocritical decree of all of those issued in respect to these people. It began with a declaration that the Crimean Tatars had been charged with treason to the motherland and that there was no basis on which this charge would be annulled. But the annullment *was* justified by the fact that a new generation that had never known the war had come of age. The greatest treachery of all was that by this decree the Crimean Tatars were deprived of the right to their own nationality. They were referred to as "citizens of Tatar nationality who previously lived in the Crimea."

This decree of political rehabilitation made the exile of the Crimean Tatars from the Crimea permanent. The second part of the decree said that citizens of Tatar nationality who had previously lived in the Crimea were permitted to reside *throughout the entire territory* of the Soviet Union, *taking into account passport regulations.* And when these passport regulations were later determined, it was written that Crimean Tatars were not permitted to settle in the Crimea. In connection with the decree, the Crimean Tatars demanded a meeting with representatives of the Politburo. The meeting actually took place: The Politburo sent a group headed by Andropov and consisting of the Prosecutor General Rudenko and the Minister of Internal Affairs, Shcholokov—all representatives of organs of police repression. The fourth member of the commission was the secretary of the Presidium of the Supreme Soviet, Georgadze.

When the meeting had convened and Andropov had started to speak, a Crimean Tatar rose and asked, "Comrade Andropov, are you here as a candidate member of the Politburo or as chairman of the KGB?"

"What's the difference?" Andropov laughed.

"There is a difference," said the Crimean Tatar. "If you are here as the chairman of the KGB, we will leave."

"It is obvious that I am here on the instructions of the Politburo and in its name."

Conversation throughout the meeting was hypocritical. Andropov and Shcholokov declared that the passport rules had no practical significance. To the question of why there was no such rule for Russians and Ukrainians, they did not give a coherent reply. The representatives of the Crimean Tatars asked whether they could call people to assembly in their respective districts in order to tell them about the talks.

"Yes, certainly," said Andropov. "I will see that instructions are issued to provide you with the necessary halls and not to hinder the conduct of the meetings."

This was a lie. The local authorities received instructions that they were forbidden to permit the Crimean Tatars to carry out their meetings. When the Crimean Tatars requested to have their meetings and referred to Andropov, the authorities declined to reply.

The Crimean Tatars subsequently presented the authorities with an ultimatum stating that if they were not allotted halls, they would assemble in the open air at Navoi Square in Tashkent—since the representatives were duty bound to report to the people. The authorities did not allot any halls and the Crimean Tatars, coming from all over Uzbekistan, held a large meeting at Navoi Square. The authorities tried to disperse them; some were detained, but the crowd surrounded the militia, and demanded that those who had been taken be freed, and they were. The authorities were unwilling to risk a conflict.

Thus not only Moscow intellectuals but also people of the Ukraine, Lithuania, and Tashkent openly demonstrated that they did not want to live under tyranny any longer. The authorities, fearful of making concessions, were always on the offensive.

After the Galanskov-Ginzberg trial we tried to consolidate and build on our success. Each person did what he wanted to do and what he felt was possible. Kostyorin and I decided to attack the prestige of our party and government leadership in the international arena: We wrote analogous letters sent off on the same day to the Soviet-initiated international meeting of Communist and Workers' parties, a meeting then only in the preparatory stages and one intended to restore Soviet leadership to the workers. Our rationale was that in the first place the Soviet leadership is extraordinarily sensitive to international public opinion; publication of one of our papers or letters in the foreign press was always worthwhile.

In the second place, exposure of the tyranny that the CPSU demonstrated after the Twentieth Congress would force the "fraternal" parties to demand that the CPSU change its internal policy. Otherwise they would be compromising themselves, exposing themselves as Stalinists. In the third place, we ourselves had not yet broken with communism. We had faith in a "real" communism and stated in our letters that we wished to help in building it.

In addition to these letters, twelve persons, among them Pyotr Yakir, Victor Krasin, Sergei Pisaryev, Kostyorin, and I sent to Budapest a telegram protesting unlawful sentences in the USSR. We received no replies to our letters and telegrams—unless the fact that my letter was bound into my indictment documents could be considered an answer. No answer despite the fact that I received an official post office notification of delivery of the letter to its addressee. When they presented the letter to me during the course of my investigation,

I asked my interrogator, "On what basis is it here with you? Why was it intercepted? After all, I wrote to the Central Committee of a fraternal party, not to an anti-Soviet organization."

"But its content was anti-Soviet."

"How could you have learned about its content? You must have opened the letter and violated my privacy of correspondence." I was shown a curious document, an official declaration by two post office employees who stated that my envelope had ripped open on a conveyor belt and that they had read the letter, seen it was anti-Soviet, and passed it along to the KGB.

However, I'd sent a copy of the letter to the Central Committee of the Italian Communist Party. It got there, but it did not get to the meeting. Surprisingly enough, this copy also turned up in my case file. When I was in Italy in 1978, I demanded that the Communist Party of Italy make a public explanation of this miracle; in reply a representative of the party spoke such rubbish that the audience became indignant and whistled him down.

While we attacked with our letters in 1968, the enemy was not sitting still with folded arms. The KGB was disturbed by the letters of protest and by the large number who had begun to speak out. They began to call these people in to give them "advice" and "friendly warnings" and called in us "veterans" as well. The machinery for frightening people was working at full capacity. I was called to the Malaya Lubyanka on February 12, 1968. While there I saw quite a few young people who had been summoned.

The reason for my summons was the September 5, 1967, publication in the newspaper *Posev* of materials that, according to a statement by the paper's editorial board, had been sent by me. I declared that regardless of whether the statement of *Posev's* editorial board was true or false, I had nothing to discuss with the KGB—because the publication of truthful information that is not a state or a military secret is not illegal, no matter what organ of the press it appears in.

All this I wrote in a letter to Andropov, which I sent to him February 19. I singled out the unlawful demands and the foolish conduct of the KGB officials who talked to me at the Malaya Lubyanka. At the time letters of this sort were in great demand in samizdat. If the KGB had not been so bureaucratized it would have refrained from summoning those who might speak out—their stories had an enormous educational significance. New members of the movement who at one point had feared the KGB began to sense that the "devil is not so awful as he is painted" and to understand that observance of the laws could be demanded of the KGB, too, that a person does not have to respond to a summons if there is no formal official notification of summons or if the formal official notification does not indicate why a person is being summoned. Many accounts of meetings with the KGB written by intelligent people focused especially on the amusing aspects of the meetings. Everyone understood the importance of laughter. A ridiculed KGB did not make one tremble.

In the meantime a related battle erupted when, acting on the September 5,1967, decree of the Presidium of the Supreme Soviet, families and groups of Tatars began to resettle in the Crimea. Some were able to get their residences registered on their passports; the majority were officially expelled, but a group of these people stayed without passports. The largest group settled in the regions nearest the Crimea, in the neighboring Ukrainian provinces and in the Krasnodar region. All besieged the government and party institutions. Those who had settled in the Kherson, Zaporozhe, and Krasnodar areas formed their own groups and sent representatives to Moscow.

Each day they came to the reception rooms of the Central Committee and of the Presidium of the Supreme Soviet and, referring to the violation of the September 5 decree, sought to be received so that the question of their residence registration could be settled.

The authorities deceived them, telling them that "instructions had been issued in localities," and they were expelled with the help of police. The Tatars kept writing and demanding what belonged to them. The literacy rate was not high among them, so before sending anything they showed it to someone like Alexei Kostyorin, who was their old friend. Upon his return in 1956 from seventeen years of imprisonment in camps and exile, he had immediately joined them in their struggle to return to their homeland.

Kostyorin had been born and raised in the Northern Caucasus, an area where many different nationalities mingle. From childhood he had seen the cruel oppression of small groups of people. Suffering from the fact that people of his own nationality, Russian, had emerged as oppressors, he, as a Russian patriot, decided to devote his life to the struggle for national equality. "The Small and the Forgotten"—the title of an article Kostyorin issued in samizdat—knew him and loved him. No matter when I visited him, he almost always had visitors from either the Northern Caucasus, the Crimea, or the Volga (Germans).

In late February 1967 Kostyorin suffered a serious heart attack. When I visited him in the hospital in mid-March, he asked me to attend and speak at a banquet the Crimean Tatars were holding in honor of his birthday. Though it was risky, I agreed to do it.

The banquet was held in a hotel in the Altai Mountains. Present were about 250 Crimean Tatars from all the resettlement areas—Central Asia, the Urals, Kazakstan, Krasnodor, the Crimea, Kherson, and Zaporozhe. They'd asked me ahead of time if they could record my speech and I'd assented. At that time only a few Crimean Tatars knew me; I don't think I knew anyone present.

The chairman of the affair praised me at length, stressing my former position as a general and emphasizing that I was Kostyorin's closest friend. I spoke first about Alexei Kostyorin and his struggle for the rights of the small peoples, particularly for the rights of the Crimean Tatars to return to their homeland. Following is the body of the speech.

"Now let me express the views of Kostyorin and myself on the immediate problems of your movement. It will soon be twenty-five years since your people were cast out of their homes, were expelled from the land of their forefathers, and were exiled onto reservations where such dreadful conditions reigned that the annihilation of the entire Crimean Tatar people appeared inevitable. But the hardy and hard-working Crimean Tatar people survived to spite their enemies.

"After having lost forty-six percent of their numbers in the forced exile disaster, they began to gather strength and to enter into battle for their own national and human rights. This struggle led to certain successes: the status of exiled deportees was lifted and a political rehabilitation of the people was achieved. True, this rehabilitaiton was carried out quietly . . . which in significant degree rendered it valueless. The majority of the Soviet people, who previously had been widely informed that the Crimean Tatars had sold the Crimea, never did learn that this 'sale' was transparent fabrication. But worst of all, the decree on political rehabilitation . . . legalized the liquidation of the Crimean Tatar nationality. Now, it appears, there are no Crimean Tatars, there are just Tatars who formerly lived in Crimea.

"This fact alone serves as the most convincing proof that your struggle not only did not achieve its goal but has led to a backward movement. You were subjected to repressions as Crimean Tatars, but now, after your 'political rehabilitation,' there is no such nationality in the world.

"A nationality has disappeared. But discrimination has remained. You did not commit the crimes for which you were expelled from the Crimea, but you are not permitted to return there now.

"Why have your people been so discriminated against? Section 123 of the Soviet Constitution reads: 'Any direct or indirect limitation on rights . . . of citizens because of their racial or national membership . . . is punishable by law.'

"Thus *the law is on your side.*" [Stormy applause]

"But still your rights are being flouted. *Why?*

"We believe that the main reason behind this is the fact that you underestimate your enemy. You think that you are dealing with honest people. But this is not so! What has been done to your people was not done by Stalin alone. And his accomplices are not only alive—but they occupy responsible positions. You are appealing to the leadership of the party and the state with conciliatory written requests. But *that which belongs to you by right should not be asked for but demanded.*" [Stormy applause and cries of agreement]

"So begin to demand. And demand not just parts, pieces, but all that was taken from you unlawfully—demand the reestablishment of the Crimean Autonomous Soviet Socialist Republic!" [Stormy applause and cries of "Hail the Crimean Autonomous Soviet Socialist Republic"]

"Don't limit your actions to the writing of petitions. Fortify them with all of those means which the Constitution provides you—the freedom of speech and of the press, of meetings, assemblies, of street marches and demonstrations.

"A newspaper is published for you in Moscow. But the people behind that newspaper do not support your movement. Take the newspaper away from them. Elect your own editorial board. And if people hinder you in doing this, boycott that newspaper and create another one—your own! A movement cannot develop normally without its own press.

"And in your struggle do not shut yourselves in a narrow nationalist shell. Establish contacts with all the progressive people of other nationalities of the Soviet Union. Do not consider your cause to be solely an internal Soviet matter. Appeal for help to the world progressive public and to international organizations. What was done to you in 1944 has a name. It was *genocide.*

"The agreement adopted by the General Assembly of the United Nations on December 9, 1948, referred to genocide as follows: '. . . actions carried out with the intent of destroying fully or in part some national, ethnic, racial or religious group . . .' by various means and in particular by intentional establishment 'for them of conditions of life which have as their purpose its complete or partial physical extermination' [of the group]. Such actions, that is, genocide, 'from the point of view of international law are a crime which is to be condemned by the civilized world and for committing which the principal persons guilty and their accomplices are subject to punishment.' As you see, *international law* is also *on your side."* [Stormy applause]

"And if you fail to solve this question inside the country you have the right to appeal to the U. N. and to the International Court.

"Stop asking! Get back that which belongs to you by right but was unlawfully taken from you!" [Stormy applause. People jumped up and cried: "The Crimean ASSR! The Crimean ASSR!"]

"And remember: In this just and noble struggle you must not allow the enemy to seize with impunity the warriors who are marching in the first ranks of your movement.

"In Central Asia there has already been a whole series of trials at which fighters for the national equality of the Crimean Tatars have been illegally convicted of false charges. Right now in Tashkent a trial of the same stature is being prepared against Enver Mametov, Yuri and Sabri Osmanov, and others. Do not permit them to be judicially repressed. Demand that the trial be public in accordance with the law. Demand and get a public trial, go to it *en masse,* and do not permit the courtroom to be packed with a specially chosen audience. Courtroom representatives of the Crimean Tatar people must be seated in the courtroom."

In ending, I delivered a toast: "To the brave and unbending fighters for national equality, to Alexei Kostyorin, to the successes of the Crimean Tatar people, and to a reunion in the Crimea, in the reestablished Crimean Autonomous Republic!"

The hall was in an uproar. You could barely make out what people were shouting, but many began to sing the "Internationale." And the Crimean Tatars did not sing it alone. All those in the hotel restaurant—customers and employees as well—joined in. I expected that someone would denounce us to the secret police—and that we would be dispersed, but we celebrated till late that night. The Crimean Tatars mingled with the restaurant customers and everyone talked about the illegal oppression of the Tatars. That evening certainly showed me how all our people longed for free speech.

In 1974, after my second imprisonment in a psychiatric asylum, Alik Ginzburg said to me, "Your speech at the celebration of Alexei Kostyorin's seventy-second birthday was an *event.*"

I laughed and told him that Rashidov, the First Secretary of the Central Committee of Uzbekistan, had had an even higher opinion of it. Speaking at a meeting of party activists of the republic he had said that the Crimean Tatars had disseminated the "anti-Soviet speech of Grigorenko in eight million copies."

Right after the banquet, the Tatars decided to announce their demands for return of the Crimea and for the restoration of autonomy at a grand public demonstration in which all Crimeans would take part. The official date for it was April 21—Lenin's birthday, which that year coincided with a Moslem holiday. A demand was made to the authorities for permission to conduct a national holiday in the important industrial center of Uzbekistan, the city of Chirchik. As usual the authorities did not reply to the public's demand, but on the appointed day thousands of Tatars streamed to Chirchik from all ends of Uzbekistan, on trains and buses and in automobiles.

The authorities undertook to disperse the demonstration. Police, firemen, and military units were brought in, and blockades were set up on all roads leading to the city. Automobiles were detained. Crimean Tatar passengers were taken out of buses and automobiles and ordered to return home. The blockade was unsuccessful. More than ten thousand people gathered in Chirchik. Police parked automobiles all over the square where the demonstration was to be held. Despite this, the demonstration began. At that point, water cannons were brought out and water mixed with chlorine and indelible dye was shot under tremendous pressure at the demonstrators.

None of the marchers ran from the water cannons—nor did they run from the police truncheons that were also unleashed upon them. And so it was that, soaked to the skin, stained and beaten, an enormous column of people marched along the streets of Chirchik chanting their slogans: "Our homeland is the Crimea. Return it to us!" "Hail to the Crimean ASSR." "Bring the law violators to justice!"

About noon Moscow time, we received a telegram from Chirchik about the events taking place there. That a telegram of this sort arrived indicated the growing power of our movement. People who worked on the lines of communication were sympathetic to us. They did not report the unusual text to the authorities and in precise execution of their duties they delivered the message in full.

I passed the message on to Alexei Kostyorin, who summoned the foreign correspondents. Reports of the events in Chirchik were broadcast on that same day.

A participant in the demonstration, Aider Bariyev, flew into Moscow that night. He arrived dressed in the same clothes in which he'd been assaulted by the water cannon, his suit covered with stains. He brought photographs of the water cannon and of the militia truncheons. Kostyorin and I held a press conference.

The next day more people arrived from Chirchik with more of the story to tell. The demonstration had gone on till late at night. The police, frightened by the possibility of a riot, had fled. With some difficulty, the Crimean Tatar leaders persuaded their people to return to their homes. During the night about three hundred of the most active Crimean Tatars were arrested, including some who had not been present at the demonstration. Eleven of those detained were tried. The nature of the trial and the unconscionable falsifications perpetrated by the prosecution were later exposed.

It is difficult to overemphasize the importance of the events in Chirchik. From that time onward the Crimean Tatar movement became united with the main current of the human rights movement in the Soviet Union and became known to the world at large.

The Crimean Tatars' heightened sense of their own worth led to a subsequent demonstration at the headquarters of the Central Committee of the CPSU in Moscow. It was scheduled for May 18, the twenty-fourth anniversary of their deportation from the Crimea. Over eight hundred people had gathered. This time the authorities were well informed of what was planned and were prepared to deal with anything that might arise. The Tatars were told that they could stay in hotels in only one district—the area of the Exhibition of Achievements of the Economy. Naturally this aroused suspicion and all tried to find places to stay elsewhere in town. However, most were forced to remain in the area designated.

A public demonstration was scheduled to take place at the Central Committee building at 11:00 A.M. on the seventeenth. At 5:00 P.M. on the sixteenth a test gathering was scheduled in the area of the hotels near the exhibition. When people began arriving, police surrounded them on all sides and, grabbing them, pushed them into automobiles. Some 200 to 250 were carted off. The rest had managed to break out of the encirclement and hide. The police planned to waylay those who would still be arriving that night and on into the morning. Kostyorin phoned me at seven that evening and reported what had taken place. I told him to advise all those who had come to him not to go back to their hotels. We would make room for some of them in our apartment and send the rest to friends.

But evidently many were shy about bothering us, and a considerable number spent the night in their hotels despite our warnings. Police arrived during the night, and many Tatars were carried off.

On May 17 at 10:00 A.M. a small group of Muscovites went to Old Square. We did not intend to participate in the demonstration. The Crimean Tatars had asked us not to. They were certain that the demonstrators would be arrested. "And you," they said, "are needed more in freedom than in prison."

But we wanted to observe what took place and we therefore arrived at the square ahead of time and sat down on park benches. We noticed a young man who looked Middle Eastern being approached by a policeman, who asked the young man to go with him. In fact, all passersby who looked Middle Eastern were being detained. Obviously the police were attempting to catch the remaining Tatars. There were many police and KGB-type men in civilian clothes in the square.

A group came into view in which I recognized several Crimean Tatars I knew. The police and plainclothesmen rushed them, examined their documents, and took them away in a bus. Another group of Tatars appeared, then another and another. All were detained and all protested to no avail. I couldn't restrain myself any longer. I walked over to the detaining area, presented my passport, and demanded to know what was going on. The police asked me to leave, but I insisted that it was my right to know why these people, who'd done nothing reprehensible, and whose documents were in order, were being detained. I was told only that I would have to ask at the forty-eighth precinct.

When more buses came, and they began to load the Tatars into them, I got in after them. The senior officer, wearing the uniform of a lieutenant colonel of police, warned me, "We are not detaining you. You are going of your own volition." When we arrived at the police station they did not permit me to remain with the Tatars and instead led me into a separate room, where they gave a police lieutenant colonel the job of ascertaining what should be done with me. They spent, in all, some eight hours—until 7:30 P.M.—finding out. At five o'clock Pyotr Yakir, Pavel Litvinov, and several others brought me some food and demanded an explanation for my detention. They were told that I was not being detained and that I would be let go as soon as certain information regarding me was clarified. Pyotr Yakir was resolute. "We will wait here for the general's release. We will go only when we can go with him. And if it drags out for more than two hours you have only yourself to blame."

What basis this threat had, I still do not know, but there is no doubt that it helped get me out of there. I was freed in less than two hours. Before Pavel and the others arrived, the question of a longer detention was brought up. The district prosecutor had been summoned and was seated alongside the officer guarding over me. It is curious that when I told the guard that it was Yakir who had been talking to him, he was astonished and asked who else there was famous. When I named Litvinov, he ran to the door. "Which one is he?" I pointed him out and he ran into the precinct office. After this everyone gathered to look at Yakir and Litvinov, just as they had all come before to look at me. Times had changed.

And what was being done, in the meantime, with the Tatars? All those detained were put into trains headed for Tashkent. Many jumped off and returned to Moscow. Moreover, the authorities had not caught them all. About seventy assembled at the alternate gathering point and marched again on Old Square. They got there at about 3:00 P.M., approached from the direction of the Moscow River embankment, not from the center as had been done previously. The police and the KGB had relaxed and one demonstrator succeeded in passing along the entire width of the square displaying a banner that read: "Communists! Return the Crimea!"

Next day (May 18) all of those who had escaped from the trains and those who had not been caught met again, at another gathering point, and from there marched on Red Square. The day before several people had succeeded in getting the permission of the Kremlin commandant to place a wreath at Lenin Mausoleum. The commandant had been caught unaware. He did not know that there was no such nationality as the Crimean Tatars. As a result about three hundred representatives of this nonexistent nationality passed through Red Square and deposited the wreath, on which was written in black on red: "To the great Lenin from the *Crimean Tatars.*"

This, too, was a demonstration.

The Tatars mourned not the "leader of the world proletariat" but their own countrymen who had perished during the deportation, and, finally, the Crimea itself.

By June 1968 we had become fascinated by what was taking place in Czechoslovakia. Czech newspapers had stopped being sold openly. Those that did manage to reach us were read until they wore out. The most significant documents produced, such as "2,000 Words," a paper that set forth a program for democratization of the Czechoslovakian Communist Party, were translated into Russian and circulated. We listened to what the infrequent tourists told us about Czechoslovakia as if it were all a fairy tale. On one occasion I met two tourists at Kostyorin's. When I arrived they were talking about how public opinion was being manifested. Before the recent trip to Moscow of the Czech party and government delegation, people collected signatures in support of the policies of Alexander Dubček, who in January had succeeded Antonín Novotny as First Secretary of the Czech Communist Party. In just a few hours more than three million signatures were collected. On hearing this, one of my comrades sighed and half-joked, "If only you would occupy us!" I laughed along with everyone else. It never occurred to me that *our* country could play the role of an occupying power.

Sympathies for Czechoslovakia were so widespread in Russia that it seemed it would be insane for the Soviet government to risk intervention in their struggle. Whenever and wherever someone spoke about the events in Czechoslovakia, and people often did, others listened with profound interest. Nonetheless, the Soviet press repeatedly tried to stimulate suspicion and mistrust of the Czech leadership. This campaign intensified after the notorious letter of the ninety-nine workers of the Czechoslovak Communist Party of Prague. Soviet-engineered, this document stated that under Dubček's leadership the party was veering away from the explicit goals of socialism.

In May I had lost my job, supposedly because of a reduction in staff, though I knew no such cutbacks were taking place. I protested my dismissal in court, but the judge rejected my suit. An appeal got me nowhere. I pondered going to Yalta to work at the vegetable warehouse. A raid of Crimean Tatars from Central Asia into the Crimea was being planned, and it would be useful for me to be there during it. As Kostyorin and I discussed this raid, we also discussed Czechoslovakia. Certainly it was necessary to take some sort of action against the petty campaign being conducted in the Soviet press. We decided to write a letter to the Czech leadership expressing our approval of its domestic policy. The letter would be transmitted via the Czech embassy in Moscow. Kostyorin wrote it with my help. In addition to the two of us, it was signed by Sergei Pisaryev, Ivan Yakhimovich, and Valery Pavlinchuk. All of us considered ourselves Communists, though Yakhimovich and I had both been expelled from the party and the question of Pavlinchuk's expulsion was about to be decided. Ivan Yakhimovich and I were chosen to take the letter to the embassy.

On the eve of our planned visit Kostyorin and I were talking and once again the question of Soviet intervention in Czechoslovakia came up. Once again we expressed our conviction that it was impossible, but something worried me. I said, "You know, Alexei, my military conscience refuses to permit me to relax. What seems most unlikely is precisely most probable. The moment you decide an event is impossible and therefore stop directing your attention to it, is the moment when it will take place. If I were the Czechs I would be prepared to repel an attack. Anyway, it should be fairly easy to defend Czechoslovakia.

"The Austrian border is safe, as is the Hungarian border. The Hungarians are so weak that they can be easily frightened off. Only the borders with the USSR, Poland, and East Germany are left, and less than a dozen roads would have to be blocked in order to halt the tank armadas. And if they were to add to that the defense of a small number of airports, there could be no surprise invasion. And without surprise the entire invasion would fail. It might even end with a total collapse of the invaders. If I were the Czechs, I would do all of that and I would also warn Brezhnev that in the event of attack they would defend themselves and declare their country to be in danger. Brezhnev may be a fool but he is not going to risk war. His only hope is in retaining the element of surprise. The Czech army is the most capable in Eastern Europe, and the people are unanimous in support of their govenrment. A military gamble in conditions like that could kill Brezhnev and his government. Czech resistance could set in motion destructive antiimperialist forces in East Germany, Poland, and yes, for that matter in the Soviet Union itself."

"If only that would happen," remarked Alexei, adding, "In that case you should write Dubček and tell him exactly what you have just told me. And transmit the letter in sealed form, and mark it PERSONAL."

I did not write the letter in the form of personal advice; I was afraid that it would turn up in the hands of the KGB. The text, I thought, should be such that I will not be charged with treason for writing it. I wrote not as though I was giving advice, but as if I was merely expressing my pleasure at the work Dubček was carrying on. I wished him all success and health and in conclusion I wrote him approximately as follows: "I do not think that genuine Communists would hinder your noble activity. Even more I do not believe in the possibility of Soviet intervention. Brezhnev is a Communist—and also a military man. He knows tht Czechoslovakia could block a Soviet invasion very easily. All that is necessary is to seize the main roads from East Germany, Poland, and the USSR, and organize defense of airdromes. Hungary can be easily stopped by a mere threat of retaliation. Brezhnev understands that all of that could cause a war which at present would be no less dangerous for the USSR than for Czechoslovakia."

Our "Letter of Five People" appeared in samizdat and in the Western press. As far as I know my personal letter to Dubček was not published, though a letter from Anatoly Marchenko to Dubček was.

Several days after the publication of his letter in the West, Anatoly was arrested and charged with a violation of passport regulations: the accusation, that he was residing in Moscow when, strictly speaking, he was registered to reside only in Aleksandrovo (about 100 kilometers away).

Residence is defined as remaining in a given place for more than three days. Anatoly knew the laws and knew also that he would not be forgiven the least violation of them. Yet in fact he never stayed in Moscow for more than two days at a time, though he worked there and his wife lived there. Larisa Bogoraz spent a large part of the year with him in Aleksandrovo. Those of us who knew Anatoly realized he had not been arrested just to "give him a good scare." This time the authorities would certainly try to "settle accounts" with him. An innocent person who has defied the terror networks' demand for conformity will survive only if he repents of the crimes he has not committed and thanks the party and the government for permitting him to live. But if this person, crippled and barely alive after torture, should retain his pride and defend his dignity, they will attempt to destroy him physically.

Anatoly was precisely this kind of person. Born into a family of workers in Siberia, he had finished eight grades of secondary school and been given a Komsomol assignment. He set off enthusiastically to labor at the "great construction projects of communism." Despite harsh living conditions, he did not return to the relative comfort of his parents' home—as so many tens of thousands of enthusiastic youths who had experienced reality at these construction projects had done. Anatoly Marchenko continued to work and to earn his own living. He might have become a highly skilled construction worker esteemed by all, perhaps even an engineer or an executive, or perhaps a party official. He *might* have, if Soviet "justice" had not taken a hand in his fate! Marchenko was first arrested and convicted under a clause of the Criminal Code that was so obviously cruel and inhumane that the Supreme Soviet of the Turkmenian Soviet Socialist Republic was forced not only to annul it but to liberate all of those sentenced under it and to annul their convictions.

In the context of his first trial Marchenko had committed no crime; he realized that himself. The undeserved conviction struck hard at his sensitive psyche. Then came the horrors of camp and his initial hurt grew into an insistent desire to leave the country in which he had been treated so harshly. Not realizing that the document for his release had already been signed he fled the camp, worked a short time near the border, and attempted to cross it but was arrested.

It's a well-known fact that criminal prosecution for an attempt at illegal border crossing is in contradiction to the generally accepted norms of the Universal Declaration of Human Rights and other treaties of international law that have been signed by our country. As Marchenko wrote in *My Testimony*, his companion Burovsky testified against him under pressure from the interrogators. As it turned out, Marchenko was charged not with illegal border-crossing but with treason to the motherland—in other words, a crime he had not committed. He was given a sentence of "less than the minimum term." But he did not understand the judge's "humanitarianism." He did not understand it because the "humane" sentence he was given was double the maximum sentence he would have received for illegal border-crossing.

He began to seek an answer in the classics of Marxism-Leninism, in literature, in communication with people, in the environment of the Mordovian political camps. His methodology for mastering Marxism-Leninism was simple: he took the complete collection of Lenin's works and studied one volume after another. Few can even imagine what a Herculean task this was for him. This person, almost a political illiterate, had to conduct his own archeological excavations in those fifty-five volumes in which the real Lenin is hidden. He did master this heritage, and he used the same method on the collected works of Marx and Engels.

When I met Marchenko in 1967 I realized at once that he was erudite in Marxism-Leninism; I had not encountered a person of such erudition in many years. His book had astonished us with its honesty, the thoroughness of its documentation, and its literary excellence.

Now he was being tried once again without basis. There was no proof that he had violated those ridiculous passport regulations. But a Soviet court can always find "proof."

"The proof," declared the judge, "lies in the fact that you work in Moscow. Your wife lives in Moscow. You are in Moscow. That means you live in Moscow. And you are not registered as a resident of Moscow."

What logic! What, then, is the status of all those thousands of other Aleksandrovo inhabitants who also work in Moscow, though they're not registered as Muscovites? What can they do, when there are no jobs in Aleksandrovo and no housing in Moscow?

Marchenko was convicted and sentenced to the maximum term under the appropriate section of the code—two years in a severe regime camp. We all knew that his term would not be limited to two years, that he would also receive a camp trial. We tried to bring this to the attention of the world public, and our prophecy came true. After two years he was again tried—in camp—and sentenced to another two years. We had estimated that they would give him ten, but this was prevented by international public opinion. The broad and persistent campaign in defense of Marchenko not only prevented the camp court from giving him a maximum sentence but prevented them from trying him a second time in camp. In order to try to undermine the campaign in his behalf, the authorities "released" Marchenko for a short time, leaving him under police supervision. Several months later they convicted him for "violation of this supervision," and he was sentenced to exile in Siberia. In Siberia they began immediately to prepare a forged case against him for alleged participation in theft of gold, but honest people informed Anatoly's friends in Moscow of this provocation. At the request of these friends, I wrote a letter to American labor leader George Meany informing him of what was happening to Marchenko. He reacted swiftly and decisively, and his action forced the Soviet authorities to drop their plan. In late 1978 Marchenko was finally freed. Thus those two years to which he had been sentenced in 1968 had stretched on and on. He and Larisa Bogoraz feel that they owe Anatoly's life to Meany, since the code clause on the theft of gold provides for the death penalty, precisely what the authorities were aiming at. Anatoly is now living in Aleksandrovo, where he brought his parents from Siberia. Offered emigration, he said: "I have too much to do in my homeland."

I was in the Crimea after Anatoly's trial in 1968. The situation there was unbelievable. The railway station, the airport, and the city parks of Simferopol were swarming with Tatars. They had even set up a tent city near the Simferopol reservoir. From morning to night their representatives besieged government and party institutions and the police, seeking just one thing—registration as residents. They were received nowhere. It is impossible for me to render the horrors that I saw. The multitude of half-naked, dirty children sleeping on the cement floor of the railway station and the airport were the fortunate. What about those who slept on the bare earth in the parks! At night it is cold there; often I heard the freezing children crying.

In any democratic country, a government that had created such a situation would not have stayed in power for even three days. To save itself it would have had to try in every way to find shelter for these people. And in a democratic country the population, even without pressure from the government, would have manifested concern for the unfortunates. But the Simferopol inhabitants did nothing. And for that matter, how could they? The authorities had warned them not to help the Tatars. Those who sold their homes to Tatars were called into the police and ordered to cancel the contract or go to prison. The authorities kept thinking up new ways to make the situation worse. They began to drive the people out of the airport and the railway station before dawn. In the parks, they doused the Tatars with water at dawn, without warning. I was outraged and wrote a letter to the head of the provincial government protesting these actions. I warned him that the people were ready to defend themselves. The Tatars took the letter from me and in one hour collected more than two thousand signatures. That same day the deputy chairman of the provincial executive committee informed those who had delivered the letter that people would be asked to leave the station and the airport only during the clean-up period. The incidents in the parks had been misunderstandings. After this, they left the people alone.

Confrontations between the two sides in Simferopol gradually assumed a routine form, with neither willing to take decisive action. There was nowhere for the Tatars to go. They had done their deed by arriving en masse in the

Crimea. When their representatives took a count in autumn 1968, it turned out that during the course of the summer over 12,000 families had been in the Crimea—from 60,000 to 70,000 persons. Now their task was to try to stay there. But Soviet hypocrisy erected as a barrier against their settlement in the Crimea even such a humanist measure as the setting of housing laws. In Moscow the minimum norm was 9 square meters per person, and in other localities it went as high as 11. For Tatars they set it at 13.25 square meters. Tatars often have as many as seven children in a family. Added to this are parents and grandparents. Thus the minimum dwelling space needed would be from 120 to 146 square meters. Since normal one-family houses have from 30 to 50 square meters, a few from 60 to 70, most Tatars were refused housing.

These poor people wandered around the Crimea seeking the impossible. From time to time they would hold demonstrations in front of the provincial party building or the provincial government building. The authorities tried not to provoke them, but now and then they would detain two or three of them and give them from ten to fifteen days each for hooliganism.

Finally the authorities began to show their teeth. In July 1968 they arrested Homer Bayev, an intelligent, calm, tactful man, a remarkable organizer who enjoyed universal esteem among his people. His arrest shocked the Crimean Tatar public. Moscow raised its voice as well. But on the whole the reaction was mild. A release had to be maneuvered, and no one seemed to be taking any step to arrange for one. I continued working calmly at the warehouse in Yalta, where I had gotten back my old job, more concerned with Czechoslovakia than with Crimean Tatar affairs. After alarming government meetings at Chierna and Tissa, I feared that we were going to attack. Then a meeting at Bratislav caused me to relax, something I scolded myself for later. The Bratislav communiqué stated almost directly, though disguised by a bit of Soviet double-talk, that we would attack; and I didn't realize it. I considered myself totally capable of deciphering party hypocrisy—but as it turned out I wasn't.

On August 21 I awakened with a feeling of alarm a few minutes before six. I turned on the radio and immediately heard the word "invasion." But I could think of nothing to do but go to work, where I encountered the sad, confused faces of my fellow workers: "Is it bad, Pyotr Grigoryevich?"

"Yes, very bad."

The older people asked me, "Does it mean war?"

In the city, the mood of the people was generally depressed. Among the resort visitors there was confusion. They didn't know whether to go home or to stay in Yalta. In the evening I wrote a letter to Pavel Litvinov, Larisa Bogoraz, Pyotr Yakir, and Alexei Kostyorin, giving my view of the events in Czechoslovakia. I enclosed an outline for a text I thought they might write, and added that I would support any action they undertook or declaration they made, and that they should telegram me immediately if I was needed in Moscow. Reshat Dzhemiliyev, a member of the Crimean Tatar rights movement, traveled to Moscow by train to deliver the letter. I waited impatiently for news from him, afraid he might be arrested en route.

Tourists were leaving Yalta and there were rumors of heavy battles in Czechoslovakia. Casualty reports arrived. Later I learned that no one was killed in battle—in fact, there were no battles. But to manipulate public opinion the authorities reported normal deaths as battle losses.

Reshat arrived at Litvinov's on the twenty-third. After reading my letter, Litvinov told him under an oath of secrecy that a demonstration had been planned for two days hence. Reshat burned with enthusiasm. He liked decisive action. Pavel cooled him off by telling him, "What you have to do is to observe what happens there. Try to recall everything you see and tell it in full to Pyotr Grigoryevich." So Reshat remained on the sidelines and watched the demonstrators go down to the execution block on Red Square and sit there and display their placards. Then from all sides KGB agents fell upon them and beat them up. Pavel, in order to stress that he had not shown any resistance, raised his hands and his briefcase above his head.

I know how difficult it must have been for Reshat with his Middle Eastern character to keep from rushing to help his friends. Indignantly he told me how they had been beaten cruelly, though they were not resisting. Victor Fainberg, a Jew, was targeted for abuse. The KGB man who assaulted him shouted, "You kike snout. I've been after you for a long time!"

After talking with Reshat on the twenty-sixth, I knew that I had to go to Moscow to help organize the defense of those who had demonstrated for Czechoslovakia. My wife, too, was in favor of returning to Moscow. I secured the wages due me and Reshat bought train tickets for us. We left Simferopol on the twenty-seventh and were in Moscow by the following day. It was an ordinary trip, though we were, of course, tailed by four incompetent plainclothes KGB agents—two husband-and-wife pairs. Because of them the train left twenty minutes after its scheduled departure time. As Zinaida said when we saw them throwing their suitcases on board, they must have overslept.

CHAPTER TWENTY-FIVE

UNDER SIEGE

In Moscow the situation was tense. The authorities had clearly gone over to the offensive. Of the seven demonstrators, the heroes of August 25—Konstantin Babitsky, Larisa Bogoraz, Natalia Gorbanyevskaya, Vadim Delon, Vladimir Dremlyuga, Pavel Litvinov, and Victor Fainberg—six were arrested. Only Natalia Gorbanyevskaya, a nursing mother, was still free. Of those arrested, Victor Fainberg was an obvious candidate for a psychiatric prison. During his detention they had knocked out his front teeth.

Victor demanded to know the name of the man who had detained him—in order to bring him to justice. The authorities, who could neither betray one of their own nor risk showing Victor with his teeth knocked out, sent him to the Serbsky Institute for diagnosis.

The investigation of the remaining five took just over a month. Another case—against Irina Belgordskaya, for participation in the campaign for the defense of Anatoly Marchenko—was being readied more slowly. In Krasnodar, a trial of the Crimean Tatar Homer Bayev was expected. Several additional arrests had been made among the Tatars. Lawyers were needed everywhere, daring lawyers capable of uttering the truth, exposing falsification, insisting on observance of the law, and demanding acquittals. There were not many of these: Kalistratova, Kaminskaya, Zolotukhin (who had defended Ginzburg), Zalessky, Ariya, Monakhov, Reznikov, and Shveidsky—these were nearly all the courageous lawyers of Moscow. For that matter, Zolotukhin really had to be left off the list—he had been forbidden to conduct juridical consultations and denied access to the court. All legal personnel had to be used very carefully, in such a way as to provide for the Muscovites and to send defense counsel to Homer Bayev, especially now that the situation of the Crimean Tatars had worsened.

In September the nights were already cold. Many Tatar families had moved to the Kherson and Zaporozhe provinces and to the Krasnodar region. They counted on advancing from there into the Crimea when spring arrived—until the authorities decided to deport those remaining in the Crimea to the Kerch Strait and further to Taman, the Northern Caucasus, the Caspian Sea area, and central Asia. This route was chosen, evidently, so that those being forcefully deported from the Crimea should not encounter those who had settled in the Ukrainian territories bordering on the Crimea. But the authorities failed to consider that the Northern Caucasus was populated by people who had also suffered forced deportation from their homelands.

As soon as the column of buses and trucks loaded with Tatars appeared in Daghestan, the local inhabitants made it their business to learn what was going on. Such indignation was aroused that the police guarding the column fled. In every village in which the columns halted, the people fed the Tatars, invited them into their homes, and advised them: "Go on back to the Crimea. We will not allow your police to follow you."

The Tatars realized that their journey could be transformed into a great propaganda crusade, and so they recalled their police escorts and continued along the route set for them. Later, participants recounted that the entire journey was one continuous propaganda meeting. Even on the ocean ferry from Baku to Krasnovodsk a propaganda meeting took place. And no one dared interrupt it.

Out of the twelve thousand Tatar families that had entered the Crimea in the summer of 1968, fewer than one thousand managed to settle there. Such numbers made the movement look like a failure. But the Tatars had accomplished the following: 1) They had been strengthened in the realization of their rights, having seen that all other peoples among whom they had passed sympathized with their struggle and that the law was on their side; they realized that the actions of the authorities were based not on the law but on tyranny; 2) They had learned to take advantage of international help, and realized that there were many kind-hearted people abroad who also were struggling for their rights in the face of tyranny; 3) Having settled in new territories—in the Ukraine and the Krasnodar region—they had acquired a broad base for future support of their cause by other peoples.

In the meantime in Moscow the trial of the heroes of August 25 began October 10, forty-six days after the demonstration. This was unheard of; with other trials, the periods of investigation often took more than a year. The short preparation time made obvious the trial's political nature.

The actions for which our friends were being prosecuted bore no relation to the criminal code section (190–3) under which they were charged. Their group action had not "crudely violated public order or involved clear-cut disobedience to the lawful demands of the representatives of the government or entailed the violation of the work of transport, state, and public institutions and enterprises."

The court knew this to be the case and it did not even try to present evidence of violations. The judges questioned the defendants on everything—except the "crimes" with which they were charged. When Volodya Dremlyuga, a quick-witted, jolly, and communicative man, was being questioned, the judge, a woman, leafing through a small notebook, asked him, "I notice some girls' names listed here. Were you living with any of them?"

"That bears no relationship to my case," Volodya replied calmly. "And even if I did, it still did not take place on a thoroughfare and could not have interfered with transport."

There was laughter in the hall. The judge rebuked Dremlyuga. He received many other rebukes, but he continued to make his witty and ironical remarks.

His behavior cost him dearly. He was the only one to get the maximum sentence under this section of the criminal code—three years of camp. In camp they added another three to the original sentence and when this term, too, came to an end, they informed him that one more case had been prepared against him and told him that if he refused to confess they would give him another seven years or maybe even ten. Volodya "repented" and after his release asked for an exit visa. Today he lives in the United States.

During the trial of Konstantin Babitsky, his wife Tatyana Mikhailovna Velikanova, was called as a witness. The judge asked, "Did you know that your husband was going to a demonstration?"

"Yes, I did."

"And you also knew that they might arrest him."

"Yes, I also knew that."

"How could you, a mother of three children, not restrain your husband from taking such a dangerous step?"

"But how could I hinder him from carrying out what he considered to be his moral duty?"

The courtroom, each occupant of which was hand-picked, fell silent after this reply. Tatyana Mikhailovna's reply was so morally superior that even such a public and even such a judge could do no more than bow their heads in the face of it.

(It was during the trial that I first met Tatyana Mikhailovna Velikanova.

She became a close friend of our family, and then came kinship—our Andrei
married her younger sister, Mariya. As these lines are being written Tanya
is in prison where she, too, awaits an unlawful trial.)

The court was most concerned with the contents of the slogans that had
been displayed by the demonstrators: "Down with the occupation of the
Czechoslovak Socialist Soviet Republic," and others. The display of slogans
is not a crime under any section of the law. But the court did not even try
to conceal the fact that the crime for which the defendants were being tried
was the protest against the occupation. The First Secretary of the Moscow
party committee, Grishin, speaking at the September meeting of party activists
in Moscow, said that the entire people had approved of the "brotherly assistance" to Czechoslovakia, and that in all Moscow, *only thirteen people* had
spoken out against the introduction of Soviet armed forces into Czechoslovakia.

While the number was small, I was overjoyed. After all, these were thirteen
isolated individuals. And any Soviet citizen who was capable of speaking out
as an individual against actions of the Soviet government, and especially such
an action as intervention, was worth many thousands.

The battle was not just inside the courtroom; it took place all around the
Proletarsky building. When we arrived in the morning, those who wanted to
be admitted to the trial were always huddled together several steps from the
building. I did not know all of these people, but I felt that they were not hostile
toward us. Many claimed to be relatives of the defendants, a sure sign that
they were spontaneous protesters. Policemen stood in front of them, and to
all their requests for admission came only one reply: "There are no empty seats
in the courtroom." It was perhaps an hour before the trial. When and how
and with whom the courtroom was filled no one knew.

Those people I knew who were experienced "dissidents" did not approach
the police but stood in a separate group. They knew there were "no seats in
the courtroom." Separately stood a rather impressive group of about fifty
young people. They were the so-called druzhinniki—auxiliary police volunteers. The police gradually pushed aside those claiming to be "relatives." Some
joined us and others, from lack of experience, moved to the side of the auxiliary
police. More and more of our people kept arriving until our numbers were
greater than the auxiliary police. One of our people came up to me and called
me aside, saying he wanted to show me what was going on in the nearby courtyards.

I went with him and, yes, he showed me something to think about. There
in the courtyards were rows and rows of automobiles in formation. In them
were seated, as if on parade, with both hands on the barrels of their carbines,
rank-and-file policemen. We passed more than ten such courtyards and everywhere saw the same picture.

I returned to our people and summoned them all into a small park opposite the court building. The auxiliary police followed. I paid no attention to them, and said, "Today we can expect provocations. The nearby courtyards are full of automobiles with armed policemen in them. I ask you not to allow yourselves to be victims of any kind of a provocation. Have nothing to do with quarrelsome people. In case of hooliganism, appeal to the official police."

No sooner had I spoken than several drunken workers, among them a woman, emerged from a small factory alongside the park. They began to pester us. The woman was particularly offensive. I approached the police and spoke directly with the senior officer present, a major. "Do you see what is going on?"

I pointed at the drunks. He halfheartedly rebuked them, and they fell silent for a short time. Then there appeared a group of workers in overalls spotted with paint. They were sober and I paid no particular attention to them, but Zinaida, who possessed a sixth sense for spotting KGB men, exclaimed, "How is it that you've pulled on workers' coveralls and failed to take off your patent leather oxfords?"

I looked at them more closely and saw that they really were wearing patent leather oxfords. Yes, and their coveralls had just been daubed with paint. Surprised at first by Zinaida's remark, the men swiftly regained their innate impudence, and one of them maliciously hissed, "You kike bitch! You should be hanged upside down from a tree till your brains fall out!"

They had good reason to be angry. We all knew who they were, and as they moved toward us we stepped back and said, "Make way for the working class."

Ultimately they were forced to retreat behind the factory and take off their camouflage suits. Then one by one they appeared again in front of the court building—in plainclothes.

For the three days of the trial they continually tried to provoke us. The situation became particularly tense on the second day. At one point we were composing a collective letter and I was reading aloud what we'd written. Suddenly someone shouted: "Look at this, Pyotr Grigoryevich!" One of our men had grasped an auxiliary policeman's wrist, and he showed us a brass knuckle the man had on. We led him over to the police, but as we approached, the auxiliary policeman got away. "He has brass knuckles on his right hand," I told the major.

"I don't see them," he objected, watching the auxiliary policeman, his brass knuckles shining, run and hide in the entryway of the court building.

It was obvious they were preparing for a melee, and they would then blame us for the weapons. We went to the nearest telegraph office—in the skyscraper on the Kotelnikov embankment—and sent a telegram to the Minister of Public Order, Shcholokov, reporting that with the compliance of the uniformed police a hooligan element was readying an assault on the people who assembled at the court building. While we were at the telegraph office, the auxiliary police provoked a certain amount of disorder and the police detained several of our people. Our entire group thereupon went to the 10th precinct, where our comrades had been taken. Our impressive number prompted the police to release those of us who had been detained. In just an hour the telegram sent to Shcholokov took effect. The police withdrew their drunken workers, and the auxiliary police began to conduct themselves more responsibly. Several people, however, including Sergei Petrovich Pisaryev, had been beaten up while we were at the telegraph office.

On October 12, the last day of the trial, both the regular police and the auxiliary police behaved as well as we could have wished. Then about 3:00 P.M. I noticed a KGB bigwig, who I had seen before talking to his men and to the regular police and the auxiliary police, leave abruptly and return. Something was underway. They had stolen from our closed automobile most of the flowers we had readied for our lawyers.

Messengers kept running from the bigwig to the telephone and bringing him notes. Yakir, Krasin, I, and a few others told our people that they must band together and not fall for any provocation.

At five o'clock the trial ended. We had difficulty handing the few flowers we had left to the lawyers and shouting out greetings to the convicted defendants as they were led away. An automobile filled with young men drove up. The bigwig loudly asked, "What about the rest?"

From the car they replied, "They'll be here right away."

"Disperse immediately!" I said to our people.

With five or six others my wife and I were among the last to go. At the first street crossing we heard behind us the squeal of brakes. Jumping back on the sidewalk, we heard, "Why did you put on the brakes? Run them down! Run them down!" It was the KGB bigwig giving orders to his driver. He had given his orders so that we could hear him. My wife replied to him with a word he deserved. Later on we learned from the auxiliary police that some men from the factories had planned an assault on us for 6:00 P.M. Blaming me for their failure to carry it out, the KGB decided that same day to teach me a lesson. After the trial I went, as on preceding days, to visit Kostyorin, who was still in the hospital. Although his spirits were good, he had not recovered from his February infarction, and I tried to see him and call him as often as possible. I left the hospital at about nine. Genrikh Altunyah, who was riding with me, called attention to a KGB operations automobile that was following us. I shrugged and replied that they had to do something, so let them ride around in a car.

When we got to my house I found Roy Medvedev there. After we had talked, I walked him to the subway with Genrikh, who fell a bit behind. I said goodbye to Roy, and turned around to see that one of my regular "tails" had attacked Genrikh. Rushing to help him, I saw the same car we had only recently been talking about drive right up on the sidewalk. There were four men in it and a fifth was standing a short distance away on the sidewalk. Three of them jumped out of the car and threw themselves on myself and Genrikh. I brought my walking stick into play and compelled them to retreat. Simultaneously they all blew police whistles and a police patrol car immediately appeared. They put us in it and drove off.

At the 7th precinct everyone was ready for our arrival. Despite the fact that it was 11:00 P.M. , the deputy chief, a police captain, was present, and he immediately proposed that Genrikh and I write an explanation of our behavior. I insisted first on an alcohol test. I could see very well that all of my "tails" were drunk, and I knew that this could be used against them later.

The usual procrastinations and pretexts commenced. Meanwhile the senior of my "tails" fell asleep. At this point Zinaida appeared and soon our friends began to arrive. The drunken group was now about to be exposed—even without alcohol tests—by witnesses. I demanded the names and addresses of those who had attacked us. The captain twisted and turned like a snake caught on a pitchfork and finally said, "Come tomorrow morning to see the precinct chief."

There was nothing more to do so we went to our homes. When I went to see the precinct chief the next morning, he told me that he had not yet sorted the case out. I went the next morning, too. He saw me approaching and ran out before I could enter, telling me as he passed that he had had an urgent call from his superiors. The third morning he refused to meet with me, and on and on. In the end he could no longer get out of giving me an explanation: "Why do you want their names? You know very well who they are. And what are you going to do with their names? They have already been punished for 'disruption of the operation.' After all, they were supposed to get you fifteen days in the cooler. And those idiots had to go and lap up the booze and ruin the whole plan."

Meanwhile life went along on its appointed course. Alexander Kostyorin died on November 10, 1968. At first we were unable to do anything at all—either to notify his friends and relatives, or to report his death to the Soviet Writers Union, of which he had been a member from the day it was founded. How surprised we were the day after, when our representatives—his niece, Irma Mikhailovna, and his friend, Pyotr Yakir—arrived at the Writers Union only to learn that everyone knew about the death and that the Writers Union had already set a time for the cremation—at 4:00 P.M. November 12, in other words, just a day later. Our representatives protested; Pyotr Yakir, for one, said, "That's enough time to burn a dead body. But not enough for us to deliver our farewells to the deceased." We were told, "You want a demonstration? We won't permit it!"

Our representatives appealed to Ilin, the Writers Union secretary. They cited the regulations for deceased veteran members of the Soviet Writers Union that an announcement must be made in the press about the death and about the place and time of the farewell to the deceased and the funeral; that an obituary must be published; that a place in the Writers Club is to be provided for the farewell; and that burial at the Novo-Devichy cemetery is to be paid for by the Literary Fund. We were denied it all.

In the end they took mercy—a bit—and changed the funeral to November 14 and agreed to have the Literary Fund pay for the hearse and the cremation. However, we were forced to reject this offer, since the Literary Fund had scheduled the arrival of the hearse and the delivery of the coffin in such a way that we would have been able to see the deceased only for those few minutes when he was on he crematorium pedestal. The officials then agreed to have the coffin set up for one hour in the morgue funeral hall and to pay for double time in the crematorium. In other words, we would be allowed to have the pedestal and the speaker's platform for half an hour. And the Literary Fund would pay for two buses in addition to the hearse. (Subsequently the Literary Fund refused to pay the bill for the buses.) We ourselves rented a dining hall for the funeral repast.

Everything seemed to have been arranged more or less decently, but several surprises awaited us on the day of the funeral. First of all, the buses carrying the funeral goers and the wreathes were stopped eight hundred meters from the morgue by the municipal traffic control service, which, by a strange set of circumstances, had set up a traffic control position at the entrance to the Botkin Hospital exactly one hour before our arrival. It was removed immediately after we left the morgue. During its entire existence it had held up our two buses, and . . . not one other thing.

The second surprise was not exactly unexpected. This was the intensified concern for our "security" by the police and officials of the KGB. Two of these people carrying light blue booklets—the KGB color—went into the room where the corpse was being kept. By 5:00 P.M. , the time agreed upon, they still had not turned over the body to us, nor at 5:10 nor even at 5:20.

We grew anxious and questioned the morgue administrator several times, but he only muttered something unintelligible and looked at us with pleading eyes. We received another surprise when our comrades who were in charge of preparing the funeral repast arrived at the morgue and reported that the dining hall we had engaged no longer was available.

Clearly the KGB was intent on breaking up the funeral. We talked the entire matter over with Kostyorin's widow, Vera Ivanovna, who decided, "If they don't issue us the body immediately, I will take it home rather than to the crematorium. We'll organize the funeral tomorrow or the day after without the help of the Literary Fund. We'll hold the memorial meeting in our courtyard."

Our conversation was overheard by a man whom some of our people had christened "the secretive man in a hat." He was, we had observed, the ringleader of Kostyorin's KGB escorts. Vera Ivanovna's alternate plans, evidently, did not suit him—and the body of the deceased was issued to us immediately. At 5:35 we placed the coffin on the pedestal and began the memorial meeting. Luckily it was an uneventful service. Kostyorin's friends formed such a close human shield around the coffin that no one dared to interfere with or to insult our sorrow.

Our movement from the morgue to the crematorium went off smoothly— except that the driver of one of the buses suddenly "forgot" how to get from Krasnaya Presnya to the Crimean Bridge and turned in the opposite direction. We had to "explain" the route to the driver. At the crematorium we saw that the courtyard was literally swarming with police and plainclothesmen who themselves were being watched over by the secretive man in a hat, who, by the way, no longer was wearing a hat, but a cap.

Some three hundred to four hundred friends of the writer had assembled in the crematorium hall in a solid mass right behind the coffin. They carried themselves with such conviction and firmness that the plainclothesmen did not dare to try to push their way into that mass but merely remained at the entrance and at a slight distance away inside the hall. Here again they tried to postpone the commencement of the funeral. But at seven our people lifted up the coffin and put it on the pedestal, and the second part of the memorial meeting began. In the middle of my speech, the loudspeaker blared out the words: "Finish it up!" Several minutes later this shout was repeated. I later learned that the man in the hat had shouted to the crematorium commandant: "Lower the coffin!" But our comrades had refused in such a way that the commandant could not really carry out the orders, and the man in the hat did not dare to repeat them.

The funeral took eighteen minutes instead of the scheduled thirty. And once again Alexei Kostyorin triumphed, not his persecutors. After decades of suffocating silence, the first free public meeting had taken place. My friend could be proud. Even in death he had inspired the democratic movement in our country.

No matter how people feel today about this meeting, at that time everyone believed that we had achieved a great victory. No one wanted to get on the buses and leave, but it made no sense to tempt fate further. Provocateurs might try to avenge their defeat. Since we had been denied the dining hall for our funeral repast, I invited everyone to come to our apartment. At this point most of our "guardians" left us. The man in the hat evidently could not imagine that forty-five square meters of floor space could accommodate many people. But all of those who had come in the two buses fit into my apartment. People filled up all the rooms, the kitchen, the bathroom, the corridor and the stair landing in front of the apartment.

Five days after Kostyorin's funeral, on November 19, the doorbell to my
apartment rang and in reply to my question, "Who's there?" I heard only
"From Tashkent!" Presuming it was a Crimean Tatar I calmly removed the
catch. The door jerked open and eleven men poured into the room, hurling
me aside in their rush. When I asked what this was about they handed me
a search warrant that read: "The investigator for particularly important cases
of the Uzbek Republic, counselor of justice Beryozovsky, has constituted in
the course of the investigation of the Crimean Tatar Bariyev and others that
there may be documents which contain slanderous fabrications directed
against the Soviet social and state structure in the apartment of P. G. Grigorenko. It has been decreed that a search is to be carried out."

The warrant had been confirmed by the Moscow prosecutor Malkov. Everything was in order—the signatures, the seals. I demanded that everyone present be introduced to me. Beryozovsky showed me his identification, and said,
"The rest are assisting me."

"Come now. We will act in accordance with the law. Let everyone introduce
himself!" I replied. When Beryozovsky objected, I showed him the relevant
section of the Criminal Procedure Code. He had to give in. It turned out that
seven of the men were Moscow KGB officials and three were "witnesses."
Beryozovsky did not know a thing about the Criminal Procedural Code. Besides being ignorant, he was extremely arrogant.

My first serious conflict with him was caused by the witnesses. Judging from
their documents, they were from another district of Moscow. I protested. I
did not know them. Witnesses to a search were supposed to know me. Otherwise, the authorities might present their own employees as unprejudiced witnesses—which was exactly what was happening here. But what could I do?
There was no one else available.

Presently another man—Lyonya Petrovsky, the grandson of the famous
Bolshevik Grigory Petrovsky—was admitted. Asked to show his documents,
Lyonya, who was employed in the Institute of Marxism-Leninism—which was
attached to the Central Committee of the CPSU—presented a pass bearing
the name of the institution written in such a way that one immediately noticed
"Central Committee of the CPSU." The KGB man who inspected it shouted,
"There's a comrade from the Central Committee of the party here. Maybe
he would consent to stay as a witness?"

Lyonya consented and I agreed. They asked me if they could use one of
their men as a second witness but I said no and demanded they take the second
witness from our apartment building. They hunted about and finally brought
in a retired man from the building next door whom I knew only slightly.

The search commenced. They dug into everything. With Lyonya's help I
amused myself by catching Beryozovsky in his ignorance of the Criminal Procedural Code. Mustafa Dzhemiliyev also sat with us. I was quite upset that

he was there, as he'd been hiding from arrest for several months. He hadn't visited me until yesterday evening, and we'd invited him to spend the night. He'd consented, and now this.

Once again there was a knock at the door. Volodya Lapin came in. They checked his documents and searched him. He was "clean." Volodya must have known I was being searched. We sat down together and he told me that he had come from the Supreme Court, where they were considering the appeal of the five convicted for the demonstration on Red Square. All of our people had been there awaiting the decision. I was supposed to have gone myself and they'd wondered where I was. Volodya had been sent to check up on me. If he didn't return immediately the others would know something was wrong.

Two hours later our friends streamed into the apartment. When the first of them arrived, the senior KGB man, Alexei Dmitriyevich Vragov, said caustically, "All right, empty your pockets. Hand over your samizdat," to which Victor Krasin replied, "Who would carry samizdat to an apartment in which a search is going on?"

"Where did you find out a search was going on here?"

"What do you mean—where did *we* find out? The whole world knows about it. The BBC and the Voice of America and the German Radio have already reported it."

To the KGB men this was unbelievable. They never did understand how England, America, and Germany knew what was going on on Komsomolsky Prospect in an apartment from which no one had departed. Our people, seeing the confused faces of the KGB men, laughed. They had all heard Yakir tell the foreign correspondents at the Supreme Court building about the search of Grigorenko's premises.

More and more people kept arriving, until the entire apartment was full. We ate, drank tea, and talked. No one paid any attention to the searchers, who were having a hard time making their way about among our friends. The rule that "during a search all persons arriving at the scene must be detained" was working against them. They were not searching for anything in particular; they were not supposed to be. They took everything I'd typed or written out in longhand, everything that had been published outside the USSR, works of Gorky, Korolenko, Shevchenko. They even took clippings from the Soviet press. When I asked Beryozovsky why they took the last, he replied, "You are keeping them. That means you need them. And if you need them we are required to take them from you."

I had recently been attempting to continue my studies of cybernetics, and all my notes and clippings were taken from me. They later were bound into my criminal case and as proof of my insanity the authorities flaunted the fact that my case file contained twenty-one volumes of anti-Soviet material. From the point of view of the case against me all of this was good for nothing. But for me personally these losses were enormous.

My second conflict with Beryozovsky arose over the typewritten copy of the memoirs of my friend Vasily Novobranets. When I demanded to know why this book was being taken, they pointed out the sentence in the author's preface: "Stalin was dead—but the poisonous seeds sown by him continue to give out shoots."

I refused to participate in the search, because documents were being confiscated that were not supposed to be confiscated under terms of the regulations on searches. I went into the most distant room to try to sleep, but I wasn't able to, for soon I heard commotion. Judging from cries that carried to my room, I understood that Mustafa Dzhemiliyev had fled. Our people blocked the access of the KGB men to the kitchen and let Mustafa down from the window on a rope made of sheets and other cloth. Unfortunately he landed badly, shattering the heel bone of his left foot. His pose resembled one that a sharpshooter might assume for firing from a kneeling position, and the KGB man who was keeping a watch on our apartment from the courtyard saw him and fled. Thus Mustafa managed to cross Komsomol Prospect and a block of apartment houses on the opposite side, run out on to the Frunze Embankment, and grab a taxi. But he did not get away. He had just managed to explain to the crowd that ran up to him who he was, when he fainted from pain.

On our insistence Mustafa was sent to the Sklifasovsky Institute, where he received emergency treatment. They put on a cast and the doctor on duty ordered him to be put in a room. The KGB man who had brought Mustafa in told the doctor, "Send him to the prison ward in the basement!"

"On what basis?" asked the doctor.

Instead of replying the KGB man showed his identification document.

"That's not a good enough reason for me," replied the doctor.

"He's a dangerous criminal."

"What crime did he commit?"

"I am not a criminal," Mustafa interjected. "I am purely and simply a Crimean Tatar and I am struggling for the right to return to the Crimea."

The doctor, a Jew by nationality, evidently knew something of this situation, and he ordered categorically, "Send him to a regular ward." And they took Mustafa away.

The KGB man tried to get permission to set up a guard over him in the ward, but the doctor refused. Thanks to this, Zinaida managed to get Mustafa released the next day and take him to our home. Such were the contradictions of our life that he lived with us for almost two months, after which he left and remained free for four more months. He was with me when I was arrested on May 7, but they did not detain him at the time. He was arrested a month later.

The search of our apartment ended in a scandal for the KGB. The true chief of the search, Alexei Dmitriyevich Vragov, got tired of the whole thing. At about eight in the evening he and Beryozovsky stuffed into a bag everything they had set aside for confiscation but had not yet listed in the protocol and also the entire contents of my desk drawers. They closed it with a seal that read "KGB-14" and Beryozovsky said to me, "Tomorrow we will invite you to the prosecutor's office in order to open up the bag and list what is in it."

"I won't come," I said calmly. "You can open it up yourselves."

"How is that?" Beryozovsky said in astonishment.

"I cannot be responsible for the contents of a bag which is with you. If you want me to participate in the opening, you must leave the bag with me." When Beryozovsky called me the next day, I told him once again that my presence there was not requisite. Realizing the position he had gotten himself into, Beryozovsky came to the apartment to ask me personally, but I remained firm. Incidentally, I knew that in my desk there was a letter from Poremsky of the NTS, the Popular Labor Alliance, an organization of anti-Communist Russian emigrés with its headquarters in West Germany. Though I had no ties with the NTS, this letter could have been used to charge me with such ties. I decided to use the KGB's mistake in order to label this particular letter as their forgery. They must have understood this, because the letter was never entered in the search protocol.

Following the search, I wrote to the Prosecutor General of the USSR, Rudenko, making the following demands: 1) That all documents confiscated from me and my two typewriters be returned immediately; 2) that all unlawful acts toward me and my family cease: shadowing, observation of my apartment with the help of special equipment, the bugging of my apartment and of my telephone line, and the opening and confiscation of my correspondence.

I knew very well there would be no answer to my letter. The system was by this time unshakeable. But now was a convenient time to show the true role of the Soviet prosecutor's office as an auxiliary organ of the KGB.

I realized, of course, that this search preceded arrest. Therefore I made my demands bluntly. I did observe tact, not out of fear, but in order not to lower my own dignity and so as not to lose the esteem of my friends. At the time I knew almost all of the well-known human rights defenders, though I had not yet established a personal acquaintance with such figures as Alexander Solzhenitsyn or with Andrei Sakharov, who had just recently appeared on the horizon of the human rights movement.

That winter, Yura Shtein had come to visit us. We knew and loved him and his family: his wife, Veronica, and their daughters, Lyena and Liliya. We were particularly entranced by the daughters and their conduct during the Soviet occupation of Czechoslovakia. The Shteins had been visiting relatives in Czechoslovakia when the Soviet forces invaded. The girls made use of their nationality and their ages—ten and twelve—in order to serve as communications contacts for the Czech resistance. Sitting on their bicycles and chatting or singing in Russian, they would pass right by roadblocks of the occupying forces and deliver Czech leaflets, reports, and instructions. Through the Shtein family we met the remarkable Russian bard Alexander Arkadyevich Galich and heard his wonderful songs. And now Yura was the herald of one more outstanding event. He'd arranged for me to talk with Solzhenitsyn, a man I'd always wanted to meet. Solzhenitsyn, he told me, wanted to see me. Yura named a village a few dozen kilometers from Ryazan, where Alexander Isayevich would be expecting me. He told me how to find the village and the house so that I would not have to make inquiries of anyone.

On the day of the meeting I left home early in the morning, though our meeting was set for late at night and the trip there would take no more than five hours. I wanted to have enough time to get rid of my tails. That day there were many; just walking to the store a half block from my apartment house I picked out three. Had they a presentiment of something? Or was I only observing more attentively today? I decided that I would try to lose them, but if I failed, I simply would not go. It was no good to lead a tail to where Solzhenitsyn was working.

It took me until five that evening to get them off my back. I went to my last check point, found them gone, and set out for the Kazan station with my ticket to Ryazan in my pocket. My friends, those who could still go about openly, had bought it early that morning and delivered it to my apartment.

I boarded a train that was not going to Ryazan and got off at the first stop, then took the Ryazan train that pulled in. For the time, it seemed, I had no tail. On the train I read, at the same time keeping my eye out for anything suspicious. There was nothing; still, no harm in taking precautions. I got off alone at a remote whistlestop, two or three stops away from Ryazan. If even one person had gotten off, I would have returned to Moscow. Another train to Ryazan arrived. I took it, and once there rushed to the bus stop. They had told me that the last bus left at midnight, and I had arrived at five to twelve. But I still was not sure that I had not brought some smart shadow along with me. After all, my disembarkation at the whistlestop might have been a stupid ploy. Any smart shadow would have avoided getting caught on that hook. He would have gone on to Ryazan and waited for me there. Therefore, I now went in a direction opposite to that which I wanted. After making several turnabouts in the area near the station I became absolutely sure that there was no one behind me and went back to the bus stop. The last bus had long since departed, but people were waiting there anyway. I did a little research and found out that there were taxis, and also truck drivers not averse to taking on a passenger. I decided to wait for a taxi. Several went by but none even stopped. Finally one did and I ran up to it. Once inside I told the driver where I wanted to go. No, he said, he wouldn't go there: it was far away and the road was not clear. I took out a thirty-ruble note, the only one in my pocket, and held it out to him: "You've got to realize, friend, that I have to get there—and tomorrow I have to be at work." He finally agreed, but warned, "Only to the first snowdrift. I won't go through snowdrifts. We'll get stuck and I have no shovel."

I had good luck. The first snowdrifts didn't appear till we were within sight of my destination. I said good night to the driver and thanked him from the bottom of my heart. He had not only delivered me there, but at the very end had generously returned to me ten rubles from the thirty I had given him. I dashed into the village and found the house immediately. But I knocked on the wrong window, the one that belonged to the woman owner. Luckily Alexander Isayevich Solzhenitsyn beat her to the window. He was determined not to let me give my name. He said, "Fyodor Petrovich? This is Pyotr Ivanovich. I'll open the door for you now. Go to the entry." He pointed to his right. Behind him I could see the silhouette of the old lady. Alexander Isayevich said something to her of which I heard only: "He's come to see me."

The doors opened, and I stepped in and fell into a strong embrace. We passed through the landlady's half of the building and emerged into a large rustic room with an enormous Russian country stove and a small nook that served as both kitchen and dining room. In the main room was a rough-hewn table, a wooden bench, and a pair of very heavy chairs. It was chilly in the room but I took my coat off anyway. Alexander Isayevich immediately noticed my light oxfords and offered to loan me some felt boots. I tried to refuse by saying, "But what about you?"

"I'm used to it." He pointed at his enormous prisoner's boots.

I had to agree to his proposal.

"Are you hungry?" he asked. "We'll eat right away."

"To be honest, I'm very hungry. I spent the whole day getting rid of my tails."

While I told him about it, he pulled a sheaf of small paper out of his jersey pocket, put it on the table next to a pencil, and began to prepare dinner.

"Do you drink?" he asked.

"Not very much, but since it's a Russian custom in honor of a meeting. . . ."

"I don't drink at all, but for the sake of our meeting, I'll transgress a bit."

I continued to look about the room, my eyes returning again and again to that pile of paper on the table. Solzhenitsyn noticed. "You're intrigued by my working tools?"

"Yes, indeed! To be perfectly frank I simply don't understand why you use paper of that size."

"I'll explain," he said and went out of the room, returning almost immediately with another pile of the same kind of paper covered with minute handwriting. The words were so dense that one of his small quarter-sheets contained as much as a typewritten, double-spaced manuscript page.

"This," he said, "is one day's work. Before I lie down to sleep I remove it from the house and I will never see it again. Whatever piles up during the day, I never leave where I work. If I have to go out, I put in my pocket both what I have written and the clean sheets as well. No matter where I live I prepare several hiding places. If a stranger appears—in particular, if he seems suspicious—everything I have written and the clean paper, too, goes into a hiding place. I stress that the clean sheets and the pencil are hidden away. My surroundings must always be not only clean but must contain no hint that I am working. For example, when you knocked—everything went into my pocket. If I had not recognized you, I would have moved everything from my pocket into a hiding place."

We ate dinner—each of us had a piece of pork fat, black bread, and an onion and barley porridge. He also brought out a flask one-third filled with spirits. We poured out several drops, added some water, and clinked glasses. It's difficult now to remember what we talked about, and for that matter it's not necessary. A conversation with a great man is invariably "recalled" in an advantageous light for oneself. I say *great;* when I think back on that night I know I had contact with a great man. At the time I didn't know much about Solzhenitsyn.

I did not like his novel, *One Day in the Life of Ivan Denisovich.* I simply failed to understand it. I perceived it as a work that glorified submissiveness. Only later on, after the uproar over the proposal to give a Lenin Prize to the book, and with the help of my wife, did I come to understand its true value. Though much spoken about, *The Cancer Ward* did not seem to me to be a masterpiece either. I had read only a few chapters from *The First Circle,* and I heard about *The Gulag Archipelago* from Solzhenitsyn himself during the evening. So the feeling of contact with a great man arose out of the encounter itself. It was not a feeling of worship; we spoke as equals. I told him about myself and he told me about himself. Most of all, he was interested in my military service. I myself was interested in his prewar life.

Our conversation continued beyond dinner, and finally Alexander Isayevich said, "It's time to sleep. Otherwise we'll be like sleepy flies tomorrow." As his guest of honor he offered me the stove on which he himself usually slept. My weak protests that he should keep this place for himself were useless. He lay down on a folding bed. For a time we lay there silently. Then one of us asked the other a question and the conversation resumed. I became uncomfortable and sat up on the edge of the stove. After a time Alexander Isayevich sat up on the cot. We talked for a long time, and then Solzhenitsyn's feet became cold and he got up and put on his boots. It began to get light and Alexander Isayevich, talking all the time, went out the back door and returned with a pail of potatoes. He went to his kitchen nook, took down a pot, poured water into it, and began to peel the potatoes. I clambered down from the stove and sat down next to him to help. We peeled and washed the potatoes, put them on the hot plate to boil, and decided to go out for a walk in the woods that began right at the landlady's garden. The sun had barely lit the horizon with crimson. The forest was silent, unmoving, clothed in snow. It was such a marvelous morning, such purely Russian nature, that I can never forget it. We talked for about an hour, absorbed in our conversation. One of us finally remembered the potatoes, and we went back to the house to find them ready. After breakfast we returned to the forest. Despite our sleepless night we both felt energetic and vigorous. We returned hungry and tired, but satisfied, heated up some pea soup and porridge, and ate and went to the bus.

We did not plot a new revolution in Russia, nor did we discuss how to remove Brezhnev and his clique from power. I never once experienced that unpleasant feeling that comes when two people suddenly have nothing to talk about and it is necessary to try and continue a conversation. We did not seek out themes. They crowded in upon us, and we parted without having exhausted them. Though I remember almost everything we said, I am going to write about only one thing, and I do so because it contains both my fault and my debt—and, as it would seem by now, a debt that cannot be paid.

Toward the end of our second walk in the woods Alexander Isayevich said, "Pyotr Grigoryevich, it is your duty before the people and before God to write the history of the last war."

In fact, the principal subject of our conversations that day was the war. Alexander Isayevich was evidently trying to clarify something for himself, and I must have been helping him in some way. I said that such a work was beyond me and told him why: "I would have to devote myself entirely to this work and that I cannot do. You see how the authorities are pressuring us. My departure from the movement might be interpreted incorrectly. It might demoralize my young comrades. I cannot sit in an ivory tower when my friends are being sent off to prison, to the executioner's block."

"You have to do it, Pyotr Grigoryevich," Solzhenitsyn insisted. "You have to deglamorize the war, show it as it really was."

He continued, speaking as if he were dictating. *"I do not see any other man who could do it.* And it is criminal for such a man to be running about to trials and composing appeals in defense of arrested persons, appeals which the authorities pay no attention to at all."

Under his influence, I promised that I would try to remove myself from current human rights affairs, but I never did nor did I have a chance to. Less than half a year after this meeting I was arrested, and I spent more than five years in an insane asylum. At the time of my arrest all of my military historical notes were confiscated. In the insane asylum they refused to let me read anything relating to military history. Evidently the KGB felt as Solzhenitsyn did. They even said so to my wife: "Military history is exactly what he should not be studying." I am not trying to defend myself. In all likelihood, I could have removed myself more decisively from routine affairs and written something about the war.

Solzhenitsyn took me to the bus stop at the village club and this conversation about my duty continued until the bus arrived. Again and again he stressed that I should and must write. The club was an old estate owner's mansion with columns. When the bus drove up, we embraced and kissed three times and I jumped on board. It was five P.M. Over fifteen hours had passed from the time we'd met. I looked back out of my bus window and saw a person who in fifteen hours of incessant conversation had become dear to me. He stood there motionless and watched the bus depart. And that is how he has remained in my memory—in his prisoner's jersey, boots, and cap with ear flaps—against the white pillars of the old mansion.

When I reached the apartment my wife said, "Well, what a fuss you caused. Your tails went crazy trying to find you. They nearly wore out the telephone. There they are ringing it right now. No doubt they saw you and want to be sure you came home. Don't answer it. I will."

She went to the phone and picked it up: "He's here! He's here! What are they paying you for anyway? How many of you there are—and you couldn't even keep track of one old man."

The person at the other end of the wire heard her out obediently—he was so pleased at my return. Next day I saw that the number of people tailing me had increased. I am not certain why this was—was it my disappearance of a day and a half, the approaching elections, or the preparations for my arrest? Ignoring the ever more frequent searches and summons of the human rights defenders to the KGB, we continued to develop and perfect our principal weapon—publicity.

In early April my wife and I were walking along Komsomol Prospect when we heard steps behind us and then a muffled voice: "Do not turn around. Listen to me carefully. A provocation is being prepared against you. Be on guard against new acquaintances." The person went off to one side, evidently into the nearest courtyard. We had no doubts that what he'd said was true. We had heard similar warnings from one of our friends and we had more than once received friendly warnings from KGB personnel. Once I received a note composed of words and letters cut from a newspaper and glued to a piece of paper. Apparently even in the KGB there were people who sympathized with us. Today they had chosen a very risky method of giving warning. In two days I received a phone call: "Pyotr Grigoryevich? I have to see you."

I am not certain how I would have reacted to that phone call if I had not received the warning on Komsomol Prospect. The unfamiliar voice sounded hostile. Trying to hide my caution, I said as calmly as I could, "Well, in that case, come and see me if it is necessary."

"What do you mean? I can't come to your place."

"Why not?"

"You certainly must know how closely your apartment house is guarded."

"Well if you know that, then you must also know that my telephone is bugged. But I am not afraid of the one or the other. I do not make any secrets of my acquaintances or my conversations."

"That doesn't suit me. I want to meet you outside your apartment building."

"Where?"

"Do you know the store on Komsomol Prospect where they buy and sell foreign things?"

"Of course I know it. It's right next to my building."

"Well, I will meet you in that store, at the counter where they sell radios."

"I would not consider going into the store. I could approach it and meet you outside, and we could go for a walk on the street."

"Well, all right," he agreed with some hesitation. "We'll meet outside the store."

"How soon can you be there? I need twenty minutes."

"No, no! Not right now. Today I only wanted to set up our meeting."

"When do you want to have it?"

"I would like it on April 19 at eleven in the morning if that suits you."

"Fine. How will I know you? Give me something by which I will recognize you."

"It's not necessary. I know you."

This was the end of the conversation. It was still days before the nineteenth. On the twelfth he called again: "You haven't forgotten our appointment?"

"I never forget my promises."

My wife and I discussed these strange phone calls. I had met with hundreds of people and never before had my meetings been accompanied by such conditions. We tried to imagine what this was all about. Of course, they were not interested in talk. What they wanted was to "catch" me at "the scene of the crime"—with someone handing to me literature, money, or directives from the NTS. Indeed, nothing even had to be actually turned over to me. All they had to do was seize us together, take both of us to be searched, and "discover" on my companion a belt like the one on Broks-Sokolov. The rest was simple. He would announce that everything in the belt was intended for me. Just try to get out of that one!

My wife and I pondered what I should do. I could not show up. Then the provocation would fail. They would know that we had suspected something was wrong and would try to get me in some other way. But we decided to keep the appointment—and to expose the provocation. Our plan was this:

Zinaida and I would go to the meeting together, arm in arm. We would approach the police agent together. Nearby a group of our friends would be waiting. As soon as the police agent identified himself—by approaching us, speaking out, greeting us—our friends, on a signal from Zinaida, would hurl themselves on the "NTS agent," seize him and turn him over to the police. To the police, not to the KGB, so that the detention would be written up in a protocol in our presence and so that a personal search of his person would be carried out in our presence and documented.

On the nineteenth at nine the agent once again called me. "Pyotr Grigoryevich, I want to remind you of our meeting once more and to ask you whether anything has changed?"

"Aren't you giving me a few too many reminders? I've already told you once that you don't have to remind me."

"Yes, yes, I know that. But I phoned you to ask you to carry something by which I can identify you. Something in your hand, for example, so I won't make a mistake."

"It would be better for you to tell me how I can recognize you. I wouldn't make a mistake."

"No, no. I know you. This is only for assurance."

"Very well. I will have today's issue of *Pravda* in my right hand."

So that the news of our plan did not spread, we reported it only at ten to our friends who had agreed to escort us. We left at ten minutes to eleven. At the commission store the atmosphere was tense. Three KGB cars were parked up against the sidewalk ready to move. KGB men darted in and out of the crowd in front of the store entrance. I immediately recognized "my" agent: he wore a gray trench coat, obviously of foreign manufacture, beneath it a gray suit and a matching necktie, and on his feet fine oxfords. His head was uncovered and he had an abundance of salt-and-pepper colored hair. His face was on the lean side and of a southern, perhaps Italian, type. He had an erect, smart figure. He was standing right where he had first proposed that we meet—at the radio counter. This place was magnificent for his purpose. It commanded an excellent view of the street and from there it would be possible to photograph beautifully everything that took place: my entering the store, my approach to the counter, my meeting with the agent. And at that point he would no doubt have pulled me over into some closed corner. But now how was he to work the whole thing backwards?—his leaving the counter and the store, and approaching me? The agent seemed to recognize me immediately but he was waiting for something, a signal from someone. Ten or fifteen minutes passed. Another KGB car rolled up. An old acquaintance got out—the very same bigwig who had organized the provocation outside the building of the Proletarsky district court during the trial of the five heroes of August 25th. Thus the KGB must have had a special section that handled only provocations.

The bigwig looked about. One of the KGB officials went up to him and reported something. He listened attentively, gave a brief order, and went to his own car. "You can go home now!" I told my friends. "The operation has been called off." And the operatives' cars began to depart, one after the other. On the way home we talked about what had happened and someone remarked that they must have guessed our intentions. Somehow I had the feeling that they had not guessed them but had been told of them. Still, I kept quiet; I could not cast suspicion on my friends.

I now felt my arrest to be imminent and I urgently worked at exposing the antipeople nature of the KGB. I wrote an open letter to Y. V. Andropov that was turned over to samizdat April 29 and in which I pointed out various activities in which the KGB was engaged: the shadowing of democratically inclined people; the clandestine opening of correspondence; searches of people who criticized the illegal actions of the authorities; the bugging of telephone lines; the dissemination of slander against honorable people via the press and the system of party propaganda; the arrangement of provocations and the creation of forged cases against peole who opposed the authorities. I used my own case to show what all that must cost the state. In shadowing me, my family, and my apartment, at least twenty persons were employed and I had counted up to twenty-six at times. But in order to make things simple I dropped the six and took a round figure of twenty. I used two hundred rubles per person per month as an average salary, even though I knew that KGB salaries, taking into account uniform allowances and so forth, were higher.

Based on my calculations I gave this total: two hundred multiplied by twenty equaled four thousand rubles—the cost of the monthly surveillance over me. In a year that was forty-eight thousand rubles. And the shadowing had been going on for almost four years. That added up to two hundred thousand rubles. For what was all this money being wasted? To hinder just one man from participating in the political life of the country! And in making my calculations I had not by any means taken everything into account. I had not included expenditures for the technical means of conducting clandestine surveillance, for apartments from which this surveillance could be conducted, for the contents of these apartments, for the costs of clandestine examination of correspondence and for servicing the apparatuses used in bugging the telephone, and for the maintenance of the KGB automobiles. I had not taken into consideration that twenty healthy men and women not only consumed what they had not produced themselves, but also did not produce anything themselves.

Three days later I disseminated in samizdat a leaflet entitled "An End to Illusions," in which I told about the KGB's provocation of Ivan Antonovich Yakhimovich, a Latvian of Polish-Russian descent. Yakhimovich was to be sent to an insane asylum without trial; at the time I wrote the letter he was imprisoned and under interrogation.

Yakhimovich was so pure, and he so naïvely believed in the "sacred ideals of communism," that it was unthinkable that he could actually be a criminal. Yet I was certain that he would be convicted. Searching for a way to prevent this, an answer came to me suddenly. It was obvious, something anyone might have thought of—anyone except those, like us, who lived in dread of the cruelty of those in power. We would gather together a group of courageous people to organize protests against illegal arrests. I began quietly to try out the idea on my friends. I did not want to frighten people away with broad purposes.

Responses to the proposal varied. It was endorsed unconditionally and immediately by Volodya Gershuni and Anatoly Yakobson. Victor Krasin and Pyotr Yakir were opposed to it, Victor more than Pyotr. We all spoke on this subject a great deal, its proponents saying that such a committee is an organization, and an organization by its very existence will have an influence; and its opponents holding that a committee would only worsen our situation. The authorities were accustomed to us as individuals, but they would attack a committee like wolves and arrest everyone in it.

We talked a great deal but never did come to an agreement. Finally I proposed that we bring more people into the discussion, reasoning that perhaps it was wrong for us, a small group, to try and make a decision for everyone.

We put together a list of the twenty or thirty most active dissidents of that period and decided to hold a meeting at my apartment. We set a day and Victor Krasin took the job of notifying people. I set the condition that there would be no preliminary preparation and that we would not even announce what question would be discussed. Let each person bring to the group only his own opinion.

As people gathered on the scheduled day my indignation started rising. Many of those whom we had mentioned at Yakir's place as participants did not appear, and on the other hand many people with whom I was little acquainted did. In addition all of them knew what the matter under discussion would be and were well aware of the nature of the disagreements. When Maiya Ulanovskaya appeared, my indignation peaked. At the time, Maiya was not a participant in the human rights movement, but, evidently out of fear, she occasionally interfered as the opponent of any decisive actions.

Once the meeting began it was obvious that the movement against the committee was strong. The only persons who joined Yakobson, Gershuni, and I were Sasha Lavut, Seryozha Kovalyev, Yulius Telesin, and one or two others. Tolya Yakobson spoke several times in defense of the proposed committee. But the main event of the evening was Maiya Ulanovskaya. Her speech could barely be called a speech at all. It was hysterics . . . the hysterics of a half-conscious person. All I can remember her saying is: "You haven't been there. You haven't been in a death row cell. . . . It's awful . . . it's unbelievable. . . .

It's incessant horror from one day to the next. . . . It's wrong to speak with them . . . but you shouldn't walk straight into their jaws." And: "It's horror . . . horror . . . horror."

After such ravings it was impossible to talk further. I proposed that we leave. Tolya Yakobson came up to me and said, "Well, Pyotr Grigoryevich, after the meeting today one or maybe both of us are going to be put in prison. The KGB obviously doesn't want the committee."

At the present time Maiya Ulanovskaya, Victor Krasin, and I are in the free world. A little more than a year ago, before he died, Anatoly Yakobson was, too. Maiya Ulanovskaya is writing her memoirs, part of which have already been published. Recently she asked my permission to make use of my letters. I didn't permit it, and I will not permit it until I am sure that they will be used only in the interests of truth. I believe that Maiya has a duty to tell the truth about that unfortunate gathering in Moscow—who invited her to it, what conversations she had and with whom before the meeting, and what put her in the state she was in when she spoke? Many strange things took place at that time, all of which somehow involve the quartet of Yakir, Krasin, Kim, and Gabai.

I am unable to doubt Pyotr Yakir's honesty in those days. I know him too well to suspect him of anything sinister. He had, however, two shortcomings that led me to suggest he leave the movement before being arrested.

The first was his excessive trustfulness, which, of course, the KGB must have noticed. If a completely unknown person came to him and told him about some actual or alleged abuses suffered at the hands of the authorities, Yakir would immediately accept him as an intimate. *Any* former prisoner was friend and brother.

Yakir's second weak point, about which the KGB must also have known, was his tendency to break down. As a boy of fourteen he had been taken from his very prosperous and highly respected family—his father, Army Commander Ion Yakir, was a hero of the Civil War and a military theoretician— and hurled into the depths of camp life. Instead of his parents' love he received beatings from the jailers and the taunts of the thieves. His seventeen years in camp and exile had left him forever terrified of the camp abyss. People failed to understand tragedy. They saw only its consequence—that the man drank. But I saw his terror and was astonished that he could overcome it to become one of the leading figures of the human rights movement. People were attracted to Pyotr Yakir and grouped themselves around him. His trust led to a situation in which he unknowingly nurtured a nest of informers and his weakness for drink led to carelessness. Still, it is important to remember that his energy, intellect, and initiative, his love and esteem for people, his communicativeness, tolerance and famous name played an enormous role in the development of the human rights movement and attracted many people—not only Muscovites—to the struggle against illegality and tyranny. His name was famous throughout the Soviet Union and everywhere it brought people to the defense of human dignity. Pyotr Yakir's accomplishments cannot be wiped out of the history of the Soviet human rights movement by any "admissions of guilt" on his part.

His fall and destruction through "admission of guilt" still puzzle and trouble me today. What I would most like to know is the role played in the affair by Pyotr's brother-in-law, the singer and songwriter Kim, and especially by Victor Krasin. I mistrusted the latter from our first encounter, but intuition is not the highest judge and therefore I kept my mistrust to myself. After Victor Krasin "admitted" to having taken money from the KGB, I asked myself whether he was attempting to conceal a more heinous sin by means of this "confession." Pyotr Yakir was such an important figure in the human rights movement that the KGB would have wanted to have someone close to him whose job it was to constantly keep an eye on him. This could not have been Gabai, who, indeed, was removed from Yakir by the KGB. The artificially created case against him was also artificially hooked up to that of Mustafa Dzhemiliyev and they were tried in Tashkent, with no connection to the trial of Yakir. And yet for many years Gabai had been the author of the documents that had been signed by Yakir alone or that Yakir signed jointly with Gabai, Kim, and others. It was as if they had wanted, by trying Gabai earlier than and separately from Yakir, to deprive Yakir of a tried and true helper and of a reliable codefendant in his own trial, one who could have fortified Yakir's spirit both during interrogation and during the trial itself.

Pyotr Yakir's interrogation and trial were combined with Victor Krasin's, even though their cases were in no way connected. Victor Krasin had never written anything either for Yakir or even for himself. He was straight out of Dostoyevsky's *The Possessed*, always running about and arranging something. All sorts of strange things happened to him. Once he was taken into custody on the street right in front of his friends and taken to an interrogator, but he returned safe and sound. Once in a gateway someone hung a black eye on him—"certainly the KGB," he said. And this was the person—the least likely of all to manifest determination and integrity—whom they chose to try with Yakir.

There was more reason for combining even Kim in one case with his brother-in-law than there was to combine Yakir with Victor Krasin. But Kim quietly left the human rights movement, and he never suffered any harm in connection with his activity, which had been quite intense.

After the meeting at my apartment organized by Victor Krasin my suspicions of him were greatly intensified. I decided it was necessary to take action without involving him, and I kept telling my friends, as if it were a gospel, "The committee must be created!"

I wrote this "gospel" as well, counting on a broad circle of samizdat readers, in an open letter to Andropov and in a leaflet in defense of Ivan Yakhimovich. These appeals turned out to be timely.

Only a little more than two weeks had passed after the notorious meeting in my apartment, when my friends created "The Organizing Group for Defense of Human Rights," which undertook not only my defense and Yakhimovich's, but that of Volodya Gershuni, who was arrested after me; the Crimean Tatars, who I had undertaken to go to Tashkent to defend; and all the others arrested after me.

Many Crimean Tatars were arrested and tried in connection with the April 21, 1968 events at Chirchik: Reshat Bairamov, Aider Bariyev, Svetlana Ametova, Munire Khalilova, Riza Umerov, Ruslan Eminov, Rollan Kadiyev, Ridvan Gafarov, Ismail Yazydzhiyev. In addition, Izzet Khairov was tried but not arrested. His case was such an obvious fake, so invented and fabricated, that it aroused indignation even among the Crimean Tatars who by then had seen everything, and they decided to really battle the trial. The Tatars began to collect signatures on a petition demanding that I be admitted as a public defender. A copy of the petition, which carried 3,200 signatures, was sent to me, and the original was sent to the court. The KGB reacted immediately. They summoned Izzet Khairov to an interrogation in the course of which they said, "Tell Grigorenko that if he shows his face in Tashkent we will arrest him." Similar warnings were received by several Crimean Tatars. Mustafa Dzhemiliyev telephoned me and said: "Pyotr Grigoryevich, I do not think this is a joke or an empty threat. Everything indicates that we must take them seriously."

After I had talked with Mustafa I called Pyotr Yakir, Tolya Yakobson, Yulius Telesin, Seryozha Kovalyev, and Sasha Lavut and asked them to come over. Those who could come did. I told them about the warning of the KGB and asked them what I should do about my trip. No one advised me to go. Yakobson expressed the most convincing objection when he said, "If we had something to use as a threat which could prevent your arrest, it would be worth the risk of going. But since we have nothing with which to scare them off, they might arrest you even against the wishes of the center. And if they do arrest you they aren't going to let you out. It is often possible to prevent an arrest, but it is impossible to free a person who has been arrested."

In reply to this I advanced just one consideration: "If we accept their unlawful ultimatum in respect to Tashkent, they will begin to forbid us journeys to other cities as well and eventually they will threaten to arrest us if we even fly out of Moscow. And then they'll tell us we can't go anywhere except to work and then they'll forbid us to leave our apartments. We cannot submit to unlawful demands."

On this note we parted. I had heard everyone else's opinion, but I had to make my own decision. While I was considering my options, a telegram dated April 30 arrived from Tashkent: "It is requisite that you appear at the municipal court for talks on speaking to the court." It was not signed, but I decided to go. I decided also to conceal my departure.

On May 2, just after the annual May Day celebrations, we celebrated our son Oleg's birthday. He was born June 2, but since we were often busy getting ready to go to the country in early June, we had established the custom of celebrating his birthday a month earlier. I decided to fly to Tashkent while the birthday party was in progress. Usually we had many guests that day. When all of them were well into the celebration I would slip out. No one except Zinaida would know I had gone, and I calculated that my departure would be unobserved. An airplane ticket had been purchased ahead of time.

CHAPTER TWENTY-SIX

PSYCHOPRISON

After saying a quiet farewell to my wife, I left the apartment. On my way to the Paveletsky station and on the train to Domodyedovo Airport I carried out several maneuvers permitting me to observe whether I was being followed. I was certain I wasn't.

Evidently the May Day celebration scattered the police agents and they had missed my departure. They would rush to try to find me the next day. Knowing this gave me a feeling of satisfaction.

I was not worried, nor did I think about how long I would be gone. In fact, I would be away for more than five years. I have described how it all began in notes I sent out of prison to my wife. She sent them to the West and the English director Leslie Wood made a film based on them. They express better than my recollections the circumstances and spirit of those events and I cite them here in slightly different form.

May 3, 1969. I arrived at the Tashkent airport in the morning and immediately went to my sister's, but she was not at home. I went to Ilyasov, a participant in the Crimean Tatar national movement, and stayed with him. There I learned that my summons to Tashkent, allegedly as a public defender at the trial, was a provocation. I decided to return to Moscow but that night I had a fever, my throat was dry, I developed an asthmatic cough, my blood pressure was high, and I had heart palpitations.

May 4. My hosts observed that their apartment was under police surveillance. "Let them keep us under surveillance," I said. "We are not criminals." But my Tashkent friends were worried.

May 5. In the evening a Crimean Tatar came in his car and offered to move me to a safer apartment. I rejected the move, both because I was ill and—mainly—because I had nothing to conceal. But taking into account my friends' concern, I did decide to hurry my return to Moscow.

May 7. In the morning someone bought me a ticket to Moscow, but not in my own name. That evening, two hours before my planned flight time, the police came to search Ilyasov's apartment. The first inside was a plainclothesman I knew from Moscow. His presence and the fact that the search warrant specified the apartment in which I was staying—without being registered, because I intended to leave—indicated that I had been under surveillance since leaving Moscow. After the search, during which nothing was found, they arrested me, presenting me with an arrest warrant under terms of section 191–4 of the Uzbek Republic criminal code (analogous to 190–1 of the Russian Republic criminal code).

May 8. I submitted an application to the prosecutor of the Uzbek Republic, Ruzemetov, with a copy to be transmitted to the Prosecutor General of the USSR, Rudenko, in which I requested a change in the way in which I was being detained. That same day, when summoned to the interrogator for questioning, I declared that I would give no testimony until normal conditions for the investigation had been instituted.

May 15. I was presented with formal charges under section 190–1 of the criminal code of the Russian Republic. "The first failure of the investigation," I thought to myself. "They counted on getting some evidence during the search and they failed. Now they have an extraordinary juridical case: 'a crime' is committed in Moscow and the Uzbek organs of public order arrest the 'criminal'; they do not detain him at Moscow's request for transport there—but themselves present him with charges, thereby adopting the pose: 'You are failing to maintain order in Moscow. Criminals commit crimes right under your noses. So now we are going to put things in order ourselves.' What a laugh!"

May 26. In connection with Ruzemetov's silence, I made a complaint to Rudenko. (I had received an empty formal bureaucratic reply signed by the deputy chief of the investigatory branch of the Uzbek prosecutor's (Nikiforov's) office that did not even make reference to the decision of the prosecutor).

May 30. I made application to Ruzemetov with a copy to Rudenko in which I demanded that my detention be terminated or that the investigation be

moved to Moscow where it belonged. I also demanded that if both these requests were refused, I should be given an appointment with my wife. If none
of these requests were satisfied I proclaimed a hunger strike.

June 2. They held a talk with me on my application of May 30. The group
was headed by Nikiforov and included the prosecutor from the directorate of
prosecutions (Naumov) and the interrogator (Berezovsky). I insisted on termination of detention—both because of the fact that, as everyone knew, I was
incapable of hiding and, most importantly, because I considered myself innocent. I had never written even one anonymous letter. Everything I had written
was true—and I had every interest in proving this to be the case. I could do
nothing to hinder the investigation since all the documents I had written were
out of my hands. As far as the place of the investigation was concerned, the
criminal procedural code states directly: it must be at the place of commission
of the crime. Nikiforov promised to report all this to the prosecutor and I
promised that if I received the prosecutor's reply within a specified period of
time, I would not begin a hunger strike.

June 9. An answer came, signed by Nikiforov, that stated: 1) It was impossible to terminate the measures of detention since I could hinder the investigation; 2) It was impossible to grant me an appointment with my wife; 3) The
investigation would take place in Uzbekistan because the majority of the witnesses were there.

June 11. I sent a declaration to Ruzemetov, with a copy to Rudenko, that
I was beginning a hunger strike on June 13. I wrote to Rudenko requesting
transfer of the investigation to Moscow and termination of detention. I demonstrated the ridiculousness of their reasons for my continued imprisonment and
for carrying out the investigation in Tashkent.

June 13. In the morning I began refusing food.

June 15. They began force-feeding. At first I was astonished that they were
doing this so soon. Then I understood: they had decided to break my will immediately. They wrapped me in a straightjacket and beat me and choked me.
They then began that tormenting procedure—the insertion of an expander in
my throat. The torment of the procedure was intensified by the fact that two
of my teeth had been filed down to the nerve before I left Moscow; the crowns
had not yet been put on.

June 16–19. Daily force-feeding. I resisted as best I could. They kept beating
and choking me. They wrenched my arms. They beat me particularly on my
wounded leg. They were especially cruel on June 17—when the documents of
the International Meeting of Communist Workers parties were signed in Moscow. The leading role in my mistreatment was played by the "Lefortovo contingent" that had been sent for me from Moscow. After each "feeding" I wrote
a declaration with a description of the tortures.

June 17. I wrote a declaration that I would continue my hunger strike as a protest against the savage treatment I was receiving.

June 19. I wrote down who I would consider the guilty parties in my death. After this the savageries ceased. They merely wrapped me in the straightjacket. I resisted. The number of jailers who assaulted me rose from five the first day to twelve on the nineteenth. The struggle lasted a long while and I usually collapsed with awful pains in my chest. But I kept resisting ever more stubbornly, hoping that my heart would give out. Exhausted, I wished for death —calculating that it would bring an exposure of tyranny.

June 20. The director of prosecutions Naumova came to my cell and let me know that they actually desired my death and were awaiting it. I was astonished and thought, "Why am I helping them? Why am I aiding in their wishes?" After she left my cell I saw in an entirely new light a conversation I'd had before my hunger strike with the chief of the investigative isolation prison of the KGB, Major Victor Moiseyevich Lysenko: "Don't even imagine that you are going to earn a big funeral. No, there won't be anything, nothing like Kostyorin's. And we'll not even let your relatives have your body. They won't even learn the precise date of your death. Maybe we'll tell them three days afterward, maybe three months later and maybe half a year later. And we aren't going to let them know the precise place of your burial, either." Considering all of that I wavered in my decision to aim at death.

June 24. I received a communication from Berezovsky that my family, in connection with my arrest, had been deprived of my pension. Perceiving this as more torture, and angered at my executioners, I made a decision.

June 25. I sent a declaration to Rudenko requesting once more that they terminate my detention, since my arrest had deprived my elderly, ill wife and invalid son of my pension, leaving them without means of subsistence.

June 27. In the evening I declared that beginning the next day I was lifting my hunger strike.

July 2. I wrote Rudenko one more letter in which on the basis of the experiences I had had since my arrest I demonstrated unlawfulness of the investigation in Uzbekistan. I had complained to him on June 26 that the Uzbek guardians of the law did not deign to reply to applications, and that I was ceasing to write to them.

July 3. I wrote to Kosygin about the cruelties and illegalities committed and asked what had led to the extension of these repressions to my family. They had been punished more cruelly than I, being left without money for food. I asked that the matter of my pension be considered.

August 6. I was informed that I was to be diagnosed by a psychiatrist. I wrote a declaration asking that on my side there be included in the committee of expert doctors Klepikov, Misyurov, and Ilyasov.

August 11. I was informed that my representatives would not be included in the committee of experts.

August 27. I was told my diagnosis: I had been declared sane. I was especially grateful for this to the chief psychiatrist of the Central-Asian military district, Colonel of Medical Services Boris Yefimovich Kagan. I was certain that he played the chief role in the decision.

August 28. I decided that to speed up the investigation I would give testimony.

August 28 to October. I was called in for interrogation eight times. In essence only one question was asked but always in reference to different documents: "Was this document composed by you? Was it typed on your typewriter? Did you disseminate it?" There were, to be sure, questions concerning other persons, but these I instantly cut off, declaring that I would reply to any questions concerning me but that on all actions of other persons I would maintain silence. The interrogator, after several unsuccessful attempts, had to take my declaration into account. I felt that the interrogator had no interest in the interrogations. He came to the interrogations unprepared. He would seize on the same documents several times. From this I drew the conclusion that I could expect one more psychiatric diagnosis. My term was coming to an end, but my case obviously was not ready. Or perhaps they wanted to prolong my term to nine months, and then more, so as to be able to hold me in prison. Tormenting doubts of a man held in complete isolation, allowed neither visits nor correspondence from his family—things I had asked for more than once. And they did not reply to complaints and declarations. In October the interrogator did not summon me once.

October 21. Before dinnertime the door of my cell—number 11 in the Tashkent isolation prison of the KGB—opened. Lysenko entered. Behind him came the duty sergeant and two more jailers. Lysenko told me that they'd been ordered to send me to Moscow.

The foregoing entry was the last note I wrote in the Tashkent prison.

I arrived at the Lefortovo prison in a semiconscious state. On admission I went through the customary frisking, the deposit of my possessions in the checkroom, and the receipt of bedding. I reached cell number 6 at about one in the morning—four, Tashkent time. Despite this they made me get up with the rest of the prisoners at 6:00 A.M.

After breakfast I was told to gather up my things and surrender all government issue items. I was then led out of my cell and frisked again. Because of the way the jailers looked at me I decided: the Serbsky Institute. A trial would be publicity. Thus they would not permit me to go to trial. They had only one way out—to label me insane. They'd been mistaken in Tashkent. Berezovsky had thought he could work up a case against me. Therefore he failed to understand the significance of the psychiatric diagnosis and had not selected the experts' commission that would have diagnosed me without fail as insane. As a result a situation had arisen that required Moscow's intervention.

I had been expecting this intervention and a second diagnosis. I knew that this time they would not take any chances but would send me directly to the institution that existed for the purpose of transforming sane people with whom the KGB was not pleased, but who had not committed any crimes, into "lunatics dangerous to society."

I emerged from the car that delivered me to the Serbsky Institute so embittered that I refused to speak with anyone. Thus my second stay there began. My first days demonstrated that fears I had were well founded.

They took me straight to solitary confinement, locked me in, and put a special guard at my door who was under instructions not to allow any of the political prisoners to get near me. Everyone else in the department—both the ordinary prisoners and the political prisoners—was registered under his own name. My name was known only to the doctors. The nurses and other personnel had been told only my first name and my patronymic. All of this put me on my guard, of course. But I firmly decided not to give any causes for psychiatric pestering and to conduct myself calmly. During my stay in solitary confinement no medical tests were conducted on me, except for the customary analyses of urine and blood. The physician, Maiya Mikhailovna Maltseva, came to talk to me on one occasion. I told her that I did not want my replies to her questions set forth in her uncontrolled transcription. "I will conduct any conversation," I said to her, "but only on the condition that I write out my own replies." Past experience had taught me that this was necessary.

Unfortunately, legitimate demands such as this one often played right into the doctors' hands. My desire to record my own answers in interrogations could be twisted by them into a manifestation of paranoia, as could my complaints about wiretapping, being tailed, and other abuses. I was beginning again a struggle against a method of repression extremely advantageous to the authorities. And this method had been "improved," made even more barbaric, since my first experience with it in 1964.

My solitary confinement came to an end within a week, and tests began. On the first day, I was invited to talk with the head of the ward, Professor Lunts. Maiya Mikhailovna Maltseva was also present. In accordance with an agreement I had reached with Lunts, after we finished talking I set forth in writing exactly what I had said. This written record is a part of the case history and speaks for itself. One item I did not write down was the question of why illegal government repressions had descended on me in 1964 and in subsequent years, which I answered by reminding Lunts of the fact that the Serbsky Institute had drawn two separate conclusions about me after my first stay. One of them, which straightforwardly diagnosed me as insane, was for the court. The other was for the government. The latter, I supposed, stated that I had been diagnosed as insane for humanitarian reasons—taking into account my services, my age, and my health—but that in actuality I was sane. The second conclusion, I said, probably had been oral.

Lunts tried to prove to me that I was mistaken, that the institute had reached only one conclusion—that I was insane. I then asked him, "How then do you explain the fact that an insane person was deprived of the pension he had earned and subjected to other cruel repressions? After all, only people who themselves have injured psyches can take such an action. But I do not want to believe that we are ruled by insane people, and therefore I insist: The government received a different conclusion than the court did. Do you not agree with me?"

Lunts only muttered, "The institute did not reach any other conclusion."

This conversation cost me dearly. The day I arrived at the institute I had felt a strange ache in the back of my head, which I'd reported. I was told that a therapist would see me the next day, but for some reason I didn't see her then; and since the therapist received patients only once a week, I had to live with this pain. Nervous tension did me in, and before the week was up the ache became unbearable and I collapsed. The night nurse measured my blood pressure and gave me a shot of magnesium and I managed to go to sleep. The day after, October 30, the ache intensified and I began to feel nauseous. The therapist finally examined me and prescribed some medicine. In a couple of days the ache diminished and the psychiatric examination was resumed.

It was conducted by a man of about my own age whom Maiya Mikhailovna addressed as "professor." One other woman was also present—evidently an assistant—and she wrote incessantly in her notebook. The conversation with this professor was ridiculous. Perhaps such a conversation is required when examining a person who has lost possession of his faculties and fallen into senile dotage. But in my case, almost anyone would immediately have seen its inappropriateness. The professor himself grasped it and seemed embarrassed, no less so than I. From past experience I knew wherein lay the essence of a psychiatric examination, and I wanted to reject it. I am not going to recount all of our conversation, but I will cite the two questions I consider the most intelligent of all that were put to me.

First, I was told to keep subtracting 17 from 200, and call out the remainder after each subtraction. I did this, but when I came to the last remainder, 13, it seemed incorrect to me and I said, "I think I made a mistake somewhere."

"Can you check it out?" asked the professor.

"Yes, of course," I replied. I divided 200 by 17 and found that 13 was indeed the correct answer.

Second, he showed me a drawing, evidently from the humor magazine *Krokodil,* of a desk behind which were sitting on one side a woman and opposite her a man, both of them looking at a man who stood by the chairman's armchair. All three were officials. In the chairman's upraised hand was a ticket for a paid resort vacation from a ticket benefit intended for workers. Beneath the drawing was the legend: "To whom shall we allot the fourth?" The professor asked me to explain the situation. So as not to insult the reader I will not cite my reply to the question. I will only note in passing that I replied with all seriousness, like a schoolchild.

After this Maiya Mikhailovna summoned me twice. I do not know what she wished to speak with me about the first time, because Lunts summoned her to his own office before she had completed the verbal preliminaries and they sent me back to the ward. During the second conversation she informed me that soon a commission would meet to discuss my case. This brought to an end my preliminary meetings with the doctors, though regular visits continued to occur twice a week. During all visits they asked the same question: "How do you feel?" My only reply was: "Just as usual."

In addition to conversations with the physicians and routine laboratory analyses, they carried out the following tests on me: an X-ray of the chest area; an X-ray of the backbone, on the basis of my own complaint; and two encephalographs. On the second occasion the encephalograph lasted two hours, though it usually takes only fifteen minutes. They brought it to an end only after I declared that I could not stand it any longer. Deep dents had been made in my hairless scalp and I had an intense headache. My feet hung off the end of the bench, swollen.

So after twenty-eight days of so-called clinical examination—from the day I arrived in the institute, October 22, to the day of the commission meeting, November 19—the only test result the commission received in addition to the materials from the Tashkent commission was my last encephalograph.

The session of the forensic psychiatric expert commission took place in a large room filled with office tables, one of which was placed in the center of the room. Behind it sat four people. In the chairman's position sat a rather young-looking, brown-haired man. He, I learned subsequently, was Morozov, the director of the Serbsky Institute of Forensic Psychiatry, and Corresponding Member of the Academy of Medical Sciences of the USSR. To his left sat Lunts. On his right was a man in a brown suit whom I have christened for the purpose of this account "the man without a doctor's smock." Opposite the chairman was Maiya Mikhailovna. They motioned me to a chair to the side of the table, near the chairman. I sat down in it and looked about. I saw many people I knew, but of my old acquaintances only Dr. Lunts and a doctor sitting by the window whom I had met in Leningrad in 1964 when the question of my release from the Leningrad Special Psychiatric Hospital was being decided were present. All the rest were ward doctors whom I had met only recently.

I realized that those behind the central table constituted the commission.

The rest were there to learn. They were seated behind the tables by the walls in the following sequence, starting at the chairman's left hand side: Zinaida Gavrilovna; Yakov Lazarevich, my Leningrad acquaintance; Lyubov Osipovna; and at the door, Albert Alexandrovich. Albert Alexandrovich was the one who escorted me back and forth to the ward. I call attention to the fact that I knew only Lunts's last name. By law the institution was supposed to give me the names of all the experts and I was supposed to have the right to exclude any with whom I was not pleased. This law had been observed in Tashkent. But here in the Serbsky Institute the insignificant prisoner did not even have the right to know the names of the high priests who were deciding his future.

The meeting was begun by the chairman: "Well, how do you feel?"

"I do not know what to answer. Probably I feel most of all like an experimental rabbit, but one capable of understanding his situation."

"No, I don't mean that. I want to know whether you feel any differently today from the way you felt when we diagnosed you in 1964."

"I do."

"How?"

"Well, at that time I could not even imagine such a trick as transforming the defendant in a criminal investigation into an insane person. I was astonished when I discovered this and I began to look upon the personnel of the institute as inveterate criminals. I believed in 1964 that I had been brought here for a diagnosis which would assure my imprisonment in an insane asylum to the end of my days. Therefore, my attitude toward all of the officials here was one of hate—and as a result I was extremely aroused, irritable, did not wish to observe any of the institute's rules, and devoted most of my time to the political enlightenment of the patients around me. By all of this I evidently made a strange impression on those around me and may have given some small cause for being considered insane."

"Lunts told me that you said that what took place at that time seemed to you as if it were in a fog," the chairman said.

"Yes, and I still say essentially the same thing. My realization of why I was here so shocked me that even today I perceive what took place as a horrible nightmare."

"What about what's happening to you now?"

"Things are different now. In the first place, psychiatric diagnosis is no longer a surprise to me. In the second place, in the years since my last incarceration I have come to know many honest psychiatrists and I realize that even in a criminal situation, human beings are employed along with the monsters. In all life situations I have decided to concern myself particularly with those who are decent. Therefore I am completely calm right now and I see around me not merely doctors but human beings as well. In turn, I hope that the experts will strive to see a human being in me as well." I smiled at him.

"Yes, but everything which you say is bound up with the events of the diagnosis itself, and after all there are actions which would compel us, even without doctors, to doubt your sanity."

"I do not know of any such actions."

"But in the protocol of the commission which determined the possibility of termination of your detention in the Leningrad Special Psychiatric Hospital it is stated that you admitted your actions to be mistaken."

"I admit the same right now."

"How is the one thing supposed to jibe with the other?"

"Very simply," I said. "Not every mistake made by a person is the result of malfunction of his psyche. My mistakes were the consequence of my incorrect political development—of unsophisticated Bolshevik and Leninist indoctrination. I believed that the only correct way was as Lenin had taught. Therefore when I encountered conflicts between what Lenin had written and life, I saw only one way out: back to Lenin. But that was wrong. During our lives changes have taken place and no one has the strength to return to 1924, let alone to 1953. We must use today as the platform from which we move ahead, making creative use of Lenin's heritage, taking into account all accumulated experience. In the past I did not understand this and that was my principal error. I first began to think about these things when I realized I was wrong in some of my actions. At the time I did not disclose my mistakes and those at the institute did not question me on that matter. Therefore, the fact that my mistakes could not be corrected by the interference of psychiatrists remained unclarified."

"How then are we to explain that after the intervention of psychiatrists you conducted yourself properly for a year or a year and a half and then once again took up your old ways?"

"Psychiatrists have no connection with my so-called 'normal' conduct. I imagine what you are alluding to is the fact that I did not write anything for dissemination?"

At this the chairman nodded, and I continued; "I did not write in 1965 and 1966 for two reasons, neither of which had anything to do with psychiatrists. The first was that I had no time. I had to work as a stevedore in two stores in order to get food for myself and my family. For those jobs I was paid a total of 132 rubles—just about what I had paid in income tax from the salary I used to receive in the military academy. The work was very hard, twelve hours each day, and I had no days off. I was therefore always exhausted. The second reason was that during this first year and a half I still hoped that I would succeed in getting the pension which I had earned and which was unlawfully taken from me. If I had succeeded in this, we would not be talking here, since back in the Leningrad Special Psychiatric Hospital I had remarked that when freed I would concentrate on writing a history of the Great War of the Fatherland. I longed to do this, but experience then showed me that the illegal repressions were rapidly increasing as time went on. I was deprived of the possibility of any employment at all and insulting illegal surveillance of me and my family was carried on at all times. These facts showed me that the time had not yet come to retreat into an ivory tower and devote myself to pure science. Until our country has a reliable defense against the tyranny from within, it is every honorable person's duty to take part in the creation of such a defense—no matter how this threatens him. I therefore joined the ranks of the warriors against tyranny. But you are mistaken when you say that I have taken up my old ways. What I have done in the last two years bears not even an outward resemblance to my old ways."

At this point I was interrupted by the man without a doctor's smock.

"What's the difference? It's only a different tactic, but it is essentially the same."

"No, the essence is different. Before, my actions were typically Bolshevik: I created a strictly conspiratorial illegal organization and disseminated illegal leaflets. Now there is no organization and there is no dissemination of illegal leaflets—but instead open, bold statements against acts of obvious tyranny, against lies and hypocrisy, against the distortion of truth. Before, there was a summons to the overthrow of the existing regime so that we could return to where Lenin had left off. Now there is a summons to liquidate the obvious ulcers of society, a struggle for strict observance of existing laws and for the realization of the constitutional rights of the people. Before, there was a call to revolution. Now there is an open struggle within the framework of what is permitted under the law—for the democratization of our public life. What common tactics or essences are shared here? Of course, if you believe the only normal Soviet person to be one who obediently bows his head before any bureaucratic tyranny then, indeed, I am 'abnormal.' I am not capable of such submissiveness—no matter how much I am beaten.

"I said then and I say again: in nineteen sixty-three through nineteen sixty-four I made mistakes. But in their correction I did not require the help of psychiatrists. In my most recent actions I also see mistakes—but again they are not such as can be corrected by psychiatrists."

"What are your current mistakes?"

"It is my impression that this is not the subject of today's conversation. To effectively analyze my recent mistakes I would have to work with people who think like me. You are not in that category, and I am incapable of speaking of all this as though I were repenting. Even if I had things to repent of, I would not do so when I had the ax hanging over my head. I consider it wrong for a person to repent under threat of punishment and death."

"Thank you, Pyotr Grigoryevich. Everything is clear to me. Do you have any questions?" the chairman directed himself to the man not wearing a smock, who during our entire conversation had remained sitting to my side, while constantly turning his face toward me but covering it with his left hand. For some reason this man interested me very much, and while talking to the chairman I kept trying to look at him. But I did not succeed. So when he declared that he had several questions I was pleased at the thought that at last I would see his face. But even when talking directly to me he managed to hide his face. Bending far down over the table, he asked his questions while looking at me out from under his left arm. I never did get a good look at him.

"How do you picture your future?" he asked.

"It's hard for me to answer that question. Right now, I cannot see beyond my trial."

"Do you mean you want to be tried?"

"Unfortunately, the answer to this question does not depend on me. I, of course, would rather have the case terminated at the stage of the preliminary investigation. But this, I repeat, does not depend on me."

"But after all, treatment can bypass a trial."

"I have no need of treatment. And I have no intention of faking illness in order to avoid responsibility. I am prepared to answer in full measure for whatever I have done."

"But if you are convicted you will be deprived of your pension . . ."

"There is a Russian proverb which says: 'A man who has lost his head doesn't cry over his hair.' Whether I am convicted or whether I am imprisoned in a special psychiatric hospital, I lose first of all my freedom. Why should I then grieve for a pension? And for that matter, why is it certain that they will convict me? I do not consider myself guilty and I will try to prove that to the court."

"Just what does that mean—that you intend to defend yourself?"

"I am not quite certain what you mean. I do not intend to lie or to be evasive. I will speak out honestly about my actions and explain them as best I can. But even if I do not succeed in proving my innocence, the maximum I can receive under the applicable code section is three years. Thus by the time the verdict comes into effect I will have only two years left to serve. So-called treatment is not going to take less time. On the other hand I will spend those years not in a sheltered prison, but in a corrective labor camp working in the fresh air and among normal people. And then too they might give me less than three years, and maybe even merely exile—there are precedents. In that case I would not lose my pension. Finally, we must not exclude the possibility of amnesty on the occasion of the hundred-year anniversary of the birth of Lenin, an amnesty which might even involve me if I am convicted. Under 'treatment' this possibility is excluded. No one grants amnesty to an insane person."

This is how my second forensic psychiatric diagnosis of 1969 and my second encounter with the Serbsky Institute of Forensic Psychiatry came to an end.

The conclusion of the institute was that I was insane. But at the time, the formal decision was not announced to me. I could only guess at the outcome—until I saw my lawyer, Sofya Vasilyevna Kalistratova.

On December 4 I pointed out that the period of sanction for my arrest had come to an end November 6. The authorities panicked and that same day carted me off to Domodyedovo and put me on an airplane. On December 5 I was once again in the isolation prison of the Uzbek Republic KGB branch. Here I made a formal declaration that until I had been presented with the sanction for lengthening my detention I would let them put me in my cell only by force. They found the sanction, dated October 21, granted by the deputy prosecutor general for a period up to December 31.

Then Sofya Vasilyevna Kalistratova arrived to defend me. We met in the prison reception room. This was the first time in nearly eight months that I had seen a face from my own world. And what a face it was! I had never seen one more beautiful. "A ray of light in the kingdom of darkness," I said to her, quoting Ostrovsky. I will never forget the tangerines and chocolates she brought to the meeting. I do not like chocolate, but the chocolate she brought me was the most delicious thing in the world.

She told me about my case and I told her about the investigation and the diagnosis. She said she would insist on a third commission of experts being present in court. She was pleased with the diagnosis of the commission of experts in Tashkent. It was competently and objectively written. The Serbsky Institute diagnosis was tendentious and incompetent. The Tashkent commission gave her a good basis for defense, but still it was difficult to hope for success. The very manner in which such cases were reviewed was tyrannous. In one trial, two mutually exclusive questions were decided, that of insanity and that of guilt. The court could not consider the first question correctly because the judges were not specialists and because they more or less had to go along with the conclusion of the experts. This conclusion was presented as part of the prosecution's case. All the court could do was rubber-stamp it. If the accused was classified as insane, there was no problem: An insane person had committed God knows what, so let him be treated. Every crime of the investigation was thereby covered up by the conclusion of a commission of experts created by the prosecution, a conclusion not subject to appeal.

Sofya Vasilyevna told me not to be too hopeful. I knew the outlook was bleak, but I also knew that she would wage a struggle. And she did. Her petition, "On the demand for supplementary medical documents by a commission of experts in court at a court session of February 3, 1970," is a document of extraordinary power.

How resoundingly she began that day: "You have two documents, dear sirs, not just one; each of them has identical force under the law and must obligatorily be considered. You, respected sirs, do not have the necessary knowledge for this and therefore you are obliged to create a third commission of experts for whom I have already chosen the candidates."

And then, between the lines: I know very well that you are not going to do anything of the sort, and that you are going to rubber-stamp the conclusions of the Serbsky Institute. And therefore from here on in I am going to destroy that conclusion and by this subject all of you to universal ridicule.

Indeed Sofya Vasilyevna was able to destroy that conclusion. Her own conclusion was as follows: "All this taken together gives a full basis for affirming that the conclusion of the in-patient commission of experts on the *insanity* of the patient is *mistaken. Everything set forth here gives the defense a basis for insistently requesting the appointment in this case of a third forensic psychiatric examination by a commission of experts for a solution to the question of the psychic state and sanity of P. G. Grigorenko.*"

"The Petition of Attorney Kalistratova" is the best example of how it is possible to struggle to a victory even while in the maw of a totalitarian monster. Both Sofya Vasilyevna and I knew that I would not be immediately removed from the hell of the insane asylums. But her petition had to be made so that the court would be compelled to face the fact of the entire Soviet system of forced treatment. Sofya Vasilyevna's document began the exposure of the foulness of Soviet psychiatry. This document was among the materials sent to western psychiatrists by Volodya Bukovsky in 1971 and it was present at the World Psychiatric Association convention in Honolulu in 1977. It acquires particular significance for me now after I have undergone examination by the most important American psychiatrists, all of whom came to the same conclusion as Sofya Vasilyevna—that I do not have any psychic illness and that I never did. Sofya Vasilyevna's document is destined to have a long life. For years and years it will be a weapon in the struggle to liquidate criminal psychiatry.

The "trial" ended February 5, 1970. Once again Sofya Vasilyevna visited me. The judge tried to refuse her this right, but she proved her right and came. The judge got back at me for this by refusing to let my wife see me on the grounds that my lawyer had been granted the visit. More than eight months had passed since I had seen Zinaida.

During Sofya Vasilyevna's second visit, we talked about the sentence, which with insane persons is called a "determination." They had "determined" that I should be given forced treatment in the Kazan Special Psychiatric Hospital. I asked Sofya Vasilyevna to ask my wife to petition Pyotr Mikhailovich Rybkin, the chief psychiatrist of the ministry of Internal Affairs, to reassign me to the Leningrad Special Psychiatric Hospital.

When Sofya Vasilyevna and I parted, I estimated that in a week or two I would be closer to Moscow. Days, weeks, and months passed, and it was only on May 11—in other words, one year and four days after my arrest—that I was transferred. I presumed I was being sent to Kazan. I traveled in a Stolypin car*in solitary confinement in an individual cell escorted by a special convoy commanded by that same Major Malyshev who had taken me to the Serbsky Institute and back. The four soldiers under his command took turns standing guard at my compartment, certainly a slap in the face of the regular convoy guard on the car. I had so longed to see the out-of-doors and nature that during every daylight hour of the entire journey I stood at the door of my compartment and looked through it and through the corridor window at the sands, the villages, and the Mohammedan graveyards, which looked like dead villages. I was such an important "insane person" that not only was I accompanied by my own personal convoy guard, but personal checkups were conducted along the way, twice each day.

We arrived in Orenburg after dark. An elderly KGB major entered the car, came up to the door of my compartment with Major Malyshev, and motioned to me through the bars. I approached him and he whispered, "Your last name?" I made a sign to him to put his ear close to my mouth and I whispered directly into it, "I don't know. Ask the major. He knows everything."

At first the captain was taken aback. Then he began to try to persuade me to tell him my name, but I walked away from the door, sat down on the bench, and ignored him.

When our train arrived in Kuibyshev, I was unloaded so that I could be put on the train for Kazan, which, as it turned out, did not leave for several days. They put me in a preliminary detention cell at the railway station. It was well lit and clean, but instead of cots it had sleeping benches. We arrived there after dinnertime, but they gave me a simple, filling meal of thick vermicelli soup with meat. After I had eaten the police chief came and said he was sorry that they would not be feeding me three times a day; that those in the preliminary detention cells are fed only once a day. I refused to accept his apology and told him, "I am not concerned with what you usually do here. I am supposed to get fed three times a day."

In an hour and a half the chief of the province KGB came and apologized for my being put in the preliminary detention cells. He said they had no suitable hospital cell in their prison, but that his own personal aide would bring

---

*The term "stolypin car"—widely used in the Soviet Union—describes a railway car fitted by the KGB for the transportation of prisoners. During the Stolypin reforms in the early part of this century before the revolution, special resettlers' railway cars were created for migration. They had two sections: one for passengers, analogous to a Soviet third-class railway car, and one for transport of livestock, agricultural tools, equipment, and so on. The migrating peasant family received a sort of home on wheels. After the Bolshevik coup d'etat there were no more resettlers and the cars were useless, until someone in the KGB (then, the Cheka) decided to use them for transportation of prisoners, whose number was growing every day. The passenger section was turned over to the guards and the cattle section was left to the prisoners. This use of the cars thereby compromised the name of one of the most remarkable of Russian reformers, P. A. Stolypin—P. G.

me breakfast, lunch, and dinner.

I have to give the devil his due. In May 1970 they had an excellent cook at the dining hall of the Kuibyshev KGB. I was served a varied and tasty menu. The fried potatoes were particularly good. Even the macaroni and vermicelli—things I had been unable to eat all my life—were cooked in such a way that I ate them with great relish. My four days in Kuibyshev were like being in a rest home. The conduct of both the KGB and the police led me to believe that they had received special instructions about me from up top.

We resumed our journey late in the evening of the fourth day. I knew right away that we were heading toward Moscow, though Malyshev kept assuring me that we were proceeding to Kazan. Perhaps my wife had gotten them to transfer me to Leningrad. In Moscow they put me up at the Butyrka prison for four days. On the fifth they sent me off via the Byelorussian station—that meant Chernyakhovsk (then called Insterburg), the main city of East Prussia, which was further from home than Kazan.

When Zinaida learned from friends of my stay at the Butyrka in Moscow, she asked to be permitted a visit. At first the authorities acted astonished at her request: "What makes you think he is in Moscow?" When they realized she really did know I was there, they promised her a visit but dragged things out until finally I was sent to Chernyakhovsk. The city's hard labor prison had been transformed into the special psychiatric hospital at which I arrived on May 28, 1970. Once again my life in the kingdom of the KGB psychiatrists commenced.

More than a year had passed since I had been arrested, and I'd spent that time in the cellars of the KGB, in prisons like other Soviet prisons—ordinary Soviet torture dungeons. But now here I was at the gates of a "hospital," a special psychiatric hospital—another chapter in the history of my "illness." Here they "treated" me for forty months, after which they sent me to an ordinary insane asylum for nine months. Here I was supposed to "complete my treatment"—to be sure, in a special ward made up of those sent there by a court determination.

What can I say about those forty-nine months? Not long before my arrest in Tashkent, in the autumn of 1968, this new arrest hovered over me and I decided that I had to prepare for it, particularly for a return to an insane asylum. Why this specifically? Because I had not violated any law and thus there was nothing for which they could try me. But to the authorities I had become a persona non grata.

I had been exposing government lies and tyranny and by this had set an example dangerous to the authorities who felt they had to scare my possible imitators and shut my mouth. I realized this and knew I had to warn the public of this imminent reprisal and expose the reasons behind it. With this purpose in mind, I wrote a brief note to my friends about the likelihood of my arrest and at the same time wrote an essay entitled "On the Special Psychiatric Hospitals," which I disseminated via samizdat. Natalia Gorbanyevskaya included it in her book *High Noon,* and from there it was reprinted in the collection *Those Punished with Insanity.* In this way it became widely known.

In my essay I wrote: "The concept of special psychiatric hospitals does not in itself contain anything bad, but there is nothing more criminal or more anti-human than our specific implementation of this idea."

Nowadays I am profoundly sorry for having written this misguided and harmful sentence. But it was how I saw the matter after my fifteen months of intitial exposure to the system of forced psychiatric "treatment." It took another five-year stay in the hands of jailers and "psychiatrists" for me to grasp that there was evil not only in the implementation of this idea but in the concept itself. The implementation depends greatly on the location of the "hospital" and on its staff. In 1964–65, I was "treated" at the Leningrad Special Psychiatric Hospital. After this the one at Chernyakhovsk seemed a real hell. I completed my "treatment" in the fifth Moscow city hospital—the "Stolby" —which has the worst of all reputations in Moscow. But to me, after Chernyakhovsk, it almost seemed like a resort. But there were things in Dnepropetrovsk that were unknown in Chernyakhovsk. And Sychyovka and particularly Blagoveshchensk are incomparably worse in terms of horrors committed than even Dnepropetrovsk.

So the implementation varies. But the variety itself is born of the original concept, which deprives the prisoners of special psychiatric hospitals of all rights. They are entirely in the power of the personnel of these "hospitals," people who need answer to no one.

In his book on the Nuremberg trial of twenty-three SS men, *Das Diktat der Menschenverachtung (The Dictatorship of Misanthropy),* Mitgerlich writes that for him the most striking thing was the merging in one person of a doctor and an SS man. He writes that "from this union came the cold inhumanity which permitted such doctors to experiment on their fellow human beings."

Where is the boundary between "simple service" in an institution that is created to suppress heterodoxy and that cultivates irresponsibility and illegality toward its patients, and the total merging of this institution with a criminal organization of political terror?

I mistakenly gave a positive value to the concept of special psychiatric hospitals, because I drew my conclusions from my stay in the one "hospital" in which I was confined during my first imprisonment. Yes, and I drew my conclusion not on the basis of the purpose of that institution, which is concealed from the eyes of outsiders, but from the composition of the body of prisoners. In order to understand the real purpose of such "hospitals" as these it is necessary to return to their origins.

The first psychiatric prison hospital was created in Kazan before World War

II for the imprisonment of dangerous political opponents of the regime—or, as they were called "enemies of the people." At the time it was said that this was a political prison and that only political prisoners were confined within it. In 1952 an analogous prison was created on Arsenal Street in Leningrad. Once again it was stated that this prison was solely for "enemies of the people."

Then Stalin died and rehabilitation commenced. The psychiatric political prisons in Kazan and Leningrad were emptied. But nature abhors a vacuum and someone at the top was unwilling to give up the concept of using psychiatry to suppress political protest. So in order to prolong the existence of both these "hospitals," a small contingent of genuinely mentally ill people who had committed serious crimes such as murder, rape, and robbery were admitted into them. Thus the cadres of the psychiatric political hospitals were preserved.

But there were those who did not wish things to come to a halt after the halfhearted measures of the Twentieth Party Congress, and who had not reconciled themselves to the attempts of the Central Committee to partially rehabilitate Stalin and the Stalinist system—in other words, people not in agreement with efforts to halt society's movement toward new life, movement that had begun only after Stalin's death. There was nothing illegal in their attempts at renewal. Indeed, they rose from the party line of the Twentieth Congress. Consequently it was impossible to try the proponents of this movement under the law. Here is where the psychiatric political hospitals come in. But they were filled with psychologically ill criminals. To clean the hospitals of this element and to replace it with only political prisoners meant to risk the accusation that psychiatric methods were being used against political dissenters.

A way out of this was swiftly found—the political prisoners would be put right in with the psychologically ill. Everything would then be in its place: there would not be, as there had been under Stalin, psychiatric hospitals solely for political prisoners. There would be merely "special psychiatric hospitals" for socially dangerous patients who required a particularly strict guard.

In the meantime the number of political prisoners whom it was undesirable to try in courts kept growing and there was not room for all of them in the two psychiatric special hospitals. To make places in these hospitals for the political prisoners by releasing those who had committed heinous crimes in a state of insanity would have exposed the whole plan. Consequently, new special psychiatric hospitals had to be created, each of which would be mostly filled with the insane but would also have a certain number of places for normal political prisoners.

A special psychiatric hospital was opened in Sychyovka in Smolensk province. Then another in Chernyakhovsk. Things moved swiftly. In the late sixties and seventies the special psychiatric hospitals sprouted like mushrooms after a rain. I know about more than ten: Kazan, Leningrad, Sychyovka, Chernyakhovsk, Dnepropetrovsk, Oryol, Sverdlovsk, Blagoveshchensk, Alma-Ata, and a "special psychiatric sanatorium" in the Poltava-Kiev area. In addition, departments for forced treatment were set up in all of the provincial psychiatric hospitals. Thus were created widescale opportunities to scatter mentally stable political prisoners among a mass of seriously ill patients.

To implement this plan it was necessary to have a cadre of doctors who could openly be told: "Classify so and so as insane," doctors with diplomas or other qualifications who would invent scientific-sounding formulations for diagnosing normal people as insane. All who have encountered this problem in the USSR agree that such criminal medical men—"doctors" and "scientists"—do exist. All those who have written on this subject recognize as chief among them Doctor of Medical Sciences Professor Daniil Romanovich Lunts (now deceased) and Corresponding Members of the Academy of Medical Sciences of the USSR, Georgi V. Morozov and Viktor M. Morozov. Member of the Academy of Medical Sciences Andrei V. Snezhnevsky is, for example, considered a kind and decent person. I myself met Snezhnevsky. He was chairman of my first experts commission and had a noble and kind appearance. Who would not be touched by this, especially in a hostile milieu? I also thought highly of Professor N. N. Timofeyev. In my case he conducted himself honestly, even courageously. He sought to get me liberated, restored to party membership and to my rank as general, and also to get me the pension to which I was legally entitled.

But it is probably wrong to judge such people on the basis of only a personal impression. The kind smile and the friendly look of Snezhnevsky did not prevent him from signing the experts commission conclusion on me, which was the equivalent of a death sentence—if not worse. And when Snezhnevsky declared to an *Izvestiya* correspondent that psychiatry in the USSR was on such a high level that *a mistake in diagnosis* by even rank-and-file psychiatrists was *"absolutely excluded,"* and that he, during his fifty years of psychiatric practice, did not know of even *one case* in which a normal person had been classified as insane, it became clear to me that he was an active participant in the forgeries of the experts commissions. Yes, and he could not have been anything else. He was the spiritual father of the present trend in psychiatric diagnosis of political prisoners, the ideologist of the expanded interpretation of schizophrenia and of other neurological illnesses.

And Professor N. N. Timofeyev appeared in quite a different light in the stories of V. Borisov and V. Fainberg. Timofeyev understood that the men before him were normal, but he made no haste in releasing them and he tried to break them. I could not and did not want to believe my friends. But when I saw Professor Timofeyev's signature beneath a false reply to Western psychiatrists, on a document that affirmed that in the USSR not a single normal person had been imprisoned in a psychiatric hospital, I realized that he was exactly the same sort as Lunts, the Morozovs, and Snezhnevsky. His attitude to me was singular and can be explained both by the vagueness of the situation after the removal of Khrushchev and also by corporate considerations—*General* Timofeyev defended *General* Grigorenko.

Thus the special psychiatric hospitals and the psychiatric experts commissions headed up by a single organ of political terror constitute a well-planned system for the classification and treatment of a particular category of normal people as lunatics.

Wouldn't it be simpler just to convict these people and to send them off to prison, camp, or exile, or maybe even to shoot them? After all, that's what was done under Stalin.

Yes, but things had changed. Now it was necessary to have at least some semblance of an accusation or an admission by the accused of his own guilt. The laws under which political prisoners are tried are not very convincing since what qualifies an action as criminal under them is extremely dubious. For example, if you keep a book with undesirable political content in your library, you can get seven years of severe regime camp plus five years of exile. You can be subjected to the same kind of punishment for oral expressions of dissatisfaction with various aspects of Soviet life. Such writings as diary entries and letters to your friends and relatives can also be qualified as criminal under these laws.

The classification as criminal of political literature, writings, and conversations depends entirely on the investigatory organs or, more simply, on the arbitrary will of the investigator.

For example, when they searched my apartment they confiscated two samizdat essays entitled "Stalin and Ivan the Terrible—Two Sides of the Same Coin," and "Stalin and Hitler—Two Sides of the Same Coin"—only because of their titles. They then confiscated all typescripts and manuscript texts they found, giving as reason the fact that they had been issued privately. Near the end of the search, they confiscated two suitcases of newspaper and magazine clippings that they believed I must have been collecting for some specific use. They even started to confiscate the Soviet magazine *Inostrannaya Literature (Foreign Literature),* until one searcher informed the rest that it was an official publication.

Among things categorically classified as subversive is everything published abroad: books of philosophy and history, the majority of works of belles lettres, religious books, and so forth.

Thus the door to jail is wide open for any thinking person in the USSR. With laws like this it would seem the authorities would need to establish special methods of repression. But Soviet state security organs have concluded that the old methods of prison and camp incarceration have lost their effectiveness. A new generation has entered the political arena and it is not infected with fear. It is a generation not of revolutionaries but of lovers of truth and justice, proponents of law and order, defenders of the inalienable rights of people, unwavering opponents of tyranny and violence. These people will not violate the laws of the country, even the laws they do not like. But they are stubborn in their defense of their lawfully established rights.

This is the tragedy of our people. Many of the most important laws of the Soviet Union are solely for show. Anyone who tries to exercise freedom of speech or of the press will be repressed, and if he then declares that our people do not possess these rights, he will be labeled anti-Soviet and a slanderer. And the government cannot openly try this person. After all, he has committed no crime. Thus it is necessary to convict this person in such a way that though there appears to be a trial, in fact there is none. Such a person must first be processed by a commission of psychiatric experts who pin on him the label "lunatic." And then he can be tried on a "lawful" basis in a closed trial at which he is not even present.

Everything happened clandestinely, and everything was faked. If the organ of terror had sentenced you to the special psychiatric hospital, the experts commission was an empty formality. They only formulated a pseudoscientific diagnosis of you—and if by chance they couldn't find an appropriate one, then they would lie. Sometimes by chance a lie was revealed. Once the Serbsky Institute director, Corresponding Member of the Academy of Medical Sciences G. B. Morozov, gave an interview to the correspondents of the magazine *Shtern* and showed them "my" case history, which he also had shown to foreign psychiatrists. This "case history" was beyond a doubt a forgery, because the *Shtern* correspondents copied from it a list of illnesses from which I never suffered. For example, I was supposed to have had cerebral thrombosis in 1952 with loss of speech and paralysis of the hand.

And take my trial in Tashkent. From the twenty-one volumes of the case file that allegedly contained three hundred criminal documents, they cited only three in court, and not one was closely examined. During the investigation, 108 witnesses were interrogated—but only 5 were present at the trial. The basic witnesses were not even summoned to the trial, since their testimony would be on my behalf. And while the testimony of the 5 who were present was not essential, none of them testified against me, either in regard to my criminal case or my alleged insanity.

Given such trial conditions, abuses are likely. And the political prisoners are not the only normal people in the special psychiatric hospitals. There are also people whom the prosecution was positive had committed a heinous crime but whose guilt they had been unable to prove. Or else the prosecution doubted that a person had committed a crime, but proof against him was so irrefutable that he was threatened with execution. And in a humanitarian sense the prosecution found it difficult to aid and abet the execution of a man who might be innocent. In a case of this sort the special psychiatric hospital could serve to cover up the failure of the investigator to complete the case.

There were also people within these institutions who were trying to escape punishment for a crime they'd committed. I knew two such. One of them, thanks to protection he received, got off with eight months in the special psychiatric hospital for a heinous crime—the corruption of a juvenile. The other was a KGB official. For beating up a policeman while drunk he was hidden by the KGB itself in the Chernyakhovsk Special Psychiatric Hospital for a lengthy examination by an experts commission. In the end he was declared sane and was freed from detention under special amnesty terms.

Sometimes these institutions were transformed into temporary dungeons. In the Leningrad Special Psychiatric Hospital I met an Azerbaidzhanian smuggler. The authorities had been trying to catch him red-handed, but he outsmarted them and the booty turned out to be two empty suitcases, at which point they decided to extract a confession from him by torture: They beat him up and then set specially trained dogs on him. He never did confess but they maimed him so badly that he could not be brought into court. He was "sentenced" to a special psychiatric hospital, where they began intensive treatment of his terrible wounds and fractures. It took more than a year before he looked relatively normal again and a second experts commission met and he was released for the duration of the investigation. I do not know his subsequent fate.

Among the normal patients of the special psychiatric hospitals were a certain number of paid informers—perhaps even KGB staff members. I met one in the Leningrad Special Psychiatric Hospital—Vasil Vasilich. I first heard about him from other patients who warned me not to talk carelessly in his presence. I ignored their warnings, having always considered this kind of talk to be a sign of delirium. I became even more firmly convinced of this when I met Vasil Vasilich. Without beating around the bush, he announced he was a senior lieutenant of the KGB. By the standards of the asylum this was a clear sign of a sick mind. We had all kinds of "high-ranking" lunatics in our section: "emperors," "kings," "generals," and even one "generalissimo." So a mere "senior lieutenant" caused me no astonishment. But he quite lucidly explained that he had been assigned here for four years with the rank of lieutenant soon after completing the KGB school. While in the hospital he had been promoted to senior lieutenant, and when he completed his term here, he would get the rank of captain. He was receiving credit for his service years—just as if he were at the front in wartime—one year for three. He told me that he could fix it so that I would never get out of here, but that he could also get me released in half a year. I laughed up my sleeve but pretended to listen seriously. However, he quickly realized that I did not believe him, and this hurt his feelings: "Very well then! You don't believe me? Just watch what I will do. In spite of everything, this next experts commission will release me and I will leave right after the commission meets, without waiting for any court decision, since I have already completed my term of service here. Anyway, another person has already arrived to take my place."

I still did not believe him. Yet I could not but be surprised by the fact that only he was able to escape punishment for all kinds of rowdy acts. Three days before the experts commission met he did things to a nurse that by rights ought to have meant he could not dream of being released. But all they did was lock him up—up till then he alone out of the whole department had walked freely about the corridor and visited other cells as he pleased—and prescribe two shots of sulfazine. The commission released him without any rebuke. Two days later he left. Before he departed, having changed to civilian clothes, he came out into the yard while our ward was having its walk—something none of those being released were permitted to do. He offered me his hand and said, "Well, now do you believe me? There are other things you don't know about that go on here. But I did you no harm."

There are other ways in which normal people get put among the insane. For example, there are those who simulate mental illness and manage to get in there through pull or bribes. These were all people who, as a rule, were deceived by the term "hospital," and who felt that anything was better than a prison or a camp. How they later repented! The regret of those who came here from camp was especially bitter. They tried and tried to prove that they had only been simulating illness. But the way back was closed. "Soviet psychiatrists do not make mistakes in diagnoses."

When people talk with me—foreign correspondents, for example—they do not ask direct questions about my sufferings in the psychiatric hospital. But in little ways they show me how much they really want to hear about this. However, I have no desire to talk at length about my experience in the hospital. I am even a bit ashamed of stressing "my experience," since I knew many who were much worse off than me.

In the ward in which they put me in late May 1970, I met a teacher from Minsk who had been there for seven years, a Pole named Genrikh Iosifovich Forpostov. He had tried to cross the border to return to his homeland but had been caught by the border guards and while under detention had expressed opinions on the Soviet system. As a result they had tried him not only for his attempt to cross the border but also for anti-Soviet propaganda. He was a very intelligent and erudite man, and, like myself, he was deprived of all opportunities to work with his mind. In addition they hindered him in all his efforts at communication. For all the years of my imprisonment, we were in the same ward. I left but he remained. Around May Day in 1975, I received a post card from him from Gomel; but he did not give his address. From this I concluded that he had been transferred from the special psychiatric hospital to the psychiatric asylum of the Ministry of Health. And if he had sent the post card from an asylum, he had been imprisoned among the mentally ill by that time for thirteen years.

Apropos, this is a reply to those who doubt the effectiveness of public protests. I spent five years and two months in prison. In that same Chernyakhovsk Special Psychiatric Prison there was a man named Paramonov who was undergoing forced treatment, having been arrested along with other sailors for participating in the Alliance for Struggle for Political Rights. Paramonov was arrested, as I was, in May 1969. By September 1973 I had been transferred for completion of forced treatment—to the psychiatric hospital of the Ministry of Health; but Paramonov spent two years more in Chernyakhovsk. It was only after Gavrilov, the former leader of the Alliance, or, in other words, the chief defendant, after serving out his six-year term in a severe regime camp, had sent a petition pointing out the inconsistency in a situation in which a rank-and-file member of the Alliance had been imprisoned longer than himself, that they finally transferred Paramonov to an ordinary asylum.

These, of course, were by no means all of the political prisoners of the Chernyakhovsk Special Psychiatric Hospital. Because I spent my entire period there in solitary confinement, I was unable to learn about many of them. In 1973 I was informed that in the Special Psychiatric Hospital there was a total of twenty-one political prisoners.

Each person's torments were different. If you happened to get a doctor who was a bit more humane things were already improved. If, as in my case, there was some sort of publicity attached to your case, things also got easier. In Chernyakhovsk, I saw orderlies and custodial staff beating individual patients. Two patients committed suicide during the years I spent there. One man hung himself and another cut his throat with a dull piece of iron—not so much cutting as tearing. There was one horrible case of vengeance. A certain patient was frequently beaten by orderlies. On leaving his job of nailing crates together, he took a hammer, found one of his tormenters, and dealt him a blow on his head. From doctors I learned that the orderly survived—as a total idiot.

The chief of the ward responded to all my protests against beatings and mistreatment of patients. Evidently he feared publicity. He was afraid I would tell my wife stories that she would in turn pass on. All the patients remarked that the atmosphere in the ward had changed since my arrival. When the court decided that I could be transferred to an ordinary asylum, I was congratulated by almost every patient, but those "chronic patients" who had spent many years in the hospital added sadly: "So now you will depart and once again everything will return to what it was before."

Forpostov, in telling about his arrival at the Chernyakhovsk Special Psychiatric Hospital, said, "It was as if I had fallen into a dark, deep pit. And I had no hope of ever making my way out of here." Forpostov had no family and so he had no connection with the outer world.

It was also impossible to "recuperate." After all, the "illness" and the "crime" of politicals are one and the same. If you say to the interrogator that there is no freedom of the press in the USSR, that means you are a slanderer, a criminal. If you say the same thing to a doctor-psychiatrist he says that this is delirium, a mental illness. If you say to the interrogator that elections should be made elections and not just theatrical productions of unanimity, that means that you are a criminal, you are against the Soviet system, you are anti-Soviet. If you repeat the same thing to a psychiatrist he will ascribe to you "concepts of reformism," and if in addition you also, and God forbid you should do so, say that things cannot go on this way for long, then they will add "prophecy" to the ever-growing list of your illnesses. And so you have a whole clump of symptoms of schizophrenia. In order to be cured of such "illnesses," you have to renounce your own convictions, trample on your own throat. You have to morally stomp on yourself.

And if you are unwilling to thus recuperate, you will be subjected to an indefinitely long "treatment"—lifelong. This gives you something to think about. Thus I am not surprised that there are persons who "repent." The alternative—imprisonment for life—is terrifying.

People advised my wife to persuade me to "repent," and these were people whom I esteemed and who themselves would probably not have "repented." But they did not feel that they had the right to demand what they would have done themselves from an old man already sufficiently wounded by life. I am grateful to my wife for not conveying their advice to me. It would only have made things more difficult. Even now I am not as surprised that anyone repented as that so few did. I do not condemn anyone who repented, and I do not feel that anyone has the right to condemn them.

It is more abnormal for a mother who has been taken from her small children to voluntarily accept life imprisonment than it is for her to return to her children by means of an untruthful "repentance." It is not her own shame—but the shame of the system that puts a mother face to face with such a choice.

I am going to dwell a little more on those details common to all special psychiatric hospitals, beginning with *the effect of medication* on patients. Much has been written about this, especially in connection with the savage impact of medication on Leonid Plyushch in the Dnepropetrovsk Special Psychiatric Hospital. Therefore I limit myself only to certain personal observations.

The most widely used medication is aminazin (similar to Thorazine), administered both internally and intramuscularly. I was astonished at the quantity prescribed to be taken internally—literally a cupped handful of pills at a time. Those who regularly took it lost the color in their palates and tongues and lost their sensation of taste. Their mouths were constantly dry and their stomachs burned. If they refused to take the pills then intramuscular injections were prescribed. When I first saw the effects of these injections I was astounded. More than once at the front I had seen buttock wounds categorized as severe. But what I saw at Chernyakhovsk and subsequently at the Fifth Moscow City Hospital was more awful than anything I had seen at the front. Both buttocks were slashed all over by the surgeon's knife. And in both hospitals, nurses in charge of the treatments explained to me that this was the result of forced injections of aminazin. The drug is not readily absorbed into one's system, and many patients' muscles refuse to accept it. Painful nodes form that prevent the patient from walking, sitting, sleeping, and that can be removed only by surgery.

The next most widely used medication was haloperidol (similar to Haldol). Those taking it cannot maintain a single position for any length of time. They jump up, run, then come to a halt and return. . . . One of the patients in the Fifth City Psychiatric Hospital, Tolya, would go into spasms each time he took this medication. He would open his mouth and could not close it for more than an hour at a time. His breathing was interrupted and his eyes bugged out. His face looked tormented and he constantly struggled with asphyxia and body tremors.

After my release from the psychiatric hospital I read a beautifully published Hungarian prospectus for haloperidol. Perhaps it is a fine medication when properly prescribed. But even the most remarkable medication can backfire when taken incorrectly.

The impact of the hospital regime on prisoners was significant. In all special psychiatric hospitals everyone is deprived of the possibility of occupying themselves with mental labor. Not only did they refuse to let me have paper, a pen, or a pencil, but they would not even permit me to keep in my cell a half-centimeter piece of pencil lead that I wanted to use to mark the margins of my own books when something in the text attracted my attention. One time the duty officer, a jailer, and a duty nurse burst into my cell, got me up, and carried out a search without telling me what they were looking for. They left without finding anything. But out in the corridor the nurse kept saying, "I saw him using it myself." After a time they reentered and asked me directly for my piece of pencil lead. Once again the nurse asserted she had seen me marking my book, and once again they searched me, but I decided not to tell them that I was not using a pencil point but my fingernail. I was afraid to tell them—they'd cut off my fingernail.

And how much trouble those books cost me! At first I was told nearly every day that I had too many books. So I went to the ward chief, taking the books with me. I demonstrated to him that not a single one was unnecessary. A new shift came on and once again I heard, "A patient is allowed to have only one book." Once again I was forced to prove that they were necessary. Finally they decided that I would be permitted to keep five books in my cell and would have to turn in the rest. This, too, I argued. In the first place, I was studying German. This meant I needed the two books that made up my text, then four volumes of the German-Russian and Russian-German dictionaries, a Russian-German phrase book, plus one literary work in German—a total of eight books. Besides this, I had decided to study mathematics logic, which meant I needed one more book, and I wanted at least one magazine of the four to which I subscribed. Thus I required in my cell twelve books at the very minimum. I had to go and prove this repeatedly.

There were all kinds of *humiliation*—dress, for example, and insults received regularly from the staff. At the same time it was believed that political prisoners should be educated at every available opportunity. The "education" was on the level of the newspapers, but our "educators" were ignoramuses. I did not have to put up with their lessons. They seemed to consider me a well-informed person and always turned to me for clarification of whatever was incomprehensible in international and domestic events. They even appealed to me for help in preparing synopses of Communist party politics. I consented to write them, and the lectures based on them were subsequently recognized by the leaders of the study groups as models.

Forpostov, however, caught it in all respects! He was the first political prisoner in Chernyakhovsk. The philistines set right to work creating a situation in which they could break him. They wanted to prove to the center that they could be entrusted with the "reeducation" of political prisoners. But Forpostov held out. The more I came to know this man, the more I realized that he was really a martyr and a hero. Though isolated he maintained a proud and independent personality through the hell of the Chernyakhovsk Special Psychiatric Hospital and thereby lightened the lot of all those who came after him. It was in particular by watching him that I learned how to fight for certain rights, for example, for books and for walks outdoors.

On the question of walks I immediately came into conflict with the staff. The dangerously insane patients were not taken out at all. When I began to demand to be taken out, in accordance with the schedule, I was told by the duty nurse and the jailer that none of the patients under guard wanted to go out for walks and that they would not consider taking out just me. I summoned the duty officer and then appealed to the chief of the ward, so they began to take me out. The schedule stated that the outdoor walk was supposed to last two hours; they would end my walk period, particularly when it was cold, after only thirty or forty minutes. We argued over this almost every day and they found every possible reason for shortening the walk periods. No matter how nauseating it was I simply had to keep on complaining. If I fell silent they would go right back to the old situation. Finally I got what I wanted. Toward the end of the second year an order was issued stating that I was to be taken out even if no one else wanted to go out. In fact they never did take me out all alone. Most of the patients under guard always chose to go out, and all of them supported me, even though the staff members kept trying to incite them against me.

The orderlies' attitude toward the prisoners included both esteem and fear.

During all the years during which I was under guard, a man named Boris Gribov was, too. Boris was aloof and seemed totally out of contact with his surroundings; he lived in some sort of an internal life of his own, conversing with himself and laughing. I had heard that before he became ill he had studied in a technical school. His family consisted of himself; his mother; and his younger sister, whom he loved dearly, and who had died suddenly. Boris had gone to the funeral, outwardly calm. After the funeral he decided to return immediately to school. His mother went to see him off. On the way there he choked her to death.

He was an athlete, still very strong when I knew him. He was nice to me, probably because of my age. I felt a deep, fatherly affection for Borya. He had one unfortunate trait—when alongside a member of the custodial staff, an orderly, or a nurse, he might strike without warning. They beat him as well, and perhaps he struck out at them because of that. He liked to sit on the floor beside or under his cot. One day, as one of the orderlies passed him, he kicked him hard in the face with his boot and badly injured him. I had directed a plea to the chief of the department earlier with a request to give the custodial personnel, the nurses, and the orderlies directions not to treat Boris in this manner. And now an incident like this!

In this case I asked the orderly whether he had really struck Borya. He responded with a challenge: "Sure it was me! So what!" I lost my temper and karate-chopped him on the throat with the side of my hand. He fell to the floor. After that they didn't touch Borya, and those criminals—in other words, the orderlies—began to treat the patients with more respect. I must say that among the orderlies there were a few decent people who were naturally sympathetic to the patients.

Insofar as the average medical staff members went, their attitude to me depended first of all on what wind was blowing from the top. The wife of the hospital chief was extremely influential. The nurses, who certainly knew how to poison daily life, played up to her. What hurt me most was when they hissed at me: "Don't get worked up!" This specific psychiatric expression referred to lunatics in whom the process of mental deterioration had sharply accelerated. All I had to do was make one remark, let's say, protesting against ending the walk ahead of time, and one of them would snap: "Don't get worked up!"

This was psychological pressure; the physical pressures were more tangible. For the first two months they confined me in a cell of six square meters with a delirious patient who had committed a heinous murder. It is not pleasant to spend the whole day staring into the face of a man who either sits motionless with a blank expression or speaks incessantly. It is even less pleasant to awaken and see this person poised over you ready to hurl himself upon you. They removed him from my cell only after I had had to tear him off me and throw him back on his cot one night at 2:00 A.M. I did not call for help, but the door to the cell was immediately opened and they took him away. What that means is that they were watching the whole struggle through the peephole, giving me the opportunity to become thoroughly frightened.

After this I remained in my cell alone until I left the hospital. They put a new lock on the cell door and stored the key in the guardroom of a different building. They nailed shut the food slot—the sliding window in the door through which meals were passed. These two measures were supposed to intensify my isolation. Their side effects were also tormenting. For example, in summer the air coming through the window was like air from an oven. Before the food slot had been nailed shut, I could signal to the jailer and he would open it. There would be some cross-ventilation in the cell and it would be easier to breathe. Now I felt like a fish on a river bank. I began to have heart paroxysms. They would not permit medication—neither validol nor nitroglycerin—in the cell. Previously when I'd had a heart paroxysm, I'd signaled for medication through the food slot, but now the door had to be opened; and the key was in the guardroom with the duty officer. When the key was needed, the duty officer might be making his rounds in the ward. Sometimes it took an hour to find him.

My isolation was unpleasant in another respect—in the use of the toilet. It was rare that I could not manage to wait to defecate. But urination was, of course, a frequent need. It might happen that by the time they found the duty officer and he came with the key I had waited too long. If this happened systematically I fell into a state of general incontinence. It got to the point where I couldn't think about anything else except not being tardy at signaling to them. Then I got to the point where I would immediately have an intolerable desire to urinate if I pressed the call button for any reason, even if I had just returned from the toilet. A conditioned reflex had been established. And how could it be otherwise? This situation went on for more than a year and a half. They could have given me a toilet in the cell. But someone evidently liked it the way it was.

One more torment was the so-called *release* commission. Twice a year the question of whom to release was allegedly decided in these commissions. In fact, nothing was decided. For one thing, the commission didn't have time. In my ward alone there were from ninety-four to ninety-eight patients. The commission would begin its work at 10:00 to 10:30 A.M. and finish by 1:30 P.M.; less than two minutes per person. And within those two minutes the commission chairman, Serbsky Institute professor Ilinsky, was supposed to diagnose the patient better than his attending physician! The physician might recommend release but Ilinsky would decide: "Continue the treatment." What magnificent erudition and how swiftly it manifested itself—an excellent illustration of Snezhnevsky's claim that Soviet psychiatry was on such a high plane that "mistakes in diagnosis were absolutely excluded."

Ilinsky had received directions from Moscow on each political prisoner. All they had to do was give him a list of those to release—and everything was clear. The rest were not to be released. Here, indeed, mistakes were impossible.

But the special hospital prisoners kept on hoping, becoming excited as early as two months before the commission. The cell for prisoners under guard would fill up and two or three more cells would be transferred to the status of prisoners kept under guard. After the commission had met, it would take another month for the prisoners to quiet down. In other words, since there were two commission meetings a year the prisoners were kept in a situation of unusual stress six months of the year.

Even the political prisoners who knew the commission was powerless could not escape this situation. No matter how brief the commission session, it always found time to talk to the political prisoners. To the young who were not yet famous, they talked rudely. And with those like me who had a name they talked ideologically.

I am never going to be able to list all the torments. But I must mention briefly one of the most heinous crimes of the system of "forced measures of a medical character"—one that underlines the antimedical nature of these measures and which none of my predecessors has touched upon: Both the sane and the rest of the patients in the special psychiatric hospitals are totally deprived of a sex life. Even in severe regime colonies and camps there are personal visits, however wretched. In the special psychiatric hospitals there are none. Young people are separated from their wives and fiancés. Families are broken up and peoples' lives are destroyed. I speak of young people, whose fate is the most tragic of all, but the elderly, too, are deprived of their last years of the joys of marriage.

Up to now I have spoken only about the torments of those who have been imprisoned in the special psychiatric hospitals. These people have families: Who has ever tried to measure their torments? What kind of suffering does a wife experience who, after having known her husband as an energetic, joyful person, suddenly encounters a dull stare and drooping shoulders? From visit to visit, she sees his intellect perish, his dear image fade forever. I find it difficult to imagine these sufferings and I believe that women feel them profoundly. I would rather suffer any torments myself than to see them visited on my wife or children.

On September 19, 1973, I had been sent to the Fifth Moscow City Psychiatric Hospital in the company of my wife and an ensign from the hospital. With customary Soviet hypocrisy the officials reported that they would be unable to give me my Tashkent prison notes, because "accidentally" the key to the safe in which they were being kept had been taken by a lieutenant who was off on holiday. But just as in Marx the "accidental occurrence" turned out to be in accordance with a natural law, I learned after being sent many false answers to my requests for them that the notes had been burned "because they had not been requested for so long an interval." At that point I sued the Chernyakhovsk hospital, without result. But at the moment of departure from that godforsaken institution, I did not worry about my notes. My wife and I had decided not to let any small details spoil our mood. We also paid no attention to the fact that the accompanying hospital ensign "forgot" to give my wife the travel money allotted for us as well as the twenty rubles withdrawn from my personal account—this being what was left out of funds sent me from home. We also tried to ignore the fact that during the entire trip this hospital ensign lived off of us.

My wife and I were totally absorbed in one another. There had been so many years of harsh separation. We sat pressed up against each other and talked. More precisely, she talked. What could I tell her? Was I to complain about what I had been through? No, this was no subject for our first meeting after such a long time. Therefore I just drank in her dear voice and tried to grasp all of what had happened out in freedom. In the course of the twenty-eight hours of travel from Chernyakhovsk to Moscow we did not shut our eyes. She told me in detail about the state of the movement, and I realized that my fears of its collapse were unfounded. While I was in the hospital, I had gauged the situation on the basis of names known to me. I knew that many had been arrested and convicted: Yakir and Krasin, Gershuni, Gabai, Mustafa and Reshat Dzhemiliyev, many Ukrainians, Lithuanians, and Crimean Tatars.

Yakobson, Telesin, Tsukerman and many others had emigrated. From all this I had deduced that the movement had totally collapsed. My own feeling of helplessness, arising from the fact that I was unable myself to struggle and was forced to be on the sidelines, intensified this feeling.

I had been extremely depressed by the "repentance" of Yakir. The KGB knows what to do. When the Yakir and Krasin press conference was broadcast they took me to the TV set. I knew that all this was show and I took a strong hold on myself. But then they asked Pyotr Yakir his opinion of my mental state. He answered, "As a non-specialist I was unable correctly to judge his mental state, and therefore all of my affirmations of his complete normality are objectively slanderous." At this I could barely hold back a cry of pain. Into what abyss must a man be hurled in order not to be able to say whether his own father is normal or insane? Pyotr Yakir had been to me a beloved son, and he had looked on me as a father. During the last half-year before my arrest it was a rare day on which we did not see each other. His kindness toward my family after my arrest bears witness to his own filial feelings for me.

And here he was declaring that he did not know whether I was normal or

insane. This was something to howl about. Even in "repenting" there must
be a boundary beyond which a man does not go. Pyotr crossed that boundary.
And he crossed it, too, without any real need. Everything else he had said was
quite enough. He could have refused to answer that question beforehand. If
he had done so, they would not have asked him it. The KGB does not stick
its neck out when there is danger in so doing.

When they led me back to my cell after the telecast, the chief of the ward,
Bobylev, my attending physician, was waiting for us in the corridor by his office. "Well," he asked me, "what's your impression?"

"Fear, a natural feeling," I responded. "But in some people in certain conditions it can overcome all other feelings. And that is unnatural."

Such memories ran through my head as Zinaida talked to me on the train.
She hid nothing and did not try to soften anything. She told me with bitterness
how much Yakir's "repentance" had hurt the movement and how hard it was
to say goodbye to Tolya Yakobson and Yulius Telesin. But then she spoke
of the coming of new people, telling me the names of everyone who had joined
the movement. I asked about a few of them and she laughed: "When you get
back you'll make their acquaintance. Before your arrest people used to say
that all of Moscow visited us, yes, and then they added, and not just Moscow.
But what used to be was nothing at all. You should see how many people come
to us now."

She talked also about the work they were undertaking and I was astonished
at the scope and form of it. Several times western youths had scattered leaflets
in Moscow in defense of our political prisoners. She spoke of Pyotr Yakir with
great warmth when telling me about the enormous amount of work that had
been put into the creation of the film *Human Rights in the USSR*.

"We ourselves," she explained, "did not believe that we would succeed. But
they managed to send the film out of the country and it is now being shown
in Europe."

She recounted all kinds of comic episodes that had occurred in connection
with filming because so many people had had to avoid surveillance all over
Moscow—groups with enormous cameras, and so on. But they had done it.

"I, too, am in it," she said, only then mentioning her own part. "And I also
succeeded in sending abroad your notes from the Tashkent dungeon. Right
now the English are making a film based on them."

She said nothing about herself. I had sent those notes to her, and she had
received them. It must not have been easy to guard them, and she risked being
arrested for having them in her possession. But Zinaida not only preserved
them, she also endowed them with life; while I was reflecting on this, she was
speaking: "These notes have been published in a special booklet called
Thoughts of an Insane Man. You owe thanks for this first to Kirill Velikanov.
He spent nearly a year gathering together your writings. After all, you didn't

keep anything yourself."

She was right. After I had written something I immediately disseminated it in samizdat and never gave thought to accumulating an archive.

She continued, "And Boris Isakovich Tsukerman and Yulius Telesin also worked on it."

Then into me there crept not only a feeling of warmth for my friends but the thought: "And you too! And you too!"

I was convinced that Zinaida Mikhailovna had managed to provide most of the material for my booklet to my friends, and I later learned that that was exactly what had happened. So it was with all Zinaida's stories. She recounted many, many stories about the movement to me but never mentioned herself. The events in which she was obviously a participant were amazing and in all of them I could see her work. For as long as I had known Zinaida she had always assisted the formation of my view of life. She had condemned my too great devotion to the system, and she had quietly and modestly suggested a realistic view of events without letting herself be overly distracted by the advantages of my position. She understood *people* and had encouraged my friendship with those who helped me to think.

Thus it was natural that now, when the system had subjected her to many cruelties, she had shown her true colors. Deprived by the government of any means of subsistence, she had not only fed her family and sent me food in the hospital but had risen to struggle against tyranny alongside the leading defenders of human rights. And I, owing my liberation to my friends both in Russia and abroad, to the Soviet defenders of human rights and to international public opinion, can only note that the central place in this struggle was taken by Zinaida Mikhailovna. Once she said to me, "It was Kostyorin who created you as you are now." Rephrasing this affirmation, I can say that my image such as it was seen by those who struggled for my liberation was created by my wife.

Absorbed in our conversations, we approached Moscow without even noticing it. Our accompanying ensign evidently decided to express his gratitude for the hospitality we had shown him and he told Zinaida Mikhialovna, "We will visit your apartment for a short time."

He had been eavesdropping as we talked. During the whole journey we had been dreaming about dropping in at our apartment, even if only for ten minutes. And he had decided to give us that joy. But how naïve we were! As the train approached the station platform, I went to the window. What I saw caused me to call out suddenly, "Zina, we're being met!"

From the compartment she answered, "Yes, yes, I forgot to tell you that I told all our friends the time of our arrival in Moscow."

"I'm not talking about that. Our 'companions' are here."

The train came to a halt and our car was surrounded by policemen. Between the police and the railway car stood about a dozen plainclothesmen, all looking very much like one another. I was first out of our car.

"Pyotr Grigoryevich, where is your escort?"

I pointed out the ensign. The officials took him off to one side for a minute and gave him a lecture. Two Volga automobiles drove straight up the track right to the station platform.

"Get in, Pyotr Grigoryevich." The ensign gestured toward one of the Volgas. "Let's be off."

"No, we are not going!" Zinaida spoke firmly. "We are not going to be off until our friends and our sons have greeted us."

But where were they? Maybe they hadn't come? Here was one of them making his way up to us. They had been held back at the end of the platform. After a time Tatyana Maximovna, Pavel Litvinov, Lena Kostyorin, our sons Andrei and Oleg, and another two dozen people, most of them unfamiliar to me, came running up. It was a joyful and passionate meeting. We embraced each other. The KGB men kept hurrying us: "We must be off!"

Finally we went to the cars. I walked arm in arm with Zina. One of the KGB men standing by a car said, "There's no place for you, Zinaida Mikhailovna."

"No place for me?" she asked, her voice full of surprise and contempt. "There's no place for one of you," she said firmly. "For me there is a place." And she opened the door of the car.

The second of the KGB men standing there began courteously to help Zinaida Mikhailovna into the car and said in an apologetic tone, "Don't pay any attention. That comrade has not been filled in. This is your place and Pyotr Grigoryevich is next to you, in the middle. I will be on his other side and Pyotr Grigoryevich's escort will be sitting up in front, next to the driver."

In general two KGB men flanked the prisoner. But here Zinaida took one of their places. I sat for the entire eighty-four kilometer trip to the Fifth City Psychiatric Hospital pressed tightly against my dear "KGB agent"—my wife. I did not hear or see the rest of them.

They did not forgive Zinaida for getting into the car. After formalities in the hospital reception room she accompanied me to my ward, during which time the car departed. When I learned of this from the nurse I immediately wrote a complaint. My wife had been listed as my escort from the medical personnel. (The ensign had been from the custodial personnel.) And they were therefore supposed to deliver her back to her residence. The only reply I received was that those to blame had been punished. Who was to blame, how he had been punished, whether he had apologized and whether there had been compensation for the material loss caused my wife, I never found out!

Life in the Fifth Moscow City Psychiatric Hospital was much better than in Chernyakhovsk. The principal improvement for me was release from solitary. For the past sixty-two months I had longed for human companionship. Here I was able to communicate with many good, normal people.

In addition, doctors of all fields of specialization were in residence at the hospital and there was all sorts of diagnostic equipment, an X-ray laboratory, various treatment laboratories, and a dental prosthetic lab. Outdoor walks lasted longer and were conducted under better conditions.

The matter of visits was also improved. This hospital was much closer to Moscow—an hour and a half away compared to twenty-eight hours for Chernyakhovsk. All my relatives and friends could visit me. (In Chernyakhovsk they had permitted only my wife and children.) Nobody sat right on top of you when you were conversing with a visitor.

Finally, the food was incomparably better. In Chernyakhovsk the food allotment had been forty-two kopecks per patient per day, whereas here it was five rubles—twelve times more.

But I was still imprisoned. In a certain sense it was even worse. I was being held as ill in a civilian hospital. The KGB could now say: "He is no longer being held by us but by the Ministry of Health system. And they too consider him to be ill."

Being in such a hospital changed things little for political prisoners. Here there existed a separate system for forced treatment, headed by a deputy chief. In our hospital it was Alexandra Kozhemyakina. All directives relating to patients under forced treatment in the Fifth Hospital came from her. She immediately took up the task of "reeducating" me.

There was no way Kozhemyakina could possibly convince me of anything; she was a total political illiterate. She also seemed to know almost nothing of medicine. She did not have the authority to release me, but because I was still deemed socially dangerous, she did have the right to send me back to a special psychiatric hospital.

After telling me this she added, "If by your conduct you manage to get sent back to a special hospital you'll never get out again."

I communicated this conversation to my wife and news of it immediately got to the West and from there to the BBC, the German Radio, and the Voice of America, and from there back to Kozhemyakina. She flew into a rage and hurled herself upon my wife. But Zinaida gave it right back to her and news of this incident, too, reached the West.

Kozhemyakina tried to bring pressure on our son Andrei, but with the same result. And she was so stupid that she blurted out to Andrei much that should have remained secret, after which she evidently received a dressing down, for she left our family in peace. However, we did not want to leave her in peace. Every day of the somewhat more than nine months I spent in this hospital consisted of a struggle for my liberation, a struggle conducted with the aid of my one and only weapon—publicity.

It was publicity that had forced them to move me from the special psychiatric hospital. But in this their intent had been perfidious. They wanted to convince the public that I really was mentally ill, that the whole scandal raised over my case was a provocation. To this end the Serbsky Institute had made up a case history of my illness—a forgery in which they inserted mention of serious organic injuries to my brain. At the time an international conference of psychiatrists was coming to an end in Yerevan and the Serbsky Institute invited participants in that conference to visit the institute and several psychiatric hospitals. Most of the participants refused this invitation on the grounds that it would be impossible to form objective conclusions on the basis of such a trip. But they did manage to assemble a group of seven persons to make the tours and it was to these persons that they showed the forged case history. It was also shown to the correspondent of the magazine *Shtern*. In addition the KGB gave this journal photographs taken in the Fifth Psychiatric Hospital. Two of the seven Western psychiatrists who visited the institute were permitted to see me.

The meeting was held in my attending physician's office. In addition to the two psychiatrists, representatives of the Serbsky Institute, the chief of the medical branch of the hospital, the chief of my own ward, N. G. Itkin, and two senior scientists from the Psychiatric Institute were present. One of the senior scientists was the translator. My wife had warned me ahead of time about the visit, stressing that I should not talk through the Psychiatric Institute's translator: "Demand your own translator," she had written to me. "I will get one."

The conversation did not take place. I demanded that my own translator be present in addition to the one chosen by the hospital, but they refused to agree to this and tried to convince me that their translator was good. It was typical that not a single one of the Western psychiatrists supported me. (My argument with the hospital officials was translated to them.) Even though everyone knew that it was folly to conduct a conversation that was to define the mental state of a patient via a possibly biased translator, and without making a tape recording of it, no one stood with me against the authorities.

However, something evidently did get through to the psychiatrists, because during a subsequent conversation with the director of the hospital they asked him when I would be released. Without even thinking about it the director told them that I would be out not later than November 19, two months after my admittance to the hospital. The date limit was seized upon by my friends in the USSR and abroad and was used in the struggle for my liberation.

It was at this time that *Shtern* published an article by the correspondent who had read my forged case history. He set everything forth in great detail and the Soviet human rights movement immediately repudiated the case history on the basis of material provided by my wife. In this way the first part of the task set for the KGB—which was to publicly prove that I was mentally ill—collapsed. To now put into effect the second part of the plan—which was to return me to the special psychiatric hospital because of an alleged worsening of my condition—would have been foolish. Because of these failures, the whole system got clogged up. November 19 passed as did all the scheduled periods for sessions of release commissions.

The release commissions in the Fifth Moscow City Psychiatric Hospital were conducted by Professor Zinaida Gavrilovna Turova, the permanent representative of the Serbsky Institute. After a series of particularly insistent broadcasts on Western radio, the chief of my own ward and Kozhemyakina, members of the release commission, in the course of one of the commission sessions finally brought pressure on Turova: "You are duty bound to examine everyone whom we present for examination!" Turova gave in and they soon summoned me.

Everything went well. When the chief of the ward returned from the commission meeting, he congratulated me on my successful appearance before the commission. But a day later, very embarrassed, he said that I had not been included in the commission's protocol. When Itkin asked Turova why this was, she said that she had not formally put me before the commission. She had only been talking with me in "a preliminary sense." One day later she reported I would be considered by the commission under the chairmanship of Margarita Feliksovna Taltse, who came and talked with me.

A month and a half later I learned that Taltse, too, had refused to decide the question of my mental state. Only in late April 1974 was the question of the chairmanship of the commission to review my case decided. They appointed a senior scientist of the Serbsky Institute, Doctor of Medical Sciences Shestakovich, the man who had asked me questions before the session of the release commission in the Leningrad Special Psychiatric Hospital on December 3, 1964. The commission session took place May 14, 1974. I had my first hearing after eight months, a period during which I should have had three.

They convened, adopted a decision to release me, and forgot about it. May passed. I learned nothing about the outcome of my court hearing. The ninth month of my stay in the Fifth Moscow City Psychiatric Hospital was coming to an end. On the twentieth Zinaida went to the court and was told only that they did not have my case. On the twenty-sixth at 8:00 A.M. they summoned me to the doctor's office, where I saw my wife and Tatyana Maximovna Litvinova sitting to the right of the doors. On my wife's knees lay a new man's shirt. I immediately realized—release! The doctor told me to go and change my clothes, but this time I was not in such a big hurry. I asked when and how this had happened—after all, the court had not had my case on the twentieth. Zinaida told me that just yesterday evening they had phoned her from the hospital and told her to come and get me at eight.

A Dr. Nefedov added that on the twenty-second they had sent him a summons to appear in court as an expert on my case. The court hearing had been held on the twenty-third. The next day was Sunday. On the twenty-fifth at five in the afternoon a KGB official had delivered a copy of the court determination and a court order stating that I was to be out of the hospital by ten the next morning. I later learned that both Solzhenitsyn and Richard Nixon had been involved in my release. At the time Nixon was getting ready for a trip to the Soviet Union, and Solzhenitsyn sent him a telegram that, according to rumors reaching the USSR, said the following: "When appeals are made to the Soviet government regarding prisoners in special psychiatric hospitals, the government replies with references to medical diagnoses, to doctors. Two such prisoners, Grigorenko and Shikhanovich, have been released by medical commissions. But the authorities continue to detain them in prison. Perhaps you can find the opportunity to petition the Soviet government to liberate at least these two persons."

Nixon was coming to Moscow on June 27. They freed Shikhanovich and me on the twenty-sixth. My friends joked about it, calling us "a gift to Nixon."

So it was that on June 26, 1974, at 10:30 A.M. in a Volga sedan belonging to one of the chiefs of the hospital we drove out of the hospital gates. As we approached Moscow, I asked my wife for my documents. She replied that she did not have them. I directed myself to Dr. Nefedov, who was in the front seat alongside the driver. He also did not have them. I demanded to be returned to the hospital: "What is this, a provocation? They'll detain me as a fugitive if I have no documents. And I'll be sent right back to the Special Psychiatric Hospital."

The doctor was nearly weeping: "I am required to deliver you home immediately. I will go immediately back to the hospital and get your documents. You have to be at home by noon."

We reached our apartment exactly at twelve and immediately I was besieged by telephone calls from Western correspondents. Then they began to visit me, one after another. Canadian radio had announced my release at 5:00 A.M.

The first wave of visitors, most of whom were foreign correspondents, had already receded when Nefedov and Litvinovna returned with my documents. I still felt ill at ease. Everything was familiar, but why was I here? After all, I was not supposed to return here. That is how profoundly, against my will, the conviction had penetrated my consciousness that I would never leave the insane asylum.

Tatyana Litvinova must have understood my state of mind. She asked, "What is it, Pyotr? Don't you believe it?"

I nodded. She said, "I can see that you are feeling your way."

I went about the apartment and because everything seemed unreal— windows without bars, lightweight doors, tables, chairs, wardrobes, chandeliers—I touched everything.

CHAPTER TWENTY-SEVEN

NO REST FOR US

During those first days after my return, our apartment was full of guests. I barely managed to meet all those who had joined the movement in my absence. We ignored warnings from the KGB that we were entertaining too much, and went on receiving visitors. But Zina and I both needed a rest. My cousin, Ilya, a physician, had invited us to visit him in Borisovka. Borisovka was five kilometers from the Azov seashore and Ilya had a car. We also had an invitation from the Tatars who had held out in the Crimea to vacation with them. We decided to accept both invitations. We would visit Ilya for a month and then go to the Crimea.

Before leaving I had to take care of my financial affairs. For five years and two months my family had not received my pension, even though by law it should have been paid them in full. The law says approximately: "If for some reason a pensioner has not received his pension, it must be paid him on his first demand." The Moscow city military commissariat had received directions regarding my pension before my arrival—and instructions from the top were more powerful than all laws taken together. They awarded me my pension starting June 26, 1974—from the day of my release, exactly as they would have

429

done with someone who had been condemned to a prison or camp term. By this they were saying that I was not ill but a criminal.

I appealed via the military commissariat hierarchy and sued in court. Both efforts were to no avail. The court initially accepted my suit, but after having received the necessary instruction, which probably was given by telephone, they returned my documents to me saying that pension cases were not within their jurisdiction.

The military commissariat hierarchy sidestepped my complaints even more effectively. They replied to everything I asked for by saying, "There is no possibility of satisfying your request." So we were preparing to leave Moscow with the one month's pension. The Solzhenitsyn Fund, which had been created during my imprisonment, came to our aid. It was, I must say, a most important achievement of the human rights movement—a material and moral support for a persecuted participant in the human rights movement and his family.

I spent most of the trip at the railway car window staring out at the landscape. Ilya met us in his car at the station in Berdyansk. In half an hour we were in Borisovka.

The village had changed greatly during the fourteen years since I had last visited it. The peasant huts had been repaired; many of them looked like city homes. There were motorcycles and a few passenger cars in the village streets. People now lived there who spoke with unfamiliar accents—resettlers, or, more precisely, evacuees or even exiles from the Ternopol area of the Western Ukraine who had already put down roots in Borisovka and had even managed to intermarry with the locals.

There were few young people in Borisovka. In the evening fifteen- and sixteen-year-olds congregated on the village street; but most of the young adults had already migrated to the city.

The outward appearance of the adults had changed. The scared look had left their eyes; they did not act as if they were afraid of something. Many had radios and listened to Radio Liberty and to Radio Free Europe without trying to hide it from their neighbors. They were not afraid of talking with me. They all knew of my odyssey, but they regarded me as one of their own. When Ilya had picked us up I had asked him, "Aren't you going to get in trouble because of me?" He replied, "What do you mean? People are going to be envious of me that I have such a cousin."

The fear induced by Stalin's terror, by collectivization, by the destruction of the kulaks, and by the famine was gradually disappearing and the very youngest generation was growing up quite without fear of and respect for the KGB. The KGB had received instructions to set up clandestine surveillance over me. But how could they do this in a village? Any stranger could be seen at a distance of ten kilometers. Thus each morning a herd of children would dash up from the district center and holler to Ilya's eight-year-old son: "Yura! Tell your people the spies are here. They're coming this way."

These were all positive phenomena. The end to fear was what our people needed most of all. But what would replace fear? So far there is no answer to this question. The people have rejected communist propaganda and do not believe what is purveyed by the Soviet media.

One day I was listening to German radio, whose broadcasts I consider the best of the Western broadcasts in the Ukrainian and Russian languages. As I listened, a collective farmer approximately my age, a relative of mine, came into the room. After listening for several minutes he said, "Why are you listening to that nonsense?" And he switched it to Radio Liberty.

"The only one worth listening to is Liberty," he said. "Those people give good, serious broadcasts. The German radio, BBC, and the Voice of America are not so different from our own. Radio Canada is even worse than ours."

I was astonished at his judgments. I had never had the opportunity to compare the various stations. He had. In the cities Radio Liberty was jammed. In the villages it could be heard, and so I, too, had a chance to compare the broadcasts. I soon became convinced that my collective farmer friend was right.

But even Radio Liberty had failed to create programs that could assist in the formation of a spiritual world for its listeners. We do not have churches; it is impossible to consider sufficient those that are set up in tiny village huts and are meant to serve entire enormous steppe districts of from twenty to thirty large villages.

What will become of those who do not know fear but have empty souls? Now this emptiness is poured full of moonshine vodka and homemade wine. But what comes after that?

That same relative who enlightened me on the radio programs asked me, "Tell me what this means! We are living in a bearable way. We are not starving. There is bread and there are things to go with bread. We are clothed. Our houses are repaired. We have furniture. Many have motorcycles and some have automobiles. Everything seems as if it should be good—but life is dreary. We have been here a whole month—and tell me, have you heard even one song? Remember when we were children and on Saturday songs rang through the whole village? But what about now? There are no songs. There is no laughter. There are no jokes."

How could I refute him? I had felt all this myself but hadn't been able to express it. I had been in the village club and I had seen those young people hanging around, and I, too, was depressed by their appearance. I, too, saw a village in which song had been killed off.

The Crimean Tatars rented a room for us right on the seashore in Yevpatoriya, just as we had asked them to. We recall with enormous gratitude their sensitivity and tact. We were left in total peace, able to rest surrounded by only our family. All this was organized so quietly that even the KGB failed to discover us for nearly a month.

We returned to Moscow in early October and began to prepare for our "day." October 16 is both my birthday and Zina's. We have an old tradition that on this day anyone who wishes can visit us without an invitation. Though it was obvious that the first such birthday after my long absence would draw many people, we decided not to end our tradition. The burden was indeed great, but volunteers came to help us prepare and serve food. The fare was not very bountiful, but there was a great deal of cordiality and sincere affection. All of our old friends were there, and there were many new ones as well—including Andrei Dmitriyevich Sakharov and Yelena Georgiyevna, his wife. He won everyone's heart with his unpretentiousness and sincerity.

It was time for me to again join in the human rights struggle. I plunged right in, meeting new people every day—Yuri Orlov and his wife, Ira; Valya and Tanya Turchin, and Igor Rostislavich Shafaryevich. My relationship with Shafaryevich is the clearest illustration of our milieu. It would have been difficult to find two people whose views differed so widely. Yet we had no difficulty conversing. More than once we changed our opinions together. I miss his quiet but urgent voice.

Meeting Father Dmitry Dudko was a tremendous occasion for me. He had come into our family when I was in the insane asylum, bringing a spirit of assurance and hope, the spirit of faith. He was a genuine spiritual shepherd, a priest no matter what he was wearing; but in his priestly garb this short, compact person looked majestic. He even seemed to emit an unearthly light. Outwardly he was quite unlike that dry little old man, my first spiritual mentor, Father Vladimir Donskoi. Still, something linked them for me: most likely their boundless faith in God and love for one's neighbor. I frequently attended services presided over by Father Dmitry, though I had to travel fifty to eighty kilometers out of Moscow to reach his church. He performed a church marriage for Zinaida and me before our departure for the United States.

I reestablished and broadened old relationships that had been strengthened by Zinaida Mikhailovna during my absence. We talked constantly of the past and of those friends who were now far away from us, on the other side of the cordon: Tolya Yakobson, Boris Tsukerman, Yulius Telesin, Alexander Yesenin-Volpin, and many others. We were particularly concerned for Tolya Yakobson, wondering how he, who loved Russia most of all, could live without it? We now know that he could not! He ended his own life.

So much was going on during this last period of my human rights struggle that I will tell only the most important events, beginning with a story about our attitude toward preparation for the Helsinki Conference, something the Soviet press was writing about a great deal at the time. I personally felt that the conference would never be held. In talking with my friends I argued that the Helsinki Conference was a feint of Soviet diplomacy that had as its purpose avoiding a peace conference. The principal problem of any peace conference is to end a state of war. In practice this means the withdrawal of all armed forces from the territories of other nations. The Soviet Union does not want to withdraw its armed forces. It wants to occupy indefinitely the territories it has seized and to maintain its occupation armies in a state of readiness for further aggression. For these reasons the Soviet Union does not need a peace conference.

The second task of a peace conference is to establish postwar boundaries between the warring states. But the only boundaries important to the Soviet Union are those that establish where the Soviet Union intends to conduct further aggression. Until the time comes when Soviet armies advance, it does not want to change these boundaries, and other boundaries do not interest it.

The other tasks of the peace conference were as follows: first, the reunification of Germany; second, the independence of the three Baltic states that were handed over by Hitler to Stalin: Estonia, Latvia, and Lithuania; and, third, the compensation to states that were transformed by the aggressors into arenas of destructive and ruinous warfare during World War II, and also the guarantee against a repetition of any such actions in the future. Specifically, the matter concerns Byelorussia, Moldavia, and the Ukraine.

In connection with the latter questions, the further question is raised as to the form of participation in the peace negotiations of the six enumerated states. The Soviet Union opposes putting such questions up for discussion. It does not wish to permit in any form the participation in peace talks of countries occupied by its armies.

Thus the position of the Soviet Union in relation to a peace conference is negative in the extreme—something which, I believe, must be clear to Western diplomats. If the West wishes peace, it must not permit its diplomats to be distracted by a conference whose only purpose is to sidetrack a peace conference. The Helsinki Conference was precisely such a sidetrack. I was convinced therefore that it would never take place.

It did, of course. August 1, 1975, will go down in history as a great victory of Soviet diplomacy and as the most shameful page in the history of Western diplomacy.

What did the Soviet Union achieve by the Helsinki Conference? It sought confirmation by an international act of law of its right to hold on to territories it had seized by force during the war, and to maintain its own armies on those territories in any strength and in any disposition. *All of this the Helsinki Final Treaty gave the Soviet Union.*

For the West everything remained precisely as it had been before Helsinki. Germany continued to be divided. The occupation of Poland, Czechoslovakia, Estonia, Latvia, Lithuania, Byelorussia, Moldavia, and the Ukraine continued. Soviet tank armies stood in the center of Europe, ready for a forward thrust into the as yet unoccupied portion of the continent. Rockets with nuclear warheads were targeted on all the basic targets of the NATO countries. The air forces were ready for attack.

To us it was evident that foreign policy successes now gave the Soviet government the opportunity to intensify its pressure against human rights inside the country. We were not impressed by the bombastic promises in the humanitarian area that were written into the conference's Concluding Act. We remembered previous international treaties in which the Soviet Union took upon itself obligations in regard to human rights but never carried them out.

But suddenly among us a person appeared who looked upon the Concluding Act differently than the rest of us. This was Corresponding Member of the Armenian Academy of Sciences, Doctor of Physical-Mathematical Sciences Yuri Fyodorovich Orlov. To me he was simply Yura.

In early 1976, because of an intensification of diabetes, I entered a hospital and left it only at the end of April. Therefore I didn't hear his opinions of the Helsinki Conference till early May, though he had begun propagandizing back in March. The essence of his views was this: "A profound connection exists between the struggle for human rights and efforts to create genuinely reliable security guarantees.

"Unlike previous declarations which contain obligations in the area of human rights, in the Helsinki Concluding Act these obligations of the Soviet government are given 'in exchange' for important political concessions by Western governments, and this has conditioned timid but nonetheless unprecedented efforts on the part of recent Western leaders to insist on the fulfillment of these obligations.

"Information about Soviet violations of human rights and about the real nature of Soviet democracy, has evidently begun to reach broad circles of Western society and has even influenced the tactics of certain Western Communist parties.

"All of this has compelled the Soviet government, disturbed by the lowering of Soviet prestige in the West, to make some concessions in relation to individuals persecuted for their convictions and well known abroad, and has in some degree stopped the obvious attack on the human rights movement in the USSR which commenced before the European Conference, halted during the Conference, and recommenced after the Conference. Right now repressions, sometimes crueler than ever, continue chiefly in those cases which for some reason we do not receive news of.

"Based on the experience of the last year, a long range extrapolation shows that: If the movement for civil rights in the USSR could broaden its work in informing the population inside the country and in informing the West; and if, at the same time, the Western public would renounce the existing unequal interpretation of the principle of noninterference and would operationally support the movement for human rights in the USSR; then the Soviet authorites would be forced to moderate their repressive policy, thereby assisting the realization of democratic rights.

"The small probability of such a development ought not to hold back efforts aimed at it, since our efforts will increase the probability."

Yura believed that we should take an official position regarding the Concluding Act. He proposed to tie the struggle for peace and international security with the struggle for human rights both by their respective activities and an organization he proposed creating. Only by this, he said, would we enter the international struggle for security and receive the support of the world public. The conversation in which he spelled out his plan took place at Andrei Dmitriyevich Sakharov's apartment. I felt ill and probably because of this I did not see anything particularly new in Yura's line of reasoning.

I didn't realize that Yura was inviting me to participate in the new organization. Therefore it was completely unexpected when he called me at home in mid-May and said, "Pyotr Grigoryevich, I would like to announce formation of the group. I am counting on you."

"Why do you want me with all my illnesses, Yura? It doesn't seem likely that I am capable nowadays of doing anything useful."

"We need your name."

"Well, if that is really so valuable, let's postpone the announcement till tomorrow."

"No, that's impossible. I am telephoning from Sakharov's apartment. The foreign correspondents are already here. If I do not announce it right now, I never will. 'Our best friends'—the KGB—have been tailing me all week."

"In that case, include me!"

Yura announced formation of the group, whose purpose was to promote fulfillment of the Helsinki agreements in the USSR. On a formal declaration were the signatures Lyudmila Alekseyeva, Mikhail Bernshtam, Yelena Bonner, Alexander Ginzburg, Pyotr Grigorenko, Doctor Alexander Korchak, Malva Landa, Anatoly Marchenko, Professor Vitaly Rubin, Anatoly Shcharansky, and Professor Yuri Orlov.

Only Yuri had understood that there was a possibility of softening the defeat of Western diplomacy. This opportunity lay in the fact that Western diplomats, in exchange for enormous political concessions, had received promises, though these were qualified promises, that human rights would be observed. If the West demanded payment of the Soviet Union for the advantages it had received, and if the group put in Western hands proof of violation by the Soviet

Union of its human rights obligations, all this would help lessen secrecy in
Soviet society and make more difficult the possibility of a sudden Soviet armed
attack.

The KGB beat me to the realization of the enormous significance of Orlov's
initiative. Even before Yura's public announcement, they had learned of his
intentions through bugging operations, and they summoned Yura in to give
him a warning. He did not respond. When they sent agents to get him, he hid.
They pursued him, catching him only after three days—that is, after his announcement. On May 15 a TASS communiqué was published entitled "A
Provocateur Warned." It was reported that "a certain Orlov" had created an
illegal anti-Soviet group for the collection and dissemination of slanderous
anti-Soviet propaganda. He had been warned that if he did not cease his activity he would be brought to criminal justice. The communiqué finally brought
me to the realization that creation of the group was a brilliant innovation in
the human rights movement. Forgetting my illness, I rushed to its defense.
I wrote a letter to the director of TASS—which I disseminated in samizdat
and which subsequently was published in the West—pointing out that TASS
was lying when it called us an underground anti-Soviet organization.

The group set to work with enormous energy. In the course of the two and
a half months from the day of its formation to the first anniversary of the Helsinki Conference, it issued seven communiqués (not counting the charter): 1)
on the persecution of Mustafa Dzhemiliyev; 2) on postal and telephone communications; 3) on conditions of imprisonment of prisoners of conscience; 4)
on divided families; 5) on the repression of religious families; 6) on security
and on cooperation (this was an evaluation of the Helsinki Conference); 7)
on the situation of former political prisoners in the USSR.

In these first months the group manifested its capability to self-perpetuate.
Soon after its creation Misha Bernshtam and Professor Vitaly Rubin left the
USSR, the former because of KGB threats. Rubin had joined the "rejection-
ists"—but after the creation of the group he was given permission to leave the
USSR. The KGB had obviously decided to destroy our group by removing
individual members from it in various ways. A third member of the group—
Doctor of Physical and Mathematic Sciences Alexander Korchak—was informed that he would be dismissed from work and expelled from the scientific
community unless he left the group. This was not an empty threat, and Korchak, who had a large family, was forced to leave. New people immediately
joined, among whom during these first months were Vladimir Slepak, Yuri
Mnyukh, Naum Meiman, Tatyana Osipova, Sofya Kalistratova, Victor Nekipelov, and Yarym Agayev.

One of the important results of the formation of the Moscow Helsinki group
was its influence on the national republics of the USSR. During that summer
and autumn the Ukrainian poet Mikola Rudenko had initiated a conversation

with me on the creation of a Ukrainian group in Kiev. We discussed the composition of the group, how it would work, and the immediate problems involved in its birth. We discussed the possible participants in depth. Mikola knew the people. I merely warned him against including people who lacked steadfastness. I was certain that the authorities would react with particular sensitivity to the creation of a Ukrainian group, since such a group could not avoid touching on the question of nationality, the most sensitive of all issues for the Soviet Union. If the matter was brought up, the authorities probably would bring particularly cruel pressure to bear on the group. Future events confirmed this apprehension, but Mikola had picked his people well. No one "repented," no one retreated—not a single one right up to the present moment.

The Ukrainian group was formed on November 9, 1976. The next evening, thugs attacked the group's temporary headquarters, throwing bricks and stones through the windows. The police were summoned but they took their time and got there only after the departure of the pogromists, who, as is usual in such cases, were not found. This beginning clearly showed what the group should be prepared for. Its initial membership was: Oles Berdnik, myself, Ivan Kandyba, Levko Lukanyenko, Miroslav Marinovich, Mikola Matusevich, Oksana Meshko, Rudenko, Nina Strokatova, and Oleksa Tikhy. Two months after the organization of the group, Petro Vins joined. Thus it just so happened that the Ukrainian group was equal in size to the Moscow group—eleven persons.

During its first month the group disseminated, in addition to its charter, two fundamental documents: Memorandum number 1, in which totals were drawn up of the violations of human rights in the Ukraine after the Helskini Conference; and Memorandum number 2, which provided a foundation for the demand that the Ukraine be included in the Belgrade Conference. The creation of the Ukrainian group was a catalyst to action in the other union republics of the USSR. Helsinki groups were formed in Lithuania, Georgia, and, after a time, Armenia.

On December 8, 1976, an explosion on the Moscow Metro killed several people. I won't affirm that this was a KGB act but the event was immediately exploited by the KGB. Victor Louis, a Soviet citizen and a correspondent for a Western newspaper who frequently underlines his ties with the KGB, publicly declared that this explosion was the work of "dissident-terrorists." Andrei Sakharov immediately spoke out against this provocatory statement. In turn, he was summoned by the Deputy Prosecutor General of the USSR, who gave him a warning.

All this was merely sour grapes. And it was sour grapes particularly because Sakharov's timely and courageous statement had hindered a campaign against the "dissidents" after the explosion. However, we still could not sit back complacently. The KGB campaign had so far been stunted, but they had put into circulation the term "dissident-terrorist," thereby connecting terrorism with dissident activity.

That same month, December 1976, the KGB raided and searched the homes of the members of the Ukrainian Helsinki group. As always, they confiscated books, manuscripts, and samizdat material. But for the first time in the post-Stalin period, they surreptitiously inserted "compromising items" into what they found. They put thirty-nine American dollars and pornographic post cards in Mikola Rudenko's things, and in Oleksa Tikhy's even a weapon (a World War II-model German rifle). During these searches they also manifested rough behavior, something not previously encountered.

The attack on the Helsinki groups had commenced. By February 1977 it was well underway and I wrote for samizdat a small booklet entitled "Our Weekdays." In it I depicted the actions of the KGB as an effort to destroy the Helsinki movement, and, based on all experiences, past and present, I gave a prognosis of events.

The publicity before the trials of the Helsinki group members was unprecedented. In light of this it was difficult for the authorities to "engineer" even run-of-the-mill trials. It became impossible for them to organize new provocations. The KGB had only enough strength to get that explosion on the Metro off its back. And as far as that went, they were unable to think up anything more intelligent than to close the case down by murdering three totally innocent people out in the remote taiga. When I spoke out on this subject in the press, I was criticized by friends who said I had nothing with which to prove my accusation since I knew about the murders only through an empty TASS report.

To these friends I say, yes, I do not have any proof of my accusations, but I also have no proof of the guilt of those shot. I am convinced that those three, whom I did not know personally, and two of whom were not even named in the TASS report, which said only that they were Armenians—were murdered and were innocent. And until such time as an unprejudiced commission investigates this crime and an unprejudiced public trial proves their guilt, I will maintain that the three Armenians were executed without cause and I will do everything within my power to convince the Soviet and world public of this. I believe that this murder was the commencement of a provocation. Why was the name of only one of the victims given—Stepan Zadikyan? His name alone was given because he had already served a term for anti-Soviet propagandizing and because he was a member of the United Armenian National Party (OANP). I do not doubt at all that this was done in order to make use of his name in future provocations against the OANP and against the human rights movement in the USSR.

After the December explosion on the Metro and searches of the Ukrainian Helsinki group's premises, similar searches took place in Lithuania and Georgia. Surveillance intensified and members of the Ukrainian group traveling to Moscow and Kiev were detained. All this charged the atmosphere around the Helsinki groups. But there was more to come.

On the morning of February 2, the *Literary Gazette* printed an article by the KGB provocateur, A. Agatov-Petrov, entitled "Liars and Pharisees," directed primarily against Alexander Ginzburg. I spent the whole day meeting with my friends and with foreign correspondents discussing the dangerous situation Ginzburg was in, and I discussed the article at length with my wife. Zinaida insisted that Ginzburg's friends and family ought to speak out and expose the slander. She hoped that a swift reaction might serve as some barrier to Ginzburg's arrest. I agreed with her, but because it was late in the day, because of my poor health, and because I was exhausted, I decided to postpone my letter till the next day. When I awoke the next morning, my wife had an outline for the letter ready. We discussed it, made corrections and gave it to be typed.

At eight in the evening our letter was handed to foreign correspondents. We were convinced that the action would forestall Ginzburg's arrest, but two hours later Tatyana Velikanova and Alexander Lavut came to the apartment and told us that it had been carried out. We had to take new measures and so began the discussions that arose every time tyranny tore someone from out of our ranks.

We passed February 4 and 5 in a state of alarm, all of us aware that other arrests were inevitable. On the fifth we learned that the leader of the Ukrainian Helsinki group, Rudenko, had been arrested in Kiev. An earlier report of the arrest in Donetsk of another member, the teacher, Oleksa Tikhy, was confirmed. On February 8 they arrested Yuri Orlov.

Yuri had traveled a complex path. When in 1956 the Twentieth Party Congress convened, he was a member of the CPSU, a candidate for a doctor's degree, and an employee of the Institute of Physics in Moscow. At the party meeting of the institute, devoted to discussion of Khrushchev's report at the congress, he delivered a convincing speech directed against Stalin's accomplices, who then were named in a resolution sent by the institute to the Central Committee of the CPSU that included a demand that the accomplices be brought to justice. The Central Committee sensed a threat to its stability in this demand and dissolved the party organization of the institute, ordering reregistration of its members.

The most active of the participants in this meeting were not reregistered, including Orlov. Several persons, Orlov among them, were expelled from the scientific community. Academician Kurchatov defended them, Orlov in particular, saying that they were the future of science. He threatened to leave science himself if they were expelled, and Khrushchev was forced to take his views into consideration—but as an obligatory condition for their return they were to be sent to the provinces. Yuri S. Orlov was sent to Yerevan.

The situation of a person who has been penalized—as Yuri Orlov had been—is common in the Soviet Union; he meets with objections in everything he does, he encounters constant problems in scientific work, he is assigned the most difficult tasks, and so on. Despite all of this Yuri Fyodorovich's scientific career was exemplary: He defended his doctor's dissertation; he was elected a corresponding member of the Academy of Sciences of the Armenian Republic; and ten years later, in 1966, he was invited to Moscow to the same Institute of Physics from which he had been expelled.

So again he was at work in Moscow, where the phenomenon of Solzhenitsyn, and then of Sakharov, had made the human rights movement an international cause. Yuri Fyodorovich Orlov was drawn into it. For participation in the movement he was fired from the institute. To this day they have refused to allow him to continue his scientific work. Not one to bow down in the face of tyranny, he has always maintained that it is impossible to separate a genuine scientist from science. His own actions confirm this. He carries out theoretical research, and writes and submits articles to the editors of learned magazines, who do not publish them. He sends them to foreign journals. He holds scientific seminars to discuss important questions. Thursday was always his seminar day, a sacred day for him. None of us ever bothered him on Thursday. In order to earn money he taught.

Now this man, whom we all admired, had been packed off into the Lefortovo prison. Though our possibilities for action on our friends' behalf were few, we nonetheless had to make use of them. First, we told the public about the arrests, and about the violation of every legality. Then we grasped, as it is said, for a straw. When Ginzburg and Rudenko were arrested, both were seriously ill, Ginzburg with pneumonia, complicated by tubercular intoxication. He had been released from the hospital only one day before his arrest and when siezed he had in his hand a sick-leave document. Mikola Rudenko was a wounded war veteran. An enormous wound in the area of his sacrum had never closed over. Covered only with a thin membrane, it was transparent enough that through it one could see the palpitations of his internal organs. He had to observe a special life style, and in prison he could not do so.

We wrote to the prosecutor of the USSR and to the prosecutor of the Ukrainian Republic, asking that the illnesses of the arrested persons be taken into consideration and that release terms unconnected with the arrest be designated for them. We wrote that we would give guarantees for them or offer bond, the amount of which could be set by the prosecutors. These petitions were signed by Yelena Bonner, myself, and Zinaida, the attorney Sofya Kalistratova, the writer Lev Kopolev, the Doctor of Physics and Mathematical Sciences Valentin Turchin, and the writer Lidiya Chukovskaya. We received no reply to the entreaty regarding Ginzburg and to the one regarding Rudenko they replied only, "It is impossible to change the measure of detention."

In the meantime the official government organ *Izvestiya* joined in the campaign against the dissidents. It published the correspondence of V. Aparin and M. Mikhailov, entitled "The Office of Mister Shimansky" (February 24, 1977), and "An Open Letter" by S. L. Lipavsky, with a postscript by D. Moryev and A. Yarilov (March 5, 1977).

The first of the articles listed a group of émigrés from the Soviet Union whom it claimed were CIA agents. There were, of course, no proofs. Lipavsky's "exposé" was written specifically to slander two more members of the Moscow Helsinki group—Vladimir Slepak and Anatoly Shcharansky. The latter, in Lipavsky's letter, was directly named as a CIA agent. Though these statements were unaccompanied by proof, they worried me greatly. I was certain that at least Shcharansky was in danger of arrest. On the ninth, I reached Shcharansky by phone at Vladimir Slepak's and suggested that we meet. Anatoly agreed to come to my apartment but added, "If, of course, you are not bothered by my 'tail.' I have a very big one." I replied that I was used to tails—even to my own. We agreed on a time.

Close to that time I went to the window and saw out on the sidewalk a group of people of which I immediately singled out Shcharansky and Slepak. At the door Anatoly joked, "Pyotr Grigoryevich, I have with me companions of two types: my own companions and companions not my own. Let mine in and keep the others out!" And, letting Vladimir Slepak and Zakhar Tesker in ahead of him, he entered and banged the door behind him. Two were left outside.

"But where did you lose the third man?" I asked. "I counted six of you on the street."

"No!" Tolya objected. "There were seven of us. Those two followed us on foot and some remained in cars. They are now carrying out surveillance of the apartment building."

We talked for two hours. It was an ordinary friendly conversation, but all through it I had the feeling of quiet anguish. The threat of Anatoly Shcharansky's arrest and my own advanced age and poor health made me think that our meeting today might be the last we would ever have.

When the group left my heart filled with grief, revulsion, and rage. Trembling with restrained wrath I shut the door and went to the window, where I saw someone dashing along the sidewalk. Soon after, my friends emerged from the entry to my house, where they'd been waiting. There were now three men accompanying them. The tight group of six moved toward Lev Tolstoi Street.

I went to a dining room window from which I could watch the street. Two sedans approached Anatoly and the others, driving right up on the sidewalk. In each there were two men, a driver and a passenger. The man I had seen running on the sidewalk stood and watched the cars turn around, while keeping an eye on the approaching group of six.

I watched my friends till they disappeared. The men following them kept right behind them as before. By violating every traffic rule, the automobiles also managed to keep up with them.

Early the next morning I received a telegram: "Dragging me to be questioned every day. Await arrest." The message was from a woman whose husband had gone on an official trip to the West and had not returned to the USSR. For his "crime" she had been deprived of her rights as a mother and for a year and a half had been detained in camp. She had been sentenced to four years but in connection with International Women's Year she had been granted amnesty. And now a new arrest was imminent. For nothing.

Less than an hour after the telegram arrived the doorbell rang. It was a man, a woman, and three young boys, and I invited them in. The man tried to tell me his story without entering the apartment, saying that he only wanted to ask my advice on a difficult situation the family had found itself in. My wife and I, knowing that an ordinary "dissident" day had begun, repeated the invitation to come in. They did, and we learned the sad story of the Voloshchuk family, headed by Alexander and Lyubov, who for eight months had been without housing or employment.

They had been living in Gorky. The husband was studying in the Agricultural Institute and the wife in the Pedagogical Institute. The authorities had not permitted Alexander to graduate from the institute and he was also unable to get work. No sooner did he manage to get a job than he was dismissed. He was not even trusted with the job of watchman. And so the family had decided to return to their native area—to the Ukraine, the Donbass. In preparation for this they officially exchanged their cooperative apartment in Gorky for an apartment in the city of Khartsyzsk in Donets Province. They secured their exchange warrant and traveled to Khartsysk. But when they got to their new residence, their apartment was already being lived in. Their former apartment in Gorky had also been occupied and they were not offered any other living space in exchange.

"Let God help you!" they were told tauntingly by every Soviet official to whom they turned for help. All of this was solely because the husband was a Baptist and the children had been brought up to believe in God. The authorities had told the wife that she would receive everything for which she was eligible if only she'd divorce her husband.

For half a year the Voloshchuks had been trying to get the rights accorded them by the Soviet Constitution, and two months ago they had become desperate and had gone to the reception room of the Supreme Soviet of the USSR and submitted petitions for renunciation of Soviet citizenship. They had turned in their passports and asked permission to go to any country of the free world. To this they received no reply. So they had come to Moscow to once again sit in the reception room of the Supreme Soviet, this time until they got a reply. They had come to tell us their plans, because they feared that they would be separated from their children and sent off to camps or insane asylums. The future proved their fears justified. Voloshchuk was taken from the reception room to an asylum and the Working Commission for Struggle Against the Use of Psychiatry for Political Purposes waged a struggle for his liberation. He was released in two weeks.

It was the fate of those of us who were called "dissidents," "renegades," and "enemies of society" to collect human grief. We had to listen every day to heart-rending stories and to watch impotently as the bureaucratic apparatus tormented innocent people. All we could do was cry out at their pain. Many people came to us for precisely that reason—they did not even have a "voice" with which to cry out themselves.

On the night of March 13 and the early morning of the fourteenth, KGB officials, headed by senior investigator Captain Yakovlev, carried out a search of Alexander Podrabinek's premises. This particular search was not at all ordinary; in my recollection there had been only one like it before—when they confiscated Solzhenitsyn's archive from an apartment. But more than anything it reminded me of the actions of a criminal covering over the traces of his crime. In order to understand why this search took place, it is necessary to look at what preceded it.

In recent years, both in the West and in our country, cases of repression with the help of psychiatry have received a great deal of publicity. Vladimir Bukovsky played a great role in this exposure when he sent material concerning the activity of the Serbsky Institute of Forensic Psychiatry to Western psychiatrists. Though he paid cruelly for this, he had cracked the dense wall of silence that had surrounded the torture chambers of psychiatric tyranny.

Bukovsky was not the first to encroach upon the inviolability of this wall. Long before him, as I have already reported, Sergei Petrovich Pisaryev made a similar attempt. Back in the fifties, immediately after the Twentieth Party Congress, he managed to bring to the attention of the Central Committee of the CPSU his declaration on criminal abuse of psychiatry; and he even achieved the creation of an authoritative commission to investigate this declaration. The public never learned anything about the noble work of this commission.

It is said that the first step is the hardest. After Bukovsky's action, the crack in the wall gradually began to widen. Together Vladimir Borisov and Victor Fainberg sent out from behind the walls of the Leningrad Special Psychiatric Hostpial a series of reports in which they demonstrated convincingly the anti-human nature of this so-called hospital and its role as one of the centers of suppression of free thought. They showed the doctors in this hospital to be criminals against humanity.

Vladimir Gershuni fearlessly did the very same thing in solitary from behind the walls of the former Oryol Central Prison, now the Oryol Special Psychiatric Hospital. Volodya Borisov and Vitya Fainberg are my friends and comrades-in-arms; but toward Volodya Gershuni, I feel besides friendship a special esteem, a sort of worship of his strength of soul.

Volodya commenced his journey to Golgotha earlier than the rest of us. While still a youth he was a fellow camp inmate of Alexander Solzhenitsyn, who devoted several sentences to Volodya in his great creation, *The Gulag Archipelago.* They were only a few sentences, but they were written in such a way that you could see Gershuni as if he were before your very eyes. While participating in the human rights movement, Gershuni actively assisted Alexander Isayevich Solzhenitsyn in gathering material for *The Gulag Archipelago.*

Volodya was arrested most recently in 1969, four months after I. Soon after his arrest our paths crossed in the Serbsky Institute. But so that we could not communicate with each other, they put him in with the criminals, whereas I was in the political prisoners ward. Despite this he managed to meet with me and to embrace me and to transmit to me at the same time— clandestinely—a chronicle of the events that had taken place during those four months when I had been in prison and he had been free. And what an astonishing memory! His "chronicle" gave not only descriptions of events but also precise dates. The Oryol Special Psychiatric Hospital paid for holding this man prisoner. Through him this institution received the exposure it both dreaded and deserved.

To my wife and to our son, Andrei, belong the principal credit for exposing the criminal activity of psychiatrists at the Chernyakhovsk Special Psychiatric Hospital. To Tatyana Khodorovich and Leonid Plyushch's wife, Tatyana Zhitnikova, belong the credit for exposing the Dnepropetrovsk Special Psychiatric Hospital.

Some individual psychiatrists spoke out. The first was Semyon Gluzman, who wrote the investigative research report entitled "A Long-Distance Diagnosis of P. Grigorenko." For this he got seven years of severe regime camp and five years of exile. The physician-psychiatrist Marina Voikhanskaya, who emigrated to the West, carried out extensive work at exposing this system. So did the physician-psychiatrist Boris Zoubok. Among our foreign friends, the publicist Peter Reddaway and psychiatrist Harry Lauber worked particularly hard and accomplished a great deal in bringing the criminal actions of Soviet psychiatry to light. At the same time that such large-scale exposures were taking place, stories about what was taking place in the special psychiatric hospitals were circulated by people who had been liberated from them—Mikhail Kukobaki, Iosif Tereli, and others.

Many of those subjected to psychiatric repressions had appealed for defense to government organs, but there was not a single case in which tales of the criminal activity were checked out.

This latest search by the KGB confirmed the connection between the psychoprisons and state security. Alexander Podrabinek had a secondary medical education and though he was only twenty-three years old at the time already had a solid record of professional work in emergency treatment. He was a sensitive man who had directed his attention to the widespread imprisonment of free-thinking Soviet citizens in psychiatric hospitals. Podrabinek understood that what was needed now was not exposure of individual incidents but a comprehensive overview of the application of psychiatry for repressive purposes. To this work he had devoted the last three years, and the result was a book-length manuscript entitled *Punitive Medicine*.

Such an enormous work could not be completed in total secrecy. In order to even begin writing the book he had to create a card file on the more than two hundred political prisoners of the special psychiatric hospitals. He had to get their photographs, copies of the relevant official instructions, and other documents. The KGB had long since established surveillance over Podrabinek and had observed him when, with all of his materials, he had gone to Yelena Bobrovich's home with his manuscript and other documents to use Bobrovich's typewriter in rewriting. In the middle of the night the searchers burst into the apartment. They were in such a rush that they had not even secured a proper search warrant. During a five-and-a-half-hour search they confiscated everything he'd brought.

That they had come for what they got, and that they knew that everything they wanted was there, is demonstrated by the fact that a simultaneous search at Podrabinek's own residence, which is customary in such a case, did not take place.

On March 15 Vladimir Slepak called to report that one hour earlier, at 6:00 P.M., Anatoly Shcharansky had been taken in the same way that they had taken Alexander Ginzburg before. Eight young thugs had hurled themselves on Shcharansky, a short, intellectual-looking man, who was obviously unarmed and who had no intention of either resisting or trying to escape, and had twisted his arms, shoved him into a car, and driven off at top speed. They had not uttered a single word or presented any warrant for arrest. Two foreign correspondents and Vladimir Slepak had been standing next to Shcharansky. They had no way of knowing whether they had witnessed an arrest or a kidnapping by terrorist bandits.

I hope I have succeeded somewhat in communicating the atmosphere in which we lived, and in which my friends live right now.

Why are the Helsinki groups so hateful to the KGB? For just one reason: They have decided to tell the truth about Soviet life. A Soviet citizen has been taught to speak in the language of official propaganda. Anyone who tells the reality of a situation and does this in simple language is proclaimed a slanderer

446 MEMOIRS

of Soviet reality. How great the differences between reality and official versions are is illustrated by the workers' letters to Stalin in the thirties and forties. While entire villages were dying from starvation, they were writing to Stalin, at his own behest, about the bountiful and happy collective farm life. Millions of starving people signed this unbelievable lie and all the newspapers published it. The USSR keeps trying to introduce this same order of things into the international arena.

The USSR pays no heed to the Universal Declaration of Human Rights but continues to declare that all of the rights of man are well observed within its borders. And the West has begun to get accustomed to this lie and to indulge it. Boris Stukalin did not hesitate in the presence of many correspondents and publishers to declare that the confiscation of more than forty publications at the recent book fair in Moscow indicated that there is no freedom of the press in the USSR.

The Helsinki groups have attacked the Soviet structure of lies; and the authorities have attempted to silence them. In Moscow, where there are diplomatic representatives and many foreign correspondents, they have acted more gently. They permitted five to emigrate: M. Berhshtam, V. Rubin, L. Alekseyev, Y. Mnyukh, and S. Polyakov. A. Korchak was forced to resign "voluntarily" from the Helsinki group by a threat to deprive him of work. I was stripped of my Soviet citizenship during a visit abroad. Four were sentenced to exile by trial—M. Landa, A. Marchenko, A. Podrabinek, and V. Slepak. Four were sentenced to imprisonment. Of that four only Felix Serebrov was given a short term of one year. The rest received long sentences: Alexander Ginzburg was given eight years of camp and five of exile; Yuri Orlov, seven of camp and five of exile; A. Shcharansky, thirteen years of prison and of camp. Victor Nekipelov, too, was arrested. Thus a group that began with eleven members lost fifteen in three years.

The Helsinki groups in the Soviet republics were attacked even more viciously. The Lithuanian, Georgian, and Armenian groups were destroyed and had to begin all over. The Ukrainian group survived—but with terrible losses! Two of its members, L. Lukanyenko and O. Tikhy, were condemned to ten years of prison and severe regime camp and five years of exile. Two others, V. Ovsiyenko and Y. Litvin, got three years of camp and five of exile. Vasil Streluyv got one and a half years of camp. P. Vins served one year of camp and was allowed to emigrate. If to these nine you add me, two more—Nina Strokatova and Yaroslav Karobinsky, who were released into emigration— and five others who were arrested and are now being prepared for trial—O. Berdnik, Pyotr Razumny, Petro and Vasil Sichko (father and son), and Vasil Streltsyv—this adds up to a loss of seventeen people. Like the Moscow group, the Ukrainian group survives only by the recruitment of new members. It must be noted that three of the repressed have returned to the Moscow group: M. Landa, F. Serebrov and A. Marchenko. The Ukrainian group has no hopes of this happening. It must count on new recruits. The cruelty of the repressions against the members of this group were calculated to frighten off new members. However, this tactic has failed so far. Not only do the Moscow and Ukrainian groups continue to operate, but the Lithuanian, Armenian, and Georgian groups are reestablishing themselves.

In concluding this story about the Helsinki groups, I have to say that their natural ally, the Western governments, in essence were no more than sideline observers of this heroic struggle.

My story is near completion, but I cannot put down my pen without speaking once again of those people with whom I fought in the post-army period of my life.

I often ask myself why emigration has been so hard for me. I would return to my motherland even if I knew that I would be taken directly to an insane asylum. Why? After all, things here are not bad for me. America is a wonderful country. Material conditions here are incomparably better than they were in the Soviet Union. And the people, I imagine, are fundamentally good, as I believe they are almost anywhere. And, as for the political system—may God grant us one like it. So what do I lack here?

What I lack is that community in which I lived in the Soviet Union whose spirit I could always feel, even in the asylum. My family and I were in constant communication with people who were in tune with us. Such people were everywhere.

One day we boarded a train in the town of Rossosh and sat in an ordinary passenger car. There were plenty of empty seats. The three of us sat in a section intended for eight. It was night, and as the train wheels clicked away we dozed off. In Voronezh we were awakened when people poured into our compartment, as they did into the rest of the car. There was a great deal of noise and confusion as everyone tried to get settled for the journey. We moved closer to each other and invited those nearby to be seated with us. Suddenly, above all this crowding and din, we heard a loud and laughing voice: "All they need to do is to shut off the toilet and give us nothing to drink, and it would be just like a Stolypin car." In reply there was friendly and understanding laughter. The train began moving and everyone gradually got settled. People started talking with us and soon a whole group who knew our names and had learned about us from the foreign radio had gathered around. One couple had no place to stay in Moscow, so we invited them to our apartment.

This was just a random crowd of people. Likewise wherever we went in Moscow and any other city we found ourselves in harmonious company. This, so to speak, is the "dissidents' republic" of Soviet society. Who are they, the citizens of this republic?

I have written about many, but there are more whom I was not able to mention. Here, I would like to express to all of them my most profound regards.

CHAPTER TWENTY-EIGHT

FAR FROM HOME

The Boeing 747, with nearly five hundred passengers aboard, lifted easily from the runway of the Frankfurt airport and climbed swiftly, headed for New York. It had only been a few hours since I, my wife, and our invalid son Oleg had said goodbye to our friends at Sheremetevo Airport. Their faces had been sad. If they did not believe in the possibility of our return, they at least hoped for it. Such a hope had arisen and gradually grown stronger within both my wife and myself.

One month had passed since we had submitted our documents to the Ministry of Internal Affairs Department of Visas and Registrations (OVIR). I was to have an operation for the removal of an adenoma and we would visit our son. We had not expected to get visas, but we needed the formal refusal. Back in March we had discovered that the KGB was manifesting "interest" in my surgery. I wanted to publicize this fact and thereby prevent them from meddling further. The authorities' refusal to give us visas would cast additional light on my information. But they gave them to us—quickly. We submitted our documents on October 27 and by November 4 our passports for travel abroad had been signed.

448

This put us on guard. We knew such speed must be significant. In all likelihood they were planning to not let us back into the country.

We considered not using the visas and discussed the possibility with our friends. Many of them wondered why we were so sure this was all a dirty trick. Perhaps the government wanted to demonstrate publicly a change in its policy in relation to freedom of movement. All advised us to use the visas but not give cause to be deprived of Soviet citizenship while we were abroad. After listening to our Moscow friends' advice, I went to Kharkhov and talked with my friends there. Thirty-seven people met with me. They unanimously supported the Muscovites' opinion.

The opinion of those we trusted and my worries about the outcome of the operation encouraged us to make the trip. Gradually our fears of my citizenship being revoked began to seem exaggerated. Therefore I enjoyed a calm and comfortable flight to New York. Everything seemed to me to be progressing smoothly.

We arrived in New York at 5:00 P.M. , on November 30, 1977, went through a simple customs examination, and then were in the embraces of our friends. How many of them there were on this benign soil! There was a brief press conference at which I declared that I viewed the issuance to us of visas as a humane act of the Soviet government and that I was prepared to pay for this with total loyalty: I would not reply to any questions of a political or human rights nature. Anyone who was interested in my views could come to Moscow when we returned. Only there would I answer such questions.

An apartment had been rented for us by the Tatars. We had a light dinner with friends—and then it was just our family. Our son, who had left Moscow three years before, was with us. I felt gratitude to the Soviet government for making this visit possible.

The next day I rested with my family, and on December 2 I went to the doctor, who recommended that I have my operation immediately.

Miracles commenced. I was in a first-class hospital—Saint Barnabas. A day after I checked in, they put me in a spacious individual room. I could not imagine getting a place at all, even a bed in the corridor, in such a short time in Moscow.

They operated December 8 after two days of tests and other preparations. I was discharged on the thirteenth. In the Soviet Union I would have had to spend no less than two months recuperating in the hospital. These long recovery periods account for the shortage of hospital beds. During the time in which our doctors operated on one person, seven patients would be processed in America. In the Soviet Union the type of operation I had is done in two stages, with two incisions. When I told my American surgeon about this he said, "We did it that way once—before the war." Nowadays American surgeons perform the operation without making an incision. When I asked him why Soviet surgeons did not do so, he said, "It's not a matter of the surgeons. Soviet surgeons have the same knowledge and experience as Americans, but they don't have our instruments—Soviet industry does not produce them and the government does not permit them to be bought abroad."

Miracles did not end here. As a sign of their support of the human rights movement in the USSR, the whole brigade of doctors—the head surgeon, Dr. Lyubomir Kuzmak, the urologist, Dr. Schoen, the therapist, Olesnitsky, and the anesthetist, Dr. Cox—carried out the operation without payment. The hospital itself took on all the expenses—$4,500.

I began to travel to other American cities. On March 9, in Boston, I visited Harvard and in the evening met with professors there. I spent the night with Andrei Amalrik. In the morning Zinaida called and said, "You have been deprived of your citizenship."

I immediately proceeded to New York, regretting every moment that I had not returned to the Soviet Union after the operation.

We had intended to spend only half our allotted time in the United States. But I had established contact with prominent American psychiatrists and had arranged to be diagnosed by them. Thus we did not depart on March 1 as we had planned. But in New York I learned that I could not have left then anyway. They had revoked my citizenship February 13, but waited until March 10 to announce it.

For what had they stripped me of citizenship? Their reason was something like this: "Grigorenko, P. G., is systematically carrying out actions which are incompatible with citizenship in the USSR. By his conduct he is doing harm to the prestige of the USSR. . . ."

Once again they had exposed the falsehood of their own allegations of my "insanity." For six and a half years they had kept me in special psychiatric hospitals affirming that I was *not responsible for my actions* at the time and that I had not been responsible for them before I had been imprisoned; at the end of my imprisonment I was sent for observation at a psychiatric clinic, indicating that I was not responsible then, either. Now it turned out that I was a malicious subverter of the prestige of the Soviet state and had been considered such all along.

I did not subvert the prestige of the state—and I also was not insane. I took part in the struggle for a just society and I fought against the falsehood that, along with terror, is the principal means by which the tyrants preserve their power. The Soviet government was born in the underground, and now that it has emerged it still loves to do its black deeds in darkness. Those who struggle for human rights are trying to drag these black deeds out into the light of day. But the government keeps trying to escape the light and so it depicts our actions as illegal and keeps trying to drive us into the underground.

But we know that in the underground you meet only rats. Those who now have power in the Soviet Union are rats who emerged from the underground.

We sought political asylum in the United States. I say "we" even though only one of us was deprived of Soviet citizenship; my wife certainly would not abandon me in an alien land just as I would not permit her to proceed without me into the teeth of the totalitarian monster. And so we remained in America, suffering our forced break with our motherland. My soul ached in particular for our ill, mentally retarded son Oleg. Without any knowledge of the language and without his Moscow friends, he was very lonely. He wept often, trying to hide his tears from us. He became especially upset after Moscow demonstrated that he and his mother were also considered exiles by taking over our Moscow apartment and expelling some relatives who were living there. After this Oleg constantly complained, "Brezhnev took my room away."

America granted us political asylum, shelter, and food. We are extremely grateful for this. But we would no doubt be even more delighted if we had the choice of returning to our friends in Moscow.

America is a country of miracles. Everything is in abundance—food and industrial goods and energy. One does not need to travel to buy anything. Even a store in a village far from the city has everything needed by the population, just as if it were a first-class store in an immense city. And all housing possesses all the urban conveniences, plus the advantages of pure air and beautiful nature. America is like a sea of light where night is turned into day. Everything is superbly organized. To sum it up, we had traveled not just to another country but to another planet. When we looked at the skyscrapers, the giant suspension bridges, the fantastic highways with junctions on several different levels, we were seeing a different world. To "catch up with America" is a stupid slogan. It is impossible to catch up. The America of today is the result of many years of freedom.

When I was young I dreamed of communism as the bright future of humanity. Somewhat later I learned by rote the following about a communist society: "From everyone in accordance with his capabilities and to each in accordance with his needs; / There is no difference between the city and the countryside, and between mental labor and physical labor."

America has achieved all that though it does not call its society communist. And America respects human rights. The story of the Soviet émigré M. Poberezhensky clearly illustrates this respect. In a letter in the New York Russian-language newspaper *Novoye Russkoye Slovo,* he recounts that on the way to the American consulate in Rome, where he was to get permission for entry into the United States, all of his documents were stolen from him. Despite this, the American consul issued him his permission to enter and asked him merely to swear on oath that what he had told them about the theft of his documents was the truth. Poberezhensky recounts further that he was allowed through New York customs without documents and given a certificate attesting to this. When an employee in the Social Security administration, to which Poberezhensky appealed several days later for help, learned that he had no documents except the certificate given him by the customs official at the airport, she took him at his word and within fifteen minutes had completed the forms for him to receive an allowance by virtue of the fact that he was over sixty-five.

I have come to love America and its kind and proud people. The individual here is truly defended—but I am in agreement with Solzhenitsyn that it is overly defended. It is so defended that it is often necessary to defend society against the individual.

In my long life, I have seen two social structures. I have seen and lived in socialism as it is described by Fyodor Dostoyevsky, Yevgeny Zamyatin, and George Orwell. And then I saw another society. It did not call itself socialist, but it set as its purpose the achievement of material prosperity. In this it was successful, but the society soon fell into a state of spiritual decline. Material abundance cannot be the end of human activity. The purpose of life is something else.

What? I do not know. But it can be sought in many places, right now in the struggle to preserve nature, to save it from the pollutants we produce so casually.

It is impossible to think about a far-reaching purpose without eliminating the danger of annihilation by nuclear catastrophe. Many feel that the danger lies in the accumulation of nuclear means of destruction. This is a convenient hypothesis for the aggressor. According to this hypothesis, you can never pinpoint a guilty party because the nonaggressive side also participates in the nuclear weapons race, in order to be prepared to repel the aggressor.

But our experience over the ages shows that war does not start over the quantity of armaments but is instead instigated. Today it is clear that there is such an instigator—the communist world headed by the Soviet Union. The customary objection to this in the West is that the Soviet Union has pursued détente. The ruling elite of the Soviet Union has been employing the tactic of détente (while not calling it by this name) for a long time now. But for as long as the Communist party has existed it has constantly been conducting war. At the same time, it employs the tactic of lessening tension—détente—only where and when it does not have the forces for a direct attack. The Bolsheviks are in a state of hostile relations with the entire world, but they strike at their enemies one at a time. In the beginning, they waged war against the old government, then with democracy and the higher classes of society, then with the democratic parties, then with the prosperous peasants and with the organized portion of the working class, then with the entire peasantry, then with the entire people of their own country, and finally with the entire world.

The West must never forget the Soviet Union's goal—world domination. It must at all times attempt to pull the teeth from the beast of prey. Without war there is only one way to do this, and that is to stand firmly in defense of the human rights defenders in communist countries, not surrendering to demagogic appeals to détente or to provacatory screams of noninterference in internal affairs.

The defense of human rights is not just an internal cause but the most important international cause. Aggression can be stopped only by defending the people's rights.